EXPLORING
Social Psychology

Third Canadian Edition

Robert A. Baron
Rensselaer Polytechnic Institute

Donn Byrne
State University of New York at Albany

Gillian Watson
University of British Columbia

Toronto

Canadian Cataloguing in Publication Data

Baron, Robert A.
    Exploring social psychology

3rd Canadian ed.
Includes bibliographical references and index.
ISBN 0-205-31631-X

1. Social psychology. I. Byrne, Donn. II. Watson, Gillian. III. Title.

HM251.B436 2001   302   C00-930736-2

Statistics Canada information is used with permission of the Minister of Industry, as Minister responsible for Statistics Canada. Information on the availability of the wide range of data from Statistics Canada can be obtained from Statistics Canada's Regional Offices, its World Wide Web site at www.statcan.ca, and its toll-free access number 1-800-263-1136.

ISBN 0-205-31631-X

Vice President, Editorial Director: Michael Young
Acquisitions Editor: Jessica Mosher
Marketing Manager: Judith Allen
Developmental Editor: Dawn du Quesnay and Lise Dupont
Production Editor: Joe Zingrone
Copy Editor: Alex Moore
Production Coordinator: Wendy Moran
Page Layout: Brian Taft/ArtPlus Limited
Permissions/Photo Research: Susan Wallace-Cox
Art Director: Julia Hall
Cover/Interior Design: Dave Murphy/ArtPlus Limited
Cover Image: Stock Illustration Source/Roxana Villa

1 2 3 4 5   05 04 03 02 01

Printed and bound in Canada.

Contents

2

SOCIAL PERCEPTION AND SOCIAL COGNITION: INTERNALIZING OUR SOCIAL WORLD   38

3

ATTITUDES: EVALUATING THE SOCIAL WORLD   84

Cornerstones

On The Applied Side

Canadian Research: On The Cutting Edge

4
SOCIAL IDENTITY: THE SELF, GENDER, AND CULTURE   120

5

PREJUDICE AND DISCRIMINATION: UNDERSTANDING THEIR NATURE, COUNTERING THEIR EFFECTS   158

6

RELATIONSHIPS: FROM ATTRACTION TO PARTING 202

7

SOCIAL INFLUENCE: CHANGING OTHERS' BEHAVIOUR 252

8

HELPING AND HARMING: PROSOCIAL BEHAVIOUR AND AGGRESSION   286

9
GROUPS AND INDIVIDUALS: THE CONSEQUENCES OF BELONGING   334

10

APPLIED SOCIAL PSYCHOLOGY: HEALTH, WORK AND LEGAL APPLICATIONS   374

Preface

Why Social Psychology is Relevant to Your Life

The authors of this book were born on different continents, in different decades, raised in very different cultures and families, are of different genders and yet where social psychology is concerned we agree on a major point—its usefulness! *Each one of us has found social psychology continuously useful in our lives.* We have used its principles literally everyday in our interactions with others, or failed to do so and been sorry. And more than that we have continued to be fascinated by this topic. We sincerely believe and hope that you, our readers, will feel the same when you have finished this course.

Social psychology is psychology as you live it—dealing with the people around you and their attitudes and prejudices; falling in love and out of it, coping with attempts to influence you, to help you or harm you, wondering why other people won't cooperate, and so on. Whatever your background and the shape of your future life, your relationships with other people will be central both at work and at home and that is the topic of this book.

The idea that *social psychology is relevant to our lives* is a basic theme for this third edition of *Exploring Social Psychology: Canadian Edition*. As in the past, we've tried to describe the findings of social psychology in Canada and internationally, in as accurate and up-to-date a manner as possible. But, we have also tried to accomplish something else—to maximize the chances that you not only see the relevance but also use social psychology in the years ahead. We have attempted in this new edition to increase the relevance of social psychology for you, the reader, in a number of ways.

Increasing the Relevance of Social Psychology by Applying it to Real Life Problems

Central to the idea that social psychology can and should be applied to our daily lives are two features: *Ideas to Take with You* and *On the Applied Side* sections.

At the end of each chapter a section labeled *Ideas to Take with You* is designed to highlight important concepts you should remember—and use—long after this course is over. In our view, you may well find these concepts useful in your own life in the years ahead. These sections include:

- Why correlation doesn't equal causation (Chapter 1)
- Minimizing the impact of errors in social cognition (Chapter 2)
- Resisting persuasion: Some useful steps (Chapter 3)
- Dealing with negative self-perceptions; recognizing and countering your own ethnocentrism (Chapter 4)
- Techniques for reducing prejudice (Chapter 5)
- How to encourage others to like you; All you need is love? (Chapter 6)
- Tactics for gaining compliance (Chapter 7)
- Being a responsive bystander (Chapter 8)
- Maximizing your own performance; minimizing social loafing by others (Chapter 9)
- Don't rush to judgment (Chapter 10)

On the Applied Side sections highlight the practical implications of social psychology—ways in which its knowledge and principles can be applied to a wide range of real-life issues and problems. Some of these topics are listed below:

- Canadian culture and its impact on social behaviour and social psychology (Chapter 1)
- Cultural differences in openness and directness of communication (Chapter 2)
- The marketing of Wayne Gretzky as an advertising spokesperson (Chapter 3)
- The motive towards self-enhancement or self-improvement in Canadian and Asian cultures (Chapter 4)
- The impact of neosexism on Canadian women in the workplace (Chapter 5)
- Does relating to others on the Internet impoverish or enhance our social lives? (Chapter 6)
- Problems when conflicts cross ethnic boundaries (Chapter 9)
- Research on the issue of gun control and the weapons effect (Chapter 10)

Increasing The Relevance of Social Psychology Through Enhancing Communication

Although it was many years ago, we can vividly recall struggling to understand the textbooks we used in our first courses in social psychology. Because we don't want you to experience the same difficulties, we have worked hard to make this book as easy to read and understand as possible. Here is an overview of the steps we've taken in this respect:

- Each chapter begins with an outline. Within the text itself, key terms are printed in **bold type like this** and are followed by a definition. These terms are also defined in a running glossary in the margins.
- To help you understand and remember what you have read, we have included brief summaries of *Key Points* at regular intervals.
- Because figures and charts contained in original research reports are often quite complex, every graph and table in this text has been specially created for it. In addition, all graphs contain special labels designed to call your attention to the key findings presented. We think that you'll find all of these illustrations easy to read and—more importantly—that they'll contribute to your understanding of social psychology.
- Finally, each chapter ends with a *Summary and Review of Key Points*. Reviewing this section can be an important aid to your studying.

Increasing The Relevance of Social Psychology for Canadian Readers

It has always been a major aim of *Exploring Social Psychology* to represent the richness and diversity of Canadian social psychology and, further, to increase the relevance of its topics to the lives of Canadian readers—something that American texts often fail to achieve.

The most obvious way in which we have attempted to do this is through the special sections called *Canadian Research: On the Cutting Edge*. These sections describe Canadian research that we believe is on the frontiers of knowledge in social psychology. This was a popular feature of previous editions and every one of these sections is new to the current edition. However, Canadian research is also represented throughout in the body of the text and in the special *Cornerstones* and *On the Applied Side* sections.

The following is just a sample of the Canadian research in this book:

- Roger Buehler and colleagues on the planning fallacy (Chapter 1)
- James Russell on cultural influences on facial expressions (Chapter 2)

- Steve Heine and Darrin Lehman on Japanese and Canadian
  responses to cognitive dissonance (Chapter 3)
- Romin Tafarodi on paradoxical self-esteem (Chapter 4)
- John Berry on acculturative stress and ethnic identity (Chapter 4)
- Francine Tougas and colleagues on neosexism (Chapter 5)
- Bob Altemeyer on right-wing authoritarianism (Chapter 5)
- John Berry on multiculturalism (Chapter 5)
- Karen and Ken Dion on cultural differences in passionate love (Chapter 6)
- Del Paulhus on the social impact of trait self-enhancement (Chapter 7)
- Lynne Jackson and Victoria Esses on attributions and religious
  fundamentalism (Chapter 8)
- Martin Daly and Margo Wilson on the evolutionary
  perspective regarding the young male syndrome (Chapter 8)
- Natalie Allen and John Meyer on organizational commitment (Chapter 9)
- Wallace Lambert on second language learning (Chapter 10)

Canadian examples are also integrated throughout the text to illustrate research material. For example:

- Historical patterns of immigration in Canada (Chapter 1)
- The remarkable recovery of RCMP Constable Laurie White (Chapter 2)
- Wayne Gretzky as an advertising spokesperson (Chapter 3)
- The racist killing of Nirmal Singh Gill by five young Canadians (Chapter 5)
- Rivalry between fans of Canadian sports teams (Chapter 5)
- Changing family patterns in Canada in the last 20 years (Chapter 6)
- Canadian men and women sharing housework (Chapter 6)
- The Ottawa bus depot shootings as an example of
  workplace aggression (Chapter 8)
- Firearm availability and homicide in Canada and internationally;
  the school shooting in Taber, Alberta (Chapter 10)

Increasing The Relevance of Social Psychology by Keeping up to Date...While Knowing Our Roots

Social psychology is a rapidly changing field, so we have always felt it crucial that this book be very current. To attain this goal, we have reorganized several chapters to take account of recent trends and findings and have thoroughly updated every chapter. The result: many of the references are from 1997-2000. We haven't neglected the foundations of our field, however; special *Cornerstones* sections describe truly classic studies in the field—ones that are fundamental to the development of major lines of research and thus have exerted a lasting impact on social psychology.

Here is an overview of the changes we have made to keep this book truly on the cutting edge.

1. *Reorganization of several chapters.* Chapter 1 has expanded coverage of methodology, with discussion of observational methods and choice of methodology. It also emphasizes the parallel yet contrasting trends of cultural and evolutionary research to a greater extent. In Chapter 7 the section on compliance has been completely reorganized around Cialdini's principles of compliance. It now also includes new material on impression management. Chapter 8 has been reorganized to include

greater representation of modern evolutionary perspectives and consideration of dispositional influences in both prosocial behaviour and aggression. It also offers new coverage of applied topics. Chapter 9 has also been reorganized and now includes the important topic of coordination in groups—cooperation, conflict, and conflict resolution—as well as having expanded coverage of fairness in groups. The applied topics in Chapter 10 now include (at the request of reviewers) applications to business and work settings, as well as coverage of medical and legal applications.

2. *Inclusion of dozens of new topics*. We have included dozens of new topics not present in the previous edition. A sample: Role of motivation in the "planning fallacy" (Chapter 1); Cultural differences in use and interpretation of indirectness in communication (Chapter 2); Accuracy of social perception (Chapter 2); Role of amount of information in the availability heuristic (Chapter 2); Thought suppression and its effects (Chapter 2); Contrasting motives for processing of persuasive messages (Chapter 3); Biased assimilation and attitude polarization in resistance to persuasion (Chapter 3); The self as an adaptive product of evolution (Chapter 4); Paradoxical self-esteem (Chapter 4); Children's perceptions of a child whose play is gender appropriate or inappropriate (Chapter 4); Prejudice and discrimination go underground: Modern racism, neosexism and covert institutional racism (Chapter 5); New information on how stereotypes exert their effects (Chapter 5); Direct and indirect effects of emotional states on attraction (Chapter 6); Relating on the Internet—new research on its effects on our social relations (Chapter 6); Self-disclosure: gender and culture differences; Cultural differences in the content of attractiveness stereotypes (Chapter 6); Impact of adult attachment styles on marital success, jealousy, and responses to unsatisfactory relationships (Chapter 6); When impression management and ingratiation fail: The "slime effect" and trait self-enhancement (Chapter 7); Role of current moods in compliance (Chapter 7); Individual differences in preferences for social influence tactics (Chapter 7); The role of "mindlessness" in the that's-not-all technique (Chapter 7); Population density and helping behaviour (Chapter 8); Genetic and experiential components of empathy (Chapter 8); The modern evolutionary perspective, the young male syndrome in warfare (Chapter 8); The general affective aggression model (Chapter 8); Narcissism, ego-threat, and aggression (Chapter 8); Nature and causes of workplace aggression (Chapter 8); Organizational commitment in times of change (Chapter 9); Coordination in groups, including cooperation and conflict (Chapter 9); Interpersonal justice (Chapter 9); Why groups fail to share information (Chapter 9); Recovered memories of childhood abuse: accurate recollections, or fictions elicited by suggestion? (Chapter 10); Genetic and personal factors in job satisfaction (Chapter 10); Organizational citizenship behaviour—helping at work (Chapter 10); Firearm availability and the weapons effect (Chapter 10).

Increasing The Relevance of Social Psychology by Reflecting Recent Trends

Additional features of this book are designed to reflect important current trends in social psychology.

1. *Interest in cultural and ethnic diversity*. Representing cultural diversity has always been a central concern of this text in an effort to reflect Canada's multiculturalism. The current edition has continued and expanded that tradition. Chapter 4, as before, contains a major section on cross-cultural psychology. In addition, throughout the book there are many sections that present information concerning differences across various cultures or between ethnic groups within a given society.

The topics these sections cover include:

In addition, culture-related discussions throughout the main text are marked by this symbol.

2 *Interest in an evolutionary or biological perspective.* Social psychologists have recently shown increased interest in the potential role of biological or genetic factors in social behaviour. We discuss this perspective at many points in the text. Just a few examples:

To help you identify this material we have marked it with this icon, designed to draw your attention to the evolutionary perspective:

3. *Evolution and culture interact.* The two trends mentioned above represent the modern form of an old dispute in psychology—sometimes termed the nature-versus-nurture controversy—the extent to which behaviour can be attributed to biological and evolved tendencies (nature) or to environmental influences (nurture). These days in social psychology interest has focused upon cultural and evolutionary explanations and, more significantly, psychologists acknowledge that *both* factors play a part in human behaviour. However, these two approaches do tend to provide very different explanations for the origins of social behaviour. At various points in this book, we will juxtapose the evolutionary and cultural approach and compare their explanations. These sections will be highlighted by placing both symbols side-by-side in the following way:

Pedagogical Features

Chapter Outline. Each chapter begins with an outline of the major topics covered.

List of Special Sections. Also featured at the beginning of each chapter is a list of the special sections (i.e., feature boxes) presented.

Key Points. To help you understand and remember what you have read, each major section is followed by a list of *Key Points*, briefly summarizing main points. Each chapter also ends with a summary and review of these key points.

Key Terms. Key terms appear in boldface type in the text and are defined in the margin.

Cornerstones. These special sections describe truly classic studies in the field—ones that are fundamental to the development of major lines of research and thus have exerted a lasting impact on social psychology.

On the Applied Side. These sections highlight the practical implications of social psychology and demonstrate ways in which its knowledge and principles can be applied to a wide range of real-life issues and problems.

Canadian Research: On the Cutting Edge. These sections describe Canadian research that we believe is on the frontiers of knowledge in social psychology.

Ideas to Take with You. Featured near the end of each chapter, these sections are designed to highlight important concepts you should remember—and use—long after this course is over.

Icons. Throughout the book there are many sections that illustrate differences across various cultures or between ethnic groups within a given society. To help you identify this material, these culture-related discussions throughout the main text are marked by the following symbol:

Social psychologists have recently shown increased interest in the potential role of biological or genetic factors in social behaviour. To help you identify these biological-related discussions, we have marked them with the follwing icon, designed to draw your attention to the evolutionary perspective:

At various points in this book, we juxtapose the evolutionary and cultural approach and compare their explanations. These sections will be highlighted by the following symbol:

Summary and Review of Key Points. Each chapter ends with a Summary and Review of Key Points. Reviewing this section is an important first step in the study process.

For More Information. Annotated suggested readings appear at the end of each chapter. These readings will be useful to you as you study and prepare essays.

Weblinks. Visit the relevant web sites at the end of each chapter for additional information and assistance with the topics covered.

Supplements to The Text

Learning Aids for Students

Companion Web Site. The purchase of this book provides you with instant access to the companion Web site for the third Canadian edition of *Exploring Social Psychology*. The Web site offers users of this text a variety of exercises to enhance the total learning experience, including practice tests, links to relevant Internet sites, and more.

Study Guide. The *Study Guide* includes chapter outlines, learning objectives, and a series of imaginative and useful exercises that will help students review and understand the material in the textbook.

Supplements for Instructors

Test Item File. A comprehensive test item file has been prepared for this edition. Available in both printed and computerized form, the file contains approximately 110 questions per chapter. Answers are referenced to the text by page number. Pearson Test Manager is a test generator designed to allow the creation of personalized exams. Test questions can be added to the Test Item File and existing questions can be edited. The Test Manager also offers an Online Testing System, which is the most efficient, time-saving examination aid on the market, allowing the instructor to administer, correct, grade, record, and return computerized exams over a variety of networks.

Instructor's Manual. An *Instructor's Manual* will be available with this edition. It will include chapter outlines and learning objectives, discussion questions, suggestions for classroom activities, a film/video list, and critical thinking and essay questions.

Acknowledgments

Some Words of Thanks from the Canadian Author

Preparing this third edition has provided plenty of examples of the relevance of social psychology. In particular, many people have cooperated and cajoled to complete it, using a variety of social influence techniques. Despite this the planning fallacy triumphed again. I have also needed, and greatly appreciated, the social support of my friends and the help of my colleagues in completing this edition.

First, many thanks to Rachel Mines who acted as researcher—and unofficial first editor—for this book. She was always available to discuss issues and offered many suggestions for new material. As is her style, she was conscientious and supportive above and beyond the call of duty.

Second, special thanks to the following reviewers of the second Canadian edition, selected by Pearson Education Canada, who offered valuable comments and suggestions for improvements, in some cases with real effort and enthusiasm: Warren Thorngate, Carleton University; Barbara Carroll, Carleton University; Heather MacDonald, Simon Fraser University; and Michael McCarrey, University of Ottawa. Many of their suggestions for new topics and material have been incorporated in this new edition.

Finally, at Pearson Education Canada (formerly Prentice Hall Allyn and Bacon), I would like to thank Nicole Lukach, Jessica Mosher, Lise Dupont, Joe Zingrone, and in particular, Dawn du Quesnay, who was unfailingly helpful—managing to balance time pressures with sympathy for authors. Also special thanks to Alex Moore who did an excellent and thorough job of copy-editing. He guided me through the various editing deadlines in a pleasant manner and was always very much involved.

About The Authors

Robert A. Baron is currently Professor of Psychology and Professor of Management at Rensselaer Polytechnic Institute. A Fellow of the APA since 1978, he received his Ph.D. from the University of Iowa (1968). Professor Baron has held faculty appointments at the University of South Carolina, Purdue University, the University of Minnesota, University of Texas, University of Washington, and Princeton University. He has received numerous awards for teaching excellence at these institutions. Professor Baron has also been a visiting Fellow at the University of Oxford (England). He served as a Program Director at the National Science Foundation from 1979 to 1981. At present, Professor Baron's major research interests focus on applying the principles and findings of social psychology to behaviour in work settings (e.g., the causes and management of organizational conflict; impact of the physical environment on task performance and productivity).

Donn Byrne holds the rank of Distinguished Professor of Psychology and is the Director of the Social-Personality Program at the University at Albany, State University of New York. He received the Ph.D. degree in 1958 from Stanford University and has held academic positions at the California State University at San Francisco, the University of Texas, and Purdue University as well as visiting professorships at the University of Hawaii and Stanford University. He received the Excellence in Research Award from the University at Albany in 1987 and the Distinguished Scientific Achievement Award from the Society for the Scientific Study of Sex in 1989. His current research interests include interpersonal attraction and the prediction of sexually coercive behaviour.

Gillian Watson was an immigrant to Canada from Britain in the 1970s, and has been interested in the cross-cultural experience ever since. Maintaining that theme, she received her first degree from McGill University in Quebec (1980), a doctorate (or D. Phil. as its called) from Oxford University in England (1985), and spent a postdoctoral year with the Department of Communication in Ottawa. Her research interests include justice, intergroup relations, and cross-cultural psychology. She is a lecturer at the University of British Columbia where she recently won an award for her teaching.

The Pearson Education Canada

companion Web site...

Your Internet companion to the most exciting, state-of-the-art educational tools on the Web!

The Pearson Education Canada Companion Web site is easy to navigate and is organized to correspond to the chapters in this textbook. The Companion Web site is comprised of six distinct, functional features:

1) **Customized Online Resources**

2) **Faculty Centre**

3) **Student Centre**

4) **Communication**

5) **Contents**

6) **About the Authors**

Explore the six areas in this Companion Web site. Students and distance learners will discover resources for indepth study, research, and communication, empowering them in their quest for greater knowledge and maximizing their potential for success in the course.

A NEW WAY TO DELIVER EDUCATIONAL CONTENT

1) Customized Online Resources

Our Companion Web sites provide instructors and students with a range of options to access, view, and exchange content.

● **Syllabus Manager** provides *instructors* with the option to create online classes and construct an online syllabus linked to specific modules in the Companion Web site.

● **Mailing lists** enable *instructors* and *students* to receive customized promotional literature.

● **Preferences** enable *students* to customize the sending of results to various recipients, and also to customize how the material is sent, e.g., as html, text, or as an attachment.

● **Help** includes an evaluation of the user's system and a tune-up area that makes updating browsers and plug-ins easier. This new feature will enhance the user's experience with Companion Web sites.

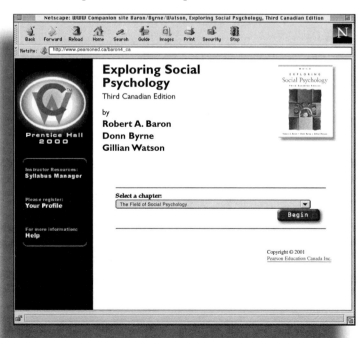

www.pearsoned.ca/baron4_ca

Pearson Education

COMPANION WEBSITE

2) Faculty Centre

This Companion Web site provides a password-protected centre featuring the Instructor's Manual that accompanies this book.

3) Student Centre

The Companion Web site offer users of *Exploring Social Psychology* a variety of exercises to enhance the total learning experience, including practice tests, links to relevant Web sites, and more. These modules are categorized according to their functionality:

● **Objectives**   ● **Essay questions**   ● **Multiple-Choice**   ● **Destinations**

The multiple-choice and essay question modules provide students with the ability to send answers to our grader and receive instant feedback on their progress through our Results Reporter. Coaching comments and references back to the text-book ensure that students take advantage of all resources available to enhance their learning experience.

Destinations provides a directory of Web sites relevant to the subject matter in each chapter.

4) Communication

Companion Web sites contain the communication tools necessary to deliver cours-es in a **Distance Learning** environment.

Communication facilities of Companion Web sites provide a key element for dis-tributed learning environments. There are two types of communication facilities currently in use in Companion Web sites:

● **Message Board** – this module takes advantage of browser technology, providing the users of each Companion Web site with a national newsgroup to post and reply to relevant course topics.

● **i-chat** – enables instructor-led group activities in real time. Using Our chat client, instructor can display Web site content while students participate in the discussion.

5) Contents

Click here to view a detailed table of contents.

6) About the Authors

Click here to find out more about the backgrounds of the authors.

7) Ordering Info

Click here to be linked to the catalogue description and the necessary ordering infor-mation for this title

The Companion Web site for this text can be found at:

www.pearsoned.ca/baron4_ca

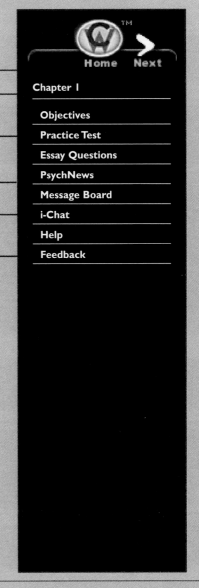

TM

Home   Next

Chapter I

Objectives

Practice Test

Essay Questions

PsychNews

Message Board

i-Chat

Help

Feedback

Note: Companion Web site content will vary slightly from site to site depending on discipline requirements.

PEARSON EDUCATION CANADA

26 Prince Andrew Place
Don Mills, Ontario M3C 2T8

To order:
Call: 1-800-567-3800
Fax: 1-800-263-7733

For samples:
Call: 1-800-850-5813
Fax: (416) 447-2819
E-mail: phabinfo.pubcanada@pearsoned.com

The Field of **Social Psychology**: How We **Think** About and **Interact** with Others

SPECIAL SECTIONS

■ The social side of life: Why it's so important

FIGURE 1.1 In our daily lives, at school or work, social interactions are an important and inevitable part of our experience. Our social behaviour and understanding can determine whether such experiences are enjoyable or difficult.

The focus of this book is the *social side* of our existence as human beings. In our opinion, this is a naturally fascinating topic, for the following basic reason: other people often play a crucial role in our lives. For example, contact with others is inevitable. Most Canadians live in an urban setting, cheek-by-jowl with hundreds or thousands of others. And in order to meet the majority of our daily goals and needs, we have to interact with people, known and unknown (see, for example, Figure 1.1). But beyond that, we often actively seek out others just for their company—we are truly "social animals" as one writer has put it (Aronson, 1994).

At different times and in different contexts, other people are the source of many of our most satisfying forms of pleasure (love, praise, help) and many of our most important forms of pain (rejection, criticism, embarrassment). In sum, it is not an exaggeration to say that our social relations with others constitute one of the most important parts of our lives. Consequently, we spend a lot of time and effort thinking about others, trying to understand them, and trying to predict their behaviour towards us.

Social psychology has been pursuing the same aim, though in a more systematic way than we do in our daily lives, through the use of basic methods of science. These methods can supply more accurate and precise information about even the most complex aspects of social behaviour than can be obtained by our own informal speculations or by resorting to the musings of poets, philosophers, playwrights, or novelists. Though such sources of social knowledge may provide us with a wealth of ideas, they

This is a small sample of the questions that are currently being studied by social psychologists, and that we'll address in this text.

TABLE 1.1 The Breadth of Social Psychology

Question	Chapter in Which it is Covered
Why do some of us always underestimate how much time a task will take?	Chapter 1
Can our expectations about someone else's behaviour actually influence how that person behaves?	Chapter 2
Can our attitudes be changed by information we don't even notice?	Chapter 3
Do women and men really differ in their behaviour? If so, why?	Chapter 4
Does Canada's policy of multiculturalism have a positive impact on ethnic relations?	Chapter 5
Why do people fall in love?	Chapter 6
If you try to boost your own image in front of others, does it make them treat you better?	Chapter 7
Why do some people just stand and stare during an emergency? Why don't they offer help?	Chapter 8
Why does workplace aggression occur?	Chapter 8
Do people accomplish more when working together or when working alone?	Chapter 9
Does your attractiveness, your gender, or your ethnicity affect how you are treated in the legal system?	Chapter 10

can be confusing or contradictory, and are rarely systematic. So we are suggesting that your understanding of the ways in which people think about and interact with others can be greatly enhanced by the study of social psychology

Because of the importance of social behaviour not only to individuals but to smooth running of society, you may be surprised to learn that a science-oriented approach is quite new. Only in the decades since World War II has social psychology developed into a really active field. Despite its recent arrival on the scene, however, social psychology has provided some very valuable knowledge about behaviour. Perhaps the breadth and potential value of the information it yields are best suggested by a list like the one in Table 1.1. Please note that the questions in the table represent only a small sample of the many topics currently being studied by social psychologists. The field is currently so diverse and so far-ranging in scope that no single list could possibly represent all of the topics it considers.

Before we turn to these intriguing topics, however, we believe it will be useful to pause briefly in order to provide you with certain background information.

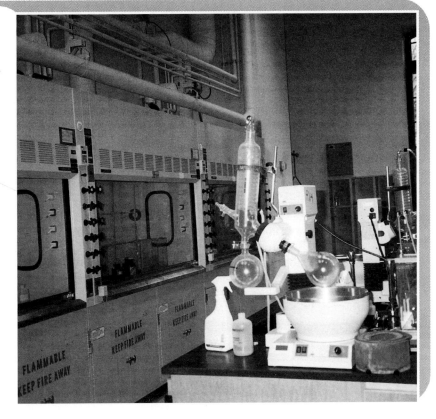

FIGURE 1.2 In fields such as social psychology, data are gathered systematically and all hypotheses are carefully tested before being accepted as accurate. In non-scientific fields, in contrast, hypotheses and assertions are accepted at face value in the absence of any systematic tests of their accuracy.

In the remainder of this chapter, then, we will focus on completing three preliminary tasks. First, we will present *a formal definition of social psychology*—our view of what it is and what it seeks to accomplish. Second, we will examine *some of the basic methods used by social psychologists in their research*. Our goal here is simple: helping you to understand just how the facts and principles presented throughout this text were obtained. Finally, we will offer *a survey of the origins and trends of social psychology*.

SOCIAL PSYCHOLOGY: A WORKING DEFINITION

Offering a formal definition of almost any field is a complex task. In the case of social psychology, this complexity is increased by two factors: (1) the field's great diversity, and (2) its rapid rate of change. Despite the broad sweep of topics they choose to study, though, most social psychologists seem to focus the bulk of their attention on one central task: Understanding how and why individuals behave, think, and feel as they do in situations involving other persons. Taking this central focus into account, our working definition of social psychology is as follows: **Social psychology** *is the scientific field that seeks to understand the nature and causes of individual behaviour and thought in social situations*. In other words, social psychology seeks to understand how we think about and interact with others. We will now clarify several aspects and implications of this definition.

Social Psychology
The scientific field that seeks to understand the nature and causes of individual behaviour and thought in social situations.

Social Psychology is Scientific in Nature

What is *science*? Many people seem to believe that this term refers only to fields such as chemistry, physics, and biology—ones that use the kind of equipment shown in Figure 1.2. If you share that view, you may find our suggestion that social psychology is a scientific discipline somewhat puzzling. How can a field that seeks to study the nature of love, the causes of aggression, and everything in between be scientific in the same sense as astronomy, biochemistry, and computer science? The answer is surprisingly simple.

In reality, the term *science* does not refer to a special group of highly advanced fields. Rather, it refers to two things: (1) a set of values, and (2) several methods that can be used to study a wide range of topics. In deciding whether a given field is or is not scientific, therefore, the critical question is: *Does it adopt these values and methods?* To the extent that it does, it is scientific in nature. To the extent that it does not, it falls outside the realm of science. We'll examine the procedures used by social psychologists in their research in detail in the next major section; here, we'll focus on the core values that all fields must adopt to be considered scientific in nature. Four of these are most important:

Accuracy: A commitment to gathering and evaluating information about the world (including social behaviour and thought) in as careful, precise, and error-free a manner as possible.

Objectivity: A commitment to obtaining and evaluating such information in a manner that is as free from bias as humanly possible.

Skepticism: A commitment to accepting findings as accurate only to the extent that they have been verified over and over again.

Open-Mindedness: A commitment to changing one's views—even views that are strongly held—if existing evidence suggests that these views are inaccurate.

Social psychology, as a field, is deeply committed to these values and applies them in its efforts to understand the nature of social behaviour and social thought. For this reason, it makes sense to describe our field as scientific in orientation. In contrast, fields that are not scientific make assertions about the world, and about people, that are not subjected to the careful testing and analysis required by the values listed above. In such fields—ones like astrology and aromatherapy—intuition, faith, and unobservable forces are considered to be sufficient.

"But why adopt the scientific approach? Isn't social psychology just common sense?" Having taught for many years (more than eighty between us!), we can almost hear you asking this question. And we understand why you might feel this way; after all, each of us has spent our entire life interacting with other persons. As a result of such experience, we are all amateur social psychologists. So why not rely on our own experience—or even on folklore and "the wisdom of the ages"—in order to understand the social side of life? Our answer is straightforward: Because such sources provide inconsistent and unreliable guides to social behaviour.

For instance, consider the following statement, suggested by common sense: "Absence makes the heart grow fonder." Do you agree? Is it true that when people are separated from those they love, they miss them and so experience increased longing for them? Many people would agree. They would answer "Yes, that's right. Let me tell you about the time I was separated from..." But now consider the following statement: "Out of sight, out of mind." How about this statement? Is it true? When people are separated from those they love, do they quickly forget them or find someone else on whom to focus their affections? As you can see, these two views—both suggested by common sense—are contradictory. The same is true for many other informal observations about human behaviour. We could go on to list others, but by now the main point is clear: Common sense often suggests a confusing and inconsistent picture of human behaviour. This is one important reason why social psychologists put their faith in the scientific method: it yields much more conclusive evidence.

But this is not the only reason why we must be wary of common sense. Another one relates to the fact that unlike Data of *Star Trek* fame, we are not perfect information-processing machines. On the contrary, as we'll note over and over again (e.g., in Chapters 2 and 5), our thinking is subject to several forms of error, or *bias*, that can lead us badly astray. In addition, our emotions often influence, or confuse, our thinking. Because of such human fallibility, we cannot rely on our own informal observation, common sense, or intuition to provide us with accurate information about social behaviour. This is why social psychologists, in their efforts to understand the social side of life, prefer to rely on the findings of carefully conducted research carried out in accordance with the methods of science. And that approach, of course, is the one we'll adopt throughout this text.

Social Psychology Focuses on the Behaviour of Individuals

Societies differ greatly in terms of their views concerning courtship and marriage; yet it is still *individuals* who fall in love. Similarly, societies vary greatly in terms of their overall levels of violence; yet it is still individuals who perform aggressive actions or refrain from doing so. The same argument applies to virtually all other aspects of social behaviour, from prejudice to helping: actions are performed by, and thoughts occur in the minds of, individuals. Because of this basic fact, the focus, in social psychology, is squarely on individuals. Social psychologists realize, of course, that individuals do not exist in isolation from social and cultural influences—far from it. But the field's major interest lies in understanding the factors that shape the actions and thoughts of individual humans in social settings. This contrasts sharply with the field of *sociology*, which you may have studied in other courses. Sociology studies some of the same topics as social psychology, but it is concerned not with the behaviour and thoughts of individuals but with large groups of persons or with society as a whole. For instance, both social psychology and sociology study the topic of violent crime. While social psychologists focus on the factors that cause specific persons to engage in such behaviour, however, sociologists are interested in comparing rates of violent crime in different segments of the society (e.g., high- and low-income groups), or in examining trends in the rate of violent crime over time.

Social Psychology Seeks to Understand the Causes of Social Behaviour and Thought

In a key sense, the heading of this section states the most central aspect of our definition, the very core of our field. What it means is that social psychologists are primarily concerned with understanding the wide range of conditions that shape the social behaviour and thought of individuals—their actions, feelings, beliefs, memories, and inferences—with respect to other persons. Obviously, a huge number of factors play a role in this regard ranging from factors within individuals, such as their cognitions and biology, to contextual factors, such as the presence of others in the immediate social surroundings, the physical environment, and the long-term social context of culture. Thus, most factors affecting social interaction can be classified into five main categories: (1) basic *cognitive* processes such as memory and reasoning—processes that underlie our thoughts, beliefs, ideas, and judgments about others; (2) *biological* aspects of our nature and genetic inheritance that are relevant to social behaviour; (3)

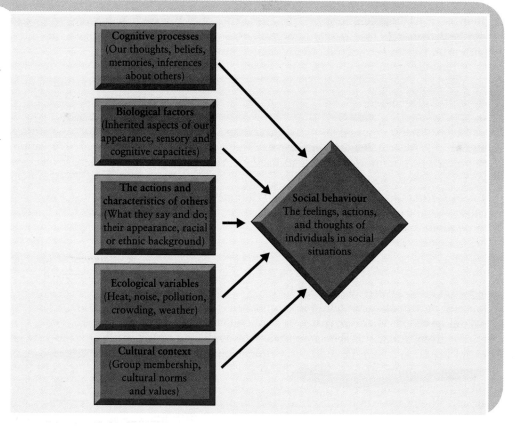

■ Social behaviour stems from many different causes

FIGURE 1.3 Among the most important of these are (1) cognitive processes, (2) biological factors; (3) the actions and characteristics of others, (4) ecological (environmental) variables; and (5) cultural context.

the actions and characteristics of *other people*; (4) *ecological* variables—direct and indirect influences of the physical environment; and (5) the *cultural* context in which social behaviour and thought occur. These categories are summarized in Figure 1.3, but a few words about each one will help clarify their essential nature.

Cognitive Processes

Suppose that you have arranged to meet a friend, and this person is late. In fact, after thirty minutes you begin to suspect that your friend will never arrive. Finally, the person does appear and says, "Sorry... I forgot all about meeting you until a few minutes ago." How will you react? Probably with considerable annoyance. Now imagine that instead, your friend says, "I'm so sorry to be late... There was a big accident, and the traffic was tied up for miles." Now how will you react? Probably with less annoyance—but not necessarily. If your friend is often late and has used this excuse before, you may be suspicious about whether this explanation is true. In contrast, if this is the first time your friend has been late, or if your friend has never used such an excuse in the past, you may accept it as true. In other words, your reactions in this situation will depend strongly upon your memories of your friend's past behaviour and your inferences about whether her or his explanation is really true. Situations like this one call attention to the fact that cognitive processes such as memory, reasoning, judgment and interpretation all play a crucial role in social behaviour.

Biological Factors

Is social behaviour influenced by biological processes and by genetic factors? Fifteen years ago most social psychologists would have answered *no*, at least with regard to genetic factors. Now, however, the pendulum of scientific opinion has swung in the other direction, and many believe that our preferences, behaviours, emotional reactions, and even cognitive abilities are affected to some extent by our biological inheritance (Buss, 1998; Nisbett, 1990).

The view that genetic factors play an important role in social behaviour is represented in social psychology by the **evolutionary perspective** (e.g., Buss, 1995; Buss & Shackelford, 1997a). This perspective suggests that natural selection can play a role in shaping various aspects of social behaviour and social thought as well as physical characteristics. *Natural selection* is the process whereby biological features or patterns of behaviour that help organisms reproduce—get their genes into the next generation—tend to spread throughout a species over time. In essence, if some characteristic that is genetically determined increases the chances that organisms will reproduce, it becomes increasingly common in succeeding generations.

Social psychologists who adopt the evolutionary perspective suggest that this process applies to at least some aspects of social behaviour. For instance, consider the question of mate preference. Evolutionary social psychologists have suggested that our preference for certain physical characteristics in a mate is predetermined by evolved genetic tendencies. The tendency to find features that suggest youth and health more attractive has evolved because it led to the selection of mates who could reproduce and, therefore, pass on that individual's genes—maximizing reproductive success (see Figure 1.4)

The evolutionary perspective has been applied extensively to the area of love relationships and sexual behaviour (as will be evident in Chapter 6 on Relationships). It has also been applied to many other aspects of social behaviour and support for its predictions is being accumulated in many recent studies (e.g., Buss, 1998; Paul, Foss, Buss, 1998). However, confirmation and support for the evolutionary perspective has not been entirely uniform (e.g., Dion & Dion, 1996; Markus & Kitayama, 1996; Tassinary & Hansen, 1998) as we shall see in subsequent sections.

Nonetheless, the evolutionary perspective is compelling and makes many intriguing predictions about social behaviour and thought. It has gained increasing recognition

Evolutionary Social Psychology An area of research that seeks to investigate the potential role of genetic factors in various aspects of social behaviour.

■ Mate preference: Do genetic factors play a role?

FIGURE 1.4 According to the evolutionary perspective, our preference for people with certain characteristics—symmetrical faces, clear skin, shiny hair—may be, in part, genetically determined. Because these characteristics are associated with reproductive capacity, a preference for them helped our ancestors get their genes into the next generation. As a result, we may be biologically "programmed" to find these characteristics attractive. (Recent findings, however, call this reasoning into question.)

in social psychology since the 1980s. Thus, we'll have reason to refer to it at several points in this book.

The Actions and Characteristics of Others

Consider the following incidents:

One second after the traffic light turns green, the driver behind you begins to honk her horn angrily.

Your professor praises a paper you wrote, describing it to the entire class as the best one he's read in several years.

At the beach, a very attractive person on a nearby blanket catches your eye and smiles at you in a very enticing manner.

Will these actions by others have any impact upon your behaviour and thought? Absolutely! So it is clear that often we are strongly affected by the actions of others.

What about the mere appearance of others rather than their actions? Now, be honest: Have you ever felt uneasy in the presence of a disabled person? Do you ever behave differently toward elderly people than toward young ones? Toward persons belonging to various racial and ethnic groups? Toward people higher in status than yourself (e.g., your boss) than toward people lower in status (e.g., children)? Your answer to some of these questions is probably *yes*, for we are often strongly affected by the visible characteristics and appearance of others. These examples illustrate the continuous influence that the presence of other people has on our behaviour, either through their actions or because of our assumptions about them. Such social influence (see Chapter 7) abounds in our everyday lives, but it will become evident that this does not always mean that we are aware of its impact on our behaviour.

Ecological Variables: Impact of the Physical Environment

Do we become more irritable and aggressive when the weather is hot and steamy than when it is cool and comfortable (Anderson, Bushman & Groom, 1997; Cohn & Rotton, 1997)? Does exposure to high levels of noise, particular types of smell (Baron, 1997), or excessive levels of crowding have any impact on whether we are likely to help? Research findings indicate that the physical environment does indeed influence our feelings, thoughts, and behaviour; so ecological variables certainly fall within the realm of modern social psychology.

Cultural Context

Social behaviour, it is important to note, does *not* occur in a cultural vacuum. On the contrary, it is often strongly affected by *cultural norms* (social rules concerning how people should behave in specific situations), membership in various groups, and shifting societal values. Whom should people marry? How many children should they have? Should they keep their emotional reactions to themselves or demonstrate them openly? How close should they stand to others when talking to them? Is it appropriate to offer gifts to professors or public officials? These are only a small sampling of the aspects of social behaviour that can be—and regularly are—influenced by cultural factors. By **culture** we simply mean the organized system of shared meanings, perceptions, and beliefs held by persons belonging to a particular group (Smith & Bond, 1993).

Every day in Canadian cities we encounter people who come from diverse cultural backgrounds. It would be difficult for most Canadians not to be aware of the importance of cultural differences in their interactions with others—and the problems this can sometimes create. Clearly, then, efforts to understand social behaviour must carefully consider cultural factors. If they do not, they stand the very real chance of being what one prominent researcher described as *experiments in a vacuum* (Tajfel,

Culture The organized system of shared meanings, perceptions, and beliefs held by persons belonging to a particular group. This often includes a particular language or system of communication, social customs and organizations, as well as artifacts and artistic products of that group.

1982)—studies that tell us little about social behaviour under real-life conditions and in real-life settings. As we'll discuss below, attention to the effects of cultural factors is an increasingly important trend in modern social psychology, one in which Canadian researchers are on the forefront.

Social Psychology: Summing Up

To conclude: Social psychology focuses mainly on understanding the causes of social behaviour and social thought—on identifying factors that shape our feelings, behaviour, and thought in social situations. It seeks to accomplish this goal through the use of scientific methods, and it takes careful note of the fact that social behaviour and thought are influenced by a wide range of cognitive, biological, social, environmental, and cultural factors.

The remaining chapters of this text are devoted to summarizing some of the key findings of social psychology. This information is naturally interesting to most of us just because we are "social animals," to use Aronson's term (1997). While we're confident you will find much of this material fascinating, we're equally sure it will surprise you. Frequently the findings of social psychology will challenge your current ideas about people and the relationships between them. It is probably safe to predict that after exposure to our field, you'll never think about social relations in quite the same way as before.

KEY POINTS

- *Social psychology* is the scientific field that seeks to understand the nature and causes of individual behaviour and thought in social situations.
- Social psychology is scientific in nature because it adopts the values and methods used in other fields of science.
- Social psychologists adopt the scientific method because "common sense" provides an unreliable guide to social behaviour, and because our thought is influenced by many potential sources of bias.
- Social psychology focuses on the behaviour of individuals and seeks to understand the causes of social behaviour and thought.
- Important causes of social behaviour and thought include cognitive processes, biological factors, other persons, the physical environment, and culture.

RESEARCH METHODS IN SOCIAL PSYCHOLOGY

Now that you know what social psychology is, it is appropriate for us to turn to another essential issue: How do social psychologists attempt to answer questions about social behaviour and social thought? How, in short, do they seek to expand our knowledge of these basic topics? To provide you with a useful overview of this process, we will touch on three related issues. First, we will describe *key methods of research* in social psychology. Then we will discuss the criteria used to *choose a methodology*. Finally, we will consider some of the complex *ethical issues* that arise in social psychological research and that, to a degree, are unique to such research.

Systematic Observation: Describing the World

One basic technique for studying social behaviour is *systematic observation*—carefully observing behaviour it as it occurs. Such observation is not the kind of informal observation we all practise from childhood on. Rather, in a scientific field such as social psychology, it is careful observation, maintaining the four core scientific values described above (accuracy, objectivity, skepticism, and open-mindedness). For example, suppose that a social psychologist wanted to find out how frequently people touch one another in different settings. The researcher could study this topic by going to shopping malls, airports, college campuses, and many other settings and observing, in those settings, who touches whom, how they touch, and with what frequency (see Figure 1.5). Such research (which has actually been conducted—see Chapter 2), would be employing what is known as **naturalistic observation**—observation of behaviour in natural settings (Linden, 1992a). Note that in such observation, the researcher would simply notice what was happening in various contexts; she or he would make no attempt to change the behaviour of the subjects being observed. In fact, such observation requires that the researcher take great pains to avoid influencing the persons in any way. Thus, the researcher would try to be as inconspicuous as possible, and might even take advantage of any naturally occurring barriers to prevent being noticed.

In recent years, social psychologists have been more frequently involved in *field research* (i.e., outside the laboratory); investigating other cultures (in *cross-cultural psychology*), or real world problems (in *applied social psychology*). It is particularly important in such areas that we understand the context and behaviour *as it naturally occurs* with little or no intervention by the researcher. For example, if as an outsider you wanted to understand violence in sports, you would do well to initially stand back and observe or read others' descriptions of this topic. *Descriptive* methods, such as observation, and the more qualitative (less numerical) data that is sometimes produced, can provide an initial broad understanding of these new social contexts. It can be useful in orienting a researcher to the important social psychological factors that need to be considered. Eventually, however, social psychologists will usually want to go beyond description to *prediction* of the relationships between events and this is where the correlational method comes in.

Naturalistic Observation A method of research in which behaviour is systematically observed in a natural setting, with the minimum amount of impact on the behaviour being observed. This method is more likely to produce descriptive data.

■ Naturalistic observation in operation

FIGURE 1.5 How frequently do people touch one another in public places? Who touches whom, and how? One way to find out would be to perform research employing naturalistic observation.

Correlation: Predicting Relationships

At various times, you have probably noticed that some events appear to be related to each other: as one changes, the other appears to change, too. For example, you might have thought you noticed that high temperatures and irritable driving (or "road rage") seem to coincide, or that your team always wins when you wear your red shirt. If your observations are correct and the two events really are related in this way, we say that they are *correlated* or that a correlation exists between them. The term *correlation* refers to a tendency for one aspect of the world to change as the other changes. Social psychologists refer to such changeable aspects of the world as *variables*, because they can take different values, so we'll use that term from now on.

From the point of view of science, the existence of a correlation between two variables can be very useful. This is so because when a correlation exists, it is possible to predict one variable from information about one or more other variables. The ability to make such *pre-*

dictions is one important goal of all branches of science, including social psychology. For instance, suppose that a correlation was observed between certain patterns of behaviour in married couples (e.g., the tendency to criticize each other harshly) and the likelihood that they would later divorce. This correlation could be very useful in predicting which couples might run into problems in their relationships and, further, it could be helpful in counselling such persons if they were attempting to save their relationship. (See Chapter 6 for a discussion of why long-term relationships sometimes fail.)

How accurately can such predictions be made? The stronger the correlation between the variables in question, the more accurate the predictions. Correlations can range from 0 to -1.00 or +1.00; the greater the departure from 0, the stronger the correlation. Positive numbers mean that as one variable increases, the other increases too. Negative numbers indicate that as one variable increases, the other decreases. For instance, there is a negative correlation between age and the amount of hair on the heads of males: the older men grow, the less hair they have.

These basic facts underlie an important method of research sometimes used by social psychologists: the **correlational method**. In this approach, social psychologists attempt to determine whether, and to what extent, different variables are related to each other. This involves making careful observations of each variable, and then performing appropriate statistical tests to determine whether and to what degree the variables are correlated. Perhaps a concrete example will help illustrate the nature of this research method.

Imagine that a social psychologist has reason to believe that the higher the temperature, the more irritable people become, and hence the greater the likelihood that they will be aggressive to others. How could research on this **hypothesis**—an as-yet-unverified prediction—be conducted? While many possibilities exist, a very basic approach would go something like this. The researcher might obtain records of daily temperatures in many different cities (one variable) and records of the number of violent crimes such as assaults and murders in these locations (the other variable). This special type of correlational method is called *archival research*, because the investigator looks in the archives, public records, for evidence of correlation. If a positive correlation were obtained, the researcher would have some evidence for a relationship between temperature and violence.

Now for the most important point: Suppose that the researcher found such a correlation (e.g., a correlation of +.26 between temperature and violent crimes); what

Correlational Method A method of research in which a scientist systematically observes two or more variables to determine whether changes in one are accompanied by changes in the other.

Hypothesis An as-yet-unverified prediction based on a theory.

■ Correlation does not equal causation

FIGURE 1.6 When one event precedes another, it is sometimes tempting to assume that the first event caused the second. As you can see from this cartoon, however, such assumptions are often on shaky ground.

could she or he conclude? That high temperatures cause violence? Perhaps; but this conclusion, reasonable as it may seem, may be totally false. Here's why: *The fact that two variables are correlated, even highly correlated, does not guarantee that there is a causal link between them—that changes in one* cause *changes in the other.* The correlation between the variables may be due to chance or random factors, as shown in Figure 1.6. In many other cases, a correlation between variables simply reflects the fact that changes in both are related to a third variable. For example, it may well be the case that as temperatures rise, individuals drink more alcohol in an effort to reduce their discomfort. It may be this factor—consumption of alcohol—rather than high temperature that actually causes an increase in aggression. In other words, alcohol consumption is related both to high temperatures (it rises as temperatures go up) and to increased aggression, but there is in fact no direct link between temperatures and violence. Research on this issue has been carried out (e.g., Anderson, Bushman, & Groom, 1997; Cohn & Rotton, 1997).

This inability to infer *causal* relationships between variables from correlational data is a major drawback for researchers. Despite this, the correlational method of research is often very useful. It can be used in natural settings, where *experimentation* would be difficult, impossible (e.g., studying passionate love), or unethical (e.g., studying the effects of emotional neglect on children's social development). Further, the correlational method is often highly efficient: a large amount of information can be obtained in a relatively short period of time. **Questionnaires** are frequently used for this purpose. The researcher carefully constructs a series of questions which are usually answered either using a *rating-scale* (where subjects circle a number or a word on the scale to indicate their answers) or in an *open-ended* manner (where subjects give the answer in their own words).

However, the fact that correlation is not conclusive with respect to cause-and-effect relationships is a serious disadvantage—one that often leads social psychologists to prefer a different method. It is to this approach that we turn next.

Questionnaires The researcher carefully constructs a series of questions which subjects will answer in an open-ended manner or using a rating scale. Questionnaires are often part of correlational research.

> ## KEY POINTS
>
> - In *systematic observation*, behaviour is carefully observed and recorded, providing a description of the world. *Naturalistic observation* involves observation conducted in the settings where the behaviour naturally occurs and with a minimum impact on the setting.
> - This method can be useful when researchers are venturing into a new field and do not wish to make too many assumptions about it.
> - In the *correlational method*, researchers measure two or more variables to determine if they are related to one another in any way. This enables us to predict one variable from information about the other.
> - The existence of even strong correlations between variables does not indicate that they are causally related to each other.

The Experimental Method: Causation and Explanation

As we have just seen, the correlational method of research is very useful from the point of view of one important goal of science: the ability to make accurate predictions. It is less useful, though, from the point of view of reaching yet another goal: *explanation.* Scientists do not merely wish to *describe* the world and *predict* relationships between variables: they want to be able to _explain_ these relationships, too. For instance, continuing with the heat-and-aggression example used above, if a link between high temperatures and crimes of violence exists, social psychologists would want to know _why_ this is so. Do high temperatures make people irritable? Do they reduce restraints against harming others? Do they get more people out on the street so that there is a greater chance people will get into fights?

In order to attain the goal of explanation, social psychologists employ a method of research known as **experimentation** or the **experimental method**. This methodology can indicate _causal_ relationships between variables and, therefore, can take the researcher one step nearer to explaining social behaviour.

Experimentation: Its Basic Nature

In its most basic form, the experimental method involves two key steps: (1) _systematic alteration_ of the presence or strength of some variable believed to affect an aspect of social behaviour or thought, and (2) _careful measurement_ of the effects of such alterations (if any). The factor systematically altered, or varied, by the researcher is termed the **independent variable**, while the aspect of behaviour measured is termed the **dependent variable**. In a simple experiment, then, different groups of participants are exposed to contrasting levels of the independent variable (such as low, moderate, and high). The researcher then carefully measures the participants' behaviour to determine whether it does in fact vary with these changes in the independent variable. If it does—and if two other conditions are also met—the researcher can tentatively conclude that the independent variable does indeed _cause_ changes in the aspect of behaviour being studied.

In an experiment on heat and aggression, the researcher could arrange for participants in the study to come to a laboratory where she or he could control the temperature (and perhaps other environmental variables as well). Temperature would then be systematically varied so that, for example, some participants in the study are exposed to comfortable conditions (temperatures of 21 to 22 degrees Celsius), others to moderately hot conditions (temperatures of 27 to 28 degrees Celsius), and still others to very hot conditions (temperatures of 32 to 33 degrees Celsius). At the same time, some measure of participants' irritability or tendency to aggress against others would also be obtained. For instance, the researcher could arrange for participants to be annoyed in some way by an assistant and then ask participants to rate this person's performance, explaining that low

Experimentation (experimental method) A method of research in which an experimenter systematically changes one or more factors (the independent variables) to determine whether such variations affect one or more other factors (dependent variables).

Independent Variable The variable that is systematically varied by the researcher in an experiment.

Dependent Variable The variable that is measured in an experiment. In social psychology, the dependent variable is some aspect of social behaviour or social thought.

■ Experimentation: A simple example

FIGURE 1.7 In this experiment participants in three different conditions were exposed to contrasting temperatures: 21–22, 27–28, and 32–33 degrees Celsius. They were annoyed by an assistant, then given an opportunity to aggress against this person. Results indicated that as temperatures rose, aggression increased. This finding provided evidence for the existence of a causal link between temperature and aggression.

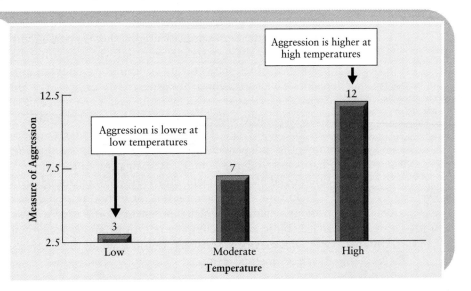

ratings would cause the assistant to lose her or his job. If results now looked like those in Figure 1.7, the researcher could conclude, at least tentatively, that high temperatures do indeed increase aggression. It's important to note that in experimentation such knowledge is obtained through direct intervention: temperature—the independent variable—is systematically changed by the researcher. In the correlational method, in contrast, variables are *not* altered in this manner; rather, naturally occurring changes in them are simply observed and recorded.

Incidentally, experiments of the type we have just described have actually been conducted. In fact, they were among the very first research studies carried out by Professor Baron (e.g., Baron, 1972a) and started a line of investigation in social psychology that has continued up to the present time (e.g., Anderson et al., 1997).

Experimentation: Two Requirements for its Success

Earlier we referred to two conditions that must be met before a researcher can conclude that changes in an independent variable have caused changes in a dependent variable. Let's consider these conditions now. The first involves what is termed **random assignment of participants to experimental conditions**. This requirement means that all participants in an experiment must have an equal chance of being exposed to each level of the independent variable. The reason for this rule is simple: If participants are not randomly assigned to each condition, it may later be impossible to determine if differences in their behaviour stem from differences they brought with them to the study, or from the impact of the independent variable, or from both. If the researcher happened to run high and low temperature conditions at different times of day—perhaps the high temperature condition in the afternoon when subjects were tired and hungry and the low temperature condition in mid-morning—then it would be difficult to tell if tiredness or temperature was responsible for the results. If, in contrast, subjects who came at either time were randomly assigned to the temperature conditions, there would be equal numbers in each condition, "cancelling out" any effects of tiredness on the results. Then any differences between the low- and high-temperature conditions could still be attributed to temperature.

The second condition essential for successful experimentation is as follows: Insofar as is possible, *all extraneous factors must be held constant*. What this means is that any other factors (apart from the independent variable) that might also affect participants' behaviour should be held at a constant level in all experimental conditions. To see why this is so, consider what will happen if, for the sake of convenience, the high and low temperature conditions are held in different laboratories. It just happens that in the high-temperature lab there is harsh lighting and an ugly pattern on the walls, but in the low-temperature lab there is softer lighting and decor. Once again, those in the high-temperature condition are more aggressive. What is the cause of this result? The aggression-increasing effects of heat, the annoying decor or possibly both factors? Once again, we can't tell; and since we can't, the value of the experiment as a source of new information about human behaviour is greatly reduced. In situations like this, and when subject characteristics have not been randomly assigned to conditions, the independent variable is said to be *confounded* with another variable—one that is not under systematic investigation in the study. When **confounding** occurs, the findings of an experiment may be largely meaningless (see Figure 1.8).

In sum, experimentation is, in several respects, the crown jewel among social psychology's methods. When experimentation is used with skill and care, it can yield results that help us answer complex questions about social behaviour and social thought. So why, you may be wondering, isn't it used all the time? As you will see below there is no "perfect" methodology.

Random Assignment of Participants to Experimental Conditions All participants in an experiment must have an equal chance of being exposed to each level of the independent variable. This ensures that differences subjects bring with them to the study are equally distributed across experimental conditions and so cannot bias results.

Confounding Confusions that occur when factors other than the independent variable in the experiment vary across experimental conditions. When confounding of variables occurs, it is impossible to determine whether results stem from the effects of the independent variable or from the effects of other variables.

FIGURE 1.8 In the experiment illustrated here, temperature—the independent variable—is confounded with another variable: the type of decor. As a result of this it is impossible to tell whether any differences between the behaviour of subjects in these two conditions stems from the independent variable, the confounding variable, or both.

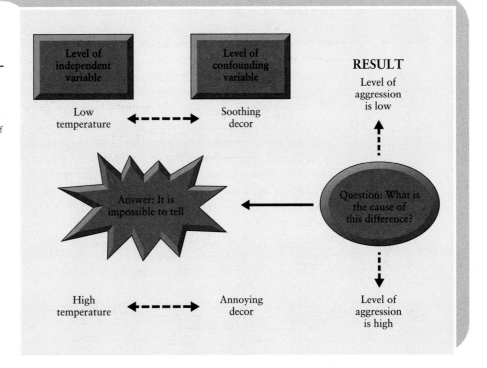

Choosing a Methodology: Description, Prediction, or Causation?

It is clear that social psychologists are faced with a wide choice of possible methods for exploring social behaviour. How is such a choice made? Unfortunately there is no easy answer—each method has its advantages and limitations. In general, descriptive research such as *systematic observation* has the advantage of involving very little intervention in the natural setting—social behaviour is observed as it spontaneously occurs in the real world. As we discussed earlier, this type of method can sometimes provide an initial overview of a behaviour in a particular social context which can be useful. The disadvantage of this type of method is that it can be particularly vulnerable to biased interpretation of data. As we will see in later chapters, a common tendency is for people to process incoming information in such a way that it is seen as supporting their expectations or beliefs. This is termed the confirmation bias—and researchers are also subject to it. Data that is descriptive, particularly when it is qualitative rather than quantitative, can more easily be interpreted to support a researcher's theory, even though he or she may be attempting to adhere to scientific principles and values.

Correlational research usually shares with descriptive research the advantage of minimal interference in the natural setting and spontaneous behaviour. Indeed there is much overlap between these two methodologies—the more quantitative type of observational research can produce correlational data. Correlation has the added benefit that if two variables are found to be related then one can be *predicted* from the other. As mentioned previously, correlational methods can produce a large quantity of data efficiently through the use, for example, of questionnaires. However this methodology has the limitation that the wording of questions can exert a strong bias on the outcomes

Confirmation Bias
The tendency to notice and remember mainly information that lends support to our views.

obtained. For example, when asked to indicate how satisfied they are with their current jobs, more than 85 percent of persons indicate that they are "satisfied" or "very satisfied." When asked whether they would choose the same job or career again, however, less than 50 percent indicate agreement. So, as experts in constructing survey questionnaires well know, it's often true that "the way you ask the question determines the answer you get." Finally, one disadvantage should be very clear to you by now—correlational research cannot provide causal information.

Experimentation has the major advantage of being able to demonstrate that one variable can *cause* changes in another and this provides greater explanatory power. Researchers can have greater control, particularly in the laboratory setting, in avoiding the *confounding* of variables, and greater precision of measurement. This allows increased confidence in the interpretation of results. Though experimentation does not, in general, suffer from the problems mentioned in relation to observation and correlation, it isn't perfect. For example, because it is often conducted in laboratory settings that are somewhat artificial and quite different from the locations in which social behaviour actually occurs, the question of **external validity** often arises—to what extent can the findings of experiments be generalized to real-life social situations and perhaps to persons different from those who participated in the research?

External Validity The extent to which findings from research can be generalized to the real world.

Another possible limitation of experimentation research is the ethical restraints that researchers are subject to. Ethical factors may prevent a researcher from conducting a study that is in fact feasible. In other words, the study could be conducted, but doing so would violate ethical standards accepted by scientists or society. Suppose, for example, that a researcher has good reason to believe that certain kinds of cigarette ads increase teenagers' tendency to start smoking. Could the researcher ethically conduct an experiment on this topic, exposing some teenagers to lots of these ads and others to none and then comparing their rates of smoking? In principle, such research is possible; but no ethical social psychologist would perform it, because it might harm some of the participants in serious ways.

It is partly because of these and related problems that social psychologists often turn from experimentation to systematic observation and the correlational method in their research. So, to underline a point: All research methods offer a mixed bag of advantages and disadvantages, and a social psychologists will choose the method that seems best for studying a particular topic or question at that time. Furthermore, it is advantageous to replicate research using a number of different methodologies and both real world (or *field*) settings as well as laboratory. It is a rule of scientific research that one study is never enough to confirm a hypothesis—there is always the possibility of some error in the research design or simply that results occurred by chance. For this reason, *replication* is always needed and confirmation through different methods can increase confidence in a researchers' conclusions. The section that follows—Canadian Research: On the Cutting Edge—illustrates some of the points we have made above in the context of research on the planning fallacy.

error

The Planning Fallacy: Why is Our Timing So Often Wrong?

Try to remember the last time you worked on a major project (for instance, a term paper). Did it take more time or less time to complete than you originally estimated? Probably, your answer is "More time...of course!" In predicting how long a given task will take, people tend to be overly optimistic; they predict that they can get the job done much sooner than actually turns out to be the case. Or, turning this around somewhat, they expect to get more done in a given period of time than they really can. You can probably recognize this tendency in your own thinking. So this tendency to make optimistic predictions about how long a given task will take—a tendency known as the **planning fallacy**—is both powerful and widespread. What features of social thought account for this common error?

Planning Fallacy
The tendency to make optimistic predictions concerning how long a given task will take for completion.

According to Canadian researcher Roger Buehler and his colleagues (Buehler, Griffin, & Ross, 1994), who have studied this tendency in detail, several factors play a role. One is that when individuals make predictions about how long it will take them to complete a given task, they enter a *planning* or *narrative* mode of thought in which they focus primarily on the future: how they will perform the task. This, in turn, prevents them from looking backward in time and remembering how long similar tasks took them in the past. As a result, one important reality check that might help them avoid being overly optimistic is removed. In addition, when individuals do consider past experience in which tasks took longer than expected, such outcomes are attributed to factors *outside their control*. The result: They fail to learn from previous experience, tending to overlook important potential obstacles, and so fall prey to the planning fallacy. These predictions have been con-

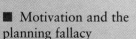

■ Motivation and the planning fallacy

FIGURE 1.9 As predicted individuals who expected a tax refund, and therefore had stronger motivation to file their forms, showed the planning fallacy to a greater extent than persons who were not expecting a refund.

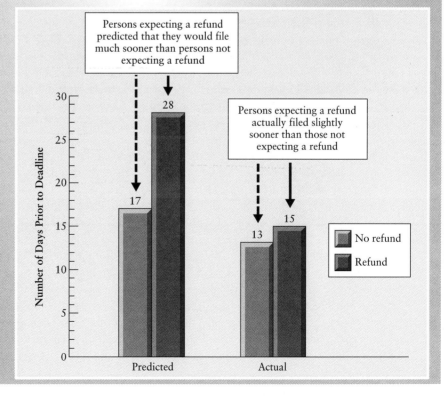

Persons expecting a refund predicted that they would file much sooner than persons not expecting a refund

Persons expecting a refund actually filed slightly sooner than those not expecting a refund

28
17
13
15

No refund
Refund

Number of Days Prior to Deadline

Predicted   Actual

firmed in several studies (e.g., Buehler et al., 1994), so they seem to provide important insights into the origins of the tendency to make optimistic predictions about task completion.

This is not the entire story, though. A recent study suggests that another factor may play an important role in the planning fallacy: *motivation* to complete a task. When predicting what will happen, individuals often guess that what will happen is what they *want* to happen (e.g., Johnson & Sherman, 1990). In cases where people are strongly motivated to complete a task, therefore, they make over-optimistic predictions concerning when this desired state of affairs will occur. To test the role of motivation in the planning fallacy, Buehler, Griffin, and MacDonald (1997) conducted a series of ingenious studies that illustrate the use of both field and laboratory-based methodologies.

Their first study was a *natural experiment*, in which they took advantage of a naturally occurring variation in the motivation to file your taxes on time—whether or not you expect to receive a refund! Buehler and his colleagues reasoned that persons expecting a *refund* would have a stronger motivation to complete their forms, and so would be overly optimistic about when they would file them—they would show the planning fallacy more often. The *independent variable* in such a study is motivation, which is determined by whether subjects expect to receive a refund (higher motivation) or not (lower motivation). Notice that in this natural experiment, the experimenters do not set the different levels of the independent variable—this occurs naturally in the field. The *dependent variable* in this study is the extent of over-optimism about the time of filing: measured as the difference between subjects' predictions of when they will file and the actual times of filing. The researcher phoned people chosen at random from the Vancouver telephone directory and asked them whether they expected to receive an income tax refund. Then they asked these individuals when, relative to the deadline, they expected to mail in their tax forms. Later, one week after the actual deadlines for submitting the forms, the researchers phoned the same persons again and asked them to indicate when their tax forms had actually been mailed.

As you can see from Figure 1.9, while all persons surveyed showed the planning fallacy, those who expected a refund were much more optimistic in their predictions than those who did not. People expecting refunds estimated that they would submit their forms 28 days before the deadline, whereas those not expecting refunds estimated that they would submit the forms about 17 days before the deadline. Both groups actually submitted their forms later than they predicted—about 15 days in advance for those expecting a refund and 13 days in advance for those not expecting one. The more motivated subjects showed a stronger planning fallacy.

Natural experiments are also sometimes called *quasi-experiments* because they do not fulfill the requirements of a true experiment. In particular, subjects in such studies are *not* randomly assigned to conditions (in this case refund or no refund). Further, there is *no* possibility of holding extraneous factors constant. Thus, the possibility of *confounding* is very high—another variable might have been varied, along with the independent variable (motivation), that could explain differences in the degree of planning fallacy over the two conditions. Perhaps the greater optimism shown has nothing to do with motivation, but is somehow a characteristic of the refund group to a greater extent than the no-refund group. Maybe the refund group typically shows overly optimistic financial planning, is therefore poorer, and is more likely to be receiving a tax or GST refund. Because such interpretation is *possible* (however far-fetched) cause-effect relationships between motivation and the planning fallacy are uncertain. For this reason, Buehler and his colleagues replicated their study in a *laboratory experiment*, using a different context for time predictions (completion of word puzzles), and using a monetary incentive for increasing motivation. Results once again indicated that those who were motivated to complete the task faster showed the planning fallacy to a greater degree. Further, researchers in this second study were able to check on the cognitions of their subjects while they were making their predictions. Those who were highly motivated to finish quickly tended to think less about past relevant experience, or to discount it, and tended to focus on the future, ignoring any impediments to completion.

To repeat points made in the previous sections: the planning fallacy studies provide an example of replication and use of a variety of methods and research contexts. The use of both field and laboratory studies to examine the planning fallacy serves to strengthen our confidence in results. While the word puzzle completion task is somewhat artificial and raises questions about *external validity*, the greater control over possible confounding in this laboratory experiment provides greater confidence that motivation plays a *causal* role in the planning fallacy. In contrast, the field study had great realism (most of us have been, or will be, motivated to complete our tax forms as soon as possible) and therefore high *external validity*, but provided less convincing causal evidence.

These results indicate that the planning fallacy can be caused by heightened motivation and that cognitions mediate this effect. In other words, individuals' estimates of when they will complete a task are influenced by their hopes and desires: they want to finish early, so they ignore past experience or future problems, and predict that they will do so. Sad to relate, however, this appears to be one of the many situations in life where wishing does not necessarily make it so. Even sadder, the planning fallacy is merely one of the cognitive biases that can lead us astray. More of such biases will be discussed in Chapter 2.

KEY POINTS

- *Experimentation* involves systematically altering one or more variables (*independent* variables) in order to determine whether these alterations affect some aspect of behaviour (*dependent* variable).

- Successful use of the experimental method requires *random assignment of participants to experimental conditions*; it also requires that the experimenter *hold constant all other factors* that might also influence behaviour so as to avoid confounding of variables.

- Advantages of systematic observation are that it can provide an initial *description* of social behaviour and that it does not interfere with behaviour as it naturally occurs. A disadvantage is that the qualitative data it often produces is vulnerable to the *confirmation bias*—a tendency to bias interpretations of information in the direction of one's expectations or beliefs.

- The correlational method has the advantage of allowing *prediction* of one variable from information about another. It also often allows us to investigate efficiently topics that are not accessible to experimentation. Its major disadvantage is that it does not allow researcher to draw causal conclusions.

- Experimentation does allow causal conclusions to be drawn and aids explanation of behaviour. However, sometimes the context of experiments is artificial, raising questions about their results' *external validity*—the extent to which findings can be generalized to the real world situation.

- Because each method has its limitations, it is recommended that replication of studies should take place using a wide range of methods.

- Using both field and laboratory methods, Beuhler and colleagues investigated our tendency to make overly optimistic predictions about how long it will take us to complete a given task, an effect known as the *planning fallacy*. It seems to stem from a focus on the future while ignoring related past events, and from motivation to have tasks completed quickly.

Ethics in Research: Consideration of Subject Rights

Deception A technique whereby researchers withhold information about the purposes or procedures of a study from persons participating in it. Deception is used in situations in which information about such matters might be expected to change subjects' behaviour, thus invalidating the results of the research.

In their use of experimentation and systematic observation, and in their reliance on comprehensive theories, social psychologists do not differ from researchers in many other fields. One technique, however, does seem to be unique to research in social psychology: **deception**. Basically, this technique involves efforts by researchers to withhold or conceal information about the purposes of a study from the persons who participate in it. The reason for using this procedure is simple: If participants know the true purposes of an investigation, their behaviour will be changed by that knowledge. The research itself will then have little chance of providing useful information.

For example, imagine that in a study designed to examine the effects of physical attractiveness on helping behaviour, participants are informed of this purpose. Will they now react differently to a highly attractive stranger than they would have in the absence of this information? Probably so; they will lean over backward to avoid being more helpful to the attractive person, to prove that they are not affected by a stranger's outward appearance.

Because of such considerations, many social psychologists believe that deception—at least on a temporary basis—is essential for their research (Suls & Rosnow, 1988). Adopting this technique is not, however, without its costs. Deceiving research participants or withholding information from them, no matter how justified, raises important ethical issues (Baumrind, 1985).

First, deception, even when temporary, may result in some type of harm to the persons exposed to it. They may experience discomfort, stress, or negative shifts in self-esteem. Second, it is possible that at least some individuals exposed to deception will resent having been led astray. They may then adopt a negative attitude toward social research generally or become suspicious of researchers (Epley & Huff, 1998; Kelman, 1967).

In short, the use of deception does pose something of a dilemma to social psychologists. On the one hand, it seems essential to their research. On the other, its use raises serious problems. How can this issue be resolved? While opinion remains somewhat divided, most social psychologists agree on the following points. First, deception should never be used to persuade people to take part in a study; withholding information or providing misleading information about what will happen in an experiment in order to induce people to take part in it is definitely not acceptable (Sigall, 1997). Second, most social psychologists agree that temporary deception is acceptable provided two basic safeguards are employed. These are **informed consent** and thorough **debriefing**. (Both procedures, by the way, are required by ethical standards published by the American Psychological Association, the professional organization for both U.S. and Canadian psychologists.)

Informed Consent A procedure by which subjects are told in advance about the activities they will perform during an experiment. The subjects then take part in the study only if they are willing to engage in such activities.

Debriefing An explanation at the conclusion of a research session in which participants are given full information about the nature of the research and the hypothesis or hypotheses under investigation.

Informed consent involves providing research participants with an as full as possible description of the procedures to be followed *prior* to their decision to participate in the study. By following this principle, researchers ensure that subjects know what they are getting into and what they will be asked to do before making a commitment to participate. In contrast, debriefing *follows* each experimental session. It consists of providing participants with a full explanation of all major aspects of a study, including its true goals and an explanation of the need for temporary deception. The guiding principle is that research participants should leave in at least as favourable or positive a state as when they arrived.

Fortunately, a growing body of evidence indicates that, together, informed consent and thorough debriefing can eliminate—or at least substantially reduce—the potential dangers of deception and any negative effects that might be experienced (Smith & Richardson, 1985). For example, most subjects view temporary deception as acceptable, do not resent its use and continue to have positive views of research

(Rogers, 1980, Sharpe, Adair & Roese, 1992). Still, it is unwise to take the safety or appropriateness of deception for granted (Rubin, 1985). Rather, it appears that the guiding principles for all researchers planning to use this procedure in their studies should be these: (1) Use deception only when it is absolutely essential to do so—when no other means for conducting a study exist; (2) always proceed with great caution; and (3) make certain that the rights, safety, and well-being of research participants come first, ahead of all other considerations.

KEY POINTS

- *Deception* involves efforts by social psychologists to withhold or conceal information about the purposes of a study from participants.
- Most social psychologists believe that temporary deception is often necessary in order to obtain valid research results.
- However, they view deception as acceptable only when important safeguards are employed: *informed consent* and thorough *debriefing*.

THE PROGRESS OF SOCIAL PSYCHOLOGY: ITS ORIGINS AND TRENDS

In order to understand the state of social psychology today we must understand its roots and the way in which it has progressed. However, any attempt to present a complete survey of the historical roots of social psychology would quickly bog us down in endless lists of names and dates. Because we definitely wish to avoid that pitfall, this discussion will be quite limited in scope, confined to developments in social psychology since the 1930s, when the modern form of social psychology began to emerge and was shaped by the times in which those early social psychologists lived.

Modern Social Psychology Emerges: The 1930s

If anyone is identified as the founder of social psychology it is Kurt Lewin who began his academic career in Germany, the birthplace of psychology as a whole. The development of social psychology might have been very different if Lewin, who was Jewish, had not been forced to leave Germany in the 1930s with the rise of the Nazi regime. He moved to the United States where the field of psychology was expanding tremendously, and was responsible for stimulating interest in social psychology, as well as enthusing a younger generation of researchers. Lewin focused on the conjunction of theory and research in our efforts to understand social behaviour. He developed his general theory of social influence (*field theory*), carried out both laboratory and field studies to test its generality, and then went on to apply his ideas to the solution of real world problems, such as community relations and working in groups (Lewin, Lippitt, & White, 1939). Quite apart from his own research, Lewin's influence on social psychology was profound, since many of his students went on to become very prominent in the field. Their names (e.g., Leon Festinger, Harold Kelley, Morton Deutsch, Stanley Schachter, John Thibaut) will feature prominently in later sections of this text. Another important milestone in the 1930s was the work of Muzafer Sherif (1935). He studied the nature and impact of

■ Extremists: Do they share certain traits?

FIGURE 1.10 Prejudice leads those who hold it to reject the members of some group simply because they belong to that group.

social norms—rules indicating how individuals ought to behave in social situations—and so contributed many insights to our understanding of pressures toward conformity. The pattern of research established by these two influential figures, combining theory development, scientific research, and the application of social psychology, is one that is reflected in current social psychology, as we shall see throughout the book.

In these years Canadian psychology was not as developed as in the United States and researchers were mostly involved in applied research. They were, for example, instrumental in developing methods for selection and classification of military personnel in wartime. This concern with applications also produced some of the first truly social psychological research in Canada—at McGill University, into the psychological effects of unemployment during the depression years, and in Toronto, into family relationships (Wright & Myers, 1982). As you can see, the early direction and focus of social psychology was very much influenced by the trends and problems of those times.

Social Psychology's Youth: The 1940s, 1950s, and 1960s

After a pause resulting from World War II, social psychology continued its growth during the late 1940s and the 1950s. During this period, the field expanded in several directions. Following Lewin's lead, researchers focused on the influence that groups and group membership exert on individual behaviour (Forsyth, 1992). And they examined the link between various personality traits and social behaviour, in, for example, noted research on the *authoritarian personality*—a cluster of traits that predispose individuals toward acceptance of extreme political ideologies such as Nazism (Adorno, et al., 1950; see Figure 1.10). Research on this issue continues to the present day in Canada (Altemeyer, 1981, 1988). Another of the significant events of this period was the development of the theory of *cognitive dissonance* (Festinger, 1957). This theory proposed that human beings dislike, and will strive to eliminate, inconsistency between their attitudes or inconsistency between their attitudes and their behaviour. While this theory alone had tremendous influence, it also signaled the beginning of an increased interest in social cognition.

The 1960s can be viewed as the time when social psychology came of age in the United States. During this turbulent decade of rapid social change, the number of social psychologists rose dramatically in Canada, Europe, and the United States, and the scope of social psychology virtually exploded. The field expanded to include practically every aspect of social interaction you might imagine. Most of the major lines of research, each represented by a chapter in this book, either began or developed during these years. In Canada, Wallace Lambert of McGill University produced his groundbreaking research on bilingualism and French immersion as we will describe in Chapter 10 (Lambert, 1967; Lambert, Gardner, Barik & Tunstall, 1963). Other Canadian social psychologists were also beginning to publish research that would later develop a distinctly Canadian flavour (e.g., Berry, 1967; Taylor & Gardner, 1969).

An Identity Crisis: The 1970s

turning pt.

The rapid pace of change did not slacken during the 1970s; if anything, it accelerated. Certainly, it was in the 1970s that Canadian social psychology fully came into its own, as researchers began to examine issues relevant to Canadian society. For example, the beginning of research on cross-cultural psychology and bilingualism had particular relevance to the development of Canada's multiculturalism policy, which was introduced in 1971. On the international front, Canadian research contributed to the expansion of many lines of study begun during the 1960s.

An important event for social psychology, beginning in this decade, was an "identity crisis" that raised basic questions about the direction of both theory and research. This crisis originated within the broader social psychological community, but was particularly strongly pursued in Europe and Canada (Israel & Tajfel, 1972; Moghaddam, 1990; Moscovici, 1972; Strickland, Aboud & Gergen, 1974; Taylor & Brown, 1979). It has been suggested that social psychology might have been responding to the social and political upheavals of the late 1960s with an ideological revolution of its own (Steiner, 1974), as well as attempting to counter the United States' domination of the field (Moghaddam, 1990).

Whatever its origins, the questions raised by this crisis alerted social psychologists to some issues of continuing importance. For example, questions were raised about whether social psychological findings were *culture-biased* because they had been largely produced in one culture—Western culture, particularly the United States (Berry, 1978). A second, and related, criticism pointed out that social psychology had tended to neglect the importance of *societal-level processes* such as cultural differences and inter-group relations (Israel & Tajfel, 1972; Taylor & Brown, 1979). A third major area of criticism involved *methodological issues*. Social psychological research has predominantly taken place in university laboratories using students as subjects, and critics questioned whether the artificial setting of a laboratory and the over-use of student subjects could produce findings that reflected the scope of real-world social behaviour (Harre & Secord, 1972; Sears, 1986). The implications of these issues continue to be debated to the present day, and the effects of the crisis can be seen in the development of topics such as cross-cultural psychology and inter-group relations. Researchers began to recognize that there was a need to increase the amount of field research, to study the behaviour of people in real-life situations as well as in the laboratory. It should be noted that laboratory research remains the dominant methodology in social psychology (Sears, 1986).

A Maturing Field: The 1980s and 1990s

As often happens following a crisis, social psychology emerged stronger and more vibrant as we moved towards the end of the century. By the 1980s, social psychology had proved itself a major player in the world of psychology—academic and student interest in this topic continued to grow. Another measure of the strength of a science is its utility: the extent to which it can be applied to real-world problems. It was in the 1980s and 90s that social psychology returned to its roots in Lewin's research and began to be widely applied. As we will describe below, the application of social psychology has expanded tremendously. Many university researchers in these decades began to extend their research interests into applied areas of social psychology. Finally, the past two decades have also been marked by the development of strong social psychological communities in countries other than the United States. In terms of the amount of research and number of researchers, the U.S. continues to dominate the world of social psychology—to be what Moghaddam (1987, 1990) called the "first world" of psychology. However, increasingly other sources of research and theory are becoming important, with the expansion of social psychology in other Western (e.g., Canada, Australia, European), as well as non-Western nations (e.g., India, Japan). This worldwide expansion has fueled interest in cross-cultural psychology (Smith & Bond, 1998; Segall, Dasen, Berry & Poortinga, 1999) and ensured that our understanding of social behaviour is beginning to have a truly international flavor.

Current and Future Trends: Beyond 2000

Earlier, we noted that the major purpose of this chapter is providing you with a framework for understanding the big picture—what social psychology is all about and how it "does its thing." Continuing with this theme, we'll now attempt to capture the current state of social psychology and trends for the future. These trends play an important role in shaping the questions and topics social psychologists study and the methods they choose for their research. Thus, they have guided the work we'll describe in the rest of this book. Four issues seem especially worthy of our attention.

■ Cognitive factors: A key determinant of social behaviour

FIGURE 1.11 Why do individuals sometimes suddenly explode and attack people with whom they have worked for years? One important cause of such behaviour is the persons' belief that they have been treated unfairly. Thus, cognitive factors play a key role in workplace violence, just as they do in virtually all forms of social behaviour.

Influence of the Cognitive Perspective

認知的

In recent decades research on the cognitive side of social psychology has grown dramatically in scope and importance. Perhaps two major focuses of this research are most representative. First, social psychologists have attempted to apply basic knowledge about *memory, reasoning, decision-making,* and *interpretation* to a broad range of social behaviours. Results of such work suggest that our thoughts about other persons and social situations play a key role in virtually *all* forms of social behaviour—from love and sexual attraction on the one hand through conflict and violence on the other. For instance, consider workplace violence, a topic that has been much in the news in recent years (see Chapter 8). Why do some individuals suddenly explode, launching deadly attacks against coworkers or bosses (see Figure 1.11)? A growing body of evidence suggests that an important part of the answer involves beliefs on the part of these persons that they have been treated *unfairly*: they haven't received the rewards they deserve, and—more important—they have not been treated with respect and courtesy (e.g., Folger & Baron, 1996; Greenberg & Alge, 1997). In short, individuals' *interpretations* of past events and situations are powerful determinants of their behaviour.

As well, there has been growing interest in the question of how we process social information—in a quick-and-dirty manner designed to reduce effort (*heuristically*), or in a more careful, effortful manner (*systematically*; e.g., Eagly & Chaiken, 1998; Killeya & Johnson, 1998). As we'll see in several later chapters (e.g., Chapters 2, 5, and 9), these differences in style of processing can strongly influence our inferences, conclusions, decisions, and judgments about others; so they are a key aspect of social cognition.

In sum, insights provided by a cognitive approach have added greatly to our understanding of many aspects of social behaviour, and this approach is definitely a major theme of social psychology as we begin a new century.

Growing Emphasis on Application: Exporting Social Psychology

A second major theme in social psychology today is continuing expansion with the *application* of social knowledge. An increasing number of social psychologists have turned their attention to questions concerning *personal health, the legal process, social behaviour in work settings, environmental issues,* and a host of other topics. In other words, there has been growing interest in attempting to apply the findings and principles of social psychology to the solution of practical problems. As mentioned above, this theme is certainly not new in the field—it is really a return to social psychology's beginnings. Kurt Lewin, one of the founders of social psychology, once remarked, "There's nothing as practical as a good theory"—by which he meant that theories of social behaviour and thought developed through systematic research often turn out to be extremely useful in solving practical problems. There seems little doubt that interest in applying the knowledge of social psychology to practical issues has increased in recent years, with many beneficial results. We'll examine this work in Chapter 10 and throughout this book in boxed sections entitled On the Applied Side. The first of these is near the end of this section; it applies the issue of cultural influence to Canada itself, asking questions about the nature of Canadian culture and its impact and influence on Canadian behaviour.

Adopting a Multicultural Perspective: Taking Account of Diversity

One of the most important of the trends in social psychology is its increasing recognition of the importance of cultural influences on social behaviour. Cultural diversity has become a fact of life in most Western countries, including Canada and the United States. In fact the ethnic composition of the Canadian population is becoming more

Patterns of immigration changed in the second half of the last century. Before 1961 the place of birth for immigrants was overwhelmingly Europe. By the 1990s the majority of those immigrating to Canada were born on continents other than Europe: particularly Asia, South and Central America, and the Caribbean.

TABLE 1.2 Changing Patterns of Immigration to Canada

Place of Birth	Period of Immigration					Total immigrant population 1996 (4.97 million)
	Before 1961	1961-70	1971-80	1981-90	1991-98	
Europe	90%	69%	36%	26%	19%	(47%)
The Americas*	6%	14%	24%	20%	15%	(16%)
Asia	3%	10%	30%	40%	51%	(27%)
Africa & The Middle East	1%	5%	9%	13%	14%	(9%)
Oceania**	1%	1%	2%	1%	1%	(1%)

Note: Numbers have been rounded.

*U.S., Central and South America, Caribbean

**Australia, New Zealand, Pacific Islands

Source: Adapted from Statistics Canada 1996 Census Nation tables **www.statcan.ca/population**; *CANISM Matrix*, 1999.

diverse. When we look at the 1996 Census figures (Statistics Canada, 1999) for those who have a single ethnic origin, the largest ethnic group is still those of European or British origin (approximately 53 percent), followed by Canadian origin (29 percent), and Asian origin (11 percent). If we take account of those who have multiple ethnic origins, then fully 64 percent of the Canadian population have some European ancestry. This suggests that European cultural influences are still predominant in Canada.

However, the pattern of immigration has changed radically since the first half of the twentieth century, as shown in Table 1.2. Europe is no longer the major source of immigrants to Canada, as it once was—of all immigrants arriving before 1961, 90 percent were from that continent. By the end of the 1990s, however, Asia had become the largest source of immigrants (51 percent of immigrants), with Europe the second largest source (19 percent of immigrants). There has been a gradual decrease of European immigration and a corresponding increase of immigrants from Asia, Africa and the Middle East, South and Central America, and the Caribbean. In the long run, this suggests increasing ethnic diversity in Canada and, as a result, more influence of non-European cultures—rather than being "eurocentric," Canada is becoming truly multicultural.

The existence of such cultural diversity raises an important question for social psychology. Is this diversity reflected in its current theory and research? We mentioned above that the majority of the world's practising social psychologists live and work in North America. As a result, a high proportion of all research in social psychology has been conducted in the United States and Canada. Can the findings of these studies be generalized to other cultures? Until the past decade, most social psychologists had assumed that the findings of their research could be generalized to other cultures, and that the processes they studied were ones operating among human beings everywhere—were universal. However, burgeoning cross-cultural research has raised some serious doubts about this assumption in many topic areas of social psychology.

It has become increasingly clear that merely assuming that basic aspects of social behaviour are much the same around the globe is not acceptable. Indeed, cross-cultural research is beginning to reveal that even basic processes may be strongly affected by cultural factors (Smith & Bond, 1998). For example, the sense of self (e.g., Heine & Lehman, 1997), causal interpretations of others' behaviour (e.g., Choi & Nisbett, 1998), and notions of romantic love (Dion & Dion, 1996) appear to differ fundamentally from one culture to another.

One cultural distinction that has emerged from cross-cultural research (Hofstede, 1980) and has received particular attention is the individualism-collectivism dimension. **Individualism** refers to a focus on individual rights and goals, individual self-determination, and the independence of the individual from others. **Collectivism**, in contrast, refers to the importance of group goals (those of the community, work, or family groups) rather than those of the individual; individuals are seen as interdependent with their groups, and importance is given to the need to maintain harmony and balance between people.

Western cultures (e.g., United States, Canada, Western Europe) tend to be more individualistic, and Eastern as well as many other non-Western cultures (e.g., in Africa, South and Central America and Southern Europe) tend to be more collectivistic. Although distinctions between cultures can be made on many dimensions (e.g., Schwartz, 1992), this particular one has proved useful in research because cultures that vary on this dimension have been shown to vary in other psychological processes from the cognitive to the interpersonal and the inter-group. Cross-cultural research presented in almost every chapter in this book will show this (see Triandis, 1990). For all these reasons social psychology has moved toward a multicultural perspective—a focus on multicultural diversity—in recent years; and it is our prediction that this trend will continue in the new millennium.

A second aspect of social diversity that social psychologists have increasingly recognized is the fact that findings obtained using one gender may not necessarily apply to the other gender. While differences between the behaviour of females and males have often been exaggerated, and appear to be quite small in most instances, some real differences in social behaviour do exist (Feingold, 1994; Oliver & Hyde, 1993). For instance, males engage in acts of physical aggression much more often than females, and this difference is greater in the absence of strong provocation. When strong provocation is present, however, the size of this difference decreases (Bettancourt & Miller, 1996). Further, females appear to engage in indirect forms of aggression (e.g., spreading rumours, ignoring people) more frequently than males (e.g., Bjorkqvist, Osterman, & Kaukiainen, 1992). Thus, studies that focus on only one gender may miss part of the total picture (see Chapter 4). This aspect of diversity is also a reality within the academic context. The proportion of females at universities has increased, and at the graduate level females now receive the majority of the advanced degrees awarded in many fields, including psychology.

In sum, modern social psychology has adopted an increasingly **multicultural perspective**—a perspective marked by recognition of the importance of cultural factors and human diversity to behaviour. We will highlight this aspect of the field in each chapter of the book with sections emphasizing cultural diversity and its effects. In addition, these sections will be marked, in the margin, by the following special symbol:

Individualism
A cultural value emphasizing the importance of individual rights and goals. Individuals are seen as independent from others.

Collectivism A cultural value emphasizing the importance of group goals. Individuals are seen as interdependent with their group.

Multicultural Perspective Focus on understanding the cultural and ethnic factors that influence social behaviour and that contribute to differences in social behaviour or social thought between various ethnic and cultural groups.

Increasing Attention to the Potential Role of Biological Factors

We should note once again the growing influence of a biological or *evolutionary* perspective in modern social psychology (e.g., Buss, 1998). While social psychologists certainly do not accept the view that the many complexities of social behaviour and social thought can be fully understood in terms of instinctive and biological processes, researchers have shown increasing interest in the potential role of biological and genetic factors. As we noted earlier, growing evidence suggests that such factors play at least some role in many forms of social behaviour—in everything from physical attraction and mate selection, to aggression and helping behaviour (see Chapters 6 and 8). Throughout the book, we will also highlight research related to this perspective using this symbol:

Biology and Culture: An Old Dispute in Modern Form

Finally, it is worth noting that the current parallel expansion of these two approaches to social behaviour (culture and biology) raises the spectre of a traditional dispute in psychology, often termed *the nature versus nurture issue*. "Nature" here refers to our *biological and instinctive* side, whereas "nurture" refers to *the influence of our environment* on our behaviour. In modern social psychological terms, it may have occurred to you that the *evolutionary* approach to social psychology does not appear to be compatible with a *multicultural* approach—if a behaviour stems from evolved instincts how can culture influence or explain it? Support for one perspective seems to preclude support for the other. From the beginnings of psychology the issue of the extent to which human behaviour is determined by our instinctive and genetic predispositions or by the influence of the world around us has been an important one. And theorists have sometimes taken extreme positions—suggesting that one or other of these factors can account entirely for the way in which we behave.

In recent years—and this is definitely the perspective of this book—psychologists acknowledge that *both* factors play a part in human behaviour and, further, that they often *interact* in influencing behaviour. Such interaction occurs, for example, when our instincts influence the environment around us, which in turn, influences the way we behave. Take the issue of aggression—our tendency to find some forms of violent activity exciting may have an instinctive and genetic basis and this may have influenced us to develop entertainments like violent sports and films. Being exposed to such violent entertainments can, in turn, increase the likelihood of an individual behaving aggressively, as we will discuss in Chapter 8. Alternatively, the way we construct our environments may also decrease the influence of instinctive predispositions—for example, we can create entertainments that foster peaceful interactions. In short, the prevailing view in social psychology today does not support the old opposition of nature *versus* nurture, but rather sees both biology *and* environment (or culture) as contributing to behaviour.

Nonetheless, these two approaches do tend to emphasize very different sources or origins of social behaviour. Just one example is their contrastive views of the origins of passionate love, as we will discuss in Chapter 6. At various points in this book, we will juxtapose the evolutionary and cultural approach and compare their explanations. These sections will be highlighted by the placement of both symbols side-by-side in the following way:

Canadian Culture: Its Impact on Social Behaviour and Social Psychology

Americans and Canadians are not the same; they are products of two very different histories, two very different situations.

Margaret Atwood , 1982, p. 392

[Canada] began as the part of British North America that did not support the [American] Revolution, and Canadians have continued to define themselves by reference to what they are not—American—rather than in terms of their own national history and tradition.

Seymour Lipset, 1990, p. 3

As these quotations (the first from a Canadian author and the second from an American social scientist) suggest, Canada has struggled to achieve a separate sense of identity—one that is different from its British roots and, perhaps more importantly, distinct from its neighbour to the south, the United States.

Social psychologists living and working in Canada have had the same problem in attempting to define a Canadian social psychology (Earn & Towson, 1986). On the one hand, historically the United States has been the dominant force in the world of psychology (Moghaddam, 1987, 1990), and the bulk of the material in this book reflects that fact. On the other hand, many Canadian social psychologists are aware, as are many of the readers, that Canadian society and the behaviour of Canadians, is somehow different. But what are these differences? And are they extensive or fundamental enough to define a Canadian character or a distinctly Canadian social psychology? In ending this first chapter, we want to explore some of these Canadian differences and to suggest the ways in which Canadian culture might influence the social behaviour of Canadians and the development of Canadian social psychology.

Multiculturalism: Canadian Cultural Diversity.
One of the most important factors distinguishing Canadian culture from the culture of the United

States is its approach towards ethnic diversity. Canada has an official policy of multiculturalism that stresses the value of cultural differences to our society and encourages groups to maintain their cultural identities—see Figure 1.12. Within that cultural context, Canada is a bilingual country: French and English being the two official languages. The idea behind multiculturalism is that the fabric of Canadian society should represent a *cultural mosaic*: that is, separate cultural groups, secure in their own identities, should come together and form a strong unified whole. The United States, in contrast, has historically emphasized assimilation of immigrant groups. The idea has been that the United States should be a *melting pot* where immigrants, within one or two generations, could assimilate (or "melt") into the American way of life.

Of course, in both countries the ideal and the reality are often quite far apart! In the United States many groups have not "melted." They continue to have separate customs, residential areas and social relationships. For example, assimilation has not occurred in areas such as Chinatown in San Francisco or in the "ghettos" of many American cities, and this can sometimes lead to ethnic conflict (e.g., the 1993 Los Angeles riots). In Canada, respect for cultural diversity has sometimes been lacking and the policy of multiculturalism is not without its critics (e.g., Bisoondath, 1994). We too have had our ethnic conflicts, and continuing regional disputes have, at times, threatened to tear holes in Canada's mosaic. Nonetheless, the large majority of Canadians support the policy of multiculturalism (Berry & Kalin, 1995) and Canada has a reputation as one of the most livable and ethnically tolerant of Western societies.

Does our multiculturalism influence the direction of Canadian social psychology? Awareness of the importance of cultural diversity has led Canadian researchers and theorists to focus more on cultural issues and relations between groups, as well as studying the effects of multiculturalism itself (e.g., Berry, 1998). Canadian social psychologists have been pioneers, and remain on the forefront, in the areas of cross-cultural psychology (e.g., Berry, Poortinga, Segall & Dasen, 1992), intergroup relations (e.g., Taylor & Moghaddam, 1994) and bilingualism (e.g., Lambert, 1969).

A Kinder, Gentler Society: Stability and Violence in Canada.

A second major factor that distinguishes Canadian culture is its relative lack of violence and greater social stability. One indicator is the rates of violent crime, which are considerably lower in Canada than in the United States. For example, in 1997 the homicide rate in Canada was 2.0 per 100 000 population, and for the United States it was 6.8—more than three times greater (Tremblay, 1999; U.S. Federal Bureau of Investigation, 1995). Given that we are such close neighbors, the size of this gap suggests a fundamental difference between Canadian and U.S. cultures.

The Canadian self-image is of a peace-loving society, and our values reflect this (as we will discuss further in Chapter 3). Canadians show greater respect for, and confidence in, their legal institutions than those in many other Western cultures (Besserer, 1998; Lipset, 1990a). In the international arena, Canada's role has traditionally been one of conciliation and peacekeeping. But we cannot become complacent. All Canadians have been aware of a number of incidents of shocking violence in recent years, from the Canadian military's torture and murder of a 16-year-old Somali boy, to the school shooting by a young man in Taber, Alberta. The publicity surrounding such incidents often adds to the view that violence in this society is escalating—and indeed the current rate of violent crime remains higher than it was ten years ago (Tremblay, 1999). However,

■ Multiculturalism in Canada

FIGURE 1.12 Canada's policy of multiculturalism encourages different ethnic groups to maintain their cultural identities. Here, celebrants in Canada's newest territory, Nunavut, appear to need little encouragement.

recent crime statistics attest to a continuing decrease in violent crime since the early 1990s (Tremblay, 1999) and stable or decreasing rates of criminal victimization over the past decade (Besserer, 1998).

Although we have a less violent society, Canadian social psychologists have still made significant contributions in the areas of aggression (e.g., Rule, 1976, 1986) and in forensic psychology (in which psychology is applied to the legal systems; e.g., Doob, 1976, 1985; Wells, 1984; Dutton, 1992). These topics will be further discussed in Chapters 8 and 10.

Communitarian Values: Canada's Sense of Community.

Seymour Lipset has suggested that differences between Canada and the United States can be traced back, in part, to the historical beginnings of both countries:

> The concern of Canada's Fathers of Confederation with 'Peace, Order, and Good Government' implies control of, and protection for the society. The parallel stress of America's Founding Fathers on 'Life, Liberty, and the Pursuit of Happiness' suggests upholding the rights of the individual.

Lipset, 1990, p. 13

As this suggests, the United States has emphasized *individual* rights and freedoms since its beginning, while in Canada relatively greater emphasis has been placed on the maintenance of peace and order in *society as a whole*. The Canadian desire for order is reflected in the relatively lower rates of violence. But further, this historical difference may have led Canadian culture to be more *communitarian*; that is, to focus "upon the cooperation of its citizens and the need to protect their welfare" (Lipset, 1990). Public opinion polls suggest that, relative to Americans, Canadians give greater support to this governmental involvement and give more weight to the importance of equality between groups in society (Lipset, 1990). Broadly, we can say that Canadian society appears to be more *communitarian* (focused on the community) and less *individualis-*

tic (focused on the individual) than the United States. We should emphasize, however, that this is only relative to the United States. According to one researcher, Canada is one of the more individualistic countries when compared with 50 others around the world (Hofstede, 1983).

In social psychology, the interest of Canadian researchers in group processes, as mentioned above, may be a result of this greater sense of community. Perhaps there has also been more emphasis on the constructive role of group relations in people's lives (Taylor & Moghaddam, 1987; Beaton, Tougas & Joly, 1996) and the impact of society upon the individual (Berry, Kim, Minde & Mok, 1987; Taylor & McKirnan, 1984).

In summary, we have suggested that Canadian culture places greater emphasis on multiculturalism, the maintenance of order, and communitarian values relative to the United States. The extent to which these values are reflected in the individual social behaviour of Canadians will vary. However, in general we do see a very marked difference in the levels of violence and support for community intervention by government among Canadians. A word of warning may be necessary here: Do not make the mistake of assuming that every Canadian is more supportive of cultural diversity, less violent and more community-minded than every American. This is simply not the case. The differences we outlined are average ones and there is considerable overlap in the behaviour and responses of the populations of both countries. Compared to other nations and cultures, these two countries and their citizens have a great deal in common.

Similarly, Canadian social psychology is not completely distinct from American, as most Canadian social psychologists agree (Rule & Wells, 1981; Earn & Towson, 1986). However, recognition of these differences has produced an interest in Canadian issues and a particularly Canadian perspective in the areas of language, culture, and group relations. Canadians have also made significant contributions to most of the topic areas of social psychology and we will endeavor to point out these contributions throughout this book.

KEY POINTS

- Kurt Lewin can be regarded as the founder of modern social psychology, setting a pattern of combining theory development, scientific and applied research.
- Social psychology expanded tremendously in the 1940s, 50s and 60s, in terms of the range of topics studies and the number of practising social psychologists.
- A crisis in social psychology in the 1970s led to a questioning of the direction of the field in terms of theory and methodology.
- As social psychology matured in the 1980s and 90s expansion continued, with the return to an emphasis on applied psychology and the growth of international social psychology.
- Current trends in social psychology include: (1) the growing influence of a *cognitive perspective*, which suggests that individuals' interpretations of social situations strongly shape their behaviour; (2) interest in *application* of the knowledge and findings of social psychology to many practical problems; (3) the adoption of a *multicultural perspective*, recognizing the importance of cultural factors; (4) a growing recognition of the potential role of *biological and genetic factors* in social behaviour and social thought.
- Canadian culture has placed a greater emphasis on cultural diversity, is more communitarian, and tends to be more stable and less violent than the United States. These cultural differences will have an impact on the social behaviour of Canadians and on the development of Canadian social psychology.

USING THIS BOOK: A ROAD MAP FOR READERS

Before concluding this introduction to the field of social psychology, we'd like to comment briefly on several features of this text. First, please note that we've taken several steps to make our text easier and more convenient for you to use. Each chapter begins with an outline of the major topics covered and ends with a summary. Important terms are printed in **boldface type like this** and are followed by a definition. This definition is also placed in the margin nearby. To help you understand and remember what you have read, each major section is followed by a list of Key Points, briefly summarizing major points. Each chapter also ends with a summary and review of these Key Points. Because figures and charts contained in original research reports are often quite complex, every graph and table in this text has been specially created for it. In addition, all graphs contain special labels designed to call your attention to the key findings presented. We think that you'll find all of these illustrations easy to read and—more importantly—that they'll contribute to your understanding of social psychology.

Second, we want to note that we've included several special sections throughout the text. These do not interrupt the flow of text materials; rather, they are presented at natural breaks in content. All are designed to highlight information we feel is especially important and interesting.

The first type of special insert is called Canadian Research: On the Cutting Edge. These sections describe Canadian research that we believe is on the frontiers of knowledge in social psychology.

The second type of special insert is called Cornerstones. These sections describe studies that initiated major lines of research in the history of social psychology, exerting a lasting influence on the field.

The third type of special section is entitled On the Applied Side. These sections highlight the practical implications of social psychology—ways in which its knowledge and principles can contribute to the solution of a wide range of practical problems.

A final type of special section, featured near the end of each chapter, relates to our belief that social psychology can and should be applied to our daily lives. These sections are labelled Ideas to Take with You. Each is designed to highlight important concepts you should remember—and use—long after this course is over. In our view you may well find these concepts useful in your own life in the years ahead.

As we noted earlier, modern social psychology is distinguished by a growing interest in social diversity and in the potential role of biological and genetic factors in human social behaviour. Topics related to these important themes are discussed at numerous points throughout the text. To help you identify them, the special symbols and [symbol] appear in the margin next to these discussions. When the contrast between these two perspectives is being emphasized, this special combined symbol is used: [symbol]

All of these features are designed to help you get the most out of your first encounter with social psychology. But, in a key sense, only you can transfer the information on the pages of this book into your own memory—and into your own life. So please do use this book. Read the summaries and chapter outlines, review the Key Points, and pay special attention to the Ideas to Take with You pages. Doing so, we believe, will improve your understanding of social psychology—and your grade, too! Finally, please think of this book as a reference source—a practical guide to social behaviour to which you can refer over and over again. In contrast to some other fields you will study, social psychology really is directly relevant to your daily life—to understanding others and to getting along better with them. Good luck—and may your first encounter with our field be one you'll enjoy and remember for many years to come.

Ideas to Take with You

Why Correlation Doesn't Equal Causation

The fact that two variables are correlated—even strongly correlated—does not necessarily mean that changes in one variable cause changes in the other. This is true because changes in both variables may actually be related to—or caused by—a third variable. Two examples:

OBSERVATION As weight increases, income increases.

POSSIBLE INTERPRETATIONS:

1. Weight gain causes increased income.

    Weight gain ——Causes——▶ Increased income

2. As people grow older, they tend to gain weight and also to earn higher incomes; both variables are actually related to age.

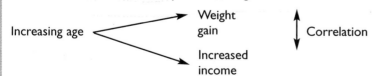

OBSERVATION The more violent television and movies people watch, the more likely they are to engage in dangerous acts of aggression.

POSSIBLE INTERPRETATIONS:

1. Exposure to media violence is one factor that increases aggression.

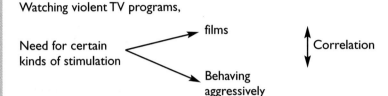

Exposure to media violence ——Causes——▶ Increased aggression

2. People who prefer a high level of stimulation have little control over their impulses; thus, they choose to watch displays of violence and also act aggressively more often than other people. Both variables are related to a need for certain kinds of stimulation.

Watching violent TV programs,

Need for certain
kinds of stimulation

films

Behaving
aggressively

Correlation

KEY CONCLUSION: EVEN IF TWO VARIABLES ARE STRONGLY CORRELATED, THIS DOES NOT NECESSARILY MEAN THAT CHANGES IN ONE CAUSE CHANGES IN THE OTHER.

Summary and Review of Key Points

Social Psychology: A Working Definition

● *Social Psychology* is the scientific field that seeks to understand the nature and causes of individual behaviour and thought in social situations.

It is scientific in nature because it adopts the values and methods used in other fields of science.

Social psychologists adopt the scientific method because "common sense" provides an unreliable guide to social behaviour, and because our thought is influenced by many potential sources of bias.

Social psychology focuses on the behaviour of individuals and seeks to understand the causes of social behaviour and thought.

Important causes of social behaviour and thought include cognitive processes, biological factors, other persons, the physical environment, and culture.

Research Methods in Social Psychology

● In *systematic observation*, behaviour is carefully observed and recorded, providing a description of the world. *Naturalistic observation* involves observation conducted in the settings where the behaviour naturally occurs and with a minimum impact on the setting.

In the *correlational method*, researchers measure two or more variables to determine if they are related to one another in any way. This enables them to predict one variable from information about the other.

The existence of even strong correlations between variables does not indicate that they are

causally related to each other.

Experimentation involves systematically altering one or more variables (*independent* variables) in order to determine whether these alterations affect some aspect of behaviour (*dependent* variable).

Successful use of the experimental method requires *random assignment of participants to experimental conditions*; it also requires that the experimenter *hold constant all other factors* that might also influence behaviour so as to avoid confounding of variables.

Advantages of systematic observation are that it can provide an initial *description* of social behaviour and that it does not interfere with behaviour as it naturally occurs. A disadvantage is that the qualitative data it often produces is vulnerable to the *confirmation bias*—a tendency to bias interpretations of information in the direction of one's expectations or beliefs.

The correlational method has the advantage of allowing *prediction* of one variable from information about another. It also often allows us to investigate efficiently topics that are not accessible to experimentation. Its major disadvantage (shared with systematic observation) is that it does not allow researcher to draw causal conclusions.

Experimentation does allow causal conclusions to be drawn and aids explanation of behaviour. However, sometimes the context of experiments is artificial, raising questions about their results' *external validity*—the extent to which findings can be generalized to the real world situation.

Because each method has its limitations, it is recommended that replication of studies should take place using a wide range of methods.

Using both field and laboratory methods, Beuhler and colleagues investigated our tendency to make overly optimistic predictions about how long it will take us to complete a given task, an effect known as the *planning fallacy*. It seems to stem from a focus on the future while ignoring related past events, and from motivation to have tasks completed quickly.

Deception involves efforts by social psychologists to withhold or conceal information about the purposes of a study from participants.

Most social psychologists believe that temporary deception is often necessary in order to obtain valid research results.

However, they view deception as acceptable only when important safeguards are employed: *informed consent* and thorough *debriefing*.

The Progress of Social Psychology

● Kurt Lewin can be regarded as the founder of modern social psychology, setting a pattern of combining theory development, scientific and applied research.

Social psychology expanded tremendously in the 1940s, 50s and 60s, in terms of the range of topics studies and the number of practising social psychologists.

A crisis in social psychology in the 1970s led to a questioning of the direction of the field in terms of theory and methodology.

As social psychology matured in the 1980s and 90s expansion continued, with a return to an emphasis on applied psychology and with the growth of international social psychology.

Current trends in social psychology include: (1) the growing influence of a *cognitive perspective*, which suggests that individuals' *interpretations* of social situations strongly shape their behaviour; (2) interest in *applications* of the knowledge and findings of social psychology to many practical problems; (3) the adoption of a *multicultural perspective*, recognizing the importance of cultural factors to behaviour; (4) a growing recognition of the potential role of *biological and genetic factors* in social behaviour and social thought.

Canadian culture has placed a greater emphasis on cultural diversity, is more communitarian, and tends to be more stable and less violent than the United States. These cultural differences will have an impact on the social behaviour of Canadians and on the development of Canadian social psychology.

For More Information

Jackson, J. M. (1993). *Social psychology, past and present*. Hillsdale, NJ: Erlbaum.

A thoughtful overview of the roots and development of social psychology. Organized around major themes in social psychological research, the book emphasizes the multidisciplinary roots of social psychology. The chapter on current trends is especially valuable.

Semin, G., & Fiedler, K. (1996). *Applied social psychology*. Thousand Oaks, CA: Sage.

How are social psychologists applying their knowledge and skills to solving practical problems? This book presents a broad and thorough overview of such efforts. Topics covered include the application of social psychology to law, the media, health, language, decision making, and survey research. A good source to consult if you want to know more about the applied aspects of social psychology.

Weblinks

www.apa.org/journals/psp.html
Journal of Personality and Social Psychology

www.spssi.org
The Society for the Psychological Study of Social Issues

www.cpa.ca
Canadian Psychological Association

www.apa.org
American Psychological Association

www.uiowa.edu/~grpproc/crisp/crisp.html
Current Research in Social Psychology

CHAPTER TWO

Social **Perception** and Social **Cognition**: Internalizing Our Social World

■ Information overload

FIGURE 2.1 All too often in social situations there is just too much social information to absorb or process. This phenomenon, called *information overload*, influences our social perceptions and social cognitions—how we see and understand the social world.

Think about a typical social situation—the party. You've arrived a little late and, as you stand on the threshold, it's obvious that things are already well underway. There's music, laughter, lights and colour, people dancing, talking, moving. Some of them glance your way, most don't even notice you, perhaps someone catches your eye and smiles enticingly. But you can only stand there for a moment or two. How can you possibly take in that buzzing mass of people, with different clothes, ways of acting, facial expressions? What does that smile mean? And how are you going to respond? At such moments you are suffering from a common problem when faced with social stimuli—**information overload**—the fact that there is frequently just too much information for you to process it properly, let alone decide how you should respond (See Figure 2.1).

The topic of the current chapter is the ways we cope as we *take in* social information and *manipulate* it, and the impact such efforts have on our social behaviour.

Information Overload Instances in which our ability to process information is exceeded.

Social Perception
The process through which we take social information in through the senses and begin to know the social world.

Social Cognition The process through which individuals use and manipulate social information. That is, they interpret, analyze, remember, and use information about the social world; a major area of research in social psychology.

The intake process is termed **social perception**—the process through which we seek social information, form impressions of others, and register or encode that information in our minds. The manipulation process is termed **social cognition**—the process through which we recall, interpret, reason, and make judgments about others. Whereas social perception is concerned with the *intake and registering* of social information, social cognition is concerned with the *use and manipulation* of social information.

Although traditionally social perception and social cognition have been seen as distinct processes, they are clearly linked and, at times, inseparable. What we perceive will influence our cognitions. So, having caught the eye of that person who smiled (your perception), your thoughts (or cognitions) about the party will be influenced. Perhaps the party will now seem much more exciting or interesting, or, if you have different priorities, you may see it as a potentially embarrassing social situation. But our cognitions (that is, our already existing beliefs and interpretations of such situations) also influence our perceptions. Clearly your interpretation of that smile as "enticing" would be based on previous social experience and knowledge. The point here is that social perception and social cognition are *interdependent processes*; that is, they both influence each other. While social perception is concerned with the intake of information, that process is influenced by the way we think about and organize our experiences. Similarly, social cognition is concerned with the use and manipulation of social information, but this information has been filtered through our selective perceptions.

To complicate these processes further, we are not always accurate or objective when faced with other people. Our social perceptions and cognitions are vulnerable to a number of systematic *biases*. Often we see what we expect or want to see, not necessarily what is there. Did that person really smile enticingly or were you just hoping too hard? You can see clearly the importance of misinterpretation here!

You may now have some inkling that social perception and cognition are complex and crucial processes, and so worthy of careful scrutiny by social psychologists. To acquaint you with the key findings of this research, we'll focus on four major topics. First, we'll examine the process of *nonverbal communication*—communication between individuals involving an unspoken language of facial expressions, eye contact, body movements, and postures (e.g., Zebrowitz, 1997). As we'll soon see, information provided by such nonverbal cues can often tell us much about others' current moods or emotions. Next, we'll examine *attribution*, the complex process through which we attempt to understand the reasons behind others' behaviour—why they have acted as they have in a given situation. Third, we'll turn to fundamental ways of coping with information overload—the use of mental shortcuts such as *schemas and heuristics*. Unfortunately, this can sometimes result in *biases* or errors in our social thought. Finally, because our emotional response to the social world is one of the factors that prevent us being objective, social psychologists are currently attempting to explore the relation between *affect and cognitions*.

Nonverbal Communication: The Unspoken Language

In many cases, social behaviour is strongly affected by temporary factors or causes. Shifting moods, fleeting emotions, fatigue, illness, various drugs—all can influence the ways in which we think and behave. Most persons, for example, are more willing to do favours for others when in a good mood than when in a bad mood (Baron & Bronfen, 1994; George, 1991). Similarly, many people are more likely to lose their tempers and lash out at others in some manner when feeling irritable than when feeling mellow (Anderson, 1989; Bell, 1992).

Because such temporary factors often exert important effects on social behaviour and thought, it is useful to know something about them. But how can we obtain knowledge about another's internal landscape? We can often still obtain revealing information about their inner feelings and reactions by paying careful attention to their *nonverbal behaviours*—changes in facial expressions, eye contact, posture, body movements, and other expressive actions. As noted by DePaulo (1992), such behaviour is relatively irrepressible—that is, difficult to control—so even when others try to conceal their inner feelings, these often leak out in many ways through nonverbal cues. So, in an important sense, nonverbal behaviours constitute a silent but eloquent language. For this reason, the meanings they convey and our efforts to interpret these are often described by the term **nonverbal communication**. Such communication is very complex, and it has been studied from many different perspectives. Here, however, we will focus on two major issues: (1) What are the basic channels through which nonverbal communication takes place? and (2) what is the role of nonverbal communication in our social perceptions and social interactions?

Nonverbal Communication Communication between individuals that does not involve the content of spoken words. It consists instead of an unspoken language of facial expressions, eye contact, and body language.

Nonverbal Communication: The Basic Channels

Researchers have identified those channels of nonverbal communication that transmit key information about our inner emotional and affective states. These seem to involve *facial expressions*, *eye contact*, *body movements* and *posture*, and *touching*.

■ Basic facial expressions

FIGURE 2.2 Facial expressions such as these provide valuable information about others' emotional states. Can you identify the emotion shown on each face?

Answers are: Top, left to right, fear, sadness; bottom, left to right, disgust, happiness, surprise.

Unmasking the Face: Facial Expressions as Clues to Others' Emotions

More than 2000 years ago, the Roman orator Cicero stated "The face is the image of the soul." By this he meant that human feelings and emotions are often reflected on the face and can be read there in specific expressions. Modern research suggests that Cicero—and many other observers of human behaviour—were correct: it *is* possible to learn much about others' current moods and feelings from their facial expressions. In fact, it appears that six different basic emotions are represented clearly, and from a very early age, on the human face: anger, fear, sadness, disgust, happiness, and surprise (Izard, 1991; Rozin, Lowrey & Ebert, 1994; see Figure 2.2). Please note: this in no way implies that human beings are capable of demonstrating only six different facial expressions. On the contrary, emotions occur in many combinations (for example, anger along with fear, surprise with happiness). Further, each of these reactions can vary greatly in strength. Thus, while there seem to be only a small number of basic themes in facial expressions, the number of variations on these themes is large.

An important issue that has concerned researchers from the beginning is the extent to which facial expressions are universal. Even Charles Darwin, after traveling around the world researching his theory of evolution, attempted to answer this particular question: Do people living in widely separated geographic areas demonstrate similar facial expressions in similar situations (Darwin, 1872; Ekman, 1989)? Would you expect someone from a remote part of the world to smile in reaction to events that made them happy, or to frown when displeased, as you do? If we found such evidence of a universal connection between facial expression and emotion, this would suggest that these responses are instinctive and are part of our evolved behaviour, as Darwin believed. However, evidence for cultural variation in facial expressions would throw doubt on this conclusion, suggesting that our cultures teach us the acceptable facial expressions of our societies.

Perhaps the most convincing evidence for universality is provided by a series of studies conducted by Ekman and Friesen (1975). These researchers traveled to isolated areas of New Guinea and asked individuals living there to imagine various emotion-provoking events—for example, your friend has come for a visit and you are happy; you find a dead animal that has been lying in the hot sun for several days, and it smells very bad. Then these subjects were asked to show by facial expressions how they would feel in each case. Their expressions were very similar to ones that a North American might show in those situations. Further, when individuals living in widely separated countries are shown photos of strangers from other cultures demonstrating anger, fear, happiness, sadness, surprise, and disgust, they are quite accurate in identifying these emotions (e.g., Ekman, 1973). These results provide convincing evidence for the universality of facial expressions, suggesting that they are instinctive, based in our evolutionary past. And this was the accepted view for some years following their publication (Ekman, 1989).

However, we should note that the accuracy of these conclusions has been questioned by Russell (1994) who has called attention to two basic issues. First, the methodology used may not always have been valid. For example, participants were asked to choose an emotion label from a list of labels provided by the researchers—a technique known as a *fixed-choice paradigm*. Russell argues that if they had been allowed to come up with their *own* labels for each facial expression they saw, participants from different cultures might have shown less consistency in identifying particular emotions. Second, results using the fixed-choice paradigms are not as consistent across cultures as has often been suggested. In fact, recognition of facial expressions by other cultures was most consistent with Western responses when individuals from that culture

The percentage of agreement with Western classifications of facial expressions is compared for (1) other Western groups, (2) non-Western literate groups who have had greater contact with the West and (3) non-Western illiterate and isolated groups who have had least contact with the West. With the exception of recognition of happiness, the less contact with the West the lower the level of agreement, suggesting that cultural socialization has an impact on recognition of facial expressions.

TABLE 2.1 Cultural Agreement About Western Classification of Facial Expressions

Median Percentage Agreement in Fixed-Choice Studies

	Facial expression					
	"Happy"	"Surprise"	"Sadness"	"Fear"	"Disgust"	"Anger"
Culture Group						
1) Western	96.4	87.5	80.5	77.5	82.6	81.2
2) Non-Western literate	89.2	79.2	76.0	65.0	65.0	63.0
3) Non-Western Illiterate, isolated	92.0	36.0	52.0	46.0	29.0	56.0

Source: Russell, 1994.

had had contact with the West. This suggests that some socialization in Western facial expressions may have taken place among subjects. (Indeed, even in remote New Guinea, many people tested had seen Western movies!) Russell's summary of findings for Western and Non-Western groups is shown in Table 2.1. As you can see, findings are most consistent with Western responses for groups that have had greater contact with the West. This evidence suggests that culture may have a greater impact on our understanding and display of facial expressions than has recently been acknowledged.

Another finding that supports an evolutionary view of facial expressions is what social psychologists describe as the *face-in-the-crowd effect* (Hansen & Hansen, 1988). We are especially sensitive to negative facial expressions on the part of others—so sensitive that we can very quickly pick out the angry face in a crowd of persons showing neutral or happy expressions. Interestingly, we are somewhat slower to identify a happy face in a crowd of angry faces (Hansen & Hansen, 1988). These findings are consistent with the view that facial expressions, and our ability to read them, may have evolved because they aid our survival. Since angry persons do indeed represent a greater threat to our safety—or survival—than happy ones, it would make sense that those who had a particular sensitivity to negative facial expressions would be better able to avoid danger and, therefore, have an increased chance to pass their genes on to the next generation.

In sum, there is evidence supporting the view that facial expressions are universal, have an instinctive basis and may, therefore, have evolved. Cross-cultural research shows substantial agreement in recognition of some facial expressions (particularly happiness) between those in widely different cultures. However, there is also evidence for cultural variation in facial expressions, as the more recent analysis from Russell suggests. Findings such as these suggest that facial expressions may not be as universal in terms of providing clear signals about underlying emotions as was previously assumed. Research continues to explore the extent to which instinct and culture determine facial expressions (e.g., Carroll & Russell, 1996; Rosenberg & Ekman, 1995), but we can be sure that *both* factors play a part. Overall, it seems safest to conclude that while facial expressions are not totally universal around the world—cultural and contextual differences do exist with respect to their precise meanings—they generally need much less "translation" than spoken languages. We will further examine cultural variations in other aspects of nonverbal communication in a later On the Applied Side section entitled "Showing Your Feelings."

Gazes and Stares: The Language of the Eyes

Have you ever had a conversation with someone who is wearing mirror-lensed glasses? If so, you know that this can be an uncomfortable situation. Since you can't see the other person's eyes, you are uncertain about how she or he is reacting. Taking note of the importance of cues provided by others' eyes, ancient poets often described the eyes as "windows to the soul." In one important sense, they were right: we do often learn much about others' feelings from their eyes. For example, we interpret a high level of gazing from another as a sign of liking or friendliness (Kleinke, 1986). In contrast, if others avoid eye contact with us, we may conclude that they are unfriendly, may be lying, or are simply shy (Zimbardo, 1977).

While a high level of eye contact from others is usually interpreted as a sign of liking or positive feelings, there is one important exception to this general rule. If another person gazes at us continuously and maintains such contact regardless of any actions we perform, she or he can be said to be staring. **Staring** is often interpreted as a sign of anger or hostility—consider the phrase "a cold stare"—and most people find

Staring A form of eye contact in which one person continues to gaze steadily at another regardless of what the recipient does.

■ Staring and road rage

FIGURE 2.3 If you encounter another driver who is showing signs of road rage—driving in a highly aggressive manner—don't stare at him or her to show your annoyance. If you do, you may cause the person to erupt in unpredictable and dangerous ways.

this particular nonverbal cue disturbing (Ellsworth & Carlsmith, 1973). In fact, we may quickly terminate social interaction with someone who stares at us and may even leave the scene (Greenbaum & Rosenfield, 1978). This is one reason why experts on road rage—highly aggressive driving by motorists, sometimes followed by actual assaults—recommend that drivers avoid eye contact with people who are disobeying traffic laws and rules of the road (e.g., B. J. Bushman, personal communication, February 18, 1998). Apparently, such persons, who are already in a highly excitable state, interpret anything approaching a stare from another driver as an aggressive act and may react accordingly (see Figure 2.3).

Body Language: Gestures, Posture, and Movements

Try this simple demonstration:

First, try to remember some incident that made you angry—the angrier the better. Think about it for about a minute.

Now try to remember another incident—one that made you feel sad—again, the sadder the better.

Compare your behaviour in the two contexts. Did you change your posture or move your hands, arms, or legs as your thoughts shifted from the first event to the second? The chances are good that you did, for our current moods or emotions are often reflected in the position, posture, and movement of our bodies. Together, such nonverbal behaviours are termed **body language**, and they too can provide us with several useful kinds of information about others.

First, as just noted, body language often reveals much about others' emotional states. Large numbers of movements—especially ones in which one part of the body does something to another part (e.g., touching, scratching, rubbing)—suggest emotional arousal. The greater the frequency of such behaviour, the higher the level of arousal or nervousness (Harrigan, et al., 1991).

Larger patterns of movement, involving the whole body, can also be informative. Such phrases as "he adopted a threatening posture" and "she greeted him with open

Body Language Cues provided by the position, posture, and movement of people's bodies or body parts.

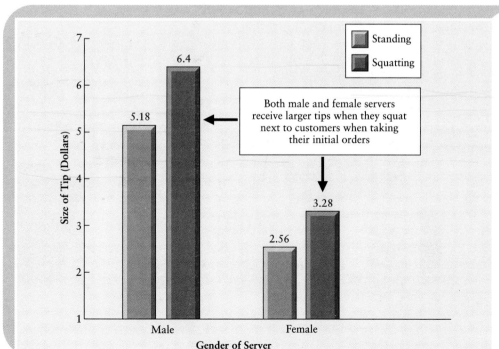

■ Body position and tipping

FIGURE 2.4 When male and female servers squatted next to customers when taking their initial (drink) orders, they received larger tips than when they remained standing.

Source: Based on data from Lynn & Mynier, 1993.

Both male and female servers receive larger tips when they squat next to customers when taking their initial orders arms" suggest that different body orientations or postures can be suggestive of contrasting emotional reactions. Aronoff, Woike, and Hyman (1992) supported this possibility by showing that the threatening characters in choreographed ballets (e.g., Macbeth) use angular poses nearly three times as often as the warm characters. In contrast, the warm characters (e.g., Romeo and Juliet) engaged in rounded poses almost four times more often. When combined with other research conducted by Aronoff et al. (1992), these findings suggest that large-scale body movements or postures can sometimes serve as an important source of information about others' emotions and traits.

Further evidence for the conclusion that body posture and movements can be an important source of information about others is provided by research conducted by Lynn and Mynier (1993). These researchers arranged for servers of both genders either to stand upright or to squat down next to customers when taking drink orders. Lynn and Mynier predicted that squatting would be interpreted as a sign of friendliness, because in this position servers would make more eye contact with customers and would be physically closer to them (Argyle, 1988). As a result, they expected servers to receive larger tips when they squatted than when they did not. As you can see from Figure 2.4, this is what happened. Regardless of servers' gender, they received larger tips when they bent down than when they did not. As shown in Figure 2.4, male servers received larger tips than female servers; but it is difficult to interpret this difference, because the males and females worked in different restaurants.

Finally, we should add that more specific information about others' feelings is often provided by gestures. Gestures fall into several categories, but perhaps the most important are *emblems*—body movements carrying specific meanings in a given culture. Do you recognize the gestures shown in Figure 2.5? In Canada and other Western countries, these movements have clear and definite meanings. In other cultures, however, they may have no meaning, or even a different meaning. For this reason, it is wise to be careful about using gestures while traveling in cultures different from your own: you may offend the people around you without meaning to do so! Even within one society, communication with those from different cultural backgrounds can be fraught with difficulties as is discussed below in the section On the Applied Side.

Touching: The Most Intimate Nonverbal Cues

Suppose that during a conversation with another person, she or he touched you briefly. How would you react? What information would this behaviour convey? The answer to both questions is, it depends. And what it depends upon is several factors relating to who does the touching (a friend or a stranger, a member of your own or of the other

■ Gesture as a nonverbal cue

FIGURE 2.5 Do you recognize the gestures here? Can you tell what they mean? In Canada and other Western cultures, each of these gestures has a specific meaning. However, they may well have no meaning, or entirely different meanings, in other cultures.

gender); the nature of this physical contact (brief or prolonged, gentle or rough); and the context in which it takes place (a business or social setting, a doctor's office). Depending on such factors, touch can suggest affection, sexual interest, dominance, caring, or even aggression. Despite such complexities, existing evidence indicates that when touching is *considered appropriate,* it often produces positive reactions in the person being touched (Alagna, Whitcher, & Fisher, 1979; Smith, Gier, & Willis, 1982). This fact is clearly illustrated by an ingenious study carried out by Crusco and Wetzel (1984) who enlisted the aid of servers working in two restaurants. They agreed to treat customers in one of three distinct ways when giving them their change: they either refrained from touching these persons in any manner, touched them briefly on the hand, or touched them for a longer period on the shoulder. Both a brief touch on the hand (about one-half second) and longer touch on the shoulder (one to one and a half seconds) significantly increased tipping over the no-touch control condition. Thus, consistent with previous findings, being touched in an innocuous, nonthreatening way seemed to generate positive rather than negative reactions among recipients.

Needless to add, touching does not always produce such effects. If it is perceived as a status or power play, or if it is too prolonged or intimate, or if it occurs in a context where touching is not viewed as appropriate (e.g., a business setting), this form of nonverbal behaviour may evoke powerful negative reactions on the part of the person being touched; it may even lead to charges of sexual harassment. So beware. Touching is a very powerful form of nonverbal communication, and should be reserved for persons we know well and for settings where this intimate form of behaviour is considered appropriate.

Reading Nonverbal Communication: How Accurate Are We?

Remember the example of the enticing smile with which we began this chapter. Now that we have surveyed the area of nonverbal communication in general, how accurate do you think you would be at interpreting such a smile? This is a question social psychologists have asked in a more general form—given that nonverbal communication occurs on so many different channels and that people are constantly changing their facial expressions and body positions, can we ever have confidence in the accuracy of our own perceptions? Surprisingly, the answer appears to be encouraging. Despite the complexity of this task and the many potential pitfalls that can lead us into error, we do seem capable of forming accurate perceptions and impressions of others based on their nonverbal communications (e.g., Berry, 1991; Gifford, 1994; Kenney et al., 1994). Moreover, this is true not only when we have had many opportunities to interact with them—for instance, teachers with their students (Madon et al., 1998). We can also form accurate perceptions of others from a very brief meeting with them; if we spend a few minutes speaking to them, see videotapes of their behaviour, or even if we see photos of their faces. On the basis of such fragmentary information, we seem capable of forming accurate impressions of where other persons stand on several basic dimensions of personality, such as submissive-dominant, agreeable-quarrelsome, and responsible-irresponsible (e.g., Kenney et al., 1994). How do we know that these first impressions are accurate? Because they correlate quite highly with ratings of the same persons provided by people who know them very well—family members, spouses, best friends (e.g., Ambady & Rosenthal, 1992; Zebrowitz & Collins, 1997)—and also with the individuals' overt behaviour (e.g., Moskowitz, 1990). One suggestion for *why* we might be able to assess an individual's qualities from appearance is that there may be an actual link between physical characteristics and psychological qualities— we may in fact show our characters in our faces for example (Zebrowitz & Collins, 1997). So the actress Lauren Bacall may be correct when she remarked (1988): "I think your whole life shows in your face and you should be proud of that."

On the **Applied Side**

Showing Your Feelings: Cultural Differences in Openness and Indirectness

Cultural differences in styles of communication can be crucial for those of us who communicate daily in a multicultural context such as Canada. We must be wary of being ethnocentric—that is, assuming that our culture's ways of communicating are used and understood by people from different cultural backgrounds. Two related aspects of communication might be of particular importance: the extent to which individuals are open and the extent to which they are indirect.

Research on facial expressions has shown that cultures vary in the degree to which they see open expressions of emotion as appropriate. For example, Japanese culture has been found to favour a more moderate level of expressiveness than that in the United States (Matsumoto & Kudoh, 1990). The Chinese have also been found to value self-restraint in expression (Bond, 1993). While both Eastern and Western cultures see smiling as related to sociability or optimism

(Albright, Malloy, Qi, & Kenny, 1997; Matsumoto & Kudoh, 1993), there are cultural differences in its appropriateness. For example, the Chinese also see smiling as indicating a lack of calmness and a lack of control (Albright et al., 1997). Similarly, research in West Sumatra (part of Indonesia) found that the Minangkabau discouraged the expression of strong, especially negative, emotions during interpersonal interactions (Levenson, Ekman, Heider, & Friesen, 1990). In general this research suggests that Western and Latin cultures are more likely to value more open displays of emotion than many Asian cultures (Markus & Kitayama, 1991). These cultural norms have been termed **display rules**—beliefs in a particular culture about when, and to what degree, various emotions should be

> **Display Rules**
> Cultural rules, or norms, about when, and to what degree, emotions should be expressed non-verbally.

Below are items from the Conversational Indirectness Scale. Subjects are asked to indicate the extent of agreement or disagreement with each statement on a 7-point scale. Individuals who are high in indirectness would agree with the first two items under each heading, but disagree with the third, reversed, item.

TABLE 2.2 Examples from the Conversational Indirectness Scale

Interpretation of others as indirect

I try to be a successful communicator by uncovering a speaker's deeper meaning.

I will often look below the surface of a person's remark in order to decide what they really mean.

I usually assume that there are no hidden meanings to what someone is saying.*

Production of indirect communication

People have to spend time thinking about my remarks in order to understand my real meaning.

My remarks often have more than one meaning.

What I mean with a remark is usually fairly obvious.*

*These items are reversed in meaning

Source: Holtgraves, T. (1997). "Styles of language use: Individual and cultural variability in conversational indirectness." *Journal of Personality and Social Psychology*, Vol. 73, No. 3, pp. 624–637. Copyright © 1997 by the American Psychological Association. Adapted with permission.

expressed (Ekman, 1972). Display rules have been shown to apply to facial expression but research on other channels of nonverbal behaviour is unclear. However, to the extent that touch or body posture and gesture are used to express emotion, it can be speculated that cultures which favour open expression of emotion will see freer use of these channels as more appropriate than cultures that favour more control of emotional expression.

A related aspect of communication that has also shown cultural variation is the directness or indirectness of verbal communication. Thomas Holtgraves (1997) devised and tested the *Conversational Indirectness Scale* which measures two dimensions of indirectness in communication: (1) interpretation—the extent to which individuals *interpret* others' conversation as having an underlying rather than an obvious meaning; and (2) production—the extent to which they *produce* such indirect communications when talking to others. Some items from this scale are shown in Table 2.2. When Holtgraves gave this scale to people from Korea and the United States systematic differences were found in both interpretation and production of indirectness as shown in Figure 2.6. Koreans showed greater indirectness in communication than Americans whether the dimension was interpretation or production.

The research discussed above suggests that those from more collectivistic cultures, particularly East Asian, tend to show more restraint and indirectness in communication compared to those in individualistic cultures such as Canada and the United States. This may be because of a greater concern for the feelings of other group members in collectivistic cultures and the importance of saving face for others (Ting-Toomey, 1988; Triandis, 1988). Indirect and more restrained communication may allow the individual to imply and infer meanings that might cause embarrassment or conflict if expressed directly. Because of a greater emphasis on the importance of expressing oneself, and the need to be independent of others, North Americans tend to value directness and openness and see restraint and indirectness as less socially desirable (Holtgraves, 1997).

In Canada, where cultural groups range from the highly expressive and direct to the highly reserved, such findings have real implications for

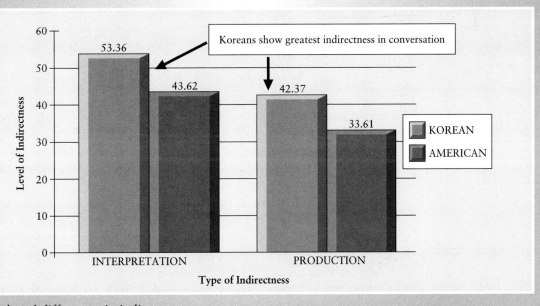

■ Cultural differences in indirectness

FIGURE 2.6 Koreans reported greater indirectness than Americans, both in terms of their *interpretation* of other's conversation and their own *production* of indirect communications.

Source: Based on Holtgraves, T. (1997).

everyday communication. A person from a more expressive cultural group might, for example, perceive the manner of someone from a reserved culture as rather unfriendly or cold; any attempts by the reserved individual at subtle indirect communication might be totally missed or even seen as somewhat manipulative (Holtgraves, 1997; Lakoff, 1977). From the perspective of a person from a more reserved cultural group, the animated emotional expression and directness of someone from another group might appear exaggerated and imposing, if not distinctly impolite (Holtgraves & Yang, 1990). These two people would find interaction with each other somewhat awkward, at least initially. You may be able to think of examples of such misunderstandings in your daily life.

Although the potential for miscommunication is very real between those from different cultures, we often manage to avoid real conflict. To some extent this may be because we make allowances for someone when we know they are from a very different background. It has been shown that we will sometimes accommodate or adapt our language to fit in with another person's (Giles, Mulac, Bradac, & Johnson, 1986). Nonetheless, misunderstandings between cultural groups are not infrequent and can have serious implications for inter-group relations. We spend many years training our children to communicate with precision grammatically in their own and other languages. Yet *styles* of communication, both verbal and nonverbal, receives little attention in education, even though there are times when they can be more important in understanding another's meaning (Mehrabian & Weiner, 1969). Those researching nonverbal communication have stressed its importance for educators (Lee, et al., 1992; Wolfgang, 1979), in courts (Blanck & Rosenthal, 1992), for those in the medical profession (Street & Buller, 1987, 1988), and in business (Graham, 1985; Lee, et al., 1992), as well as in social interaction. As one group of researchers has commented,

> *The success of intercultural interactions depends on the willingness to learn about specific cultural differences in nonverbal behaviours and messages, and on the patience required to attribute cultural transgressions to culture, rather than to the intention of the individual*

Lee, et al., 1992, p. 249

It is only if we are all willing to make such efforts that we can hope to reduce multicultural miscommunications.

KEY POINTS

- *Social perception* is concerned with the intake of social information and *social cognition* involves the use and manipulation of such information. These two processes interact in determining the way in which we internalize our social world.

- In order to understand others' emotional states, we often rely on *nonverbal communication*—an unspoken language of facial expressions, eye contact, and body movements and postures.

- Facial expressions appear to have a genetic or instinctive basis but are also influenced by cultural factors. They often provide useful information about others' emotional states. Useful information is also provided by eye contact, *body language*, and touching.

- Growing evidence suggests that our perceptions of nonverbal communication are actually quite accurate. One explanation is that actual links may exist between the way people look (their physical characteristics) and their psychological traits.

- Cultures vary in the extent to which they encourage open emotional expression and directness in verbal communication. *Display rules* specify the extent to which emotional dispays are seen as appropriate.

ATTRIBUTION: UNDERSTANDING THE CAUSES OF OTHERS' BEHAVIOUR

Nonverbal communication can be useful in beginning to understand others. Yet eventually, like the dog in Figure 2.7, we will want to know more, to understand others' lasting traits and to know the causes behind their behaviour—*why* they have acted as they have. The process through which we seek such information is known as attribution. More formally, **attribution** refers to our efforts to understand the causes behind others' behaviour and, on some occasions, the causes behind our behaviour, too. Attribution has been a topic of major interest in social psychology for several decades (e.g., Graham & Folkes, 1990; Heider, 1958; Jones, 1990).

> **Attribution** The process through which we seek to identify the causes of others' behaviour and so gain knowledge of their stable traits and dispositions.

Theories of Attribution: How We Understand the Social World

Because attribution is complex, many theories have been proposed to explain its operation (e.g., Gilbert, Pelham, & Srull, 1988; Trope, 1986). Here, we will focus on three that have been especially influential.

The Theory of Correspondent Inferences: When Behaviour Corresponds to Character

The first of these theories—Jones and Davis's (1965) *theory of correspondent inference*—asks how we use information about others' behaviour as a basis for inferring that they possess various traits or characteristics. How can we be sure that someone's behaviour reflects their character? According to Jones and Davis's theory (Jones & Davis, 1965; Jones & McGillis, 1976), we accomplish this difficult task by focusing our attention on certain types of actions—those most likely to prove informative.

First, we consider only behaviours that seem to have been *freely chosen*. We tend to ignore or at least discount behaviours that were somehow forced on the person in question. Second, we pay careful attention to actions that produce what Jones and Davis refer to as **noncommon effects**—effects that can be caused by one specific factor but not by others. (Don't confuse this word with uncommon, which simply means infrequent.) Why are actions that produce noncommon effects informative? Because they allow us to zero in on the causes of others' behaviour. Perhaps a concrete example will help.

> **Noncommon Effects** Effects produced by a particular cause that could not be produced by any other apparent cause.

Imagine that one of your casual friends has just gotten engaged. Her future spouse is very handsome, has a great personality, is wildly in love with your friend, and is very rich. What can you learn about her from her decision to marry this man? Not much. There are so many good reasons that you can't choose among them. In contrast, imagine that your friend's fiance is very handsome but that he treats her with indifference and is known to be extremely boring; also, he has no visible means of support and intends to live on your friend's salary. Does the fact that she is marrying him tell you anything about her personal characteristics? Definitely. You can probably conclude that she places more importance on physical attractiveness in a husband than on personality or wealth. As you can see from this example, we can usually learn more about others from actions on their part that show noncommon effects than from ones that do not.

■ "Why?": A basic question in social perception

FIGURE 2.7 Like the dog shown in this cartoon, we often want to understand why other people behave as they do.

Finally, Jones and Davis suggest that we also pay greater attention to actions by others that are *low in social desirability* than to actions that are high on this dimension. In other words, we learn more about others' traits or characteristics from actions they perform that are somehow out of the ordinary than from actions that are very much like those performed by most other persons.

In sum, according to the theory proposed by Jones and Davis, we are most likely to conclude that others' behaviour reflects their stable traits (i.e., we are likely to reach accurate or *correspondent inferences* about them) when that behaviour (1) occurs by choice; (2) yields distinctive, noncommon effects; and (3) is low in social desirability.

Kelley's Theory of Causal Attributions: How We Answer the Question *Why*?

Consider the following events:

You receive a much lower grade on an exam than you were expecting.

You phone one of your friends repeatedly and leave messages on her answering machine, but she never returns your calls.

What question would arise in your mind in each of these situations? The answer is clear: *Why?* You would want to know *why* your grade was so low and *why* your friend wouldn't return your calls. In countless life situations, this is the central attributional task we face. We want to know why other people have acted as they have, or why events have turned out in a particular way. Such knowledge is crucial, for only if we understand the causes behind others' actions can we adjust our own actions accordingly and hope to make sense out of the social world. Obviously, the number of specific causes behind others' behaviour is large. To make the task more manageable, therefore, we often begin with a preliminary question: Did others' behaviour stem mainly from *internal causes* (their own characteristics, motives, intentions); mainly from *external causes* (some aspect of the social or physical world); or from a combination of the two? For example, did you receive a lower grade than expected because you didn't study enough (an internal cause), because the questions were difficult and tricky (an external cause), or, perhaps, because of both factors. Revealing insights into how we carry out this initial attributional task are provided by a theory proposed by Kelley (Kelley, 1972; Kelley & Michela, 1980).

According to Kelley, in our attempts to answer the question why about others' behaviour, we focus on information relating to three major dimensions. First, we consider **consensus**—the extent to which others react to some stimulus or event in the same manner as the person we are considering. The higher the proportion of other people who react in the same way, the higher the consensus. Second, we consider **consistency**—the extent to which the person in whose behaviour we are interested reacts to the stimulus or event in the same way on other occasions. In other words, consistency relates to the extent to which the person's behaviour is unvarying over time. And third, we examine **distinctiveness**—the extent to which the person reacts in the same manner to other, different stimuli or events. (Be careful not to confuse consistency and distinctiveness. Consistency refers to similar reactions to a given stimulus or event at *different times*. Distinctiveness refers to similar reactions to *different stimuli* or events. If an individual reacts in the same way to a wide range of stimuli, distinctiveness is said be low.)

Kelley's theory suggests that we are most likely to attribute another's behaviour to *external causes* under conditions in which consensus, consistency, and distinctiveness are all high. In contrast, we are most likely to attribute another's behaviour to *internal causes* under conditions in which consensus and distinctiveness are low, but consistency is high. Finally, we usually attribute behaviour to a combination of internal and external factors when other combinations of information apply. Perhaps a concrete example will help illustrate the reasonable nature of these suggestions.

Consensus The extent to which actions by one person are also shown by others.

Consistency The extent to which an individual responds to a given stimulus or situation in the same way on different occasions (i.e., across time).

Distinctiveness The extent to which an individual responds in a similar manner to different stimuli or different situations.

An incident in 1988 caused many Canadians to ask the question *why*? Canadian sprinter Ben Johnson won the Olympic gold medal in the 100-metre dash, beating his closest American rival, Carl Lewis. He was hailed as a hero and Canada celebrated with him. You can imagine the dismay when the next day Ben Johnson was stripped of his gold medal because he had tested positive for the use of steroids. An official investigation was launched in Canada (the Dubin Inquiry) to answer the question why this had happened. According to Kelley's theory, the answer would depend on information relating to the three factors mentioned above. And certainly the Dubin Inquiry was interested in whether other athletes had taken steroids at the Olympics (consensus information), whether Ben Johnson had taken steroids before other athletic events (consistency information), and his honesty in general (distinctiveness information). However, for the sake of illustration, let's go beyond the facts and imagine that the following conditions had prevailed at such an inquiry:

1. No other Canadian athlete was found to have taken steroids at the Olympics (*consensus is low*).

2. The athlete being investigated was found to have taken steroids before other international athletic events (*consistency is high*).

3. The athlete was known to have cheated in other competitive situations (*distinctiveness is low*).

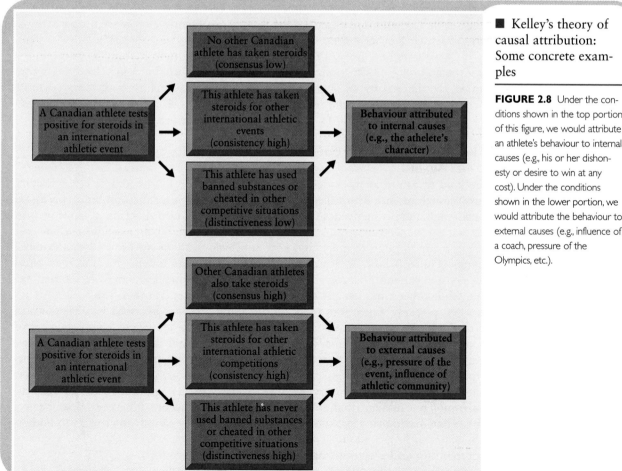

■ Kelley's theory of causal attribution: Some concrete examples

FIGURE 2.8 Under the conditions shown in the top portion of this figure, we would attribute an athlete's behaviour to internal causes (e.g., his or her dishonesty or desire to win at any cost). Under the conditions shown in the lower portion, we would attribute the behaviour to external causes (e.g., influence of a coach, pressure of the Olympics, etc.).

In this case, Kelley's theory suggests that an *internal attribution* would have been made: the athlete would have caused his own downfall (see the upper portion of Figure 2.8).

To continue our with our illustration, now imagine that different conditions had prevailed:

1. Many other Canadian athletes were found to have taken steroids at the Olympics (*consensus is high*).

2. The athlete being investigated was found to have taken steroids before other international athletic events (*consistency is high*).

3. The athlete was not known to act dishonestly in other competitive situations (*distinctiveness is high*).

Here, Kelley would predict that attribution would be made to external causes—the pressure of the Olympics or the context of international athletics, and, indeed, some commentators did draw this conclusion in the Ben Johnson case (refer to the lower portion of Figure 2.8).

In fact, the Dubin Inquiry actually attributed blame to both Johnson and his coach Charlie Francis, as well as calling for tougher standards in Canadian athletics organizations. This may well be due to the fact that Johnson had initially lied when asked about his actions and his honesty was, therefore, in question (making distinctiveness lower). Also, only a few athletes came forward and admitted to taking steroids (making consensus only moderate). In this kind of situation, Kelley's theory suggests that attribution would be made to a combination of internal and external causes—which is exactly what happened.

As we noted earlier, Kelley's theory is reasonable; and it seems applicable to a wide range of social situations. Further, basic aspects of the theory have been confirmed by the results of many different studies (e.g., Harvey & Weary, 1989; McArthur, 1972). We should note, though, that research on the theory also suggests the need for certain extensions. Some of these are described below.

When Do We Engage in Causal Attribution? The Path of Least Resistance Strikes Again

The kind of causal analysis described by Kelley requires considerable effort. Paying close enough attention to others' behaviour to gather information about consensus, consistency, and distinctiveness can be quite difficult. Given this fact, it is not surprising that people tend to avoid such cognitive work whenever they can. Often, they are all too ready to jump to quick and easy conclusions about the causes behind others' actions (Lupfer, Clark, & Hutcherson, 1990). They can do this because they know from past experience that certain kinds of behaviour generally stem from internal factors, while other kinds usually derive from external ones (Hansen, 1980).

So, precisely when does the kind of careful analysis described by Kelley occur? Primarily under three conditions: (1) when people are confronted with unexpected events (ones they cannot readily explain in terms of what they already know about a specific situation or person, or about people generally); (2) when they encounter unpleasant outcomes or events; and (3) when the events are important enough to them that the effort seems necessary. In sum, Kelley's theory appears to be an accurate description of causal attribution when such attribution occurs. It may not describe people's behaviour in many situations, though, because they simply don't want to bother.

Augmenting and Discounting: Multiple Potential Causes

Imagine you hear about an 18-month-old child who has fallen from a suspension bridge in a park while being carried by her mother. Your first reaction might be sympathy for the mother but you also couldn't help but wonder *why* this had happened. Perhaps the mother had slipped; even so, how could she be that careless? Then imagine that you hear a whole series of contradictory "facts" through the media: the police are investigating this incident; the mother says she slipped and hurt her ankle; the child's father has accused the mother of deliberately dropping the child; the parents are going through an acrimonious divorce; the mother claims the father was malicious; the child had Down's Syndrome and, lacking muscle tone, may have slipped; the mother had tried to have the child adopted before the incident occurred and was emotionally stressed. Confused? Not sure who or what to blame? Perhaps you feel that each new piece of information just serves to undermine the confidence you had in previous information.

This example sounds as if it comes from a soap opera but is in fact based on a real incident that occurred in the Capilano Canyon in Vancouver in September 1999—and you may recall that the child survived the 80 metre drop with barely a scratch! For our purposes, it illustrates a general principle in attribution, termed the **discounting principle**, which holds that when multiple possible causes are present, the weight placed upon one particular cause is lessened. That is, we tend to *discount* the importance of any potential cause of behaviour to the extent that other potential causes also exist (Kelley, 1972).

Discounting Principle The tendency to attach less importance to one potential cause of some behaviour when other potential causes are also present.

■ The augmenting principle in action

FIGURE 2.9 RCMP Constable Laurie White returns to duty ten months after being shot and seriously injured while investigating a crime. Her reinstatement to full status in only ten months demonstrated her bravery and determination, but her achievement is seen as more remarkable when we realize that she had to cope with the amputation of her right leg.

Now imagine a somewhat different situation: A young Royal Canadian Mounted Police constable is shot in the leg while investigating a crime. You feel sad when later you read that she has had to have most of her right leg amputated and, despite bravery and determination, her career is almost certainly at an end. Incredibly, ten months later you hear that she has been reinstated to active service after passing the rigorous RCMP test of physical ability with flying colours: she can not only walk but also run, climb, and cycle, as well as any other RCMP officer is required to. Now what do you think of her bravery and determination? Most probably that it is of heroic proportions.

This example, again based on a real incident (see Figure 2.9), illustrates a second attributional principle—the **augmenting principle**. It suggests that when a factor that might facilitate a given behaviour (e.g., her determination and bravery) and a factor that might inhibit it (e.g., the amputation) are both present and the behaviour actually occurs, we assign added weight to the facilitative factor (e.g., her bravery and determination become heroic). We do so because that factor has succeeded in producing the behaviour even in the face of an important inhibitory barrier.

A growing body of evidence suggests that both augmenting and discounting play an important role in attribution, especially when we can't observe others' actions over extended periods or in several situations (i.e., when information about consistency and distinctiveness is lacking). Thus, both augmenting and discounting should be taken into account when we apply Kelley's theory.

> **Augmenting Principle** The tendency to attach greater importance to a potential cause of behaviour if the behaviour occurs despite the presence of other, inhibitory causes.

Weiner's model of causal attribution

While we are often very interested in knowing whether others' behaviour stemmed mainly from internal or external causes, this is not the entire story according to Bernard Weiner (1985, 1995). In addition, we are also concerned with two other questions: (1) Are the causal factors that influence someone's behaviour likely to be *stable* over time or to change? And (2) are these factors *controllable*—can the individual change or influence them if she or he wishes to (Weiner, 1993, 1995)? These dimensions are independent of the internal-external dimension, which is termed *locus* in this theory, referring to the location of the cause—whether internal or external to the actor. For instance, some internal causes of behaviour, such as personality traits and temperament, tend to be quite stable over time (e.g., Miles & Carey, 1997). In contrast, other internal causes can and often do change greatly—for instance, motives, health, and fatigue. Similarly, some internal causes are controllable; individuals can, if they wish, learn to hold their tempers in check. Other internal causes, such as chronic illnesses or disabilities, are not. A large body of evidence indicates that in trying to understand the causes behind others' behaviour, we do take note of all three of these dimensions—internal-external, stable-unstable, and controllable-uncontrollable (Weiner, 1985, 1995). Moreover, our thinking in this respect strongly influences our conclusions concerning important matters, such as whether others are personally responsible for their own actions. A very dramatic illustration of this fact is provided by an ingenious study conducted recently by Graham, Weiner, and Zucker (1997).

These researchers approached male and female passers-by on a large urban college campus as well as in public places such as shopping malls, supermarkets, libraries, and parks. They asked these individuals a series of questions concerning an event that was much in the news at the time: the alleged murder by O. J. Simpson of his wife and her male friend. (Simpson was acquitted of the murder in his criminal trial, but later lost a civil suit relating to the same alleged crimes.) Overall, predictions derived from Weiner's attribution theory were confirmed: to the extent that Simpson's behaviour

- In order to obtain information about others' lasting traits, motives, and intentions, we often engage in *attribution*—efforts to understand why others have acted as they have.

- According to Jones and Davis's *theory of correspondent inference*, we attempt to infer others' traits from observing certain aspects of their behaviour—especially behaviour that is freely chosen, produces *noncommon effects*, and is low in social desirability.

- According to Kelley's *theory of causal attribution*, we are interested in the question of whether others' behaviour stemmed from internal or external causes. To answer this question, we focus on information relating to *consensus*, *consistency*, and *distinctiveness*.

- When two or more potential causes of another person's behaviour exist, we tend to downplay the importance of each—an effect known as the *discounting principle*. When a cause that facilitates a behaviour and a cause that inhibits it both exist but the behaviour still occurs, we assign added weight to the facilitative factor—the *augmenting principle*.

- Weiner's theory of attribution suggests that in addition to the internal-external dimension of attribution, termed *locus*, we are also interested in the extent to which causal factors are *stable* or changeable over time, and *controllable*, or can be influenced by the individual. These additional dimensions relate to the assignment of personal responsibility.

was seen as stemming from factors under his control, he was held more responsible for the crimes, viewed less sympathetically by participants, and assigned harsher punishment (see Figure 2.10).

These findings and those of many other studies (e.g., Schlenker et al., 1994) suggest that when trying to decide whether others should be held responsible for their actions, we do focus on more than just the locus of causality of such factors (whether they are internal or external in nature): we consider their stability and controllability, too. Thus, extending Kelley's theory to include these variables appears to be a very useful step.

Attribution: Some Basic Sources of Bias

Our discussion of attribution so far seems to imply that it is a highly rational process in which individuals seeking to identify the causes of others' behaviour follow orderly cognitive steps. In general, this is so. We should note, however, that attribution is also subject to several forms of bias—tendencies that can lead us into serious errors concerning the causes of others' behaviour. Several of these errors are described below.

The Fundamental Attribution Error: Overestimating the Role of Dispositional Causes

Imagine that you witness the following scene. A man arrives at a meeting 40 minutes late. On entering, he drops his notes all over the floor. While he is trying to pick them up, his glasses fall off and break. Later he spills coffee all over the desk. How would you explain these events? The chances are good that you would reach conclusions such as these: this person is disorganized, clumsy, and generally incompetent. Are such attributions accurate? Perhaps. But it is also possible that the man was late because of

■ The role of attributions in recommended punishment

FIGURE 2.10 When individuals believe that a crime has stemmed from factors that could be controlled, they experience high levels of anger and low levels of sympathy for the criminal. They then hold the person responsible for the crime and recommend punishment designed to make this person suffer or to deter others from the same crime. In contrast, when they view the crime as stemming from uncontrollable factors, they report less anger and more sympathy toward the criminal, hold this person less responsible for the crime, and recommend punishment focused on rehabilitation.

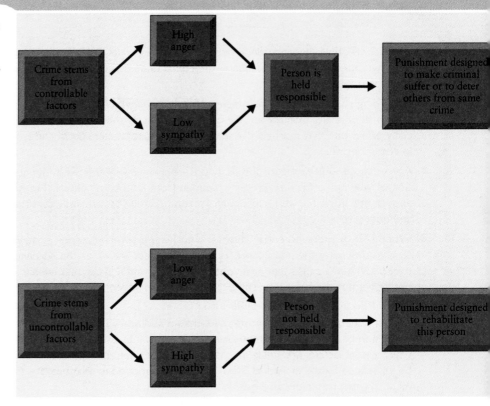

Fundamental Attribution Error The tendency to overestimate the impact of dispositional (internal) causes on others' behaviour.

unavoidable delays at the airport, dropped his notes because they were printed on very slick paper, and spilled the coffee because the cup was too hot to hold. That you would be less likely to consider such potential causes reflects what is often termed the **fundamental attribution error** (or *correspondence bias*)—our strong tendency to explain others' actions in terms of dispositional (internal) causes, even in the face of clear situational (external) causes (e.g., Gilbert & Malone, 1995). In short, we tend to perceive others as acting as they do because they are "that kind of person," rather than because of the many situational factors that may have affected their behaviour.

This tendency to overemphasize dispositional causes while underestimating the impact of situational ones seems to arise from the fact that when we observe another person's behaviour, we tend to focus on his or her actions. The context in which these actions occur often fades into the background or we tend not to adjust our first impression to allow for the impact of external events (Gilbert & Malone, 1995). As a result, the potential impact of situational causes receives less attention. A second possibility is that we do notice such situational factors but tend to assign them insufficient weight (Gilbert & Jones, 1986).

Whatever the basis for the fundamental attribution error, it has important implications. For example, it suggests that even if individuals are made aware of the situational forces that adversely affect disadvantaged groups in a society (e.g., poor diet, shattered family life), they may still perceive these persons as "bad" and responsible for their own plight. In such cases, the fundamental attribution error can have serious social consequences.

Interestingly, growing evidence suggests that while our tendency to attribute others' actions to dispositional causes is robust, it weakens over time (e.g., Burger, 1991; Burger & Pavelich, 1993; Frank & Gilovich, 1989). In other words, while we tend to attribute others' actions to internal causes soon after they have occurred, we take

---

58   **Exploring Social Psychology**

greater and greater account of situational (external) causes as time passes. Apparently the fundamental attribution error decreases over time because the accessibility of personal information diminishes more rapidly than the accessibility of situational information (Burger, 1991).

The Actor-Observer Effect: You Fell; I Was Pushed

Another and closely related type of attributional bias can be readily illustrated. Imagine that while walking along the street, you see someone stumble and fall down. How would you explain this behaviour? Probably in terms of internal characteristics. You might assume that the person is clumsy. Now, suppose the same thing happens to *you*; would you explain your own behaviour in the same terms? Probably not. Instead, you might well assume that you tripped because of situational causes—wet pavement, slippery shoes, and so on.

This tendency to attribute our own behaviour to external or situational causes, but that of others to internal ones, is known as the **actor-observer effect** (Jones & Nisbett, 1971) and has been observed in many different studies (e.g., Frank & Gilovich, 1989). It seems to stem in part from the fact that we are quite aware of the situational factors affecting our own actions but, as outside observers, are less aware of such factors when we focus on the actions of others. Thus, we tend to perceive our own behaviour as arising largely from situational causes but the behaviour of others as deriving mainly from their traits or dispositions.

Actor-observer Effect The tendency to attribute our own behaviour mainly to situational causes but the behaviour of others mainly to internal (dispositional) causes.

The Self-Serving Bias: I Can Do No Wrong; You Can Do No Right

Suppose that you write a term paper for one of your courses. When you get it back you find the following comment on the first page: "An *excellent* paper—one of the best I've read in years. A+." To what will you attribute this success? If you are like most people, you will likely explain your success in terms of internal causes—your high level of talent, the tremendous amount of effort you invested in writing the paper, and so on.

Now, in contrast, imagine that when you get your paper back, this comment is written on it: "Horrible paper—one of the worst I've read in years. D-." How will you interpret this outcome? In all likelihood, you will be sorely tempted to focus mainly on external (situational) factors—the difficulty of the task, your professor's unreasonable standards, and so on.

This tendency to attribute positive outcomes to internal causes but negative ones to external factors is known as the **self-serving bias**, and it can have a powerful effect on social relations (Brown & Rogers, 1991; Miller & Ross, 1975).

Self-serving Bias The tendency to attribute our own behaviour mainly to situational causes but the behaviour of others mainly to internal (dispositional) causes.

Why does this bias in our attributions occur? Several possibilities have been suggested, but most of these can be classified into two categories: cognitive and motivational explanations. The cognitive model suggests that the self-serving bias stems primarily from certain tendencies in the way we process social information (Ross, 1977). Specifically, it suggests that we attribute positive outcomes to internal causes but negative ones to external causes because we *expect* to succeed, and we have a stronger tendency to attribute expected outcomes to internal causes than to external causes. In contrast, the motivational explanation suggests that the self-serving bias stems from our need to protect and enhance our self-esteem, or the related desire to look good in the eyes of others (Greenberg, Pyszczynski, & Solomon, 1982). Both cognitive and motivational factors may well play a role in this type of attributional error, though recent evidence has shown support for the latter (Brown and Rogers, 1991).

Some of the most interesting evidence to emerge from cross-cultural psychology has suggested that frequency of these biases may, at least in part, stem from cultural individualism. As we will see in the next section, the self-serving bias as well as the fundamental attribution error may not be the universal tendencies they were assumed to be. In fact, they appear to be much less common in non-Western cultures.

Cultural Styles of Attribution: The Socialization of Explanations

Over the last decade research has begun to accumulate indicating that cultural factors may have an important impact on attribution processes. Research suggests that processes of social cognition and perception, as revealed in Western social psychology, may not be universal. Specifically, this work suggests that cultural and subcultural groups socialize their members toward certain types of explanation or *cultural styles of attribution* (e.g., Crittenden, 1996; Guimond, Begin, & Palmer, 1989; Guimond & Palmer, 1996; Miller, 1984; Morris & Peng, 1994). One cultural difference that has been the focus of interest has been the dimension of individualism-collectivism (see Chapter 1). Cultural groups that are individualistic (e.g., North America, Northern and Western Europe, Australia, and New Zealand) will tend to focus on the individual as self-determining and, thus, as causing his or her own outcomes. This focus on the individual may have led to a consequent neglect of external factors, as we have seen in the *fundamental attribution error*. Similarly, the *self-serving bias* in attribution may stem from an individualistic need for maintenance and enhancement of self-esteem (Heine & Lehman, 1995). The question is raised—Will such patterns be found in collectivistic cultural groups? Collectivistic cultures (e.g., Asia, India, and South America), which tend to see the individual as interdependent with his or her group and subordinate to it, may give greater emphasis to external causes of individual behaviour. Three sets of studies nicely illustrate the challenge that this recent research has presented to the traditional Western view of attribution processes.

A study investigating the fundamental attribution error was carried out by Joan Miller (1984). She asked subjects in India (a collectivistic culture) and the United States (an individualistic culture) to recount real-life instances of other people's prosocial and antisocial behaviour and to explain why these occurred. Subjects in each culture were of four age groups: 8 years, 11 years, 15 years, and adult. Their explanations for these

Miller (1984) found that internal attribution increased with the age of subjects in the United States but not in India. In contrast, external attribution increased with age in India but not in the United States.

TABLE 2.3 Internal and external attribution in the United States and India

	Percentage of Attributions to Internal Causes		Percentage of Attributions to External Causes	
	U.S.A.[*]	India	U.S.A.	India[*]
Adult	40.0	18.5	18.0	40.5
15 years	20.5	12.5	30.0	31.0
11 years	14.0	11.0	20.5	28.0
8 years	10.5	9.5	23.5	23.0

*only these two sets of results showed a significant increase with age

Source: Based on Miller, 1984.

real-life incidents were coded according to whether they attributed the behaviour to internal (dispositional) factors or to external (contextual) factors. Results are shown in Table 2.3. Just looking at the results for the Adult group, it is clear that Indians do not make the fundamental attribution error—if anything, their attributional patterns bias toward the external. However, more interesting is the pattern of change over the different age groups. American subjects make more internal attributions as they get older and Indian subjects make more external attributions as they approach adulthood. This developmental trend suggests a gradual socialization in the cultural styles of attribution appropriate in each country. Such findings must be interpreted cautiously because this is a cross-sectional study and other factors, such as different influences on the generations, might account for the different patterns of attribution over the age groups. However, Miller's results are certainly in line with the notion of cultural socialization of attributional processes.

Turning to the self-serving bias, a number of studies have shown that this tendency is very much less frequent in collectivistic cultures (see Smith & Bond, 1998). In one study, Canadian children between 8 and 10 years from an Indian-Asian background used internal attribution to the same extent whether they were explaining their own success or failure, whereas their European-origin counterparts showed the expected patterns of internal attribution for their own success and external attribution for their own failure (Fry & Ghosh, 1980). The tendency for those from more collectivistic cultural origins to make fewer internal attributions when they succeed (and often more internal attributions for failure) has been shown to occur among Chinese (Bond, Leung, & Wan, 1982; Crittenden, 1991; Lee & Seligman, 1997) and Japanese (Kashima & Triandis, 1986). When the pattern of attributions is reversed from that expected in the self-serving bias this has been termed a *self-effacement* or *modesty bias*—the individual will make internal attribution for failure and external for success—and again this has been shown more frequently among those from collectivistic backgrounds (e.g., Mizokawa & Ryckman, 1990; Wan & Bond, 1982). Further, Chinese students who used this style of attribution were liked more by their peers than those who did not (Bond, et al, 1982), suggesting that such attributions are an important part of social relations.

To summarize, cross-cultural research has shown that those from more collectivistic cultures either do not use the self-serving bias and the fundamental attribution error, or use them less than North Americans. Further, the development patterns shown in Miller's study (1984) suggest that children are being increasingly socialized towards adoption of differing cultural styles of attribution, reflecting the prevailing individualism or collectivism of the social group concerned.

Studies by Guimond and colleagues (Guimond, Begin, and Palmer, 1989; Guimond & Palmer, 1996) demonstrated that attributional styles can be learned by showing that Canadian students' attributional patterns were influenced by their academic major. In particular, when asked to explain poverty and unemployment, students in the social sciences (where the approach tends to focus on external factors) made more external attributions than students in the natural sciences and business studies (where the approach is more likely to focus on internal factors). Further, this difference tended to be more marked the longer students had been involved in education, suggesting that attributional styles were being gradually learned as part of the topic of study.

Applications of Attribution Theory: Insights and Interventions

As mentioned in Chapter 1, Kurt Lewin, one of the founders of modern social psychology, remarked that "There's nothing as practical as a good theory." By this he meant that once we obtain scientific understanding of some aspect of social behaviour or social thought, we can, potentially, put this knowledge to practical use. Where attribution theory is concerned, this has definitely been the case. As basic knowledge about attribution has grown, so too has the range of practical problems to which such knowledge has been applied (Graham & Folkes, 1990). Here, we'll examine two important, and especially timely, applications of attribution theory.

Attribution and Depression

Depression is the most common psychological disorder. In fact, it has been estimated that almost half of all human beings experience this problem at some time during their lives (e.g., Blazer et al., 1994). Although many factors play a role in depression, one that has received increasing attention is what might be termed a *self-defeating pattern of attributions*. In contrast to most people who show the self-serving bias described above, depressed individuals tend to adopt an opposite pattern. They attribute negative outcomes to lasting (stable), internal causes such as their own traits or lack of ability, but attribute positive outcomes to temporary (unstable), external causes such as good luck or special favours from others (see Figure 2.11). As a result, such persons perceive that they have little or no control over what happens to them—they are mere chips in the winds of unpredictable fate. Little wonder that they become depressed and may give up on life.

Fortunately, several forms of therapy that focus on changing such attributions have been developed, and these appear to be quite successful (e.g., Bruder et al., 1997; Robinson, Berman, & Neimeyer, 1990). These new forms of therapy focus on getting depressed persons to change their attributions—to take personal credit for successful outcomes, to stop blaming themselves for negative outcomes (especially ones that can't be avoided), and to view at least some failures as the result of external factors beyond their control. These new forms of therapy do not explore repressed urges, inner conflicts, or traumatic events during childhood, but they do seem to help. Attribution theory provides the basis for these new forms of treatment, so it has certainly proved very useful in this respect.

Attribution and Rape: Blaming Innocent Victims

In a survey of sexual violence in 44 Canadian universities (Dekeseredy & Kelly, 1993), almost 1 in 10 women (9.8 percent) reported having been raped in conditions where physical force, or the threat of it, was used to coerce them. Further, 29 percent of female students indicated that they had suffered some form of sexual abuse in the past year. Clearly, these are frightening statistics. Perhaps even more unsettling, however, is the strong tendency of many persons to hold rape victims responsible for this crime (Fischer,

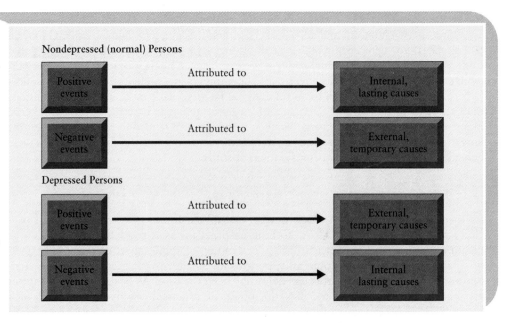

■ Attribution and depression

FIGURE 2.11

While most persons show a tendency to attribute positive events to internal, lasting causes and negative events to external, temporary causes, depressed persons show precisely the opposite pattern. They attribute negative outcomes to lasting, internal causes (e.g., their own traits or lack of ability) but attribute positive outcomes to temporary, external causes (e.g., good luck).

1986; Shotland & Goodstein, 1983). "She must have led him on." "What was she doing in a bar or on the street at that hour of the night, anyway? She was asking for trouble!" These are the kind of comments frequently heard in conversations concerning media reports of rapes. From the perspective of attribution theory, in short, blame is often attributed to victims as much as, or even more than, to perpetrators. As you might guess, men are more likely to make such attributions than women (Cowan & Curtis, 1994); but women, too, often show some tendency to attribute responsibility for rape to its victims.

What accounts for this tendency? One possibility involves what has been termed *belief in a just world*—our desire to assume that the world is basically a fair place (Lerner, 1980). According to this reasoning, if a woman is sexually assaulted, then she "must" have done something to deserve it; thinking the opposite—that she is a completely blameless victim—is too threatening an idea for some persons to consider. Put another way, believing that totally blameless individuals can be made to suffer such degradation is very threatening, so some people find comfort from such thoughts by concluding that rape victims are not blameless and must somehow have invited the assault.

Indirect support for this view is provided by the findings of a recent study conducted by Bell, Kuriloff, and Lottes (1994). These researchers asked male and female college students to read one of four descriptions of a rape. In two cases, the woman was attacked by a stranger. In two other incidents, the woman was raped by a man whom she was dating. After reading one of these incidents, participants were asked to rate the extent to which the victim was responsible for the crime. As you can see from Figure 2.12, both males and females blamed the victim to a greater extent when she knew the rapist (someone she dated) than when the rapist was a stranger. In addition, while males attributed greater blame to the victim than females, both genders seemed to hold her responsible, to some degree, for the assault.

These findings, and those of many other studies (e.g., Cowan & Curtis, 1994), have important implications with respect to rape prevention and can help in the development of programs designed to educate men and women. Such efforts are already under way, but only time—and additional data—will reveal their impact.

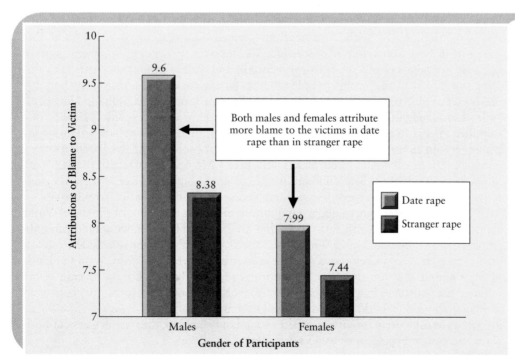

■ Attributions about Rape: Some unsettling findings

FIGURE 2.12 Both males and females blamed the victim of a rape to a greater extent when she knew the rapist (date rape) than when the rapist was a stranger.

Source: Based on data from Bell, Kuriloff, & Lottes, 1994.

- Attribution is subject to many potential sources of error. One of the most important of these is the *fundamental attribution error*, sometimes called the correspondence bias, which is the tendency to explain others' actions as stemming from internal dispositions even in the presence of situational causes.

- Two other attributional errors are the *actor-observer effect*—the tendency to attribute our own behaviour to external (situational) causes but that of others to internal causes—and the *self-serving bias*—the tendency to attribute our own positive outcomes to internal causes but negative ones to external causes.

- The strength of the fundamental attribution error and the self-serving bias differs across cultures, being stronger in Western, individualistic societies than in Asian, collectivistic cultures. Research suggests that *cultural styles of attribution* may be learned during socialization.

- Attribution theory has been applied to many practical problems. Depressed persons often show a pattern of attributions opposite to that of the self-serving bias: they attribute positive events to external causes and negative ones to internal causes. The victims of rape are often held partly responsible for this crime—it is assumed that they somehow "asked for trouble." Such tendencies seem to stem partly from our *belief in a just world*.

SCHEMAS, HEURISTICS, AND BIASES: COPING WITH INFORMATION OVERLOAD

Despite evidence that our perceptions or nonverbal communications are often accurate, we are not always the rational and efficient thinkers that we would like to be. Three key characteristics of social cognition contribute to this. First, we are often faced with excessive amounts of social information—termed *information overload*—and this forces us to be *selective* in our processing. We impose organization upon information (e.g., we use schemas and social categorization), and we use mental shortcuts in evaluating this information. Second, people often prefer the path of least resistance, and this preference applies to cognitive, as well as to physical, efforts. In fact, it is a guiding principle of social cognition: All things being equal, most of us will attempt to *minimize our cognitive efforts* (e.g., Fiske & Taylor, 1991). Third, human beings are definitely not computers. In films and books we have attempted to portray the totally emotionless and logical individual who rarely makes a mistake—Mr. Spock or Data of the *Star Trek* series for example. But, being human, we are *fallible*—highly fallible—where the cognitive side of life is concerned. Social thought is certainly no exception to this rule.

In sum, our attempts to understand others and make sense out of the social world sometimes involve selectivity, little effort and are fallible. However, we should carefully emphasize the following point: While such aspects of social thought sometimes result in errors, they are also, in key respects, quite *adaptive*. They help us to focus on the kinds of information that are usually most informative, and they reduce the overall effort required for understanding our complex social world. Further, they sometimes help us to feel good about our world or ourselves and to maintain a consistent world-view. So, as is true of virtually every important aspect of human behaviour, these tendencies cut both ways and can be beneficial as well as detrimental.

Our discussion of these cognitive processes will first examine *schemas*. These mental structures or frameworks allow us to organize large amounts of diverse information in an efficient manner (Fiske & Taylor, 1991). Second, we'll turn to *heuristics*, cognitive shortcuts and strategies that help us to make decisions quickly and easily. Third, we'll examine several *biases in social cognition*—tendencies to pay more attention to some kinds of information than to others, sometimes leading to conclusions that are less than accurate. Finally, we will examine the impact of *affect*—our current feelings or moods— on social cognition. Obviously, we are emotional as well as cognitive beings and these two aspects of our mental processes have an impact upon each other (e.g., Forgas, 1994).

Schemas: Organizing Social Information

One key finding of research on social cognition is this: Our thoughts about the social world are definitely not a mixture of random ideas and knowledge. On the contrary, information we have acquired through experience is organized into cognitive structures known as **schemas** (e.g., Fiske & Taylor, 1991; Wyer & Srull, 1994). In a sense, schemas can be thought of as "mental scaffolds"—cognitive structures that hold and organize information. Schemas are important because, once formed, they exert powerful effects on the processing of information related to them. For example, they influence which aspects of the social world are selected for attention, what information is entered into memory, what is later retrieved from memory storage, and how it is interpreted (Wyer & Srull, 1994).

Schemas Organized collections of beliefs and feelings about some aspect of the world. Schemas operate like mental scaffolds, providing structure for the interpretation and organization of new information we encounter.

In these respects schemas play a key role in our understanding of other persons, ourselves, and the social world generally. Their main function is to help us cope with information overload by speeding up the processes of social cognition. However, on the down side, because schemas focus our attention on *particular* aspects of incoming information, some other information about the social world is lost. Let's turn to some examples of schemas so that you can understand how they work.

One key type of schema that helps us understand others is the *person schema*, a mental framework suggesting that certain traits and behaviours go together and that individuals having them represent a certain type.

A second kind of schema relates to specific social roles—*role schemas*. These schemas contain information about how persons playing specific roles generally act, and what they are like. For example, consider your role schema for professors. You expect professors to stand in front of the room; to talk about the topic of the course; to answer questions from students, prepare exams, and so on. You don't expect them to try to sell you a product or to do magic tricks; such actions are definitely not part of your role schema for professors.

A third type of schema involves mental frameworks relating to specific situations. Such schemas relate to events, or sequences of events, and are known as *scripts*. They indicate what is expected to happen in a given setting. For example, when you walk into a restaurant, you expect someone to greet you and either lead you to a seat or put your name on a list. Then you expect a server to come to your table to offer drinks and to take your order. Next on the agenda is the appearance of the food, followed, ultimately, by the bill. Once established, scripts save us a great deal of mental effort, because they tell us what to expect, how other persons are likely to behave, and what will happen next in a wide range of social situations. (We'll consider another, and very important, type of schema—the self-schema—in Chapter 4.)

As mentioned, schemas have an important influence on basic aspects of social cognition (Wyer & Srull, 1994). With respect to *attention*, schemas often act as a kind of filter: only information consistent with them "registers" and enters our consciousness. Information that does not fit with our schemas is often ignored (Fiske, 1993), unless it is so extreme that we can't help but notice it. And even then, it is often discounted as "the exception that proves the rule." In the *encoding* process the effects of schemas are more complex. Existing evidence indicates that once schemas have been formed, information consistent with them is easier to remember than information that is inconsistent. Earlier in the process, however, when schemas are first being formed, information *inconsistent* with them may be more readily noticed and thus encoded (e.g., Stangor & Ruble, 1989). Finally, schemas also influence what information is *retrieved* from memory. To the extent that schemas are activated when we are trying to recall some information, they determine precisely what information is actually brought to mind—in general, information that is part of these schemas or at least consistent with them (e.g., Conway & Ross, 1984).

Perseverance Effect
The tendency for beliefs and schemas to remain unchanged even in the face of contradictory information.

We should quickly add, however, that there is a serious downside to schemas too. By influencing what we notice, enter into memory, and later remember, schemas can produce distortions in our understanding of the social world. Research findings indicate that schemas are often very resistant to change—they show a strong **perseverance effect**, remaining unchanged even in the face of contradictory information (e.g., Ross et al., 1975).

For a discussion of an even more unsettling effect of schemas—the fact that they can often be *self-confirming*—please see the Cornerstones section below.

Cornerstones

Evidence for the Self-Confirming Nature of Schemas: The Self-Fulfilling Prophecy

In 1999, Statistics Canada asked teachers and parents of elementary students about their expectations for the children's educational futures. Whereas 60 percent of parents at the lowest income level expected their children to become university graduates, teachers of these same children expected fewer than 20 percent of them to graduate from university. The perceptions of parents in higher income brackets and the teachers of their children did not show as great a disparity. On hearing of these findings a coordinator of parent programs for the Toronto School Board was quoted as saying, "If someone feels you are not capable, you do not feel capable and you do not perform well" (Galt, 1999). The coordinator is suggesting that if teachers have low expectations of their students, this will be fulfilled in their students' results—see Figure 2.13. But can a teacher's expectations have such a profound effect?

Research suggests that they can. Schemas can influence expectations and produce such effects, which are sometimes described as **self-fulfilling prophecies**—predictions

Self-fulfilling Prophecies Predictions that, in a sense, make themselves come true.

that, in a sense, make themselves come true. The first evidence for such effects was provided by Robert Rosenthal and Lenore Jacobson (1968) during the turbulent 1960s. During that period there was growing concern over the possibility that teachers' beliefs about minority students—their schemas for such youngsters—were causing them to treat such children differently (less favourably) than majority-group students, and that as a result the minority-group students were falling farther and farther behind. No, the teachers weren't overtly prejudiced; rather, their behaviour was shaped by their expectations and beliefs—their schemas for different racial or ethnic groups.

To gather evidence on the possible occurrence of such effects, Rosenthal and Jacobson conducted an ingenious study that exerted a profound effect on subsequent research in social psychology. They went to an elementary school in San Francisco and administered an IQ test to all students. They then told the teachers that some of the students had scored very high and were about to bloom academically. In fact, this was not true: the researchers chose the names of these students randomly. But Rosenthal and Jacobson predicted that this information might change teachers' expectations (and schemas) about these children, and hence their behaviour toward them. Teachers were not given such information about other students, who constituted a control group.

To check on their prediction, Rosenthal and Jacobson returned eight months later and tested both groups of children once again. Results were clear—and dramatic: Those who had been described as "bloomers" to their teachers showed significantly larger gains on the IQ test than those in the control group. In short, teachers' beliefs about the students had operated in a self-fulfilling manner: the students teachers believed would bloom academically actually did so.

How did such effects occur? In part, through the impact of schemas on the teachers' behaviour. Further research (Rosenthal, 1994) indicated that teachers gave the bloomers more personal atten-

tion, more challenging tasks, more and better feedback, and more opportunities to respond in class. In short, the teachers acted in ways that benefited the students they expected to bloom, and as a result, these youngsters really did.

As a result of this early research, social psychologists began to search for other self-confirming effects of schemas in many settings—in education, therapy, and business, to name just a few. They soon uncovered much evidence that schemas do often shape behaviour in ways that lead to their confirmation. For example, they soon found that teachers' lower expectations for minority students or females often undermined the confidence of these groups and actually contributed to poorer performance by them (e.g., Sadker & Sadker, 1994). So the research conducted by Rosenthal and Jacobson has had far-reaching effects and can be viewed as one important cornerstone of research in our field.

■ The self-fulfilling prophecy

FIGURE 2.13 Research suggests that teachers' expectations about their students can act as *self-fulfilling prophecies*—can influence students' behaviour in the direction expected. In the light of Statistics Canada findings that teachers have much lower expectations of children from low-income families, we can anticipate that such children will in fact achieve less.

- Research on social cognition suggests that our thinking is not always accurate or rational. We cope with *information overload* by being selective, we minimize our cognitive effort and we are fallible.
- One source of such effects is *schemas*—mental frameworks centring around a specific theme that help us to organize social information.
- Schemas can relate to persons, events, or situations. Once formed, schemas exert powerful effects on what we notice (attention), enter into memory (encoding), and later remember (retrieval). Even in the face of disconfirming information schemas tend to persist, showing the *perseverance effect*.
- Schemas can also exert self-confirming effects—the *self-fulfilling prophecy*—causing us to behave in ways that confirm them.

Heuristics: Cognitive Shortcuts

In many cases, people adopt strategies to help them make social judgments in the face of information overload. To be successful, such strategies must have two properties. First, they must provide a quick and simple way of dealing with large amounts of social information. Second, they must work—they must be reasonably accurate much of the time.

Heuristics Rules or principles that allow individuals to make social judgments rapidly and with reduced effort.

While many potential shortcuts for reducing mental effort exist, the ones that have received the most attention with respect to social cognition are **heuristics**—simple decision-making rules we often use to make inferences or draw conclusions quickly and easily. To understand how heuristics work, consider an analogy. Suppose you want to estimate the dimensions of a room but don't have a tape measure. What will you do? One possibility is to pace off the length and width of the room by placing one foot almost exactly in front of the other. Since the distance from the heel to the toe of an adult's foot is approximately 12 inches, you will be able to get rough estimates of the room's dimensions through this "quick-and-dirty" method.

In a similar manner, we make use of many different mental heuristics in our efforts to think about and use social information. Two of these that are used frequently in everyday life are known as *representativeness* and *availability*. These heuristics can also lead to a number of biases or fallacies (false reasoning or conclusions).

Representativeness: Judging by Resemblance

Imagine that you have just met your neighbour for the first time. On the basis of a brief conversation with her, you determine that she is very neat in her habits, has a good vocabulary, reads many books, is somewhat shy, and dresses conservatively. Later you realize that she did not mention what she does for a living. Is she a business executive, a librarian, a server, a lawyer, or a dancer? One quick way of making a guess is to compare her with other members of each of these occupations; simply ask yourself how well she resembles persons you have met in each of these fields. If you proceed in this fashion, you may well conclude that she is a librarian. After all, her traits seem to resemble the traits many people associate with librarians more closely than the traits of dancers, lawyers, or servers. In this instance, you would be using the **representativeness heuristic**. In other words, you would make your judgment on the basis of a relatively simple rule: *The more similar an individual is to "typical" members of a given group, the more likely he or she is to also belong to that group.*

Representativeness Heuristic A strategy for making judgments based on the extent to which current stimuli or events resemble ones we view as being typical.

Such judgment rules are developed because of their utility, so the representativeness heuristic often leads to accurate conclusions. As you probably know from your experience, however, there are exceptions to this general rule. Some librarians are extroverted and lead exciting social lives; some dancers are shy and read lots of books. And some professors (believe it or not) climb mountains, practise sky-diving, and even run for political office in their spare time. Because of such exceptions, the representativeness heuristic, although useful, can lead to serious errors in at least some instances. In addition, and perhaps more importantly, reliance on this heuristic can lead us to overlook other types of information that could potentially be very useful. The most important type is information relating to *base rates*—the frequency with which some event or pattern occurs in the general population. The tendency to overlook such information when relying on the representativeness heuristic was illustrated some years ago by a famous study carried out by Tversky and Kahneman (1973).

Participants in this study were told that an imaginary person named Jack had been selected from a group of 100 men. They were then asked to guess the probability that Jack was an engineer. Some participants were told that 30 of the 100 men were engineers (thus, the base rate for engineers was 30 percent). Others were told that 70 of the men were engineers. Half of the subjects received no further information. The other half, however, also received a personal description of Jack that either resembled the common stereotype of engineers (e.g., they are practical, like to work with numbers, etc.) or did not. When participants in the study received only information relating to base rates, their estimates of the likelihood that Jack was an engineer reflected this information: They thought it more likely that Jack was an engineer when the base rate was 70 percent than when it was 30 percent. However, when they received personal information about Jack, they tended to ignore this important information. They made their estimates primarily on the basis of whether Jack seemed to resemble their stereotype of an engineer: That is, in terms of representativeness alone. This tendency to ignore useful base rate information is known as the **base rate fallacy**.

Base Rate Fallacy The tendency to ignore or underuse information relating to base rates—the relative frequency with which conditions, events, or stimuli actually occur.

Availability: What Comes to Mind First?

Which is more common—words that start with the letter *k* (e.g., king) or words with *k* as the third letter (e.g., *awkward*)? Tversky and Kahneman (1982) put this question to more than 100 people. Their findings were revealing. In English there are more than twice as many words with *k* in third place as there are with *k* in first place. Yet despite this fact, most of the subjects guessed incorrectly. Why was this the case? In part, because of their use of another heuristic—availability. According to this heuristic, the easier it is to bring instances of some group or category to mind, the more prevalent or important these are judged to be. This heuristic, too, makes good sense: After all, events or objects that are common are usually easier to think of than ones that are less common, because we have had more experience with them. But relying on availability in making such judgments can also lead to errors, such as the one involving words with the letter *k*. In this and many other situations, the fact that information is easy to remember does not guarantee that it is important or common. Yet our subjective feeling that something is easy to remember may lead us to assume that it is important (Schwartz, et al., 1991). To the extent that this assumption is correct then the availability heuristic can be useful.

However, it can also lead us to erroneous conclusions and one of these may be the **false consensus effect**, the tendency to assume that other people agree with you to a greater extent than is actually true. This effect can be explained as resulting from the availability heuristic because often the information we have about others' behaviour is biased either by our selective recall of instances in which others agree with our perspective or perhaps from knowing others who are similar to ourselves. Research in Chapter 6 will show that our friends do in fact tend to have

False Consensus Effect The tendency to assume that others behave or think as we do to a greater extent than is actually true.

attitudes similar to ourselves. Whatever its roots, the false consensus effect has been observed in many different contexts. For example, in one study high school boys who smoked estimated that 51 percent of their fellow male students smoked, but nonsmoking boys estimated that only 38 percent smoked (Sherman, Presson, & Chassin, 1984). In a similar manner, students tend to overestimate the proportion of other students who agree with their attitudes about drugs, abortion, seat belt use, university policies, politics, and even Ritz crackers (Nisbett & Kunda, 1985; Suls, Wan, & Sanders, 1988). In short, the false consensus effect is quite common (although in an absolute sense, it is not very large).

Interestingly, research suggests that there is more to the availability heuristic than merely the subjective *ease* with which relevant information comes to mind. In addition, the *amount* of information we can bring to mind seems to matter (e.g., Schwarz et al., 1991b). The more information we can think of, the greater its impact on our judgments. Which of these two factors is more important? The answer appears to depend on the kind of judgment we are making. If it is one involving emotions or feelings, we tend to rely on the "ease" rule; if it is one involving facts

■ The false consensus effect

FIGURE 2.14 While research proves friends do tend to have similar attitudes, the false consensus effect means that there is a tendency to assume that other people agree with you to a greater extent than is actually true.

or information, we tend to rely more on the "amount" rule. This pattern has been demonstrated clearly in studies by Rothman and Hardin (1997) who showed that in making judgments about our own group (the one to which we belong; know as an *ingroup* to social psychologists), we tend to focus on facts or information; thus, the more information we can bring to mind, the stronger its impact on our judgments. In contrast, when making judgments about other groups (*outgroups*, as they are termed in social psychology), we tend to focus more on emotions or feelings and so will rely more on the ease-with-which-it-comes-to-mind rule.

So the availability heuristic seems to include two different rules for judging the importance of information: how easily it comes to mind, and how much we can remember. And which of these rules we follow depends strongly on the kind of judgment we are making.

KEY POINTS

- *Heuristics* help us cope with information overload by making decisions in a quick and relatively effortless manner.
- The *representativeness* heuristic, in which we make judgments about others based on how typical they are, can lead to the *base rate fallacy*.
- The *availability* heuristic is used to make judgments based on the ease and amount of information we can bring to mind. One error that may stem from this heuristic is the *false consensus effect*.

Errors in Social Cognition: Why We Are Fallible

We have already seen that in our attempts to cope with information overload through the use of schemas and heuristics, we sometimes jump to inaccurate or biased conclusions (e.g., the base rate fallacy and the false consensus effect). In this section we will extend this exploration of our inaccuracies by looking at a number of systematic biases in social cognition. You will notice that while these biases can lead us to erroneous conclusions, they can also sometimes be adaptive and useful, helping us to interpret and respond to the social world. There are numerous instances of cognitive biases (e.g., Rozin & Nemeroff, 1990; Wilson & Schooler, 1991; Zusne & Jones, 1989): we will focus on some notable recent examples.

Optimistic Biases: Looking at the Future Through Rose-Coloured Glasses

When we look toward the future, particularly our own, we sometimes tend to be more optimistic than is warranted. A robust example of such a tendency is termed **unrealistic optimism**—the tendency to believe that you are more likely to experience positive events, and less likely to experience negative events, than similar others. This bias is a common and robust one, particularly where negative life events (e.g., losing your job, becoming alcoholic, getting AIDS) are concerned (Perloff, 1983; Perloff & Fetzer, 1986; Weinstein, 1982, 1984). One review estimated that at least 121 studies had demonstrated this phenomenon (Taylor & Brown, 1994). You may be thinking that in your case optimism about the future is not unrealistic. After all, perhaps you are doing very well in your education; perhaps your character and behaviour are such that you feel you can avoid many of life's pitfalls. Indeed, you may have a rosy future ahead of you. However, before you feel too complacent, be aware that research shows that this is how most students feel. That is, the average student believes that his or her future

Unrealistic Optimism The tendency to believe that we are more likely to experience positive life events and less likely to experience negative life events, than similar others.

will be better than the average student of the same age and gender—and statistically it is not possible for the average to be greater than average! For this reason, and because it seems such a common response, this kind of optimism can be considered truly unrealistic. The unrealistic optimism bias has been explained as part of a broader inclination to be *self-enhancing*: to see ourselves and our lives somewhat more positively than reality might dictate. We should note here that recent research has raised questions about the universality of this effect. Cross-cultural research is beginning to suggest that, as with other self-enhancing biases, unrealistic optimism may not be as common in other cultures as it is in North America (Heine & Lehman, 1995).

A second optimistic bias can be seen in public as well as private life. The *planning fallacy*, described in Chapter 1, is our tendency to make optimistic predictions about the completion of a task. In public life examples abound, from the completion (or incompletion) of the Olympic Stadium in Montreal in 1976 to the government inquiry into the Red Cross handling of HIV-tainted blood in the late 1990s. All too often, public officials and professionals seem to underestimate the time (and cost) of building projects, social programs, government inquiries—to name a few. Perhaps this is understandable when we consider the complexities of such plans. But as we saw, many people in their private lives make the same error, in situations where more detailed knowledge of past performance and current temporal limitations is available. Researchers show that we are more likely to fall victim to this bias when we are highly motivated to finish a task (Buehler et al., 1994).

Counterfactual Thinking: Considering "What Might Have Been"

Imagine the following events:

> *Ms. Caution never picks up hitchhikers. Yesterday, however, she gave a stranger a ride. He repaid her kindness by robbing her.*

Now, in contrast, consider the following events:

> *Ms. Risk frequently picks up hitchhikers. Yesterday, she gave a stranger a ride. He repaid her kindness by robbing her.*

Which of these two persons will experience greater regret? If you answered "Ms. Caution, of course," your thinking in this instance is very much like that of other persons. An overwhelming majority of respondents identify Ms. Caution as feeling more regretful (Kahneman & Miller, 1986). Why is this the case? Both individuals have suffered precisely the same negative outcome: They have been robbed. In most general terms, it appears that our reactions to events depend not only on the events themselves but on what these events bring to mind (Miller, Turnbull, & McFarland, 1990)—the extent to which we can think of the possibility of alternative events and outcomes. This process is termed **counterfactual thinking**. It appears to occur in part because it is easier to imagine alternatives to unusual behaviour, such as Ms. Caution's picking up the hitchhiker, than it is to imagine alternatives to usual, normal behaviour (e.g., Ms. Risk's picking up the hitchhiker). So, we conclude that Ms. Caution experienced more regret because it is easier to imagine her acting in a different way—sticking to her rule—than it is to imagine Ms. Risk acting differently. This is not to suggest, however, that Ms. Risk would not feel regret in a real-life situation (see Davis, Lehman, Wortman, Silver, & Thompson, 1994). Rather, it suggests that we, as observers, find it easier to generate counterfactual alternatives to Ms. Caution's behaviour because it is unusual for her.

This reasoning leads to the prediction that negative outcomes that follow unusual behaviour will generate more sympathy and be seen as deserving more com-

Counterfactual Thinking The tendency to evaluate events by thinking about alternatives to them (e.g., "What might have been"). The more readily such alternative events or outcomes come to mind, the stronger our reactions to the events that actually occurred.

pensation than ones that follow usual behaviour. Precisely such effects have been demonstrated in many recent studies (Kahneman & Tversky, 1982; Macrae, 1992; Miller and McFarland, 1986).

Neal Roese (1997), a social psychologist who has conducted many studies on counterfactual thinking, suggests that engaging in such thought can yield a wide range of effects, some of which are beneficial and some of which are costly to the persons involved (e.g., Roese & Maniar, 1997). For instance, counterfactual thinking can, depending on its focus, yield either boosts to or reductions in our current moods. If individuals engage in *upward counterfactual thinking*, comparing their current outcomes with more favourable ones they can imagine, or positive opportunities they might have missed, the result may be strong feelings of dissatisfaction or envy, especially if they do not feel capable of obtaining better outcomes in the future (Medvec & Savitsky,1997; Sanna, 1997). For instance, Olympic athletes who win a silver medal but imagine winning a gold one experience such reactions (e.g., Medvec, Madey, & Gilovich, 1995). Alternatively, if individuals engage in *downward counterfactual thinking*, comparing their current outcomes with less favourable ones, or if they contemplate various ways in which disappointing results could have occurred and positive ones could have been missed, they may experience positive feelings of satisfaction or hopefulness. Such reactions have been found among Olympic athletes who win bronze medals, and who therefore imagine what it would be like to have won no medal whatsoever (e.g., Gleicher et al., 1995). In sum, engaging in counterfactual thought can strongly influence affective states.

In addition to affecting emotional states, counterfactual thinking can provide individuals with increased understanding of the causal factors that contributed to the negative or disappointing outcomes they experienced—enhanced insight into *why* these outcomes occurred. Such information, in turn, can assist people in planning changes in behaviour or new strategies that can improve their future performance (e.g., McMullen, Markman, & Gavanski, 1995; Roese, 1997). Engaging in counterfactual thinking may be one technique that assists individuals in learning from past experience and in profiting from their mistakes. (Figure 2.15 presents a summary of all these potential effects.)

In sum, imagining what might have been in a given situation can yield many effects, ranging from despair and intense regret on the one hand, through hopefulness

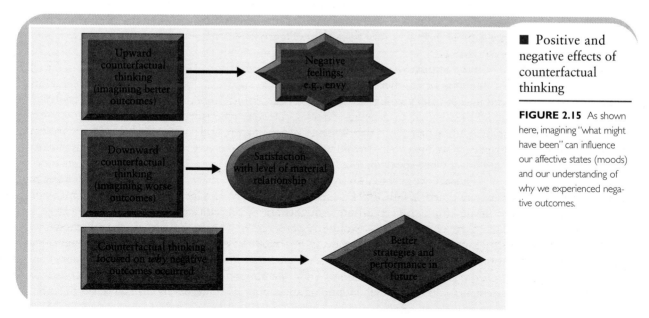

■ Positive and negative effects of counterfactual thinking

FIGURE 2.15 As shown here, imagining "what might have been" can influence our affective states (moods) and our understanding of why we experienced negative outcomes.

and increased determination to do better on the other. Our tendency to think not only about what is but also about what might be, therefore, can have far-reaching effects on many aspects of our social thought and social behaviour.

Rational Versus Intuitive Processing

Imagine the following situation: You are shown two bowls containing red jelly beans and white jelly beans. One holds a single red bean and nine white ones; the other bowl holds ten reds and ninety whites. Further, imagine that you will win money each time you select (blindfolded) a red bean. From which bowl would you prefer to draw? Rationally, it makes no difference: the chances of winning are exactly 10 percent in both cases. But if you are like most people, you'd prefer the bowl with one hundred beans. In fact, in several studies, more than two-thirds of the participants given this choice preferred the bowl with the larger number of jelly beans—and, even more surprisingly, they were willing to pay money to guarantee this choice (Kirkpatrick & Epstein, 1992). In a sense, it's hard to imagine a clearer illustration of the fact that our thinking is far from perfectly rational in many situations.

What accounts for this and related findings? A model of cognition proposed by Epstein and his colleagues (e.g., Denes-Raj & Epstein, 1994; Epstein, 1994) offers one explanation. According to this model, known as **cognitive-experiential self-theory** (or CEST), our efforts to understand the world around us proceed in two distinct ways. One of these is deliberate, rational thinking, which follows basic rules of logic. The other is a more intuitive system that operates in a more automatic, holistic manner—a kind of do-it-by-hunches-or-intuition kind of approach. CEST suggests that we tend to use these contrasting styles of thought in different kinds of situations. Rational thinking is used in situations involving analytical thought—for example, when we are solving mathematical problems. Intuitive thinking is used in many other situations, including most social ones. In other words, when we try to understand others' behaviour, we often revert to intuitive, gut-level thinking.

So why do we choose the bowl with more jelly beans, even though the chances of winning are the same as for the smaller bowl with fewer beans? CEST suggests that in situations such as this where our emotions are involved, the intuitive system is dominant. We know, rationally, that the odds of winning are the same in both cases; but we *feel* that we have a better chance of winning when there are ten red jelly beans rather than only one. The same kind of intuitive thought is often involved when people gamble or buy lottery tickets (see Figure 2.16).

Thought Suppression: Why Avoidance Sometimes Backfires

At one time or another, everyone has tried to suppress certain thoughts—to keep ideas and images from coming into consciousness. For example, a person on a diet may try to avoid thinking about delicious desserts, someone who is trying to quit smoking may try to avoid thoughts about the pleasures of lighting up, and someone who is nervous about giving a speech may try to avoid thinking about all the ways in which he or she risks looking foolish while speaking to a large audience. (See Figure 2.17 for another example.)

How do we accomplish such, and what are the effects of this process? According to Daniel Wegner (1992b, 1994), a social psychologist who has studied **thought suppression** in detail, efforts to keep certain thoughts out of consciousness involve two components. First, there is an automatic *monitoring process*, which searches for evidence that unwanted thoughts are about to intrude. When such thoughts are detected by the monitoring component, a second process, which is more effortful and less automatic (i.e., more controlled), swings into operation. This *operating process* involves effortful, conscious attempts to distract oneself by finding something else to think about. In a sense, the mon-

■ Intuitive processing in action

FIGURE 2.16 Gambling behaviour is seldom rational. Sales of relatively low-priced lottery tickets usually far exceed sales of more expensive lottery tickets, even though the odds of winning are often greater in the latter case. Apart from the price, the greater sale of low-priced tickets is often due to our intuitions. Many people feel intuitively that they have a greater chance of winning if they buy several low-priced tickets rather than one higher-priced ticket. This is an example of *intuition*, or hunch-based thought.

itoring process is an "early warning" system that tells the person unwanted thoughts are present, and the second process is an active prevention system that keeps such thoughts out of consciousness through distraction.

Under normal circumstances, the two processes do a good job of suppressing unwanted thoughts. When information overload occurs or when individuals are fatigued, however, the monitoring process continues to identify unwanted thoughts but the operating process no longer has the resources to keep them from entering consciousness. The result: The individual actually experiences a pronounced *rebound* effect in which the unwanted thoughts occur at an even higher rate than was true before efforts to suppress them began. Further, individuals who are high in *reactance*— those who react very negatively to perceived threats to their personal freedom—may be especially at risk for such effects. Such persons often reject advice or suggestions from others because they want to do their own thing, so they may find instructions to suppress certain thoughts hard to follow (Kelly & Nauta, 1997).

The operation of the two processes described by Wegner (1992a, 1994) has been confirmed in many different studies (e.g., Wegner & Zanakos, 1994) and with respect to thoughts ranging from strange or unusual images (e.g., a white elephant) to thoughts about old romantic flames (Wegner & Gold, 1995). So this model of thought suppression appears to be an accurate one.

■ Thought suppression: Harder than it seems!

FIGURE 2.17 As the cartoon character has discovered, when told not to think about something (e.g., some activity or object), many people find that this is precisely what they do think about.

KEY POINTS

- Systematic biases in our social cognitions can result in erroneous conclusions about the social world, but they can also be adaptive at times.

- Optimistic biases can occur when individuals show *unrealistic optimism*, seeing their own future as more optimistic than those of comparable others, or the *planning fallacy*, making overly optimistic predictions about how long it will take to complete a given task.

- In many situations, individuals imagine "what might have been"—they engage in *counterfactual thinking*. Such thinking can affect our sympathy for persons who have experienced negative outcomes and can cause us to experience strong regret over missed opportunities.

- Counterfactual thinking can also strongly influence our affective states. And it may increase our understanding of why we experienced negative outcomes; in this way, such thought can help us to improve our performance in the future.

- Growing evidence related to *cognitive-experiential self-theory* (CEST) suggests that we rely largely on intuitive rather than rational processing when we think about other persons or social situations.

- Individuals often engage in *thought suppression*, trying to prevent themselves from thinking about undesirable topics. Although efforts at thought suppression are often successful, sometimes they result in a *rebound* effect, in which such thoughts actually increase in frequency. Persons high in *reactance* are more likely to experience a rebound effect.

AFFECT AND COGNITION: THE INTERPLAY BETWEEN OUR FEELINGS AND OUR THOUGHTS

An important area of research in social psychology involves efforts to investigate the interplay between *affect*, our current moods or feelings, and *cognition*—the ways in which we process social information (Forgas, 1994; Isen & Baron, 1991). We say *interplay*, because the relationship is very much a two-way street: our feelings and moods exert strong effects on several aspects of cognition, and cognition, in turn, exerts strong effects on our feelings and moods (e.g., Seta, Hayes, & Seta, 1994).

The Influences of Affect on Cognition

Does being in a positive or negative mood influence the way we think? Informal observation suggests that this is indeed the case. As one old song puts it, when we are happy, "We see the world through rose-coloured glasses"—everything takes on a positive tinge. And most people are aware of the fact that they think differently when feeling happy than when they are depressed. For example, when we are experiencing positive feelings (affect), difficult tasks or situations seem easier to perform or deal with than when we are experiencing negative feelings. Are these subjective impressions correct? Growing evidence suggests that they are—that our current affective states do indeed have important effects on how we process social information (Bower, 1991; Clore, Schwarz, & Conway, 1993; Isen & Baron, 1991).

For example, evidence indicates that while positive emotions or feelings are certainly enjoyable, they may reduce our tendency to think carefully or systematically, unless we are specifically (and highly) motivated to do so (e.g., Bodenhausen, Kramer, & Susser, 1994; Mackie & Worth, 1989). Why do such effects occur? One explanation is provided by a theory known as the **cognitive tuning model** (Schwarz, 1990). This theory suggests that positive affective states, such as those induced by seeing another person smile, inform us that the current situation is safe and therefore doesn't require careful attention or processing of information. In contrast, negative affective states, such as those induced by seeing another person frown, signal us that the situation is potentially dangerous and that we had better pay careful attention to what's happening.

Applying this model to facial expressions leads to the following intriguing prediction: If another person smiles while presenting information to us (for example, while giving a speech), we may be less likely to think carefully and systematically about the content of the speech than if this person shows a neutral facial expression or frowns in anger (Ottati, Terkildsen, and Hubbard, 1997).

Another general finding about the influence of affect on cognition is what is termed the **mood-congruent judgment effect**, the finding that there is often a match between our mood and our social judgment. When we are in a positive mood, we tend to think pleasant thoughts and have happy memories; when we are in a negative mood, we tend to think unpleasant thoughts and remember negative information (Seta, Hayes, & Seta, 1994). So, for example, in one recent study using members of sororities and fraternities at a large university (Mayer & Hanson, 1995), individuals' moods predicted their judgments about the probability of positive and negative events (e.g., the threat of nuclear war) and their judgments about people in social categories (e.g., the typical worker). Changes in participants' moods over time were closely related to changes in their social cognition. The mood-congruent judgment effect also has practical implications. For

Cognitive Tuning Model Theory suggesting that positive affective states inform us that the current situation is safe and doesn't require careful thought. In contrast, negative affective states signal that the situation is potentially dangerous and requires careful processing.

Mood-congruent Judgment Effect The finding that there is often a good match between our current mood and the social judgments that we make.

example, physicians have been shown to be more creative (often a requirement for that profession) when in a good mood than in a neutral mood (Estrada, Isen, & Young, 1995). Also, it has been found that when interviewers are in a good mood, they tend to assign higher ratings to job applicants (Baron, 1987, 1993, 1995)—temporary fluctuations in mood might even, therefore, influence the course of someone's career.

The Affect Infusion Model: How Affect Influences Cognition

Before concluding, we should address one final issue: *How*, precisely, does affect influence cognition? Through what mechanisms do our feelings influence our thought? A theory proposed by Forgas (1995), known as the **affect infusion model** (or **AIM**), offers revealing answers. According to Forgas (1995a), affect influences social thought and, ultimately, social judgments through two major mechanisms. First, affect serves to *prime* (i.e., trigger) similar or related cognitive categories. When we are in a good mood, positive feelings serve to prime positive associations and memories; when we are in a bad mood, in contrast, negative feelings tend to prime mainly negative associations and memories (Bower, 1991; Erber, 1991).

Second, affect may influence cognition by acting as a *heuristic cue*—a quick way for us to infer our reactions to a specific person, event, or stimulus. According to this *affect-as-information* mechanism (Clore et al., 1993), when asked to make a judgment about something in the social world, we examine our feelings and then respond accordingly. If we are in a good mood, we conclude: "I like it" or "I'm favourable toward it." If we are in a bad mood, we conclude: "I don't like it" or "I'm against it." In other words, we ask ourselves: "How do I feel about it?" and use our current affective state to answer this question—*even if it is unrelated to the object, person, or event itself*. An example of this was mentioned earlier—interviewers' moods can influence their ratings of job applicants, even if the moods have nothing to do with these applicants (Baron, 1995).

The findings of many different studies lend support to the view that affective states can influence judgments and decisions through both of these mechanisms (e.g., Clore et al., 1994; Forgas, 1993). The key remaining question, however, is this: Precisely *when* do such effects occur? When do our current moods strongly influence our thoughts, judgments, and decisions? AIM offers a surprising answer. It suggests that the likelihood of affect infusion is *higher* when individuals engage in careful, effortful thought about some issue or topic than when they engage in simpler and relatively "automatic" modes of thought. Relatively simple modes of thought occur in situations where individuals make judgments or decisions by recalling previous evaluations or they are strongly motivated to reach a particular conclusion; in such situations the individual is not motivated to engage in a detailed analysis of all available information. According to AIM, current moods are unlikely to exert strong effects in these instances, because these kinds of thinking are so rapid and lacking in effort that there is little opportunity for current moods to enter the picture (see Figure 2.18).

Careful, reasoned thought, however, presents a markedly different picture. Here, individuals engage in active effortful processing of information, often with the goal of transforming this information (the raw materials of cognition) into something new (Forgas, 1995a). According to AIM, when individuals engage in such thought, affect infusion has ample opportunity to occur. When such thought is relatively unimportant to the persons performing it and they do not feel compelled to seek maximum accuracy, affect infusion will occur primarily through the *affect-as-information mechanism* described above. In contrast, when such thought is important or personally relevant to the persons performing it and they do feel compelled to examine all pertinent infor-

Affect Infusion Model (AIM) Theory explaining how affect influences social thought and social judgment through either a heuristic or priming mechanism.

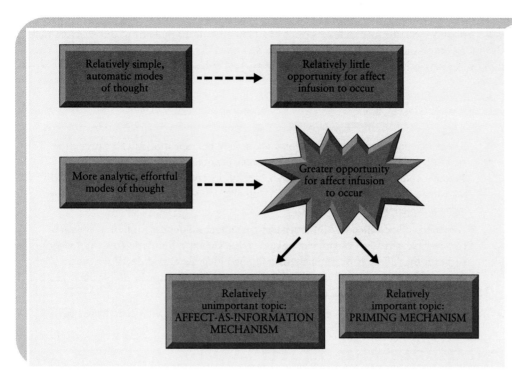

FIGURE 2.18 The affect infusion model, or AIM, (Forgas, 1995a) makes a somewhat surprising prediction: It suggests that our affective states are more likely to influence our social judgments and decisions when we engage in careful analytic thought than when we engage in simpler and more automatic modes of thought.

mation, affect infusion will occur primarily through the *priming mechanism*. In both cases, the main point—and the one that is certainly counterintuitive—remains the same: Current moods are more likely to influence judgments and decisions when individuals engage in active, effortful thought about issues, for example, when they are attempting to form an impression of another person or to evaluate him or her very carefully (Forgas, 1995a).

The results of many studies offer support for these suggestions (e.g., Forgas, 1998b; Forgas & Fiedler, 1996; Sedikides, 1995), so it appears that AIM provides a useful framework for understanding how and when our affective states influence our thought and social judgments.

Reciprocal Influence of Cognition on Affect

Finally, we should mention once again that the influence of affect on cognition is *reciprocal*: our thought processes also influence our feelings. We have seen a number of instances in this chapter where our interpretation of social information can contribute to an emotional response. Research indicates that the impact of cognition on affect can be as powerful as the effects mentioned above. First, the activation of *schemas*, particularly where they contain a strong affective component, can generate emotion. An example is the activation of negative stereotypes that can produce the emotions of hatred, as we will see in Chapter 5 on prejudice. Second, our thoughts can often influence our reactions to emotion-provoking events. For example, our interpretation of another's inconsiderate behaviour can determine whether we become angry with that person or instead interpret this as due to stress and feel more tolerant. Chapter 8 contains many examples of the way cognition influences aggression and anger. Finally, our *expectations* can influence our reactions to an event or situation. Often such expectancies shape our perceptions and our feelings about a new situation or stimulus (e.g., Wilson, et al, 1989). For example, if you expect to dislike candied grasshoppers the first time you try them, you will probably feel disgust before you even taste them. Expectations have even been shown to shape our memories, such that we recall events as more (or less) pleasant than they were, depending on our anticipation of them (Wilson & Klaaren, 1992).

KEY POINTS

● Affect influences cognition in several ways. Our current moods can cause us to react positively or negatively to new stimuli, including other persons. Positive affective states can act as a signal that careful processing is unnecessary according to the *cognitive tuning model*. Affect can also influence judgments through the *mood judgment congruence effect*.

● The *affect infusion model* (AIM) suggests that affect influences cognition through two mechanisms—through priming and by serving as a heuristic cue. AIM also suggests that affect is more likely to influence judgments and decisions when individuals engage in analytic thought than when they engage in simpler and relatively automatic modes of thought.

● Cognitions also influence emotions through our schemas, interpretations, and expectations of social situations.

Ideas to Take with You

Minimizing the Impact of Errors in Social Cognition

Attribution and social cognition are subject to many errors, and these can prove quite costly both to you and to the people with whom you interact. Thus, it's well worth the effort to avoid such pitfalls. Here are our suggestions for recognizing—and minimizing—several important cognitive errors.

The Fundamental Attribution Error.
We have a strong tendency to attribute others' behaviour to internal (dispositional) causes even when strong external (situational) factors that might have influenced their behaviour are present. To reduce this error, always try to put yourself in the shoes of the person whose behaviour you are trying to explain. In other words, try to see the world through their eyes. If you do, you will often realize that from their perspective there are many external factors that played a role in their behaviour.

The Self-Serving Bias: "I'm good; you're lucky."
Perhaps the strongest attributional error we make is that of attributing our own positive outcomes to internal causes such as our own abilities or effort but our negative outcomes to external factors such as luck or forces beyond our control. This can lead us to overestimate our own contributions to group projects, thus producing unnecessary friction with others. It can also reduce the chances that we will learn something valuable from negative outcomes—for instance, how we might do better the next time. You can help minimize this error simply by being aware of it; once you know it exists, you may realize that not all your positive outcomes stem from internal causes, and that you may have played a role in producing negative ones. In addition, try to remember that other people are subject to the same bias; they, too, instinctively want to take credit for positive outcomes but to shift the blame for negative ones to external causes—such as you!

The Planning Fallacy.

Often, we underestimate the amount of time it will take us to complete a task. The stronger our motivation to be done with the task, the stronger this effect. Next time you have a deadline, allow what seems like too much time for it to be completed and you will probably finish it on time.

Thought Suppression: Trying to Keep Certain Thoughts Out of Consciousness.

In many situations we try to suppress thoughts that we believe will get us into trouble. For example, dieters try to suppress thoughts of delicious foods, and people trying to quit smoking try to avoid thinking about the pleasure of lighting up. Unfortunately, trying to suppress such thoughts often causes the thoughts to intrude more than they would otherwise do.

Summary and Review of Key Points

Nonverbal Communication:
The Unspoken Language

● *Social perception* is concerned with the intake of social information and *social cognition* involves the use and manipulation of such information. These two processes interact in determining the way in which we internalize our social world.

In order to understand others' emotional states, we often rely on *nonverbal communication*—an unspoken language of facial expressions, eye contact, and body movements and postures.

Facial expressions appear to have a genetic or instinctive basis but are also influenced by cultural factors. They often provide useful information about others' emotional states. Useful information is also provided by eye contact, body language, and touching.

Facial expressions influence our affective states, and hence important aspects of social thought. The *cognitive tuning model* suggests that when others smile, we interpret this as a sign that we do not need to think carefully about what they are saying. When they frown, however, we sense that careful thought about their words *is* required.

Growing evidence suggests that our perceptions of nonverbal communication are actually quite accurate. One explanation is that actual links may exist between the way people look (their physical characteristics) and their psychological traits; also our social perceptions may exert a self-fulfilling effect, causing people to behave in ways that confirm our expectations.

Cultures vary in the extent to which they encourage open emotional expression and directness in verbal communication. *Display rules* specify the extent to which emotional dispays are seen as appropriate.

Attribution: Understanding the Causes of Others' Behaviour

● In order to obtain information about others' lasting traits, motives, and intentions, we often engage in *attribution*—efforts to understand why others have acted as they have.

According to Jones and Davis's *theory of correspondent inference*, we attempt to infer others' traits from observing certain aspects of their behaviour—especially behaviour that is freely chosen, produces *noncommon effects*, and is low in social desirability.

According to Kelley's *theory of causal attribution*, we are interested in the question of whether others' behaviour stemmed from internal or external causes. To answer this question, we focus on information relating to *consensus*, *consistency*, and *distinctiveness*.

When two or more potential causes of another person's behaviour exist, we tend to downplay the importance of each—an effect known as the *discounting principle*. When a cause that facilitates a behaviour and a cause that inhibits it both exist but the behaviour still occurs, we assign added weight to the facilitative factor—the *augmenting principle*.

Weiner's *theory of attribution* suggests that in addition to the internal-external dimension of attribution, termed *locus*, we are also interested in the extent to which causal factors are *stable* or changeable over time, and controllable, or can be influenced by the individual. These additional dimensions relate to the assignment of personal responsibility.

Attribution is subject to many potential sources of error. One of the most important of these is the *fundamental attribution error*, sometimes called the correspondence bias, which is the tendency to explain others' actions as stemming from internal dispositions even in the presence of situational causes.

Two other attributional errors are the *actor-observer effect*—the tendency to attribute our own behaviour to external (situational) causes but that of others to internal causes—and the *self-serving bias*—the tendency to attribute our own positive outcomes to internal causes but negative ones to external causes.

The strength of the fundamental attribution error and the self-serving bias differs across cultures, being stronger in Western, individualistic societies than in Asian, collectivistic cultures. Research suggests that *cultural styles of attribution* may be learned during socialization.

Attribution theory has been applied to many practical problems. Depressed persons often show a pattern of attributions opposite to that of the self-serving bias: they attribute positive events to external causes and negative ones to internal causes. The victims of rape are often held partly responsible for this crime—it is assumed that they somehow "asked for trouble." Such tendencies seem to stem partly from our *belief in a just world*.

Schemas, Heuristics and Biases: Coping with Information Overload

● Research on social cognition suggests that our thinking is not always accurate or rational. We cope with *information overload* by being selective, we minimize our cognitive effort and we are fallible.

One source of such effects is *schemas*—mental frameworks centring around a specific theme that help us to organize social information.

Schemas can relate to persons, events, or situations. Once formed, schemas exert powerful effects on what we notice (attention), enter into memory (encoding), and later remember (retrieval). Even in the face of disconfirming information schemas tend to persist, showing the *perseverance effect*.

Schemas can also exert self-confirming effects—the *self-fulfilling prophecy*—causing us to behave in ways that confirm them.

Heuristics help us cope with information overload by making decisions in a quick and relatively effortless manner.

The *representativeness* heuristic, in which we make judgments about others based on how typical they are, can lead to the base rate fallacy.

The *availability* heuristic is used to make judgments based on the ease and amount of information we can bring to mind. One error that may stem from this heuristic is the *false consensus effect*.

Systematic biases in our social cognitions can result in erroneous conclusions about the social world, but they can also be adaptive at times.

Optimistic biases can occur when individuals show *unrealistic optimism*, seeing their own future as more optimistic than those of comparable others, or the *planning fallacy*, making overly optimistic predictions about how long it will take to complete a given task.

In many situations, individuals imagine "what might have been"—they engage in *counterfactual thinking*. Such thinking can affect our sympathy for persons who have experienced negative outcomes and can cause us to experience strong regret over missed opportunities.

Counterfactual thinking can also strongly influence our affective states. And it may increase our understanding of why we experienced negative outcomes; in this way, such thought can help us to improve our performance in the future.

Growing evidence related to *cognitive-experiential self-theory* (CEST) suggests that we rely largely on intuitive rather than rational processing when we think about other persons or social situations.

Individuals often engage in *thought suppression*, trying to prevent themselves from thinking about undesirable topics. Although efforts at thought suppression are often successful, sometimes they result in a *rebound* effect, in which such thoughts actually increase in frequency. Persons high in *reactance* are more likely to experience a rebound effect.

Affect and Cognition: How Feelings Shape Thought and Thought Shapes Feelings

● Affect influences cognition in several ways. Our current moods can cause us to react positively or negatively to new stimuli, including other persons. Positive affective states can act as a signal that careful processing is unnecessary according to the *cognitive tuning model*. Affect can also influence judgments through the *mood judgment congruence effect*.

The *affect infusion model* (AIM) suggests that affect influences cognition through two mechanisms—through priming and by serving as a heuristic cue. AIM also suggests that affect is more likely to influence judgments and decisions when individuals engage in analytic thought than when they engage in simpler and relatively automatic modes of thought.

Cognitions also influence emotions through our schemas, interpretations and expectations of social situations.

For More Information

Kenny, D. A. (1994). *Interpersonal perception: A social relations analysis.* New York: Guilford.

This well-written and relatively brief book provides an excellent overview of what social psychologists have discovered about many different aspects of interpersonal perception. The book focuses on the key questions of how we see other people, how we see ourselves, and how we think we are seen by others. All in all, a very thoughtful and useful volume.

Malandro, L. A., Barker, L., & Barker, D. A. (1994). *Nonverbal communication* (3rd ed). New York: Random House.

A basic and very readable text that examines all aspects of nonverbal communication. Body movements and gestures, facial expression, eye contact, touching, smell, and voice characteristics are among the topics considered.

Forgas, J. P. (Ed.). (1991). *Emotion and social judgments.* Elmsford, NY: Pergamon Press.

Chapters in this volume deal with the complex interplay between affect and cognition. The many ways in which our feelings can influence our social judgments are carefully examined by experts in this field.

Roese, N. J., & Olson, J. M. (Eds.). (1997). *What might have been: The social psychology of counterfactual thinking.* Mahwah, NJ: Erlbaum.

This book focuses on counterfactual thinking in specific situations. The nature of such thought and its effects are examined from many different perspectives by social psychologists who have studied this fascinating topic.

Weblinks

www.psy.anu.edu.au/Social
Social Psychology page at Australian National University

www.acs.ohio-state.edu/units/psych/s-psych/socnelab.htm
Social Neuroscience homepage

wizard.ucr.edu/~kmcneill/social1.htm
Social Psychology—Research and Experimental Methodologies

www.ai.univie.ac.at/archives/Psycoloquy/1998.V 9/0068.html
"The Bet on Bias: A Foregone Conclusion?" by Joachim Krueger, Brown University

exp.kyb.tuebingen.mpg.de/web-experiment
"Feeling and Thinking: The Role of Affect in Social Cognition"—International Symposium on Affect and Cognition

Attitudes: Evaluating the Social World

FIGURE 3.1 Do you have any reactions—favourable or unfavourable—to the person shown here? If so, you hold attitudes toward the person.

At any one time, a range of important issues is being hotly debated in the public forum. In Canada today issues such as the state of our education system, the preservation of the wilderness, Quebec politics, or the treatment of young offenders continue to provide fodder for headlines in the media and discussions over the kitchen table. Whenever one of these topics is raised, opinions seem to differ—just listen to a local radio phone-in program. You might find yourself wondering why, after this amount of public debate, such issues have not been resolved. Why do people continue to oppose each other so vehemently? How can people, often with the same level of knowledge and ability, reach such opposing conclusions? How can they be persuaded to agree? Many social psychologists would suggest that in order to answer these questions—and truly understand why people hold the views they do—it would be necessary to consider the topic of *attitudes*.

Attitudes have been a central concept in social psychology since its earliest days (e.g., Allport & Hartman, 1924) and for good reason: they shape both our social perceptions and our social behaviour (Pratkanis, Breckler, & Greenwald, 1989). But what, precisely, are they? **Attitudes** refer to *our evaluations of virtually any aspect of the social world* (e.g., Fazio & Roskos-Ewoldsen, 1994; Tesser & Martin, 1996), the extent to which we have favourable or unfavourable reactions to issues, ideas, persons, social groups, objects—any and every element of the social world (see Figure 3.1). They are more enduring than passing preferences—once formed they tend to persist and are often strongly resistant to change, especially if they are strongly related to the interests or outcomes of the persons who hold them (e.g., Crano, 1997).

The importance of attitudes to social psychology stems from their two major features. First, as we have just noted, they strongly influence our social thought—the

Attitudes
Evaluations of various aspects of the social world.

ways in which we think about and process many kinds of social information. In fact, growing evidence suggests that when defined as evaluations of the world around us, attitudes may represent a very basic aspect of all forms of thought. Indeed, the tendency to categorize stimuli as positive or negative appears to be the initial step in our information processing (e.g., Ito & Cacioppo, 1999). Recent evidence suggests, for instance, that negative stimuli (e.g., a photo of a mutilated face) produce larger event-related potentials in our brains (changes in electrical activity) than do positive stimuli (e.g., a photo of a sports car; Ito, Larsen, Smith, & Cacioppo, 1998). The effects of attitudes on the processing of social information have been a key theme of recent research on attitudes, and we will examine such research carefully here (e.g., Eagly & Chaiken, 1998).

Second, it has been widely assumed, attitudes strongly affect behaviour. Do you believe that abortion is wrong and should be outlawed? Then you may join a demonstration against it. Do you hold a negative attitude toward the current prime minister or the premier of your province? Then you may not vote for those persons or their parties in the next election. If attitudes influence behaviour, then knowing something about them can help us predict people's behaviour in a wide range of contexts. As we'll see in Chapter 6, we also hold attitudes toward specific persons—for example, we like them or dislike them. Clearly, such attitudes can play a crucial role in our relations with these persons.

Now that we've described the basic features of attitudes, we can turn to the wealth of information about them uncovered by social psychologists. In order to provide you with a useful overview of this intriguing body of knowledge, we'll proceed as follows. First, we'll examine the process through which attitudes are *formed* or *developed*. Next, we'll consider the relationship between attitudes and behaviour. This link is more complex than you might expect, so be prepared for some surprises. Third, we'll examine how attitudes are sometimes changed through persuasion and related processes. The word sometimes should be emphasized, for as we'll note in another section, changing attitudes that are important to those who hold them is far from easy. Finally, we'll consider cognitive dissonance—an internal state with far-reaching implications for social behaviour and social thought that, surprisingly, sometimes leads individuals to change their own attitudes in the absence of external pressure to do so.

ATTITUDE FORMATION: HOW WE COME TO HOLD THE VIEWS WE DO

What are your views about gun control? Affirmative action? Aboriginal hunting and fishing rights? Sexual harassment? The film *The Blair Witch Project*? Pizza? Almost certainly, you have views—attitudes—about all of these. But where, precisely, did these attitudes come from? Were you born with them? Or did you acquire them as a result of various life experiences? Most people—and most social psychologists—accept the view that attitudes are learned, and most of our discussion of this issue will focus on the processes through which attitudes are acquired. But please take note: We would be remiss if we did not mention that a small but growing body of evidence suggests that attitudes may be influenced by genetic factors, too. We'll describe some of the evidence for this surprising idea below.

Social Learning The process through which we acquire new information, forms of behaviour, or attitudes from other persons.

Social Learning: Acquiring Attitudes From Others

One important source of our attitudes is obvious: we acquire them from other persons through the process of **social learning**. In other words, many of our views are acquired in situations where we interact with others or merely observe their behaviour. Social learning occurs through several processes.

Classical Conditioning: Learning Based on Association

It is a basic principle of psychology that when one stimulus regularly precedes another, the one that occurs first may soon become a signal for the one that occurs second. In other words, when the first stimulus occurs, individuals expect that the second will soon follow. As a result, they gradually acquire the same kind of reactions to the first stimulus as they show to the second stimulus, especially if the second is one that induces fairly strong and automatic reactions. For instance, consider a woman whose shower emits a low hum just before the hot water runs out and turns into an icy stream. At first, she may show little reaction to the hum. After the hum is followed by freezing water on several occasions, though, she may well experience strong emotional arousal (fear!) when it occurs. After all, it is a signal for what will soon follow—icy cold water.

What does this process, which is known as **classical conditioning**, have to do with attitude formation? Potentially, quite a lot. To see how this process might influence attitudes under real-life conditions, imagine the following scene. A young child sees her mother frown and show other signs of displeasure each time the mother encounters a member of a particular ethnic group. At first, the child is neutral toward members of this group and their visible characteristics (e.g., skin colour, style of dress, accent). After these cues are paired with the mother's negative emotional reactions many times, how-

Classical Conditioning A basic form of learning in which one stimulus, initially neutral, acquires the capacity to evoke reactions through repeated pairing with another stimulus. In a sense, one stimulus becomes a signal for the presentation or occurrence of the other.

■ Classical Conditioning of Attitudes

FIGURE 3.2 Initially, a young child has little or no emotional reaction to the visible characteristics of members of some minority group. If she sees her mother showing signs of negative reactions when in the presence of these persons, however, she too may gradually acquire negative reactions to them, through the process of classical conditioning.

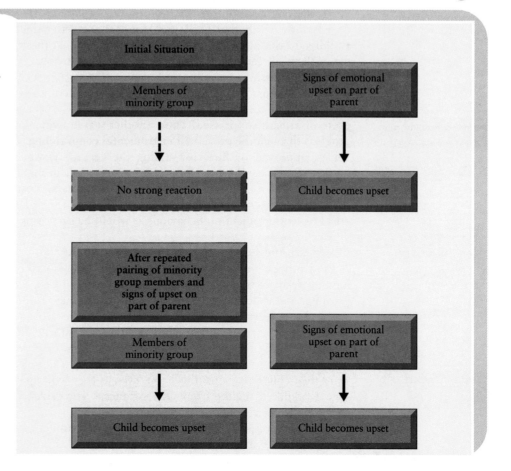

ever, classical conditioning occurs; the child comes to react negatively to these stimuli, and to members of this ethnic group (see Figure 3.2). The result: The child acquires a negative attitude toward such persons—an attitude that may form the core of a full-blown ethnic prejudice. (We'll examine prejudice in detail in Chapter 5.)

Interestingly, studies indicate that classical conditioning can occur below the level of conscious awareness—even when people are not aware of the stimuli that serve as the basis for this kind of conditioning. For instance, in one experiment on this topic (Krosnick et al., 1992), students saw photos of a stranger engaged in routine daily activities such as shopping in a grocery store or walking into her apartment. While these photos were shown, other photos known to induce either positive or negative feelings were presented very briefly—so briefly that participants were not aware of their presence. One group of research participants was exposed to photos that induced positive feelings (e.g., a bridal couple, people playing cards and laughing); another group was exposed to photos that induced negative feelings (e.g., open-heart surgery, a werewolf). Later, both groups expressed their attitudes toward the stranger. Results indicated that even though participants were unaware of the second group of photos (the ones presented very briefly), these stimuli significantly influenced their attitudes toward the stranger. Those exposed to the positive photos reported more favourable attitudes toward this person than those exposed to the negative photos. These findings suggest that attitudes can be influenced by **subliminal conditioning**—classical conditioning that occurs in the absence of conscious awareness of the stimuli involved.

Instrumental Conditioning: Learning to Hold The "Right" Views

Have you ever heard a three-year-old state, with great conviction, that she is a Liberal or a Reformer? Or that Fords (or Hondas) are better than Chevrolets (or Toyotas)? Children of this age have little understanding of what these statements mean. Yet they make them all the same. Why? The answer is obvious: They have been praised or rewarded in various ways by their parents for stating such views. As we're sure you know, behaviours that are followed by positive outcomes are strengthened and tend to be repeated. In contrast, behaviours that are followed by negative outcomes are weakened, or at least suppressed. Thus, another way in which attitudes are acquired from others is through the process of **instrumental conditioning**. By rewarding children with smiles, approval, or hugs for stating the "right" views—the ones they themselves favour—parents and other adults play an active role in shaping youngsters' attitudes. It is for this reason that until they reach their teen years, most children express political, religious, and social views highly similar to those of their families. Given the powerful effect of reinforcement on behaviour, it would be surprising if they did not.

Observational Learning: Learning by Example

A third process through which attitudes are formed can operate even when parents have no desire to transmit specific views to their children. This process is **observational learning**, and it occurs when individuals acquire new forms of behaviour or thought simply by observing the actions of others. Where attitude formation is concerned, observational learning appears to play an important role. In many cases, children hear their parents say things not intended for their ears, or observe their parents engaging in actions the parents tell them not to perform. For example, parents who smoke often warn their children against this habit, even as they light up (see Figure 3.3). What message do children acquire from such instances? The evidence is clear: They often learn to do as their parents do, not as they say.

In addition, of course, both children and adults often acquire attitudes from exposure to the mass media—television, magazines, films, and so on. For instance,

Subliminal Conditioning Classical conditioning that occurs through exposure to stimuli that are below individuals' threshold of conscious awareness.

Instrumental Conditioning A basic form of learning in which responses that lead to positive outcomes or permit avoidance of negative outcomes are strengthened. Also known as operant conditioning.

Observational Learning or Modeling A basic form of learning in which individuals acquire new forms of behaviour or thought through observing and imitating others.

FIGURE 3.3 Children learn
many things through observation, including attitudes their
parents may not want the
children to acquire, such as a
positive view of smoking.

the characters in many films today now make liberal use of four-letter words that in
the past were considered unacceptable. The result: Persons under the age of thirty,
who have grown up watching such films, don't find these words as objectionable as
older persons.

Social Comparison and Attitude Formation

While many attitudes are formed through social learning, this is not the only way in
which they are acquired. Another mechanism involves **social comparison**—our tendency to compare ourselves with others in order to determine whether our view of
social reality is that correct (Festinger, 1954). To the extent that our views agree with
those of others, we conclude that our ideas and attitudes are accurate; after all, if others hold the same views, the views must be right! Because of the operation of this
process, we often change our attitudes so as to hold views closer to those of others.
On some occasions, moreover, the process of social comparison may contribute to the
formation of new attitudes, ones we didn't previously hold. For example, imagine that
you heard individuals you like and respect expressing negative views toward a group
with whom you've had no contact. Would this influence your views? While it's tempting to say, "Of course not! I wouldn't form any opinions without seeing for myself!"
research findings indicate that hearing others state negative views might actually influence you to adopt similar attitudes—without ever meeting a member of the group in
question (e.g., Shaver, 1993). Such effects are clearly demonstrated in one Canadian
study by Maio, Esses, and Bell (1994).

These researchers presented visitors to the Ontario Science Centre with information about a fictitious group (the Camarians) that was, supposedly, about to immigrate
to Canada. Subjects received either favourable or unfavourable information about this
imaginary group: they learned that people in England had assigned them high ratings
in terms of personality traits and values or that they had been assigned low ratings.
Participants who received the favourable social information about this fictitious group
expressed more favourable attitudes toward them than those who received negative
information, and showed greater willingness to allow them to immigrate to Canada.
Remember: these differences were based entirely on social information received by

Social Comparison
The process through
which we compare
ourselves to others in
order to determine
whether our view of
social reality is or is
not correct.

participants; they had never met a Camarian. Findings such as these indicate that often our attitudes are shaped by social information from others, coupled with our own desire to be similar to people we like or respect. The cultural groups with which we have contact can often be an important source of such social information. We will next consider the role of culture in influencing attitudes.

Cultural Factors: The Role of Cultural Values

Cultural background can also influence attitude formation (Davidson & Thompson, 1980). In the previous chapter we saw that culture can play a part in many forms of social cognition (Smith & Bond, 1998). When considering cultural differences in this area, researchers have often examined broader *cultural values* rather than specific attitudes.

Values Broad and abstract principles of life. They contain our moral beliefs and our standards of conduct.

Values are broad and abstract principles of life. They contain our moral beliefs and our standards of conduct. Where they differ from attitudes is in their generality or abstractness (Schwartz, 1992). For example, the *value of equality* is nonspecific—it does not relate to one particular type of event or object as an attitude does. Rather, it guides our thinking or actions over a broad range of situations. A value such as

---

Four dimensions of cultural values emerged from Hofstede's research in 40 countries (1980). These dimensions are described below together with samples of questionnaire items for each dimension.

TABLE 3.1 Four dimensions of cultural values

Individualism/Collectivism

Description: Valuing loosely knit social relations in which individuals are expected to care only for themselves and their immediate families versus tightly knit relations in which they can expect their wider ingroup (e.g., extended family, clan) to look after them in exchange for unquestioning loyalty.

Questionnaire Items: Responses of "very" here indicate high individualism.

How important is it to you to have a job that leaves you sufficient time for your personal or family life?

How important is it to you to have considerable freedom to adapt your own approach to the job?

Power Distance

Description: Accepting an unequal distribution of power in institutions as legitimate versus illegitimate (from the viewpoint of the less powerful person).

Questionnaire Item: A response of "frequently" here indicates high power distance.

How frequently, in your experience, does the following problem occur: employees being afraid to express their disagreement with their managers?

Uncertainty Avoidance

Description: Feeling uncomfortable or comfortable with uncertainty and ambiguity and therefore valuing or devaluing beliefs and institutions that provide certainty and conformity.

Questionnaire Item: A response of "strongly agree" here indicates high uncertainty avoidance.

Company rules should not be broken, even if the employee thinks it is in the company's best interest.

Masculinity/Femininity

Description: Valuing achievement, heroism, assertiveness, and material success versus relationships, modesty, caring for the weak, and interpersonal harmony.

Questionnaire Items: An answer of "very" to the first question indicates high masculinity; an answer of "very" to the second question indicates high femininity.

How important is it to you to get the recognition you deserve when you do a good job?

How important is it to you to work with people who cooperate well with one another?

Source: Adapted from Hofstede, 1980; Smith & Bond, 1998; Smith & Schwartz, 1997.

equality may guide your attitudes to many issues from welfare and affirmative action programs to whether professors should be called by their first names. There is evidence that values are translated into action via our attitudes. That is, values may determine attitudes, which in turn may determine behaviour (Homer and Kahle, 1988).

Values can also be culturally transmitted through processes of social learning and shaped by social comparison at home, in school, and among our friends. Major studies comparing values of over 50 nations have found measurable differences between the values of those from different cultures (Hofstede, 1980; Schwartz, 1992). Findings of Hofstede's study (1980), for example, showed that Canadians and Americans had very similar rankings in three out of four values—see Table 3.1. They were similar in showing high *individualism* (focus on individual choice rather than group goals), low *power distance* (little value on hierarchical relationships), and low *uncertainty avoidance* (placed little value on stability and order). A difference did occur for one value related to *achievement orientation* (termed *masculinity* by Hofstede)—Americans showed a higher ranking for this value than Canadians. However, both countries' responses differed markedly from those of a number of other cultures, particularly the more collectivistic cultures of South America, Africa, and Asia. The cultural value dimension of individualism-collectivism has emerged as an important one in social psychological research (Triandis, 1995) and Hofstede also points out that this dimension correlates negatively with the power distance dimension. Western cultures (in North American, North and West Europe and Australia) tended to be high on individualism and low on power distance, whereas Latin American and Asian cultures show the reverse pattern: low on individualism and high on power distance (Smith & Bond, 1998).

Despite some underlying similarities, Canada and the United States do show differences on important values, as we saw in Chapter 1. Seymour Lipset has pointed out that Canadians are less likely to endorse the value of liberty or freedom than Americans and more likely to endorse the value of equality between groups, supporting his opinion that Canada is a more community-minded or *communitarian* culture (CARA-Gallup, 1983; Lipset, 1989, 1990). Some research has also indicated value differences between French- and Anglo-Canadians. For example, in the 1983 CARA-Gallup poll French-Canadians were consistently further from Americans than Anglo-Canadians in their support of basic values: that is, they were more likely to endorse the value of equality, and less likely to endorse liberty and independence for the individual.

Those who monitor recent trends in Canadian social values agree that there have been important changes in values among Canadians, particularly those aged roughly 15 to 29 years, (Adams, 1997; Armstrong, 1996; Bibby, 1995; Foote, 1996; Sauve, 1994). One commentator has even suggested this shift in values amounts to a "social revolution" (Adams, 1997). There appear to be three major trends: *greater individualism*, a *devaluing of institutions* in Canada, and *greater diversity*. First, Canadians seem to be becoming somewhat less communitarian, or group-oriented, and more individualistic. Adams (1997) suggests that the emerging values of the current generation reveal this individualism: placing greater importance on personal autonomy, hedonism (the valuing of pleasure), and a quest for personal meaning or spiritual fulfillment. There has also been a general decline in membership of many community and religious groups (e.g., a 27 percent decrease in membership in religious organizations since 1975; Bibby, 1995). Second, accompanying this decreasing group-orientation in Canada is a devaluing of institutions and their leaders. For example, only 16 percent of Canadians express "a great deal" or "quite a lot" of confidence in the House of Commons (Gallup, 1993, cited in Sauve, 1994). In addition, from 1985 to 1995 there was a drop in the proportion of Canadians expressing confidence in the leaders of institutions such as the federal government (5 percent drop), the court system (14 percent drop) and the police (7 percent drop; Bibby, 1995). There has also been a decline in endorsement of the idea of a "cultural mosaic," from 56 percent in 1985 to 44 percent in 1995 (Bibby, 1995). Finally, a trend toward diversity is mentioned by researchers—a greater diversity in values (Adams, 1997), and an acceptance of greater variety in attitudes, lifestyles, and forms of family life (Bibby, 1995).

Despite claims of a "social revolution," most of these trends described here are gradual and many of the more traditional and compassionate Canadian values continue to predominate in the population as a whole. For example, over 70 percent of Canadians continue to place a high value on kindness, concern for others, and politeness, and Canadians maintain a belief that the underprivileged in society have a right to medicare (96 percent) and an adequate income (84 percent; Bibby, 1995).

One final note: these findings do not begin to address the extensive value differences among subcultural groups in Canada. If we assume that everyone, whatever their background, endorses mainstream values, we are being ethnocentric. And further, we are in danger of neglecting important value dimensions of other groups in society such as those from Eastern cultures. This is an issue that will be discussed further in Chapter 4 when we look at issues in *cross-cultural psychology*.

Genetic Factors: Some Surprising Recent Findings

Can we inherit our attitudes—or, at least, a propensity to develop certain attitudes about various topics or issues? At first glance, most people would answer with an emphatic *no*. While we readily believe that genetic factors can shape our height, eye colour, and other physical characteristics, the idea that such factors might also influence our thinking—including our preferences and our views—seems strange to say the least. Yet if we remember that thought occurs within the brain and that brain structure, like every other part of our physical being, is certainly influenced by genetic factors, the idea of genetic influences on attitudes becomes, perhaps, a little easier to imagine. And in fact, a small but growing body of empirical evidence indicates that genetic factors may play some small role in attitudes (e.g., Arvey et al., 1989; Keller et al., 1992; Hershberger, Lichtenstein, & Knox, 1994).

Most of this evidence involves comparisons between identical (monozygotic) and nonidentical (dizygotic) twins. Since identical twins share the same genetic inheritance,

■ Identical twins separated very early in life: Often, their attitudes are very similar

FIGURE 3.4 The attitudes of identical twins separated very early in life correlate more highly than those of nonidentical twins or unrelated persons. This finding provides support for the view that attitudes are influenced by genetic factors, at least to some extent.

while nonidentical twins do not, higher correlations between the attitudes of the identical twins would suggest that genetic factors play a role in shaping such attitudes. This is precisely what has been found: The attitudes of identical twins do correlate more highly than those of nonidentical twins (e.g., Waller et al., 1990). Moreover, this is the case even if the twins have been separated early in life and raised in sharply contrasting environments from then on (see Figure 3.4; Bouchard et al., 1992; Hershberger, Lichtenstein, & Knox, 1994). Under these conditions, greater similarity in the attitudes of identical twins than in the attitudes of other persons can't be attributed to similarity in environmental factors.

Additional results suggest, not surprisingly, that genetic factors play a stronger role in shaping some attitudes than others—in other words, that some attitudes are more *heritable* than others. While it is too early to reach definite conclusions, some findings seem to suggest that attitudes involving gut-level preferences (e.g., a preference for certain kinds of music) may be more strongly influenced by genetic factors than attitudes that are more "cognitive" in nature (e.g., attitudes about abstract principles or about situations and objects with which individuals have had little direct experience; Tesser, 1993). In addition, it appears that attitudes that are highly heritable may be more difficult to change than ones that are not, and that highly heritable attitudes may exert stronger effects on behaviour (e.g., Crealia & Tesser, 1998). For instance, we seem to like strangers who express attitudes similar to ours more when these attitudes are highly heritable than when they are less heritable (Tesser, 1993). We'll return to these points in a later discussion of the effects of attitudes on behaviour.

But how, we can almost hear you asking, can such effects occur—how can genetic factors influence attitudes? One possibility is that genetic factors influence more general dispositions, such as the tendency to experience mainly positive or negative affect—to be in a positive or negative mood most of the time (George, 1990). Such tendencies, in turn, could then influence evaluations of many aspects of the social world. Only time, and further research, will allow us to determine whether, and how, genetic factors influence attitudes. But given that such factors appear to influence many other aspects of social behaviour and social thought, ranging from our choice of romantic partners through aggression (e.g., Buss, 1999), the idea that attitudes, too, may be subject to such influences is not improbable.

KEY POINTS

- *Attitudes* are evaluations of any aspects of the social world.
- Attitudes are often acquired from other persons through *social learning*. Such learning can involve *classical conditioning*, *instrumental conditioning*, or *observational learning*.
- Attitudes are also formed on the basis of *social comparison*—our tendency to compare ourselves with others to determine whether our view of social reality is or is not correct. In order to be similar to others we like or admire, we often accept the attitudes they hold.
- Culture can play a part in the transmission of *values*—broad and abstract principles of life. The cultural value dimension of individualism-collectivism has emerged as an important distinction.
- Studies conducted with identical twins suggest that attitudes may also be influenced by genetic factors, although the strength of such effects varies greatly for different attitudes.

ATTITUDES AND BEHAVIOUR: WHEN ARE THEY LINKED?

Do our attitudes influence our behaviour? Your first answer is likely to be, "Of course." After all, you can remember many incidents in which your own actions were strongly shaped by your opinions. You may be surprised to learn, therefore, that until quite recently, evidence concerning the strength of the link between attitudes and behaviour was far from conclusive. Many studies seemed to suggest that this relationship was sometimes more apparent than real. The classic study by LaPiere that triggered interest in this issue is featured in the Cornerstones section below.

Cornerstones

Attitudes Versus Actions: "No we don't admit that kind of person—unless they show up at the door!"

It was 1930, and all over the world, the bottom had dropped out of the economy. But Richard LaPiere, a social psychologist at Stanford University, wasn't interested in economics: he was concerned, in his research, with the link between attitudes and behaviour. At the time, social psychologists generally defined attitudes largely in terms of behaviour—as a set of tendencies or pre-

dispositions to behave in certain ways in social situations (Allport, 1924). Thus, they assumed that attitudes were generally reflected in overt behaviour. LaPiere, however, was not so certain. In particular, he wondered whether persons holding various prejudices—negative attitudes toward the members of various social groups (see Chapter 5)—would demonstrate these actions in their

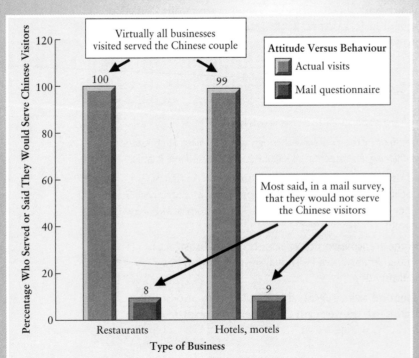

■ Evidence that attitudes don't always influence behaviour

FIGURE 3.5 Virtually all restaurants, hotels, and motels visited by LaPiere and a young Chinese couple offered courteous service. When asked through the mail whether they would serve Chinese visitors, however, more than 90 percent said no. These findings suggest that there is sometimes a sizable gap between attitudes and behaviour.

Source: Based on data from LaPiere, 1934.

overt behaviour. To find out, he adopted a novel technique. For more than two years LaPiere traveled around the United States with a young Chinese couple. During these travels, they stopped at 184 restaurants and 66 hotels and "tourist camps" (predecessors of the modern motel). In the overwhelming majority of the cases, they were treated with courtesy and consideration. In fact, they were refused service only once; and in most cases they received what LaPiere (1934) described as an average to above-average level of treatment.

Now, however, the study gets really interesting. After the travels were complete, LaPiere wrote to all the businesses where he and the Chinese couple had stayed or dined, and asked whether they would offer service to Chinese visitors. The results were nothing short of astonishing: Out of the 128 establishments that responded, 92 percent of the restaurants and 91 percent of the hotels said no. In short, there was a tremendous gap between the attitudes expressed by these businesses (generally, by their owners or managers), and what they had done when confronted with live, in-the-flesh Chinese guests (see Figure 3.5). Similar attitudes were expressed by hotels and restaurants LaPiere did not visit, so the sample appears to have been a representative one.

What accounts for these findings? LaPiere himself noted that the young couple with whom he traveled spoke English well and—as he put it—were "skillful smilers." In other words, they were attractive and friendly. Faced with such persons, the owners of businesses ignored their own prejudiced attitudes and, far from rejecting such guests, welcomed them with courtesy. In fact, LaPiere reported that in the only "yes" letter he received from motels they had visited, the owner noted that she would be glad to accept Chinese guests, since she had enjoyed a pleasant visit from a Chinese gentleman and his sweet wife the previous summer!

Putting such factors aside, LaPiere (1934) interpreted his results as indicating that there is often a sizable gap between attitudes and behaviour—between what people say and what they actually do. This classic study, and related findings reported in later decades (e.g., Wicker, 1969), led social psychologists to focus a great deal of attention on the questions of *when* and *how* attitudes predict behaviour. In this respect, LaPiere's study, conducted so long ago and with methods so different from the rigorous ones used in modern research, exerted a strong and lasting impact on our field.

When Do Attitudes Influence Behaviour? Specificity, Strength, Accessibility, and Other Factors

Research on the question of *when* attitudes influence behaviour has uncovered several different factors that serve as what social psychologists term *moderators*—factors that influence the extent to which attitudes affect behaviour. We'll now consider two of the most important of these moderators: aspects of the situation and aspects of attitudes themselves.

Aspects of the Situation: Factors That Prevent Us From Expressing Our Attitudes

Have you ever been in the following situation? You are in a restaurant eating with a group of friends, and when the food arrives, there's something wrong—for instance, it's not what you ordered or it's cold. Yet when the server asks, "How is everything?" you and your friends all answer: "Fine." Why don't you express your true reactions? In other words, why doesn't your behaviour in this situation reflect your underlying attitudes? In this and many other contexts, *situational constraints* moderate the relationship between attitudes and behaviour: they prevent attitudes from being expressed in overt behaviour (e.g., Ajzen & Fishbein, 1980; Fazio & Roskos-Ewoldsen, 1994).

Situational factors can influence the link between attitudes and behaviour in one additional way worth noting. In general, we tend to prefer situations that allow us to express our attitudes in our behaviour. In other words, we often choose to enter and spend time in situations in which what we say and what we do can coincide (Snyder & Ickes, 1985). Indeed, because individuals tend to choose situations where they can engage in behaviours consistent with their attitudes, the attitudes themselves may be strengthened by this overt expression and so become even better predictors of behaviour (DeBono & Snyder, 1995). In sum, the relationship between attitudes and situations may be a two-way street. Situational pressures shape the extent to which attitudes can be expressed in overt actions; but in addition, attitudes determine whether individuals enter various situations. In order to understand the link between attitudes and behaviour, then, we must carefully consider both sets of factors.

Aspects of Attitudes Themselves

While the situation may limit our action, attitudes themselves also differ in ways that can affect the attitude-behaviour link. You know yourself that if a particular attitude or value is very close to your heart—perhaps related to important political or religious views—it would be very difficult to ignore it in a relevant situation. In fact, this could make you very uncomfortable, as we will discuss in the section of cognitive dissonance. So some types of attitude are more likely to influence behaviour than others.

Attitude Origins

One such factor has to do with how attitudes are formed in the first place. Considerable evidence indicates that attitudes formed on the basis of direct experience often exert stronger effects on behaviour than ones formed indirectly, through hearsay. Apparently attitudes formed on the basis of direct experience tend to be stronger and easier to bring to mind, or more accessible. Both strength and accessibility are factors that increase the impact of attitudes on behaviour.

Attitude Strength

Clearly one of the most important factors in attitude involves what is typically termed the *strength* of the attitudes in question. The stronger attitudes are, the greater their impact on behaviour (Petkova, Ajzen, & Driver, 1995). The term strength, however, includes several components: the extremity or *intensity* of an attitude (how strong is the emotional reaction provoked by the attitude object); *knowledge* (how much an individual knows about the attitude object); and its *importance* (the extent to which an individual cares deeply about and is personally affected by the attitude). Research findings indicate that all these components play a role in attitude strength and that all are related (Krosnick et al., 1993; Kraus, 1995).

Importance is a major component of attitude strength—the extent to which an individual cares about the attitude (Krosnick, 1988). And one of the key determinants of such importance is what social psychologists term *vested interest*—the extent to which the attitude is personally relevant to the individual who holds it, in that the object or issue to which it refers has important consequences for this person. The results of many studies indicate that the greater such vested interest, the stronger the impact of the attitude on behaviour (e.g., Crano, 1995, 1997; Crano & Prislin, 1995). For instance, in one famous study on this issue, Sivacek and Crano (1982) telephoned students at a large university and asked them if they would participate in a campaign against raising the legal age for drinking alcohol from eighteen to twenty-one. As you might have guessed response depended on age. Forty-seven percent of the students who were under twenty-one, and therefore had a vested interest, agreed to take part in the campaign, whereas only twelve percent of those in older age groups did so.

Attitude Specificity

A third aspect of attitudes themselves that influences their relationship to behaviour is *attitude specificity*—the extent to which attitudes are focused on specific objects or situations rather than on general ones. For example, you may have a general attitude toward religion (e.g., you believe that it is important for everyone to have religious convictions as opposed to not having them); in addition, you may have several specific attitudes about various aspects of religion—for instance, about the importance of attending services every week (this is important or unimportant) or about wearing a religious symbol (it's something I like to do—or don't like to do). Research findings indicate that the attitude–behaviour link is stronger when attitudes and behaviours are measured at the same level of specificity. For instance, we'd probably be more accurate in predicting whether you'll go to services this week from your attitude about the importance of attending services than from your attitude about religion generally. On the other hand, we'd probably be more accurate in predicting your willingness to take action to protect religious freedoms from your general attitude toward religion than from your attitude about wearing religious jewelry (Fazio & Roskos-Ewoldsen, 1994). So attitude specificity, too, is an important moderator of the attitude–behaviour link.

In sum, as we noted earlier, existing evidence suggests that attitudes really *do* affect behaviour (e.g., Petty & Krosnick, 1995). However, the strength of this link is strongly determined by many different factors—situational constraints that permit or do not permit us to give overt expression to our attitudes, as well as several aspects of attitudes themselves (e.g., their origins, strength, and specificity, among others).

How Do Attitudes Influence Behaviour? Intentions, Willingness, and Action

Understanding *when* attitudes influence behaviour is an important topic. But, as we noted in Chapter 1, social psychologists are interested not only in the *when* of social thought and behaviour but in the *why* and how as well. So it should come as no surprise that researchers have also tried to understand how attitudes influence behaviour. Work on this issue points to the conclusion that in fact there are several basic mechanisms through which attitudes shape behaviour.

Attitudes, Reasoned Thought, and Behaviour

The first of these mechanisms operates in situations where we give careful, deliberate thought to our attitudes and their implications for our behaviour. Insights into the nature of this process are provided by the *theory of reasoned action* (and a later version of this framework known as the **theory of planned behaviour**), proposed by Ajzen and Fishbein (1980; Ajzen, 1991). This theory suggests that the decision to engage in a particular behaviour is the result of a rational process that is goal-oriented and that follows a logical sequence. In this process we consider our behavioural options, evaluate the consequences or outcomes of each, and reach a decision to act or not to act. That decision is then reflected in our *behavioural intentions*, which, according to Fishbein, Ajzen, and many other researchers are often strong predictors of how we will act in a given situation (Ajzen, 1987). Perhaps a specific example will help illustrate the very reasonable nature of this idea.

Suppose a student is considering body piercing—for instance, wearing a nose ornament. Will she actually take this action? According to Ajzen and Fishbein, the answer depends on her intentions; and these, in turn, are strongly influenced by three key factors. The first factor is the person's attitudes toward the behaviour in question. If the student really dislikes pain and the idea of someone sticking a needle through her nose, her intention to engage in such behaviour may be weak. The second factor is the person's beliefs about how others will evaluate this action (this factor is known as *subjective norms*). If the student thinks that others will approve of body piercing, her intention to perform it may be strengthened. If she believes that others will disapprove of it,

Theory of Planned Behaviour A theory of how attitudes guide behaviour suggesting that individuals consider the implications of their actions before deciding to perform various behaviours. An earlier version was known as the *theory of reasoned action*.

her intentions may be weakened. Finally, intentions are also influenced by *perceived behavioural control*—the extent to which a person perceives a behaviour as hard or easy to accomplish. If it is viewed as difficult, intentions are weaker than if it is viewed as easy to perform. Together, these factors influence intentions; and intentions are the best single predictor of an individual's behaviour.

Attitudes and Immediate Behavioural Reactions

The model described above seems to be quite accurate in situations where we have the time and opportunity to reflect carefully on various actions. But what about situations in which we have to act quickly or when our actions are impulsive rather than reasoned? According to one theory—Fazio's **attitude-to-behaviour process model**—when we don't have time for careful thought, attitudes influence behaviour in a more direct and seemingly automatic manner (Fazio, 1989; Fazio & Roskos-Ewoldsen, 1994). The process, illustrated in Figure 3.6, is initiated when an event activates an attitude, making your attitude more accessible to you. Once activated, the attitude influences your perceptions of the attitude object. At the same time, your knowledge about what's appropriate in a given situation (your knowledge of various *social norms*) is also activated. Together, the attitude and this stored knowledge shape your definition of the situation; and it is this definition, or perception of the situation, that influences your behaviour. Let's consider a concrete example.

Imagine that a panhandler approaches you on the street. What happens? This event triggers your attitude toward panhandlers and also your understanding of how people are expected to behave on public streets. Together, these factors influence your definition (perception) of the event, which might be "Oh no, another one of those worthless bums!" or "Gee, these homeless people have it rough!" Your definition of the event then shapes your behaviour. Several studies provide support for this model, so it seems to offer a useful explanation of how attitudes influence behaviour in some situations (e.g., Bargh, 1997; Dovidio et al., 1996).

In sum, it appears that attitudes affect our behaviour through at least two mechanisms, and that these operate under somewhat contrasting conditions. When we have time to engage in careful, reasoned thought, we can weigh all the alternatives and

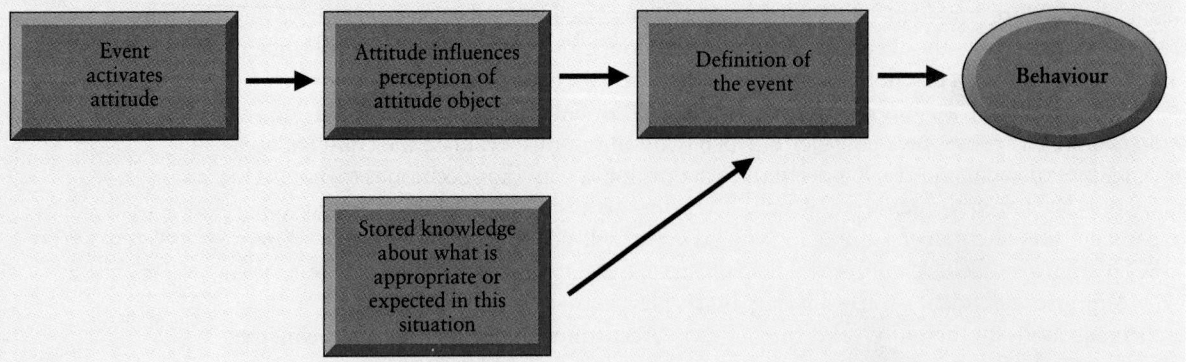

Attitude-to-behaviour Process Model A model of how attitudes guide behaviour that emphasizes the influence of both attitudes and stored knowledge of what is appropriate in a given situation on an individual's definition of the present situation. This definition, in turn, influences overt behaviour.

■ Fazio's attitude-to-behaviour process model

FIGURE 3.6 According to one recent model, in situations where we don't have time to engage in careful, reasoned thought, attitudes guide behaviour in the manner shown here.

Source: Based on suggestions by Fazio, 1989, and Fazio & Roskos-Ewoldsen, 1994.

decide, quite deliberately, how to act. Under the hectic conditions of everyday life, however, we often don't have time for this kind of deliberate weighing of alternatives; in such cases, our attitudes seem to shape our perceptions of the situation and thus our immediate behavioural reactions to them.

■ Persuasion in everyday life

FIGURE 3.7 Like the characters in this cartoon, we are often bombarded with persuasive messages. How can we decide which are worth noticing?

PERSUASION: THE PROCESS OF CHANGING ATTITUDES

How many times during the past 24 hours has someone, or some organization, tried to change your attitudes? If you stop and think for a moment you may be surprised at the result, for it is clear that every day we are bombarded with countless efforts of this type—see Figure 3.7. Newspaper and magazine ads, radio and television commercials, political speeches, appeals from charitable organizations—the list seems almost endless. To what extent are such attempts at **persuasion**—efforts to change our attitudes through the use of various kinds of messages—successful? And what factors determine whether they succeed or fail? It is to these issues that we turn next.

Persuasion The process through which one or more persons attempt to alter the attitudes of one or more others.

Persuasion: The Early Approach

In most cases, efforts at persuasion involve the following elements: some source (a communicator) directs some type of message (the communication) to a person or group (the audience). Taking note of this fact, much early research on persuasion coming from Yale University (Hovland, Janis, & Kelley, 1953), focused on these key elements of the process of communication. This approach yielded many interesting findings, among the most consistent—having stood the test of time—are those summarized in Table 3.2. Advertisers today are still using the principles of persuasive communication that the Yale University researchers discovered. As you can see in Table 3.2, the communicator can be important in persuasion and the perfect spokesperson for your product is often someone for whom advertisers search far and wide. The following On the Applied Side box discusses a figure who is arguably Canada's perfect spokesperson.

Investigating aspects of the communication process that increase persuasion, Hovland and colleagues at Yale focused on the source of the communication (the *communicator*), the persuasive *message* itself, and the recipient of that message (the *audience*)—or *who* said *what* to *whom*.

TABLE 3.2 Persuasion: The early approach

Factors that increase effectiveness of a persuasive communication:

Communicator	Message	Audience
Credibility Includes expertise, trustworthiness, and sincerity (e.g., Hovland & Weiss, 1951)	**Non-obvious persuasion** Messages that do not seem too obvious in their attempt to influence (e.g., Walster & Festinger, 1962)	**Low or moderate self-esteem** Early research suggested that people with low self-esteem are more persuadable, but recent research suggests it is those with moderate self-esteem (e.g., Janis, 1954; Rhodes & Wood, 1992)
Attractiveness Includes good looks, popularity and likeability (e.g., Hovland et al., 1953)	**Both sides of the issue** Presenting both sides of an issue is more effective, especially if the audience is knowledgeable about the issues and you can refute an opponent's perspective (e.g., Lumsdaine & Janis, 1953)	**Younger age groups** Younger individuals are more persuadable compared to adults over 25 (e.g., Sears, 1981)
Speaks rapidly Rapid speech seems to suggest expertise (e.g., Miller et al., 1976)	**Arousing emotion** Strong emotion can enhance persuasion; use of fear is effective if the level is moderate and ways to avoid the feared situation are included (e.g., Leventhal, Stinger & Jones, 1965; Rodgers, 1984)	

On the **Applied Side**

The Marketing of a Sports Hero: Wayne Gretzky— Ideal Canadian Spokesperson?

The early approach to persuasion emphasized the importance of the *communicator* of a persuasive message—see Table 3.2. Recognizing this, public and private organizations search for the perfect figurehead for their ideas or products, and in Canada Wayne Gretzky is perhaps the ideal representative whatever your message. Let's look at the qualities that create the "marketing magnetism of No. 99" as the *Globe and Mail's Report on Business* put it and which enabled him to earn more than $15 million in 1998 (MacDonald & Waldie, 1999).

■ Canada's ideal spokesperson

FIGURE 3.8 There's hardly a person in Canada who does not recognize Wayne Gretzky. In fact he has all, or almost all, the characteristics of an effective communicator.

First of all there is no doubt about his *attractiveness*—he is one of the most well known Canadian public figures—few could fail to recognize that face (see Figure 3.8). Essentially this stems from his hockey record. He is considered the "Great One" because of that record and this has made his *popularity* immeasurable in Canada. According to the corporate communications manager of the Hudson's Bay Company, they chose Gretzky to endorse a new line of menswear because they "wanted to work with a Canadian icon, somebody who Canadians admired" (MacDonald & Waldie, 1999). However, he has other qualities which add to his attractiveness. He has fresh-faced *good looks* and an engaging lopsided grin. The hint of shyness in his manner and his becoming modesty fit with Canadian values and make him all the more *likable*.

The other important quality for a spokesperson is *credibility*—he or she must be believable—and research tells us this stems from such factors as expertise, trustworthiness and sincerity (e.g., Hovland & Weiss, 1951). Gretzky certainly has *expertise* in the area of hockey and has been the spokesman for hockey equipment manufacturers both in the United States and Canada. He is seen as a boy from small-town Canada, and a family man, as well as having an impeccable reputation both on and off the ice—"He's always proven himself to be a very good hometown boy," the mayor of Brantford, Ontario, his home town, is quoted as saying (MacDonald & Waldie, 1999). We have also seen Gretzky giving his time and endorsement to community organizations such as Canadian literacy campaigns. Such characteristics increase our sense that he is a *trustworthy* and *sincere* individual and his simple unassuming manner adds to this impression. In fact you can see that Wayne Gretzky has almost all the features that research from the traditional approach confirmed as increasing the persuasiveness of a communicator. The only quality he appears to lack is that of being fast-talking. However, as this might well detract from his sincerity or likability, that is hardly a disadvantage.

One negative note was struck more recently which may be the result of the marketers' clumsy attempt at *non-obvious persuasion*—see Table 3.2. With retirement from hockey in 1999, we heard that Gretzky was suffering from arthritis and would become a spokesperson for the Arthritis Society. However, when the expected announcement was shown on television, it included a plug for a well-known painkiller. Perhaps the manufacturers were hoping that the mention of their product would appear spontaneous and unsolicited and *not*, therefore, part of a persuasive attempt. If so, they failed badly and for a while slightly tarnished Mr. Gretzky's image in the media.

In the long run though, the credibility of that image will almost certainly outweigh such setbacks. Neither does the *Globe and Mail* expect his retirement to decrease his appeal to advertisers. As his hometown mayor said: "He's got the kind of name and reputation that lives on long after his playing days are over" (MacDonald & Waldie, 1999).

Persuasion: The Cognitive Approach

The early approach to understanding persuasion has certainly been useful; it provided a wealth of insights into factors that influence persuasion. It did not, however, offer a coherent account of how people change their attitudes in response to persuasive messages. This issue has been brought into sharp focus in a more modern approach to understanding the nature of persuasion known as the cognitive perspective (Petty, Cacioppo, Strathman & Priester, 1994; 1986; Eagly & Chaiken, 1998). This approach rests firmly on social psychology's increasingly sophisticated understanding of the nature of social thought—in this case how we process (absorb, interpret and evaluate) the information contained in persuasive messages. What happens when individuals receive a persuasive message? According to the cognitive approach, that depends upon whether the individual subjects the message to systematic processing, thinking carefully about it, or uses more simple heuristic processing.

The Elaboration Likelihood Model: Two Routes To Persuasion

The most influential theory from this perspective, **the elaboration likelihood model (ELM)**, suggests that two different cognitive routes to persuasion are possible, reflecting whether the recipient elaborates upon—thinks carefully about—a persuasive message. The first of these is known as the **central route**, and it involves *systematic processing*—careful consideration of message content, the ideas it contains, and so on. Such processing is quite effortful and absorbs much of our information-processing capacity. The second approach, known as the **peripheral route**, involves *heuristic processing*—the use of simple rules of thumb or mental shortcuts—such as the belief that "experts can be trusted" or the idea that "if it makes me feel good, I'm in favour of it." This kind of processing is much less effortful and allows us to react to persuasive messages in an automatic manner, like the character in the cartoon in Figure 3.7 earlier. It occurs in response to *persuasion cues* in the message that evoke various mental shortcuts (e.g., beautiful models who evoke the "What's beautiful is good and worth listening to" heuristic). This model is summarized in Figure 3.9.

When do we engage in each of these two distinct modes of thought? The answer, in part, is that it depends upon our capacity and our motivation to process the persuasive message. Briefly, we use the central route (systematic processing) when our capacity to process information relating to the persuasive message is high (e.g., when we have lots of knowledge about the subject or lots of time to engage in such

Elaboration Likelihood Model (of persuasion) A theory suggesting that persuasion can occur in either of two distinct ways, differing in the amount of cognitive effort or elaboration they require.

Central Route (to persuasion) Attitude change resulting from systematic processing of information presented in persuasive messages.

Peripheral Route (to persuasion) Attitude change that occurs in response to persuasion cues—information concerning the expertise or status of would-be persuaders.

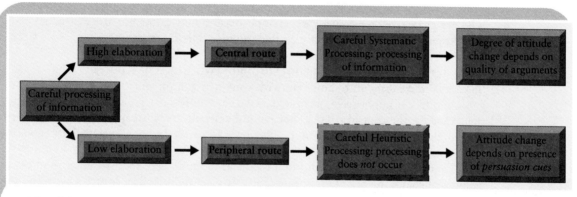

■ The elaboration likelihood model

FIGURE 3.9 According to the elaboration likelihood model, persuasion can occur in either of two distinct ways. Individuals can engage in careful, systematic processing of the information contained in persuasive messages, in which case persuasion occurs through the central route (upper pathway). Alternatively, individuals may think very little about the message itself and instead respond largely to more superficial persuasion cues. In this case persuasion occurs through the peripheral route (lower pathway).

Source: Based on suggestions by Petty & Cacioppo, 1986.

thought) or when we are motivated to do so—when the issue is important to us, when we believe it is important to form an accurate view, and so on (e.g., Maheswaran & Chaiken, 1991; Petty & Cacioppo, 1990). In contrast, we use the peripheral route (heuristic processing) when we lack the ability or capacity to process more carefully (we must make up our minds very quickly, we have little knowledge about the issue, and so on) or when our motivation to perform such cognitive work is low (the issue is unimportant to us or has little potential effect on us, and so on). Advertisers, politicians, salespersons, and others wishing to change our attitudes prefer to push us into the heuristic mode of processing because, for reasons we'll describe below, it is often easier to change our attitudes when we think in this mode than when we engage in more careful and systematic processing.

Earlier, we noted that the discovery of these two contrasting modes of processing provided an important key to understanding the process of persuasion. The existence of these two modes of thought has helped us solve many intriguing puzzles. For instance, it has been found that when persuasive messages are not interesting or relevant to individuals, the amount of persuasion they produce is *not* strongly influenced by the quality of the arguments they contain. But when such messages are highly relevant to individuals, they are much more successful in inducing persuasion if the arguments they contain are strong and convincing. Can you see why this so? According to modern theories such as the ELM, when relevance is low, individuals tend to process messages through the heuristic mode, by means of cognitive shortcuts. Thus, argument quality has little impact on them. In contrast, when relevance is high, they process persuasive messages through the systematic (central) route, and in this mode, argument quality is important (e.g., Petty & Cacioppo, 1990).

Similarly, the systematic-versus-heuristic distinction helps explain why people are more easily persuaded when they are somehow distracted—in a sense, asked to do two things at once—than when they are not. Under these conditions, the capacity to process the information in a persuasive message is limited, so people adopt the heuristic mode of thought. If the message contains the "right" persuasion cues (e.g., communicators who are attractive or seemingly expert), persuasion may occur because distracted people respond to these cues and not to the arguments being presented.

Long Term Effects of Persuasion Through Two Kinds of Routes

Since it is more difficult to come up with convincing arguments than it is to find gorgeous models, it might seem, at first glance, that would-be persuaders shouldn't waste their time on the central route. They should concentrate, instead, on producing persuasion through the peripheral route. However, research findings suggest that there are some definite disadvantages to such a strategy.

First, attitudes changed through the central route seem to last longer than ones changed through the peripheral route (Petty & Cacioppo, 1986). Initially, both routes to persuasion may produce similar levels of attitude change; but later, change produced through the peripheral route tends to disappear. Given that persuasion via the central route involves careful thought and changes in cognitive structures, this finding is hardly surprising. Second, it appears that attitude change produced by means of the central route is more resistant to later attempts at persuasion than change produced through the peripheral route (Petty et al., 1994). And finally, attitudes changed by the central route are more closely related to behaviour than attitudes changed via the peripheral route. All these differences seem to be related to the fact that change induced through the central route represents a real shift in the way people think about a particular attitude object—a reorganization of the cognitive structure relating to this object. This reorganization will also produce greater *attitude strength* and, as we saw earlier, strong attitudes tend to influence behaviour more than weak ones. In contrast, change induced through the peripheral route seems to reflect a response to current conditions or stimuli—a whim of the moment if you will; once these current stimuli are gone, the change they induce, too, may disappear. So the message for would-be persuaders is clear: short-term results can be attained through flash and sizzle; but if the goal is that of producing lasting change in recipients' attitudes, then there may be no substitute for well-reasoned arguments presented in a clear and forceful manner.

In sum, the ELM offers important insights into persuasion. It explains how our cognitive processes interact with the persuasive message to induce attitude change. Further, it calls attention to the fact that persuasion can occur along either of two distinctly different cognitive routes, depending upon individual characteristics and differences that affect cognitive processing of information. Clearly, such models constitute a marked advance in our understanding of this important process.

Cultural Values and Persuasion Cues

The possibility that persuasion cues that are particularly resonant with the values of one cultural group have little significance for another was investigated by Han and Shavitt (1994).

These researchers compared the persuasive messages in advertisements from the United States (an individualistic culture) and Korea (a collectivistic culture) in two pairs of comparable magazines. Some of the different slogans are shown in Table 3.3. They found greater individualism in American advertisements which had slogans related to individuality, self-reliance, competition (e.g., "You, only better," "A leader among leaders"). Korean advertisements, in contrast, showed greater collectivism with slogans emphasizing the family or group well-being and harmony (e.g., "The dream of prosperity for all of us," "Your business success: Harmonization with Sunkyong"). These researchers then went on to show that American subjects were more persuaded by slogans presenting individualistic cues and Korean subjects were more persuaded when the advertisements presented collectivistic cues.

Han and Shavitt (1994) examined advertisements in American and Korean magazines. Slogans varied in whether they made individualistic appeals or collectivistic appeals.

TABLE 3.3 Individualistic and collectivistic advertising

Individualistic Slogans	Collectivistic Slogans
The art of being unique	We have a way of bringing people together
She's got a style all her own	We share our love with seven wonderful children
Alive with pleasure	The dream of prosperity for all of us
Self-esteem	Celebrating a half-century of partnership
My own natural color's come back; only better, much better	We devote ourselves to contractors
You, only better	Sharing is beautiful
A quick return for your investment	Your business success: Harmonization with Sunkyong
A leader among leaders	Our family agrees with the selection of home-furnishings
With this new look I'm ready for my new role	Ringing out the news of business friendships that really work
Make your way through the crowd	Successful partnerships

Source: Based on Han & Shavitt, 1994.

This study suggests that the cultural values of the audience may be important to persuasion. The persuasion cues used in advertisements in Canada tend to emphasize individualistic values and as such may have less impact on Canadians from collectivistic cultural groups than those from individualistic cultural groups. Perhaps more importantly, a focus on individual concerns and personal benefits may be seen as immoral by those who have collectivisitic values (Smith & Bond, 1998; Triandis, 1994). Such persons might not merely find individualistic appeals uninteresting, but they might even find them *repellent*. If research confirms such suggestions, persuaders, from product manufacturers to public health campaigners and politicians, will need to tailor their campaigns to include both collectivistic and individualistic messages.

KEY POINTS

- Early research on *persuasion*—efforts to change attitudes through the use of messages—focused primarily on characteristics of the communicator (e.g., expertise, attractiveness), the message (e.g., one-sidedness versus two-sidedness), and the audience.

- More recent research has focused on the cognitive processes that play a role in persuasion. Research related to the *elaboration likelihood model (ELM)* suggests that we process persuasive messages in two distinct ways: through systematic processing with the *central route*, which involves careful attention to message content, or through heuristic processing route, with the *peripheral*, which involves the use of mental shortcuts (e.g., "experts are usually right").

- Research suggests that in the long-term, central route persuasion might be more resistant to change, and that cultural values may play a part in the effectiveness of peripheral route persuasion.

WHEN ATTITUDE CHANGE FAILS: RESISTANCE TO PERSUASION

Given the frequency with which we are exposed to persuasive messages, one point is clear: If we changed our attitudes in response to even a small fraction of these messages, we would soon be in a sorrowful state. Our views on a wide range of issues would change from day to day or even from hour to hour; and, reflecting this fact, our behaviour too would show a strange pattern of shifts and reversals. Obviously, this does not happen. Despite all the charm, charisma, and expertise that would-be persuaders can muster, our attitudes remain remarkably stable. Rather than being pushovers where persuasion is concerned, we are a tough sell and can withstand even powerful efforts to change our attitudes. Why? What factors provide us with such impressive ability to resist? We will now describe several of these.

Reactance: Protecting Our Personal Freedom

Have you ever found yourself becoming irritated at one of the "motivational" speakers on television or a salesperson who tries too hard? You begin to feel "brow-beaten" and feel that you want to find holes in their every argument. You may, in fact, turn off your television or escape from the salesperson. This is an example of what social psychologists term **reactance**—the negative reactions we experience when we conclude that someone is trying to limit our personal freedom by getting us to do what they want us to do. Research findings suggest that in such situations we often change our attitudes (or behaviour) in a direction exactly opposite to that being urged on us—an effect known as *negative attitude change* (Brehm, 1966; Rhodewalt & Davison, 1983). Indeed, so strong is the desire to resist excessive influence that in some cases individuals shift away from a view someone is advocating even if it is one they would otherwise normally accept!

The existence of reactance is one main reason why hard-sell attempts at persuasion often fail. When individuals perceive such appeals as direct threats to their personal freedom (or to their image of being a free and independent human being), they are strongly motivated to resist. And such resistance, in turn, virtually guarantees that many would-be persuaders are doomed to fail.

Forewarning: Prior Knowledge of Persuasive Intent

On many occasions when we receive a persuasive message, we know full well that it is designed to change our views. Indeed, situations in which a communicator manages to catch us completely unprepared are quite rare. Does such advance knowledge or **forewarning** of persuasive intent help us to resist? Research evidence suggests that it does (e.g., Cialdini & Petty, 1979; Johnson, 1994). When we know that a speech, taped message, or written appeal is designed to alter our views, we are often less likely to be affected by it than if we do not possess such knowledge. The basis for such beneficial effects seems to lie in the impact that forewarning has on key cognitive

Reactance Negative reactions to perceived threats to one's personal freedom. Reactance often increases resistance to persuasion.

Forewarning Advance knowledge that one is about to become the target of an attempt at persuasion. Forewarning often increases resistance to the persuasion that follows.

processes. When we receive a persuasive message, especially one contrary to our current views, we often formulate *counterarguments* against it. Knowing about the content of such a message in advance provides us with extra time in which to prepare our defences. In addition, forewarning also provides us with more time in which to recall relevant facts and information from memory—facts that may prove useful in refuting a persuasive message (Wood, 1982). Such effects are more likely to occur with respect to attitudes we consider to be important (Krosnick, 1989), but they occur to a smaller degree even for attitudes we view as fairly trivial. For these reasons, to be forewarned is to be forearmed where persuasion is concerned.

Selective Avoidance

Still another way in which we resist attempts at persuasion is through **selective avoidance**, a tendency to direct our attention away from information that challenges our existing attitudes. In the context of social cognition (see Chapter 2), selective avoidance is one way in which attitudes (a type of schema) guide the processing of new information. For example, consider the act of television viewing. People do not simply sit in front of the tube and absorb whatever the media decide to dish out. Instead, they channel surf, push the mute button, or cognitively tune out when confronted with information contrary to their existing views. The opposite effect occurs as well: When we encounter information that supports our views, we tend to give it increased attention. We stop changing channels and listen carefully. Together, these tendencies to ignore or avoid information that contradicts our attitudes while actively seeking information consistent with them constitute the two sides of *selective exposure*—deliberate efforts to obtain information that supports our views. Through this mechanism, we often protect our current attitudes against persuasion and assure that they remain largely intact for long periods.

Selective Avoidance A tendency to direct one's attention away from information that challenges existing attitudes. Such avoidance increases resistance to persuasion.

Biased Assimilation and Attitude Polarization

Selective avoidance is not, however, the only way in which we protect our attitudes from efforts to change them. In addition, we often engage in **biased assimilation**—evaluating information that disconfirms our existing views as less convincing and less reliable than information that confirms our existing views (e.g., Lord, Ross, & Lepper, 1979; Miller et al., 1993). And to put the icing on the cake, we also show an effect known as **attitude polarization**—a tendency to evaluate mixed evidence or information in such a way that it strengthens our initial views and makes them more extreme (e.g., Pomeranz et al., 1995). As a result of these two tendencies, our attitudes really *do* seem to be beyond the reach of many efforts to change them; and, as we've noted at several other points in this chapter, they tend to persist even when we are confronted with new information that strongly challenges them.

Evidence for the powerful nature of biased assimilation and attitude polarization is provided by many studies, but one of the clearest of these was conducted by Munro and Ditto (1997). These researchers first selected two groups of participants—one group strongly prejudiced toward homosexuals and another group low in prejudice toward homosexuals. Then they exposed both groups to the results of two scientific studies, one that supported common negative stereotypes of homosexuals (e.g., that they suffer from more psychological disorders than heterosexuals) and one that refuted such views. As participants received this mixed information, they rated the quality of each of the scientific studies and indicated how convincing they found it to be. In addition, they reported on how each study made them feel (its impact on their current affective state) and on their general attitudes about homosexuals. Munro and Ditto (1997) predicted that participants

Biased Assimilation The tendency to evaluate information that disconfirms our existing views as less convincing or reliable than information that confirms these views.

Attitude Polarization The tendency to evaluate mixed evidence or information in such a way that it strengthens our initial views and makes them more extreme.

FIGURE 3.10 As shown here, persons who were strongly prejudiced toward homosexuals rated information that confirmed their negative stereotypes of this group as more convincing than information that refuted such stereotypes. The opposite was true for persons low in prejudice against homosexuals.

Source: Based on data from Munro & Ditto, 1997.

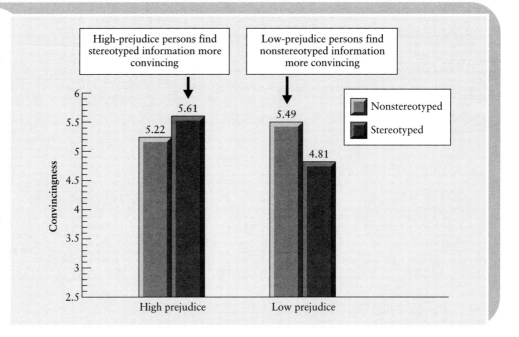

would rate information that contradicted their current views about homosexuals as being less reliable or convincing than information that confirmed their current views; and, as you can see from Figure 3.10, this is precisely what happened. Highly prejudiced persons rated the study that confirmed the negative stereotype of homosexuals (and thus their own attitudes) as more convincing than the study that refuted the negative stereotype, and the opposite was true for persons low in prejudice against homosexuals. In addition, participants reported more negative feelings when confronted with information inconsistent with their current views than when confronted with information consistent with their current views. Moreover, such affective reactions seemed to play a key role in biased assimilation; when the effects of such changes in current mood were removed statistically, biased assimilation, too, was eliminated.

Some evidence for attitude polarization was also obtained. Although participants' attitudes did not become more extreme after they read the mixed evidence presented in the two studies, they perceived that their views had shifted in this manner. In other words, highly prejudiced persons believed that the studies caused them to become more prejudiced, while less prejudiced persons believed that the studies caused them to become less prejudiced.

The findings reported by Munro and Ditto (1997) and other researchers (e.g., Giner-Sorolla & Chaiken, 1997; Miller et al, 1993) point to another reason why efforts at persuasion often fail. When individuals receive information that disagrees with their current views they tend to react with annoyance and contempt, and they quickly discount such input as biased. In addition, other research (e.g., Duck, Terry, & Hogg, 1998; Vallone, Ross, & Lepper, 1985) indicates that people may also tend to perceive the *source* of such information, not just the information itself, as biased—an effect known as the *hostile media bias*, as in "Media coverage that disagrees with my views is biased!" (e.g., Duck, Terry, & Hogg, 1997). To the extent that such effects occur, even strong arguments are rejected, and there is little chance that attitude change will occur. Please see the Ideas to Take with You section featured at the end of the chapter for our advice on how to resist persuasion.

- Our attitudes tend to remain quite stable despite many efforts to change them. Several factors contribute to such resistance to persuasion. One such factor is *reactance*—negative reactions to efforts by others to reduce or limit our personal freedom. When we interpret efforts at persuasion as producing such effects, we reject them and may even adopt views opposite to these being urged upon us.

- Resistance to persuasion is often increased by *forewarning*, the knowledge that someone is trying to change our attitudes, and by *selective avoidance*, the tendency to avoid exposure to information that contradicts our views.

- Two additional processes, *biased assimilation* and *attitude polarization*, also play a role in resistance to persuasion. Biased assimilation is our tendency to evaluate information that contradicts our attitudes as less reliable or convincing than information that confirms our current views. Attitude polarization is the tendency to interpret mixed evidence in ways that strengthen our existing views and make them more extreme.

COGNITIVE DISSONANCE: HOW WE SOMETIMES CHANGE OUR OWN ATTITUDES

Suppose that you have very strong feelings about the need to protect the environment and have always tried to behave in environmentally sound ways: recycling, getting involved in the environmental movement, and refusing to drive a car even though this is inconvenient—you live a long way from school and work. Now, however, a family member is offering you his old car at virtually no cost. Of course, you should refuse. But it's the middle of winter and you have just taken on extra hours at work, which makes your schedule very tight. A car would make life so much more simple and those long, cold waits at the bus stop would be a thing of the past! You accept this generous offer, telling yourself this is just a temporary state of affairs. However, six months later, in the middle of summer, you still have the car. One day you meet a friend who is involved in the environmental movement and is shocked that you own a car after your previously strong stand on this issue. You find yourself explaining at length that this is only a temporary situation, it's an absolute necessity with your very busy lifestyle, and it doesn't imply that your beliefs about the environment have changed. But afterward, you find yourself feeling very uncomfortable—somehow these justifications rang hollow, even in your own ears. What accounts for this discomfort? You have just become aware that your behaviour is clearly inconsistent with your attitudes—now you are also questioning your own commitment to the environment. Social psychologists term this kind of discomfort **cognitive dissonance** (Festinger, 1957).

This is the feeling, usually unpleasant, that arises when we discover inconsistency between two of our attitudes or between our attitudes and our behaviour (see Figure 3.11). There are many causes of dissonance. It can occur when individuals must choose between two attractive alternatives, for example, rejecting one job, school, or lover in favour of another. This rejection is inconsistent with the positive features of the rejected option. Most relevant to our present discussion, though, is the fact that dissonance is generated whenever individuals say things they don't mean or behave in ways that are inconsistent with their underlying attitudes or values. In such cases, the dissonance

Cognitive Dissonance An unpleasant internal state that results when individuals notice inconsistency between two or more of their attitudes or between their attitudes and their behaviour.

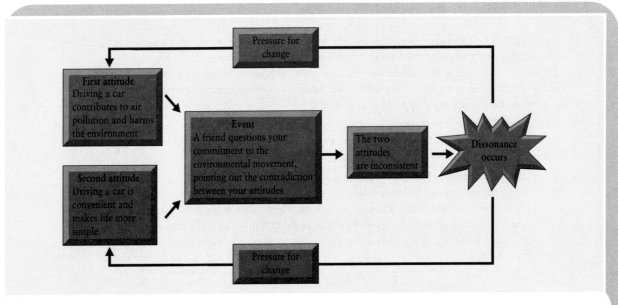

■ Dissonance and attitude change

FIGURE 3.11 When individuals notice that two attitudes they hold are somehow inconsistent, cognitive dissonance occurs. This process generates pressures to change one or both of the attitudes involved.

produced can sometimes have a startling effect: It can lead the people involved to change their attitudes so that these more closely reflect their words and deeds. In other words, saying or doing things that are inconsistent with their own attitudes sometimes causes people to *change the attitudes themselves*. How can this be so? Read on.

Dissonance and Attitude Change: The Effects of Induced Compliance

There are many occasions in everyday life when we must say or do things inconsistent with our real attitudes. For example, your friend has a new haircut and asks you how you like it. You really hate it but know your friend has to walk around with it for at least a few weeks. What do you say? Probably something like "Nice, really nice." Similarly, imagine that at an important meeting your boss turns to you and asks your opinion of her new plan. Since you value your relationship with her (and your job!) you praise the plan, even though you realize it has serious problems. In these and countless other situations, our actions and our attitudes are inconsistent. What happens in these situations, which social psychologists describe as involving **induced compliance** (or *forced compliance*)? This term derives from the fact that in such incidents we are induced or forced by circumstances to say or do things contrary to our real views.

Since dissonance is an unpleasant state (Elliot & Devine, 1994), people who experience it are motivated to reduce it. So something has to give (change). The theory focuses on three basic mechanisms.

First, individuals can use *actual change* of their attitudes or their behaviour so that they are now consistent with each other. For example, you may convince yourself that your boss's plan is actually better than you thought or, in the first example, you might decide to sell your car to bring your behaviour in line with your environmental attitudes.

Induced Compliance
Situations in which individuals are somehow induced to say or do things inconsistent with their true attitudes; also known as *forced compliance*.

Second, dissonance can be reduced by acquiring *new information*—information that is consistent with the attitudes or actions that, at first blush, seem inconsistent. For example, you might eagerly read a news report claiming that cars contribute relatively little to air pollution compared to industrial chemicals (ignoring the fact that this report was sponsored by a major car manufacturer).

Finally, dissonance can be reduced by *minimizing the importance* of the inconsistency. This is termed **trivialization**—when we conclude that the attitudes or behaviours in question are not important, so the inconsistency itself is trivial. Until recently, the conditions under which this means of dissonance reduction will be used had been subject to relatively little research. Simon and her colleagues (Simon, Greenberg, & Brehm, 1995) found that trivialization was most often used if individuals had been made aware of their real attitude before they acted in a counterattitudinal way (e.g., students were asked to think about their attitude toward comprehensive final exams—almost always a negative attitude—before writing an essay in support of such exams). It seems that if we have been made aware of a strongly felt attitude, then changing it becomes difficult and trivialization is often an easier alternative. The students mentioned above could hardly ignore their attitudes. However, they might dismiss the importance of the issue of comprehensive exams or of writing the counterattitudinal essay. Similarly, in our original example, you might find it difficult to change your attitudes toward environmental issues, having just reconfirmed their importance to your friend. In this situation, you might well focus on how seldom you drive and, therefore, how little you contribute to air pollution. In this way, driving a car is trivialized and its inconsistency with your beliefs minimized.

All of these strategies can be viewed as *direct* approaches to dissonance reduction: they focus on the attitudes–behaviour discrepancies that are causing the dissonance. Research by Steele and his colleagues (e.g., Steele, 1988; Steele & Lui, 1983), however, indicates that dissonance can also be reduced through *indirect* tactics—ones that leave the basic discrepancy between attitudes and behaviour intact but reduce the unpleasant negative feelings generated by dissonance. According to Steele (1988), adoption of such indirect routes to dissonance reduction is most likely to occur when an attitude–behaviour discrepancy involves important attitudes or self-beliefs. Under these conditions, Steele suggests (e.g., Steele, Spencer, & Lynch, 1993), individuals experiencing dissonance may focus not so much on reducing the gap between their attitudes and their behaviour as on *self-affirmation*—restoring positive self-evaluations that are threatened by the dissonance (e.g., Elliot & Devine, 1994; Tesser, Martin, & Cornell, 1996). How

Trivialization The conclusion that the attitudes or behaviours in question are not important, so the inconsistency itself is trivial.

■ Reducing dissonance: The indirect route

FIGURE 3.12 The results of many studies indicate that it is not necessary to reduce discrepancy between attitudes and behaviour to reduce dissonance. Other indirect routes exist, ranging from self-affirmation through engaging in enjoyable or distracting activities as shown here.

can they accomplish this goal? By focusing on their positive self-attributes—good things about themselves (e.g., Steele, 1988). For instance, in the original example, you might focus on what a caring person you are in general. You have given many hours to helping your friends as well as regularly volunteering to help the elderly. Contemplating these positive actions would help reduce the discomfort produced by your failure to act in a way consistent with your pro-environmental attitudes.

Other research suggests that almost anything we do that reduces our discomfort and negative affect can sometimes succeed in reducing cognitive dissonance—everything from consuming alcohol (e.g., Steele, Southwick, & Critchlow, 1981) to engaging in distracting activities that take one's mind off the dissonance (e.g., Zanna & Aziza, 1976) to simple expressions of positive affect (see Figure 3.12; Cooper, Fazio, & Rhodewalt, 1978).

Thus, dissonance can be reduced in many different ways—through indirect tactics as well as through direct ones focused on reducing the attitude–behaviour discrepancy. In general, the principle behind our choice of these dissonance reduction techniques is "Whenever possible, take the path of least resistance." As we saw in Chapter 2, this seems to be a guiding principle for many aspects of human behaviour, including social thought. Our choice may also be a function of what's available and the specific context in which dissonance occurs (e.g., Fried & Aronson, 1995). So we will seek to reduce dissonance by changing whatever it is easiest and possible to change and sometimes that is our attitude itself.

Dissonance and the Less-Leads-To-More Effect

Social psychologists generally agree that the *induced compliance effect* is a fact: When individuals say or do things they don't believe, they often experience a need to bring their attitudes into line with these actions. There is one complication in this process we have not yet considered, however: How strong are the reasons for engaging in

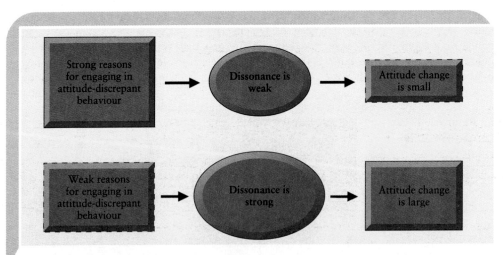

■ Why less (smaller inducements) often leads to more (greater attitude change) after attitude-discrepant behaviour

FIGURE 3.13 When individuals have strong reasons for engaging in attitude-discrepant behaviour, they experience relatively small amounts of dissonance and relatively weak pressure to change their attitudes. However, when individuals have weak reasons for engaging in attitude-discrepant behaviour, they experience larger amounts of dissonance and stronger pressure to change their attitudes. The result: Less (smaller rewards) leads to more (greater amount of attitude change).

counterattitudinal actions? If these reasons are quite strong, little or no dissonance will be generated. After all, if the last person to disagree with your boss publicly was fired on the spot, you would have strong grounds for praising her plan even if you don't like it. But what if good, convincing reasons for engaging in such actions are lacking? Under these conditions, dissonance will be stronger, for you must confront the fact that you said or did something you didn't believe *even though you had no strong or clear basis for doing so*. In short, dissonance theory points to the unexpected prediction that the weaker the reasons for engaging in counterattitudinal behaviour, the stronger the dissonance generated, and hence the greater the pressure to change one's attitudes, as shown in Figure 3.13. Social psychologists often refer to this paradoxical prediction as the **less-leads-to-more effect**: The more inducements there are for engaging in attitude-discrepant behaviour, the weaker the pressures toward attitude change.

Surprising as it may seem, this effect has been confirmed in many different studies (e.g., Riess & Schlenker, 1977). For example, in the first and most famous of these experiments (Festinger & Carlsmith, 1959), subjects were offered either a small reward (one dollar) or a large one (20 dollars) for telling another person that some dull tasks they had just performed were very interesting. (One of the tasks consisted of placing spools on a tray, dumping them out, and repeating the process several times.) After engaging in this attitude-discrepant behaviour (telling another subject the tasks were interesting when they knew full well that they were not), participants were asked to indicate their own liking for the tasks. As predicted by the less-leads-to-more effect, subjects actually reported greater liking for the dull tasks when they had received the small reward than when they had received the large one.

While the less-leads-to-more effect has been confirmed many times, we should note that it does not occur under all conditions. Rather, it seems to happen only when several conditions exist (Cooper & Scher, 1994). First, this effect occurs only in situations in which people believe that they have a choice as to whether or not to perform the attitude-discrepant behaviour. Second, small rewards lead to greater attitude change only when people believe that they are personally responsible for both the chosen course of action and any negative effects it produces. And third, the less-leads-to-more effect occurs only when people view the reward they receive as a well-deserved payment for services rendered, not as a bribe. Since these conditions do often exist, however, the strategy of offering others just barely enough to induce them to say or do things contrary to their true attitudes can often be an effective technique for inducing attitude change.

Dissonance as a Tool for Beneficial Changes in Behaviour

As we move into the twenty-first century, public health campaigns have been successful at increasing awareness of many of the most immediate dangers in our everyday environment (e.g., Carey, Morrison-Beedy, & Johnson, 1997); so most people have generally favourable attitudes toward using seat belts, quitting smoking, losing weight, and engaging in safe sex. Yet, as you well know, these attitudes are often not translated into overt actions: people continue to drive without seat belts, to smoke, and so on. What's needed, in other words, is not so much changes in attitudes as shifts in overt behaviour. Can dissonance be useful in promoting such beneficial changes? A growing body of evidence suggests that it can (e.g., Gibbons, Eggleston, & Benthin, 1997; Stone et al., 1994b), especially when it is used to generate feelings of **hypocrisy**—awareness that one is publicly advocating some attitude or behaviour but then acting in a way that is inconsistent with these attitudes or behaviour. Under these conditions, several researchers have reasoned (e.g., Aronson, Fried, & Stone, 1991), an individual should experience strong feeling of dissonance. Moreover, these feelings should be so

Less-leads-to-more Effect The fact that offering individuals small rewards for engaging in counterattitudinal behaviour often produces more dissonance, and so more attitude change, than offering them larger rewards.

Hypocrisy Publicly advocating some attitude or behaviour and then acting in a way that is inconsistent with this espoused attitude or behaviour.

intense that adopting indirect modes of dissonance reduction (e.g., distracting oneself or bolstering one's ego by thinking about or engaging in other positively evaluated behaviours) would not do the trick: only actions that reduce dissonance directly, removing the discrepancy between one's words and deeds, would be effective.

These predictions have been tested and confirmed in several studies where the behaviour in question was using safe sex methods to prevent transmission of HIV—a particularly important topic for young people today (Stone et al 1994b; 1997). Such findings suggest that using dissonance to generate awareness of hypocrisy can indeed be a powerful tool for changing people's behaviour in desirable ways—ones that protect their health and safety. To be maximally effective, however, such procedures must involve several elements: The persons in question must publicly advocate the desired behaviours (e.g., using condoms, wearing safety belts), must be induced to think about their own failures to show these behaviours in the past, and must be given access to direct means for reducing their dissonance. When these conditions are met, beneficial changes in behaviour can definitely follow.

Do people all around the world experience dissonance? Or is the experience of dissonance—and its effects—influenced by cultural factors? For information on this issue, please see the Canadian Research: On the Cutting Edge section that follows.

Canadian Research: On the Cutting Edge

Is Dissonance Culture-Bound? Evidence from a Cross-National Study

Human beings, dissonance theory contends, dislike inconsistency. They feel uncomfortable when they perceive inconsistency in their attitudes or behaviour, and this often leads them to engage in active efforts to reduce it. As we have already seen, a large body of evidence offers support for these ideas, so dissonance theory has long been seen as providing important insights into several aspects of social thought. There is one major fly in this ointment, however: the vast majority of studies on dissonance have been conducted in North America and Western Europe. Does cognitive dissonance exist and operate in the same manner in other countries? A few studies have examined this question (e.g., Takata & Hashimoto, 1973; Yoshida, 1977), but the findings of this work have been inconsistent; some studies have suggested that dissonance operates in the same way everywhere, while others have called this generality into question.

Fortunately, important new insights into the effects of cultural factors on dissonance have recently been provided by Steve Heine and Darrin Lehman of the University of British Columbia (1997). Drawing on past research suggesting that dissonance often springs from inconsistencies in attitudes and behaviour that threaten individuals' positive view of themselves (*self-affirmation theory*), Heine and Lehman (1997) reasoned that dissonance might actually be less likely to occur and to influence attitudes in some cultures than in others. Specifically, these researchers suggested that after making a choice between closely ranked alternatives, persons from cultures such as those in Canada and the United States would be more likely to experience dissonance than persons from cultures such as those in Japan and other Asian countries. Why? Because in Western cultures the self is linked to individual actions, such as making correct decisions. Thus, after making a choice, individuals in Western cultures often experience considerable dissonance (termed *post-decision dissonance*) because of the potential threat to the self posed by the possibility of having made a wrong decision. In many Asian cultures, in contrast, the self is not as closely linked to individual actions or choices. Rather, it is more strongly tied to roles and status—to an individual's place in society and the obligations this involves (see Figure 3.14). Thus, persons in Asian cultures should be less likely to perceive the possibility of making an incorrect decision as a threat to their self, and so also less likely to experience dissonance.

To test this reasoning, Heine and Lehman (1997) had both Canadian students and Japanese students temporarily living in Canada choose from a group of 40 CDs the 10 CDs that they would most like to own. The participants also evaluated how much they would like each of these 10 CDs. At this point, participants were told that they could actually have either the CD they ranked fifth or the one they ranked sixth. After making their choices, participants rated the two CDs once again. Previous research on post-decision dissonance suggests that in order to reduce dissonance, individuals who make such

decisions often downrate the item they didn't choose while raising their ratings of the item they did choose—an effect known as *spreading of alternatives* (e.g., Steele et al., 1993). The researchers predicted that such effects would be stronger for Canadians than for Japanese participants, and this is precisely what happened. The Canadian students showed the spreading of alternatives effect which results from dissonance reduction to a significant degree; the Japanese students did not.

These findings suggest that cultural factors do indeed influence the operation of dissonance. While all human beings are made somewhat uneasy by inconsistencies between their attitudes or inconsistencies between their attitudes and their behaviour, the intensity of such reactions, the precise conditions under which they occur, and the strategies used to reduce them may all be influenced by cultural factors. Even with respect to very basic aspects of social thought, then, it is essential to take careful account of cultural diversity.

■ Cultural factors in the occurrence of dissonance

FIGURE 3.14 In Western cultures, the self is linked closely to individual actions or choices. In many Asian cultures, however, the self is more strongly tied to roles and status—to an individual's place in society and the obligations this involves. For these reasons, post-decision dissonance may be stronger for persons from Western cultures than for persons from several Asian cultures. This prediction has recently been confirmed (Heine & Lehman, 1997).

KEY POINTS

- *Cognitive dissonance* is an unpleasant state that occurs when we notice discrepancies between our attitudes or between our attitudes and behaviour.
- Dissonance often occurs in situations involving *induced compliance*—ones in which we are induced by external factors to say or do things that are inconsistent with our true attitudes.

- In such situations, attitude change is maximum when we have reasons that are barely sufficient to get us to engage in attitude-discrepant behaviour. Stronger reasons (or larger rewards) produce less attitude change—the *less-leads-to-more effect*.

- Inducing individuals to advocate certain attitudes or behaviours and then reminding them of their *hypocrisy*—the fact that they haven't always behaved in ways consistent with these views—can be a powerful tool for inducing dissonance and thus promoting beneficial changes in behaviour.

- Dissonance appears to be a universal aspect of social thought, but the conditions under which it occurs and the tactics individuals choose to reduce it appear to be influenced by cultural factors.

Ideas to Take with You

Resisting Persuasion: Some Useful Steps

Each day we are exposed to many attempts to change our attitudes. Advertisers, politicians, charities all seek to exert this kind of influence upon us. How can you resist such efforts, which are often highly skilled? Here are some suggestions, based on the research findings of social psychology.

View Attempts at Persuasion as Assaults on Your Personal Freedom.
No one likes being told what to do, but in a sense this is precisely what would-be persuaders are trying to do when they attempt to change your attitudes. So when you are on the receiving end of such appeals, remind yourself that you are in charge of your own life and that there's no reason to listen to or accept what advertisers, politicians, and the like tell you.

Recognize Attempts at Persuasion When You See Them.
Knowing that someone is trying to persuade you—being *forewarned*—is often useful from the point of view of resisting efforts at persuasion. So whenever you encounter someone or some organization that seeks to influence your views, remind yourself that no matter how charming or friendly they are, persuasion is their goal. This will help you resist.

Remind Yourself of Your Own Views and of How These Differ from the Ones Being Urged upon You.
While *biased assimilation*—the tendency to perceive views different from our own as unconvincing and unreliable—can prevent us from absorbing potentially useful information, it is also a useful means for resisting persuasion. When others present views different from your own as part of a persuasive appeal, focus on how different these ideas are from those you hold. The rest will often take care of itself!

Summary and Review of Key Points

Attitude Formation: How We Come to Hold The Views We Do

- *Attitudes* are evaluations of any aspects of the social world.

  Attitudes are often acquired from other persons through *social learning*. Such learning can involve *classical conditioning*, *instrumental conditioning*, or *observational learning*.

  Attitudes are also formed on the basis of *social comparison*—our tendency to compare ourselves with others to determine whether our view of social reality is or is not correct. In order to be similar to others we like or admire, we often accept the attitudes they hold.

Culture can play a part in the transmission of *values*—broad and abstract principles of life. The cultural value dimension of individualism-collectivism has emerged as an important distinction.

Studies conducted with identical twins suggest that attitudes may also be influenced by genetic factors, although the strength of such effects varies greatly for different attitudes.

Attitudes and Behaviour: When Are They Linked?

● Several factors serve as moderators of the link between attitudes and behaviour, affecting the strength of this relationship. *Situational constraints* may prevent us from expressing our attitudes overtly. In addition, we tend to prefer situations that allow us to express our *attitudes*, and this may further strengthen these views.

Several aspects of attitudes themselves also moderate the attitude–behaviour link. These *include attitude origins* (how attitudes were formed*), attitude strength* (which includes attitude accessibility and importance), and *attitude specificity.*

Attitudes seem to influence behaviour through several mechanisms. The *theory of planned behaviour* suggests that when we can give careful thought to our attitudes, intentions derived from our attitudes strongly predict behaviour.

In situations where we can't engage in such deliberate thought, the *attitude-to-behaviour process model* suggests that attitudes influence behaviour by shaping our perceptions of the situation. In addition, willingness and prototypes affect the attitude–behaviour link.

Persuasion: The Process of Changing Attitudes

● Early research on *persuasion*—efforts to change attitudes through the use of messages—focused primarily on characteristics of the communicator (e.g., expertise, attractiveness), the message (e.g., one-sidedness versus two-sidedness), and the audience.

More recent research has focused on the cognitive processes that play a role in persuasion. Research related to the *elaboration likelihood model* (ELM) suggests that we process persuasive messages in two distinct ways: through systematic processing with the *central route*, which involves careful attention to message content, or through heuristic processing with the *peripheral route*, which involves the use of mental shortcuts (e.g., "experts are usually right").

Research suggests that in the long-term, central route persuasion might be more resistant to change, and that cultural values may play a part in the effectiveness of peripheral route persuasion.

When Attitude Change Fails: Resistance to Persuasion

● Our attitudes tend to remain quite stable despite many efforts to change them. Several factors contribute to such resistance to persuasion. One such factor is *reactance*—negative reactions to efforts by others to reduce or limit our personal freedom. When we interpret efforts at persuasion as producing such effects, we reject them and may even adopt views opposite to these being urged upon us.

Resistance to persuasion is often increased by *forewarning*, the knowledge that someone is trying to change our attitudes and by *selective avoidance*, the tendency to avoid exposure to information that contradicts our views.

Two additional processes, *biased assimilation* and *attitude polarization*, also play a role in resistance to persuasion. Biased assimilation is our tendency to evaluate information that contradicts our attitudes as less reliable or convincing than information that confirms our current views. Attitude polarization is the tendency to interpret mixed evidence in ways that strengthen our existing views and make them more extreme.

Cognitive Dissonance: Why Our Behaviour Can Sometimes Influence Our Attitudes

Cognitive dissonance is an unpleasant state that occurs when we notice discrepancies between our attitudes or between our attitudes and behaviour.

Dissonance often occurs in situations involving *induced compliance*—ones in which we are induced by external factors to say or do things that are inconsistent with our true attitudes.

In such situations, attitude change is maximum when we have reasons that are barely sufficient to get us to engage in attitude-discrepant behaviour. Stronger reasons (or larger rewards) produce less attitude change—the *less-leads-to-more effect.*

Inducing individuals to advocate certain attitudes or behaviours and then reminding them of their hypocrisy—the fact that they haven't always behaved in ways consistent with these views—can be a powerful tool for inducing dissonance and thus promoting beneficial changes in behaviour.

Dissonance appears to be a universal aspect of social thought, but the conditions under which it occurs and the tactics individuals choose to reduce it appear to be influenced by cultural factors.

For More **Information**

Eagly, A. H., Wood, W., & Chaiken, S. (1996). *Principles of persuasion*. In E. T. Higgins & A. W. Kruglanski (Eds.), *Social psychology: Handbook of basic principles* (pp. 702–742). New York: Guilford Press.

Two experts on the process of persuasion provide an insightful overview of the findings of recent research on this important topic.

Gollwitzer, P. M., & Barth, J. A. (1996). *The psychology of action: Linking motivation and cognition in behavior*. New York: Guilford Press.

A collection of insightful chapters focused on recent efforts by social psychologists to understand one of the essential puzzles of life: why other people behave the way they do.

Shavitt, S., & Brock, T. C. (1994). *Persuasion: Psychological insights and perspectives*. Boston: Allyn and Bacon.

Explores all aspects of persuasion. The chapters on when and how attitudes influence behaviour, on cognitive dissonance, and on the cognitive perspective on persuasion are all excellent.

Weblinks

www.iicm.edu/jucs_4_3/application_and_assess ment_of/paper.html

"Application and Assessment of Cognitive-Dissonance Theory in the Learning Process" by Esma Aimeur, University of Montreal

www.freeminds.org/psych/propfail.htm

"When Prophecies Fail: A Sociological Perspective on Failed Expectation in the Watchtower Society" by Randall Watters

www.nldline.com/clikeman.htm

"Right Hemispheric Dysfunction in Nonverbal Learning Disabilities: Social, Academic, and Adaptive Functioning in Children and Adults" by Margaret Semrud-Clikeman, University of Georgia

cognitrn.psych.indiana.edu/rgoldsto/papers.html

Selected papers and abstracts by cognitive psychologist Robert Goldstone

paradigm.soci.brocku.ca:80/~lward

George Herbert Mead page

Social Identity: The **Self**, **Gender**, and **Culture**

"I was a ruthless, driven, unfeeling son of a bitch—and it worked out extremely well."

■ Symbolic self-awareness

FIGURE 4.1 The gentleman in this cartoon is demonstrating an abstract representation of the self which he is able to communicate to others through language. Humans may be the only species able to do this, but it evidently doesn't make us necessarily better beings.

Understanding the origins and nature of the sense of self has been seen as important from the beginnings of psychology (Cooley, 1902; James, 1890). Early theories (James, 1890) suggest that the sense of self has its origins in our relationships with others, and that it has both internal components (such as our values and feelings or "inner sensibilities") and external components (such as our social position and our possessions). As we will see, these early views are very much reflected in today's theories and research.

Extending earlier conceptions, Sedikides and Skowronski (1997) propose that the self evolved as an adaptive characteristic. The first aspect to evolve was *subjective self-awareness*; this involves the ability of the organism to differentiate itself to some degree from its physical and social environment. Most animals share this characteristic, which makes it possible to survive (Damasio, 1994; Lewis, 1992). Over time, *objective self-awareness* developed among primates; this term refers to the organism's capacity to be the object of its own attention (Gallup, 1994), to be aware of its own state of mind (Cheney & Seyfarth, 1992), and "to know it knows, to remember it remembers" (Lewis, 1992, p. 124). Only humans seem to have developed the third level of self-functioning—*symbolic self-awareness*—which permits adults of our species to form an abstract cognitive representation of self through language—though hopefully not like the man in the cartoon in Figure 4.1. This representation, in turn, makes it possible for us to communicate, form relationships, set goals, evaluate outcomes, develop self-related attitudes, and defend

ourselves against threatening communications. Throughout each person's life, interactions with others in multiple contexts continue to influence and to modify the specific contents of that person's self-identity.

The sense of self that emerges from our interactions with others combines both the private or internal person and the more public or social person who identifies with various groups—including cultural, racial, religious, political, gender, age, and occupational groups, to name just a few. The private self provides us with a sense of *personal identity*, while the more public self provides us with a sense of *social identity* (Tajfel & Turner, 1979; Deaux, et al., 1995). It should be emphasized, however, that these different aspects of our identity combine in the overall sense of self, or *general self-concept* (Byrne & Shavelson, 1996; Roberts & Donahue, 1994). In this chapter we will discuss these two major aspects of the self. First, we will describe some of the crucial elements of the *personal* self, including self-concept, self-esteem, self-focusing and self-monitoring. Second, we will turn to the more *social* aspects of the self, concentrating on gender and the sense of cultural or ethnic identity, which is so important to a Canadian context. Finally, we will look at the area of *cross-cultural psychology* that has begun to provide insights into the extensive influence of culture on social behaviour. This work has led us to question some long-cherished assumptions about social behaviour.

PERSONAL IDENTITY: ASPECTS OF THE PRIVATE SELF

In this first part of the chapter we will review current knowledge about the self from the point of view of social cognition (see Chapter 2). This perspective has focused on the self as an organizational framework that influences our processing of information, as well as our own motivations, emotional states, and feelings of well-being (Klein, Loftus, & Burton, 1989; Van Hook & Higgins, 1988). From this perspective, the self is the centre of each person's cognitive and social universe.

The Cognitive Organization of the Self-Concept

Who are you? Before you read further, try to give twenty different answers to that question.

Investigating the content of a person's self-concept, questions such as "Who are you?" and "Who am I?" have been asked for more than a hundred years as psychologists, beginning with William James (1890), have endeavored to determine the specific content of the individual self-concept (Ziller, 1990).

Rentsch and Heffner (1994) utilized this technique when they asked more than two hundred college students to give repeated answers to the question "Who are you?" The investigators analyzed the responses statistically in order to determine the basic categories of self as perceived by the research participants. The study rested on the assumption that while the *overall structure* of the self-concept is the same for everyone, each person possesses a unique self-concept with *specific content*. The students described themselves on the basis of eight categories (or factors): e.g., Internalized Beliefs; Self Awareness; Interests and Activities; Social Differentiation; Interpersonal Attributes; and Ascribed Characteristics. Some of these categories refer to some aspects of social identity (I am a Canadian; I am a man), whereas others refer to personal attributes (I am a good person; I like modern art). One goal for social psychologists is to establish a clear picture or blueprint of the self-structure. If you answered the question about yourself, did you also include personal and social aspects? The results of this research suggest that you would include both, showing an overall structure similar to other students, although the specific content of your items would be unique to you.

The Self-Schema

A schema is an organized collection of beliefs and feelings about some aspect of the world. Each of us has a self-schema in which our self-knowledge is organized (Markus & Nurius, 1986). That is, the **self-schema** is a cognitive framework that guides the way we process information about ourselves. Self-schemas reflect all of our past self-relevant experiences; all of our current knowledge and existing memories about ourselves; and what we expect to be like in the future. A person's self-schema is the sum of everything that individual knows or can imagine about her or himself and it can play a role in guiding our behaviour (Kendzierski & Whitaker, 1997). If you see yourself as a helpful person, this may guide you toward a career in the helping professions.

Because the self is the centre of each person's social universe and our self-schemas tend to be well developed, it follows that we should do a better job of processing information that is relevant to ourselves than any other kind of information. Self-relevant information should be more likely to capture our attention, to be entered into memory, and to be recalled (Higgins & Bargh, 1987). These hypotheses have been confirmed in studies of memory in which words deliberately made relevant to self ("Does this word describe you?") were later recalled more easily than words not made relevant ("Is this word printed in big letters?"). This tendency for information related to the self to be most readily processed and remembered is known as the **self-reference effect**.

Some investigators have pursued the question of just *how* self-relevant information is processed more efficiently. Klein and Loftus (1988) reasoned that that recall

Self-schema An organized collection of beliefs and feelings about the self.

Self-reference Effect The tendency for information related to the self to be processed more efficiently (in several respects) than other forms of information.

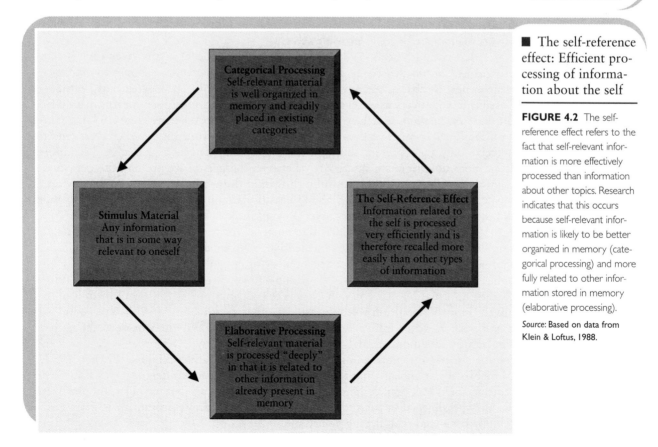

■ The self-reference effect: Efficient processing of information about the self

FIGURE 4.2 The self-reference effect refers to the fact that self-relevant information is more effectively processed than information about other topics. Research indicates that this occurs because self-relevant information is likely to be better organized in memory (categorical processing) and more fully related to other information stored in memory (elaborative processing).

Source: Based on data from Klein & Loftus, 1988.

could be facilitated in one of two ways. First, you are likely to spend more time thinking about words or events that are relevant to yourself than about any other words or events. By doing so, you are engaging in *elaborative processing*, which connects new material to existing information that is already stored in memory. Second, self-relevant material is likely to be well organized in your memory; as a result, new self-relevant information can easily be placed in categories that are already present—a phenomenon known as *categorical processing*. That is analogous to having a filing system already set up and ready for new material to be inserted in the appropriate folders. In a test of the effects of these two types of processing, Klein and Loftus (1988) encouraged research participants to engage in elaborative processing of words ("think of a definition of each") or to engage in categorical processing of the words ("think about a personal experience related to each"). By comparing how well the participants remembered the words afterward, the investigators were able to show that we deal with self-relevant material very efficiently because it is based on both elaborative and categorical processing. In sum, we think more about whatever is relevant to ourselves, and we also categorize such material effectively. As a result, we are able to recall self-relevant information much better than information unrelated to ourselves. These processes are summarized in Figure 4.2.

The Changing Self-Concept

When people speak about themselves, they often assume stability and the absence of change. Despite this, most of us realize that we can and do change. You are not the same person you were 10 years ago, and you can safely assume that 10 years from now you will not be exactly the same person you are today. Your daydreaming fantasies are likely to involve how you might change once you get out of school, get married, enter a career, make more money, or move to a new location. So, along with a self-concept, we are also aware of other **possible selves**.

Possible Selves
Mental representations of what we might become, or should become, in the future.

Markus and Nurius (1986) suggest that a self-concept at any given time is actually just a *working self-concept*, one that is open to change in response to new experiences, new feedback, and new self-relevant information. The existence of alternative possible selves affects us in several ways. The image of a future self may have an effect on one's *motivation*, as when a decision is made to spend more time studying or to stop smoking. Though you may have a clear image of your future self, others tend to perceive only your present self, and the *discrepancy* can be a source of discomfort. Even more upsetting is a discrepancy between the person we are and the person we want to be (Higgins, 1990). Research show that those who are characteristically optimistic have higher expectations about actually attaining a positive possible self than did those who are pessimistic (Carver, Reynolds, & Scheier, 1994).

People also differ in whether they imagine many possible alternatives or only a very limited number. Research by Niedenthal, Setterlund, and Wherry (1992) indicated that people who have a very limited number of possible future selves are emotionally vulnerable to relevant feedback. For example, if you are considering 20 possible future careers, information that you don't have the necessary ability for one of them is of relatively limited importance—there are 19 other possibilities. If you have only one career goal, however, information indicating a lack of ability may be devastating. In a similar way, the more strongly and the more exclusively a person identifies with the role of athlete, the more emotionally upsetting is an athletic injury (Brewer, 1993). More broadly, it appears that those who can envision many different selves adjust better to setbacks (Morgan & Janoff-Bulman, 1994). It seems that having a complex view of one's possible selves (assuming that they are realistically grounded) is more emotionally beneficial than having a very simple view.

■ Self-concept: Role-specific self-concepts

FIGURE 4.3 When Roberts and Donahue (1994) asked women to describe themselves with respect to several characteristics, they produced different self-descriptions in different roles (worker, wife, friend, daughter), indicating role-specific self-concepts. In other words, one's self-concept differs to some extent in different interpersonal situations. The women nevertheless showed some consistency from role to role, indicating some continuity of the self-concept.

A change in occupation status can lead to a radical altering of the self-concept. One example is the negative effects on a person's self-concept when he or she loses a job and suddenly has a new social identity—unemployed (Sheeran & Abraham, 1994). The opposite experience—entering a new occupation—also leads to changes in the self-concept; for example, new police officers are found to develop new views of themselves (Stradling, Crowe, & Tuohy, 1993). Even greater changes occur when an individual joins the armed forces and is thrust into combat. This experience can lead to many self-relevant problems, including confusion about "Who am I?" ("Am I a civilian or a military person?"), confusion about time perspective ("I was too young to feel so old"), interpersonal and work-related problems, and the development of a negative self-identity (Silverstein, 1994).

Changing social relationship contexts can also affect the self-concept. For example, just thinking about a significant other leads research participants to shift their self-descriptions to reflect the way they are when they're with this other person (Hinkley & Andersen, 1996). The self-perceptions and interpersonal perceptions of same-sex college roommates change as they interact overtime (McNulty & Swann, 1994). Researchers propose that the self acts as an "architect" in shaping and determining the reactions of others, but that then the self is also altered by how others react. Given the fact that mutual influences occur in pairs of roommates, it seems very likely that this process is even stronger in close relationships such as friendship and marriage.

Rather than the self's undergoing change in a social context, a different interpretation is possible. That is, it may be that each person has a central core self plus many different *social selves* that are activated by different people in different social interactions. Roberts and Donahue (1994) pursued this question with a sample of middle-aged women by assessing several of their *role-specific* self-concepts as well as their *general* self-concepts. The role-specific concepts for each individual were worker, wife, friend, and daughter (see Figure 4.3). The women were asked to describe themselves in these different roles with respect to positive affect, competence, and dependability. As hypothesized, self-conceptions differed across roles, indicating the existence of role-specific self-concepts. However, there was also an underlying consistency for individuals as they shifted from role to role. For example, although different levels of positive affect might be shown in one role than another, an individual might have a higher average level of positive affect across all roles than most people do. This consistent difference across roles reflects the operation of a general self-concept.

KEY POINTS

- The self can be conceived as combining our *personal identity*—the private aspects of the self, and our *social identity*—the more public and socially embedded sense of self.
- Cognitive information related to the self is organized into a *self-schema*. This organization helps us to process information about ourselves more efficiently than other types of information—*the self-reference effect*. The processing is both *elaborative* and *categorical*.
- In addition to our current self-concept, there are many possible different and better selves that we can envision in the future.
- Self-concept changes with age, but also in response to feedback, changes in one's environment or occupational status, and interactions with others.

Self-Esteem: Attitudes About Oneself

Self-esteem The self-evaluations made by each individual; the general attitude a person holds about himself or herself.

Perhaps the most important attitude each person holds is his or her attitude about self, an evaluation that we label **self-esteem** (James, 1890). If you were asked right now to evaluate yourself on a scale of 1 to 10 (with 1 indicating an extremely negative evaluation and 10 an extremely positive one), what number do you think would best describe your attitude toward yourself? Keep your answer in mind as you read the following section.

Having *high self-esteem* means that an individual likes himself or herself. Such evaluations are based in part on the opinions of others and in part on specific experiences. As we will see in Chapter 6, these attitudes about self may begin with the earliest interactions between an infant and a caregiver. Cultural differences also influence what is important to one's self-esteem. For example, harmony in interpersonal relationships is an essential element in collectivist cultures, whereas self-worth is all-important in individualistic cultures (Kwan, Bond, & Singelis, 1997).

Though most of the research on self-esteem is focused on a global indication of self-evaluation, it is also clear that people subdivide aspects of their self. For example, you may rate yourself very highly on being able to dance and very low on being able to speak French. Because of such subdividing, you can have very positive attitudes about some aspects of yourself and very negative attitudes about other aspects. Your overall, global self-esteem can be conceptualized as the combination of the relative number and relative intensity of these positive and negative self-evaluations (Marsh, 1993, 1995; Pelham, 1995a, 1995b). Beyond that, however, specific self-evaluations predict *cognitive* reactions to success and failure (e.g., how you *explain* them) whereas global self-esteem predicts *emotional* reactions to such outcomes (e.g., how you *feel* about them; Dutton & Brown, 1997). It also matters whether one's "good" and "bad" qualities are common or rare. The lowest level of self-esteem is found among those who perceive their liked characteristics to be quite common and their unliked characteristics to be relatively rare (Ditto & Griffin, 1993).

Self-Esteem and Social Comparison

As we saw in Chapter 3, attitudes can be formed through *social comparison*—and attitudes toward the self are no exception. Social comparison is a common means of self-evaluation (Brown et al., 1992) and this is especially true of individuals who are low in self-esteem (Wayment & Taylor, 1995). Depending on your comparison group, specific successes and failures may contribute to high or low self-evaluations or be completely irrelevant. For example, Osborne (1995) points out that despite better academic performance among whites than among African-Americans in U.S. schools, global self-esteem is significantly higher for the latter group. The apparent reason: Among whites, academic success and failure are related to self-evaluation more than they are among African-Americans. In the earliest grades, both racial groups indicate a connection between grades and self-esteem; but by the tenth grade, the relationship tends to drop dramatically for African-Americans, especially males (Steele, 1992). For them, the comparison groups affecting self-esteem seem to involve not classmates engaging in academic activities, but other people and different activities.

Although such social comparisons are relatively complex, the general underlying principle is that any experience that creates a positive mood raises self-esteem, whereas a negative mood lowers self-esteem (Esses, 1989). Consider three possible comparison groups: strangers, ingroup peers, and people who are very close to you.

The effect of discovering someone worse off than yourself (a *downward comparison*) can help or hurt your self-esteem depending on the comparison group. A downward comparison with a stranger, has a positive effect on your mood and raises your self-esteem (Crocker, 1993): "She's fatter than I am, so I feel better about myself." This is termed a *contrast effect* because you have emphasized the *difference* between yourself and another person. However, contrast effects do not always result in a rise in self-esteem (Reis, Gerrard, & Gibbons, 1993). A downward comparison with a member of your ingroup also results in a positive contrast effect: "I can draw better than any of my classmates." This is the kind of boost to self-esteem experienced by a big frog in a little pond (McFarland & Buehler, 1995). But when someone very close to you exhibits inferior qualities, this has a negative effect on your self-esteem; because this kind of downward comparison means that you are associated with the inadequacy: "My best friend is emotionally disturbed (so maybe I'm a little off myself)." This is termed an *assimilation effect* because you have emphasized the *similarity* between yourself and another person.

Analogous differences occur when you observe others better off than yourself. An *upward comparison* can be a matter of indifference if the comparison is with distant strangers: "I could never play chess as well as the Russian champion, but who cares?" If, however, the upward comparison is with your usual comparison ingroup, their superiority makes you feel depressed and lowers your self-esteem (Major, Sciacchitano, & Crocker, 1993). The contrast effect here is a negative one: "I'm the worst tennis player in the tenth grade." Finally, social comparison with someone with

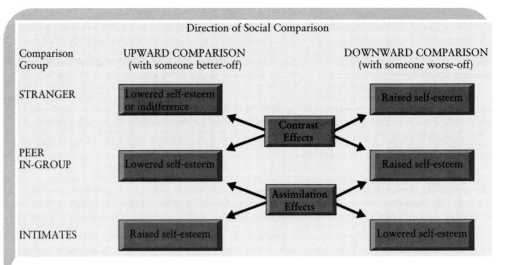

Direction of Social Comparison

Comparison Group	UPWARD COMPARISON (with someone better-off)	DOWNWARD COMPARISON (with someone worse-off)
STRANGER	Lowered self-esteem or indifference	Raised self-esteem
PEER IN-GROUP	Lowered self-esteem	Raised self-esteem
INTIMATES	Raised self-esteem	Lowered self-esteem

Contrast Effects

Assimilation Effects

■ A summary of the effects of social comparison on self-esteem: It depends on the comparison group

FIGURE 4.4 When you compare yourself with others, the effects on your self-esteem depend upon the particular comparison group you are using—whether it's a stranger, your peer ingroup, or someone close to you (an intimate). We will tend to emphasize the similarity between ourselves and those close to us (an *assimilation effect*) which can have a positive impact on self-esteem if that person is superior to you, but a negative impact if they aren't. If we are emphasizing the difference (a *contrast effect*) between ourselves and our peer group, or between ourselves and a stranger, then *upward comparison* tends to result in lowered self-esteem (or indifference to a distant stranger). However, when we see ourselves as superior to those persons (a *downward comparison*) this raises our self-esteem.

qualities superior to your own can enhance your self-esteem, if that person is someone to whom you feel close—this time an assimilation effect has a positive impact on self-esteem (Pelham & Wachsmuth, 1995): "My brother won the tennis tournament, and that makes me look good." These effects of social comparison are summarized in Figure 4.4.

The Effects of High Versus Low Self-Esteem

Research consistently indicates that high self-esteem is beneficial while low self-esteem has many negative consequences (Leary, Schreindorfer, & Haupt, 1995). For example, a negative self-evaluation is associated with less adequate social skills (Olmstead et al., 1991), loneliness (McWhirter, 1997), and depression (Jex, Cvetanovski, & Allen, 1994). As will be discussed in Chapter 10, low self-esteem is one of the psychological factors that can weaken the body's immune system, while high self-esteem helps ward off infections and illness (Strauman, Lemieux, & Coe, 1993). There is even some evidence that as self-esteem goes up, serotonin levels in the blood increase, and that the result is decreased likelihood of impulsivity and aggressiveness (Wright, 1995). Similarly, some research indicates that *unrealistically positive* self-esteem can temporarily benefit one's mental health (Taylor & Brown, 1988); more generally, however, research indicates that accurate self-evaluation is preferable in the long run (Colvin, Block, & Funder, 1995).

While depression is associated with low self-esteem, such negative emotions are associated even more strongly with *variable self-esteem*. That is, people whose self-evaluations fluctuate up and down in response to changes in the situation are the ones most likely to become depressed (Butler, Hokanson, & Flynn, 1994). The reason seems to be that anyone whose self-esteem is strongly affected by minor occurrences has a less stable base of self-worth than people whose self-esteem remains relatively constant (Kernis et al., 1998). High, stable self-esteem acts as a buffer when negative events occur (Wiener, Muczyk, & Martin, 1992). Besides depression, other characteristics are also related to variable self-esteem. For example, self-centred, narcissistic individuals are especially affected by negative interpersonal experiences (Rhodewalt, Madrian, & Cheney, 1998).

Short-term changes in self-esteem can be brought about fairly easily. In the laboratory, when participants are given false feedback about how well they did on a personality test, self-esteem goes up (Greenberg et al., 1992). Similarly, interpersonal feedback indicating acceptance or rejection by others can raise or lower one's self-evaluation (Leary et al., 1998). A familiar, but important, effect is based on clothing: self-esteem increases when people like the clothes they are wearing (Kwon, 1994). It is even possible to bring about such changes by directing your thoughts toward positive or negative content. For example, simply thinking about desirable versus undesirable aspects of oneself can, respectively, raise or lower self-esteem (McGuire & McGuire, 1996).

Self-esteem can also influence our behaviour. For example, lowered self-esteem can result in decreased effort on a task following failure (Tafarodi & Vu, 1997). Research has even suggests that the performance of medical doctors can be influenced in part by their self-esteem. Huang (1998) proposed that medical practices vary as a function of doctors' self-esteem in conjunction with perceptions of **self-efficacy**: a person's evaluation of his or her ability in a particular domain. He tested this proposal among resident physicians at a large teaching hospital in southern Taiwan. The greater the physicians' feelings of self-efficacy, the less stress they experienced when they were uncertain about reaching a diagnosis or prescribing a specific treatment. And the less stress they felt, the more effective and efficient were their medical practices. In addition, the higher the self-esteem of these doctors, the better their medical practices. The investigator proposed that medical education should include an emphasis on developing self-esteem, self-efficacy, and effective ways to cope with the stress of uncertainty.

One major perspective, influenced by the work of therapist Carl Rogers (1951; Rogers & Dymond, 1954), is that self-esteem is essentially related to **self-ideal discrepancies** (i.e., discrepancies between the perception of the actual self and the ideal self—the way you feel you should be). The greater the discrepancy, the lower the self-esteem and the greater the depression an individual shows (Higgins, 1987, 1989); and this discrepancy tends to remain stable over time, even though the specific content may change (Strauman, 1996). Notice that it is a person's *subjective perception* of this discrepancy that is important rather than any objective standard or estimate. It's a positive experience to receive feedback indicating that some aspects of our ideal self are functioning well, and a negative one to receive evidence that we are not living up to our ideal (Eisenstadt & Leppe, 1994). An interesting kind of discrepancy in a person's self-concept, *paradoxical self-esteem*, is described in Canadian Research: On the Cutting Edge, below.

Is it common to adjust our perceptions in order to protect self-esteem? Most people are, in fact, attuned to do just this. Research has shown that, when given a choice, we will often seek out *self-enhancing* information rather than accurate information (Sedikides, 1993; Tesser, 1988). Students who receive a favourable outcome—such as a good test score—are likely to internalize the result and take credit for being intelligent or for working hard (Burke, Hunt, & Bickford, 1985). An unfavourable outcome is more likely to be attributed to external factors (such as "the room was too hot" or "the instructor was unfair"). If this point seems familiar, it is because in Chapter 2 we discussed taking credit for favourable outcomes and looking elsewhere for the cause

Self-efficacy A person's evaluation of his or her ability or competency to perform a task, reach a goal, or overcome an obstacle.

Self-ideal Discrepancies Discrepancies between the perception of the actual self (the way you see yourself) and the ideal self (the way you feel you should be).

of unfavourable events as *attributional biases*. Many common attributional biases serve to enhance or protect self-esteem. However, there are some cultures where use of such *self-serving biases* in attribution is much less common than in the West, as we saw in Chapter 2. Further, the tendency to be self-enhancing has also been shown to vary with culture, as we will discuss later in this chapter.

Canadian Research: On the Cutting Edge

Paradoxical Self-Esteem: When Self-Liking and Competence Diverge

Occasionally, individuals have a discrepant self-concept of a particularly puzzling kind. This occurs when perceptions of your own competence and your own self-worth are very much at odds with each other. The term used by Romin Tafarodi (1998) of the University of Toronto for this phenomenon is **paradoxical self-esteem**, which occurs when perceptions of *self-competence* and *self-liking* are strongly discrepant. Paradoxical self-esteem can occur for someone who has low self-worth (termed *paradoxical low self-esteem*) or for someone who has high self-worth (termed *paradoxical high self-esteem*). For example, a person might be admired by others because of her achievements, and even acknowledge that she is very capable (be high in self-competence), and yet really dislike herself (have paradoxical low self-esteem). In contrast, someone might be seen by those around him as incompetent, and might see himself in the same way, and yet feel strong self-liking (paradoxical high self-esteem). Note that there is a *real* basis for the individual's sense of competence, and it is assumed that others would agree with the individual's own assessment. For most people, their senses of competence and self-worth are in accord, so it is the rare person who shows enduring paradoxical self-esteem—less that 10 percent of students in Tafarodi's research (1998).

The real puzzle with this phenomenon is how it is maintained, and research indicates that it is not just a passing state for some people (Bednar, Wells, & Peterson, 1989). We mentioned above that usually self-esteem varies with feedback from others— if others rate us positively we feel better about ourselves, if they rate us negatively our self-esteem

Paradoxical Self-esteem When perceptions of self-competence and self-liking are discrepant.

goes down. However, this does not seem to occur for those with long-term paradoxical self-esteem. Individuals with paradoxical self-esteem will continually receive social feedback that is discrepant with their self-liking: those with paradoxical high self-esteem will receive feedback that they are incompetent, while those with paradoxical low self-esteem will receive feedback that they are competent. Yet their self-liking does not respond to this feedback. How can this occur?

Tafarodi (1998) suggests that *biased processing of self-relevant information* is at the root of the maintenance of paradoxical self-esteem. This could be achieved for paradoxical individuals if they had a strong bias to selectively process self-relevant information that was *consistent* with their self-liking. For example, the person with paradoxical low self-esteem might selectively notice, remember, and recall only self-information that was negative, while ignoring any positive information. It is not unusual for people to show biased processing of self-relevant information (e.g., the self-enhancing bias). However, this bias would have to be particularly strong for *paradoxicals* in order to minimize the impact of feedback from others that constantly contradicts their self-view.

Tafarodi put these ideas to the test in one study of selective memory bias (1998). Undergraduates, previously screened as either paradoxical or nonparadoxical and either high or low in self-liking, were shown a list of trait words—single word descriptions of positive and negative personality characteristics. In one condition they were told that these words were taken from an assessment of their own personality that had been given during screening (*self-relevant condition*). In a second condition subjects were told that the trait adjectives were from the personality assessment of another student (*non-self-relevant condition*). All subjects were told that they should read the words and that they might later be asked about the meaning of these traits to them. A surprise test of memory for these trait words was later administered. If Tafarodi's ideas were to receive support, then we would expect that subjects with paradoxical self-esteem would show a stronger selective bias in memory for traits consistent with their self-liking than would subjects with non-paradoxical self-esteem. And this strong bias should be shown only when trait words were relevant to the self (self-relevant condition) because it is then that the self-view might be challenged.

Results confirmed expectations—a stronger selectivity memory bias was shown by paradoxicals, but only in the self-relevant condition. Findings for the self-relevant condition are shown in Figure 4.5. You can see that those who have paradoxical low self-esteem show greater recall for negative self-relevant traits than positive ones. Further, this memory bias is larger for the low paradoxical subjects than the non-paradoxical. Similarly, among subjects who have high self-liking, the paradoxical individuals show a much greater bias for recall of positive self-relevant information over negative.

A second study demonstrated that paradoxical individuals showed greater bias in their interpretation of conversation than non-paradoxical individuals (Tafarodi, 1998), tending to interpret others' conversation as showing positive response to the self if the individual had high self-liking and as showing negative response to the self if the individual had low self-liking.

Together these two studies demonstrate that those with paradoxical self-esteem bias their cognitions more strongly than normal in a direction that enables them to maintain their discrepant self-view. However, a question that still remains is the source of such stubborn self-liking or self-loathing in the face of others' constant contradictions. Although research has not yet addressed this issue, Tafarodi suggests that this may reflect a particularly strong early experience with primary caregivers such as parents. Perhaps, for example, a vivid sense of self-liking—if formed early enough because of loving treatment from our parents—so strongly colours our emotions and cognitions that it is resistant to later external influence or even our own perceptions of ourselves as incompetent. This speculation relates to research we will discuss in Chapter 6, showing that early parent-child *attachment patterns* can have a lasting effect on a person's social interactions.

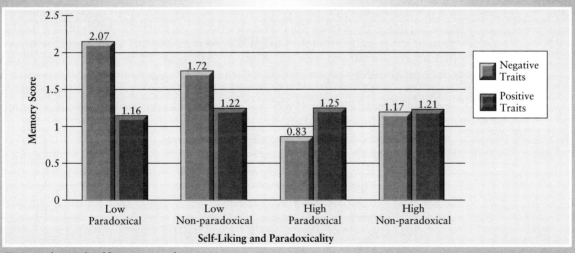

■ Paradoxical self-esteem and memory

FIGURE 4.5 Those who had paradoxical self-esteem showed a stronger selectivity memory bias than non-paradoxicals. Subjects who had paradoxical low self-esteem (disliked themselves, despite being competent) remembered many more negative trait words than positive. Those who had paradoxical high self-esteem (liked themselves, despite being incompetent) remembered more positive trait words than negative. Subjects who were not paradoxical in their self-esteem did not show such large discrepancies, whether they had high or low self-esteem.

Self-Focusing: Awareness of the Self

So far we have examined several aspects of the self, including the way knowledge about the self is organized in the self-schema and the way one's self-esteem varies. We now examine the self in a slightly different way. **Self-focusing** refers to the centrality at a given moment of an individual's sense of self. The extent to which you are self-focused is indicated by the degree to which your attention is directed inward toward yourself as opposed to outward toward the environment (Fiske & Taylor, 1991).

Situational factors have a strong effect on self-focusing, and even simple instructions can determine where one focuses. For example, right now, please think about the ceiling in your room. If you did so, your focus was away from yourself. Now, please think about the most positive aspects of yourself. If you did, you just engaged in self-focusing. Self-focusing also occurs when such environmental cues as a mirror or a video camera are present (Fenigstein & Abrams, 1993).

Recalling relevant past events and processing relevant current information are required for self-focusing to occur (Dixon & Baumeister, 1991; Klein, Loftus, & Burton, 1989). A question such as "Where were you born?" directs you to retrieve factual information about yourself. A question such as "How would you describe your relationship with your parents?" can elicit relatively simple or relatively complex judgments about yourself. The tendency to focus on oneself increases between childhood and adolescence (Ullman, 1987), and some adults consistently self-focus more than others (Dana, Lalwani, & Duvall, 1997).

A brief period of self-focusing can improve insight. After deliberately spending a few minutes thinking about themselves, research participants show increased accuracy in judging social feedback (Hixon & Swann, 1993). This ability to change one's focus can be seen as part of the more general process of *self-regulation* of one's thoughts (Macrae, Bodenhausen, & Milne, 1998). Darwin (1871) recognized the importance of such mental activity when he said that "the highest possible stage in moral culture is when we recognize that we ought to control our thoughts" (p. 123). So the key is not simply to self-focus but to control and regulate the content of the thought processes. On a long-term basis, for example, continued self-focusing can simply involve replaying the same thoughts over and over rather than making progress toward self-awareness and understanding (Conway et al., 1993).

And sometimes focusing away from oneself is the best thing to do. For example, external focusing is helpful in improving the affective state of someone who is depressed (Lyubomirsky & Nolen-Hoeksema, 1995). If you are not depressed, however, the direction of focus has no effect on your feelings (Nix et al., 1995).

Self-focusing Self-awareness; the directing of attention toward some aspect of oneself as opposed to outward toward the environment.

The ability to self-focus can be part of a very useful coping strategy in which a person responds to stressful situations by managing his or her affective state and thinking about ways to solve problems (Taylor et al., 1998). In effect, people who cope this way are able to envision possibilities for the future and develop plans to bring about those possibilities. Evidence suggests that a positive mood greatly facilitates the processing of goal-relevant information (Aspinwall, 1998).

Self-Monitoring: Focusing on Internal Versus External Factors as the Basis of Behaviour

The idea of self-monitoring was first conceptualized by Snyder (1974) and his colleagues (Gangestad & Snyder, 1985; Snyder & Ickes, 1985). Note that **self-monitoring** is a special case of self-focusing in that it refers to the extent to which individuals focus on internal aspects of the self or on external situations as the basis for how they behave. *High self-monitors* will tend to regulate their behaviour on the basis of external events such as the reactions of other people, while *low self-monitors* will regulate behaviour on the basis of internal factors such as their own beliefs, attitudes, and interests. Low self-monitors will tend to be more consistent across situations, whereas high self-monitors change in response to situational demands (Koestner, Bernieri, & Zuckerman, 1992)—the high self-monitor is often a "social chameleon."

One way to think about self-monitoring is in terms of differences in responding to social situations (Hoyle & Sowards, 1993). A high self-monitor analyzes a social situation by assessing the relationship between his or her public self and what is socially appropriate in the setting, then strives to alter the public self to match the situation. In contrast, a low self-monitor analyzes a social situation by assessing the relationship between his or her private self and personal standards of behaviour, then strives to alter the situation to match the private self.

Snyder proposed that high self-monitors must engage in role-playing, because they want to be positively evaluated by others. To gain acceptance, they mold their behaviour to fit the audience—a useful characteristic for politicians, salespeople, and actors. You might think about that the next time you watch a political candidate in action, interact with a successful salesperson, or observe a stage actor. Items from Snyder's *Self-Monitoring Scale* are shown in Table 4.1.

Other behaviours associated with differences in self-monitoring. Guided by the general idea that self-monitoring is related to focusing either on the external audience or on internal values, social psychologists have examined a variety of behavioural differences among those high and low on this dispositional variable. For

Self-monitoring The degree to which an individual regulates his or her behaviour on the basis of the external situation and the reactions of others (high self-monitors) or on the basis of internal factors such as beliefs, attitudes, and values (low self-monitors).

On Snyder's Self-Monitoring Scale, respondents answer each item by indicating whether it is true or false with respect to themselves. On the sample items presented here, high self-monitors would tend to agree with the first two and to disagree with the second two.

TABLE 4.1 Measuring self-monitoring behaviour: Items from the self-monitoring scale

When I am uncertain how to act in social situations, I look to the behaviour of others for cues.

In different situations and with different people, I often act like very different persons.

My behaviour is usually an expression of my true inner feelings, attitudes, and beliefs.

I would not change my opinions (or the way I do things) to please someone else or to win their favour.

Source: Based on information in Snyder, 1974.

example, high self-monitors tend to speak in the third person (he, she, his, her, their, etc.), but low self-monitors use the first person (I, me, my, mine, etc.) (Ickes, Reidhead, & Patterson, 1986). DeBono and Packer (1991) found that highs respond best to advertising that is image-based ("Heineken—you're moving up") and lows to quality-based ads ("Heineken—you can taste the difference"), as described in Figure 4.6.

In interpersonal behaviour as well, high self-monitors choose companions on the basis of external qualities (how well they play tennis, for example), whereas low self-monitors make choices on the basis of how much they like the other person (Snyder, Gangestad, & Simpson, 1983). Even in romantic relationships, low self-monitors are more committed to the other individual (and so have fewer and longer-lasting relationships), while high self-monitors are attuned to the situation, thus engaging in more and relatively

■ Image versus quality in advertising

FIGURE 4.6 Advertising that stresses the image of the product is most appealing to high self-monitors, because they are attuned to externals such as other people's attitudes. Advertising that stresses the quality of the product is most appealing to low self-monitors, because they are attuned to internals such as values and beliefs.

briefer relationships (Snyder & Simpson, 1984). When dating, low self-monitors do so for intrinsic reasons, such as having similar interests, while high self-monitors report extrinsic reasons, such as the other person's having the right connections (Jones, 1993).

A less negative characterization of high self-monitors has been offered by Howells (1993). He found that high self-monitors have more positive personality characteristics than lows, in that they are more sociable, affectionate, energetic, sensitive, open, and intellectually curious. This finding suggests that the interpersonal differences between highs and lows could be based on the fact that low self-monitors lack the necessary social skills and confidence to be able to deal with people successfully. High self-monitors are also high in self-esteem, and their monitoring behaviour may simply be a way to maintain good feelings about themselves, to make themselves likable (Leary et al., 1995), and to regulate their own emotional state (Graziano & Bryant, 1998). Interestingly, either extremely high or extremely low self-monitors are more neurotic and less well adjusted than those falling in the middle of this dimension (Miller & Thayer, 1989).

What are the origins of these different behaviours? Only a limited amount of research has dealt with this question, but Gangestad and Simpson (1993) provide evidence indicating genetic differences between high and low monitors. Among questionnaire items answered in a more similar way by identical than by nonidentical twins are those items involving having an ability to imitate others, trying to impress or entertain people, playing charades, and being able to lie. All four of these behaviours are more likely for high than low self-monitors, and all are more similar in identical twins than in fraternal twins.

SOCIAL IDENTITY: THE SELF IN A SOCIAL CONTEXT

Early psychological theorists of the self suggested that the self is essentially social. For example, other people, friends, family, and ancestors were seen by William James (1890) as an important part of the self. Further, the development of a sense of self was seen as occurring only through interaction with others and with society by George Herbert Mead and other *symbolic interactionist* theorists (Cooley, 1902/1964; Mead, 1934). This view has endured, and today those who take a *sociocultural perspective* see the self as "property of the culture" (Sampson, 1991, p. 212). It is this social side of our identity on which we will focus in this second section of the chapter, specifically, our *gender identity* and our *cultural identity*.

Social Identity Theory: The Importance of a Group-Based Sense of Self

Social Identity Theory The theoretical approach that stresses the importance of a person's social identity to the self-concept. Individuals are motivated to achieve or maintain a positive and distinctive social identity.

Social Identity The group-based aspects of an individual's self-definition, derived from membership in and identification with social groups.

Personal Identity The unique aspects of the individual's internal and private self-definition.

One of the most influential theories to emerge from European social psychology since the "crisis" of the 1970s is **social identity theory** (Tajfel, 1978; 1982; Tajfel & Turner, 1979). Social identity theorists have stressed that group belonging is a major contributor to the individual's self-concept. Your **social identity** is that part of your self-concept derived from membership in, and identification with, social groups. It is distinguished from **personal identity**, which is the unique and individual aspects of your self-concept. In other words, social identity is the part of your sense of self that comes from the knowledge that you are part of particular groups in society. Some of these groups are chosen by you, such as when you decide to become a student at one particular college or decide to join a club. But membership in other groups is involuntary or ascribed: you are born into them or assigned them by your society. For example, we do not choose our gender group, age group or cultural background. By an accident of birth you may be a young, male, Italian-Canadian or a middle-aged, female, Anglo-Canadian. Notice that the group-title (e.g., Italian-Canadian) is one that is defined by the society in which you live. You may or may not identify yourself in that way. However, it is almost impossible not to be aware that such designations are of social significance in Canada—whether you like it or not, others often identify you in that way.

Often our sense of self-worth is tied to our group-membership or group-identification (Crocker et al., 1994; Tajfel, 1982). For example, sports-fans' self-esteem will rise and fall with the success or failure of their team (Hirt, Zillman, Erickson, & Kennedy, 1992). In line with this, a fundamental assumption of social identity theory is that we *strive to maintain or achieve a positive and distinctive social identity*. First, we are concerned that our group can be distinguished from other groups—this is what gives us an identity. So for example, when the North American Free Trade Agreement (NAFTA) was signed in 1993, there were fears expressed that Canada would suffer the loss of its distinctive identity through economic and cultural domination by the United

■ Social identity: The importance of your group

FIGURE 4.7 Many Canadians have felt the need to maintain a distinctive Canadian identity.

States (see Figure 4.7). Second, as well as being distinctive, we are also concerned that our groups are positively evaluated, relative to other groups in society.

In order to establish whether our group has a positive or a negative social identity, we use *intergroup social comparison*. We compare the status and respect of our group with other groups in society. If you want a measure of how important group status can be to the individual, think how strongly you react when you hear someone in a public setting say something negative about a group to which you belong, particularly if that group is an important one to you. For example, if you feel strongly about being Canadian and you heard someone from another country running down Canada: perhaps calling the country "dull and characterless." Now, if you are like many Canadians, your hackles would begin to rise. That statement would have implications for you—and you were just about to be given a negative social identity.

The importance of social identity is evident here, and you can see some of its ramifications. In the example above, you can imagine that you might have the urge to defend Canada, by describing its positive qualities. Further, you might want to point out that the speaker's own country had a few problems, too. This is just what social identity suggests: An individual who has a negative social identity is motivated to improve it. This often involves a clash of competing identities with other groups and can lead to prejudice and conflict. Social identity theorists would characterize the numerous nationalist movements and ethnic conflicts that have occurred around the world as examples of the struggle for a separate and positively evaluated social identity (e.g., Taylor & Moghaddam, 1987). We will discuss the implications of social identity to the area of prejudice and discrimination in the next chapter (Chapter 5).

KEY POINTS

- *Social identity theory* suggests that the groups to which we belong form an important part of our identity. We are motivated to achieve a positive and distinctive social identity.
- *Social identity* refers to an individual's group-based self-concept, whereas personal identity refers to the unique and individual aspects of a person's self-concept.

Gender as a Crucial Aspect of Social Identity

It seems the most pervasive aspect of social identity derives from categorizing ourselves as either female or male. That is, you may or may not pay much attention to your ethnic identity or your social class but it would be extremely rare to find someone who was unaware and unconcerned about being a male versus being a female. In hundreds and hundreds of ways, we are reminded each day of our gender by how we dress, how we act, and how others respond to us.

The terms *sex* and *gender* are often used to mean the same thing. In our discussion, however, we follow the terminology of those in the field (e.g., Beckwith, 1994) who distinguish them in the following way. **Sex** is defined in *biological* terms as the anatomical and physiological differences between males and females that are genetically determined. **Gender** refers to everything else associated with one's sex, including the roles, behaviours, preferences, and other attributes that define what it means to be a male or a female in a given *culture*. Please note that the specific definitions used here are not universally accepted by those actively working in this field (e.g., Deaux, 1993b; Gentile, 1993; Unger & Crawford, 1993).

Sex Maleness or femaleness as determined by genetic factors present at conception that result in anatomical and physiological differences.

Gender The attributes, behaviours, personality characteristics, and expectancies associated with a person's biological sex in a given culture.

Gender Identity

Gender Identity The sex (male or female) that a person identifies as his or her own; usually, though not always, corresponds to the person's biological sex.

Each of us has a **gender identity** in that a key part of our self-perception involves the label "male" or "female." For the vast majority of people, biological sex and gender identity correspond, though there is a small proportion of the population in which gender identity differs from sex.

What is the origin of our gender identity? Though all differences in the behaviour of men and women were once assumed to be biological givens, it now seems very likely that many "typical" masculine and feminine characteristics are in fact acquired (Bem, 1984). *Gender schema theory* was formulated by Bem (1981, 1983). She suggested that children have a "generalized readiness" to organize information about the self in a way that is based on cultural definitions of appropriate male and female attributes. Once a young child learns to apply the label "girl" or "boy" to herself or himself, the stage is set for the child to learn the "appropriate" roles that accompany these labels. As childhood

■ Gender and toys: Are the preferences built-in or acquired?

FIGURE 4.8 It is obvious that boys and girls play with different toys in different ways. While these gender differences could be based on physiological differences, it seems more likely that cultural influences from advertising to peer modeling are responsible. Whatever the explanation, parents such as the father depicted here find it extremely difficult to avoid playthings that "reinforce preconceived gender roles."

progresses, **sex typing** occurs when children learn in detail the stereotypes associated with maleness or femaleness in their culture. We learn such stereotypes from our parents, our media and our peers and they affect our judgments of each other from an early age. In Israel, fifth- and sixth-grade boys who were shown a videotape of a boy their age playing a feminine game (jump-rope) with girls attributed stereotypic feminine traits to the boy and they judged him to be low in popularity (Lobel, 1994). A boy observed playing a masculine game with other boys was perceived as the more masculine and popular. In another study, children and adolescents both agreed that nine-month-old infants given the name "Mary" and "Karen" (whether the infants were actually female or not) were smaller, more beautiful, nicer, and softer than when the same infants were given the names "Stephen" and "Matthew" (Vogel, Lake, Evans, & Karraker, 1991). It seems clear that the stereotypes associated with each gender determine our perceptions of them even when they are still infants! Modern parents sometimes attempt to resist such stereotyping for their children, with varying levels of success—see Figure 4.8. They may find themselves in a losing battle when their offspring respond to advertising and to what their friends have.

Generally, children are rewarded for engaging in gender-appropriate behaviour and discouraged (or ridiculed) when they engage in gender-inappropriate behaviour. Consider,

Sex Typing Acquisition of the attributes associated with being a male or female in a given culture.

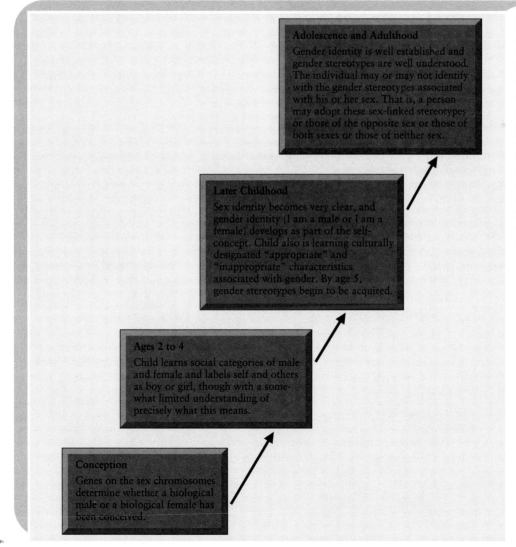

■ The developmental aspects of gender

FIGURE 4.9 Beginning with the genetic determination of sex at conception, each of us progresses through developmental stages in which we learn to label self and others as male or female, internalize gender identity as part of our self-concepts, learn our culture's gender stereotypes, and eventually adopt gender roles that may or may not match these stereotypes.

Adolescence and Adulthood
Gender identity is well established and gender stereotypes are well understood. The individual may or may not identify with the gender stereotypes associated with his or her sex. That is, a person may adopt these sex-linked stereotypes or those of the opposite sex or those of both sexes or those of neither sex.

Later Childhood
Sex identity becomes very clear, and gender identity (I am a male or I am a female) develops as part of the self-concept. Child also is learning culturally designated "appropriate" and "inappropriate" characteristics associated with gender. By age 5, gender stereotypes begin to be acquired.

Ages 2 to 4
Child learns social categories of male and female and labels self and others as boy or girl, though with a somewhat limited understanding of precisely what this means.

Conception
Genes on the sex chromosomes determine whether a biological male or a biological female has been conceived.

for example, the probable response to a little girl who requests a doll for Christmas versus the response to a little boy who makes the same request. On the basis of how adults, older siblings, and others respond, a little girl learns that wanting a doll is acceptable but wanting boxing gloves is not, while a little boy learns that for him boxing gloves are cute but a doll is unacceptable. As the years pass, the lessons are well learned, and by the time they reach the sixth grade, the overwhelming majority of children have learned the prevailing gender stereotypes (Carter & McCloskey, 1984). Even people who disagree with the stereotypes know what is considered suitable for each gender and what constitutes out-of-role behaviour. This developmental progression is outlined in Figure 4.9.

The specific content of these stereotypes about masculinity and femininity in our culture and the possibility of nonstereotyped behaviour are presented in the following Cornerstones section.

Cornerstones

Bem's Concept of Psychological Androgyny as an Alternative to Masculinity versus Femininity

More than two decades ago, Sandra Bem (1974, 1975) produced a new theoretical formulation and a measuring device that revolutionized how gender is conceptualized and studied. At the time she began this work, most people (including psychologists) assumed that masculinity and femininity represented the opposite ends of a single dimension. Thus, each person was relatively masculine and therefore not feminine or relatively feminine and therefore not masculine. Of course, many people actually do fit into just one of these two categories (Kagan, 1964; Kohlberg, 1966). And a person who fits a masculine or feminine stereotype is motivated to behave in ways consistent with the gender role he or she has learned: small children are not the only ones encouraged to conform to stereotypes, and "inappropriate" gender behaviour is strongly discouraged.

Bem rejected the idea of a single dimension and suggested that various personal characteristics associated with masculinity and femininity lie on two separate dimensions: one ranging from low to high masculinity and the other ranging from low to high femininity. In this conceptualization, many individuals may actually be high on characteristics associated with both genders. For example a person could be competitive (supposedly masculine) and also sensitive to the needs of others (supposedly feminine). A person who combines tradition-

al masculine characteristics with traditional feminine ones is considered to be **androgynous**.

To identify masculine, feminine, and androgynous individuals, the **Bem Sex-Role Inventory (BSRI)** was developed. Note that in the terminology used in this chapter, this measure would be labeled the "Bem *Gender*-Role Inventory." Research participants identified more than 400 positive characteristics as being socially desirable for men and/or for women. The final measure contains 20 items desirable for males but not for females, 20 items desirable for females but not desirable for males, and 20 that are equally desirable for males and females. The male and female items are shown in Table 4.2. Note that additional studies have indicated very little change in these gender stereotypes over time (Martin, 1987; Raty & Snellman, 1992).

A person taking the BSRI indicates, for all 60 items, how accurate each one is as a description of herself or himself. On the basis of the items that are selected as self-descriptive, the individual is classi-

Androgyny In studies of gender, the tendency to report having both traditionally "masculine" and traditionally "feminine" characteristics.

Bem Sex-Role Inventory (BSRI) Bem's measure of the extent to which an individual's self-description is characterized by traditional masculinity, traditional femininity, a mixture of the two (androgyny), or neither (undifferentiated).

fied as a particular *sex-typed* (gender-typed) individual. The possibilities are a sex-typed masculine male or feminine female, a *reverse-typed* individual (a masculine female or feminine male), an *androgynous* individual of either gender, or an *undifferentiated type* who has few characteristics of either gender. Research indicates that about a third of males fit the masculine gender type, and about the same proportion of females fit the feminine gender type. About one out of three males is androgynous, as are a third of females. The undifferentiated and cross-gender categories make up the rest. This classification indicates *gender-role identification*, or the extent to which an individual does or does not identify with the culture's gender stereotypes.

Research has been consistent with the implication that "androgyny is good." For example, compared to gender-typed individuals, androgynous men and women were found to be better liked (Major, Carnevale, & Deaux, 1981); better adjust-ed (Orlofsky & O'Heron, 1987; Williams & D'Alessandro, 1994); more adaptable to situational demands (Prager & Bailey, 1985); more flexible in coping with stress (McCall & Struthers, 1994); more comfortable with their sexuality (Garcia, 1982); more satisfied interpersonally (Rosenzweig & Daley, 1989); and, in an elderly sample, more satisfied with their lives (Dean-Church & Gilroy, 1993). Spouses report happier marriages when both partners are androgynous than is true for any other combination of roles (Zammichieli, Gilroy, & Sherman, 1988). Further, sexual satisfaction is greater if one or both partners is androgynous than if both are sex-typed (Safir et al., 1982).

Further, extreme adherence to traditional gender roles is often found to be associated with relationship problems. For example, men who identify with the extreme masculine role behave more violently and aggressively than men who perceive themselves as having some feminine characteristics

A person taking the *Bem Sex-Role Inventory* rates a series of characteristics in terms of how well they describe him or her. Those items shown here are the ones that are perceived as more characteristic of males than of females or vice versa. That is, they represent pervasive gender stereotypes in our culture.

TABLE 4.2 Gender stereotypes identified by Bem

Characteristics of the Male Stereotype	Characteristics of the Female Stereotype
acts as a leader	affectionate
aggressive	cheerful
ambitious	childlike
analytical	compassionate
assertive	does not use harsh language
athletic	eager to soothe hurt feelings
competitive	feminine
defends own beliefs	flatterable
dominant	gentle
forceful	gullible
has leadership abilities	loves children
independent	loyal
individualistic	sensitive to the needs of others
makes decisions easily	shy
masculine	soft-spoken
self-reliant	sympathetic
self-sufficient	tender
strong personality	understanding
willing to take a stand	warm
willing to take risks	yielding

Source: Based on information in Bem, 1974.

(Finn, 1986). Among adolescent males, high masculinity is associated with having multiple sexual partners, the view that men and women are adversaries, low condom use, and the belief that getting a partner pregnant is a positive indication of one's masculinity (Pleck, Sonenstein, & Ku, 1993). Both men and women who endorse a purely feminine role are lower in self-esteem than either masculine or androgynous individuals (Lau, 1989).

Currently there is increasing recognition of the multifaceted nature of sexuality and sexual- or gender-identity. Recently, Bem (1995, p. 334) borrowed an analogy from anthropologist Kathryn March to make a more general point:

"Sex is to gender as light is to colour." That is, sex and light are physical phenomena, whereas gender and colour are culturally based categories that arbitrarily divide sex and light into designated groups. With colour, some cultures have only two categories, others three, while in the North America there are Crayola boxes with 256 different hues, each with its own assigned name. With respect to gender, the reverse is true. We have traditionally emphasized only two genders, whereas other cultures have had Crayola boxes of possibilities ranging from bisexuality to an array of heterosexual and homosexual roles and lifestyles.

Gender and Self-Perception

Gender differences in self-perception are commonly found. Compared to men, women are much more likely to be concerned about their body image (Pliner, Chaiken, & Flett, 1990), to express dissatisfaction about their bodies (Heinberg & Thompson, 1992) and physical appearance in general (Hagborg, 1993), to develop eating disorders (Forston & Stanton, 1992; Hamilton, Falconer, & Greenberg, 1992), and to become depressed (Strickland, 1992). Obesity is a special issue for women. When males blame them for being overweight ("It's your own fault"), women are likely to accept this evaluation. When an overweight woman is viewed as an unacceptable date by a male, instead of being mad at him and attributing the problem to his prejudice, she is more likely to blame herself (Crocker, Cornwell, & Major, 1993). Even though obese women tend to attribute rejection in the workplace as caused by unfair biases, romantic rejection is perceived to be justified (Crocker & Major, 1993).

Why is appearance a major problem for women? Possibly because from infancy on, others respond to appearance differently on the basis of gender. Even parents discriminate against overweight daughters (but not overweight sons) with respect to providing financial support for college (Crandall, 1995). To the extent that young men express any appearance anxiety, it is a relatively mild dissatisfaction about not measuring up to the body-builder muscular ideal of male attractiveness (Davis, Brewer, & Weinstein, 1993).

Consider for a moment the day-to-day negative effects of the special emphasis our society places on the physical attractiveness of women in general and on specific anatomical details such as breast size (Thompson & Tantleff, 1992). One consequence is that women often are vulnerable and easily upset when their appearance becomes an issue (Mori & Morey, 1991). For example, after looking at magazine pictures showing ultrathin models, undergraduate women respond with feeling of depression, stress, guilt, shame, insecurity, and dissatisfaction with their own bodies (Stice & Shaw, 1994). As they age, women are perceived as increasingly less feminine, though men are not viewed as becoming less masculine with age (Deutsch, Zalenski, & Clark, 1986).

The cultural basis of this dramatic difference in self-perceptions between men and women is strongly suggested by the fact that such problems are much more common in Western industrialized nations than in developing countries. Even within the United States, Canada, and the United Kingdom, women of Asian and African descent have fewer eating disorders than Caucasian women. Caucasian females are also more likely to view themselves as overweight and to evaluate their bodies negatively. White women denigrate overweight women much more than black women do (Hebl & Heatherton, 1998). One possible explanation is that men of Asian and African descent are less concerned about the weight of their romantic partners. Whatever the reason, white women have more weight concerns than their non-white counterparts. Comparing white and Asian female students aged 14 to 22 in London schools, Wardle and colleagues (1993) found that both groups had the same ideals about appearance (thin is good). Nevertheless, white females differed from Asian females in wanting to lose weight, being actively involved in trying to lose weight, and weighing themselves more frequently—even when their current size and weight did not differ from those of their Asian classmates. Among the thinnest participants, more white than Asian females said that they felt "fat."

Beyond appearance, other self-perceptions also differ for men and women. On self-report measures, women describe themselves as more anxious, gregarious, trusting, and nurturing than men, while men describe themselves as more assertive than women (Feingold, 1994). Compared to men, women respond with greater emotional intensity, as indicated by self-reports and by physiological assessment (Grossman & Wood, 1993). Some evidence suggests that the explanation for such gender differences rests on differences in the specific areas of the brain used by men and women in thinking and responding to emotional cues (Gur, 1995; Kolata, 1995; Shaywitz & Shaywitz, 1995).

We have focused on the contribution of gender to a sense of self. While our biology (our sex) certainly contributes to our sense of femaleness or maleness, it is the social side of this aspect of our self-concept that has been the concern here. In short, we can say that the society in which we are raised, its beliefs and stereotypes, plays a large part in determining our gender identity: one of the earliest and most fundamental aspects of our social identity. We will now turn to the contribution of cultural and ethnic background to social identity.

KEY POINTS

- One important aspect of social identity is *gender*—the societal expectations associated with a person's *biological sex*. Children develop a sense *of gender identity*, a sense of maleness or femaleness, as part of the self-concept. This usually includes some sex typing of behaviour as children learn the culturally appropriate forms of behaviour for their gender.

- Research on *androgyny*, using the *Bem Sex-Role Inventory (or BSRI)*, has provided evidence that those who are androgynous (have both traditionally masculine and feminine traits) tend to be more adaptable than those who adhere strongly to traditional gender roles.

- Gender differences in self-perception are common, particularly differences in perception of *body image*. Typically, females tend to be more concerned about many aspects of physical appearance than males. One possible reason is the greater emphasis society places on physical attractiveness in women.

Cultural Influences on Identity: Ethnicity and Interdependence

One of the most important aspects of a person's social identity is his or her cultural background. But before we examine its relationship to the self, we should clarify the meaning of culture. *Culture* is defined as the organized system of shared meanings, perceptions, and beliefs held by persons belonging to a particular group. The shared understanding of a

Culture The organized system of shared meaning, perceptions, and beliefs held by persons belonging to a particular group. This often includes a particular language or system of communication, social customs and organization, as well as artifacts and artistic products of the group.

Ethnic Identity The part of an individual's social identity that is derived from membership in, or identification with, a particular cultural or racial group.

culture is often communicated among members by a shared language, or for some sub-cultural groups it is a particular jargon, a specialized way of speaking. For example, anyone who has become "computer-literate" knows the specialized language of "RAM," "down-loading," and "hard-drives." Culture is also expressed in social customs, cultural artifacts and products (from buildings to eating implements and food), and artistic works. In Canada, for example, French-Canadian culture has its own system of communication, which has evolved with marked differences from the language spoken in France and has produced its own artistic traditions and cuisine. The shared understanding of a culture is passed from generation to generation and it both shapes, and is shaped by, each successive generation. As Moghaddam, Taylor, and Wright (1993) put it: "In essence, humans have an interactive relationship with culture: we create and shape culture, and are in turn influenced by our own cultural products" (1993, p. 3).

Ethnic Identity

At the individual level, a person's identification with a cultural or racial group is often termed **ethnic identity**—that part of someone's social identity that is derived from membership in, or identification with, a particular ethnic group. When individuals are from a minority cultural group, developing a sense of ethnic identity can be problematic. Adolescents sometimes find that reconciliation of their own cultural group with that of the larger society is difficult (Ethier & Deaux, 1994; Spencer & Markstrom-Adams, 1990). Phinney (1990) has described four styles of resolving the dilemma of whether to identify with one's own cultural group or the mainstream culture: These are shown in Table 4.3.

Canadian research has demonstrated that these identifications have important consequences. For example, John Berry (1976) examined *acculturative stress* (a reduction in health status related to contact between cultural groups) among members of 10 native samples across Canada. In eight of these groups it was found that those who

---

Those who identify strongly with their own cultural group but have little contact with the mainstream culture have a *separated identity*; individuals who abandon their own cultural ties and identify with the mainstream culture are termed *assimilated*; identification with mainstream culture as well as one's own cultural group is termed having an *integrated identity* (or *bicultural identity*); and, finally, those who do not value identification with either cultural group have a *marginal identity*.

TABLE 4.3 Four strategies for coping with ethnic identity in a multicultural context

		Value of Identification with Own Cultural Group	
		High	**Low**
Value of Relationship or Identification with Mainstream Culture	**High**	INTEGRATED Identity	ASSIMILATED Identity
	Low	SEPARATED Identity	MARGINAL Identity

Source: Adapted from Berry & Sam, 1998; Phinney, 1990.

believed in *integration* or in *assimilation* showed less acculturative stress than those who had *separatist* beliefs. It is not surprising that a person who has separatist beliefs, or a *separated identity*, might find contact with the mainstream culture unwelcome and, therefore, stressful. In contrast, for an integrated or assimilated individual, contact would be more welcome and less stressful. Further, more recent research has suggested that those who have a strong ethnic identity with their own cultural group tend to have higher self-esteem and cope better in a multicultural context but only if they also have a positive attitude to the mainstream culture (LaFromboise, Coleman, & Gerton, 1993; Phinney, 1991; Sanchez & Fernandez, 1993).

Another Canadian study demonstrated that these identifications are also related to cross-cultural contact. Dona (1991; Dona & Berry, 1994) found that refugees from Central America who had an integrated identity had greater contact with Canadian society than those who had a separated identity. In addition, both integrated and separated refugees spent more time with other Central Americans than those who were assimilated to mainstream Canadian society.

Cultural Influences on the Self: The Effects of Individualism or Collectivism

Though it is commonly assumed that one's self-concept is formed in the context of social interactions, the implications of this proposal are difficult to appreciate within a single culture. When we look across cultures or subcultures, however, aspects of the self that are based on social factors become much more obvious. This impact goes beyond identification with a particular ethnic group, to fundamental differences in perception of how self is related to the social world and others.

Two researchers who have written extensively about the importance of culture to the self are Markus and Kitayama (1991a, 1991b). Reviewing a considerable body of research conducted in Asian countries, they have concluded that there are fundamental differences in Eastern and Western conceptions of the self. The **independent conception of the self** is of an individual who is separate and distinct from other individuals and from the social and physical environment. Those who have an independent sense of self will see themselves as autonomous and tend to strive to achieve individuality and uniqueness. Their behaviour will tend to be influenced by reference to their own thoughts, feelings, and beliefs. This has been characterized as a construal of the self that is common in *individualistic* cultures such as Canada, the United States and Britain. Independence tends to be seen as the right, and even the healthy, way to be in Western culture. We believe someone should "stand on your own two feet," "think for yourself," "don't follow the crowd," "be true to yourself," but this may not be how most non-Western cultures conceptualize the self (Geertz, 1974).

In contrast, the **interdependent conception of the self** views it as fundamentally connected to others and to the environment: the self is integrated into the social context. Those who have an interdependent sense of self will strive for acceptance, attempt to fit in with others and to maintain harmonious relations. Their behaviour will be more likely to be influenced by the thoughts, feelings, and actions of significant others. This construal of the self is more typical of *collectivistic* cultures in Asia, Africa, South America, and Southern Europe (see also, Smith & Bond, 1998; Triandis, 1989).

Research has begun to confirm these cultural distinctions in fundamental self-concept. Cousins (1989) found greater context-dependence in the self-concepts of students from Japan (a collectivistic culture) compared to those from the United States (an individualistic culture). His subjects were asked to complete the "Who am I?" or Twenty Statements Test mentioned at the beginning of the chapter. However, a second version of this test was provided for a second group of subjects, asking them to answer the same question in various contexts (e.g., at home, at school, with close friends). As

Independent Conception of the Self The self is viewed as separate and distinct from other individuals and from the environment. The individual will tend to be seen as autonomous and unique. This construal of the self is typical of Western cultures.

Interdependent Conception of the Self The self is viewed as fundamentally connected to others and to the environment: the self is integrated into the social context. Such individuals will strive for acceptance and to maintain harmonious relations with others. This construal of the self is more typical of non-Western cultures.

■ The independent and interdependent self in context and context-free

FIGURE 4.10 When asked "Who am I?" without any accompanying social context, students in the United States described themselves in terms of personal attributes to a greater extent than students in Japan. However, when the students were asked the same question with respect to specific social contexts (e.g., "Who am I at home...at school...with close friends..."), Japanese students were more likely to describe themselves in terms of personal attributes. These findings suggest the American self-concept tends to be more independent of social context, whereas the Japanese self-concept tends to be more interdependent with the social context in which the self is considered.

Source: Based on data from Cousins, 1989.

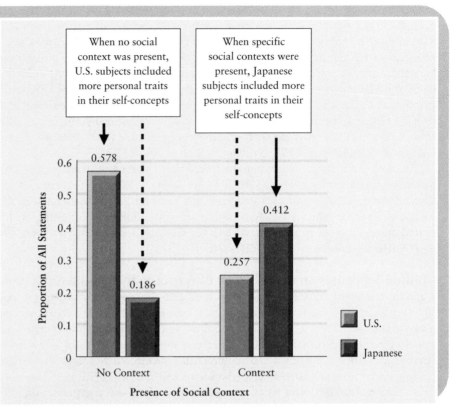

shown in Figure 4.10, when no context was provided, American students included more abstract and context-free personal trait statements (such as "I am lazy" or "I am sociable") compared to the Japanese. In fact, when there was no context provided, Japanese students often spontaneously provided one for their behaviour (e.g. "I am one who plays *mah-jongg* on Friday nights"). However, when a specific context was provided, the findings were reversed: Japanese students produced more personal trait statements than American students. That is, the Japanese self-concept was more bound to particular contexts, whereas the American self-concept was more independent of social context. Broader applications of the independent-interdependent distinction are discussed in the following On the Applied Side section.

On the **Applied Side**

Self-Enhancement or Self-Improvement? It Depends on Culture

Western psychology has often made the assumption that the mentally healthy individual has high self-esteem (Rogers, 1951) and further, that this individual's self-esteem is robust and self-maintaining. To facilitate this, the use of **self-enhancing biases**, which help to bolster the self-esteem of individuals, is often seen as beneficial, at least in moderation (e.g., Fiske &

> **Self-enhancing Biases** Any cognitive bias that serves to enhance the positive self-view of the person using it. Examples are the self-serving bias and unrealistic optimism.

Taylor, 1991). But how would such ideas apply to those with an interdependent self-concept? After all, their priority may not be maintenance of a positive self-concept but maintenance of the group and its needs. For example, Lebra (1976) has suggested that Japanese individuals experience themselves as "fractions" who do not become whole until they fit into and belong within a group (as cited in Heine & Lehman, 1995). Would self-enhancement be as important for such individuals?

Recently, Kitayama and his colleagues (1997) proposed that people raised in Western, individualistic cultures learn that everyday life presents repeated opportunities for *self-enhancement*. In contrast, for those in Eastern, collectivistic cultures, everyday life is believed to present opportunities for self-criticism and thus *self-improvement*.

In comparing the behaviour of college students in Japan and the United States, the investigators found the expected differences between

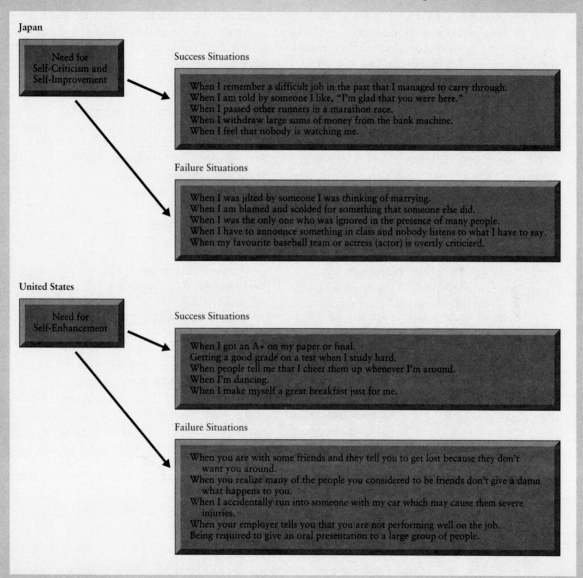

Japan

Need for Self-Criticism and Self-Improvement

Success Situations

When I remember a difficult job in the past that I managed to carry through.
When I am told by someone I like, "I'm glad that you were here."
When I passed other runners in a marathon race.
When I withdraw large sums of money from the bank machine.
When I feel that nobody is watching me.

Failure Situations

When I was jilted by someone I was thinking of marrying.
When I am blamed and scolded for something that someone else did.
When I was the only one who was ignored in the presence of many people.
When I have to announce something in class and nobody listens to what I have to say.
When my favourite baseball team or actress (actor) is overtly criticized.

United States

Need for Self-Enhancement

Success Situations

When I got an A+ on my paper or final.
Getting a good grade on a test when I study hard.
When people tell me that I cheer them up whenever I'm around.
When I'm dancing.
When I make myself a great breakfast just for me.

Failure Situations

When you are with some friends and they tell you to get lost because they don't want you around.
When you realize many of the people you considered to be friends don't give a damn what happens to you.
When I accidentally run into someone with my car which may cause them severe injuries.
When your employer tells you that you are not performing well on the job.
Being required to give an oral presentation to a large group of people.

■ Success and failure in collectivistic and individualist cultures.

FIGURE 4.11 Cultural differences result in differences in self-concept. In a collectivistic culture such as Japan, self-criticism is the norm, while in an individualist culture such as the United States, self-enhancement is the norm. This difference leads to different interpretations of what constitutes success and failure and to different behaviour.

Source: Based on information in Kitayama et al., 1997.

self-enhancing Americans and self-criticizing Japanese. In addition, students in the two countries differ when they indicate the types of situations that raise their self-esteem (success) or lower it (failure). As shown in Figure 4.11, Americans tend to emphasize the individual and Japanese the group as most relevant.

Evidence is accumulating that self-enhancement may be prevalent in Western but not in Eastern cultures. Across many studies, North Americans are found to express unrealistically optimistic self-evaluations (Regan, Snyder, & Kassin, 1995) and to show self-serving attributional biases (see Chapter 2), while Japanese do neither. In a similar way, Chinese college students in Hong Kong are much less self-enhancing than comparable students in Canada (Yik, Bond, & Paulhus, 1998). Heine and Lehman (1997b) raised the possibility that in Asian cultures, self-enhancement might be replaced by group enhancement. A comparison of Canadian and Japanese students revealed, however, that the latter not only engage in self-criticism but ingroup criticism as well. For example, Japanese participants evaluated their family members and their universities less positively than Canadians did. In effect, in individualistic cultures there is the assumption that "We're number one!" whereas in collectivist cultures the assumption is that "We could do better if we made sufficient effort."

It is worth noting, however, that even within an individualistic culture, self-enhancement and more critical self-assessment each occur under specific circumstances. For example, students in the Western world want favourable feedback about unchangeable aspects of themselves, but they are willing to receive accurate, unfavourable feedback about a characteristic that can be improved (Dunning, 1995). Analogously, self-enhancement sometimes occurs even within a collectivist culture, but only in a modest and non-obvious way. For example, Japanese students prefer the letters in their own names and the numbers corresponding to the month and day of their birth over other letters and other numbers (Kitayama & Karasawa, 1997).

Finally, Heine and Lehman (1995) have suggested that while self-enhancing biases may be adaptive for the individual who is required to function independently of others, this may not apply to those who function interdependently. If you have to "stand on your own two feet" then you had better feel good about who you are. However, to separate yourself from others, even in a positive, self-enhancing way, implies alienation from the group for the interdependent individual and a loss of a sense of self. In line with this suggestion one study found that for Japanese subjects the strongest feelings of well-being were related not to individual pride and a sense of achievement (as they were with Americans) but to a sense of *acceptance* from others (Kitayama, Markus & Kurokawa, 1994, in Heine & Lehman, 1995).

Western views of the "healthy" individual have begun to be more inclusive of cultural differences in the sense of self and this has implications for clinical psychologists and therapists attempting to help individuals who have psychological difficulties (e.g., Tanaka-Matsumi & Draguns, 1997). As our society becomes increasingly multicultural, understanding of cultural differences is crucial. This is the task of cross-cultural psychology, which we discuss in the next section.

KEY POINTS

- *Cultural groups* are an important source of social identity and can determine our understanding of the self. We gain our ethnic identity from the cultural or racial group to which we belong. Contact with other cultural groups in a multicultural society can create problems for the development of an individual's *ethnic identity*.

- Cultures can vary in terms of whether they have an *independent* or *interdependent* conception of the self and this has implications for the extent to which individuals show self-enhancing or self-improvement tendencies.

CROSS-CULTURAL PSYCHOLOGY: COMPARING CULTURES

Since the 1970s, social psychologists have begun systematically to examine social behaviour in different cultures. This is the task of **cross-cultural psychology**, which is defined as "the systematic study of behaviour and experience as it occurs in different cultures, is influenced by culture, or results in changes in existing culture" (Triandis, 1980, p.1). Cross-cultural psychology, therefore, is concerned with differences between cultures in behaviour and experience, the way in which culture influences behaviour and experience, and with changes in culture. This task involves more than simple replication of studies first carried out in the United States, followed by examination of any differences found. The cross-cultural approach has required a fundamental rethinking of theory and research in psychology. We will examine some of the original theoretical concepts that have emerged from cross-cultural psychology. These concepts lay the groundwork for research in cross-cultural psychology.

> **Cross-cultural Psychology** The branch of psychology concerned with the systematic study of cultural differences, cultural influences, and cultural changes in behaviour.

Ethnocentrism: Seeing Things From Your Culture's Perspective

If you have travelled to a foreign country or spent time with people from another cultural group, you may have found yourself thinking that their customs were strange or, perhaps, that their food was odd and their accents funny. If so, you were displaying **ethnocentrism**. This term was first used in 1906 by William Sumner and was defined by him as: "the view of things in which one's own group is the centre of everything and all others are scaled and rated with reference to it" (in Brewer, 1986, p. 88). That is, the culture in which you were raised tends to be seen as the "centre of everything," the norm, and, by comparison, other cultural groups are seen as "abnormal" or "wrong"—they don't quite do things in the right way. Beyond this, ethnocentrism can often make us deride other groups' customs as ridiculous, or make us feel morally superior. In sum, ethnocentrism is the cultural equivalent of *egocentrism*. When we say that someone is egocentric, we mean that they only see things from their own point of view. Someone who is ethnocentric only sees things from the perspective of their own culture. Adorno and colleagues (1950) developed an *Ethnocentrism Scale* for use with European-Americans in the post-war years. The following items from this scale can give you an idea of ethnocentrism of that time:

> **Ethnocentrism** Evaluating other cultures from the perspective of your own. Your own group standards are used as the norm and other groups are then seen as "abnormal" or "wrong."

> America may not be perfect, but the American way has brought us about as close as human beings can get to a perfect society.

> The people who raise all the talk about putting Negroes on the same level as whites are mostly radical agitators trying to stir up conflict.

> Certain religious sects who refuse to salute the flag should be forced to conform to such patriotic action, or else be abolished.

A highly ethnocentric European-American of the 1950s would strongly agree with such statements. It is obvious from these scale items that strong ethnocentrism is a part of prejudice, and this will be further discussed in the next chapter.

You may not be strongly ethnocentric, but there are few people who have not at times seen things from their culture's perspective, taken pride in their group's superiorities, or ridiculed the ways of other groups. Many Canadians believe that they live in the best country in the world—by comparison, other countries just don't match up. Social psychology itself may have been guilty of ethnocentrism (or "euro-centrism") when it overgeneralized its theories and findings based on a largely European-American population to other non-Western subcultures within that society or to other nations.

Etic versus Emic: A Universal or Cultural Perspective?

Etic A finding or concept that appears to be consistent across cultures; that is, it is universal.

Emic A finding or concept that differs between cultures; that is, it is culturally specific.

A distinction made by Canadian John Berry (1969) has proved very useful for examining ethnocentric biases in social psychology. He suggested that social psychological research and findings can be approached in two different ways. An **etic** analysis of social behaviour focuses on universal factors—ones that apply across all cultures. For example, all cultures have family relations or a set of cultural norms. An **emic** analysis focuses upon factors that are culturally specific—that vary between cultures and have specific meaning within a particular culture. For example, the concepts of "masculinity" or "the self," as we saw above, have different meanings in different cultures.

The importance of this distinction is in its implications for social-psychological research. An etic analysis has often led researchers to assume that their measures, or the distinctions they made between variables, were of equal significance in another culture. Research in other cultures merely replicated that in the West, using the same measures. It was assumed that the psychological concepts and distinctions of Western research would hold in other cultures (Smith & Bond, 1998). Berry terms this approach to research an *imposed etic*. That is, such research *imposed* Western values and concepts as if they were universal. We have seen, in relation to the self, that we cannot make assumptions of universality of meaning between cultures. For example, when another of Adorno et al.'s scales (the "F" scale, 1950) was used in Turkey, items in the scale did not correlate with each other as they had in the U.S. testing. This suggests that the meaning of scale items was less closely related in a Turkish context (Kagitcibasi, 1970). Many concepts used in research have been assumed to be etic when in fact there are many emic variations.

Indigenous Psychology A psychological discipline that arises from within a particular culture, adequately representing naturally occurring psychological processes and distinctions of that culture.

Increasing awareness of this danger has led to a call for indigenous psychologies by Canadian psychologists (e.g., Adair, 1992, 1996; Berry, 1989; Segall, Dasen, Berry, & Poortinga, 1999), non-Western psychologists (e.g., Moghaddam, 1990; Sinha, 1988, 1996), as well as those in the interdisciplinary area of cultural psychology (e.g., Shweder, 1990; Shweder & Sullivan, 1993). An **indigenous psychology** would be one arising from within a particular culture and that adequately represents that culture (Adair, 1996). It would examine psychological issues that naturally arise in a culture and would make culturally relevant distinctions. A comparison of indigenous findings from many different cultures could then identify universal or etic factors: ones that were common to all cultures. John Berry has termed this approach a *derived etic*: universals are derived from culturally valid indigenous research, rather than being assumed or imposed by Western researchers. Although there has been tremendous expansion in some Asian countries (e.g., Pandey, Sinha, & Bhawuk, 1996), as yet, a well-developed indigenous psychology has not been achieved, except of course in Western culture. As you can imagine, it is no small task to build the sufficiently large and scientifically convincing literature that is necessary. We are just at the beginning of this process, as the next section will discuss.

Cross-Cultural Research in Social Psychology: Its State of Development

Throughout this book we have presented current cross-cultural research in most of the topic areas of social psychology. And this is just a small selection of the research that has been completed, and is currently being carried out (e.g., Berry, Poortinga, & Pandey, 1997). Such research reflects the tremendous expansion of interest in cultural issues within the discipline, and its findings are fascinating for those of us who live in a multicultural society. However, this research is just at the beginning stages and is not without difficulties.

Currently, the focus for understanding cultural differences is the *individualism-collectivism* value dimension. Research from this perspective has proved very fruitful (Kim, 1994; Triandis, 1995): cultural groups whose values differ along this dimension have also shown differences in a wide range of psychologically significant behaviours and responses. However, it should be noted that focusing on one dichotomous distinction between cultures is almost certainly an oversimplification. For example, there are many subtle differences between cultures that have collectivistic values, as there are between individualistic cultures. Further, there are other value dimensions upon which cultures differ, and research has not yet explored their importance, as Schwartz commented (1992) after his cross national study of values—see Table 4.4.

Many Western researchers are attempting to meet the challenge presented by cross-cultural research. However, various pitfalls are possible for Western researchers and these must be avoided if ethnocentrism is to be eliminated. John Berry and colleagues (Berry, et al,

Schwartz has pointed out that the individualism–collectivism dimension is not the only important value distinction between cultures (1992). Using concepts derived from both Western and non-Western cultures, his data from research in 20 countries around the world revealed 10 different value-clusters.

TABLE 4.4 Beyond individualism–collectivism: Should cross-cultural psychology investigate a broader range of value differences?

1. *Self-direction*: independent thought and action, choosing, creating, exploring.

2. *Stimulation*: need for variety, excitement, challenge in life.

3. *Hedonism*: seeking pleasure, enjoying life.

4. *Achievement*: success through competence, gaining social approval.

5. *Power*: attaining social status and prestige, control, or dominance over others and over resources.

6. *Security*: safety, harmony, stability of society, relationships, and self.

7. *Conformity*: restraint of actions, inclinations, and impulses that would upset others or violate social expectations.

8. *Tradition*: respect, commitment, and acceptance of customs.

9. *Benevolence*: preservation and enhancement of the welfare of other people (e.g., forgiveness, helpfulness, honesty, loyalty).

10. *Universalism*: appreciation and tolerance for all people and for nature (e.g., equality, protecting environment, world at peace).

Source: Value Across Many Cultures from "The universal content and structure of values," by Schwartz, S.H. in *Advances in Experimental Social Psychology*, Volume 25. Copyright © 1992 by Academic Press. Reproduced by permission of the publisher.

1992) have identified four levels of research where ethnocentrism has tended to occur:

1. The selection of items and stimuli in a measurement instrument (e.g., a test).

2. The choice of instruments and procedures used in research.

3. The definition of theoretical concepts.

4. The choice of topics for research.

At the first level, items used in tests of psychological characteristics are sometimes culturally biased. An example is tests of intelligence and other tests of general cognitive abilities that have been shown to have items that test knowledge specific to particular cultural groups (e.g., Berk, 1982; Poortinga, 1971; Poortinga & Foden, 1975). An example at the second level is the use of measures developed in the West when carrying out cross-cultural research. For example, early cross-cultural studies of values (e.g. Hofstede, 1980) or styles of love (e.g. Philbrick, 1987; Philbrick & Opolot, 1980) used questionnaires developed in North America. The use of such measures may fail to tap into indigenous concepts significant within non-Western cultures. At the third level, theories developed in Western psychology may not seem appropriate when imported into other cultures. This has been recognized in India, which is one of the non-Western cultures that has moved toward indigenisation of psychology (e.g., Sinha, 1996). In that context, it has been seen as necessary for theory to develop its own character appropriate to Indian culture (Sinha, 1986). Finally, the choice of topics of research may be biased by issues important to the West. For example, the need for individuals to develop high self-esteem has been the impetus behind many research studies in the West (e.g., Coopersmith, 1967; Marsh, 1993). But individual self-esteem is not considered as so important in cultures that see individuals as interdependent, as we saw in the previous section (Heine & Lehman, 1995, 1996, 1997; Kitayama, et al, 1997).

Western researchers are increasingly aware of these kinds of problems in research and, through collaboration with colleagues in other cultures, have begun to adapt and extend their measures and theories. However, the efforts of Western psychology alone are insufficient to ensure that social psychology avoids ethnocentrism. Indigenous psychology is needed to identify issues relevant to particular cultures, and to develop culturally relevant theory and measurement instruments.

Literature on indigenous psychology has suggested that there are stages of development through which *indigenisation* evolves (Adair, 1996; Sinha, 1984). Initially, psychologists in a non-Western culture may begin to become aware of the limitations of Western models of psychology as applied to their culture. This initial stage is characterized by identification of *cultural differences* between own culture and Western findings. As there is increasing acknowledgment within the culture of a need to address its own psychological issues, research begins to explore *local psychological variables* and to make comparisons between non-Western cultures. Finally, research begins to test *indigenous theory* that has developed based upon interpretation of previous findings. At the current time, such indigenous psychology is hardly beyond the stage of recognition of the need to address its own psychological issues (see Kim, 1990; Pandey, et al., 1996). Further, typically fewer resources are available within such cultures for the tremendous amount of research needed (Moghaddam, 1990). Again this suggests that collaboration between Western and non-Western psychologists may be necessary, something that has been welcomed by both parties.

In sum, the findings of cross-cultural research have challenged many of the cherished and long-accepted assumptions of social psychology, as you have already seen in these first four chapters of the book. Its implications for social psychology are profound. We can no longer assume that our findings are universally applicable until extensive cross-cultural research has been carried out. The discussion above may make this seem a daunting task. Yet it is a very exciting one that has been greeted with enthusiasm by many researchers around the world.

While cross-cultural psychology has questioned some cherished and long-accepted assumptions of social psychology, it has also opened up new vistas. For example, this approach has already produced new dimensions for understanding social behaviour and some methodological innovations. It may eventually provide a way of distinguishing the universal (etic) from the cultural (emic) and ultimately deepen our understanding of the scope of human nature (Matsumoto, 1994).

KEY POINTS

- *Cross-cultural psychology* investigates the influence of culture, cultural differences and cultural change. If we are raised in one culture, we can suffer from *ethnocentrism* and evaluate other cultural groups from the perspective of our own.

- Social psychology has tended to have a somewhat *ethnocentric* perspective in understanding social behaviour. It has tended to assume that it is studying *etic* factors—universal factors—when in fact it is studying factors which are specific to Western culture—that is, they are *emic* or culturally specific factors.

- Cross-cultural psychology is a developing field and is invaluable in expanding our understanding of social behaviour. Currently, there is recognition of possible ethnocentrism in research when Western theory and methods are applied to other cultures without *indigenous input*.

- Two developments promise to be fruitful in the future: (1) the development of indigenous psychologies from within particular cultures; and (2) an increase in collaboration between Western and non-Western psychology.

Ideas to Take with You

Dealing with Negative Self-Perceptions

A very consistent and pervasive difference between men and women in Western societies involves the way they perceive and evaluate their appearance. Beginning in adolescence, women are much more concerned about body image than men. Changing this isn't easy but you can start with yourself.

Be Realistic About the Importance of Appearance.

"Be realistic" is obviously easier to say than to accept. By definition, most of us lie outside of the top one-tenth of one percent of the population who are represented in professional sports, modelling, or movie stardom. If you decide you are imperfect because you are not in such a category, you will spend many unhappy hours brooding about not reaching an impossible goal. Also, as you will discover in Chapter 6, the adage that "you can't judge a book by its cover" is true. The most attractive individuals in the world do not differ from the rest of us in intelligence, creativity, character, kindness, or anything else that matters—except in the fact that they are liked on the basis of their looks. Think of the most unkind, dishonest, and totally detestable human being you know. Would you find that person more acceptable if he or she suddenly acquired a very attractive face and body? If you meet an attractive person for the first time, try to remember that appearance gives you no information at all about this individual.

Ask Yourself How Important Your Weight Is To Others.

Women in Canada and other Western nations are often obsessed with their weight. Do you know how much you should weigh on the basis of height–weight charts? If you fit within those norms, are you satisfied? Or do you want to weigh less? Why? Do other people perceive you as underweight, average, or overweight? How much do you think you would have to lose or to gain for anyone to notice? Some of us know that you can work hard to lose ten pounds or so, only to find that no one has a clue unless you tell them. You may think about your weight a lot and about fatness/thinness as you observe others, but other people are not obsessed with your weight! They don't care nearly as much as you do.

Recognizing and Countering Your Own Ethnocentrism

Next time you find yourself critical of the way other cultural groups respond to the social world—perhaps they display too much emotion, or too little; perhaps their practises or clothing seem ridiculous—stop and realize that you are being ethnocentric, assuming that your group's customs are the normal and the right ones.

Learn About Other Cultures.

One way to counter such tendencies is through education about cultural differences and you are already doing that! Learning to understand about different cultural views of the world is interesting as well as enlightening. It can help you to become aware that there are many different ways of being human and each culture's solution, including your own, has its advantages and disadvantages.

Try To See Things From Other Cultures' Perspectives.

Another way to counter ethnocentrism is to visualize things from the perspective of other cultural groups. This is being empathic and of course must be based in real understanding of their culture. One way to achieve this is to mix with and make friends from other cultural groups. This is always an experience that broadens your mind. You can then begin to appreciate the richness of your multicultural society.

Summary and Review of Key Points

Personal Identity: Aspects of the Private Self

● The self can be conceived as combining our *personal identity*—the private aspects of the self, and our *social identity*—the more public and socially embedded sense of self.

Cognitive information related to the self is organized into a *self-schema*. This organization helps us to process information about ourselves more efficiently than other types of information—*the self-reference effect*. The processing is both *elaborative* and *categorical*.

In addition to our current self-concept, there are many possible different and better selves that we can envision in the future.

Self-concept changes with age, but also in response to feedback, changes in one's environment or occupational status, and interactions with others.

Self-esteem consists of self-evaluation, or the attitudes we hold about ourselves in general and in specific domains. It is based in part on social comparison processes.

There are many positive benefits associated with high as opposed to low self-esteem, and to having a small, as opposed to a large, discrepancy between the actual and ideal self—termed a *self-ideal discrepancy*. However, *variable self-esteem* has even more negative consequences than low self-esteem.

Generally, our self-esteem is influenced by social factors such as *social comparison* and other people's evaluation of us. However, individuals who have *paradoxical self-esteem*—where self-liking and perceptions of self-competence are discrepant—show strongly biased cognitive processing which allow them to be impervious to outside opinion.

Self-focusing refers to the extent to which an individual is directing attention toward the self or toward the external world.

Self-monitoring refers to a dispositional tendency to regulate behaviour on the basis of external factors (high self-monitoring) or on the basis of internal beliefs and values (low self-monitoring).

Differences in self-monitoring tendencies influence speech patterns, response to advertising content, and interpersonal behaviour. Individual levels of self-monitoring are based in part on genetic factors.

Social Identity: The Self in a Social Context

● *Social identity theory* suggests that the groups to which we belong form an important part of our identity. We are motivated to achieve a positive and distinctive social identity.

Social identity refers to an individual's group-based self-concept, where as personal identity refers to the unique and individual aspects of a person's self-concept.

One important aspect of social identity is *gender*—the societal expectations associated with a person's *biological sex*. Children develop a sense of *gender identity*, a sense of maleness or femaleness, as part of the self-concept. This usually includes some sex typing of behaviour as children learn the culturally appropriate forms of behaviour for their gender.

Research on *androgyny*, using the *Bem Sex-Role Inventory (or BSRI)*, has provided evidence that those who are androgynous (have both traditionally masculine and feminine traits) tend to be more adaptable than those who adhere strongly to traditional gender roles.

Gender differences in self-perception are common, particularly differences in perception of *body image*. Typically, females tend to be more concerned about many aspects of physical appearance than males. One possible reason is the greater emphasis society places on physical attractiveness in women.

Cultural groups are an important source of social identity and can determine our understanding of the self. We gain our ethnic identity from the cultural or racial group to which we belong. Contact with other cultural groups in a multicultural society can create problems for the development of an *ethnic identity*.

Cultures can vary in terms of whether they have an *independent* or *interdependent* conception of the self and this has implications for the extent to which individuals show self-enhancing or self-improvement tendencies.

Cross-Cultural Psychology: Comparing Cultures

● *Cross-cultural psychology* investigates the influence of culture, cultural differences and cultural change. If we are raised in one culture, we can suffer from *ethnocentrism* and evaluate other cultural groups from the perspective of our own.

Social psychology has tended to have a somewhat *ethnocentric* perspective in understanding social behaviour. It has tended to assume that it is studying *etic* factors—universal factors—when in fact it is studying factors which are specific to Western culture—that is, they are *emic* or culturally specific factors.

Cross-cultural psychology is a developing field and is invaluable in expanding our understanding of social behaviour. Currently, there is recognition of possible ethnocentrism in research when Western theory and methods are applied to other cultures without *indigenous input*.

Two developments promise to be fruitful in the future: (1) the development of indigenous psychologies from within particular cultures; and (2) an increase in collaboration between Western and non-Western psychology.

For More **Information**

Bednar, R. L., Wells, M. G., & Peterson, S. R. (1992). *Self-esteem: Paradoxes and innovations in clinical theory and practice*. Washington, DC: American Psychological Association.

A description of a therapeutic process that focuses on the client's self-esteem as a central concern. The therapist emphasizes the situations in which the individual constructs his or her self-evaluations, and the client learns to face problems rather than avoid them. The goal is improved self-esteem and the attendant reduction of various maladaptive symptoms.

Oskamp, S., & Costanzo, M. (Eds.) (1993). *Gender issues in social psychology*. Newbury Park, CA: Sage.

A collection of chapters by leading experts on a wide range of gender issues.

Smith, P. B., & Bond, M. H. (1998). *Social psychology across cultures*. 2nd edition. Boston: Allyn & Bacon.

This excellent book provides a critical analysis and a summary of cross-cultural research in many of the major areas of social psychology.

Triandis, H. C. (1995). *Individualism and collectivism*. Boulder, CO: Westview.

An up-to-date review and discussion of ideas and research related to the individualism-collectivism dimension.

Weblinks

www.fit.edu/CampusLife/clubs-org/iaccp
The International Association for Cross-Cultural Psychology

www.spsp.org
Society for Personality and Social Psychology

pmc.psych.nwu.edu/personality
The Personality Project

www.uku.fi/laitokset/sospsyk/esopsy.html
Social Psychology Department, University of Kuopio, Finland

www.sil.org/sil/roster/headland-t/ee-intro.htm
"Etics and Emics: The Insider/Outsider Debate" by Thomas Headland

CHAPTER FIVE

Prejudice and Discrimination:
Understanding Their Nature, Countering Their Effects

SPECIAL SECTIONS

■ The effects of prejudice and discrimination in Canadian society

FIGURE 5.1 Prejudice and discrimination are some of the most destructive forces in our multicultural society; combating this is one of the most important tasks our society confronts.

Virtually everyone reading this chapter has experience of prejudice or discrimination. You may have been the victim of spiteful remarks about your race, gender, or physical attributes, or perhaps you were systematically excluded by a group on the same basis. If so, you know about prejudice and discrimination from the receiving end. And, if you are like many victims, this has left a lasting and painful memory.

On the other hand, you may have been the perpetrator of prejudice or discrimination. You may have made a negative assumption about someone based on their gender, ethnicity, age, or appearance and excluded them for that reason. Perhaps you have repeated a joke that contains racist or sexist stereotypes, or laughed at one. If so, then you know about prejudice and discrimination from the other side—as a perpetrator. In contrast to the experiences of victims, being the perpetrator does not lead to emotional scars—at least for you. In fact, you have probably dismissed any suggestion that you could be a "bigot"—it is almost certainly inconsistent with your self-concept. You

were "just having a little fun;" you probably "didn't mean anything by it." The point here is that none of us is immune from the experience of prejudice and discrimination as either victim or perpetrator, or, often, both. Even if you are the (very rare) person who has been neither victim nor perpetrator, you have certainly observed its destructive effects in society as a whole.

A quick review of the past millennium indicates that prejudice and discrimination have often, alas, been part of human society. As the new millennium begins in Canada, we continue to have distressing examples of its effects. Recently in British Columbia five young men between 18- and 26-years-old, who had been in the Canadian military, were convicted of the beating and killing of a 65-year-old man. They had belonged to white racist groups and this man was a Sikh who was about to open his temple. Conflict between Native and Non-native Canadians over fishing and hunting rights continues and sometimes becomes violent (see Figure 5.1).

But what, precisely, is *prejudice*, and how does it differ from another term with which we are also, unfortunately, too familiar—*discrimination*? What factors contribute to the existence of prejudice and discrimination? And perhaps even more important, how can these negative forces in human society be reduced? Given the great diversity of the human species, plus the fact that contact among people of different racial, ethnic, and national backgrounds is increasing, these are vital questions and ones with which we surely must grapple. In fact, it does not seem too extreme to suggest that combating prejudice and discrimination is one of the most crucial tasks confronting humanity today. The alternative—permitting them to exist unchecked—seems to condemn us to an ever-rising tide of hatred and violence. If nothing else, then, social psychology's commitment to understanding, and combating, prejudice and discrimination seems more timely than ever.

First, we'll examine the nature of both prejudice and discrimination, indicating what these concepts are and how they differ. Second, we will consider the causes of prejudice and discrimination—why they occur and what makes them so intense and so persistent. Third, we will look at the responses of victims of prejudice and discrimination. Finally, we will explore various strategies for reducing prejudice and discrimination.

PREJUDICE AND DISCRIMINATION: THEIR NATURE AND FORMS

In everyday speech, the terms *prejudice* and *discrimination* are used interchangeably. Are they really the same? Most social psychologists draw a clear distinction between them. **Prejudice** refers to a special type of attitude—generally, a negative one—toward the members of some social group. In contrast, **discrimination** refers to negative actions toward those individuals. Since this is an important difference, let's consider it more closely.

Prejudice: Choosing Whom To Hate

We'll begin with a more precise definition: *Prejudice* is an attitude (usually negative) toward the members of some group, based solely on their membership in that group. In other words, a person who is prejudiced toward some social group tends to evaluate its members in a specific manner (usually negatively) merely because they belong to that group. Their individual traits or behaviour play little role; they are disliked (or, in a few cases, liked) simply because they belong to a specific social group.

Prejudice Negative attitudes toward the members of specific social groups.

Discrimination Negative behaviours directed toward members of social groups who are the object of prejudice.

When prejudice is defined as a special type of attitude, two important implications follow. First, our *cognitions* are involved. As we noted in Chapter 3, attitudes often function as *schemas*—cognitive frameworks for organizing, interpreting, and recalling information (Fiske & Taylor, 1991). Thus, individuals who are prejudiced toward particular groups tend to process information about these groups differently from the way they process information about other groups: Prejudiced individuals take longer or pay closer attention to material related to the prejudice. One example: Racially prejudiced persons take significantly longer than persons who are not racially prejudiced to decide whether strangers whose racial identity is ambiguous belong to one racial category or another (Blascovich et al., 1997). Information consistent with their prejudiced views often receives more attention, is rehearsed more frequently, and, as a result, tends to be remembered more accurately than information that is not consistent with these views (Bodenhausen, 1988; Judd, Ryan, & Park, 1991). To the extent that this happens, prejudice becomes a kind of closed cognitive loop, and, in the absence of truly dramatic experiences that refute its accuracy, it can only grow stronger over time. Prejudice may also involve other aspects of cognition such as beliefs and expectations about members of these groups—specifically, *stereotypes* suggesting that all members of these groups demonstrate certain characteristics and behave in certain ways.

Second, if prejudice is a negative attitude, then negative feelings or *emotions* are shown by prejudiced persons when they are in the presence of, or merely thinking about, members of the groups they dislike (Bodenhausen, Kramer, & Susser, 1994). These emotional reactions are shown very clearly in research conducted by Vanman and his colleagues (Vanman et al., 1997). In this investigation, white participants of both genders were asked to imagine working on several cooperative tasks (e.g., a team running race, a debate team competition, a team research project, or team participation on a game show) with a partner who was either white or black. While participants were imagining these situations, the researchers made recordings of electrical activity in their facial muscles—muscles related to smiling and to frowning. Despite the fact that participants actually reported more positive attitudes toward their partners when these persons were supposedly black than when they were supposedly white, their muscle movements belied these assertions. Facial muscles showed more activity indicative of negative emotional reactions when subject's imagined partner was black than when this person was white. In a follow-up study, white participants known to be high or low in racial prejudice were shown photos of white and black strangers. Activity from their facial muscles indicated that for the low-prejudiced persons there was no difference in muscle activity for white and black strangers. For highly prejudiced persons, however, activity patterns indicative of less positive and more negative feelings occurred. So, to repeat: Prejudice can strongly influence affective reactions toward other persons.

KEY POINTS

- *Prejudice* is an attitude (usually negative) toward members of some social group based solely on their membership in that group.
- Prejudice, like other attitudes, influences our processing of social information. In addition, prejudice influences our beliefs about persons belonging to various groups, and our feelings about them.

Discrimination: Prejudice In Action

Attitudes, we noted in Chapter 3, are not always reflected in overt action—far from it. Prejudice is definitely no exception to this rule. In many cases, persons holding negative attitudes toward the members of various groups cannot express these views directly. Laws, social pressure, fear of retaliation—all serve to deter them from putting their prejudiced views into open practice. Further, those who are prejudiced may restrain themselves from overt actions that might violate their own standards and cause guilt (Devine & Monteith, 1993; Monteith, 1996). In fact the incidence of blatant *discrimination* may have decreased in recent years in North America (e.g., Swim, Aikin, Hall, & Hunter, 1995; Tougas, Brown, Beaton, & Joly, 1995). However, such restraining forces are sometimes absent. Then the negative beliefs and feelings referred to above may find expression in overt actions. Such discriminatory behaviours can take many forms and is often quite subtle. At relatively mild levels it involves simple avoidance— prejudiced persons simply avoid or minimize contact with the objects of their dislike (Henry, 1995). While such discrimination may seem relatively benign, it can sometimes have serious consequences for its victims. For example, recent studies indicate that sizable proportions of health-care professionals (physicians, nurses, hospital workers) report spending less time with AIDS patients than with people suffering from other illnesses (Gordin et al., 1987, Hunter & Ross, 1991). Clearly, such discrimination can add to the pain and suffering of the victims. At stronger levels, discrimination can produce exclusion from jobs, educational opportunities, or neighborhoods. Finally, in the most extreme cases, prejudice leads to overt forms of aggression against its targets and even to the destruction of groups in society. We have all seen disturbing film of the results of "ethnic cleansing," historically in World War II or, more recently, in Chechnya, the former Yugoslavia, and Rwanda, to name just some examples.

Prejudice and Discrimination Go Underground

As public disapproval of overt prejudice and discrimination increases and, further, is enforced in our legal system, the prejudiced person goes underground. They may be reluctant to express their feelings and beliefs, except among the like-minded. Yet there is evidence that their negative attitudes still manage to influence their behaviour. How is this achieved? One answer involves the use of subtle forms of discrimination—ones that permit their users to conceal the underlying negative views from which they stem. We'll focus on two major examples that have been studied in recent years: *modern racism* and *neosexism*.

The New Racism

Modern Racism
Subtle forms of prejudice and discrimination against other (usually minority) ethnic groups. This involves apparent support for egalitarian principles while also denying continued discrimination against minorities, showing antagonism towards minority demands and resentment against any preferential treatment designed to redress past imbalances.

At one time, many people felt no qualms about expressing openly racist beliefs. They would state they viewed members of minority groups as inferior in various ways, and that they would consider moving away if persons belonging to these groups took up residence in their neighborhoods (Sears, 1988). Now, of course, very few persons would openly state such views. Does this mean that racism, a particularly virulent form of prejudice and discrimination, has disappeared? While many social psychologists would argue that this is the case (e.g., Martin & Parker, 1995), others would contend that in fact, all that has happened is that "old-fashioned" racism (read "blatant" for "old-fashioned") has been replaced by more subtle forms, which these researchers term **modern racism**. What is such racism like? Swim and her colleagues (Swim, et al., 1995) have recently gathered data indicating that this new variety of racism focuses on three major components: (1) denial that there is continuing dis-

Some examples of institutional racism from Canada's history.

TABLE 5.1 Institutional racism in Canadian history

Restriction or denial of immigration. At the end of the last century, Chinese men were encouraged to emigrate to Canada to help build the great railway that links this country. With the railway completed, in 1886 a head tax of $50 was imposed on all Chinese immigrants. When this did not stem the tide of immigrants, it was increased—to $500 by 1903—effectively preventing many families from being united. Finally, in 1923 the Chinese Immigration Act was passed prohibiting all Chinese immigration.

Restriction of educational opportunities. From 1920 to the 1950s and 60s, it was mandatory for Native children to be sent away from their often remote homes to special residential schools. There they were discouraged from maintaining their own cultural heritage. If they spoke their own language or practised their own customs they were punished. Laws had also been passed banning important Native ceremonies such as the *potlach*. The effect of this program was to severely disrupt the Native culture and way of life. Family relationships were destroyed by enforced separation for two or three generations, and today communities are still recovering.

Control of property ownership/Restriction of movement. Subsequent to the Japanese attack on Pearl Harbor in December, 1941, 23 000 Canadian residents of Japanese descent were placed in intern-

ment camps. Their property was placed in the hands of the "Custodian of Enemy Alien Property" and later sold at well below market prices. Approximately 75 percent of these people were Canadian citizens. Again, this government action was clearly discriminatory. People of German descent did not receive this harsh treatment although Germany was also an enemy of Canada during World War II.

Denial of franchise and employment opportunities. Canadians of Chinese descent did not receive the vote until 1947. Canadians of Japanese descent did not receive the vote until 1949. Note that for both groups immigration had begun as early as the 1880s. The Inuit first received the federal vote in 1962 and Status Indians first received the vote in 1960. A person who could not vote could not hold public office, could not be in the public service and was prevented from entering many professions such as law and pharmacy.

Restriction of education and housing facilities. Until 1942, McGill University entrance requirements were a 65 percent average for Jews, but a 50 percent average for non-Jews. The law authorizing segregated schools was not repealed until 1965. As late as 1973, residential property deeds in Vancouver's affluent "British Properties" stipulated that no person of Asiatic or African ancestry could stay on the premises overnight unless he or she was a servant.

Source: Barrett (1987) and others.

crimination against minorities; (2) antagonism to the demands of minorities for equal treatment; and (3) resentment about special favours for minority groups. As you can readily see, such views are certainly different from those involved in "old-fashioned" racism, but they can still be very damaging to the victims. For example, as noted by Swim et al. (1995), modern racism may influence the likelihood of voting for a minority. So—and we want to emphasize this point strongly—despite the fact that blatant forms of racism have diminished sharply in this and many other countries, this repulsive and damaging form of prejudice is still very much alive and represents a serious problem in many societies.

Covert Institutional Racism

Historians of racism in Canada suggest that it has an *institutional* origin; historically, it was a part of the "institutional framework" of this society—built into its system of social stratification and legitimized by regulations, laws and established customs (Barrett, 1987; Kinsella, 1994; Sher, 1983). As Stanley Barrett concluded from his analysis of racism and racist groups in Canada:

> My argument is that racism—quite apart from the formally organized [racist] groups—has been institutionalized into Canadian society since the country's beginning. The right wing, including the most extreme racists and anti-semites, simply represent a more crystallized and overt form of a broader phenomenon (Barrett, 1987, p.4).

Evelyn Kallen (1995) has described institutional racism in Canada as having occurred in six areas of society: through restriction or denial of (1) immigration, (2) educational opportunities, (3) property or land ownership and use, (4) employment opportunities, (5) the franchise (i.e. the right to vote), and (6) housing. Some examples of these types of institutional racism from Canadian history are shown in Table 5.1. The examples shown can be thought of as *overt institutional racism*: that is, discrimination that is explicit in the laws and regulations of a society. However, not all institutional racism is as obvious as this. **Covert institutional racism** exists when ethnic discrimination is not openly approved in an institution, but nonetheless is present. This latter type of racism can perhaps be thought of as the institutional form of *modern racism*. It is often difficult to detect, or to prove and tends to become evident when certain ethnic groups are systematically (though unofficially) excluded from certain areas of social, economic, or political life in a country.

Covert Institutional Racism exists when ethnic discrimination is not openly approved in an institution, but nonetheless is present.

In Canada today, *overt* institutional racism is rare. Human rights legislation specifically prohibits discrimination against individuals or groups on the basis of race and ethnicity, sex, religion, age, and disability. However, we should not make the mistake of thinking that this has eliminated problems of racial discrimination in this country. Covert institutional racism does occur. In March 1997, the Human Rights Commission rendered a landmark decision against a government department, Health Canada, stating that it had discriminated against visible minority employees. That is, members of visible minority groups systematically failed to achieve promotion, despite suitable qualifications and work records. Health Canada was ordered to promote more of such employees to senior management positions within the following six months. Such cases of covert institutional racism tend to occur not because of any deliberate policy on the part of an organization, but because those in management positions use their power to exclude or otherwise discriminate against people from other ethnic groups. The institution itself turns a blind eye or is unaware that discrimination is occurring.

Two field studies in Toronto indicate that governmental organizations are not the only places in which covert institutional racism can occur. Henry and her colleagues (Henry, 1999; Henry & Ginzberg, 1985) had researchers pose as job applicants for positions advertised in newspapers. The approach was either on the telephone or in person. Applicants on the telephone had a standard Canadian accent, a European-origin foreign accent, a West Indian accent, or an Indo-Pakistani accent. Those who applied in person were either black or white. In the first study, there was considerable discrimination against non-white subjects whether they applied by phone or in person. For example, when applying in person, the jobs offered to white applicants outnumbered those offered to black applicants by a ratio of 3 to 1, although their résumés were exactly the same. Although in the second study carried out about five years later (Henry, 1999), discrimination against the in-person applicants was not found, applicants on the telephone were still discriminated against and to the same extent as in the first study. That is, the non-white applicants were about twice as likely to be told that the job was no longer available than the white applicants.

In sum, although great progress has been made in Canada in terms of overt institutional racism, we cannot be complacent. It appears that the covert form of institutional racism is still common.

Neosexism

Sexism (prejudice and discrimination based on gender) has been widely investigated since the 1970s (Bem, 1995; Cameron, 1977; Eagley, 1995). It should be emphasized that *both* sexes have been negatively affected by *sexism*—the personal and professional limitations that traditional sex roles impose. Both males and females have felt the pressure to conform to the social definition of their gender behaviour and have found it difficult to step beyond the traditional occupational roles open to each sex. However, as mentioned in Chapter 4, these limitations have been much greater for women: They have been excluded from economic and political power; they have been the subject of stronger negative stereotypes; and they have faced overt discrimination in many areas of life, such as work, education, and government (Fisher, 1992; Heilman, Block, & Lucas, 1992). For this reason most research has focused upon the effects of sexism on women.

Parallel to the findings of the work on *modern racism*, research has noted a decrease in overt forms of sexism towards women (e.g., Kahn & Crosby, 1985; Sutton & Moore, 1985) and a new form of sexism has been investigated termed **neosexism**—subtle forms of prejudice and discrimination against women, defined by its major researchers as a "manifestation of a conflict between egalitarian values and residual negative feelings towards women" (Tougas, Brown, Beaton & Joly, 1995, p. 843). According to their analysis the "old-fashioned" form of sexism, based on the presumed inferiority of women to men (Cameron, 1977), has been supplanted by this new form (see Figure 5.2). They suggest that because social norms in our society are largely egalitarian and changes in the law have made overt discrimination more difficult, the expression of sexist attitudes has become more covert. As we will see in the following On the Applied Side section, there is evidence that neoxsexism may contribute to *maintaining* inequalities in the workplace.

> **Sexism** Prejudice or discrimination based upon gender.

> **Neosexism** Subtle forms of prejudice and discrimination against women produced by a conflict between egalitarian values and residual negative feelings towards women.

■ From sexism to neosexism

FIGURE 5.2 As old fashioned forms of *sexism* decrease, a new form—*neosexism*—has emerged. It usually manifests itself more subtly than shown here.

"That was a fine report, Barbara. But since the sexes speak different languages, I probably didn't understand a word of it."

Women in the Workplace: Does Neosexism Have an Impact?

During the past 20 years human rights legislation made occupational discrimination on the basis of gender illegal (in the *Human Rights Act*, 1985). However, given the evidence of covert institutional racism mentioned above, we might expect that sexism or *neosexism* will continue to have an impact in the workforce. Is there any evidence to support this suggestion?

First the good news: the world of work has certainly improved for women in Canada. For example, in 1951 only 24 percent of women in Canada were in the labour force, whereas by 1996 this had risen to 57 percent (Creese & Beagan, 1999). Even within the past 20 years women's average education and earnings have increased: In 1981 only 10.8 percent of women (16.5 percent of men) between the ages of 25-44 years had a degree, but in 1996 the figure was 18.5 percent (for men 18.4 percent); in that same time period when salaries tended to make little progress, women's average salary rose by 6.3 percent adjusted for inflation (MacKinnon, 1999). At the psychological level research has shown that attitudes to women in the work place have improved (Kahn & Crosby, 1985). For example, there are more positive stereotypes of women in the workplace (Eagly & Mladinic, 1994) and in one study, the proportion of men expressing negative attitudes towards female executives declined from 41 percent in 1965 to 5 percent in 1985 (Sutton & Moore, 1985).

An example of the gradual nature of women's gains in the workforce is the recent Federal Court decision in October 1999 relating to the issue of *equal pay for work of equal value*. Section 11 of the *Human Rights Act (1985)* states that there should be equal pay for work which requires equal levels (though not necessarily the same type) of four factors: skill, responsibility, effort, and working conditions (Canadian Human Rights Commission, 1999). Historically, jobs in which the majority of employees were female have tended to receive less pay than male-dominated jobs even though they were equal on the basis of these four criteria. The recent Federal Court's decision urged that the Canadian government should no longer delay its settlement with its own employees. This decision affects 200 000 employees in largely female-dominated positions (clerks, secretaries and librarians) who have been underpaid in comparison to those in male-dominated positions. However, enacting its own legislation has taken the government more than eleven years. In his ruling, Justice John Evans suggested that this issue had "dragged on for far too long and at far too great a cost" and that "justice unduly delayed in this context is indeed likely to be justice denied" (*Globe and Mail*, Oct. 20, 1999).

Despite real gains in women's position in the workforce, change has come slowly and inequalities still abound. By 1996 in Canada, the same proportion of men and women were achieving an undergraduate degree (roughly 18.5 percent), but the incomes they achieved were not parallel, as shown in Table 5.2. Overall, women in full-time work earn 73 percent of salary of their male counterparts. Even when those with the same level of education or within the same occupation are compared, men earn considerably more than women. Further, the range of occupations held by women is narrower than for men, with women remaining concentrated in occupations that have lower pay and less social prestige. Two-thirds of all Canadian women in the workforce are in only four occupational sectors: clerical, service, sales and nursing (Creese & Beagan, 1999). And we can see from Table 5.2 that even in those traditionally female occupations—sometimes called "pink collar" occupations—men earn more than women. Also note that the wage gap tends to be smaller for higher status occupations, though it is still present.

Women in High Status Occupations.

There has also been an increasing proportion of working women in Canada who attain high status positions such as managerial and professional occupations: for example, only 23 percent of women in the workforce were in such positions in 1971, whereas there were 34.5 percent in 1991 (Baer, 1999). But women tend to be under-represented in the upper ranks of management: In 1995 they made up only 12.3 percent of upper management and 44.3 percent of middle and lower management positions; in 1997 only 10 of the top 500 companies in Canada were run by women (Wells, 1997)—see Figure 5.3. for an example of one of these exceptional women. These facts have led many authors to suggest the existence of a *glass ceiling*—a final barrier that prevents females, as a group, from reaching the top positions in many companies (e.g., Glass Ceiling Commission, 1995). More formally, the **glass ceiling** has been defined as "those artificial barriers based on attitudinal or organizational bias that prevent qualified individuals from advancing upward in their organization" (U.S.

Glass Ceiling Subtle barriers basesd on attitudinal or institutional bias that prevent qualified females from advancing to top-level positions. The glass ceiling can be seen as one form of neosexism.

Department of Labor, 1992). Is this barrier real? And if so, why does it exist? Research evidence on these issues is beginning to accumulate, and some tentative answers can be suggested.

First, a glass ceiling does not appear to be the result of blatant and overt efforts to keep women out of male domains (Powell & Butterfield, 1994). Rather, as the concept of *neosexism* suggests, more subtle factors seem to produce this effect. For example, females may receive fewer opportunities to develop their skills and competency than males—opportunities that prepare them for top-level jobs (Ohlott, Ruderman, & McCauley, 1994). For instance, females report fewer chances than males to take part in projects that increase their visibility or widen the scope of their responsibilities. In short, they are not given the kind of work assignments that teach them new skills and, at the same time, permit them to demonstrate their competence. In addition, females report encountering more obstacles in their jobs: they note that it is harder to find personal support, that they are often left out of

The wage gap for Canadian women and men in full-time work, 1995.

TABLE 5.2 The wage gap in Canada

| | Average Annual Earnings | | Women's Earnings as a percentage of Men's |
	Women	Men	
Educational Level			
High School Graduates	$25 760	$35 650	72.3%
University Graduates	$42 584	$55 976	76.1%
Occupation			
Clerical	$26 414	$33 641	78.5%
Sales	$25 600	$38 033	67.3%
Service	$19 734	$31 539	62.6%
Managerial/Administration	$36 583	$52 561	69.6%
Teaching	$40 568	$49 814	81.0%
Medicine/Health	$36 671	$61 375	59.7%
Natural Sciences	$41 253	$49 259	90.0%
Total Workforce	**$29 700**	**$41 610**	**73.1%**

Source: Statistics Canada, "Earnings of Men and Women in 1995," Catalogue No. 13-217, Tables 1 and 5, and "The Labour Force Annual Averages," Catalogue No. 71-220, 1996.

important networks, and that they have to fight hard to be recognized for excellent work (Ohlott et al., 1994).

Second, neosexism in the attitudes of those in the workplace also has an impact. Research in Canada has shown that when male managers in a federal agency felt *threatened* by an increased representation of women in management, this increased the likelihood that they endorsed neosexist views. Further, the greater their neosexism the more likely managers were to downgrade women's qualifications and competence in comparison to men's and the less willing they were to personally mentor or support women in management (Beaton, Tougas & Joly, 1996).

Subordinates also make distinctions in their evaluations of female and male leaders. First, although subordinates often say much the same things to female and male leaders, research findings indicate that they actually demonstrate more negative nonverbal behaviours toward female leaders (Butler & Geis, 1990). Moreover, such differences occur even when individuals strongly deny any bias against females. In a meta-analysis of existing evidence on this issue, Eagly, Makhijani, and Klonsky (1992) found

that overall, female leaders received somewhat lower evaluations than male leaders, though there was an improvement from earlier research results (Butler & Geis, 1990). Students are even found to evaluate professors differently on the basis of gender (Burns-Glover & Veith, 1995): apparently, it is desirable for a male professor to be enterprising, self-confident, stable, and steady, whereas a female professor should be jolly and talkative.

A third source of barriers to women's occupational achievement may be unintentional limits that women place upon themselves. For example, Pratto and her colleagues (1997) provide evidence that one factor contributing to continued inequalities is gender differences in *self-selection* for various occupations. That is women themselves are more likely to select "pink collar" occupations even when no barriers exist. Tannen (1994) stresses the additional importance of gender differences in communication styles. For example, women are not as likely as men to brag about their accomplishments; as a result, they often fail to receive the appropriate credit when their work is exceptionally good (Tannen, 1995). Further, research has found that a woman is more likely than a man to expect

■ Canadian women in upper management

FIGURE 5.3 Women tend to be under-represented in upper management positions in Canada. Of the top 500 Canadian companies, only 10 of them are run by women. One of these women is shown here—Bobbie Gaunt, CEO of Ford Canada.

(Jackson, Gardner & Sullivan, 1992), or believe that she deserves (Janoff-Bulman & Wade, 1996), a lower salary. Even in carrying out a laboratory task, women suggest lower pay for themselves than men do (Desmarais & Curtis, 1997).

Some recent findings can be viewed as suggesting that the glass ceiling can be, if not shattered, at least cracked. The clearest evidence in this respect has been reported by Lyness and Thompson (1997) in their large scale study of female and male executives in a sizeable company. The median salary of women in this study was close to $170 000 (U.S.)! So these women could be considered to have already passed through the glass ceiling. The findings showed few differences between male and female executives in terms of salaries and bonuses, their past developmental opportunities and their ability to fit into the male-dominated organizational culture. Females did, however, supervise fewer subordinates—a sign, perhaps, that they had less power or authority. They also had more career interruptions, and reported more obstacles (e.g., difficulty trying to influence other people without the needed

authority to back up such attempts). Finally, when asked to estimate their future career opportunities, the females responded less optimistically than the males. Given that the two groups were carefully and closely matched in many respects other than gender, these differences suggest that while the glass ceiling may have been breached, a second, higher ceiling may still exist and operate against even exceptional women.

Taken together, these findings suggest that the glass ceiling is indeed real, and that it stems from factors suggestive of neosexism—lingering forms of prejudice and discrimination towards females. While the glass ceiling may be melting in some organizations, its presence in many work settings appears to be an additional subtle barrier to female achievement.

In sum, major gains have occurred in many work settings in recent years, and at least some of these changes appear to be ones that have lessened, if not eliminated, barriers to females' success. However, covert forms of discrimination still exist and appear to have very real impacts in women's lives at the economic and psychological level.

KEY POINTS

- *Discrimination* involves negative actions, based on prejudice, toward members of various social groups.
- While *blatant* discrimination has clearly decreased in Western societies, more subtle forms such as *modern racism*, *covert institutional racism,* and *neosexism* persist.
- There have been improvements for women in the workplace with increases in their qualification, pay, and promotion to higher status positions.
- Nonetheless, subtle barriers, often termed the *glass ceiling*, are still evident in the continuing wage gap and the few women in upper management.

THE ORIGINS OF PREJUDICE: CONTRASTING PERSPECTIVES

That prejudice exists is all too obvious. The question of why it occurs, however, is more complex. Why do so many people hold negative views about members of particular social groups? What factors or conditions foster such attitudes and lead to their persistence? The answers to these questions are not simple. As with many complex forms of social behaviour, a simple explanation for the existence of prejudice will not suffice. Prejudice exists and is maintained at many different social levels: from the societal to the individual. And the theoretical views of prejudice reflect this. We will begin at the societal level, examining institutional origins of prejudice. Next we will explore prejudice in intergroup relations. This level of explanation looks to conflict between social groups in society as the source of prejudice. A third level of explanation points to socialization processes or social learning of prejudice from many sources in an individual's life, from parents and peers, to education and the media. Finally, at the individual level, we can point to limitations in our own cognitive processes as, at the least, maintaining existing prejudices. Further, individual personality characteristics have also been suggested to incline some people toward prejudice. In particular, one of the earliest approaches was to study the authoritarian personality (Adorno, et al., 1950).

At this point, we should note that these different approaches should not be regarded as competing or conflicting explanations. Rather, they view the same phenomenon from different perspectives. Each of these perspectives is necessary to fully understand the complexities of prejudice and, as we will see in the section on "Challenging Prejudice," each of them is necessary in order to combat prejudice in society.

Intergroup Conflict: Competition and Categorization as Sources of Prejudice

Competition as a Source of Prejudice

It is an axiom of life that the things people value most—good jobs, nice homes, high status—are always in short supply. There's never quite enough to go around. This fact serves as the foundation for what is perhaps the oldest explanation of prejudice—**realistic conflict theory** (e.g., Bobo, 1983). According to this view, prejudice stems from competition among social groups over valued commodities or opportunities. In short, prejudice develops out of the struggle over jobs, adequate housing, good schools, and other desirable outcomes. The theory further suggests that as such competition continues, the members of the groups involved come to view each other in increasingly negative terms (White, 1977). They label one another as "enemies," view their own group as morally superior, and draw the boundaries between themselves and their opponents ever more firmly. The result, of course, is that what starts out as simple competition relatively free from hatred gradually develops into full-scale emotion-laden prejudice (refer to Figure 5.4).

Evidence from several different studies seems to confirm the occurrence of this process: As competition persists, the individuals or groups involved come to perceive each other in increasingly negative ways. Even worse, such competition

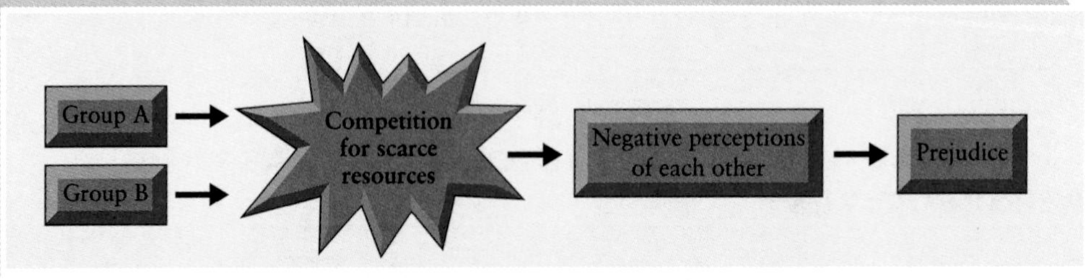

Realistic Conflict Theory The view that prejudice sometimes stems from direct competition among social groups over scarce and valued resources.

■ Realistic conflict theory: When conflict leads to prejudice

FIGURE 5.4 According to realistic conflict theory, competition between social groups for scarce resources can lead each side to view the other in increasingly negative terms. If the process continues, they may ultimately form strong prejudices toward one another.

often leads to direct and open conflict. A very dramatic demonstration of this principle in operation is provided by a well-known field study conducted by Sherif and his colleagues (Sherif et al, 1961).

For this unusual study, the researchers sent 11-year-old boys to a special summer camp in a remote area where, free from external influences, the nature of conflict and its role in prejudice could be carefully studied. When the boys arrived at the camp (named The Robber's Cave in honour of a nearby cave that was once, supposedly, used by robbers), they were divided into two separate groups and assigned to cabins located quite far apart. For one week, the campers in each group lived and played together, engaging in such enjoyable activities as hiking, swimming, and other sports. During this initial phase, the boys quickly developed strong attachments to their own groups. They chose names for their teams (Rattlers and Eagles), stencilled them on their shirts, and made up flags with their groups' symbols on them.

At this point, the second phase of the study began. The boys in both groups were told that they would now engage in a series of competitions. The winning team would receive a trophy, and its members would earn prizes (pocket knives and medals). Since these were prizes the boys strongly desired, the stage was set for intense competition. Would such conflict generate prejudice? The answer was quick in coming. As the boys competed, the tension between the groups rose. At first it was limited to verbal taunts and name-calling, but soon it escalated into more direct acts—for example, the Eagles burned the Rattlers' flag. The next day the Rattlers struck back by attacking the rival group's cabin, overturning beds, tearing out mosquito netting, and seizing personal property. Such actions continued until the researchers intervened to prevent serious trouble. At the same time, the two groups voiced increasingly negative views of each other. They labeled their opponents "bums" and "cowards," while heaping praise on their own group at every turn. In short, after only two weeks of conflict, the groups showed all the key components of strong prejudice toward each other.

Fortunately, the story had a happy ending. In the study's final phase, Sherif and his colleagues attempted to reduce the negative reactions described above. Merely increasing the amount of contact between the groups failed to accomplish this goal; indeed, it seemed to fan the flames of anger. But when conditions were altered so that the groups found it necessary to work together to reach *superordinate goals*—ones they both desired—dramatic changes occurred. After the boys worked together to restore their water supply (previously sabotaged by the researchers), pooled their funds to rent a movie, and jointly repaired a broken-down truck, tensions between the groups largely vanished. In fact, after six days of such experiences the boundaries between the groups virtually dissolved, and many cross-group friendships were established.

There are, of course, major limitations to this research. The study took place over a relatively short period of time; the camp setting was a special one; all participants were boys; and perhaps most important, the boys were quite homogeneous in background—they did not belong to different racial, ethnic, or social groups. Despite these restrictions, however, the findings reported by Sherif and his colleagues are compelling. They offer a chilling picture of how what begins as rational competition over scarce resources can quickly escalate into full-scale conflict, which then in turn fosters the accompanying negative attitudes toward opponents that form the core of prejudice.

The research reported by Sherif and his colleagues is viewed as a classic in the study of prejudice. Yet it was not the first, nor the most dramatic, study of the relationship between conflict and prejudice conducted by social psychologists. That honour goes to a much earlier, and much more disturbing, investigation conducted by Hovland and Sears (1940)—a study described in detail in the Cornerstones section below.

The Economics of Racial Violence: Do Bad Times Fan the Flames of Prejudice?

In 1939, several psychologists published an influential book entitled *Frustration and Aggression* (Dollard et al., 1939). In this book they suggested that aggression often stems from frustration—interference with goal-directed behaviour. In other words, aggression often occurs in situations where people are prevented from getting what they want. As we'll see in Chapter 8, this hypothesis is only partially correct. Frustration can sometimes lead to aggression, but it is definitely not the only, or the most important, cause of such behaviour.

In any case, the *frustration–aggression hypothesis* stimulated a great deal of research in psychology, and some of this work was concerned with prejudice. The basic reasoning was as follows: When groups are competing for scarce resources, they come to view one another as potential or actual sources of frustration. After all, if "they" get the jobs, the housing, and other benefits, then "we" don't. The result, it was reasoned, is not simply negative attitudes toward opposing groups; in addition, strong tendencies to aggress against them may also be generated.

Although this possible link between conflict, prejudice, and aggression was studied in several different ways, the most chilling findings were reported by Carl I. Hovland and Robert R. Sears (1940)—two psychologists who made important contributions to social psychology in several different areas (e.g., in the study of attitudes and persuasion; see Chapter 3). These researchers hypothesized that economic conditions provide a measure of frustration, with "bad times" being high in frustration for many people and "good times" somewhat lower. They reasoned that if this

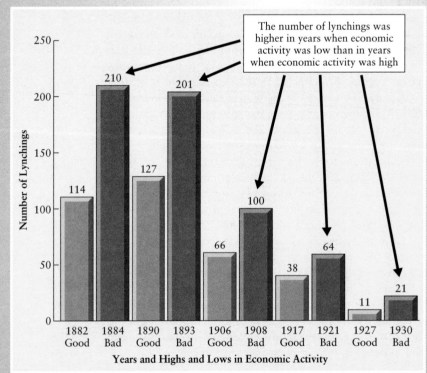

■ Racial violence and economic conditions

FIGURE 5.5 As shown here, the number of lynchings in the United States—primarily of African-Americans and mainly in southern states—varied with economic conditions. Lynchings increased when times were bad, but decreased when economic conditions improved. These findings provide indirect support for the direct conflict model of prejudice.

Source: Based on data from Hovland & Sears, 1940.

is so, then racially motivated acts of violence such as lynchings should be higher when economic conditions are poor than when they are good. To test this unsettling hypothesis, Hovland and Sears obtained data on the number of lynchings in the United States in each year between 1882 and 1930. Most of these lynchings (a total of 4761) occurred in 14 southern states, and most (though not all) of the victims were African-Americans. Next, Hovland and Sears (1940) related the number of lynchings in each year to two economic indexes: the farm value of cotton (the total value of cotton produced that year) and the per-acre value of cotton. Because cotton played a major role in the economies of the states where most lynchings occurred, Hovland and Sears assumed that these measures would provide a good overview of economic conditions in those states.

As you can see from Figure 5.5 , results were both clear and dramatic: The number of lynchings rose when economic conditions declined, and fell when economic conditions improved. Hovland and Sears (1940, p. 307) interpreted these findings as reflecting *displaced aggression*: since farmers could not aggress against the factors that were causing their frustration (e.g., a lack of rainfall), they aggressed against African-Americans—a group they disliked and that was, at that time, relatively defenceless. This process has also been termed *scapegoating*: taking one's frustrations out on the easiest, if not legitimate, target (Allport, 1954). Today most social psychologists prefer a somewhat different interpretation—one suggesting that competition for scarce economic resources increases when times are bad, and that this increased competition intensifies racial prejudice. Lynchings and other violence then result from increased prejudice rather than from displaced aggression.

Regardless of the precise mechanisms involved, however, Hovland and Sears' study was important for several reasons. First, it demonstrated an important link between economic conditions and racial violence—a finding that has been confirmed with more sophisticated modern research methods (Hepworth & West, 1988). Clearly, this relationship is relevant to government programs designed to improve economic conditions for disadvantaged persons, many of whom are the victims of racial or ethnic prejudice. Second, this research provided a dramatic illustration of the value of applying psychological theory to important real-life events. Finally, it showed how important social problems can be investigated by means of *archival data*—existing records of social and economic events. In these and other ways, Hovland and Sears's research paved the way for further and more sophisticated investigations of the roots of prejudice—research that has continued without interruption ever since.

Social Identity and Social Categorization as a Source of Prejudice

A second perspective that points to conflict between groups as the source of prejudice is based on Tajfel's *social identity theory* (Tajfel & Turner, 1979; Tajfel, 1970). This time the conflict is not over material concerns such as housing or jobs. Rather, as you will recall from our discussion of this theory in Chapter 4, Tajfel suggests that groups compete for a *distinctive and positive social identity*: to be esteemed and valued by other groups in society. This is essentially a desire for one's own group to be seen as both different from, and better than, other groups. Obviously, not all groups can achieve this desirable position in society. However, when they attempt this, the conflict in social perceptions that arises, termed *social competition*, results in prejudice.

Initiating this process is the cognitive mechanisms of **social categorization**. In order to cope with the overload of social information, we classify the social world into groups along socially important dimensions. Such distinctions are based on many dimensions, including ethnicity, religion, gender, age, occupation, income, to name a few. But we go beyond mere categorization and identify—*us* and *them*. We identify the groups to which we belong (usually termed the **ingroup**) and the groups to which we do not belong (the **outgroup**).

Social Categorization Our tendency to divide the social world into two separate categories: our ingroup ("us") and various outgroups ("them").

Ingroup The social group to which an individual perceives herself or himself as belonging ("us").

Outgroup Any group other than the one to which individuals perceive themselves as belonging ("them").

If the process of dividing the social world into "us" and "them" stopped there, it would have little bearing on prejudice. Unfortunately, however, it does not. Our desire for a positive social identity leads to sharply contrasting feelings and beliefs about members of one's ingroup and members of various outgroups. Persons in the former ("us") category are viewed in favourable terms, while those in the latter ("them") category are perceived more negatively. This tendency even extends to extraneous attributes of the ingroup and outgroup. For example, individuals tend to perceive their own country's products as being of higher quality and more reliable than another country's, even when they are of the same standard—this tendency is termed the *country-of-origin effect* (Peterson & Jolibert, 1995). Outgroup members are assumed to possess more undesirable traits, are perceived as being more alike (i.e., more homogeneous) than members of the ingroup, and are often strongly disliked (Judd, Ryan, & Park, 1991; Lambert, 1995; Linville & Fischer, 1993). In total, this process of ingroup-outgroup bias has been called the **us-versus-them effect**.

The ingroup-outgroup distinction also affects *attribution*—the ways in which we explain the actions of persons belonging to these two categories. Specifically, we tend to attribute desirable behaviours by members of our ingroup to stable, internal causes (e.g., their admirable traits), but attribute desirable behaviours by members of outgroups to transitory factors or to external causes—we "explain away" positive attributes outcomes of outgroups (Hewstone, 1990). This tendency to make more favourable and flattering attributions about members of one's own group than about members of other groups is sometimes described as the **ultimate attribution error**, since it carries the self-serving bias we described in Chapter 2 into the area of intergroup relations—with potentially devastating effects.

That strong tendencies exist to divide the social world into these contrasting groups has been demonstrated in many studies (e.g., Stephan, 1985; Tajfel, 1982;

The Us-versus-Them Effect The tendency to show bias towards the ingroup and against the outgroup. It is suggested that this is an inevitable outcome of social categorization and identification of ingroups and outgroups.

Ultimate Attribution Error The tendency to make more favourable and flattering attributions about members of one's own group than about members of other groups.

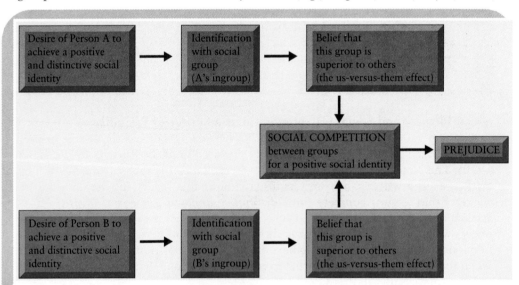

■ Why social identity and social categorization processes sometimes lead to prejudice

FIGURE 5.6 According to Tajfel's social identity theory (1982), prejudice sometimes arises out of social competition. This process reflects the desire of individuals to achieve a positive and distinctive social identity by identifying with groups they view as desirable or superior. Since the members of many groups have the same desire, conflict between them occurs. Prejudice then follows from this clash of social perceptions.

Source: Based on suggestions by Tajfel, 1982.

Turner et al., 1987). In these investigations, participants generally expressed more negative attitudes toward members of outgroups and treated them less favourably than members of their own group. Further, these patterns held true even when these categories were purely arbitrary and had no existence beyond the experiment, and when the persons involved never met face to face.

But why, precisely, does the us-versus-them effect occur? Why does the definition of others as outgroup members lead us to view them in biased and mainly negative ways? Tajfel and his colleagues (e.g., Tajfel, 1982) suggest that social identity processes are the key. Individuals seek to enhance their self-esteem by becoming identified with specific social groups. This tactic can succeed, however, only to the extent that the persons involved perceive their groups as somehow distinctive and superior to other, competing groups. Since all individuals are subject to the same forces, the final result is inevitable: Each group seeks to view itself as somehow better than its rivals, and prejudice arises out of this clash of social perceptions, termed *social competition* (see Figure 5.6).

Convincing evidence that such group biases do occur has been provided by numerous studies (e.g., Hewstone, 1990; Mullen, Brown & Smith, 1992). For example, an ingenious study conducted by Fein and Spencer (1997) tested the prediction that outgroup evaluation is related to self-esteem. These researchers asked male and female students to evaluate the personality and job qualifications of a job candidate. Information and a photo attached to the application indicated that she was either Jewish or Italian. Before making their evaluations, participants received feedback from a bogus IQ test indicating that they had scored either very high (93rd percentile) or very poorly (47th percentile). Fein and Spencer (1997) predicted that after receiving positive feedback, participants would have little reason to derogate either job applicant. After the negative feedback, however, their self-concept would be threatened, so they would tend to derogate (downrate) the job applicant when she was described as being Jewish. This latter prediction was based on the fact that a negative stereotype for Jewish females ("Jewish American princesses" or JAPs) existed at the college where the research was conducted. Results strongly confirmed these predictions.

But did putting down the Jewish job applicant actually enhance participants' self-esteem? To see if this was so, Fein and Spencer had the students complete a measure of self-esteem twice: at the start of the study, and again after evaluating the job applicant. Results were clear: Those who had received negative feedback and downrated the Jewish applicant did in fact show the largest gain in self-esteem. Together with other studies (e.g., Meindl & Lerner, 1985) these results offer strong support for the view that disparaging an outgroup can boost self-esteem as social identity theory suggests. Thus, it appears that our tendency to divide the social world into two opposing camps often plays a role in the development of of prejudice.

A second study explored whether *distinctiveness* was related to outgroup evaluation. As we will see in Chapter 6, similarity often leads to liking: the more similar we perceive others as being to ourselves, the more we tend to like them. This has been termed the *similarity-attraction hypothesis*. Does this apply to the distinction between ingroups and outgroups? At first glance it might seem that this would be the case. But social identity theory points to another possibility: Learning that outgroup members are similar to us in various ways could threaten our self-esteem and cause us to evaluate these persons even more negatively (e.g., Tajfel, 1982). After all, if our group is similar to another then our *distinctiveness* is lost and perhaps with that goes our entire sense of social identity.

Several countries that emerged when the former Soviet Union collapsed offer a unique location in which to test these effects, because before 1991 they were all part of the same nation. Thus, in a sense, they were part of a single ingroup. Since that date,

■ When ingroups become outgroups

FIGURE 5.7 Before 1991 Russians, Moldavians, Ukrainians, and Georgians all belonged to one country—the Soviet Union. Since that time, the areas these groups come from have become independent countries and so, to an extent, these groups are now outgroups for one another.

however, these countries have been independent and, as such, have become each other's outgroups and, further, may actually be hostile to each other (see Figure 5.7). Henderson-King and his colleagues (1997) asked several hundred students at a large Russian university to rate the traits of three outgroups: Ukrainians, Moldavians, and Georgians. Ratings were made on such dimensions as hostility, friendliness, intelligence, and greed. In addition, participants rated the extent to which each of these groups was similar to their own ingroup (Russians). Finally, participants also rated the extent to which these three outgroups posed a threat to Russia, either externally or internally (as contributors to violence within Russia's borders).

Results showed whether similarity to outgroups led to attraction or not depended upon whether an outgroup was seen as a threat. Outgroups that posed little or no threat to Russia (Ukrainians and Moldavians) were rated favourably (i.e., less ingroup bias was shown), the more they were perceived as similar to Russians. For outgroups that posed a threat (Georgians), however, perceived similarity resulted in less favourable evaluations. So, in sum, it appears that our reactions to outgroups are a function of both their degree of perceived similarity to us and the threat they seem to pose. As noted by Henderson-King and his colleagues (1997), these findings have implications not only for social groups within a given culture but, perhaps, for international relations as well.

Early Experience: The Role of Social Learning

A third explanation for prejudice is one you will not find surprising: it suggests that prejudice is *learned* and that it develops in much the same manner, and through the same basic processes, as other attitudes (refer to our discussion in Chapter 3). According to this **social learning view**, children acquire negative attitudes toward various social groups through processes of *classical conditioning*, *instrumental conditioning*, and *modelling*.

An example of *classical conditioning* is the way in which we come to associate particular groups with certain characteristics through exposure to the media. We may never have met a single member of a particular ethnic or regional group, yet we might have developed negative reactions toward that group, or at least the impression that we know their characteristics, merely because through television or films they have been repeatedly presented in a particular way. In classical conditioning terms, the originally neutral stimulus of that group has been repeatedly paired with emotion-provoking stimuli and we have learned to respond to the group with a similar emotional response. For example, until quite recently members of some ethnic minority groups were shown infrequently in movies or television. Further, when they did appear, they were usually cast in low-status, comic or victim roles. Given repeated exposure to such material over the years, it is not surprising that many children came to believe that members of these groups were inferior, powerless, or merely to be pitied rather than respected. And many groups in society are still under-represented in the media, though gradual changes are occurring (Weigel, Loomis, & Soja, 1980; Weigel, Kim, & Frost, 1995). Such processes are often very subtle. We may not even be aware that learning has taken place until we experience surprise on first meeting an individual from the group who does not fulfill our expectations.

The processes of *modeling* and *instrumental conditioning* of prejudice attitudes often occur together for children. We may hear influential people in our lives such as parents, peers, or a media hero, express prejudiced views. These individuals are likely to be seen as role models and, if that is the case, we are likely to imitate their behaviour by adopting such attitudes ourselves. Subsequently, the social reinforcement we are given (direct praise, approval, or acceptance by others) for expression of such prejudices, will entrench them in our cognitive repertoire. As we will see in the next section on cognition, once such attitudes are formed, they may be difficult to overcome because they tend to be self-confirming.

To this point, we have talked as if social learning only occurs in childhood. This is, of course, a crucially important period for the development of prejudices. However, we should emphasize that social learning occurs throughout our lives. The subtle influences of the media continue to make an impression upon us. In addition, although as adults we may be less malleable, nonetheless we are still open to the influence of social norms around us (Pettigrew, 1969). As we will see in Chapter 7, most people choose to conform to the *social norms* of groups to which they belong. Even if we disagree with someone expressing open hostility toward a group, it can be very difficult to stand out against the crowd and openly object if everyone else appears to agree. As social learning theory suggests, until social punishments are evident for prejudiced attitudes, our own failure to respond in a proactive way can often ensure the persistence of prejudice.

> **Social Learning View** The view that prejudice is learned—acquired through direct and vicarious experiences—in much the same manner as other attitudes.

Social Cognition: Its Role in Maintaining Prejudice

This source of prejudice is in some ways the most unsettling of all. It involves the possibility that prejudice stems, at least in part, from basic aspects of each individual's social cognition—how we think about other persons. We will now consider several forms of evidence pointing to this conclusion.

Stereotypes: What They Are and How They Operate

Consider the following groups: Chinese-Canadians, French-Canadians, homosexuals, Jews. Suppose you were asked to list the traits that are most characteristic of each. Would you experience much difficulty? Probably you would not. You would be able to construct quite easily a list of traits for each group. Moreover, you could do this *even for groups with which you have had limited personal contact.* Why? The reason involves the existence and operation of **stereotypes**. As we saw earlier, these are cognitive frameworks suggest that all members of a social group demonstrate certain characteristics and behave in certain ways. As noted by Judd, Ryan, and Park (1991), stereotypes involve generalizations about the typical or "modal" characteristics of members of various social groups. That is, they suggest that all members of such groups possess certain traits, at least to a degree. Once a stereotype is activated, these traits come readily to mind; hence the ease with which you could construct the lists described above (Higgins & Bargh, 1987).

Like other cognitive frameworks or *schemas*, stereotypes exert strong effects on the ways in which we process social information. For example, information relevant to a particular stereotype is processed more quickly than information unrelated to it (Dovidio, Evans, & Tyler, 1986). Similarly, stereotypes lead the persons holding them to pay attention to specific types of information—usually, information consistent with the stereotypes. Alternatively, if information inconsistent with a stereotype does manage to enter consciousness, we may actively refute it, perhaps by recalling facts and information that are consistent with the stereotype (O'Sullivan & Durso, 1984). For instance, research findings indicate that when we encounter information about someone who belongs to a group about which we have a stereotype and this information is inconsistent with the stereotype, we draw *tacit inferences* (conclusions and ideas not contained in the information) that change the meaning of this information to make it consistent with the stereotype (e.g., Kunda & Sherman-Williams, 1993; Dunning & Sherman, 1997).

Such effects can occur for a wide range of stereotypes—for instance, ones relating to gender, ethnicity or roles—and occur when the information relating to a stereotype is first encountered. Together, these findings led Dunning and Sherman (1997, p. 459), to describe stereotypes as "inferential prisons"—once they are formed, stereotypes shape our perceptions of other persons so that we interpret new information about these persons as confirming our stereotypes even if this not the case (see Figure 5.8).

Stereotypes Beliefs to the effect that all members of specific social groups share certain traits or characteristics. Stereotypes are cognitive frameworks that strongly influence the processing of incoming social information.

■ Stereotypes: Inferential prisons?

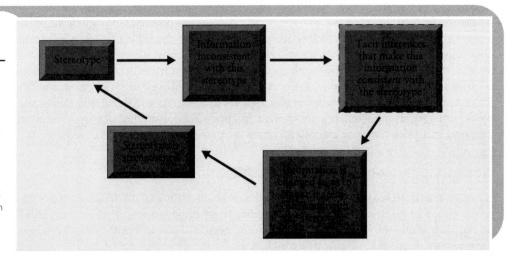

FIGURE 5.8 Once stereotypes exist, they strongly influence the way we process information relating to them. When we encounter information inconsistent with a stereotype, for instance, we formulate tacit inferences that make the information seem to fit with the stereotype rather than change the stereotype.

Stereotypes and Prejudice

That stereotypes exist and exert strong effects on social thought is clear. But are they closely related to prejudice? Surprisingly, until recently, evidence for the existence of this link was not as strong or clear as you might guess (e.g., Dovidio et al., 1996). Recent research using sophisticated techniques for measuring both stereotypes and prejudice, however, has yielded stronger results. For instance, consider a study by Kawakami and her colleagues (Kawakami et al., 1998).

These researchers exposed students at the University of Toronto to words designed to *prime* (activate) either racial stereotypes or no stereotypes: "Black," "White," and the letters CCC. These words were presented either for 0.3 seconds, a period too short to allow for controlled (i.e., careful) processing, or for 2.0 seconds, a period long enough for such processing to occur. Shortly after each of these words appeared on a computer screen, a second word that was related to a positive or negative racial stereotype for blacks appeared. Examples of words related to positive stereotypes included *athlete, musical, hip, funny, cool*; examples of words related to negative stereotypes included *aggressive, angry, poverty, criminal, welfare*. Participants were asked to say this second word out loud as quickly as possible. It was reasoned that the faster they said the stereotype-related words, the stronger the activation of racial stereotypes.

Kawakami and her colleagues (1998) predicted that if stereotypes are related to prejudice, then high- and low-prejudiced persons would differ in their responses to the stereotype-related words. Specifically, highly prejudiced persons would respond more quickly to stereotype-related words following the prime "Black" but more quickly to non-stereotype-related words following the prime "White." In contrast, no differences of this type would occur among low-prejudiced persons. To test this reasoning, the researchers obtained a measure of participants' racial prejudice. As shown in Figure 5.9, their hypothesis was confirmed.

These results, and those of other studies (Lepore & Brown, 1997), suggest that stereotypes are indeed linked to prejudice. In other words, negative attitudes we hold toward various social groups can serve to activate negative stereotypes about them. Because these stereotypes then influence our processing of new information about such

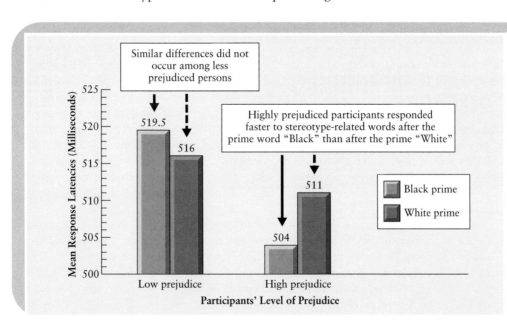

■ Evidence that stereotypes are related to prejudice

FIGURE 5.9 Highly prejudiced persons responded more quickly to words related to the stereotype for African-Canadians after seeing the word (prime) "Black" than the word "White." In contrast, similar differences did not occur among low-prejudiced persons.

Source: Based on data from Kawakami, Dion, & Dovidio, 1998.

groups toward confirming the stereotypes, an especially vicious circle in which prejudice activates stereotypes and stereotypes strengthen prejudice can occur—with dire consequences for the targets of prejudice. As we noted at the start of this section, cognitive sources of prejudice are indeed, in some ways, the most disturbing of all.

KEY POINTS

- The *social learning* perspective suggests that *early experience* can lead to prejudice when children are trained to hate various groups.
- Prejudice sometimes stems from basic aspects of social cognition—the ways in which we process social information.
- *Stereotypes* are cognitive frameworks suggesting that all persons belonging to a social group show similar characteristics. Stereotypes strongly influence social thought. For instance, when activated, they lead us to draw *tacit inferences* about others that then make information which is inconsistent with stereotypes seem to be consistent with them.
- Recent findings indicate that stereotypes are closely linked to prejudice; for example, highly prejudiced persons respond more quickly to stereotype-related words than less prejudiced persons.

Other Cognitive Mechanisms of Prejudice

Illusory correlations: Perceiving relationships that aren't there.

Consider the following information: (1) there are 1000 members of Group A but only 100 members of Group B; (2) 100 members of Group A were arrested by the police last year, and 10 members of Group B were arrested. Suppose you were asked to evaluate the criminal tendencies of these two groups: would your ratings of them differ? Your first answer is probably "of course not—why should they?" After all, the rate of criminal behaviour is equal in the two groups (10 percent in both cases). Yet a large body of evidence suggests that you might actually assign a less favourable rating to Group B (Hamilton & Sherman, 1989; Mullen & Johnson, 1990). Why? The answer seems to involve what social psychologists term *distinctiveness-based illusory correlations*, or, more simply, **illusory correlations**: the perception of a stronger relationship between two variables than actually exists. In this case, you might perceive a correlation between membership in one of these groups and the tendency to commit criminal acts. Illusory correlations seem to stem, at least in part, from the fact that infrequent events are highly distinctive. Thus, when two relatively infrequent events occur together, or when they later become linked in our minds (McConnell, Sherman, & Hamilton, 1994), we tend to perceive that they are correlated. Being arrested and belonging to Group B are both relatively infrequent events, so we perceive a stronger correlation between them than we do between being arrested and belonging to Group A (which is 10 times as large).

Illusory Correlations Perceptions of stronger associations between variables than actually exist. This comes about because each variable is distinctive and their apparent correlation is readily entered into and retrieved from memory.

What do illusory correlations have to do with prejudice? A great deal. For example, in the 1990s in Canada visible minorities represented only 10 percent of the population (Esses & Gardner, 1996). So in most social contexts they would be distinctive. Violent crimes is also a relatively rare occurrence for most people. Thus, when majority-group individuals read or hear about a violent crime committed by someone from a visible minority-group, two relatively infrequent stimuli co-occur. As a result, an illusory corre-

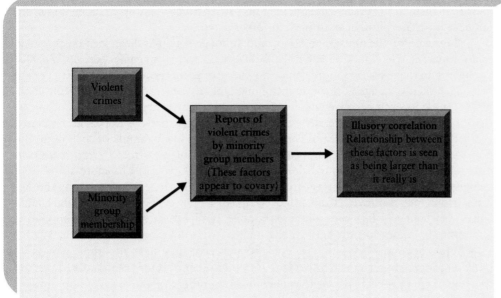

FIGURE 5.10 When two relatively rare or infrequent events seem to covary, they are often perceived as being correlated to a greater extent than is actually the case; this is an illusory correlation. In the example shown here, an illusory correlation between race and violent crime results from the fact that for many majority-group persons both such crimes and minority group members are relatively infrequent (and therefore distinctive) phenomena. Hence, many perceive these two factors as more closely linked than they really are.

lation may emerge, suggesting a stronger link between race and violent behaviour than is warranted. Further, illusory correlations also lead people to ignore the many factors that may be responsible for such relationships and that have nothing whatsoever to do with race or ethnic background (e.g., poverty, discrimination, growing up in a highly violent environment, and so on; please see Figure 5.10).

A large number of studies offer support for this *distinctiveness-based* interpretation of illusory correlations (Hamilton et al., 1989; Stroessner, Hamilton, & Mackie, 1992). However, other research findings indicate that this interpretation should be modified in at least one important respect. Apparently, it is not crucial that information be distinctive when it is first encountered; rather, information can become distinctive at later times and produce illusory correlations when this occurs (McConnell, Sherman, & Hamilton, 1994). It seems that we review and reconsider social information again and again, in the light of new input. As a result of this process, information that was not highly distinctive when it was first encountered may become distinctive at a later time. And if it does, it may then exert unduly strong effects on judgments relating to it; in other words, it may serve as a source of illusory correlation. In practical terms, this means that even if individuals don't extensively encode negative information about minority group members when they first receive it, they may go back and do so in the light of new and perhaps even more attention-getting news coverage of negative events. Then such information may produce illusory correlations: the tendency to overestimate the rate of negative behaviours among minority groups.

Outgroup homogeneity: "They're all the same"—or are they?

One remark people with a strong prejudice toward some group often make goes something like this: "You know what they're like; they're all the same." What such comments imply, of course, is that the members of some outgroup are much more similar to one another (i.e., are more homogeneous) than the members of one's own ingroup. This tendency to perceive persons belonging to groups other than one's own as all alike is known as the **illusion of outgroup homogeneity** (Linville et al., 1989). The mirror image of this tendency is known as the *ingroup differentiation hypothesis*—the

Illusion of Outgroup Homogeneity The tendency to perceive persons belonging to groups other than one's own as all alike.

view that we tend to perceive members of our own groups as showing much larger differences from one another than those of other groups.

Existence of the illusion of outgroup homogeneity has been demonstrated in many different contexts. For example, individuals tend to perceive persons older or younger than themselves as more similar to one another in terms of personal traits than persons in their own age group—an intriguing type of "generation gap" (Linville et al., 1989). Students even perceive students from another university as more homogeneous than those at their own university—especially when these persons appear to be biased against them (Rothgerber, 1997). Perhaps the most chilling example of such outgroup homogeneity effects, however, appears in the context of *cross-racial facial identification*—the tendency for persons belonging to one racial group to be more accurate in recognizing the faces of strangers from their own group than strangers from another racial group (e.g., Bothwell, Brigham, & Malpass, 1989; see Figure 5.11). In the United States this tendency has been observed among both blacks and whites, although it appears to be somewhat stronger among whites (Anthony, Cooper, & Mullen, 1992).

What accounts for our tendency to perceive members of other groups as more homogeneous than members of our own group? One explanation may be that we have a great deal of experience with members of our own group, and so are exposed to a wider range of individual variation within that group. In contrast, we generally have much less experience with members of other groups, and

■ Cross-racial facial identification: The illusion of outgroup homogeneity strikes again

FIGURE 5.11 Look at the photos shown here. If you are Asian, would you find it easier to recognize the strangers in the bottom row than those in the top row? If you are white, would the reverse be true? A large body of research evidence suggests that in fact most people find it easier to recognize strangers from their own racial or ethnic group.

hence less exposure to their individual variations (e.g., Linville et al., 1989). Whatever the precise basis for its existence (see, e.g., Lee & Ottati, 1993), the tendency to perceive other groups as more homogeneous than our own can play an important role in prejudice and in the persistence of negative stereotypes. Once we conclude that members of some disliked group are "all alike," there is little reason to seek contact with them—we expect to learn nothing from such encounters, and we also expect them to be unpleasant. So the illusion of outgroup homogeneity provides yet another basis for both the development and the persistence of prejudice.

The Authoritarian Personality

One of the earliest approaches to prejudice was Adorno and colleagues' (1950) work on the *authoritarian personality*. This approach focused on a type of highly conventional individual who was submissive to strong leaders and threatened by those in society who were different or unconventional. High authoritarians were found particularly likely to be racially prejudiced and homophobic.

Current research in this area is dominated by the work of Bob Altemeyer in Manitoba (1981; 1988). He has carried out a thorough revision and validation of the original scales, which are now much more reliable and measure what is termed **right-wing authoritarianism (RWA)**. The right-wing authoritarianism scale measures three basic attitudinal clusters. Those who are high in right-wing authoritarianism will show: (1) *authoritarian submission*, a high degree of submissiveness to figures of authority who are perceived as legitimate and established; (2) *authoritarian aggression*, a general aggressiveness toward various people (often minorities, the unconventional and socially deviant) when it appears that such aggression is sanctioned by established authority; and (3) *conventionalism*, a high degree of adherence to social values and customs that are perceived as endorsed by society and established authorities.

The term "right wing" as it is used here does not imply a necessarily conservative political perspective. In general, Altemeyer does not find a very strong relationship between political allegiance and the RWA score. Extensive studies have found that high scores in right-wing authoritarianism correlate with ethnic and racial prejudice, acceptance of government high-handedness or illegality (e.g., illegal wire-taps and intimidation of opponents), endorsement of severe punishment for law-breakers, and religious orthodoxy and fundamentalism.

Right-wing Authoritarianism (RWA) The tendency to be particularly vulnerable to prejudice and show submissiveness to figures of authority, aggression towards nonconformists or those who are different and who hold conventional values.

KEY POINTS

- Other cognitive sources of prejudice include *illusory correlations*—overestimations of the strength of relationships between social categories and negative behaviours, and the *illusion of outgroup homogeneity*—the tendency to perceive outgroups as more homogeneous than our own ingroup.
- Individuals who have personalities high in *right-wing authoritarianism* show a propensity towards prejudice against minority groups in society.

RESPONSES OF THE VICTIMS OF PREJUDICE

As well as understanding the sources of prejudice and discrimination, we must also attempt to understand its impact. How do the targets of prejudice cope with such treatment? What impact does it have on their self-concepts, self-esteem, and identification with their own group? These are the kinds of questions that have been raised with increasing frequency in recent years. However, it is to early writings on this topic that we can turn for an overview.

Types of Possible Responses to Prejudice and Discrimination

An early and influential theoretical approach to prejudice was presented in Gordon Allport's book, *The Nature of Prejudice* (1954). Among the topics considered was the responses of victims of prejudice. Allport described a broad range of possible responses from passivity to aggression against the source of prejudice. However, these responses were classified into two fundamental types based on whether the victim attributed blame for prejudice and discrimination internally or externally. An **intropunitive response** turns the blame for victimization inward, on the self or on the victim's group. Thus, intropunitive defences against others' prejudice include self-hatred, aggression against or denial of one's own group, sympathy for other victims, clowning (a form of self-ridicule), or neuroticism and passive withdrawal. In contrast, an **extrapunitive response** turns the blame for victimization outward, upon other individuals or groups. Specific extrapunitive defences are prejudice, aggression, and obsessive suspicion of outgroups, fighting back and militancy, strengthening of ingroup ties, and increased striving for self-improvement.

A second early perspective comes from social identity theory (Tajfel, 1982; Tajfel & Turner, 1979). Social identity theory suggests that those who have a negative social identity (i.e., their group is perceived and evaluated negatively by other groups in society) can respond in one of three ways: (1) acceptance and passivity; (2) personal improvement strategies; and (3) group improvement strategies. Individuals may accept the negative view of their group and not attempt personal or group change, though it is suggested that they will feel resentment towards more advantaged groups in society. Those who are motivated to improve their social identity can use *personal strategies* or *group-based strategies*. Examples of personal strategies are attempting personal upward mobility (termed a *social mobility* strategy) or perhaps leaving one's own group. Group-based strategies for improvement of social identity will be used when individuals can see the possibility of change in the structural relations between groups in society (termed *social change* strategies). Use of such strategies improves an individual's social identity through improvement of the whole group's position in society. For example, groups may attempt to change the negative social definition of their own characteristics, or they may directly challenge and compete with more advantaged groups in society. This is something that African-American groups did in the 1960s and 1970s when they challenged the current negative view and position of their group in the United States. One slogan that emerged from this movement was "black is beautiful," which clearly aimed to redefine the negative view of their characteristics.

Recent extensions of the social identity approach have distinguished between two types of group-based strategy for responding to prejudice and discrimination: either *supporting* group reponses or *organizing* them yourself—the latter is seen as more effort and is therefore less likely (Louis & Taylor, 1999). In addition, responses have been classified as *normative* and *antinormative* (Louis & Taylor, 1999; Wright,

Intropunitive Response A response of the victim of prejudice and discrimination that turns the blame inward towards the self or the victim's group.

Extrapunitive Response A response of the victim of prejudice and discrimination that turns the blame outward, towards other individuals or groups.

Taylor & Moghaddam, 1990). Normative responses are those that come within the bounds of acceptable social responses from the perspective of the dominant group, whereas antinormative responses tend to be socially unacceptable ranging from unpleasant to immoral or illegal. Examples of this latter type of response would be organizing an illegal strike, or getting around a discriminatory barrier to employment by lying about your background. Research has generally shown that antinormative and collective responses are most likely to occur when discrimination is extreme (e.g., Lalonde & Cameron, 1994; Lalonde, Majumder, & Parris, 1995; Wright, Taylor & Moghaddam, 1990)

These broad categories provide a useful way of organizing and understanding the varied responses of victims of prejudice. While Allport (1954) classified these responses on the basis of attribution of blame (internal or external), social identity theorists (Tajfel, 1982; Tajfel & Turner, 1979) distinguished between personal and group-based strategies.

Research on Victim Responses to Prejudice

Responding to a Negative Stereotype

Recent research shows that those who are the victims of prejudice can be particularly sensitive to the possibility of being negatively stereotyped. This is known as **stereotype threat**—the threat, perceived by persons who are the target of stereotypes, that they will be evaluated in terms of these stereotypes (Steele, 1997). Concerns about stereotype threat may disrupt task performance in many contexts. For example, in one recent study on this possibility, Croizet and Claire (1998) had persons from high or low socioeconomic backgrounds work on a test that was described either as a measure of their intellectual ability or as a measure of the role of attention in memory. The researchers predicted that when the test was described as one of intellectual ability, this would induce anxiety about stereotype threat among persons from low socioeconomic background, who would fear that they would be evaluated in terms of a negative stereotype. Thus, individuals from low socioeconomic background would actually perform worse on the test than those from high socioeconomic background. When the test was described as a measure of attention, however, such differences would not occur. Results offered clear support for these predictions. Findings such as these suggest that the existence of stereotypes can indeed have harmful effects on the persons to whom they apply—effects that are quite distinct from those generated by discrimination against such persons.

Interestingly, it is not only those who suffer persistent prejudice who anticipate the possibility of being negatively stereotyped. Jacquie Vorauer and colleagues at the University of Manitoba (Vorauer, Main & O'Connell, 1998) found that white Canadians anticipated negative views of themselves from Aboriginal Canadians. Further, such *meta-stereotypes* (perceptions of negative stereotyping from another group) had an impact on anticipated interaction with Aboriginal individuals. White students who had more extensive meta-stereotypes expected to enjoy interaction less and to experience greater negative emotion. Indeed when simulated interaction did occur with an Aboriginal person, high-prejudice white students were more likely than low-prejudice white students to believe that they had been negatively stereotyped by their Aboriginal interactant.

In a series of early laboratory experiments carried out in a Canadian context (Dion, 1975; Dion & Earn, 1975), members of minority groups were given the impression that they had been the victim of discrimination by members of the majority group. Their emotional responses and endorsement of ingroup stereotypes were measured. Members of visible minorities (e.g., the Chinese) responded to discrimination by denying negative

Stereotype Threat
The threat perceived by persons who are the target of stereotypes that they will be evaluated in terms of these stereotypes.

aspects of their stereotype. In contrast, those whose minority status was less visible, or constant, (e.g., Jews and women) responded by increasing identification with positive aspects of their stereotype. Emotional and self-esteem measures were more frequently *extrapunitive* than intropunitive. For example, victims of discrimination showed greater aggression and less social affection toward majority-group members, as well as an increase in egotism. These studies also failed to find any negative effects on self-esteem among subjects. However, among the few *intropunitive* responses shown were greater sadness and anxiety on the part of those believing they had been victimized.

The laboratory studies described above may be somewhat lacking in *external validity*, by taking place in an artificial laboratory setting, and involving simulation rather than real interaction with outgroup members. Real-life long-term discrimination can have the effect of gradually eroding its victim's self-esteem (Clark & Clark, 1947). For examination of the victims of prejudice in their social context, we can turn to field studies.

Focusing on One's Group, Not Oneself, as the Target of Prejudice and Discrimination

An intriguing finding from recent research in the area of victim responses is that members of minority groups often perceive higher levels of discrimination as directed at their group as a whole than at themselves personally (Crosby, 1982, 1984; Guimond & Dubé-Simard, 1983; Taylor, Wright, Moghaddam, & Lalonde, 1990). It is as if individuals are saying, "My group as a whole has been treated badly, but personally I've been lucky enough to avoid such treatment." While it is possible that an occasional individual from a group that is the target of widespread discrimination may be lucky enough to avoid this treatment, it is not possible that this is the typical experience of its members. The question then arises—why do group members typically perceive themselves (or present themselves) in this way?

Crosby (1982), for example, found that when asked about their working life, women expressed some resentment and bitterness about "women's employment situation." However, they did not generally feel discriminated against personally at work. This *personal/group discrimination discrepancy* (Taylor et al., 1990) has been shown among Canadian cultural groups such as Francophone *Québécois* (Guimond & Dubé-Simard, 1983), Anglophone *Québécois* (Taylor, Wong-Rieger, McKirnan, & Bercusson, 1982), and more recently among Haitian and Indian women immigrants to Quebec (Taylor et al., 1990). In the latter study, despite the fact that fairly high levels of personal discrimination were reported, particularly by the Haitian subjects, both groups of subjects saw greater racial and cultural discrimination directed at their group in general than at themselves personally.

A number of explanations have been put forward for this discrepancy (Crosby, 1982; Taylor et al., 1990). One is that individuals may be motivated to deny the discrimination that they have experienced, presumably because this protects them from perceived threat, shame in front of others, or lowered self-esteem (Taylor et al., 1990). Or, similarly, they may see it as less appropriate to complain about their own personal situation than about that of the group as a whole (Crosby, 1982).

A second explanation has pointed to differences in the cognitive processes of social comparison or group-identification that may occur when someone is asked about discrimination toward the self or toward the group as a whole. When a person is asked about discriminative treatment of his or her group, this directs attention toward the individual's group-based identity and may lead to comparisons of the whole group with other groups in society (a process of intergroup social comparison). For example, when asked about women's situation in general (as in Crosby's study,

1982), the obvious source of comparison is men in general. However, when asked about discrimination against the self, attention may be more focused upon personal identity, and evaluation may involve comparison of the self with other individuals within one's group (a process of intragroup social comparison). Such differences in identification and social comparison will lead to different sources of information being accessed and, therefore, to differing estimates of levels of discrimination for the self and the group as a whole.

Racial Identification as a Response to Victimization

One crucial effect of exposure to racial prejudice is heightened **racial identification**. When others exclude you from their schools, offices, and neighborhoods, assume that you possess stereotyped traits, and describe your physical characteristics in negative terms, one obvious effect is to make you, as an individual, conscious of your own membership in a specific racial group. That this is part of the experience of many visible minority group members is apparent (e.g., Asante, 1980; Williams, 1976). But what, precisely, does racial identification involve? Is it an all-or-nothing process in which individuals conclude that they belong to a particular racial group and to no other? Modern conceptions of racial identification suggest that this is not so (Hilliard, 1985). Based on her research, Sanders Thompson (1988, 1991) developed what is perhaps the most influential current model of this process, suggesting that racial identification of African-Americans involves three key aspects: physical, psychological, and sociocultural components (see Figure 5.12). Results indicated that by far the most important predictor of all three aspects of racial identification was the extent to which respondents had personal experience with racial prejudice. The greater such experience, the stronger their racial identification. In general, demographic factors such as age, income, and education were less important (although they did seem to play a role in the psychological aspect of racial identification). Not surprisingly, conflicts within one's own family related to skin colour or social class significantly predicted physical racial identification.

Racial Identification The process through which individuals (especially those belonging to minority groups) acquire identification with their own racial group. Current models of racial identification suggest that it involves physical, psychological, and sociocultural components.

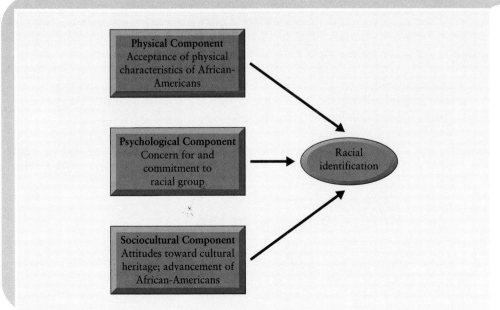

■ Racial identification: Basic components

FIGURE 5.12 According to a model proposed by Sanders Thompson (1990, 1991), racial identification involves three major components: physical, psychological, and sociocultural.

Source: Based on suggestions by Sanders Thompson, 1990, 1991.

- Theorists have distinguished between *intropunitive* responses of victims, which involve self-blame, and *extrapunitive* responses, which involve other-blame. Further, responses can be classified as responses aimed at *personal* improvement or at *group-based* improvement. In addition, responses can be regarded as normative—taking socially acceptable paths, or antinormative—using means that are unacceptable to the dominant group.

- Research has demonstrated that the victims of prejudice respond to *stereotype threat*—the threat of being stereotyped—in a variety of ways. They can perform more badly on a task, anticipate less enjoyment from interaction, or change self-presentations and affect.

- Reported levels of discrimination also vary as a function of whether victims are focusing on their group as a whole or themselves personally, with group levels reported to be higher.

- Modern theories of *racial identification* propose that such identification consists of several distinct components, including physical, psychological, and sociocultural identification.

CHALLENGING PREJUDICE: WHY IT IS NOT ALWAYS INEVITABLE

Whatever the specific origins of prejudice, there can be no doubt about the following point: Prejudice is a brutal, negative force in human society. Wherever and whenever it occurs, it is a drain on precious human resources. So reducing prejudice and countering its effects are important tasks—and especially crucial at a time when world population exceeds 5.5 billion and the potential harm stemming from irrational hatred is greater than ever before. Do any effective strategies for accomplishing these goals—for lessening the impact of prejudice—exist? Fortunately, they do; and while they cannot totally eliminate prejudice or discrimination, these strategies can make a substantial dent in the problem. Several of these tactics will now be reviewed, ranging from intervention at the group and societal level to attempts to change our individual cognitions. We begin with societal or institutional intervention in the following Canadian Research: On the Cutting Edge section.

Canadian Research: On the Cutting Edge

Putting Multiculturalism to the Test

Canada's *policy of multiculturalism* represents an ambitious attempt to combat prejudice and discrimination at the institutional level. Canada is one of the only countries in the world that has an official *multiculturalism policy*, encouraging ethnic groups to maintain their own cultural heritage while participating fully in the larger society. When introduced in 1971, the policy statement suggested that

> National unity, if it is to mean anything in the deeply personal sense must be founded in confidence in one's own individual identity; out of this can grow respect for that of others and a willingness to share ideas, attitudes and assumptions (quoted in Kalin & Berry, 1994).

This statement is expressed in social psychological terms, assuming that the promotion of multiculturalism would increase the confidence of individuals in their own cultural identity. In turn, this greater confidence would lead to increased respect for the identity of other cultural groups and a willingness to interact and communicate.

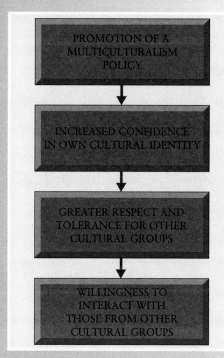

■ The multiculturalism hypothesis

FIGURE 5.13 The *multiculturalism hypothesis* suggests that promotion of a policy of multiculturalism, which encourages the maintenance of ethnic identity while participating in the larger society, will lead to increased confidence in an individual's sense of identity. From this will stem an increased respect and tolerance for other ethnic groups and, in turn, a willingness to interact and communicate with them.

Multiculturalism Hypothesis The assumption that the promotion of multiculturalism will increase the confidence of individuals in their own cultural identity, which in turn will lead to increased respect for the identity of other cultural groups and increased interaction with them.

This suggestion has been termed the "multiculturalism assumption" (Kalin & Berry, 1994) or the **multiculturalism hypothesis**—see Figure 5.13 (Lambert, Mermigis, & Taylor, 1986).

The Debate Over Multiculturalism.

Thirty years after its introduction, is Canada's multiculturalism policy fulfilling its promise? The answer to that question is still being debated. There are those who suggest that this policy merely maintains divisions between people rather than bringing unity (e.g., Bissoondath, 1995). Further, sociologist Reginald Bibby suggests that the Canadian public is losing confidence in multiculturalism and moving toward a preference for the American "melting pot" over the Canadian "mosaic" (Bibby, 1990). His findings indicate that, whereas in 1985 56 percent of Canadians preferred the "mosaic" and only 28 percent the "melting pot," in 1995 44 percent supported the "mosaic" and 40 percent the "melting pot" (Bibby, 1995).

On the other hand, social psychological research conducted by John Berry and his colleagues comes to a more positive conclusion (see Berry, 1999). Two national surveys of attitudes to multiculturalism and Canadian ethnic groups have been carried out, one in 1974 (Berry, Kalin & Taylor, 1977) and one in 1991 (Berry & Kalin, 1995). Findings in the most recent survey of over 3000 Canadians were supportive of multiculturalism, as shown in Figure 5.14. Further, support for multicultural programs and ideology had increased since the 1974 survey. Support for multiculturalism programs had increased from 69 percent in 1974, to 94 percent in 1991. Although not as large, there was also an increase in those supporting multicultural ideology: 64 percent in 1974, to 69 percent in 1991.

Testing the Multiculturalism Hypothesis.

More directly relevant to the multiculturalism hypothesis are questions about the relationship between cultural identity, tolerance for other groups, and willingness to interact or communi-

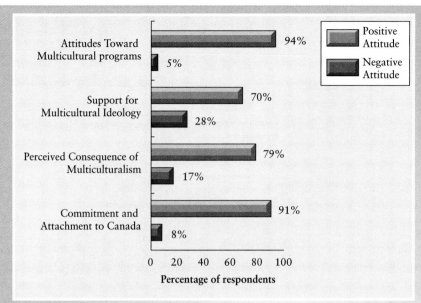

Attitudes Toward Multicultural programs — 94% Positive / 5% Negative
Support for Multicultural Ideology — 70% Positive / 28% Negative
Perceived Consequence of Multiculturalism — 79% Positive / 17% Negative
Commitment and Attachment to Canada — 91% Positive / 8% Negative

Positive Attitude
Negative Attitude

0 20 40 60 80 100
Percentage of respondents

■ Social psychological research finds support for multiculturalism in Canada

FIGURE 5.14 A 1991 national survey found that most Canadians were supportive of multicultural programs and multicultural ideology, as well as seeing multiculturalism as having positive consequences.

Source: Based on Berry & Kalin, 1995.

cate. While it is not possible to establish a causal relationship between these variables from this survey, it can provide correlational support. In terms of cultural identity, the 1991 survey (Kalin & Berry, 1995), found that most respondents (64 percent) felt a strong sense of identity as "Canadian." Compared to the 1974 survey, the 1991 results showed an increase in self-identity as "Canadian" and a decrease in ethnic identity (e.g., Italian-Canadian or Italian) or provincial identity (e.g., *Québécois* or Manitoban). Further, those with a Canadian or an ethnic identity tended to be somewhat more tolerant of other cultural groups than were those with a provincial identity. Nonetheless, ratings of tolerance were in the moderately high range for all groups (means ranged from 5.5 to 5.1 on a 7-point scale). Tolerance was also positively correlated with levels of comfort when interacting with those from other groups (Berry & Kalin, 1995). That is, those who scored higher on measures of tolerance also reported feeling more "comfortable being around" people from other ethnic groups. Once again, comfort ratings were generally in the moderately high range for all groups (means ranged from 5.3 to almost 5.5 on a 7-point scale). These results are generally supportive of the multiculturalism hypothesis.

Areas of Concern in Intergroup Relations.
While the bulk of findings from this survey were encouraging, it also revealed some areas of con-

cern for Canadian intergroup relations. First, all groups, with the exception of South Asians, showed some ingroup favouritism: They had more positive attitudes towards their own group than other groups and were most comfortable interacting with the ingroup. Second, not all groups were equally accepted. There was generally a higher level of tolerance and comfort with those of European origin (British, French and Italian ethnic groups were rated highest) than with those of non-European origin (Arabs, Muslims, Indo-Pakistanis, and Sikhs were given lowest ratings). Finally, on a number of measures, those of French origin (especially in Quebec) showed differences from the rest of the sample. They displayed greatest preference for the ingroup, least self-identity as Canadian (32 percent), and greatest provincial identity (i.e., *Québécois*, 47 percent). In addition, those of French origin in Quebec had the lowest ratings of commitment and attachment to Canada. Results in these three areas indicate potential, and ongoing problems for intergroup relations in Canada.

In total, the results of the 1991 survey suggest considerable support not only for Canada's policy of multiculturalism, but also for the multiculturalism hypothesis itself. However, we should emphasize that the *causal* role of multiculturalism in combatting prejudice cannot be definitively established by such survey results. These and other results (see Berry & Kalin, 1994) generally demonstrate *corre-*

lational relationships of a high or moderate level, in the direction predicted by the multiculturalism hypothesis. However, not all such results are supportive (e.g., Lambert, Mermigis, & Taylor, 1986). In addition, the multiculturalism policy is only *one* effort in the complex process of combatting prejudice and discrimination.

In 1998 John Berry won the Donald O. Hebb Award for Distinguished Contribution to Psychology as a Science. In his address when receiving this award, he emphasized that while public policy can have an impact on the psychological processes of prejudice and intercultural relations, this influence can be reciprocal. That is, psychological research, such as the work described above, can contribute to public policy-making by increasing our understanding of the complex psychological mechanisms that inform ethnic relations in a multicultural society (Berry, 1999).

Changing Relations Between Groups

Direct Intergroup Contact

We often have little contact with other cultural groups or minorities, particularly if we hold strong prejudices against them. For example, a study carried out in Toronto found that only 18 percent of those who described themselves as "very prejudiced" had had close contact with minority groups, whereas over 56 percent of those who were "very tolerant" had had such close contact (Henry, 1978). This state of affairs raises an intriguing question: Can prejudice be reduced by somehow increasing the degree of contact between different groups? The idea that it can is known as the **contact hypothesis**, and there are several good reasons for predicting that such a strategy might prove effective (Pettigrew, 1981). First, increased contact between persons from different groups can lead to growing recognition of similarities between them. As we will see in Chapter 6, perceived similarity can generate enhanced mutual attraction. Second, while stereotypes are resistant to change, they can be altered when sufficient information inconsistent with them is encountered or when individuals meet a sufficient number of "exceptions" to their stereotypes (Kunda & Oleson, 1995). Third, increased contact may help to counter the illusion of outgroup homogeneity described earlier. For these reasons it seems possible that direct intergroup contact may be one effective means of combating prejudice. Is it?

A large number of studies, both in the laboratory and in the field, have investigated the contact hypothesis (Cook, 1985; Kalin & Berry, 1982; Stephan, 1985). This accumulated evidence has confirmed that intergroup contact can reduce prejudice, but only under certain conditions.

First, the groups interacting must be roughly equal in social, economic, or task-related status. If they differ sharply in such respects, communication may be difficult and prejudice can actually be increased by contact. Second, the contact situation must involve cooperation and interdependence so that the groups work toward shared goals (as in the famous Robber's Cave experiment described earlier in the chapter). Third, contact between the groups must be informal so that they can get to know one another as individuals. Fourth, contact must occur in a setting in which existing norms favour group equality. Fifth, the groups must interact in ways that permit disconfirmation of negative stereotyped beliefs about one another. And sixth, the persons involved must view one another as typical of their respective groups; only then will they generalize their pleasant contacts to other persons or situations (Wilder, 1984).

When contact between initially hostile groups occurs under these conditions, prejudice between them does seem to decrease (Cook, 1985; Riordan, 1978). Such effects have been observed in the United States, where increased contact between

Contact Hypothesis
The view that increased contact between members of various social groups can be effective in reducing prejudice between them. Such efforts seem to succeed only when contact takes place under specific, favourable conditions.

African-Americans and whites has been found to reduce prejudice between them (Aronson, Bridgeman, & Geffner, 1978), and in many other nations as well. For example, increased school contact between Jews of Middle Eastern origin and Jews of European or American origin tends to reduce ingroup bias among Israeli soldiers (Schwarzwald, Amir, & Crain, 1992).

On the basis of these findings, it seems reasonable to suggest that, when used with care, direct group contact can be an effective tool for combating cross-group hostility and prejudice. When people get to know one another, it seems, many of the anxieties, stereotypes, and false perceptions that have previously kept them apart seem to melt in the warmth of new friendships.

Recently, however, a modified version of the contact hypothesis, known as the *extended contact hypothesis*, has helped to reverse these gloomy conclusions.

The **extended contact hypothesis** suggests that direct contact between persons from different groups is not essential for reducing prejudice between them. In fact, such beneficial effects can be produced if the persons in question merely know that persons in their own group have formed close friendship with persons from the other group (e.g., Pettigrew, 1997; Wright et al., 1997). How can knowledge of such cross-group friendship help to reduce prejudice? In several different ways. For instance, knowledge of such friendship can indicate that contact with outgroup members is acceptable—that the norms of one's own group are not so anti-outgroup as one might initially have believed. Similarly, knowing that members of one's own group enjoy close friendships with members of an outgroup can help to reduce anxiety about interacting with them: if someone we know enjoys such contact, why shouldn't we? Third, the existence of such cross-group friendships suggests that members of an outgroup don't necessarily dislike members of our own ingroup. Finally, such friendships can indirectly generate increased empathy and understanding between groups; in other words, we don't necessarily have to experience personal contact with persons from an outgroup to feel more positively toward them—learning that members of our own ingroup have had such experiences can be sufficient.

A growing body of research evidence provides support for the accuracy of this reasoning, and for the extended contact hypothesis. For instance, in one investigation of this hypothesis (Pettigrew, 1997), almost 4000 people living in several European countries completed a questionnaire that measured the extent to which these people had friendships with, and were prejudiced towards, others outside their own cultural group. Results offered striking support for the benefits of intergroup friendships. The greater the number of cross-group friendships participants reported, the lower their prejudice toward various outgroups and the more favourable their beliefs about immigration into their country. In addition, the greater their experience with intergroup friendships, the more positive their feelings toward many other groups—including ones with which they had experienced little or no contact. This latter finding is very important, for it suggests that reductions in prejudice produced by friendships with persons from one outgroup may generalize to other outgroups as well, providing some support for the extended contact hypothesis.

Additional support for the value of intergroup friendships is provided by laboratory as well as survey research. For example, in one ingenious study, Wright and his colleagues (1997) arranged for students to participate in a situation similar in certain respects to the Robber's Cave experiment. Briefly, the researchers divided the students into teams which went through consecutive periods of team-building and competition. After the first round of competition two team members from each team engaged in an exercise designed to create strong feelings of friendship and liking toward opposing team members.

Extended Contact Hypothesis A view suggesting that simply knowing that members of one's own group have formed close friendships with members of an outgroup can reduce prejudice against this group.

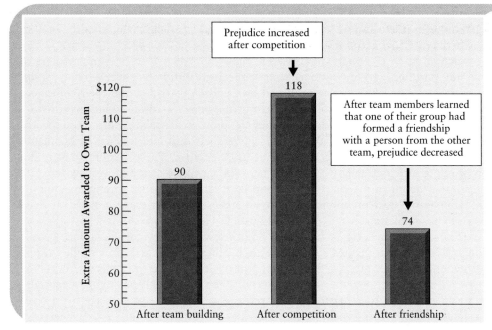

FIGURE 5.15 When members of opposing teams learned that a person on their own team had formed a friendship with a person from the other team, their prejudice toward the opposing group decreased. For example, as shown here, they showed less tendency to take more than their fair share of a financial prize.

Source: Based on data from Wright et al., 1997.

During the experiment (which lasted all day), participants completed measures of their reactions to the other team on several occasions—after the initial team-building phase, after the first set of competitions, and again after the two team members who formed a friendship returned to the team. It was predicted that the comments these persons made to their teammates about their new intergroup friendship would reduce prejudice toward the opposing team, and this is what happened (see Figure 5.15). Similar results occurred for ratings of the quality of the interactions between the groups and for ratings of the other team with respect to several traits (e.g., friendliness, warmth).

In sum, it appears that contact between persons belonging to different groups can be a highly effective means for reducing prejudice between them, especially if these contacts develop into friendships. Moreover, the beneficial effects of such friendships can readily spread to other persons who have not themselves experienced such contacts: simply knowing about them can be enough. So in this respect, at least, English essayist Joseph Addison appears to have been correct when he stated, more than two centuries ago (1794) that "The greatest sweetener of human life is friendship."

Recategorization: Redrawing the Group Boundaries

Normally, the sports teams of large cities in Canada are great rivals. Think of the historical opposition between the Toronto Maple Leafs and Montreal Canadiens. Fans of each team jeer at opponents and take pleasure in their defeat by another team. It is not uncommon for such rivalries to lead to fights between supporters. Given the long-term histories of antagonism between city teams, it is astonishing to see those same antagonists suddenly united in cheering for the same team—if one of them is in the finals against an American team. When the Vancouver Canucks were in the Stanley Cup finals against the New York Rangers, all of Canada was cheering them on. When the Toronto Blue Jays won the World Series, young baseball fans in Vancouver paraded up and down Robson Street shouting "We're number one!"

What has happened? In terms of the principles discussed in this chapter, the fans have shifted the location of the boundary between "us" and "them." When the normal season is continuing, the boundary is between cities. However, when a single Canadian team is left in the finals competing with an American team, then the boundary is between Canada and the United States.

Such shifts in the boundary between "us" and "them" are a common part of social life. Can this kind of boundary shift or **recategorization** be used to reduce prejudice in other contexts? A theory proposed by Gaertner, Dovidio, and their colleagues (1989, 1993) suggests that it can. This theory, known as the **common ingroup identity model,** suggests that when individuals belonging to different social groups come to view themselves as members of a *single social entity,* their attitudes toward each other—toward former outgroup members—become more positive. These favourable attitudes then promote increased positive contacts between members of the previously separate groups, and this in turn reduces intergroup bias still further. In short, weakening or eliminating initial us-them boundaries starts a process that carries the persons involved toward major reductions in prejudice and hostility (see Figure 5.16).

How can this process be launched? In other words, how can we induce people belonging to different groups to perceive each other as members of a single group? Gaertner and his colleagues (1990) suggest that one crucial factor in this process is the experience of working together cooperatively. When individuals belonging to initially distinct groups work together toward shared goals, they come to perceive themselves as a single social entity. Then feelings of bias or hostility toward the former outgroup—toward "them"—seem to fade away, taking prejudice with them. Such effects have been demonstrated in several labouratory studies (e.g., Brewer et al., 1987; Gaertner et al., 1989, 1990). In addition, they have been observed in a field study carried out by Gaertner, Dovidio, and their associates (1993).

This investigation was conducted in a multicultural high school in the United States. Students in the school came from many different backgrounds— African-American, Chinese, Hispanic, Japanese, Korean, Vietnamese, and Caucasian. More than 1300 students completed a survey designed to measure their perceptions of factors that had been shown in previous research to influence the effects of increased intergroup contact (e.g., equal status, cooperative interdependence, norms supportive of friendly intergroup contact). Other items on the survey measured students' perceptions of the extent to which the student body at the school was a single group, consisted of distinct groups, or was composed of separate individuals. Finally, students also completed items designed to measure their feelings toward both their ingroup and various outgroups.

Recategorization
Shifts in the boundary between an individual's ingroup ("us") and some outgroup ("them"), causing persons formerly viewed as outgroup members now to be viewed as belonging to the ingroup.

Common Ingroup Identity Model A theory suggesting that to the extent individuals in different groups view themselves as members of a single social entity, positive contacts between groups will increase and intergroup bias will be reduced.

■ The common ingroup identity model

FIGURE 5.16 The common ingroup identity model suggests that when individuals belonging to different groups come to perceive themselves as members of a single group, their attitudes toward each other become more positive. This increases contact between members of the groups, which reduces intergroup bias still further.

Source: Based on suggestions by Gaertner, Dovidio, et al., 1990, 1993.

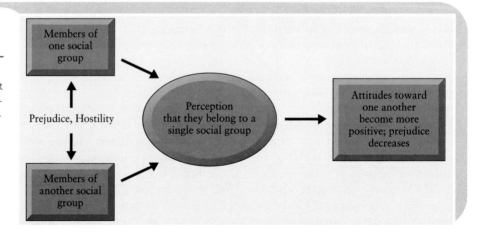

Results offered strong support for the common ingroup identity model. First, as predicted, perceptions of cooperative interdependence between students from different groups were positively related to the students' belief that the student body was a single group. In other words, the more students reported experiencing cooperative interactions with persons from other groups, the weaker the us-versus-them boundaries they reported. Similarly, the greater the extent to which the students felt as though they belonged to a single group, the more positive their feelings toward outgroup members.

When combined with the results of laboratory studies, these findings suggest that efforts to induce persons belonging to different groups to engage in *recategorization*—specifically, shifting the boundary between "us" and "them" so as to include persons previously excluded—can be an important step toward the reduction of many forms of prejudice. We should hasten to add, however, that broadening the "us" category to include groups that were previously excluded does not eliminate the human tendency to enhance our own self-identity by cognitively boosting our own group while belittling others (Tajfel, 1982). This seems to be a basic tendency that cannot be entirely eliminated. However, recategorization can certainly reduce prejudice in some contexts, and any reduction in such blanket negative reactions is a definite plus in ongoing social life.

KEY POINTS

- Social psychologists believe that prejudice is not inevitable; it can be reduced by several techniques.
- Canada's major institutional intervention is its policy of multiculturalism. The *multiculturalism hypothesis*, which assumes that confidence in cultural identification will lead to improved relations with other ethnic groups, has received some support.
- As the *contact hypothesis* suggests, direct intergroup contact also seems to be helpful, provided that the contact occurs under appropriate conditions. Recent research on the *extended contact hypothesis* suggests that improvements can be shown even when the contact is more indirect.
- Another useful technique, *recategorization*, involves somehow inducing individuals to shift the boundary between "us" and "them" so that former outgroup members are included in the ingroup, providing a *common ingroup identity*.

Breaking the Cycle of Prejudice: On Learning Not to Hate

Few persons would suggest that children are born with prejudices firmly in place. Rather, most would contend that bigots are made, not born. Social psychologists share this view: they believe that children acquire prejudice from their parents, other adults, their peers, and—as we noted earlier—the mass media. Given this fact, one useful technique for reducing prejudice follows logically: somehow, we must discourage parents and other adults from training children in bigotry.

Having stated this principle, we must now admit that putting it into practice is far from simple. How can we induce parents who are themselves highly prejudiced to encourage unbiased views among their children (see Figure 5.17)? One possibility involves calling parents' attention to their own prejudiced views. Few persons are willing to describe themselves as prejudiced; instead, they view their own negative attitudes

■ Breaking the cycle of hate

FIGURE 5.17 Three crouching teenage skinheads salute at a rally, with one of them holding a knife. Note the swastika on the hanging flag. Do highly prejudiced parents produce the majority of these belligerent kids? Can such parents be encouraged to raise children who do not share their bigotry? In this case it may be a difficult task, but progress can be made if the parents realize that holding prejudiced views can adversely affect their children's future prospects in a society that is becoming more culturally and ethnically diverse.

toward various groups as entirely justified. A key initial step, therefore, would be to convince parents that the problem exists. Once people come face to face with their own prejudices, many do seem willing to modify their words and behaviour so as to encourage lower levels of prejudice among their children. True, some extreme fanatics actually want to turn their children into hate-filled copies of themselves. Most people, however, recognize that we live in a world of increasing diversity and that this environment calls for a higher degree of tolerance than ever before.

Another argument that can be used to shift parents in the direction of teaching their children tolerance rather than prejudice lies in the fact that prejudice harms not only those who are its victims but those who hold such views as well (Dovidio & Gaertner, 1993; Jussim, 1991). Persons who are prejudiced, it appears, live in a world filled with needless fears, anxieties, and anger. They fear attack from presumably dangerous social groups; they worry about the health risks stemming from contact with such groups; and they experience anger and emotional turmoil over what they view as unjustified incursions by these groups into their neighborhoods, schools, or offices. In other words, their enjoyment of everyday activities and life itself is reduced by their own prejudice (Harris et al., 1992). Of course, offsetting such costs is the boost in self-esteem prejudiced persons sometimes feel when they derogate or scapegoat outgroup members (see our earlier discussion of this topic; Branscombe & Wann, 1994; Fein & Spenser, 1997). Overall, though, it is clear that persons holding intense racial and ethnic prejudices suffer many harmful effects from these views. Most parents want to do everything in their power to further their children's well-being, so calling these costs to parents' attention may help discourage them from transmitting prejudiced views to their offspring.

Cognitive Interventions: When Stereotypes Become Less Compelling

It is generally assumed that the effects of stereotyping on social relations are negative and indeed, much research has supported this view. However, Don Taylor at McGill University has suggested that, in the context of intergroup relations, stereotyping is not *always* destructive (1981; Taylor & Moghaddam, 1987). His *intergroup stereotyping model* explores both negative and positive forms of stereotyping and suggests that when groups are not in conflict, intergroup stereotyping can have a constructive effect on intergroup relations. How can this occur? First, Taylor points out that the content of stereotypes is not necessarily negative. For example, groups with high status are often viewed positively by other groups in society (e.g., Berry, Kalin, & Taylor, 1977; Berry & Kalin, 1995; Kalin & Berry, 1996). Frequently, groups will also characterize themselves positively. Kirby and Gardner (1973), for instance, found that English-Canadians stereotyped themselves as "clean, intelligent, good, and modern." Second, he suggests that such positive stereotypes help to create a distinct identity for a group. Building on notions of social identity theory, Taylor's model then suggests that if groups wish to maintain a distinctive and positive social identity, they will welcome stereotyping to the extext that it has two qualities: (1) it is perceived as accurate by the group itself; and (2) it is positively evaluated by others. Thus, in the context of intergroup relations we have to consider the positivity and accuracy of each group's stereotypes of other groups and of themselves.

The implications of this model for intergroup relations in Canada are that stereotyping need not be a destructive force. When groups are in conflict, then this is reflected in their negative stereotyping of each other. However, if groups understand and respect each other, stereotyping can, at times, provide the positive and distinctive identity for which groups strive (Tajfel, 1982).

Throughout this chapter, we have noted that stereotypes play an important role in prejudice. The tendency to think about others in terms of their membership in various groups or categories (known as *category-driven processing*) appears to be a key factor in the occurrence and persistence of several forms of prejudice. If this is so, then interventions designed to reduce the impact of stereotypes may prove highly effective in reducing prejudice and discrimination. How can this goal be attained? Several techniques seem to be effective.

First, the impact of stereotypes can be reduced if individuals are encouraged to think carefully about others—to pay attention to their unique characteristics rather than to their membership in various groups. Research findings indicate that such *attribute-driven processing* can be encouraged even by such simple procedures as informing individuals that their own outcomes or rewards in a situation will be affected by another's performance, or telling them that it is very important to be accurate in forming an impression of another person. Under these conditions, individuals are motivated to be accurate, and this reduces their tendency to rely on stereotypes (Neuberg, 1989).

Second, and more surprising, the impact of stereotypes can sometimes be reduced by techniques based on the principle of attribution (see Chapter 2; Mackie et al., 1992). How do such procedures work? Several are based on the fact that often we make inferences about others on the basis of their outcomes, while ignoring factors that might have produced these outcomes (Allison, Worth, & King, 1990).

Now let's apply this to prejudice, and to the task of countering stereotypes. Suppose you learned that a woman was promoted to a high-level managerial job in a large company. The outcome is clear: she was promoted. Would this outcome influence your estimations of her talent or motivation? Again, the chances are good that it would—and crucially, that this would be the case *even if you learned that her company has a strong affirmative action program and actively seeks to promote women and minorities*. In cases such as this, our tendency to base our inferences about others on their outcomes can lead us to conclusions that are *counterstereotypic* in nature; and the result may be a weakening of the stereotypes involved. Effects of this type have been reported in several different studies (e.g., Mackie et al., 1992), and they suggest a complex, but effective, means of weakening various stereotypes.

This technique, of course, has important implications for efforts to counter the effects of prejudice through *affirmative action programs*. These programs are designed to improve the outcomes of various disadvantaged groups by increasing the chances that they will obtain such benefits as jobs and promotions. To the extent that such outcomes improve, perceptions of the characteristics of these groups, too, may improve although, as we noted earlier, this is not always the case.

KEY POINTS

- One way to reduce prejudice is to change children's early experiences by encouraging parents and others to transmit to them accepting rather than prejudiced attitudes.
- Cognitive interventions, such as inducing individuals to focus on others' specific traits and outcomes rather than on their group membership helps reduce the impact of stereotyping.

Ideas to Take with You

Techniques for Reducing Prejudice
Prejudice is an all-too-common part of social life, but most social psychologists believe that it can be reduced—it is not inevitable. Here are some techniques that seem to work.

Teaching Children Acceptance Instead of Bigotry.
If children are taught from an early age to respect all groups—including ones very different from their own—prejudice can be nipped in the bud, so to speak.

Increased Intergroup Contact—or Merely Knowledge That it Occurs.
Recent findings indicate that if people merely know that friendly contacts occur between members of their own group and members of various outgroups, their prejudice toward these groups can be sharply reduced.

Recategorization.
Once individuals mentally include people they once excluded from their ingroup within it, prejudice toward them may disappear. Reminding people that they are part of larger groups—for instance, that they are all Americans, Canadians, or even human beings—can help accomplish this kind of recategorization.

Undermining Stereotypes.
Stereotypes suggest that all persons belonging to specific social groups are alike—that they share the same characteristics. Such beliefs can be weakened if people are encouraged to think about others as individuals, not simply as members of social groups. Also, some evidence suggests that affirmative action programs may actually encourage positive perceptions of the persons who benefit from them, and so serve to counter prejudice by undermining stereotypes.

Summary and Review of Key Points

Prejudice and Discrimination:
Their Nature and Origins

● *Prejudice* is an attitude (usually negative) toward members of some social group based solely on their membership in that group.

Prejudice, like other attitudes, influences our processing of social information. In addition, prejudice influences our beliefs about persons belonging to various groups, and our feelings about them.

Discrimination involves negative actions, based on prejudice, toward members of various social groups.

While *blatant* discrimination has clearly decreased in Western societies, more subtle forms such as *modern racism*, *covert institutional racism* and *neosexism* persist.

There have been improvements for women in the workplace with increases in their qualification, pay, and promotion to higher status positions.

Nonetheless, subtle barriers, often termed the *glass ceiling*, are still evident in the continuing wage gap and the few women in upper management.

The Origins of Prejudice:
Contrasting Perspectives

● Prejudice stems from several different sources. *Realistic conflict theory* suggests that one of these is direct intergroup conflict—situations in which social groups compete for the same scarce resources.

Social identity theory suggests that the desire of social groups for a positive and distinctive identity can provide the impetus for social categorization, and that prejudice stems directly from our strong tendencies to divide the social world into two camps, "us" and "them"—the *us-versus-them effect*.

Recent findings indicate that perceived similarity to an outgroup can reduce prejudice toward its members unless the group is viewed as a threat.

The social learning perspective suggests that *early experience* can lead to prejudice when children are trained to hate various groups.

Prejudice sometimes stems from basic aspects of social cognition—the ways in which we process social information.

Stereotypes are cognitive frameworks suggesting that all persons belonging to a social group show similar characteristics. Stereotypes strongly influence social thought. For instance, when activated, they lead us to draw *tacit inferences* about others that then make information which is inconsistent with stereotypes seem to be consistent with them.

Recent findings indicate that stereotypes are closely linked to prejudice; for example, highly prejudiced persons respond more quickly to stereotype-related words than less prejudiced persons.

Other cognitive sources of prejudice include *illusory correlations*—overestimations of the strength of relationships between social categories and negative behaviours, and the *illusion of outgroup homogeneity*—the tendency to perceive outgroups as more homogeneous than our own ingroup.

Individuals who have personalities high in *right-wing authoritarianism* show a propensity towards prejudice against minority groups in society.

Responses of the Victims of Prejudice

● Theorists have distinguished between *intropunitive* responses of victims, which involve self-blame, and *extrapunitive* responses, which involve other-blame. Further, responses can be classified as responses aimed at *personal* improvement or at *group-based* improvement. In addition, responses can be regarded as normative—taking socially acceptable paths, or antinormative—using means that are unacceptable to the dominant group.

Research has demonstrated that the victims of prejudice respond to stereotype threat—the threat of being stereotyped—in a variety of ways. They can perform more badly on a task, anticipate less enjoyment from interaction, or change self-presentations and affect.

Reported levels of discrimination also vary as a function of whether victims are focusing on their group as a whole or themselves personally, with group levels reported to be higher.

Modern theories of racial identification propose that such identification consists of several distinct components, including physical, psychological, and sociocultural identification.

Challenging Prejudice: Why it is Not Always Inevitable

● Social psychologists believe that prejudice is not inevitable; it can be reduced by several techniques.

Canada's major institutional intervention is its policy of multiculturalism. The *multiculturalism hypothesis*, which assumes that confidence in cultural identification will lead to improved relations with other ethnic groups, has received some support.

As the *contact hypothesis* suggests, direct intergroup contact also seems to be helpful, provided that the contact occurs under appropriate conditions. Recent research on the *extended contact hypothesis* suggests that improvements can be shown even when the contact is more indirect.

Another useful technique, *recategorization*, involves somehow inducing individuals to shift the boundary between "us" and "them" so that former outgroup members are included in the ingroup, providing a *common ingroup identity*.

One way to reduce prejudice is to change children's early experiences by encouraging parents and others to transmit to them accepting rather than prejudiced attitudes.

Cognitive interventions, such as inducing individuals to focus on others' specific traits and outcomes rather than on their group membership helps reduce the impact of stereotyping.

For More Information

Zanna, M. P., & Olson, J. M. (1994). *The psychology of prejudice: The Ontario symposium on personality and social psychology* (Vol. 7). Mahwah, NJ: Erlbaum.

Thought-provoking chapters by Canadian experts in the fields of stereotypes, intergroup conflict, and attitudes. Together, the authors present a very comprehensive view of what social psychologists have discovered about the origins and effects of prejudice.

Henry, F., Tator, C., Mattis, W., & Rees, T. (1995). *The colour of democracy: Racism in Canadian society*. Toronto: Harcourt Brace.

An assessment of racism in Canada today from a long-time researcher in the field of social anthropology. This book examines racism in each of Canada's major institutions and is full of striking examples and research.

Taylor, D. M., & Moghaddam, F. (1990). Theories of intergroup relations: International social psychological perspectives. New York: Praeger.

An critical examination of social psychological theories of intergroup relations. This book provides detailed descriptions of realistic conflict theory and social identity theory, as well as additional related theories.

Oskamp, S., & Costanzo, M. (Eds.). (1993). *Gender issues in contemporary society*. Newbury Park, CA: Sage.

Leading experts on all aspects of gender contribute chapters to this book. The discussions of gender stereotyping and discrimination are closely related to topics covered in this chapter.

Weblinks

www.cpa.ca/cjbsnew/1996/ful_kalin2.html
"Interethnic Attitudes in Canada: Ethnocentrism, Consensual Hierarchy and Reciprocity" by Kalin, Berry, Queen's University

www.ceifo.su.se/en/Proj/icsey.htm
International Comparative Studies of Ethnocultural Youth Page from the Centre for Migration and Ethnic Relations, Stockholm, Sweden

www.Trinity.Edu/~mkearl/race.html
Race and Ethnicity Web resources

www.acusd.edu/ethics/race.html
Literature and Web resources on race, ethnicity, and multiculturalism

php.indiana.edu/~heise/Download.html
Analyzing Social Interaction

Relationships:
From Attraction to Parting

SPECIAL SECTIONS

FIGURE 6.1 In interpersonal interactions, we like very much to receive positive evaluations of any kind and dislike very much receiving negative evaluations of any kind. Such evaluations are are more powerful determinants of attraction than similarity or anything else. Except in rare circumstances, even "something helpful" is likely to be resented if it implies criticism.

"Do you mind if I say something helpful about your personality?"

I t is a testament to our essentially *social* nature that relationships provide us with some of the most wonderful experiences of our lives, as well as some of the most painful. In all societies throughout history relationships have typically been seen as crucial for an individual—including family and close friends, as well as the pivotal experience of falling in love. And despite changes in values and attitudes about relationships most people, whatever their culture, expect to go through the processes of making friends, meeting a mate, establishing long term relationships and perhaps becoming parents. However, we are all aware, after exposure to films and novels as well as to real-life experiences, that this isn't always easy—often families feud, friendships fade, and love can turn to hate—sometimes "love hurts." Still, despite negative examples, other people are important to us and we tend to maintain our hopes about what relationships can and should be.

Levinger (1980) has described relationships as passing through five possible stages: (1) *initial attraction*; (2) *building a relationship*; (3) *continuation*; and—for some—(4) *deterioration*; and (5) *ending*. This chapter will follow this outline, beginning with the initial attraction and building stages of the relationship. The majority of the research on relationships, until recent years, has concentrated on these first two stages, under the heading of **interpersonal attraction**. This area is concerned with the initial steps involved in establishing relationships.

We will first describe the initial factors involved in becoming acquainted. This process is often only indirectly related to the personality characteristics of the people involved. Rather, chance and external factors seem more likely to play a role at the ini-

Interpersonal Attraction The degree to which we like other individuals. Interpersonal attraction varies along a dimension ranging from strong liking on one extreme to strong dislike on the other.

tial stage of relationships: such as close *physical proximity* and *observable characteristics* of the other person (physical attractiveness, skin colour, height, clothing, and so forth). Internal processes also contribute, such as cognitive processes that occur while we are *forming an impression* of someone else, the emotions or *affect* we feel, and our own *need for affiliation*.

Once interaction begins, interpersonal attraction is strongly determined by the extent to which the two people discover that they are *similar* in various attitudes, beliefs, values, and interests. That attraction can become stronger if liking is mutual. This is the power of *reciprocity*: we tend to like those who provide us with positive evaluations (see Figure 6.1).

If relationships are to progress to the *continuation* stage, then *love* often provides the emotional underpinning in the long term. Research has tended to focus on romantic or *passionate love* but we will also consider the many different forms that love can take.

Contrary to the impression from fairy tales—remember the line "and they all lived happily ever after"—maintenance of long-term intimate relationships is not easy. As the final two stages of relationship in the Levinger model (1980) suggest, *deterioration* and *ending* can occur. This is not to suggest that relationships inevitably reach this point. However, few relationships are entirely trouble-free, and it is often our response to problems that determines whether the relationship continues or ends. Therefore, we'll also consider troubled relationships, how problems arise and the effects of dissolution.

INTERPERSONAL ATTRACTION: BECOMING ACQUAINTED

There are over 30 million people in Canada today, and several thousand of them could conceivably become your friends. That is exceedingly unlikely to happen, however; any one of us is likely to become aware of, interact with, and get to know only a tiny percentage of these individuals. Of those in this relatively small subgroup, only a few will become acquaintances, fewer still will become friends, while most will remain strangers. What determines awareness, interaction, and differential attraction? Let's begin with our physical surroundings. Seemingly unimportant environmental details constitute an important and often overlooked initial determinant of those we are likely to meet. Simply stated, two people tend to become acquainted if they are brought into regular contact. Such contact is primarily based on physical **proximity** (or closeness), and proximity is most often a function of the location and design of such ordinary aspects of the environment as dormitory rooms and hallways, classroom seats, sidewalks, and our workplaces.

Proximity In attraction research, the closeness between two individuals' residences, classroom seats, work areas, and so on. The closer the physical distance, the greater the probability of the individuals' coming into regular contact and thus experiencing repeated exposure.

Physical Proximity

Friendships often begin because of a series of unplanned encounters that are controlled by the physical details of the immediate environment. On the basis of these casual, accidental contacts, each person begins to recognize the other. At this point it is common for people to exchange greetings when they see one another and to exchange remarks about the weather or whatever. This positive response to a familiar face can be observed even among infants. They are, for example, more likely to smile when exposed to a photograph of someone they have seen before than in response to a stranger's picture (Brooks-Gunn & Lewis, 1981).

The first empirical data suggesting a *proximity effect* were provided by sociological studies in the 1930s, which demonstrated that prior to marriage most couples had lived within the same neighborhood (Bossard, 1932; Davie & Reeves, 1939). Later studies in student residences, where individuals or couples had been randomly assigned to units, showed similar effects of proximity. Most friendships occurred among those who were on the same or adjacent floors in dormitories, or within seven metres of each other in apartments (e.g., Evans & Wilson, 1949; Festinger, Schachter, & Back, 1950).

Classroom investigations permit more precise study of such effects, because seats can be assigned and the amount of contact in this setting is limited to specific days and times. Once again, classroom friendships are clearly determined by where each person is seated. Those sitting side by side are most likely to become acquainted. When students are seated alphabetically, friendships form between those whose last names begin with the same or a nearby letter (Segal, 1974). Among other implications, those given a corner seat or a seat on the end of a row make fewer friends (Maisonneuve, Palmade, & Fourment, 1952). So, the total number of friends you make in a class depends in part on where you sit. If you have someone sitting on your right and someone on your left, you are likely to make two friends, whereas a seat on the end of a row yields the likelihood of only one new friend (Byrne & Buehler, 1955). Further, if the instructor changes seat assignments once or twice during the semester, each student becomes acquainted with additional classmates (Byrne, 1961). It also follows that those who want to maintain privacy can select a seat accordingly. The back of the room as far from others as possible is most likely to deter acquaintances being formed (Pedersen, 1994).

Why Does Proximity Lead To Attraction?

To some extent, we are affected by proximity because we tend to avoid strangers unless we are forced to come in contact because of where we live, where we are seated in a classroom, and so forth. But there is another, more basic, reason. As Zajonc (1968) and his colleagues have reported, **repeated exposure** to a new stimulus (frequent contact with that stimulus) leads to a more and more positive evaluation of the stimulus—as long as the initial reaction is not an extremely negative one. Whether the stimulus is a drawing, a word in an unknown foreign language, a new product being advertised, a political candidate, or a stranger, the greater the exposure, the more positive the response (Moreland & Zajonc, 1982). Something familiar is preferable to something new and strange. As an even less obvious example, faculty and staff on a college campus not only correctly identify but prefer buildings close to the one in which they work, compared to more distant buildings (Johnson & Byrne, 1996). Apparently, the more often one sees a building, the better one likes that building. The general idea is that we respond with at least mild discomfort to anything or anyone new. With repeated exposure we become desensitized, anxiety decreases, and that which was new becomes *familiar*.

In a test of how repeated exposure operates in a college classroom, Moreland and Beach (1992) found that as the number of exposures to a fellow student increases, the greater the attraction toward that person. At the end of a semester, these researchers asked students in a large college course to evaluate four different female classmates (actually, experimental assistants). One of these women never attended the class, one attended 4 times, one 10 times, and one 15 times. To control for other variables that might influence attraction, the experimenters selected assistants who were similar in appearance, and they instructed the assistants not to interact with any of the actual students, in or out of class. As shown in Figure 6.2, attraction toward these strangers increased as the number of classroom exposures increased; thus, the effect of repeated exposure was clearly evident.

Repeated Exposure
Frequent contact with a stimulus. According to Zajonc's theory of repeated exposure, as the number of contacts with any neutral or mildly positive stimulus increases, the evaluation of that stimulus becomes increasingly positive.

■ Classroom contacts and attraction

FIGURE 6.2 When female experimental assistants pretended to be students and sat quietly in a large college classroom without interacting with the professor or with fellow students, the attraction of the class members toward each assistant increased as the number of days of her class attendance increased. Attraction was least toward the assistant who never attended the class and greatest toward the individual who attended the class 15 times.

Source: Based on data from Moreland & Beach, 1992.

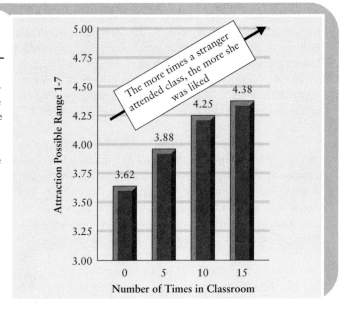

Note that proximity is not 100 percent effective in fostering attraction. Repeated exposure to a stranger who behaves in an unpleasant fashion leads to more and more dislike (Swap, 1977). Even a stranger who is not unpleasant can be evaluated negatively if proximity involves interference with your need for **privacy**: your need to limit others' knowledge of your personal life (Larson & Bell, 1988). Sometimes you prefer to be by yourself rather than with another person—no matter who that person is. At such times, too much proximity can be aversive.

Physical proximity may have brought us close to a stranger and increased the odds that we might form a relationship, but our initial response to others is also strongly influenced by their *observable characteristics:* such as race, sex, age, height, physique, accent, clothing, and so forth. Among the most pervasive of these characteristics is physical attractiveness.

> **Privacy** The need to limit how much other people know about one's past, present, or future activities.

KEY POINTS

- Relationships can be seen as passing through five possible stages: (1) *initial attraction*, (2) *building a relationship*, (3) *continuation*, (4) *deterioration* and (5) *ending*.

- The term *interpersonal attraction* refers to the attitudes we form about other people, expressed along a dimension ranging from like to dislike, based on feelings ranging from extremely positive to extremely negative.

- One's initial contact with others is very often based on *proximity* resulting from such physical aspects of the environment as classroom seating assignments, the location of residences, and how a workplace is arranged.

- Proximity leads to *repeated exposure* to some individuals in one's environment; repeated exposure tends to result in positive affect, and positive affect results in attraction.

Responding to Observable Characteristics: External Cues to Attraction

When we like—or dislike—someone at first sight, it is an indication that we have observed something about that person that appears to provide information about him or her. You may tend to like a stranger simply on the basis of a superficial resemblance to someone else you know and like (Andersen & Baum, 1994). In other instances, the cue may not be related to a specific person in your past but to a subgroup of people to whom you respond positively—the stranger has a Newfoundland accent, for example, and you have a fondness for Newfoundlanders. As discussed in Chapter 5, stereotypes are poor predictors of behaviour, but we nevertheless find ourselves reacting to other people on the basis of associated affect and incorrect assumptions based on superficial characteristics. Among the numerous examples of this tendency to be guided by affect and stereotypes is one's reaction to appearance, so we will examine the pervasive effects of **physical attractiveness**—the facial and bodily characteristics that people in a given culture regard as visually appealing (or unappealing). Both sexes respond strongly to the physical attractiveness of those they meet (Collins & Zebrowitz, 1995; Hatfield & Sprecher, 1986), though males are more responsive to female attractiveness than females are to male attractiveness (Feingold, 1990, 1992b; Pierce, 1992). Also, individuals differ in the importance they attach to physical appearance (Cash & Jacobi, 1992).

Physical Attractiveness Combination of facial and bodily characteristics that is perceived as aesthetically appealing by members of a given culture at a given time.

Explanations for the Importance of Physical Appearance

Why should physical appearance have such an impact on attraction? For one thing, attractive individuals arouse positive affect (Johnston & Oliver-Rodriguez, 1997; Kenrick et al., 1993), and we shall see in a later section that positive affect results in attraction. But, going back a step, why does physical attractiveness arouse positive affect? According to *evolutionary theory*, the reason that female beauty appeals to men is because it is associated with health and reproductive fitness. This approach suggests that when men were attracted to women whose appearance suggested youth and health and hence fertility, reproductive success became more likely (Johnston & Franklin, 1993). Thus, over hundreds of thousands of years, attraction to female appearance proved to be a crucial male preference that increased the odds of the man's genes being passed on to the next generation. There are various pieces of indirect supporting evidence for this explanation. For example, Singh (1993) has found that men are sensitive to a woman's waist-to-hip ratio. The smaller a woman's waist relative to her hips, Singh found, the more she is preferred by men and rated by them as attractive, healthy, and well built to bear children—though Tassinary and Hansen (1998) provide evidence indicating many exceptions to that generalization. In addition, Singh (1995) has shown that waist-to-hip ratio is also important in the attractiveness of men to women. Women of quite varied ages, educational backgrounds, and income levels rated line drawings of men most favourably when they were in the normal range rather than being underweight or overweight.

The idea that beauty equals youth and good health is appealing, and research shows that attractive strangers are rated as being healthier than unattractive ones. Nevertheless, there is actually *no relationship* between the attractiveness of males and females and their health—either during adolescence or adulthood (Kalick et al., 1998). A related question that has not yet been investigated is whether attractiveness is related to fertility or to the health of offspring.

The evolutionary approach also suggests that considerations involving attractiveness and fertility differ for men and women, because women have a relatively limited age span in which reproduction is possible, whereas males ordinarily can reproduce from puberty into old age. From a female perspective then, male youthfulness is not a prerequisite for successful reproduction. Instead, it is in the woman's best interest to choose a male who has the ability (and the inclination) to provide resources and protection for his mate and their children (Kenrick et al., 1994).

An interesting way to investigate such gender differences is to examine personal ads placed by males and females who are seeking a romantic partner. It is generally found that women stress their appearance and men stress their material resources (Deaux & Hanna, 1984; Harrison & Saeed, 1977). In a more recent study, Baize and Schroeder (1995) went a step farther by looking at the number of replies each ad received. In other words, do some factors in the ads attract more potential mates than others? Gender differences were found that are consistent with predictions based on evolutionary theory. For example, a personal ad placed by a man was most effective if it indicated a mature, rich, educated individual. In ads placed by a woman, the only ad content related to its effectiveness was *age*—the younger the more replies.

While such results are consistent with evolutionary theory, they could also be argued to be consistent with *cultural psychology*. Those who write or respond to such ads may simply be reflecting widespread cultural beliefs about what is most appealing in the opposite sex. That is, the personal ads could reflect our social learning rather than our innate tendencies.

Cross-cultural research suggests that the existence of positive stereotypes about attractiveness is universal, however, the specific content of the stereotypes depends on the culture (Dion, Pak, & Dion, 1990). For example, in a collectivistic culture such as Korea, attractiveness is assumed to be associated with integrity and concern for others; these attributes do not appear among the traits stereotypically associated with attractiveness among individualistic North Americans (Wheeler & Kim, 1997). Even so, there is agreement across cultures that attractiveness indicates social competence, adjustment, intelligence, and sexual warmth.

Beliefs About Attractiveness

We tend to have stereotypic beliefs about attractiveness. Research findings show that people tend to believe that attractive men and women are also more poised, interesting, sociable, independent, dominant, exciting, sexy, well adjusted, socially skilled, and successful than those who are unattractive (Dion & Dion, 1987; Moore, Graziano, & Miller, 1987). Handsome men are perceived as more masculine and beautiful women as more feminine than their less attractive counterparts (Gillen, 1981). Attractiveness even affects judgments about how a stranger became HIV-positive (Agnew & Thompson, 1994). Essays identified as the work of attractive students are evaluated more positively than those whose authors were identified as unattractive (Cash & Trimer, 1984). Attractiveness among adults aged 60 to 93 is also assumed to indicate positive personality traits (Johnson & Pittenger, 1984). Altogether, as social psychologists discovered almost three decades ago, people assume that "what is beautiful is good" (Dion, Berscheid, & Hatfield, 1972).

Most of the stereotypes based on appearance are quite wrong (Feingold, 1992; Kenealy et al., 1991). The only characteristics actually associated with attractiveness are those related to popularity (Johnstone, Frame, & Bouman, 1992; Reis, Nezlek, & Wheeler, 1989) and good interpersonal skills (O'Grady, 1989). Further, the more positive a person's self-rating of attractiveness, the stronger his or her feelings of subjective well-being (Diener, Wolsic, & Fujita, 1995). Presumably, these differences based on appearance develop primarily because attractive individuals are liked and treated nicely by others from their earliest years, while those who are unattractive receive less-favourable treatment (Reis, Nezlek, & Wheeler, 1980). Attractive individuals are no more likely to have high self-esteem than the less attractive (Kenealy et al., 1991). A possible reason that good-looking people don't necessarily evaluate themselves highly, is that when you are very attractive, you tend to believe that others value you *only* for your appearance (Major, Carrington, & Carnevale, 1984).

Given the pervasive effects of attractiveness, it follows that many people may worry about their appearance. Canadian researchers Dion, Dion, and Keelan (1990) investigated *appearance anxiety*, defined as apprehension concerning one's physical appearance and the evaluations made by others. Among college students, women indicate more appearance anxiety than men, and high scores on this test are associated with experiencing social anxiety, feeling unattractive in childhood, and having had fewer dates in high school. This anxiety is not necessarily justified. People are not very accurate at estimating their own attractiveness as judged by others. Men (but not women) have been found to overestimate how good they look (Gabriel, Critelli, & Ee, 1994).

A few negative attributes are associated with being attractive. Many people believe that beautiful women are more vain and materialistic than unattractive ones (Cash & Duncan, 1984). Attractiveness is a plus for males running for political office, but not for female candidates (Sigelman et al., 1986), possibly because elected officials are not "supposed" to be feminine. Though attractiveness is believed to lead to success, people often assume that the resulting good fortune is undeserved and simply based on looks (Kalick, 1988). Recently Smeaton, (1998) found that undergraduate women perceived attractive males as posing a greater risk of sexually transmitted disease than unattractive ones. Presumably, women assume that attractive men have had more sexual partners than those who are unattractive.

The Physical Constituents of Attractiveness

It is difficult to identify the precise cues that determine judgments of relative attractiveness. One line of research found that women perceived as most attractive have either childlike features (large, widely spaced eyes and a small nose and chin) or "mature" features (prominent cheekbones, narrow cheeks, high eyebrows, large pupils, and a big smile). These same two facial types were perceived as equally attractive among white, African-American, and Asian women (Cunningham, 1986, 1991; Cunningham, Barbee & Pike, 1990). Men perceived as most attractive are those who have big eyes, prominent cheek bones and rugged chins (Hatfield & Rapson, 1996). Research shows that people tend to agree extremely well about who is or is not attractive, even across racial and ethnic lines (Cunningham et al., 1995). However, there is also evidence of cultural variation across time in what has been considered attractive, particularly in terms of whether the waif-like or rounded female shape is considered most desirable (Banner, 1983; Hatfield & Rapson, 1996).

Langlois and Roggman (1990) took a very different approach to determine what is meant by attractiveness. They began with photographs of faces, then produced computer-generated pictures that combined several faces into one. That is, the image in each photo was transformed into a series of numbers representing shades of gray, the numbers were averaged across the group of pictures, and the result was translated back into a photo—see Figure 6.3. For both men and women, a composite face was rated as more attractive than most of the individual faces that went into making it. Further, the more faces that were used to make the composite, the more attractive the result. These investigators concluded that, for most people, an attractive face is simply one whose components represent the arithmetic mean of the details of many faces (Langlois, Roggman, & Musselman, 1994). One possible reason for this is that the average of multiple individual faces is perceived as more *familiar* than any of the actual faces, and, as we saw earlier, familiar stimuli receive a more positive evaluation.

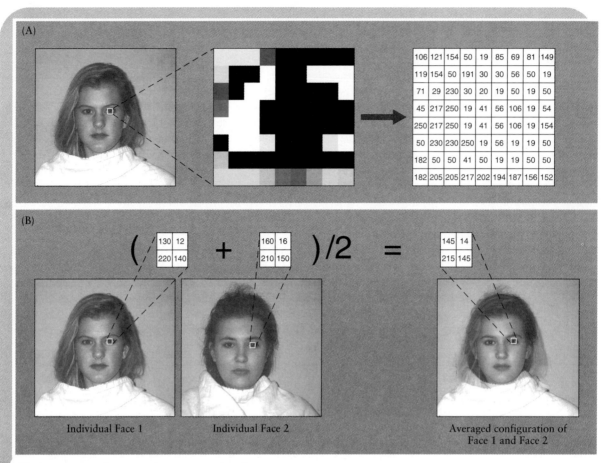

■ An average face equals an attractive face

FIGURE 6.3 In order to create a picture of an average face, a black and white photograph is translated into a series of numbers that represent shades of gray, a process know as digitizing, as shown in A. These numerical values from several different faces are then averaged, and the resulting numbers are transformed back into a photograph, as shown in B. An average face is rated as more attractive than the individual faces that were combined to create it. And the more faces that are combined to make the average one, the more attractive the resulting face.

Source: Langlois, Roggman, & Musselman, 1994.

In sum, research overwhelmingly indicates that the *external* appearance and behaviours of those we meet have a strong impact on our initial attraction to them. We have seen that cognitive stereotyping and emotional responses can result from our assessment of another person's physical appearance. Research has, therefore, also been interested in those *internal* cognitive and emotional responses of the observer. We will next consider the cognitive process of *impression formation* and the role of *affect* in interpersonal attraction.

KEY POINTS

● Interpersonal attraction and interpersonal judgments are strongly influenced by various observable characteristics of those we meet, including *physical attractiveness*.

- Evolutionary theory suggests that the features we find attractive in others are those associated with *reproductive success*. Other research suggests that cultural beliefs have a strong impact on our stereotypes of attractiveness.
- People are found to like and to make positive attributions about attractive men and women of all ages, despite the fact that assumptions based on appearance are usually inaccurate.
- Research has begun to identify some of the constituents of attractiveness, although there is also cultural variation. A computer-generated average face is more attractive, perhaps because of its generic familiarity.

Impression Formation: The Cognitive Basis of Attraction

First impressions, it is widely held, are very important in attraction. Most of us assume that the initial impressions we make on others will shape the course of our future dealings with them in crucial ways. Further, we believe that such impressions may be quite resistant to change, even in the face of later contradictory information. For these reasons, most people prepare very carefully for first dates, job interviews, and other situations in which they will meet others for the first time. Are these commonsense assumptions about the nature of first impressions accurate? The answer provided by several decades of research is at least a qualified yes (e.g., Anderson, 1981; Wyer, et al., 1994).

The first systematic research on this issue were now-classic studies carried out by Asch (1946). He used a straightforward procedure in which subjects in two different groups were given one of the following descriptions of a hypothetical person:

> intelligent-skillful-industrious-warm-determined-practical-cautious
> intelligent-skillful-industrious-cold-determined-practical-cautious

As you can see, the lists differ only with respect to two words: warm and cold. Persons who read the list containing *warm* were much more likely to view the stranger as generous, happy, good-natured, sociable, popular, and altruistic than were people who read the list containing *cold*. The words warm and cold, Asch suggested, were central traits—ones that would strongly shape overall impressions of the stranger and colour the other adjectives in the list.

As a result of this and further studies, Asch concluded that **impression formation** involves more than simply adding individual traits together. The effects of traits interact such that the meaning of one trait will influence our understanding of others. In this way, the order of traits was important because the first adjectives that subjects read changed the meaning of the ones they read later. Having learned that someone was intelligent and industrious, they interpreted the later more negative adjectives within this favourable context. Thus, the fact that the hypothetical person was critical implied that this person made good use of his or her intelligence. In contrast, having learned that the imaginary person was envious and stubborn, subjects interpreted the fact that she or he was also intelligent as suggestive of calculating shrewdness.

More recent research has extended that of Asch by focusing on how different types of information is combined in impression formation. For example, researchers have identified the factors that influence the relative weight we place on various types of information. Among the most important factors identified were these: (1) source of the input—information from sources we trust or admire is weighted more heavily than information from sources we distrust (Rosenbaum & Levin, 1969); (2) whether the information is positive or negative in nature—we tend to weight negative information about others more heavily than positive information (Mellers, Richards, & Birnbaum, 1992); (3) the extent to which the information describes behaviour or traits that are

Impression Formation The process through which we form impressions of others.

unusual or extreme—the more unusual, the greater the weight placed on information; (4) the sequence of input—as Asch found, information received first is weighted more heavily than information received later (this is known as a *primacy effect*).

A growing body of evidence also suggests that the nature of impressions may shift as we gain increasing experience with another person (e.g., Budesheim & Bonnelle, 1998; Klein et al., 1992; Klein & Loftus, 1993). At first, our impression of someone we have just met consists largely of *exemplars* (concrete examples of behaviours they have performed). Later, as our experience with this person increases, our impression comes to consist mainly of mental *abstractions* (mental summaries or generalizations) derived from many observations of the person's behaviour (Sherman & Klein, 1994).

In sum, research on impression formation, both early and recent, emphasizes the *cognitive basis of attraction*. The task itself often seems effortless, but research by social psychologists indicates that a lot is going on beneath the surface. In the next chapter (Chapter 7) on the topic of social influence we will look at the other side of the coin—*impression management*—how individuals attempt to influence or *manage* the impression they make on others. The ability to create a favourable impression, as you might imagine, often increases your ability to influence other people.

As we saw in previous chapters, cognitive processes are often influenced by emotion. An early study exploring this interplay is described in the following Cornerstones section.

Cornerstones

The Capilano Bridge Experiment: Cognition and Emotion in Attraction

In the early 1970s, Don Dutton and Arthur Aron, working at the University of British Columbia, were interested in a fundamental mechanism of attraction—the fact that it is often associated with intense emotional arousal. Further, in line with the expansion of interest in cognition at that time, they were interested in the possibility that our cognitions might lead us to misinterpret or mislabel our emotions. In fact, their *mislabeling hypothesis* suggested that if you were in a state of emotional arousal when you met an attractive potential partner, this arousal might be attributed to the attractive person—you would misinterpret your arousal as due to the person in front of you and conclude that you were strongly attracted.

They were able to take advantage of a field setting nearby where arousal was naturally varied (see Figure 6.4). The Capilano Canyon near Vancouver is a popular tourist attraction. It contains two types of bridge: one a suspension bridge, 1.5 metres wide and swaying 80 metres above a

rocky canyon, and the other a broader bridge only 3 metres above a calm and shallow stream. The researchers could be assured that people crossing the Capilano suspension bridge would feel consid-

■ Attraction on the Capilano Bridge

FIGURE 6.4 Dutton and Aron's classic research might suggest that people crossing this bridge have an increased likelihood of being attracted to others because of the increased emotional arousal that its great height induces.

erably more arousal (fear) than those on the lower bridge. If the mislabeling hypothesis were correct, Dutton and Aron predicted that those crossing the suspension bridge (high arousal group) would be more likely to experience attraction if they encountered a potential partner, than those crossing the low bridge (low arousal group).

An attractive female interviewer asked males coming off both bridges if they would fill out a questionnaire, supposedly for her class psychology project concerned with the effects of scenic beauty on creativity. They were asked to write a small passage about an ambiguous picture presented to them, and then the interviewer offered each subject her telephone number in case they wanted more information about the study. We should also mention that the experiment was repeated with a male interviewer questioning male subjects.

Results supported the hypothesis: Men in the high arousal (suspension bridge) group showed greater sexual imagery in their written passages and were more than three times as likely to call the female interviewer than men in the low arousal (low bridge) group. Results for the male interviewer showed no significant difference between the high and low arousal conditions: the presence of a potential partner was necessary before arousal was interpreted as sexual attraction.

This study, now a classic in the attraction literature, demonstrated the importance of emotion, or affect, to the process of attraction, and the interplay of affect and cognition in our understanding of a social situation—evidently cognitive *mislabeling* of our emotions can occur in the highly charged field of sexual attraction. Since this study, research into the subtleties of affect in interpersonal attraction has expanded tremendously as you will see below.

Affect as the Basis of Attraction

Our social nature also means that other people often provoke an emotional reaction in us and certainly emotion is a common part of our relationships. As we saw above our emotions can strongly influence attraction, whether they are provoked by another person or not (Berry & Hansen, 1996; Erber, 1991; Forgas, 1995; Zajonc & McIntosh, 1992). The two most important characteristics of affect are its *intensity* (the strength of the emotion) and *direction* (whether the emotion is positive or negative). Positive emotions such as excitement were once thought to fall at one end of a single continuum, with negative emotions such as anxiety falling at the opposite end. Research indicates, however, that positive and negative emotions represent two separate and independent dimensions that are reflected in people's self-ratings of their feelings (Byrne & Smeaton, 1998) and in the different brain structures that are activated by positive and negative emotions (George et al., 1995). This means that you can experience a mixture of positive and negative feelings, and that one sort of emotion can increase without the other necessarily decreasing (Barrett & Russell, 1998; Goldstein & Strube, 1994).

Experiments consistently indicate that positive feelings lead to positive evaluations of others—liking—while negative feelings lead to negative evaluations—disliking (Dovidio et al., 1995). Affect can influence attraction in two different ways. A *direct effect* occurs when another person says or does something that makes you feel good or bad; the obvious result is that you like an individual who makes you feel good and dislike one who makes you feel bad (Downey & Damhave, 1991; Shapiro, Baumeister, Kessler, 1991). It is not very surprising that you prefer a person who brightens your day with a compliment and dislike one who brings you down with an insulting remark. An *associated effect* is much less obvious; it occurs when another person is simply present when your feelings happen to be positive or negative (for some reason unrelated to that person), but you still tend to evaluate him or her on the basis of your own affective state. For example, if you meet someone on your way to visit your dentist, you are less inclined to like him or her than if you met the person on your way to a long-anticipated new movie.

One example of the *direct effect* of emotions comes from the research of Kleinke and colleagues (Kleinke, Meeker, & Staneski, 1986) who have investigated the kinds of things people say when they try to interact with someone they don't know. Many people attempt to be amusing by saying something cute or flippant—"Hi I'm easy, are you?"—presumably hoping to elicit positive affect and to be liked. Unfortunately, the most common emotional response to such attempted cleverness in research was negative, the opposite of what was intended. In contrast, a positive affective response was much more common when the opening line is either direct ("Would you like to dance?") or innocuous ("Where are you from?"). The most positive response in laboratory research (Kleinke & Dean, 1990) and in a real singles bar (Cunningham, 1989) was toward a person saying something simple and direct, the most negative was toward someone using a cute or flippant line, and innocuous lines were evaluated as between these two. It might be helpful to know the nonverbal indications of such annoyance. Women demonstrate their rejection by, among other things, yawning, frowning, attending to their nails, and staring at the ceiling. These and other "silent brush-offs" were identified in a field study of singles bars in St. Louis by psychologist Monica Moore (O'Neil, 1998). Cute and flippant lines lead to such brush-offs whereas simple and innocuous lines lead to further interaction. The lesson is that those who try to be too cute often manage turn people off.

The *associated effect* of emotion occurs when our positive and negative feelings are aroused by events having nothing directly to do with the other person (Johnston & Short, 1993). If another person just happens to be there when your feelings are good, you tend to like him or her; if that person is present when your feelings are bad, you tend to feel dislike (Byrne & Clore, 1970). The general idea is based on classical conditioning. In Chapter 3 we described how attitudes in general can be acquired through classical conditioning; whenever an attitude object is paired with a stimulus that evokes positive or negative affect, the observer develops positive or negative attitudes toward the object. In the same way, researchers have prompted attraction or dislike toward a stranger by pairing the stranger's photograph with pleasant or unpleasant pictures presented subliminally (Krosnick et al., 1992). In analogous experiments, emotions have been aroused by such manipulations as pleasant versus unpleasant background music (May & Hamilton, 1980), good versus bad news on the radio (Kaplan, 1981), and pleasant versus unpleasant room lighting (Baron, Rea, & Daniels, 1992). In these and numerous other experiments, positive affect resulted in positive evaluations (liking) by participants experiencing positive emotions and negative evaluations (disliking) by participants experiencing negative emotions.

Whatever the source of an individual's emotional state, happy feelings lead to liking, but if that person feels unhappy, he or she likes other people less well and evaluates them in negative terms (Dovidio, Gaertner, Isen, & Lowrance, 1995). When you consider the importance of affect and the ease with which it is conditioned to previously neutral targets, you can see that interpersonal behaviour is often quite predictable, even though it is not always entirely reasonable. For example, Rozin, Millman, and Nemeroff (1986) point out that even a brief contact between a neutral object and something that arouses affect can transfer the emotional response to the neutral object. In one study of this process, a laundered shirt that had been worn by a disliked person was rated as less desirable than a laundered shirt that had been worn by a liked person. Though the shirts did not actually differ, one elicited a positive response and the other a negative response on the basis of learned associations.

Emotions can also go on to influence interpersonal behaviour as well as attraction responses (Clark & Watson, 1988). Cunningham (1988) induced happy or sad feelings in male subjects (some saw movies and others received false evaluations), then sent the subjects to a waiting room in which a female confederate was seated. The males in a positive mood communicated with the female stranger more and disclosed more about themselves than did those in a negative mood.

The Affect-Centred Model of Attraction

The **affect-centred model of attraction** (Byrne, 1992) can provide an overview of the role of both cognitive and affective processes in attraction. As shown in Figure 6.5, affective responses toward another person can result from *associated* environmental events (such as pleasant or unpleasant music) or *directly* from the person themselves. For example, you may find pleasure in looking at someone you find beautiful, or the person might say something you like. Cognitive processing of all available information also takes place. Because this information (including impressions, stereotypes, beliefs, and factual knowledge) can be affectively arousing, it contributes to the affect and in turn to the total evaluative response. Ultimately, this will lead to a behavioural response to the person which can be verbal or nonverbal: you might avoid the person and look away or turn towards them and begin to talk.

If two people are brought into repeated contact by proximity and if both form positive impressions of each other, experiencing relatively positive affect, they are at a transition point. They may simply remain superficial acquaintances who nod and perhaps say hello when they happen to see one another. Another possibility is that they may begin to converse from time to time, learn each other's names, and begin to exchange information about themselves, thus becoming close acquaintances. Which alternative is chosen may depend on the *affiliation need* of each individual.

Affect-Centred Model of Attraction A conceptual framework in which attraction is assumed to be based on positive and negative emotions. These emotions can be aroused directly by another person, simply associated with that person, and/or mediated by cognitive processes.

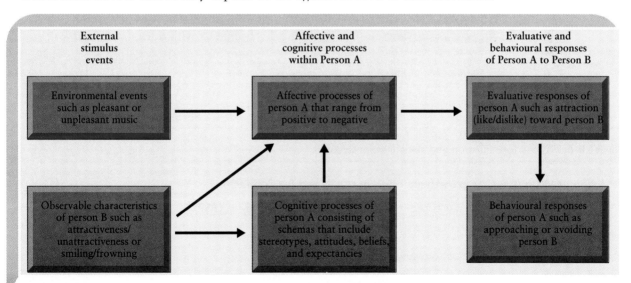

■ The affect-centred model of attraction

FIGURE 6.5 Essentially, attraction to a given person is based on affective responses that are aroused by various events (e.g., pleasant versus unpleasant music), by relatively stable characteristics of the person (e.g., physical appearance), and by changeable characteristics of the person (e.g., smiling versus frowning). Some of the person's characteristics have a relatively direct effect on one's emotional responses (e.g., flattering comments or hostile insults); other characteristics must be processed cognitively in ways that activate schemas involving stereotypes, attitudes, beliefs, and expectancies (e.g., attractiveness, race, similarities and differences, etc.). The net affective state leads to an evaluative response along a dimension ranging from liking to disliking and to approach or avoidant behaviour consistent with the evaluation.

Source: Based on material in Byrne, 1992.

- Research on *impression formation*—the process through which we form impressions of others—suggests that first impressions are indeed important. Complex cognitive processes are involved such as the weighting of different information about others and the use of exemplars and abstractions.

- Positive and negative affective states can influence attraction either through *direct effects* (when the other person is responsible for the positive or negative emotion) or through indirect or *associated effects* (when the emotion is created by a different source, but the other person happens to be associated with it). Sometimes *mislabelling* of emotion generated indirectly occurs, as in the Capilano Bridge experiment.

- The *affect-centred model of attraction* provides an integration of the role of both cognition and affect in attraction. It specifies that attraction is determined by direct and associated sources of affect, only mediated by cognitive processes.

The Affiliation Need: The Motive to Relate to Others

Most people spend a large part of their free time interacting with other people. Recent research indicates that the tendency to affiliate has a neurobiological basis (Rowe, 1996), possibly derived from the fact that our prehistoric ancestors who formed interpersonal relationships thereby improved their chances for survival and thus for passing on their genes to us (Wright, 1984).

Need for Affiliation
The motive to seek interpersonal relationships.

People differ, of course, in the strength of this **need for affiliation**, and such differences constitute a relatively stable *trait* (or *disposition*). Hill (1987) suggests that there are four basic motives for affiliation. He proposes that affiliation is based on the *need for social comparison* (to reduce uncomfortable feelings of uncertainty), the *need for positive stimulation* (for interesting, lively contact with others), the *need for social*

Over the years, investigators have found differences in interpersonal behaviour that are associated with measures of affiliation need. Consistent with Murray's (1938) original definition of this disposition, an individual's need for affiliation is related to the tendency to form friendships and to socialize, to interact closely with others, to cooperate and communicate with others in a friendly way, and to fall in love.

TABLE 6.1 Need for affiliation and social responsiveness

Individuals Who Are Comparatively High in the Need for Affiliation:

Write more letters and make more local telephone calls (Lansing & Heyns, 1959).

Laugh more and remain physically close to others (McAdams, 1979).

Avoid making negative comments to fellow workers (Exline, 1962).

Desire more dates per week and are more likely to be emotionally involved in a relationship (Morrison, 1954).

Are more likely to express a desire to marry right after college (Bickman, 1975).

Engage in fewer antisocial or negative acts with fellow workers.
Spend less time alone (Constantian, 1981).

Are more likely to be described by other people as likable, natural, and enthusiastic (McAdams, 1979).

■ Affiliation under conditions of stress

FIGURE 6.6 Affiliation is a common response to the stress of an emergency situation or disaster, such as the 1998 ice storm in Eastern Canada. Contact with others allows us to compare our response and reduces our anxiety.

support (for companionship when problems arise), and the *need for attention* (for praise and admiration from others). People seem to seek the amount of social contact that is optimal for them, preferring to be alone part of the time and in social situations part of the time (O'Connor & Rosenblood, 1996).

Beginning with the early work of Murray (1938), psychologists have investigated behavioural differences in those high and low in the need to affiliate. Some of these findings are summarized in Table 6.1.

Though people differ in their need to interact with others, external events can also arouse this motive. You have probably been in certain situations in which total strangers began to talk to one another during the excitement of a special event like a New Year celebration or a festival (Byrne, 1991). Humphriss (1989) provided an account of a California earthquake in which a dreadful natural disaster that destroyed many homes led neighbours to unite in an unusually friendly atmosphere. In a similar way, in 1998 a crippling ice storm hit parts of Canada, northern New England and New York; fallen trees blocked roads and downed power lines, leaving residents without electricity for an extended period—see Figure 6.6. People in the affected area gathered in Red Cross shelters and other facilities in a surprisingly cheerful atmosphere of shared companionship. In addition, people who suffered less damage volunteered to deliver food, baby formula, bottled water, pasta, bread, peanut butter, generators, and other supplies to those in need (Benjamin, 1998).

Affiliation and Social Comparison

The underlying reason for responding to a stressful situation with affiliative behaviour was first recognized in the 1950s in the work of Asch (1954) and Schachter (1959). In that decade Leon Festinger developed his influential **theory of social comparison** (1954). He hypothesized that each human being has a drive to evaluate his or her opinions and

Theory of Social Comparison Festinger's influential theory of our tendency to evaluate our opinions and abilities based on comparison with other people and our preference for making comparisons with others similar to ourselves.

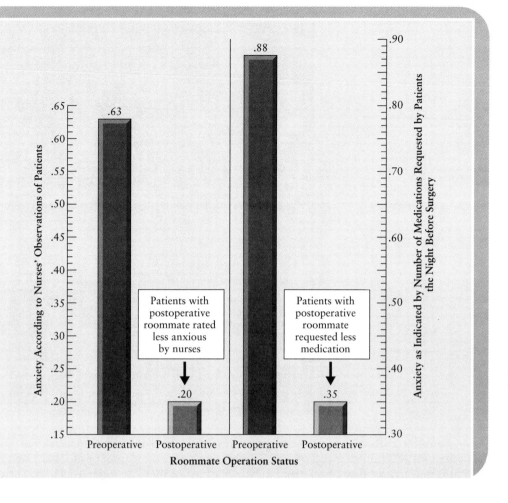

The beneficial effects of affiliation

FIGURE 6.7 When surgical patients are given the opportunity to interact with another patient who can provide both emotional and cognitive clarity about the operation and its effects, they experience less anxiety before the operation and are able to leave the hospital more quickly after the operation.

Source: Based on data in Kulik, Mahler, & Moore, 1996.

abilities. While we will turn to objective criteria whenever possible, there are types of opinion or ability for which there are no objective standards. In this case, we use our social world as the bases for evaluation by comparing our own opinions and abilities with those of other people. That is, we make a *social comparison*. Further, we generally prefer to make such comparisons with others who are similar to ourselves. You cannot evaluate yourself very accurately if you compare yourself with someone who is too different from you.

In Chapter 3 we saw the way that social comparison can contribute to attitude formation. However, these ideas have also been important to our understanding of affiliation processes, particularly when we are fearful or anxious. In Schachter's classic (1959) investigations, for example, some participants were told they would receive painful electric shocks, while others expected to receive only mild, tickling electrical stimulation. As they waited anxiously for this (nonexistent) procedure to begin, the participants were asked to indicate whether they preferred to remain alone or to spend the time with others. Many of those expecting pain preferred to wait with other participants, while those not expecting pain wanted to wait alone or expressed no preference. And Schachter concluded that the affiliative motive of his fearful participants was based on a need for social comparison: We want to compare our own anxieties with others who are in the same position. As he said, "misery doesn't love just any kind of company, it loves only miserable company" (Schachter, 1959, p. 24).

Evidence for the positive effects of such social comparison-based affiliation is provided by a study of patients before and after coronary bypass surgery (Kulik, Mahler, & Moore, 1996). Patients showed greatest affiliative behaviour (talking and asking for information) if their roommate was also a cardiac patient and if the individual was postoperative (rather than preoperative). Note that it is this type of roommate who would give more opportunity for social comparison and calming of fears. In addition, patients having this opportunity experienced beneficial effects, as shown in Figure 6.7

We should remember that social comparison is just one of a number of motives for affiliation as Hill's model above suggests (1987). Often we are drawn to other people not because we seek comfort and support but because they are enjoyable—they can provide positive stimulation and attention.

KEY POINTS

- Individuals high, as opposed to low, in *need for affiliation* are more likely to engage in establishing and maintaining interpersonal relationships and are more interpersonally skilled.

- People can be differentiated with respect to their reasons for wanting to affiliate, and these reasons lead to different types of affiliative behaviour oriented toward different goals.

- When unusual circumstances, such as natural disasters, arise, people are likely to affiliate with others. Research related to the *theory of social comparison* suggests that we affiliate when anxious in order to compare our reactions with those of others; often this results in positive effects.

BUILDING A RELATIONSHIP: SELF-DISCLOSURE, SIMILARITY AND RECIPROCITY

What have we learned about attraction so far? Briefly, we know once two people are brought together by physical proximity, the probability that they will like each other and establish some kind of relationship is increased if each (1) evaluates the appearance of the other favourably, (2) forms a positive first impression, (3) is in a positive emotional state, and (4) is motivated by affiliative needs. The next steps toward interpersonal intimacy involve communication. Three crucial aspects of this communication are the degree to which the acquaintances reveal information about themselves (show *self-disclosure*), discover areas of *similarity* and the extent to which they show *reciprocity* in positive evaluations of one another.

Self-Disclosure: Growing Intimacy

One of the most important parts of building a relationship is conversation. As individuals begin to interact they communicate information about themselves that is increasingly personal. This process of **self-disclosure** usually proceeds from communication of relatively superficial information about their occupation, background, preferences, to progressively more intimate details of their lives, such as their relationships, their opinions and beliefs, their feelings and perhaps their personal problems (Altman

Self-Disclosure The revelation of personal information about the self to another person. Seen as an integral part of the growing intimacy between two people who are becoming friends.

& Taylor, 1973; Jourard, 1968). In developing friendships, the progress towards greater intimacy tends to occur through reciprocal exchanges. One individual will disclose something at a more intimate level about themselves and the other person will reciprocate with greater intimacy. Many studies have confirmed that self-disclosure generally increases liking (Collins & Miller, 1994). When strangers are asked to engage in relationship-building activities such as self-disclosure in a laboratory interaction, they later express greater feelings of closeness (Aron et al., 1997). But this is only true if it is appropriate within the relationship (Miller, 1990). When one individual discloses too much, too soon relative to their interactant, he or she is not liked to the same extent and is sometimes seen as maladjusted (Chaiken & Derlega, 1974).

Gender and Cultural Differences in Self-Disclosure

You might have wondered if there are gender or culture differences in self-disclosure. After all, we mentioned in previous chapters that cultures differ in expressiveness and men have traditionally been raised to be more "strong and silent" than women.

A meta-analysis, reviewing more that 200 studies of self-disclosure (Dindia & Allen, 1992) confirms the stereotype—women are more willing to self-disclose than men, though the difference is not as great as the stereotype would suggest and depends on the type of relationship. In same-sex friendships, women friends do disclose more to each other than male friends. Women view talking and sharing personal confidences as an important and enjoyable part of the relationship, whereas men place greater emphasis on shared activities (Caldwell & Peplau, 1982). With opposite sex relationships, particularly those of romantic partners or spouses, the self-disclosure differences between men and women are smaller. Both sexes expect some disclosure in such intimate relationships and there tends to be quite high and equal levels of disclosure among university couples (Rands & Levinger, 1979; Rubin, Hill, Peplau & Dunkel Schetter, 1980).

Investigation of culture differences has centred on the individualistic-collectivistic dimension of cultural values. However, results are unclear. In some studies those in collective cultures show greater self-disclosure. In others it is those from individualistic cultures. For example, in one study, Hong Kong Chinese showed greater self-disclosure than Americans (Wheeler, Reis & Bond, 1989). However, other studies have found that Americans or British subjects (individualistic cultures) showed greater self-disclosure than those from various collectivistic cultures—Japan (Barlund, 1989), Korea (Won-Doornink, 1985) or Singapore (Goodwin & Lee, 1994).

The resolution to these contradictory findings may rest in differences in cultural norms about *who* one should disclose towards. First, the results of research may depend upon cultural norms about disclosure to same- and opposite-sex friends. For example, in most Western cultures it is the norm for men to direct most of their self-disclosures towards the women in their lives rather than to same-sex friends. In many collective cultures, in contrast, where the roles of men and women are more separated, the norm for males is to confide in same-sex friends rather than opposite sex, particularly before marriage. When this was put to the test comparing male student from Hong Kong and Jordan with American students, results showed that indeed the male students from collective cultures were more disclosing to other males than were American (Reis & Wheeler, 1991).

Second, the results of research may also depend on whether the culture studied makes sharp distinctions in norms of self-disclosure between ingroups and outgroups. The work of Gudykunst has shown that students from Japan, Hong Kong and Taiwan showed more intimate disclosing communications with ingroup members than with outgroup individuals (Gudykunst, Gao, Schmidt, et al., 1992). However, Americans did not differ in the degree of disclosure to ingroups and outgroups. It is therefore possible that the contradictory research did not take account of these two normative patterns—cultural norms about disclosure to opposite- and same-sex interactants and about disclosure to ingroup and outgroup members.

Similarity: We Like Those Most Like Ourselves

Over 20 centuries ago, Aristotle described the nature of friendship and hypothesized that people who agree with one another become friends, while those with dissimilar attitudes do not. In books and movies opposites may attract, but in real life birds of a feather flock together. As tennis pro Bjorn Borg said of his new wife, "She's a great woman. She's just like me" (Milestones, 1989).

Attitude Similarity and Attraction

When people interact, their conversation often involves the expression of their attitudes about whatever topics come up—school, music, television shows, politics, religion, and so on. As people talk, each person indicates his or her likes and dislikes (Hatfield &

"Sorry, we're all cat people. The dog people are in that boat over there."

■ People usually like similar others and dislike dissimilar others

FIGURE 6.8 Most people most of the time respond to similar people with positive affect, attraction, and the desire to associate with them; dissimilar people generally evoke the opposite responses. Fortunately, these reactions do not ordinarily extend to segregating lifeboats on the basis of relative preference for cats versus dogs.

Rapson, 1992; Kent, Davis, & Shapiro, 1981). Often people discover as they talk that they share the same attitudes about a range of topics. Research has specifically shown that each individual in the interaction responds to the other on the basis of the **proportion of similar attitudes** that are expressed. For example, we are equally attracted to someone who has views like our own on 2 of the 4 topics we discuss or on 50 of the 100 topics we discuss; the proportion is 0.50 in each instance. The higher the proportion of similar attitudes, the greater the liking (Byrne & Nelson, 1965).

Critics have questioned one or more aspects of the concept of similarity-attraction (Bochner, 1991; Rosenbaum 1986; Sunnafrank, 1992). One of the most challenging criticisms was offered by Rosenbaum, (1986) with his **repulsion hypothesis**. Simply stated, he proposed that dissimilar attitudes decrease attraction but that similar attitudes have no effect—see Figure 6.8. He pointed out that in most studies participants respond to a stranger who expresses both similar and dissimilar attitudes. Though it has been assumed that each type of attitude influences attraction, Rosenbaum suggested otherwise. In effect, he assumed that people like whomever they meet, but are gradually repulsed if the other person expresses dissimilar attitudes. His hypothesis that similar attitudes are irrelevant was, however, shown to be incorrect in an experiment in which the number of dissimilar attitudes remained the same in each of three conditions, while the number of similar attitudes varied (Smeaton, Byrne, & Murnen, 1989). The repulsion hypothesis predicts no difference in attraction across the conditions, because their only difference consisted of varying numbers of similar attitudes. The proportion hypothesis, in contrast, predicts that attraction will differ across conditions, because the proportion of similar attitudes varies. The repulsion hypothesis was found to be incorrect, and the proportion hypothesis was confirmed.

Rosenbaum's proposal was of value, however, in leading to additional research. And this research does indicate a slightly greater effect for dissimilar attitudes than for similar ones (Chapman, 1992), in part because most people assume that a stranger, especially an attractive one (Miyake & Zuckerman, 1993), holds attitudes similar to their own (Hoyle, 1993; Krueger & Clement, 1994). This assumption of widespread agreement with one's own views—sometimes labeled the *false consensus effect* (Alicke & Largo, 1995)—applies to both important and unimportant topics and occurs among people of all ages (Fabrigar & Krosnick, 1995; Tan & Singh, 1995). It is because agreement is expected that we will find disagreement surprising and it will have more impact on our evaluation of another person (Singh & Tan, 1992; Smeaton et al., 1995).

The wide-ranging generality of the similarity-attraction relationship holds for college students and high school dropouts; for children and senior citizens; and for students representing a variety of cultures, including India, Japan, and Mexico as well as the United States (Byrne et al., 1971). Even on the Internet, people using e-mail exchange lists are likely to seek out others who share their views and to exclude those with dissimilar views (Schwartz, 1994). There is only limited evidence indicating that individual differences in personality can modify how we respond to attitude similarity. The best example involves need for affiliation. Individuals differing in this need respond about the same to a dissimilar stranger, but those high in affiliation need are more positive toward a similar stranger than are individuals low in affiliation need, as shown in studies in the United States and Singapore (Kwan, 1998).

In total, however, research continues to confirm the importance of similarity in attraction. As Duck and Barnes (1992) point out, the similarity-attraction relationship resembles the history of the *Titanic* in reverse; many are sure it will sink, but it remains afloat. And this is true even when we sail it between cultures.

Proportion of Similar Attitudes The number of topics on which two individuals hold the same views in relation to the total number of topics on which they compare their views. Expressed as a percentage or proportion: the number of topics on which there is agreement divided by the total number of total topics discussed.

Repulsion Hypothesis Rosenbaum's proposal that attraction is not enhanced by similar attitudes; instead, people initially respond positively to others but are repulsed by the discovery of dissimilar attitudes.

Why Do We Care About Similarity?

Three possible explanations have been offered as to why people respond emotionally to the similar and dissimilar attitudes expressed by others.

The oldest formulation, **balance theory** (Heider, 1958), rests on the concept that humans organize their likes and dislikes in a symmetrical way. *Balance* exists when two people like each other and agree about some topic (Newcomb, 1961). When they like each other and disagree, however, an unpleasant state of *imbalance* is created (Orive, 1988). Each person attempts to restore balance through such means as changing attitudes, convincing the other person to change attitudes, or reducing liking (Monsour, Betty, & Kurzweil, 1993). When two people dislike each other, they are in a state of *nonbalance* and each is indifferent about the other's attitudes.

While balance theory leads to a number of interesting predictions about how people will respond to agreement and disagreement, it really doesn't explain why such information is important. A convincing answer is provided by Festinger's (1954) *social comparison theory*, which we discussed earlier. In effect, you compare your attitudes with those of other people because that is the only way to evaluate what you believe to be true. You turn to others to obtain **consensual validation** of your views about the world. According to this theory, described earlier, when someone agrees with you, the agreement validates your views—provides "evidence" that you are correct. Not surprisingly, you like the person who makes you feel good about yourself. Disagreement has just the opposite effect and suggests that perhaps you have faulty judgment, are not too bright, and have poor taste. Such information makes you feel bad about yourself, and you dislike the other person. As discussed in Chapter 4, this idea fits with the evidence of a tendency to seek self-enhancement.

In a broader sense, however, the positive response to similarity of all kinds could be a very general one. According to one Canadian researcher, it may be based on a biological tendency to respond most positively to those who are genetically similar to ourselves and most negatively to those who are genetically different (Rushton, 1989, 1990). From this perspective, we act so as to maximize the survival of our own genes as well as the survival of the genes of whoever is most like us. We will explore some of the consequences of the positive response to similarity in the following section.

Matching Each Other: Liking Others Who Are Like Yourself

Whether or not the evolutionary explanation for a similarity effect is the basic one, it is true that attraction is affected by many types of interpersonal similarity. Though it is commonly believed that "opposites attract," research overwhelmingly indicates that similarity is the rule.

Sir Francis Galton first determined that "like marries like" in 1870, but the **matching hypothesis** became a matter of interest to social psychologists in the context of research on physical attractiveness (Berscheid et al., 1971). The idea is that romantic partners tend to pair off on the basis of being similar in physical attractiveness. See Figure 6.9. Not only are dating couples similar in attractiveness, but married couples are, too (Zajonc et al., 1987). Observers usually react negatively when they perceive couples who are "mismatched." The dissimilar couples are rated as having less ability, being less likable, and having a less satisfactory relationship than couples who are similar in attractiveness (Forgas, 1993).

It is perhaps more surprising, but matching for attractiveness also occurs in same-sex friendships, for men as well as women (Cash & Derlega, 1978; McKillip & Reidel, 1983). Also surprising is the fact that two individuals assigned as college roommates will be less satisfied if they are dissimilar in attractiveness than if they are similar (Carli,

Balance Theory
Theory that specifies the relationships among (1) an individual's liking for another person, (2) his or her attitude about a given topic, and (3) the other person's perceived attitude about the same topic.

Consensual Validation The perceived validation of one's views that is provided when someone else expresses identical views.

Matching Hypothesis The proposal that individuals are attracted to one another as friends, romantic partners, or spouses on the basis of similar attributes—physical attractiveness, age, race, personality characteristics, or social assets such as wealth, education, or power.

■ The matching hypothesis: Selecting a similar partner

FIGURE 6.9 Research indicates that the matching hypothesis is correct. People tend to choose friends, lovers, and spouses who are similar to themselves in physical attractiveness.

Ganley, & Pierce-Otay, 1991). The dissatisfaction is expressed by the more attractive of the two, apparently because the less attractive roommate is believed to be unacceptable to outside friends and hence an obstacle to the attractive student's social life.

Beyond attitude and appearance similarity, numerous studies have reported that similarity and perceived similarity on a wide variety of specific characteristics are associated with attraction (Hogg, Cooper-Shaw, & Holzworth, 1993). For example, college students who choose their roommates do so in part because the two individuals are similar in sociability (Joiner, 1994). Among other similarity findings are the positive effects on attraction of being alike in expressing emotions (Alliger & Williams, 1991); smoking marijuana (Eisenman, 1985); belonging to a given religion (Kandel, 1978); having similar self-concepts (LaPrelle et al., 1990); smoking, drinking, and engaging in premarital sex (Rodgers, Billy, & Udry, 1984); accepting traditional gender roles (Smith, Byrne, & Fielding, 1995); and being morning versus evening people (Watts, 1982).

Reciprocity in Attraction: Mutual Liking

Having discovered similarities a final confirmation is needed for a relationship to be established—the discovery that your liking of another is *reciprocated* by the other person (Condon & Crano, 1988). Almost everyone is pleased to receive such feedback. In contrast, unreciprocated liking—or worse, unrequited love—is very upsetting (Coleman, Jussim, & Abraham, 1987). Often, even an inaccurate positive evaluation (Swann et al., 1987) is well received.

The first signs of mutual liking are often nonverbal (see the discussion of nonverbal cues in Chapter 2). For example, when a woman converses with a man while maintaining eye contact and leaning toward him, he often interprets her behaviour (sometimes incorrectly) as an indication that she likes him, and so he may be attracted to her (Gold, Ryckman, & Mosley, 1984). As we saw above, reciprocal exchange of *self-disclosure* increases intimacy, in part because it increases the feeling of being liked and trusted (Derlega & Grzelak, 1979).

It seems very clear that we like those who like us or who we believe like us. You may find it useful to consider several techniques that should lead people to like you, as outlined in the Ideas to Take with You feature at the end of the chapter. In the following chapter we will see that knowledge that liking tends to be reciprocated can be used as a technique of social influence—through flattery and ingratiation.

KEY POINTS

- One of the factors determining attraction is *similarity* of attitudes, beliefs, values, and interests. Though dissimilarity has a greater impact on attraction than similarity, we respond to both. The higher the *proportion of similar attitudes* (including beliefs, values, etc.) the greater the attraction.
- Explanations of the similarity effect include *balance theory*, the need for *consensual validation*, and the importance of genetic similarity.
- As the *matching hypothesis* suggests, people are most attracted to others who resemble them on a wide variety of dimensions. That is, we like, become friends with, date, and marry those who are similar to us.
- We also like other people who *reciprocate* our positive evaluations of them, either in what they say or in what they do; and we tend to dislike others who evaluate us negatively. In a great many situations, flattery will get you everywhere.

FROM LIKING TO LOVING: MOVING BEYOND CASUAL FRIENDSHIPS

Moving from acquaintance to romantic relationships, social psychological research in recent years has provided considerable information about what is involved in romance, love, and sexual intimacy. Note that as a relationship develops, each of these three components may or may not be involved; and they may take place simultaneously or in any sequence. Also, it is generally true that people who are successful in making friends and establishing close friendships are likely to be successful in forming romantic relationships (Connolly & Johnson, 1996).

Most of the following discussion will be based on research with heterosexual relationships, because most psychological research has dealt with such relationships. However, within the last two decades, as relationship research has become more diverse generally—focusing on a wider range of types of relationship—it has also begun to take account of sexual orientation. Where research has compared sexual ori-

■ Dating behaviour: Having fun and acting nice

FIGURE 6.10 When two people are falling in love, they tend to engage in enjoyable activities, seek only compliments and positive evaluations from each other, experience positive illusions about each other and about the relationship, and behave as nicely as possible.

Source: The New Yorker, January 18, 1998, p. 37.

S.GROSS

"You certainly know how to show a girl a good time."

entations, the major differences found are not between gay and straight relationships but between the responses of males and females, regardless of their sexual orientation (Duffy & Rusbult, 1986; Kurdek, 1996, 1998; Peplau, Veniegas & Campbell, 1996). Although research continues, at this stage it is probably safe to say that the commonalities between gay and straight relationships are greater than the differences—the ecstasies and agonies of love are ones to which we can all relate.

There are a number of differences between a friendship and a romantic relationship. Aron et al. (1989) point out that many people fall in love, but that there is no analogous experience of "falling in friendship." Although the initial contact may occur in similar ways, there is the special problem of how to initiate a romance. College undergraduates say that they hesitate to "make the first move" because they fear rejection, but at the same time they interpret a partner's hesitation as indicating a lack of interest. For example they are often the focus for more social anxiety than in friendship formation (Snell, 1998). It is particularly important to be accepted—to like and to be liked. People go out to have a good time, and they are on their best behaviour (see Figure 6.10). Judgments are very often unrealistic, because each individual is searching for uncomplicated, totally positive feedback from the partner (Simpson, Ickes, & Blackstone, 1995).

Another way to describe romance, then, is to say that such relationships are built in part on fantasy and positive illusions and that such illusions actually help to create better relationships (Martz et al., 1998; Murray & Holmes, 1997; Murray, Holmes, & Griffin, 1996). Perceptions of one's partner tend to be biased; the other person is perceived as being more like one's ideal self (see Chapter 4) than is actually the case (Klohnen & Mendelsohn, 1998). Actually, it is not as important to be accurate about a romantic partner as to be *confident* that one is accurate (Swann & Gill, 1997). One consequence of these tendencies is that, in both the United States and the Netherlands, for example, couples judge their own relationships to be more positive than the relationships other people have (Van Lange & Rusbult, 1995). As other investigators note, the feeling is that "most relationships are good, but ours is best" (Buunk & van der Eijnden, 1997). Another sort of illusion is *belief in romantic destiny*—the conviction that two people are either meant for each other (or that they are not). If a relationship begins positively, it is likely to be maintained for a longer period of time among those who hold this belief (Knee, 1998). That is, if two people care for each other, and believe they were meant to be together, such beliefs can help hold the relationship together.

Passionate Love: The Basis of Romantic Relationships

Love can take many forms, but it is passionate love that is the focus of popular songs and has been the topic of most research (Hendricks & Hendricks, 1986). As we saw, proximity and similarity are major determinants of friendship. Love, in contrast, is much more likely to be precipitated by desirable aspects of the other person, such as an attractive appearance, pleasing personality, and reciprocal liking (Lamm, Wiesmann, & Keller, 1998). It is even possible to love someone who does not love you. This one-way flow of affection is known as *unrequited love*. In one large survey about 60 percent of respondents said that they had had such an experience within the past two years (Bringle & Winnick, 1992). Men in late adolescence and early adulthood report more instances of unrequited love than women do, and more instances of unrequited than of mutual love (Hill, Blakemore, & Drumm, 1997). The incidence of love that is not recip-rocated is greatest among those whose attachment style is *preoccupied*—the individual feels ambivalent and insecure about relationships (Aron, Aron, & Allen, 1998). When unrequited love develops, the one who loves in vain feels rejected and loses self-esteem, while the one who fails to respond to the other's love feels guilty (Baumeister, Wotman, & Stillwell, 1993).

In any event, romance often begins as a sudden, intense, all-consuming response to another person. Phrases such as *falling head over heels in love* imply that love is an accident—something like slipping on a banana peel (Solomon, 1981). This kind of interpersonal response is labeled **passionate love** (Hatfield, 1988), one of several varieties of love that have been identified. A person experiencing passionate love tends to be preoccupied with his or her partner—and to perceive the love object as being perfect. Responses include sexual attraction, physiological arousal, the desire to be in constant contact, despair at the thought of the relationship ending, and the intense need to be loved in return. Hatfield and Sprecher (1986) developed the Passionate Love Scale to measure this emotion, with items such as "I would feel deep despair if _____ left me" and "For me, _____ is the perfect romantic partner."

Under the "right" conditions, passionate love can arise suddenly and without warning. Even a brief contact with a stranger can sometimes lead to love at first sight (Averill & Boothroyd, 1977). When two opposite-sex strangers in a laboratory exper-iment are simply asked to gaze into each other's eyes for two minutes, they are likely to report feelings of passionate love for each other (Kellerman, Lewis, & Laird, 1989). What is the explanation for this seemingly irrational response?

Passionate Love An intense and often unreal-istic emotional response to another person. When two individuals respond to one another in this way, they interpret their feelings as "true love," while observers often label their response as "infatuation."

Cultural and Evolutionary Explanations for Passionate Love

Do we fall in love because our culture has taught us to expect this to happen or because this is an inbuilt and instinctive response? This is essentially the distinction between the sociocultural approach to passionate relationships and the evolutionary approach. How much do our cultures and biology contribute to the experience of passionate love?

Culture's Contribution to Passionate Love

In an explanation that focuses on the cultural contribution to passionate love, Hatfield and Walster's (1981) **three-factor theory of passionate love** suggests that three condi-tions are necessary (see Figure 6.11). First, you must learn what love is and develop

Three-Factor Theory of Passionate Love
This theory suggests that for passionate love to develop an individual must (1) come from a cultural background that teaches about love, (2) be in the presence of another person considered an appropriate love object by the culture, and (3) be physiologically aroused.

the expectation that it will happen to you (Dion & Dion, 1988). Beginning in early childhood, most of us are exposed to the idea that people fall in love and get married. Remember *Snow White* and *Cinderella*. If you were raised on such stories, how much did they shape your own expectations about love? The second condition required for the occurrence of passionate love is the presence of a culturally appropriate target person with whom one can fall in love. Social learning theorists propose that we have been taught by parents, movies, books, songs, and peers to seek an attractive partner of the opposite sex—someone similar to ourselves in most respects. Thus, we base our romantic choices on culturally prescribed criteria.

The third requirement for passionate love is that a state of emotional arousal occur while the love object is present. If arousal occurs in the presence of an attractive person of the opposite sex, attraction, romantic feelings, and sexual desire often result. The Capilano Bridge experiment (Dutton & Aron, 1974) described earlier demonstrated that this arousal can involve the states as fear, and in other research it has been frustration and anger (Driscoll, Davis, & Lipetz, 1972). In such cases the term "passionate love" is simply a misattribution. When the arousal involves sexual excitement (Istvan, Griffitt, & Weidner, 1983), being "in love" may be a more accurate label for one's aroused state. Though it has long been assumed that romantic love was invented in medieval Europe, some psychologists, historians, and anthropologists have recently become convinced that it is a universal phenomenon (Gray, 1993; Hatfield & Rapson, 1993).

The Biological Contribution to Passionate Love

A second explanation of passionate love's apparently universal presence is based on *evolutionary theory* (Buss & Schmitt, 1993; Fisher, 1992). About four or five million years ago, our ancestors began to walk in an upright position and forage for whatever food could be carried back to a safe shelter. The survival of our species depended on reproductive success (Buss, 1994). That is, men and women had to be sexually attracted and also willing to invest time and effort in feeding and protecting their offspring. These two different but equally crucial aspects of reproductive success—sexuality and commitment—were enhanced among those humans whose physiology led them to seek and

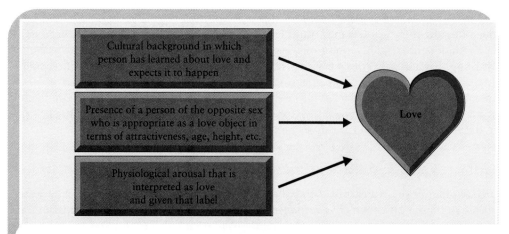

■ Love-oriented culture + love object + arousal = love

FIGURE 6.11 According to the three-factor theory of passionate love, love is likely to occur when three conditions are met. If you live in a culture that teaches you what love is, meet someone who is an appropriate love object, and are physiologically aroused, you may very well interpret your aroused state as indicating love. This process underlies the behaviour that has led to such familiar phrases as "love at first sight," "love is blind," and "head over heels in love." Sadly enough, passionate love is not likely to last, and enduring love requires a more realistic foundation.

enjoy not only sexual satisfaction but also bonding between male and female and between parent and child. Note that animal research provides evidence of the effect of brain chemistry on pair bonding (Rensberger, 1993). With emotional attachments motivated by physiological underpinnings, early human male-female pairs became more than simply sex partners—they also liked and trusted one another and divided up the necessary tasks into hunting and gathering food versus caring for the children. Thus, according to this scenario, love enhances *reproductive success*. As a consequence, today's humans are genetically primed to seek sex, fall in love, and care for their children. Brain chemistry may underlie monogamy (Insel & Carter, 1995), and most young married adults expect their relationship to be a monogamous one (Wiederman & Allgeier, 1996).

Keep in mind that even if this evolutionary explanation is accurate, cultural influences can still overcome people's tendencies to fall in love; guide these tendencies into quite specific and varied forms; and even add new elements based on stories, religious practices, and the laws societies enact (Allgeier & Wiederman, 1994). In any event, Elaine Hatfield, who has been studying relationships for the past thirty years, concludes that both factors contribute to passionate love (Hatfield & Rapson, 1996).

KEY POINTS

- Romantic relationships differ from friendships in a number of ways. They tend to involve a number of illusions about the partner and the relationship.

- The basis for romantic relationships is often *passionate love*, an intense, overpowering emotional experience. The *three-factor theory* emphasizes the role of cultural socialization in passionate love, while evolutionary theory stresses its biological or genetic basis.

Cultural Differences in Passionate Love

The issue of culture differences in passionate love has been addressed by Canadian researchers Karen and Ken Dion. They suggest that different value orientations on the individualism-collectivism dimension will affect how people conceptualize love and intimacy (Dion & Dion, 1993). The idea of romantic or passionate love as the most important basis for marital relationships is seen as a particularly individualistic one: emphasizing the personal satisfaction and excitement to be gained from the relationship. However, in collectivistic societies where group benefits take precedence over individual, the personal satisfaction of romantic love will be less important. Here we find that family involvement in the choice of a partner is more likely, with a focus on how marital partners will benefit the extended family.

Their review of the literature (Dion and Dion, 1996) suggests that the younger generation in many of the developed Asian countries (e.g., Japan and Taiwan) is turning to more individualistic conceptions of romantic love. Further, we can expect that within a predominantly individualistic but multicultural society, such as Canada, there will be variations between subgroups in the extent to which they endorse the predominant values. In addition, there will be intergenerational differences as a function of exposure to Canadian society—that is, the extent of acculturation. Research is beginning to accumulate in support of these suggestions.

Typically research shows that those in collectivistic countries are less likely to endorse romantic or passionate love styles than those in individualistic countries. For example, a study of college students in Japan, Germany, and the United States found that

Japanese students placed much less value on romantic love than students in the two Western countries and they also saw being in love as a state of having primarily negative connotations—being in a dazed state and feeling jealous (Simmons, Von Kolke, & Shimizu, 1986). Within Canada, Dion & Dion (1993) found greater endorsement of friendship love among Chinese-Canadians than among European-Canadians. Chinese residents of Hong Kong place greater stress on the importance of *yuan*, the idea that love is predestined and a matter of fate. Belief in yuan is associated with logical and selfless love styles, which are fairly uncommon among Westerners (Goodwin & Findlay, 1997).

Those from Western cultures also tend to see romantic love as the basis for marriage (Hatfield & Rapson, 1996). Research has used the question "If a man (woman) had all the other qualities you desired, would you marry this person if you were not in love with him (her)?" to examine the importance of passionate love in marriage to those in different cultures. In one study of 11 cultures (Levine, Sato, Hashimoto & Verna, 1994), those from the United States and England overwhelmingly answered "No" to this question as would be expected from those in an individualistic society. In contrast, in India, Thailand, and Pakistan, traditionally collectivistic societies, the majority answered "Yes." Interestingly, around 60 percent of subjects from Japan and the Phillipines answered "No." Dion and Dion suggest that this endorsement of love as the basis for marriage in Japan and Philippines reflects an intergenerational difference in these cultures. The subjects for this study were largely students in their early twenties and appear to be becoming Westernized in their values. Yang (1986) has suggested a similar trend among the young Chinese of Hong Kong and Taiwan. He describes this generation as turning away from a "social orientation" and toward the "individual orientation" of the West: putting greater emphasis on personal gratification and self-expression.

The Many Forms of Love: Beyond Passion

Passionate love may be a common experience, but it is too intense to be maintained indefinitely. Love that is totally based on emotion is sufficiently fragile that simply being asked to think about a relationship and answer questions about it can interfere with one's feelings of love (Wilson & Kraft, 1993). Passionate love seems to thrive best when our fantasies are not interrupted by detailed, rational examination.

Other kinds of love can, however, be long lasting and able to survive rational inspection. Hatfield (1988, p. 205) describes companionate love as the "affection we feel for those with whom our lives are deeply entwined." Unlike passionate love, **companionate love** is based on a very close friendship in which two people are attracted, have a great deal in common, care about each other's well-being, and express mutual liking and respect (Caspi & Herbener, 1990). This is a kind of love that can sustain a relationship over time—even though it does not lend itself to many songs and movies.

Hendrick and Hendrick (1986) extended the conception of love by adding four additional "love styles" to passionate and companionate love, as shown in Table 6.2. Among the research findings involving the six love styles are indications that men embrace both passionate love (*eros*) and game-playing love (*ludus*) more than women, while the reverse gender difference is found for companionate or friendship love (*storge*), logical love (*pragma*), and possessive love (*mania*) (Hendrick et al., 1984). Women high in possessive love report high levels of verbal and physical aggression in their dating relationships (Bookwala, Frieze, & Grote, 1994). Game-playing love is most characteristic of those who are concerned with themselves and their own independence (Dion & Dion, 1991); this is considered the least satisfactory style, because it leads to multiple sexual partners, unhappy relationships, loneliness, and coercive sexual behaviour (Hensley, 1996; Kalichman et al., 1993; Rotenberg & Korol, 1995).

Companionate Love
Feelings of love that are based on friendship, mutual attraction, common interests, mutual respect, and concern for each other's happiness and welfare.

Hendrick and Hendrick (1986) have proposed six distinct varieties of love. These include passionate and companionate (friendship) love, but they add four other possibilities. This table indicates the six "love styles" and presents sample items from a scale designed to measure each of them. People differ in the kind of love they feel, so the question of love style is a crucial issue for a couple attempting to work out a relationship that is satisfying to both.

TABLE 6.2 How do I love thee? Six possible ways

Basic Love Styles	Sample Test Item
Eros: Passionate Love	My lover and I were attracted to each other immediately after we first met.
Storge: Friendship Love	Love is really a deep friendship, not a mysterious, mystical emotion.
Ludus: Game-playing Love	I have sometimes had to keep two of my lovers from finding out about each other.
Mania: Possessive Love	I cannot relax if I suspect that my lover is with someone else.
Pragma: Logical Love	It is best to love someone with a similar background.
Agape: Selfless Love	I would rather suffer myself than let my lover suffer.

Very religious individuals are likely to be highest in friendship, logical, and selfless love (Hendrick & Hendrick, 1987). And in general, romantic partners tend to have similar love styles (Hendrick, Hendrick, & Adler, 1988; Morrow, Clark, & Brock, 1995).

Still another major conceptualization of love is Sternberg's (1986, 1988a, 1988b) **triangular model of love**, which is depicted in Figure 6.12. This formulation suggests that each love relationship contains three basic components that are present in varying degrees for different couples (Aron & Westbay, 1996). One component is **intimacy**—the closeness two people feel and the strength of the bond that holds them together. Partners high in intimacy are concerned with each other's welfare and happiness, and they value, like, count on, and understand one another. The second component, **passion**, is based on romance, physical attraction, and sexuality. **Decision/commitment** is the third component, representing cognitive factors such as the decision that you love the other person and the commitment to maintain the relationship. Actual lovers subjectively experience these three components as overlapping and related aspects of love. When all three components are present for a couple, the relationship is likely to be a long-lasting one (Whitley, 1993); and when all three components are strong and equally balanced, the result is consummate love.

Now that we have discussed the many varieties of love, you may find it useful to think about some of the love-related issues that are raised in the Ideas to Take with You feature near the end of the chapter.

Triangular Model of Love Sternberg's formulation that conceptualizes love relationships in terms of the relative emphasis placed on intimacy, passion, and decision/commitment.

Intimacy In Sternberg's triangular model of love, the closeness or bondedness of two partners.

Passion In Sternberg's triangular model of love, the sexual drives and sexual arousal associated with an interpersonal relationship.

Decision/Commitment In Sternberg's triangular model of love, the cognitive elements involved in deciding to form a relationship and in being committed to it.

KEY POINTS

- There are cultural differences in attitudes to passionate love. Those from individualistic cultures tend to value and see it as the basis for marriage to a greater extent.
- Love can take many forms. A close, caring friendship is labeled *companionate love*—a less intense and more lasting state than passionate love. Hendrick and Hendrick describe six love styles.
- Sternberg's *triangular model of love* describes love as a blend of three possible components: intimacy, passion, and decision/commitment.

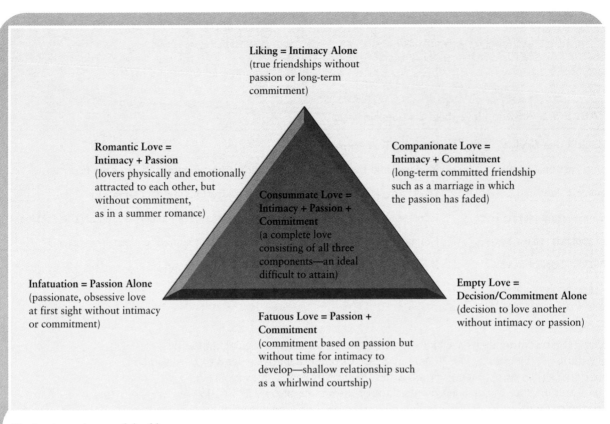

Liking = Intimacy Alone
(true friendships without passion or long-term commitment)

Romantic Love =
Intimacy + Passion
(lovers physically and emotionally attracted to each other, but without commitment, as in a summer romance)

Companionate Love =
Intimacy + Commitment
(long-term committed friendship such as a marriage in which the passion has faded)

Consummate Love =
Intimacy + Passion + Commitment
(a complete love consisting of all three components—an ideal difficult to attain)

Infatuation = Passion Alone
(passionate, obsessive love at first sight without intimacy or commitment)

Empty Love =
Decision/Commitment Alone
(decision to love another without intimacy or passion)

Fatuous Love = Passion + Commitment
(commitment based on passion but without time for intimacy to develop—shallow relationship such as a whirlwind courtship)

■ A triangular model of love

FIGURE 6.12 Robert Sternberg conceptualizes love as a triangle with three basic components: intimacy, passion, and decision/commitment. Love can be based on any one of these alone, on combinations of any two components, or on all three. There are seven quite different types of relationships, depending on which components are combined.

Source: Adapted from Sternberg, 1986, 1988.

LONG-TERM CLOSE RELATIONSHIPS

When college students are asked to identify the one person in the world to whom they feel most close, they describe one of three types of relationship (Berscheid, Snyder, & Omoto, 1989). Some (14 percent) specify a family member, 36 percent identify a friend, and almost half (47 percent) name a romantic partner. Canadian undergraduates reported close attachment relationships with an average of about five individuals, including family members, romantic partners, and friends (Trinke & Bartholomew, 1997). At the basis of any close relationship are the individuals' *attachment styles*, the enduring patterns of relating that individuals show.

Adult Attachment Patterns

Observations of different infant-mother attachment styles led Hazan and Shaver (1990) to propose that adults follow similar attachment patterns in forming relationships with their peers in romantic or friendship relationships. A recent model developed by Kim Bartholomew of Simon Fraser University is the **four-category model of adult attachment** (Bartholomew, 1990, 1993; Bartholomew & Horowitz, 1991). Basing her model on the original writings of John Bowlby on attachment in children (1973), Bartholomew proposes that adult attachment patterns can be conceptualized as derived from two related dimensions: (1) The positivity of the individual's model of the self (the extent to which the individual's self-concept is characterized by anxiety related to the self); and (2) the positivity of the individual's model of others in general (the extent to which the orientation to others is avoidant). Table 6.3 shows the four categories of adult attachment that result from these two dimensions: *secure, preoccupied, dismissing, and fearful-avoidant*. Beneath each one is the description used in research to define that particular type of attachment to others in general (Griffin & Bartholomew, 1994). Most people, rather than showing a single type of response pattern, display elements of two or more (Bartholomew & Horowitz, 1991). Of these attachment styles, only the secure style is likely to enable individuals to form long-lasting, committed, satisfying relationships (Shaver & Brennan, 1992). Research indicates that self-reports of cold or inconsistent relationships with one's parents are associated with later avoidant and/or preoccupied romantic attachments, whereas parental relationships described as warm are associated with secure romantic attachments (Bringle & Bagby, 1992).

Four-category Model of Adult Attachment Bartholomew's theory of adult attachment styles, in which a person's pattern of relationships with others stems from the individual's model of the self (positive or negative) and model of others (positive or negative). These two dimensions produce four categories of attachment style: secure, preoccupied, dismissing and fearful-avoidant.

Attachment Style and Relating

It is generally true that attachment style is most likely to influence social interaction when such interaction are with those who are close or potentially close to you (Pietromonaco & Barrett, 1997). Research shows that *secure* individuals express trust in their partners (Mikulincer, 1998b) and are able to engage in collaborative problem solving with their partners (Lopez et al., 1997). It has been argued that a secure attach-

The pattern of attachment that adults demonstrate depends on the positivity of their model of the self and the positivity of their model of others.

TABLE 6.3 The four-category theory of adult attachment

| | **Model of Self** | |
	Positive (Low Anxiety)	Negative (High Anxiety)
Model of Others — Positive (Low Avoidance)	**Secure Pattern** "It's easy for me to become emotionally close to others. I am comfortable depending on them and having them depend on me. I don't worry about being alone or having others not accept me."	**Preoccupied Pattern** "I want to be completely emotionally intimate with others, but I often find that others are reluctant to get as close as I would like. I am uncomfortable being without close relationships, but I sometimes worry that others don't value me as much as I value them."
Model of Others — Negative (High Avoidance)	**Dissmissing Pattern** "I am comfortable without close emotional relationships. It is very important to me to feel independent and self-sufficient, and I prefer not to depend on others or have others depend on me."	**Fearful-Avoidant Pattern** "I am uncomfortable getting close to others. I want emotionally close relationships, but I find it difficult to trust others completely, or to depend on them. I worry that I will be hurt if I allow myself to become too close to others."

Source: Based on Bartholomew & Horowitz, 1991.

ment style is roughly equivalent to the concept of androgyny that was described in Chapter 4—an ideal combination of masculine and feminine characteristics (Shaver et al., 1996). A person with a secure style tends not only to have a warm relationship with parents (Bringle & Bagby, 1992) but (in adulthood) to describe both his or her original and his or her new family in positive and nonpunitive terms (Diehl et al., 1998; Levy, Blatt, & Shaver, 1998) and to provide warmth and security for his or her own offspring (Scher & Mayseless, 1994). Compared to the people with other attachment styles, secure individuals are less prone to becoming angry, attribute less hostile intent to others, and expect more positive and constructive outcomes when an angry interaction occurs (Mikulincer, 1998a). Altogether, such individuals get along well with people, feel close to their parents, and express positive feelings about relationships (McGowan et al., 1999b). Compared to people with other attachment styles, secure individuals have a more balanced, complex, and coherent self-concept (Mikulincer, 1995). As you might guess from the descriptions of the four attachment styles, people prefer a secure romantic partner over any of the other three, regardless of their own attachment style (Chappell & Davis, 1998; Latty-Mann & Davis, 1996).

College students who are *fearful-avoidant* describe their parents as punitive and malicious (Levy et al., 1998). Among the characteristics of these individuals is a high level of hostility and a failure to realize when they are becoming angry (Mikulincer, 1998a). Also, fearful-avoidant individuals report less intimacy and enjoyment in interacting with the opposite sex (Tidwell, Reis, & Shaver, 1996), more jealousy, and a greater likelihood of using alcohol to reduce anxiety in social situations (McGowan et al., 1999b).

Preoccupied persons, along with those who are fearful-avoidant, are prone to feelings of shame in their relationships (Lopez et al., 1997). In responding to events in a relationship, preoccupied individuals interpret what is going on in more negative ways than do secure individuals, report more emotional distress, and expect more conflict (Collins, 1996). Both *dismissing* and fearful-avoidant individuals evaluate relationships in negative terms, tend to avoid face-to-face interactions in favour of impersonal contacts such as e-mail, and are more likely to drink alone (McGowan et al., 1999b).

Close Friendships

Close Friendship A relationship in which two people spend a great deal of time together, interact in a variety of situations, exclude others from the relationship, and provide emotional support to each other.

Beginning in childhood, most of us establish casual friendships with peers of our own age with whom we share common interests. We are also likely to establish a **close friendship**, usually with just one person. The transition from simply being acquainted with another person to being that person's friend is a gradual process that depends on a series of incidents or signs of mutual liking—making a nice gesture, reciprocating a favour, sharing moments of closeness, and so on (Lydon, Jamieson, & Holmes, 1997). Those in a close relationship are less likely to lie to each other—unless the lie is specifically intended to make the other person feel better (DePaulo & Kashy, 1998) and less likely to brag (Tice et al., 1995). Once established, a close friendship, compared to a casual relationship, results in the two individuals spending more time together, interacting in more varied situations, excluding others from the relationship, and providing mutual emotional support (Kenney & Kashy, 1994). Not surprisingly, close friends become increasingly accurate in their descriptions of each other's personality (Paulhus and Bruce (1992).

Closeness in a relationship means self-disclosure, support, and shared interests (Laurenceau, Barrett, & Pietromonaco, 1998; Parks & Floyd, 1996). People are most satisfied with their best friends if they are approachable, open-minded, active, industrious, and emotionally balanced (Cole & Bradac, 1996). A casual friend is someone who is "fun to be with," while a close friend is valued for generosity, sensitivity, and honesty (Urbanski, 1992). The establishment of close friendships has also been found to be related to attachment styles. Even in childhood and adolescence, those who have a secure attachment style are more likely to have a close friend and show superior social skills (Cooper, Shaver, & Collins, 1998; Shulman, Elicker, & Stroufe, 1994).

There are benefits to having close friends. For example, adults who have such a friend at work are more satisfied with their jobs (Winstead et al., 1995). The downside is that it is painful to lose or to be separated from a highly valued friend. Anticipating imminent separation from their best friend, graduating seniors report more intense emotional involvement with friends than is true for students not facing graduation (Fredrickson, 1995).

Gender differences in friendship are found. For example, women report having more close friends than do men (Fredrickson, 1995). Topics of conversation also differ (Martin, 1997). Common topics in a male-male conversation are women, sports, fighting, being trapped in a relationship, and alcohol consumption. Topics often associated with female-female conversations are relationships, men, clothes, problems with roommates, and giving or receiving presents.

The amount of research being devoted to adult friendships is increasing in recent years (Adams & Blieszner, 1994). Topics being investigated are lifelong friendships (Matthews, 1986; Whaley & Rubenstein, 1994), cross-sex friendships (Gaines, 1994), and friendship in the lives of gays and lesbians (Nardi & Sherrod, 1994). Recently interest has turned to friendship formation on the Internet. One question raised is whether the proliferation of Internet relationships will enrich our social lives or reduce our connections with those around us. The following On the Applied Side section discusses this issue.

KEY POINTS

- Adults' *attachment styles* reflects their feelings of anxiety and avoidance about relationships. This conceptualization yields four attachment styles that are labeled *secure, dismissing, fearful-avoidant*, and *preoccupied*. Individuals who are secure are best able to form long-lasting, committed, satisfying relationships.

- Friendships develop slowly but can last life long, with close friends providing each other with understanding and many other benefits.

On the **Applied Side**

Relating on the Net: Connection or Isolation?

In Canada, 36 percent of all households have at least one member who uses the Internet, and this figure rises each year. These users are most likely to have higher than average income and education, and to be below 55 years of age (Dickinson & Ellison, 1999). While the Internet enables us to have wider access to people we could not possibly meet through face-to-face contact, it is also a new form of interacting. For social psychologists this provides an intriguing context for studying relationship formation. And although the amount of research involving hard data is still quite limited, there is already controversy about whether the effect of the Internet on our social lives is positive—enriching our connections to others—or negative—leading to impoverishment of our social lives and greater isolation (Parks & Floyd, 1996).

Those who suggest a positive social impact of Internet use point to the fact that many common barriers to communication have less impact on the Net—barriers such as physical remoteness, being stigmatized due to a disability, social class and convention, and stereotyping and the preconceptions it produces. From this perspective the context of Internet communication is seen as a great liberalizer and equalizer of interpersonal relations. Further, it creates opportunities for everyone to form a wider variety of contacts with people from around the world and at many different levels of society. From its supporters' perspective, this can only be regarded as a beneficial outcome of Internet use, broadening people's social lives (e.g., Beninger, 1987; Berry, 1993; Pool, 1983; Rheingold, 1993).

Those who take a more negative view see many of these social benefits as illusory (e.g., Civin, 1999). They claim that while the individual may have a wider circle of contacts, relationships formed on the Net will tend to be more shallow and less developed. Why might that occur? For a start, there is a loss of relational and nonverbal cues when interacting on the Net (Culnan & Markus, 1987). See Table 6.4 for nonverbal sub-stitutes used on the Net. There is the lack of physical proximity, limiting the possibility of using observable characteristics of a person—their behaviour, appearance and facial expression—to understand them and the state of your relationship. It has been suggested that this loss of essential emotional information makes communication on-line more impersonal, and often more nonconforming, than face-to-face communication (Kiesler, Siegal & McGuire, 1984; Rice & Love, 1987). Because your on-line interactant is often depersonalized (you are less aware of him or her as an individual) and you too are equally anonymous, this can result in flouting of the normal social rules (Joinson, 1998; Noonan, 1998). Further, on-line relationships are seldom seen as providing the full range of practical and emotional support that those in your immediate social circle can, for example, someone to help you move or give you a hug when you are sad. In addition, extensive Internet use might detract from the investment of time and effort into local relation-

---

Research has shown that much of the communication on the Internet is social in nature. However, an essential part of the normal communication process is lost in this medium. We cannot observe or hear the emotional state of our interactants. Internet users have developed a series of symbols to compensate for this termed *smileys* (sideways faces with a variety of expressions) and *emoticons* (non-pictorial hints about the writer's feelings or actions).

TABLE 6.4 On the Internet, emotions are indicated by smileys and emoticons

Some Common Smileys (turn book on side to view)	The Approximate Meaning
:-) or :)	Feeling pleasant or happy
:-(or : (	Feeling sad or miserable
(:-(	Very unhappy and frowning
:->	Sarcastically intended
;-(	Crying "I'm so unhappy!"
;-) or ,-)	Winking "Don't take me seriously"
:-o or 8-o	Uh-oh! or Omigod!
:-@	AHHHH! screaming

Some Common Emoticons (indicates the expression or action of the sender)	
<grin>	Same as happy smiley
<sigh>	Sigh!
88	Love and kisses
_\,,/	I love you (an imitation of the ASL sign)
::	e.g. :: hits own head against wall :: Action markers

Source: Levine, Reinhold & Levine Young, 1999; Helwig's Smiley Dictionary, www.cg.tuwien.ac.at/~helwig/smileys.html

ships with family, friends and community, and those relationships may suffer.

On the one hand the Internet can provide a wider range of social possibilities, in a context that may create less social anxiety (because others cannot directly assess any physical or social limitations you have) and so make relating easier. On the other hand the relationships formed may be shallower and increase individuals' isolation with respect to their immediate social environment. This has been termed the "Internet paradox" by Robert Kraut and colleagues (Kraut, Patterson, Lundmark, Kiesler, Mukhopadhyay & Scherlis, 1998).

Kraut and colleagues point out that the positions described above are too often based on anecdote or theorizing rather than research data, particularly research examining long-term effects (1998). Their own study examined the social impact of Internet use over a two year period. At the beginning of the study subjects were not Internet users, but as part of the study they were provided with the hard- and software that enabled them to go on-line. Changes in *social involvement* and *psychological well-being* were measured before and after long-term Internet use. The degree of social involvement referred to subjects' family communication, social support and the size of their social circle in their immediate environment rather than on the Net. Measures of psychological well-being included loneliness, depression and degree of stress.

If Internet use enriched subjects' social lives rather than impoverished them, those using it more often should show less loneliness, and continued healthy relations in their local community. Subjects did in fact use the Internet chiefly for social purposes, such as communicating in chat and news groups and by e-mail. However, the major results provided support for the impoverishment view: the greater the subjects' use of the Internet the less their social involvement and the worse their psychological well-being. Those who used the Internet more frequently socialized less with family and local friends and, in addition, were more lonely and depressed.

Other studies by Parks and colleagues have looked at the nature of the relationships that develop on the Net and found moderate levels of depth, interdependence and commitment in relationships such as those among members of news groups (Parks & Floyd, 1996) and "Moos"— social interaction fantasy games (Parks & Roberts, 1998). Communication contexts became more varied as interpersonal relationships developed—people often e-mailed each other, spoke on the telephone and even met face-to-face. Their research also indicates that the quality of the on-line relationship varies with the particular Internet context and the length of contact of the users. However, *off-line* relationships were more developed and richer than those in the virtual world of the Net, whatever the context (Parks & Roberts, 1998).

The research reported above has led to heated debate (e.g., Kiesler & Kraut, 1999; Rierdan, 1999; Silverman, 1999) and we can expect such discussions to continue. Until a larger body of data has been gathered we cannot come to any final conclusion about the ultimate effect of Internet use on our social lives. While there is no doubt worthwhile relationships can be developed on the Net, Kraut's research suggests that the danger is that these relationships can become substitutes for higher quality, face-to-face relationships in our daily lives.

Marital and Family Relationships

It is clear that patterns of marital and family relationships are slowly changing in Canada. Census figures show that between 1971 and 1996 the marriage rate fell from 8.9 to 5.3 and divorce rates almost doubled from 1.3 to 2.5 per 1000 population (Che-Alford, Allen, & Butlin, 1994; Statistics Canada, 1999). In addition, the proportion of couples living common-law doubled between 1981 and 1996. However, it should be noted that marriage and family (defined by Statistics Canada in this case as married couples or common-law couples, with or without children, or single

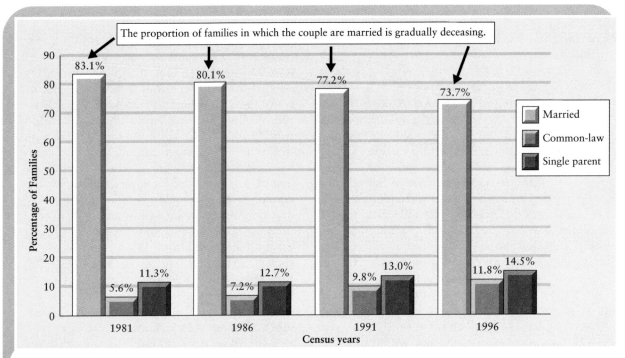

The proportion of families in which the couple are married is gradually deceasing.

■ Changing family structure in Canada

FIGURE 6.13 The structure of family life in Canada has been changing gradually. Since 1981, the proportion of all families in which the couples were married decreased by almost 10 percent, while the proportion of unmarried couples and single parents increased by the same amount. However, marriage remains the preferred form of family life in Canada.

Source: Based on Che-Alford, Allan & Butlin, Statistics Canada, 1994; www.statcan.com, Statistics Canada, January, 2000: *1996 Census Nation Tables.*

parents and children) are still by far the most preferred form of living arrangement. Figure 6.13 shows the changes in family structure in the period from 1981 to 1996. There are gradual decreases in marriage and increases in common-law relationships and in single-parent families. Although the proportion of single parent families is increasing, the proportion of male heads of those families has not increased: today the gender breakdown still remains around 17 percent male and 83 percent female, exactly it was in 1981.

Family life in Canada has slowly evolved from the extended family, common at the beginning of the twentieth century, to the two-parent "nuclear" family of the mid-twentieth century that remains the dominant form today. Perhaps diversity in family life will be the hallmark of the twenty-first century. For the present, however, we can say that the "traditional" family is still the preferred form of relationship: Today in Canada 86 percent of the husband-wife couples are married and 77 percent of families with children still contain both a father and a mother (Statistics Canada, 1999).

Most of the research in this area in social psychology has focused on marriage, although increasingly it is investigating common-law and same-sex couples (e.g., Kurdek, 1993, 1996). One of life's greatest challenges continues to be finding happiness in such relationships and discovering how to avoid dispute or break-up.

Similarity and Marriage

Not surprisingly, almost a century of research consistently indicates that spouses are similar in their attitudes, values, interests, and other attributes (e.g., Pearson & Lee, 1903; Schuster & Elderton, 1906; Smith et al., 1993). Interestingly, a longitudinal study of couples from the time they were engaged through twenty years of marriage indicated very little change in the degree of similarity over the entire period (Caspi, Herbener, & Ozer, 1992). In other words, similar people marry, and the similarity neither increases nor decreases over time.

Similarity is very important, but there are two problems that are often overlooked: (1) It is easy enough to find a potential mate who is similar to oneself in many respects, but practically impossible to find one who is *exactly* similar. So the two individuals will always have to learn to accept various differences and adjust to them; and (2) it is common at the beginning of a relationship to overlook or minimize some important areas of dissimilarity because of the many other factors, such as attractiveness, sexual passion, wealth or status, that can influence the choice of a partner. The dissimilarities may seem trivial at the beginning of a marriage, but over time other factors can fade or become less important. At that point the various differences may unexpectedly become extremely important and a source of dissatisfaction in the marriage.

Relationship Patterns Among Married Couples

A common question for married couples and for those studying married couples is the degree to which the partners are content with their relationship. Do people ever live happily ever after? Or are they often disappointed by the realities of spending a lifetime with a given spouse? Let's look at a few of the factors that influence marital satisfaction.

Surveys of married partners consistently indicate that sexual interactions become less frequent over time, and the most rapid decline occurs during the first four years of marriage (Udry, 1980). Nevertheless, 41 percent of all married couples

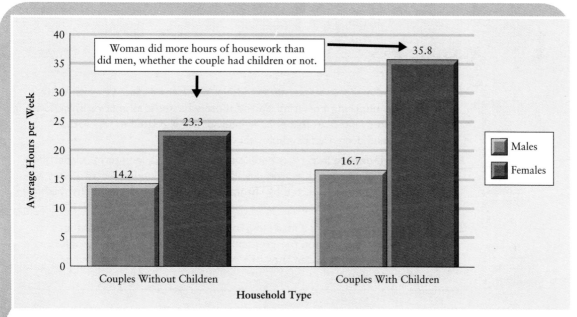

■ Hours of housework among Canadian couples

FIGURE 6.14 As more and more Canadian households contain dual-career families, the issue of who does what in the house becomes increasingly relevant. The *General Social Survey* of Statistics Canada (1992) found that women do considerably more housework than men. Of course, overall more women stay home and have fewer hours of paid external employment relative to men. But even when these factors are controlled statistically, women's hours of housework are still much greater than men's.

Source: Adapted from McQuillan & Belle, 1999; Statistics Canada, *General Social Survey*, 1992.

have sex twice a week or more often, whereas only 23 percent of single individuals have sex that frequently. Cohabiting couples are the most sexually active category, however, in that 56 percent have sex at least twice a week (Laumann et al., 1994; Michael et al., 1994). One reason, of course, is that unmarried couples who live together are usually within the early years of their sexual relationship. With respect to the relationship in general and to sexuality specifically, parenthood can create problems (Alexander & Higgins, 1993; Hackel & Ruble, 1992), although the majority of parents also report they enjoy the experience (Feldman & Nash, 1984). With multiple children, women report less and men report more marital satisfaction (Grote, Frieze, & Stone, 1996). Becoming a parent is also accompanied by a decrease in feelings of passionate love (Tucker & Aron, 1993).

It is not surprising that passionate love tends to decrease over the years (Tucker & Aron, 1993), but Aron and Henkemeyer (1995) found that women who still felt passionate love after the passage of several years were more satisfied with their marriages than women who no longer had these feelings. Male satisfaction with the marriage was unrelated to feelings of passionate love. For both men and women, satisfaction is related to behaviour that suggests companionate love—sharing activities, exchanging ideas, laughing together, and working together on projects (Lauer & Lauer, 1985).

A major task for both spouses is discovering how best to adjust to the demands of a two-career family (Gilbert, 1993; Helson & Roberts, 1992). One major issue in many households is housework. As shown in Figure 6.14, when Canadian couples have no children, women do over 60 percent more housework than men, and the gap is even wider when children enter the picture. Even when the number of hours of outside employment is controlled for, women still contributed over 50 percent more hours of housework than men (McQuillan & Belle, 1999). In fact, compared to heterosexual and gay couples, only lesbian pairs seem able to share household labour in a fair manner (Kurdek, 1993).

KEY POINTS

- Research on the effects of Internet friendships produces dispute between those who see it as enriching a person's life and those who see it as impoverishing. One longitudinal study indicates that greater Internet use is related to less social involvement and decreased psychological well-being.

- Despite a high divorce rate, most people marry or form a long-term relationship. Similarity between partners in attitudes, values, interests, and other attributes is greater than would be expected by chance, and the greater the similarity the more satisfying the relationship.

- Relationship patterns among married people change over times in term of the frequency of marital sex and the predominance of passionate love. Couples must often cope with the demands of a two-career family and with the pressures of child-rearing.

TROUBLED RELATIONSHIPS: FROM DISSATISFACTION TO DISSOLUTION

People usually enter long-term relationships with high hopes. So, each year in Canada about 160 000 couples marry and most of them are convinced that their marriage will last. However, in each year another 75 000 couples divorce. As Figure 6.15 suggests, people can change after they become partners, and many people seem to be nicer during courtship than they are as spouses. Maintaining a relationship is a never-ending job (Harvey & Omarzu, 1997), and success is not guaranteed. Whatever the problem, solutions may be possible, but couples differ in how well they deal with them. In this section, we will explore some major sources of conflict, possible ways to prevent or resolve problems, and some of the consequences of a broken relationship.

Problems in Relationships, and Possible Solutions

What happens to transform a loving romantic relationship into one characterized by unhappiness, dissatisfaction, and—sometimes—hate? People who believe they are ideally suited for one another can discover that there are negative as well as positive elements in the relationship. Studies of married couples indicate that most report having disagreements regularly (from more than once a week to monthly), while only 1.2 percent say they *never* have disagreements (McGonagle, Kessler, & Schilling, 1992).

Discovering Dissimilarities
The genders tend to have different sources of dissatisfaction in the relationship. While some behaviours are equally upsetting to both sexes (for example, unfaithfulness), others are more annoying to one sex than to the other. Buss (1989a) asked several hundred men and women to describe the source of their conflicts with a romantic partner. Generally, women become upset if their partners are not loving and gently protective, while men become upset if their partners reject them sexually or ignore them.

Because no partner (including oneself) is perfect, spouses who once believed that they were ideally suited for each other almost inevitably come to realize that there are negative as well as positive elements in the relationship. Spouses greatly overestimate how much they are in agreement about most matters (Byrne & Blaylock, 1963), and they are then disappointed when they discover that their views actually differ (Sillars et al., 1994). *Secure* individuals are most accurate in perceiving how similar they are to another individual, while those who are *fearful-avoidant* underestimate and those who are preoccupied overestimate similarity (Mikulincer, Orbach, & Iavnieli, 1998).

Even personal characteristics that once seemed to be especially positive attributes of the future spouse can become a primary reason for disliking him or her as time passes (Felmlee, 1995; Pines, 1997). For example, dissimilarity from oneself may seem interesting and intriguing in a romantic partner, but this can eventually become a source of distress and dislike. Early in the relationship, some things the other person says or does may seem cute. Later on, what was

"It's as though everything nice about you had been just some kind of introductory offer."

■ Relationship problems

FIGURE 6.15 One of the many potential problems in long-term relationships is that one or both individuals may eventually begin to behave less nicely than they did early in the relationship. If each person could continue over time to be as nice and considerate in interacting with a partner as was true on their first date, many problems could be avoided.

once cute becomes annoying. Felmlee's (1998) research suggests that if you are drawn to someone because that person is very different from yourself or even unique, chances are good that disenchantment will set in over time. One obvious solution is for two individuals to know as much as possible about one another early in the relationship (Byrne & Murnen, 1988).

Destructive Forms of Behaviour and Communication

Problems in a relationship are often accompanied by increases in abusive or destructive communications and behaviours. Even in the most healthy relationships conflicts arise. When people take the time to consider the long-term consequences for the relationship, a constructive response is more likely to follow (Yovetich & Rusbult, 1994). For example, when one partner makes the effort to apologize for something that was said or done and the other makes the effort to indicate forgiveness, they have engaged in constructive behaviour (Azar, 1997; McCullough, Worthington, & Rachal, 1997). Less obviously, those who learn simply to give in are more likely to have happy, stable marriages (Maugh, 1998). Marital disagreement is not a sport in which you need to score points or win every time. Couples interact in a more favourable way if each individual responds to the other person's need to maintain a positive self-evaluation (Mendolia, Beach, & Tesser, 1996) and works to understand the partner's perspective when problems arise (Arriaga & Rusbult, 1998). The most general characteristic of people who deal well with interpersonal conflict is agreeableness (Graziano, Jensen-Campbell, & Hair, 1996).

Destructive patterns of communication can arise over time when partners shift from providing one another with positive evaluations to words and deeds that indicate negative evaluations. Dating couples and newlyweds frequently express their positive feelings about one another. Gradually, however, quite different expressions of feeling occur. It is easy enough to think (or say), "I don't have to tell you I love you; I married you, didn't I?" Other indications of love can also fade away, as in "You don't bring me flowers anymore." Miller (1991) suggests that we become rude and impolite to intimate partners for three reasons. (1) In an intimate relationship there is more opportunity to discover a mate's many trivial imperfections than in other relationships, in part because each person feels confident of being accepted by the partner, feels less need for impression management, and so relaxes and becomes "himself" or "herself." (2) When the other person's flaws become apparent, misplaced expectations lead each spouse naively to assume that the other will change for the better; it is frustrating and annoying when change doesn't occur—and it usually doesn't. (3) It is easy enough to stop complimenting and rewarding a partner because of *lack of motivation*. It requires less effort and less thought to be selfish and impolite than to be socially skillful and thoughtful. We save that for others. This kind of shift is characteristic of unsuccessful relationships.

A person's attachment styles has been found to relate to the occurrence of abusive behaviour in a relationship. Dutton, Bartholomew and colleagues (Dutton, Saunders, Starzomski & Bartholomew, 1994) explored the relationship between adult attachment patterns (using Bartholomew's model of adult attachments, see Table 6.5) and abusive behaviour between couples. Verbal and physical abuse were least likely for those with a secure attachment style (positive image of self and others) and most likely for those with a fearful-avoidant style (negative image of self and others). A weaker relationship was found between a preoccupied style (negative image of self, but positive image of others) and abuse, but a dismissing pattern (positive image of self, negative image of others) was unrelated to abusiveness. Once again, research indicates that attachment patterns are related to success in adult relationships (Carnelley, Pietromonaco, & Jaffe, 1996; Radecki-Bush, Farrell, & Bush, 1993).

Jealousy: A Special Threat

Jealousy is a person's reaction to a perceived threat to the continuity or quality of a relationship (DeSteno & Salovey, 1994). The possibility of attraction toward someone new is a common problem in relationships, and jealousy is the usual response of one's partner (White & Mullen, 1990). Among the negative emotions aroused by jealousy are suspicion, rejection, hostility, and anger (Smith, Kim, & Parrott, 1988). Jealousy endangers a relationship. An individual who is dependent on a relationship, cares deeply about it, or is low in self-esteem is most likely to become jealous (Salovey & Rodin, 1991; White & Mullen, 1989). Jealousy also precipitates a decrease in self-esteem (Mathes, Adams, & Davies, 1985). Much like passionate love in reverse, jealousy elicits a flood of all-consuming negative thoughts, feelings, and behaviours (Pines & Aronson, 1983). Men and women also differ: Men become more jealous in response to sexual infidelity, while women's jealousy is stronger in response to indications of a partner's emotional commitment to someone else.

Jealousy The thoughts, feelings, and actions that arise when a relationship is threatened by a real or imagined rival for a partner's affection.

Taking an evolutionary perspective, Buss (1989) has proposed that such responses occur because of built-in differences between men and women. For reasons based on evolutionary pressures, women seek a mate who will be loving and protective, and women become especially upset by any indication that a partner is not affectionate or not eager to provide protection. It is suggested that men, however, primarily seek a young, healthy partner who is able to reproduce, and they become especially upset by sexual rejection. Consequently, although jealousy is a common problem in relationships (Buunk, 1995; Sharpsteen, 1995), the reason for jealousy differs as a function of gender. The evolutionary perspective also suggests that a rival's potential threat is based on these gender differences. Males are most troubled by a male rival who is dominant and powerful while females are most threatened by a female rival who is young and physically attractive (Dijkstra & Buunk, 1998). Support for the evolutionary explanation of these differences is strengthened by the finding that the same gender differences are found cross-culturally, in the Netherlands, Germany, and the United States (Buunk, 1995).

Jealousy has also been studied from the perspective of *attachment effects* (Sharpsteen & Kirkpatrick, 1997). Securely attached individuals tend to express anger toward the partner but to maintain the relationship. Those with a fearful-avoidant style tend to express anger and blame toward the outsider rather than the partner, while preoccupied individuals resist expressing any anger based on jealousy. In response to feeling jealous, preoccupied individuals express the most negative affect, whereas dismissing individuals report the least fear and unhappiness (Guerrero, 1998).

Though a lot of marital research focuses on problems, it should be remembered that still more marriages succeed than fail. A successful long-term relationship seems to involve an emphasis on friendship, commitment, similarity, and efforts to create positive affect (Adams & Jones, 1997; Lauer & Lauer, 1985). Older couples who remain together express more positive affect than younger and middle-aged couples (Levenson, Cartensen, & Gottman, 1994), perhaps because people get smarter and mellower about relationships as they grow older (Locke, 1995).

KEY POINT

- Problems and conflicts arise in long-term relationships. Among the common difficulties are dissimilarities between the partners, changes in costs and benefits, destructive forms of interaction, and *jealousy*.

Breaking Up Is Hard To Do

Social psychologists have become increasingly interested in understanding the last two stages in the relationship process: *deterioration* and *ending*. Friendships often fade away quietly when friends move to new locations or develop new interests (Rose, 1984). When love is involved, however, it is very difficult to drift apart peacefully. Instead, painful emotions are aroused, feelings are hurt, and anger can become intense.

Romantic relationships don't end easily because they involve the investment of one's time, the exchange of powerful rewards, and commitment (Simpson, 1987). If an acceptable substitute is readily available, the loss of a partner is less traumatic than when one is simply cast adrift (Jemmott, Ashby, & Lindenfeld, 1989).

Responding to Relationship Problems

Men and women differ in how they cope with a failed relationship. Women confide in their friends, whereas men tend to start a new relationship as quickly as possible (Sorenson et al., 1993). Divorce is, of course, a stressful experience for almost anyone; but, compared to persons with insecure attachment styles, an individual with a secure style experiences less distress and has a greater ability to cope (Birnbaum et al., 1997).

Rusbult and Zembrodt (1983) have pointed out that people respond either *actively* or *passively* to an unhappy partnership. To summarize the alternatives they suggest, an active response can involve ending the relationship (*exit*—"Here's the name of my lawyer; I'm filing for divorce") or working to improve it (*voice*—"I believe we should give marital counseling a try"). Passively, one can simply wait for improvement (*loyalty*—"I'll stand by my partner until things get better") or wait for the inevitable breakup (*neglect*—"I just won't do anything until the situation gets totally impossible"). These alternatives are diagrammed in Figure 6.16. If the goal is

■ Cost and benefits of a marital relationship

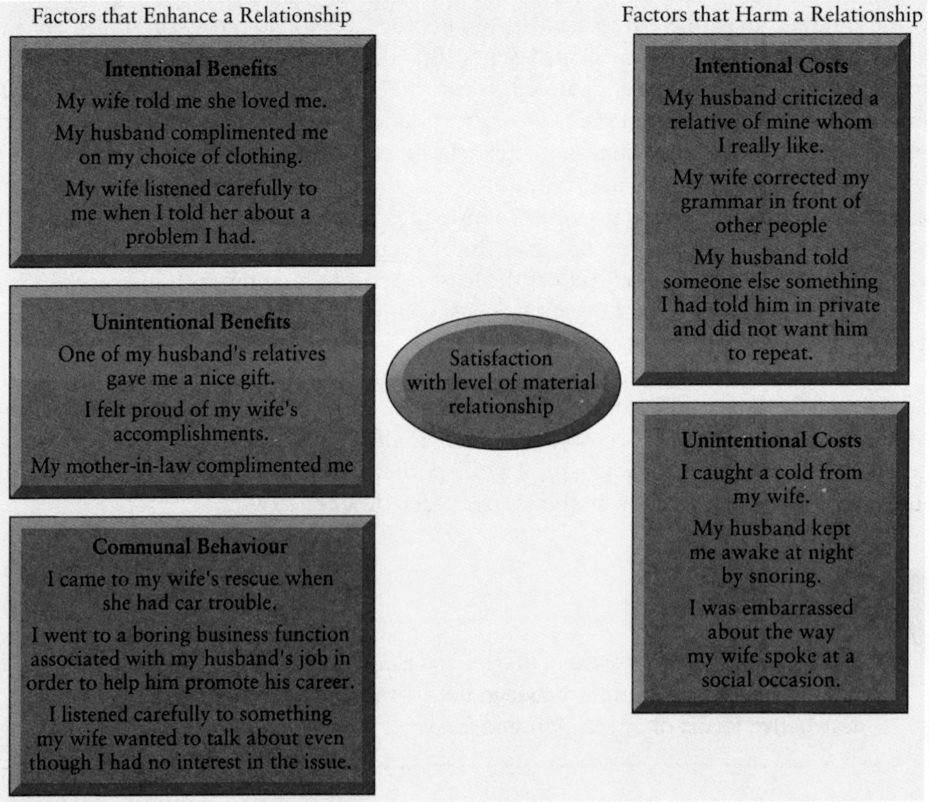

FIGURE 6.16 One approach to understanding relationship success and failure is to examine the relative costs and benefits. Clark and Grote (1998) developed a measure to asses intentional and unintenional costs and benefits in a marital relationship. In addition, they added a fifth category of "costs" (communal behaviour) that actually function as benefits. Marital satisfaction is believed to depend on the relative number of costs and benefits spouses experience in the marriage. Samples of some of the test items are shown here.

Source: Based on information in Clark & Grote, 1983.

Factors that Enhance a Relationship

Intentional Benefits
My wife told me she loved me.
My husband complimented me on my choice of clothing.
My wife listened carefully to me when I told her about a problem I had.

Unintentional Benefits
One of my husband's relatives gave me a nice gift.
I felt proud of my wife's accomplishments.
My mother-in-law complimented me

Communal Behaviour
I came to my wife's rescue when she had car trouble.
I went to a boring business function associated with my husband's job in order to help him promote his career.
I listened carefully to something my wife wanted to talk about even though I had no interest in the issue.

Satisfaction with level of material relationship

Factors that Harm a Relationship

Intentional Costs
My husband criticized a relative of mine whom I really like.
My wife corrected my grammar in front of other people
My husband told someone else something I had told him in private and did not want him to repeat.

Unintentional Costs
I caught a cold from my wife.
My husband kept me awake at night by snoring.
I was embarrassed about the way my wife spoke at a social occasion.

to maintain a relationship, exit and neglect are clearly the least constructive and voice the most constructive choice. Compared to secure individuals, those who are insecure are more likely to react with exit and neglect and less likely to react with voice. Loyalty tends to go unnoticed or to be misinterpreted: often, when people say that they have responded with loyalty, their partners perceive them as being uninterested or unaware (Drigotas, Whitney, & Rusbult, 1995).

Among quite divergent types of couples (college students, older spouses, gays, lesbians), men and women with high self-esteem tend to respond to relationship failure by exiting, while low self-esteem is often associated with passive neglect (Rusbult, Morrow, & Johnson, 1990). The more dependent a person is on the relationship, the less he or she is motivated to dissolve it (Drigotas & Rusbult, 1992), even in response to physical abuse (Rusbult & Martz, 1995).

The Importance of Commitment

Although it is very difficult to reverse a deteriorating relationship, couples can sometimes remain together despite their difficulties, particularly if they show **commitment**—the tendency to feel attached to a relationship and behave in ways that maintain it. As researchers began to study relationships over the long term, this concept emerged as central. We saw commitment as one element in the *triangular model of love* and Sternberg (1988) has suggested that the long-term marital relationship will be maintained by feelings of intimacy and commitment (or *companionate love*) rather than intimacy and passion (or *romantic love*). Caryl Rusbult's *investment model of commitment* (1981, 1983) describes the components of commitment. It suggest that commitment will be high and relationships more likely to last if: (1) the partnership provides satisfaction and comes up to each persons standards of expectation; (2) alternative lovers are not available; and (3) each person has invested a great deal of themselves and their life in the relationship (Rusbult, Martz, & Agnew, 1998). The greater such investments the greater the costs for the individual if the relationship ends. The cartoon in Figure 6.18 suggests that commitment may be in short supply in relationships these days!

Commitment A tendency to feel attached to, and to behave in such a way as to maintain, a long-term relationship.

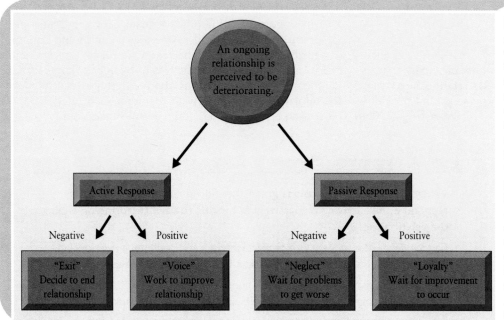

■ Alternative responses to a troubled relationship

FIGURE 6.17 When a relationship is beginning to fail, the partners can respond in either an active or a passive way. Either way, a partner can take a positive or a negative approach. Assuming the best, a partner can work actively to improve the situation or wait passively in the hope that improvement will simply occur. Assuming the worst, a partner can actively end the relationship or passively wait for it to fall apart. If the relationship is not hopeless, the adaptive response is an active, positive one.

Source: Based on suggestions by Rusbult & Zembrodt, 1983.

BIZARRO   By Dan Piraro

Do you promise to love & cherish each other until it's inconvenient, or you're tired of it, or somebody more exciting comes along, or it's just not fun anymore?...

■ Commitment in long-term relationships: In short supply?

FIGURE 6.18 Researchers have studied the constituents of commitment. According to Caryl Rusbult's investment model, commitment will be higher if a relationship provides satisfaction and comes up to expectations, if partners have invested a great deal of themselves and their lives, and when they do not have alternative relationships available. However, these factors don't seem to be a part of marriage for the couple in this cartoon!

Breakup and Divorce

Although about 84 percent of Canadians have been married by the age of 34 years (Kerr & Ram, 1994), almost 40 percent of those marriages will end in divorce, with the average duration of the marriage being 11 years (Che-Alford et al., 1994; *Canadian Social Trends*, 1994).

Longitudinal research on the dissolution of long-term relationships can indicate how important each of the problems discussed above are in determining whether couples break up. Kurdek (1993) obtained data from 222 newlywed couples each year for five years. Over that period, 64 of the couples dissolved their marriages. Several psychological factors were found to predict marital outcome. Associated with marital failure were dissimilarities in spouses' need for independence, in the value they placed on attachment, and in their motives for marriage. Further, breakup was associated with decreased positivity and problematic handling of conflict. These and other factors (each present at the time of the marriage) permitted a fairly accurate prediction of which couples would and would not remain married. A very similar pattern was shown in a five-year study of gay and lesbian relationships (Kurdek, 1996). Such findings suggest the possibility that couples planning a long-term relationship might find it valuable to be interviewed, tested, and counselled about the likelihood that their relationship will have problems.

Social psychologists, as well as other behavioural scientists, are focusing more and more attention on the study of long-term close relationships (Duck & Barnes, 1992; Morgan & White, 1993; Werner, Altman, & Brown, 1992) and from increasingly diverse perspectives (Hatfield & Rapson, 1996; Kurdek, 1996). Given the importance of family, friendship, love, and marriage to most people, social psychology's continuing attempt to discover what makes close relationships thrive, and how problems arise, is one of its most significant tasks. It is to be hoped that research on relationships can help people make better decisions about entering romantic partnerships and provide needed information about how to maintain such relationships. The Ideas to Take With You section below also has some useful suggestions.

> **KEY POINTS**
>
> ● When dissatisfaction becomes great, the individuals involved generally respond either actively or passively in moving toward restoring or ending the relationship.
>
> ● *Commitment*—the tendency to feel attached to and maintain a relationship—emerges as an important factor that can help people avoid breakup.
>
> ● Problems that partners bring to a relationship often appear to be the cause of breakup, including decreases in positivity and poor problem coping skills.

Ideas to Take with You

How to Encourage Others to Like You

Most of us would much rather be liked than disliked, and yet many of us have trouble getting to know other people and establishing friendly relationships. The suggestions outlined here are based on social psychological research, and you may find them helpful. If, of course, you don't want to be liked and prefer to be left alone, just do the opposite.

Control Proximity Factors.
Whenever possible, play an active role in arranging the ordinarily accidental contacts that control who becomes acquainted with whom. In the classroom, for example, sit beside others and avoid seats on the end of rows or in the corners. After a while, if you haven't become acquainted with those sitting near you, move to a new location and start over.

Create Positive Affect.
In situations where you hope to make friends, do whatever you can to create a pleasant mood. Depending on the situation, this could involve playing pleasant music, finding upbeat conversational topics, providing something good to eat and drink, as well as being nice yourself. It's as easy to be nice as to be obnoxious, and "nice" includes saying sincerely positive things to others. Compliments, praise, congratulations, and positive evaluations are almost always guaranteed to create a favourable impression; insults, criticisms, derogatory remarks, and negative evaluations are almost always guaranteed to cause discomfort.

Make the Most of Your Appearance and Look Beyond Appearances.
Because observable characteristics play an important role in how others react to you, anything you can do to improve your physical appearance and outward manner can be helpful. Without becoming obsessed about it, there are multiple ways to improve how you look and (much more easily) to improve whatever you say or do that pleases or offends others. On the other hand, try very hard to overcome inaccurate stereotypes based on superficial characteristics that may influence your response to others.

Stress Similarities and Minimize Differences.
Remember that people respond well to agreement and similarity. You don't need to deceive anyone about your own views or beliefs or interests, but there is absolutely no need to emphasize and dwell on areas of dissimilarity when you can find areas of similarity instead. No one likes to have their beliefs and values continually challenged (and potentially threatened), so approach disagreements in an open-minded and nondogmatic way. At the same time, try to make sense of the views of others without becoming threatened and defensive yourself. Keep in mind that agreement need not mean you are correct, and disagreement need not mean you are wrong.

All You Need Is Love?

There are few (if any) words that appear more often in songs, stories, movies, fairy tales, and in our everyday lives than "love." But the messages they give you about the nature of love can be confusing and contradictory. You might find it more helpful to consider some of the issues raised in social psychological research.

Emotional Arousal Is Not Necessarily Love.
When you encounter someone who appeals to you, it is easy to mistake a variety of arousal states as indicating love. As Elaine Hatfield has said, we often fall in lust and interpret it as love. Think of various things that may occur on a date (from kissing to watching a horror film to riding a roller coaster) that can potentially elicit arousal and lead to mislabeling. If you find

yourself surging with emotion and decide that you must be madly in love, pause and think about pinpointing alternative explanations for what you may be feeling. Give yourself time for sober second thoughts.

What Do You Know about This Person?
None of us has an acceptable and effective way to go about getting to know someone else in depth. And don't assume because you feel strongly about someone that they must be similar to you. We can't prepare detailed questionnaires for potential dates, lovers, or spouses to fill out. A simple but reasonable alternative is for two people to learn as much as they can about each other by talking, writing, chatting on-line, or whatever else they find comfortable. And each person should be aware of issues that are of special personal importance—from religion to politics, or from sex to parenthood. Ask. That may seem awkward, but it's better to be a little awkward now than to be surprised or hurt later on.

Summary and Review of Key Points

Interpersonal Attraction:
Becoming Acquainted

● Relationships can be seen as passing through five possible stages: (1) *initial attraction*, (2) *building a relationship*, (3) *continuation*, (4) *deterioration* and (5) *ending*.

The term *interpersonal attraction* refers to the attitudes we form about other people, expressed along a dimension ranging from like to dislike, based on feelings ranging from extremely positive to extremely negative.

One's initial contact with others is very often based on *proximity* resulting from such physical aspects of the environment as classroom seating assignments, the location of residences, and how a workplace is arranged.

Proximity leads to *repeated exposure* to some individuals in one's environment; repeated exposure tends to result in positive affect, and positive affect results in attraction.

Interpersonal attraction and interpersonal judgments are strongly influenced by various observable characteristics of those we meet, including *physical attractiveness*.

Evolutionary theory suggests that the features we find attractive in others are those associated with *reproductive success*. Other research suggests that cultural beliefs have a strong impact on our stereotypes of attractiveness.

People are found to like and to make positive attributions about attractive men and women of all ages, despite the fact that assumptions based on appearance are usually inaccurate.

Research has begun to identify some of the constituents of attractiveness, although there is also cultural variation. A computer-generated average face is more attractive, perhaps because of its generic familiarity.

Research on *impression formation*—the process through which we form impressions of others—suggests that first impressions are indeed important. Complex cognitive processes are involved such as the weighting of different information about others and the use of exemplars and abstractions.

Positive and negative affective states can influence attraction either through *direct effects* (when the other person is responsible for the positive or negative emotion) or through indirect or *associated effects* (when the emotion is created by a different source, but the other person happens to be associated with it). Sometimes *mislabelling* of emotion generated indirectly occurs, as in the Capilano Bridge experiment.

The *affect-centred model of attraction* provides an integration of the role of both cognition and affect in attraction. It specifies that attraction is determined by direct and associated sources of affect, only mediated by cognitive processes.

Individuals high, as opposed to low, in *need for affiliation* are more likely to engage in establishing and maintaining interpersonal relationships and are more interpersonally skilled.

People can be differentiated with respect to their reasons for wanting to affiliate, and these reasons lead to different types of affiliative behaviour oriented toward different goals.

When unusual circumstances, such as natural disasters, arise, people are likely to affiliate with others.

Research related to the theory of social comparison suggests that we affiliate when anxious in order to compare our reactions with those of others; often this results in positive effects.

Building a Relationship: Self-Disclosure, Similarity and Reciprocity

● Relationship building involves increasingly close communication between individuals. One essential part of this process is *self-disclosure* as interactants reveal increasingly personal information about themselves to the other person.

Research shows that women disclose somewhat more than men, particularly to same-sex friends. Comparison of individualistic and collectivist cultures produces conflicting research results. This may be because such behaviour depends upon cultural norms about the appropriateness of disclosure to same- or opposite-sex interactants and to ingroup or outgroup members.

One of the factors determining attraction is *similarity* of attitudes, beliefs, values, and interests. Though dissimilarity has a greater impact on attraction than similarity, we respond to both. The higher the *proportion of similar attitudes* (including beliefs, beliefs, values, etc.) the greater the attraction.

Explanations of the similarity effect include *balance theory*, the need for *consensual validation*, and the importance of genetic similarity.

As the *matching hypothesis* suggests, people are most attracted to others who resemble them on a wide variety of dimensions. That is, we like, become friends with, date, and marry those who are similar to us.

We also like other people who *reciprocate* our positive evaluations of them, either in what they say or in what they do; and we tend to dislike others who evaluate us negatively. In a great many situations, flattery will get you everywhere.

From Liking to Loving:
Moving Beyond Casual Friendships

● Romantic relationships differ from friendships in a number of ways. They tend to involve a number of illusions about the partner and the relationship.

The basis for romantic relationships is often *passionate love*, an intense, overpowering emotional experience. The *three-factor theory* emphasizes the role of cultural socialization in passionate love, while evolutionary theory stresses its biological or genetic basis.

There are cultural differences in attitudes to passionate love. Those from individualistic cultures tend to value and see it as the basis for marriage to a greater extent.

Love can take many forms. A close, caring friendship with a romantic partner is labeled *companionate love*—a less intense and more lasting state than passionate love. Hendrick and Hendrick describe six love styles.

Sternberg's *triangular model of love* describes love as a blend of three possible components: intimacy, passion, and decision/commitment.

Long-Term Close Relationships

● Adults' *attachment styles* reflects their feelings of anxiety and avoidance about relationships. This conceptualization yields four attachment styles that are labeled *secure*, *dismissing*, *fearful-avoidant*, and *preoccupied*. Individuals who are secure are best able to form long-lasting, committed, satisfying relationships.

Friendships develop slowly but can last life long, with *close friends* providing each other with understanding and many other benefits.

Research on the effects of Internet friendships produces dispute between those who see it as enriching a person's life and those who see it as impoverishing. One longitudinal study indicates that greater Internet use is related to less social involvement and decreased psychological well-being.

Despite a high divorce rate, most people marry or form a long-term relationship. Similarity between long-term partners in attitudes, values, interests, and other attributes is greater than would be expected by chance, and the greater the similarity the more satisfying the relationship.

Relationship patterns among married people change over time in terms of the frequency of marital sex and the predominance of passionate love. Couples must often cope with the demands of a two-career family and with the pressures of child-rearing.

Troubled Relationships:
From Dissatisfaction to Dissolution

● Problems and conflicts arise in long-term relationships. Among the common difficulties are dissimilarities between the partners, changes in costs and benefits, destructive forms of interaction, and *jealousy*.

When dissatisfaction becomes great, the individuals involved generally respond either actively or passively in moving toward restoring or ending the relationship.

Commitment—the tendency to feel attached to and maintain a relationship—emerges as an important factor that can help people avoid breakup.

Problems that partners bring to a relationship often appear to be the cause of break-up, including decreases in positivity and poor problem coping skills.

For More Information

Duck, S. (1994). *Meaningful relationships: Talking, sense, and relating*. Thousand Oaks, CA: Sage.

A leading investigator and theorist in the field of interpersonal behaviour, Steve Duck describes how relationships are a constant challenge, requiring continued effort and maintenance.

Hatfield, E., & Rapson, R. L. (1996). *Love and sex: Cross-cultural perspectives*. New York: Allyn & Bacon.

This very readable book was coauthored by a social psychologist and her historian husband. It examines love, sexuality, and relationships with particular emphasis on cultural and historical differences.

Hendrick, S. S., & Hendrick, C. (1992). *Romantic love*. Newbury Park, CA: Sage.

Two psychologists who are at the forefront in investigating the phenomenon of love bring together what is known on the subject. They combine material from psychologists, sociologists, historians, and philosophers in dealing with the history of love, love in close relationships, love styles, and the way love affects our everyday lives.

Gurdin, J. B. (1996). *Amitie/friendship: An investigation into cross-cultural styles in Canada and the United States*. Bethesda, MD: Austin & Winefield.

This book has been described as a landmark contemporary comparative study of friendship. Using data from surveys, participant observations, and small group research, the author describes how friendships are affected by ethnicity, gender, class, marital status, and age.

Gottman, J. M. (1993). *What predicts divorce? The relationship between marital processes and marital outcomes*. Hillsdale, NJ: Erlbaum.

This book covers research on marriage and divorce. The emphasis is on predicting marital success and failure, but the author also presents theory and recommendations about how to achieve a stable marriage.

Weblinks

www.isspr.org
International Society for the Study of Personal Relationships

www.apa.org/journals/amp/amp5391017.html
"Internet Paradox: A Social Technology That Reduces Social Involvement and Psychological Well-Being?" by Kraut, Lundmark, Carnegie Mellon University

www.soc.hawaii.edu/leonj/leonj/leonpsy/cyber.html
"Cyber-Psychology: Principles of Creating Virtual Presence" by Leon James, University of Hawaii

www.neoteny.org/a/femalesexualselection.html
Female Sexual Selection

www.massey.ac.nz/~i75202/lecture5/lect599.htm
Male and Female Mate Choice

Social Influence:

Changing Others' Behaviour

SPECIAL SECTIONS

"Sometimes I wish they'd never perfected setless television."

FIGURE 7.1 While efforts to change our attitudes and behaviour haven't yet reached this stage, they are becoming increasingly sophisticated—and perhaps effective.

I don't know about you, but I (Robert Baron) almost never answer my phone anymore. Instead, I let my answering machine take the call, and only pick up the receiver if it's someone I know or with whom I wish to speak. Why do I do this? Not because I'm unfriendly; almost everyone who knows me would say that just the opposite is true. Rather, I have adopted this strategy to protect myself from literally dozens of calls each day from people trying to sell me something or to get me to make a donation to some cause or vote for their candidate. In short, I screen my calls so that I can avoid many attempts at **social influence**—efforts by others to change my attitudes, beliefs, perceptions, or behaviour (Cialdini, 1994). Unfortunately, such efforts at social influence are an extremely common fact of life in today's world; and while they haven't yet reached the level shown in Figure 7.1, they do seem to be increasingly frequent and intrusive.

Where social influence is concerned, however, we dish it out as well as receive it. How many times each day do you try to influence others—friends, roommates, family members, romantic partners? If you are like most people, you practise many forms of social influence each day. Consider my own daily life. I have no trouble getting up in the morning, but my wife does; so my day often starts with gentle efforts on my part to coax her out of bed. As the hours pass, I find myself using social influence in many other contexts. I ask one of my colleagues if she'll take over my class while I am away at a conference; I ask the server at lunch to toast the bread on my sandwich and to hold the mayonnaise; I drop my car off for servicing and ask if I can have it back by 4:00 p.m.; I plead with my daughter to drive carefully when she goes to visit her boyfriend...and so it goes, all day long.

Because of its importance in our daily lives, social influence has long been a central topic of research in social psychology. We have already considered some of this

Social Influence
Efforts on the part of one person to alter the behaviour or attitudes of one or more others.

work in Chapter 3, where we examined the process of persuasion. Here, we'll expand on that earlier discussion by examining many other aspects of social influence. First, we'll focus on the topic of *conformity*—changing one's attitudes or behaviour in order to go along with the crowd, to act the same as other persons in one's group or society. As we'll soon see, pressures toward conformity can be amazingly strong and hard to resist. Next, we'll turn to *compliance*—efforts to get others to say yes to various requests. Finally, we'll examine *obedience*—a form of social influence in which one person simply orders one or more others to do what they want.

CONFORMITY: GROUP INFLUENCE IN ACTION

Conformity A type of social influence in which individuals change their attitudes or behaviour in order to adhere to existing social norms.

Social Norms Rules indicating how individuals are expected to behave in specific social situations.

Have you ever found yourself in a situation in which you felt that you stuck out like the proverbial sore thumb? If so, you have already had direct experience with pressures toward **conformity**. In such situations, you probably experienced a strong desire to "get back into line"—to fit in with the other people around you. Such pressures toward conformity stem from the fact that in many contexts, there are spoken or unspoken rules indicating how we should or ought to behave. These rules are known as **social norms**. In some instances, norms can be both detailed and precise. For instance, governments generally function through constitutions and written laws and athletic contests are usually regulated by written rules. Signs in many public places (e.g., along highways, in parks, and at airports) frequently describe expected behaviour in considerable detail—see Figure 7.2.

In contrast, other norms are unspoken or implicit. Most of us obey such unwritten rules as "Don't stand too close to strangers on elevators if you can help it" and "Don't arrive at parties or other social gatherings exactly on time." Similarly, we are often strongly influenced by current and rapidly changing standards of dress, speech, and personal grooming. Regardless of whether social norms are explicit or implicit, one fact is clear: *Most people obey them most of the time.* For example, few persons

■ Social norms: Regulators of everyday life

FIGURE 7.2 Social norms tell us what we should do (or not do) in a given situation. They are often stated explicitly in signs like these.

visit restaurants without leaving a tip for their server. And virtually everyone, regardless of personal political beliefs, stands when the national anthem of their country is played at sports events or other public gatherings.

Although social norms restrict an individuals options—prevent people from "doing their own thing"—there is a strong basis for the existence of so much conformity. Without conformity we would quickly find ourselves facing social chaos. Imagine what would happen outside movie theaters or voting booths or at supermarket checkout counters if people did not follow the simple rule, "Form a line and wait your turn." Given that strong pressures toward conformity do exist in many settings, it is surprising to learn that conformity, as a social process, was not the subject of systematic investigation by social psychologists until the 1950s. At that time Solomon Asch (1951) carried out a series of experiments that yielded dramatic results. In fact, the results obtained by Asch were so strong and so surprising that they quickly captured the attention of both social psychologists and the general public. This research is described in the Cornerstones section below.

Corner stones

Conformity Pressure: The Irresistible Social Force?

Imagine that just before an important math exam, you discover that your answer to a homework problem—a problem of the type that will be on the test—is different from that obtained by one of your friends. How do you react? Probably with mild concern. Now imagine that you learn that a second person's answer, too, is different from yours. To make matters worse, it agrees with the answer reported by the first person. How do you feel now? The chances are good that your anxiety will be considerable. Next, you discover that a third person agrees with the other two. At this point, you know that you are in big trouble. Which answer should you accept? Yours or the one obtained by your three friends? The exam is about to start, so you have to decide quickly.

Life is filled with such dilemmas—instances in which we discover that our own judgments, actions, or conclusions are different from those reached by other persons. What do we do in such situations? Important insights into our behaviour in such cases was provided by a series of studies conducted by Solomon Asch (1951, 1955)—studies that are considered to be true classics in social psychology. In his research, Asch asked participants to respond to a series of simple perceptual problems such as the one in Figure 7.3. On each problem they indicated which of three comparison lines matched a standard line in length. Several other persons (usually six to eight) were also present during the session; but, unknown to the real participant, all were accomplices of the

■ Asch's line judgment task: An example

FIGURE 7.3 Participants in Asch's research were asked to report their judgments on problems such as this one. On each problem, they indicated which of the comparison lines (1, 2, or 3) best matched the standard line in length.

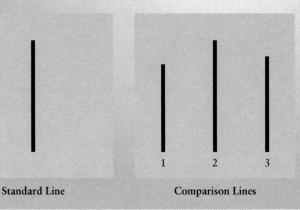

Standard Line   Comparison Lines

1   2   3

experimenter. On certain occasions known as critical trials (12 out of the 18 problems) the accomplices offered answers that were clearly wrong: they unanimously chose the wrong line as a match for the standard line. Moreover, they stated their answers before the participant responded. Thus, on these critical trials, the participants faced the type of dilemma described above. Should they go along with the other persons present or stick to their own judgments? A large majority of the participants in Asch's research opted for conformity. Indeed, in several different studies, fully 76 percent of those tested went along with the group's false answers at least once; in fact, they voiced their agreement with these errors about 37 percent of the time. In contrast, only five percent of the subjects in a control group, who responded to the same problems in the absence of any accomplices, made such errors.

Of course, there were large individual differences in this respect. Almost 25 percent of the participants never yielded to the group pressure. At the other extreme were persons who went along with the majority nearly all the time. When Asch questioned them, some of these persons stated "I am wrong, they are right"—they had little confidence in their own judgment. Others, however, said they felt that the other persons present were the victims of some sort of optical illusion, or were merely sheep following the responses of the first person. Nevertheless, when it was their turn to speak, these participants still went along with the group.

In further studies, Asch (1951, 1956) investigated the effects of shattering the group's unanimity by having one of the accomplices break with the others. In one study, this person gave the correct answer, becoming an "ally" of the real participant; in another, he chose an answer in between the one given by the group and the correct one; and in a third, he chose an answer that was even more incorrect than that chosen by the majority. In the latter two conditions, in other words, he broke from the group but still disagreed with the real participant. Results indicated that conformity was reduced under all three conditions. However, somewhat surprisingly, this reduction was greatest when the dissenting accomplice expressed views even more extreme (and wrong) than the majority. Together, these findings suggest that it is the unanimity of the group that is crucial: once that unanimity is broken, no matter how, resisting group pressure becomes much easier.

One more aspect of Asch's research is important to mention. In later studies, he repeated his basic procedure, but with one important change: Instead of stating their answers out loud, participants wrote them on a piece of paper. As you might guess, conformity dropped sharply. This finding points to the importance of distinguishing between public conformity—doing or saying what others around us say or do—and private acceptance—actually coming to feel or think as others do. Often, it appears, we follow social norms overtly, but don't actually change our private views (Maas & Clark, 1984). This distinction between public conformity and private acceptance is an important one, and we'll have reason to comment on it at several points in this book.

Asch's research was the catalyst for a flurry of activity in social psychology, as many other researchers rushed to investigate the nature of conformity, to identify factors that influence its impact, and to establish its limits (e.g., Crutchfield, 1955; Deutsch & Gerard, 1955). Indeed, such research is still continuing today, and is still adding to our understanding of this crucial form of social influence (e.g., Buehler & Griffin, 1994; Reno, Cialdini, & Kallgren, 1993). Clearly, then, Asch's early studies of conformity constitute an important cornerstone of social psychology—one with a lasting impact upon the field.

KEY POINTS

- *Social influence*—efforts by one or more persons to change the attitudes or behaviour of one or more others—is a common part of life.

- Most people behave in accordance with *social norms* most of the time; in other words, they show strong tendencies towards *conformity*.
- Conformity was first systematically studied by Solomon Asch, whose classic research indicated that many persons will yield to social pressure from a *unanimous* group.

Factors Affecting Conformity: Determinants of Whether We "Go Along"

Asch's research demonstrated the existence of powerful pressures toward conformity, but even a moment's reflection suggests that conformity does not occur to the same degree in all settings. For instance, body piercing and tattoos are really in vogue right now (see Figure 7.4), with the result that many teenagers and some young adults experience strong pressures to adorn themselves in these ways. Yet despite this fact, many are not tattooed or pierced. Why? In other words, what factors determine the extent to which individuals yield to conformity pressure or resist it? Many variables seem to play a role, however, we will focus on five that have been considered important: (1) *cohesiveness*—degree of attraction to the group or persons exerting influence; (2) *group size and unanimity*—how many persons are exerting influence; (3) the *type of social norm* involved in the influence attempt; (4) the effect of *cultural background*; (5) *gender differences* in conformity.

Cohesiveness With respect to conformity, the degree of attraction felt by an individual toward an influencing group.

Cohesiveness and Conformity: Accepting Influence From Those We Like

Let's return to the craze for body piercing. Recently, this fashion has moved into a new phase; not content to wear simple rings or jewels, some young people are having much larger items attached to their bodies, including artificial horns—which presumably give them that "devil-may-care" look they've always wanted (Leonard, 1998)! Suppose that this fashion suddenly appeared in your own neighborhood. Further, imagine that the people who adopted it were the most popular and admired in the entire area. Would their adoption of this new style lead to its rapid spread? Perhaps; in any case, the fact that they adopted it would tempt many persons to do the same. But now suppose that instead, the only ones who adopted the new fad were the unpopular people in your neighborhood—people who were viewed as losers and weird. Would their adoption of the new fashion lead to its rapid expansion? Probably not; after all, who would want to be like them?

This example illustrates one factor that plays an important role where conformity is concerned: **cohesiveness**, which can be defined as the degree of attraction felt by individuals toward some group. When cohesiveness is high—when we like and admire some group of persons—pressures toward conformity are magnified. After all, we know that one way of gaining the acceptance of such persons is to be like them in various ways, even if this involves alterations in our own anatomy. When cohesiveness is low, on the other hand, pressures toward

■ What factors influence conformity?

FIGURE 7.4 These days body piercing is popular among some groups. When any fad occurs there are strong conformity pressures on group members. Yet there are many who have no peircings at all. Why? What factors determine the extent to which individuals will yield to conformity pressure or resist it?

conformity are also low; why should we change our behaviour to be like other people we don't especially like or admire? Research findings indicate that cohesiveness exerts strong effects on conformity (Crandall, 1988; Latané & L'Herrou, 1996), so it is definitely one important determinant of the extent to which we yield to this type of social pressure.

Group Size and Unanimity

A second factor that exerts important effects on the tendency to conform is the *size* of the influencing group. Asch (1956) and other early researchers (e.g., Gerard, Wilhelmy, & Conolley, 1968) found that conformity increased with group size, but only up to about three members; beyond that point, it appeared to level off or even decrease. More recent research, however, has failed to confirm these early findings (e.g., Bond & Smith, 1996). Instead, these later studies have found that conformity tends to increase with group size up to eight group members and beyond. So it appears that the larger the group, the greater our tendency to go along with it, even if this means behaving in ways different from the ones we'd really prefer.

However, it is also important that the group members agree. In Asch's early research, and in many later studies of conformity, subjects were exposed to social pressure from a *unanimous* group. Under those conditions, most subjects yielded to social pressure. But when another person present broke with the majority, conformity was reduced (Asch, 1951, 1956). Later studies found that conformity is reduced even when the ally in nonconformity is inaccurate or someone not competent in the present situation. For example, in one study, involving visual judgements, conformity was reduced even by a partner who wore thick glasses and could not see the relevant stimuli (Allen & Levine, 1971). These and other findings suggest that almost any form of *social support* can help a person resist social pressure.

Type of Social Norm: What We Should Do Versus What We Actually Do

Social norms, we have already seen, can be formal or informal in nature—as different as rules printed on large signs and informal guidelines such as "Don't leave your shopping cart in the middle of a parking spot outside a supermarket." This is not the only way in which norms differ, however. Another important distinction is that between **descriptive norms** and **injunctive norms** (e.g., Cialdini, Kallgren, & Reno, 1991; Reno, Cialdini, & Kallgren, 1993). Descriptive norms are ones simply indicating what most people do in a given situation. They influence behaviour by informing us about what is generally seen as effective or adaptive behaviour in that situation. In contrast, injunctive norms specify what *ought* to be done—what is approved or disapproved behaviour in a given situation. Both kinds of norms can exert strong effects upon behaviour; for instance, teenagers' beliefs about the extent to which their friends drive while under the influence of alcohol are strongly related to their own tendency to engage in this risky and illegal behaviour (Brown, 1998). However, Cialdini and his colleagues believe that in certain situations—especially ones in which antisocial behaviour (behaviour not approved of by a given group or society) is likely to occur—injunctive norms may exert somewhat stronger effects. This is true for two reasons. First, such norms tend to shift attention away from how people are acting in a particular situation (e.g., littering) to how they should be behaving (e.g., putting trash into containers). Second, such norms may activate the social motive to do what's right in a given situation regardless of what others have done.

Cialdini and his colleagues have tested this prediction in several studies, and have obtained evidence that confirms it. For example, in one of these studies (Reno,

Descriptive Norms
Norms that simply indicate what most people do in a given situation.

Injunctive Norms
Norms specifying what ought to be done—what is approved of or disapproved of behaviour in a given situation.

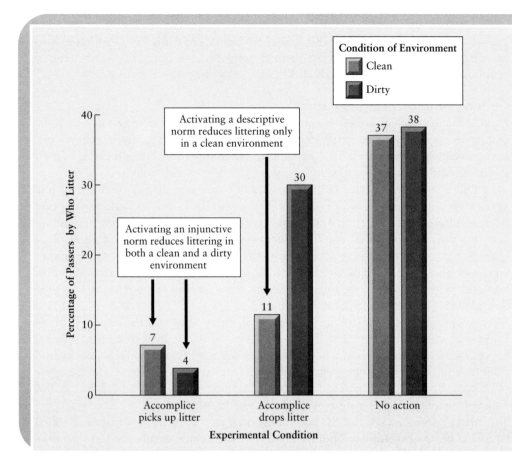

Condition of Environment
- Clean
- Dirty

Activating a descriptive norm reduces littering only in a clean environment

Activating an injunctive norm reduces littering in both a clean and a dirty environment

Percentage of Passers by Who Litter

40 —
30 —
20 —
10 —
0 —

7   4   11   30   37   38

Accomplice picks up litter | Accomplice drops litter | No action

Experimental Condition

■ The effects of injunctive and descriptive social norms

FIGURE 7.5 When passersby saw a stranger pick litter from the ground (activation of an injunctive norm), they were less likely to litter themselves in both a dirty and a clean environment. In contrast, when they saw another person drop litter onto the ground (activation of a descriptive norm), they were less likely to litter themselves only in a clean environment.

Source: Based on data from Reno, Cialdini, & Kallgren, 1993.

Cialdini, & Kallgren, 1993), individuals crossing a parking lot encountered an accomplice walking toward them. In one condition, this person carried a bag from a fast-food restaurant and dropped it on the ground. In another, this person was not carrying anything but actually stopped to pick up a fast-food bag dropped by someone else. The researchers reasoned that seeing someone drop a bag would activate a descriptive norm—information about what other people did in this situation. In contrast, seeing another person actually pick litter up from the ground would remind participants of society's disapproval of littering, and so would activate an injunctive norm against littering. Another variable in the study was whether the environment was already littered with trash or newly cleaned by the researchers. To test the effects of these norms on behaviour, Reno and his colleagues (1993) observed what participants did with a handbill that had been placed on the windshield of their car. The researchers predicted that the descriptive norm would reduce people's tendency to litter when the environment was clean (because it would indicate the bag-dropper was out of line) but not when it was dirty, but that the injunctive norm would reduce littering in both conditions. As you can see from Figure 7.5, this is exactly what happened.

These findings, and those of other studies, suggest that both descriptive and injunctive social norms do exist, and that the two types may influence our behaviour through somewhat different mechanisms. A practical implication of this finding is that efforts to change people's behaviour should focus on activating the type of norm most likely to succeed. In situations in which most people already behave in a prosocial manner, calling their attention to this fact—activating a descriptive norm—may further strengthen this tendency. But in situations in which many people do not behave in a prosocial manner, activating an injunctive norm (and so reminding people of how they should behave) may be more effective.

Cultural Differences in Conformity

Beyond factors such as cohesiveness, group size, and norms, another more enduring feature of group influence is the importance of *culture*. That is, some cultures may encourage greater conformity in their members than others and such socialization differences could be expected to have lasting influence upon individuals.

One of the earliest cross-cultural studies of conformity was carried out by John Berry (1967) of Queen's University. He reasoned that the extent of conformity expected in a culture would be related to its means of subsistence. Specifically, agricultural communities tend to be very interdependent because the cooperation of all members is needed in order to achieve successful food production. Therefore, these cultures would emphasize conformity to group needs. In contrast, where subsistence involves hunting, food is usually available throughout the year and the hunter can be more independent of others in the community.

Adapting Asch's (1950) line-judgment task, Berry compared the responses of two traditional cultural groups: the Temne (farmers) and the Inuit (hunters). He had hypothesized that greater conformity would be shown by Temne subjects than by Inuit subjects and results confirmed the hypothesis. Later studies confirmed the high level of independence in perceptual judgments among other hunting cultures, for example among Canadian Native groups (Berry & Annis, 1974).

Berry's study was one of the earliest in social psychology to compare individualist and collectivistic cultures (though these terms were not widely used at that time) and to suggest that social influence and conformity vary along this cultural dimension. But his work goes further in suggesting that the origins of such cultural differences are in a society's means of survival: If subsistence requires a high level of cooperation, then greater conformity may be required of individuals in that culture.

More recently, Smith and Bond (1996) have conducted a meta-analysis of 133 studies drawn from 17 countries that replicated Asch's classic study. They found strong evidence for the impact of cultural values on conformity, specifically differences in individualism and collectivism. Individuals from collectivistic cultures (e.g., China, Japan, Zimbabwe) tend to conform more than did individuals from individualistic societies (e.g., the United Kingdom, Holland, or the United States) and this was true regardless of the size of the influencing group (see Figure 7.6).

It also appears that collectivists make a stronger distinction between ingroup and outgroup membership (e.g., friends and family versus strangers). Because their identity is more strongly rooted in their group membership, they tend to be more cooperative and helpful to ingroup members and more competitive with outgroup members. In a study with Japanese students, Williams and Sogon (1984) found a greater rate of conformity for students who knew each other and a lower rate for unacquainted students. Conformity rates also tend to be higher among individuals who share some strong link with the other group member. For instance, conformity was especially high among students (particularly if they believed that they were all students in the same area of study) and among minority groups (Abrams et al., 1990; Chandra, 1973; Perrin & Spencer, 1981).

In summary, an accumulation of studies (e.g., Hamilton & Sanders, 1995) sug-

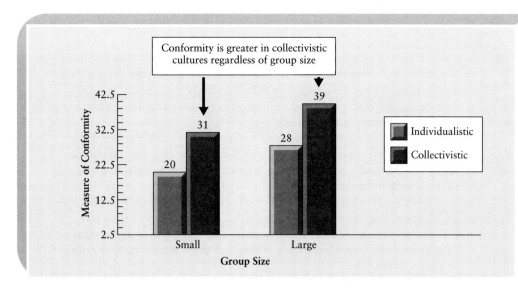

■ Culture and conformity

FIGURE 7.6 A recent review of existing evidence suggests that conformity is higher in collectivistic cultures (that emphasize being part of the group) than in individualistic cultures (that emphasize individuality). This appears to be true regardless of whether the influencing groups are small or large.

Source: Based on data from Bond & Smith, 1996.

gest that conformity may be better understood when we consider the interdependence of individuals in a culture, or even within a subculture of a larger society. The more one's fate is interdependent with that of others, the greater the likelihood of conformity occurring (Smith & Bond, 1998).

Gender Differences in Conformity: More Apparent Than Real

Early investigations suggested that females are more susceptible than males to conformity pressures and other forms of social influence (e.g., Crutchfield, 1955). More recent investigations (e.g., Eagly & Carli, 1981), however, have called these conclusions into questions. It now appears that early studies used materials and tasks more familiar to males than to females and so placed females at a disadvantage in terms of susceptibility to conformity pressure. Sistrunk and McDavid (1971) found evidence that when females were less familiar with the items (i.e., giving opinions about sports), they did in fact show greater yielding to group pressure. However, when the tables were turned so that the items were less familiar to males (i.e., opinions on fashion), it was they who showed greater conformity. So in efforts to compare females and males in terms of susceptibility to social pressure, we must be on guard against confounding gender with an additional unrelated factor—familiarity with the items or tasks used in the research.

Another reason that many persons continue to believe that females are more conforming than males is because females still frequently occupy lower-status positions in society, and low-status persons tend to conform to a greater degree than high-status persons. Support for this reasoning has been obtained in several studies conducted by Eagly and her colleagues (e.g., Steffen & Eagly, 1985). For instance, in one such study, Eagly and Wood (1982) asked men and women to read a brief story in which one business employee attempted to influence the views of another employee of the opposite sex. Participants were asked to indicate the extent to which they thought the target person would be influenced. In the absence of any information about relative status, participants predicted greater yielding by females than by males. When information on status (e.g., job titles) was presented, they predicted greater yielding by low-status individuals, *regardless of their gender*. Findings such as these add further support to the view that in general, all other things being equal, there are no appreciable differences between females and males in terms of susceptibility to social pressure.

- Many factors determine whether, and to what extent, conformity occurs. These include *cohesiveness*, or the degree of attraction felt by an individual toward some group; *group size* and *unanimity*; and type of social norm—*descriptive or injunctive*—operating in that situation.
- Some cultures place greater emphasis on the need for conformity among members and this appears to derive from the need for cooperation in order to survive. Generally, there is more pressure to conform in collective cultures to those in an individual's ingroup.
- Early investigations suggested that females are more susceptible to conformity pressures than males. It now appears that it is not gender *per se*, but unfamiliarity with a situation and low status that can increase conformity. When these factors are controlled in research there appear to be no overall gender differences.

The Basis of Conformity: Why We Often "Go Along"

As we have just seen, several factors determine whether and to what extent conformity occurs. Yet this does not alter the essential point: Conformity is a basic fact of social life. Most people conform to the norms of their groups or societies most of the time. Why? Why do people so often choose to go along with these social rules or expectations instead of combating them? The answer seems to centre primarily on two powerful needs possessed by all human beings: the desire to be liked or accepted by others and the desire to be right (Insko, 1985)—plus cognitive processes that lead us to view conformity as fully justified after it has occurred (e.g., Griffin & Buehler, 1993).

The Desire To Be Liked: Normative Social Influence

How can we get others to like us? This is one of the eternal puzzles of social life. As we will discuss later in this chapter, there are many tactics that are effective in this regard. One of the most successful, though, is to appear to be as similar to others as possible. From our earliest days, we learn that agreeing with the persons around us and behaving much as they do causes them to like us. Parents, teachers, friends, and others often heap praise and approval on us for demonstrating such similarity (refer to our discussion of attitude formation in Chapter 3). One important reason we conform, therefore, is simple: we have learned that doing so can yield the approval and acceptance we strongly crave. This source of social influence—and especially of conformity—is known as **normative social influence**, since it involves altering our behaviour to meet others' expectations. Clearly, it is a common aspect of daily life.

Normative Social Influence Social influence based on the individual's desire to be liked or accepted by other persons.

The Desire To Be Right: Informational Social Influence

If you want to know your weight, you can step on to a scale. Similarly, if you want to know the dimensions of a room, you can measure them directly. But how can you establish the "accuracy" of your own political or social views or decide which hairstyle suits you best? There are no simple physical tests or measuring devices for answering these questions. Yet most of us have just as strong a desire to be correct about such matters as about questions relating to the physical world. The solution is obvious: to answer these questions, or at least to obtain information about them, we must turn to other people. We use their opinions and their actions as guides for our own. Obviously, such reliance on others can be another source of conformity, for in an important sense, other people's actions and opinions define social reality for us. This source of social influence is known as **informational social influence**, since it is based on our tendency to depend on others as a source of information about many aspects of the social world.

Information Social Influencer Social influence based on the desire to be correct (i.e., to posses accurate perceptions of the social world).

Because our motivation to be correct or accurate is very strong, informational social influence is a very powerful source of conformity. However, as you might expect, this is most likely to be true in situations in which the motivation to be accurate is high (the outcome is *important* to us) yet we are highly *uncertain* about what is "correct" or "accurate." That this is so was clearly illustrated in a study conducted by Robert S. Baron, Vandello, and Brunsman (1996). (Robert S. Baron is not the Robert Baron who is a coauthor of this text.) These researchers found that when the motivation to be accurate was high (the task was described as important), research participants showed a greater tendency to conform to the judgments of others when they were uncertain about the correct answer (the task they were given was difficult) than when they had confidence in their own judgments (the task was easy). However, when motivation to be accurate was low (the task was described as unimportant), no such differences occurred.

Together, normative and informational social influence provide a strong basis for our tendency to conform—to act in accordance with existing social norms. In short, there is nothing mysterious about the compelling and pervasive occurrence of conformity; it stems directly from basic needs and motives that can be fulfilled only when we do indeed decide to "go along" with others.

Justifying Conformity: The Cognitive Consequences of Going Along With the Group

Asch (1951, 1955) reported that some people who conform do so without any reservations: they conclude that they are wrong and the others are right. For these people, conforming poses only a very temporary dilemma at most. But for many other persons, the decision to yield to group pressure and do as others do is more complex. Such persons feel that their own judgment is correct, but at the same time they don't want to be different; so they behave in ways that are inconsistent with their private beliefs. What are the effects of conformity on such persons? Research findings (e.g., Buehler & Griffin, 1994; Griffin & Buehler, 1993) suggest that one effect may involve a tendency for people—while maintaining their original judgment—to alter their perceptions of the situation so that conformity appears, in fact, to be justified. As Canadian-born economist and diplomat John Kenneth Galbraith stated, "Faced with the choice between changing one's mind and proving that there is no need to do so, almost everyone gets busy on the proof!" (cited in Buehler & Griffin, 1994, p. 993).

Given these results, an interesting question arises: Will this same pattern occur in all cultures? In cultures that value individuals' individual choice backed by rational analysis of available information (e.g., Canada and many Western countries), such effects would be expected to occur: people feel a strong need to explain why they conformed. In cultures that place greater value on group judgments and on avoiding disagreements with others, however, the pressures toward such cognitive self-justification may be weaker (Bond & Smith, 1996). As noted by Buehler and Griffin (1994), this is an intriguing issue well deserving of further study.

- Two important motives seem to underlie our tendency to conform: the desire to be liked by those we like or respect and the desire to be right or accurate. These two motives are reflected in two distinct types of social influence, *normative social influence* and *informational social influence*.

- Once we show conformity in a given situation, we tend to view our conforming as justified, even if it has required us to behave in ways contrary to our true beliefs.

Resisting Conformity: Individuality and Control

Having read this discussion of normative and informational social influence, you may now have the distinct impression that pressures toward conformity are all but impossible to resist. If that's so, take heart. While such pressures are indeed powerful, they are definitely not irresistible. In many cases, individuals—or groups of individuals—decide to dig in their heels and say *no*. This was certainly true in Asch's research, where, as you may recall, most of the subjects yielded to social pressure, but only part of the time. On many occasions they stuck to their own judgments, even in the face of a disagreeing, unanimous majority. What accounts for this ability to resist even powerful pressures toward conformity? Research findings point to two key factors.

First, as you probably already realize, many people have a strong desire to maintain their uniqueness or *individuality*. People want to be like others, but not to the extent that they lose their personal identity. In other words, along with the needs to be right and to be liked, many of us possess a desire for **individuation**—for being distinguished in some respects from others (e.g., Maslach, Santee, & Wade, 1987; Snyder & Fromkin, 1980). The result is that most people want to be similar to others generally, but don't want to be exactly like the people around them. In short, they want to hold on to at least a modicum of individuality (e.g., Snyder & Endelman, 1979). It is partly because of this motive that individuals sometimes choose to disagree with others or to act in unusual or even bizarre ways. They realize that such behaviour may be costly in terms of gaining the approval or acceptance of others, but their desire to maintain a unique identity is simply stronger than various inducements to conformity.

Another reason why individuals often choose to resist group pressure involves their desire to maintain *control* over the events in their lives (e.g., Burger, 1992; Daubman, 1993). Most persons want to believe that they can determine what happens to them, and yielding to social pressure sometimes runs counter to this desire. After all, going along with a group implies behaving in ways one might not ordinarily choose; and this, in turn, can be viewed as a restriction of personal freedom and control. The results of many studies suggest that the stronger an individual's need for personal control, the less likely he or she is to yield to social pressure; so this factor, too, appears to be an important one where resisting conformity is concerned.

In sum, two motives, the desire to retain our individuality and the desire to keep control over our own lives, serve to counter the motives that tend to increase conformity—our desires to be liked and to be accurate. Whether we conform in a given situation, then, depends on the relative strength of these various motives and the interplay between them.

Minority Influence: Why The Majority Doesn't Always Rule

As we have just noted, individuals can—and often do—resist group pressure (Wolfe, 1985). Lone dissenters or small minorities can dig in their heels and refuse to go along.

Individuation
Differentiation of oneself from others by emphasis on one's uniqueness or individuality.

Yet even this is not the total story; in addition, there are cases in which such persons or groups can turn the tables on the majority and *exert* rather than merely *receive* social influence. History provides numerous examples of such events. Such giants of the scientific world as Galileo, Pasteur, and Freud faced virtually unanimous majorities who rejected their views in harsh terms. Yet over time they won growing numbers of colleagues to their side until, ultimately, their opinions prevailed. More recent examples of minorities influencing majorities are provided by the success of environmentalists. Initially such persons were viewed as wild-eyed radicals operating at the fringes of society. Over time, however, they have succeeded in changing strongly held attitudes and laws, with the result that society itself has been altered through their efforts.

When do minorities succeed in exerting social influence on majorities? Research findings suggest that they are most likely to be successful under certain conditions (Kruglanski & Mackie, 1991; Moscovici, 1985).

First, the members of such groups must be *consistent* in their opposition to majority opinions. If they waffle or show signs of yielding to the majority view, their impact is reduced. Second, in order for a minority to affect a larger majority, its members must avoid appearing rigid and dogmatic (Mugny, 1975). A minority that merely repeats the same position over and over again is less persuasive than one that demonstrates a degree of *flexibility* in its stance. Third, the general social context in which a minority operates is important. If a minority argues for a position that is consistent *with current social trends* (e.g., conservative views at a time of growing conservatism), its chances of influencing a majority are greater than if it argues for a position that is out of step with such trends.

Of course, even when these conditions are met, minorities face a tough uphill fight. The power of majorities is great, especially in ambiguous or complex social situations; in such situations majorities are viewed as more reliable sources of information about what is true than are minorities. In other words, majorities function as an important source of both informational and normative social influence (Wood et al., 1996). Why then, are minorities sometimes able to get their message across?

One possibility is that when people are confronted with a minority stating views that they don't initially accept, they are puzzled and exert cognitive effort to understand why these people hold their views and why they are willing to take a strong stand against the majority (Nemeth, 1995; Vonk & van Knippenberg, 1995). In other words, vocal and deeply committed minorities can induce members of the majority to engage in *systematic processing* with respect to the messages and information they provide (e.g., Smith, Tindale, & Dugoni, 1996; Wood et al., 1996). Another, and related, possibility is that when people believe they are part of a minority, they themselves engage in more careful (systematic) thought about their views. As a result, they generate stronger arguments; and this contributes to their success in influencing the majority.

Evidence for precisely these kinds of effects is provided by an experiment conducted by Zdaniuk and Levine (1996). These researchers led participants in a discussion group of five students to believe that they were either in a minority of one, or had varying degrees of support for their opinion (on comprehensive exams for graduates). They predicted that when participants in the study believed they were part of a minority, they would anticipate strong group pressure against them; as a result, they would think more systematically about the issue (and generate more thoughts). As you can see from Figure 7.7, this is precisely what happened. Participants who were led to believe that they were part of a minority perceived that they would face greater social pressure and generated more initial thoughts about the examination issue than participants who thought they were part of a majority.

If minorities do the cognitive work necessary to generate strong and persuasive arguments for their views, it seems possible that during actual group debates minori-

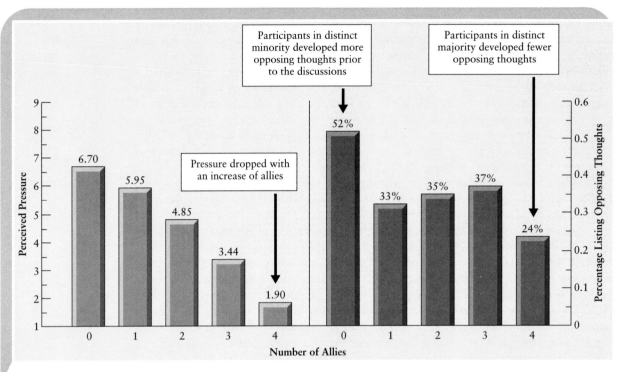

Participants in distinct minority developed more opposing thoughts prior to the discussions

Participants in distinct majority developed fewer opposing thoughts

Pressure dropped with an increase of allies

■ Systematic thought: One reason why minorities sometimes prevail

FIGURE 7.7 When research participants were told that they were part of a minority, they anticipated stronger social pressure to change their views (left-hand graph). In addition, they generated more thoughts about their position and so, presumably, were better prepared to defend it (right-hand graph). These findings suggest that minorities often engage in more systematic thought about their views than the majority, and this may give them an important edge when they confront the majority.

Source: Based on data from Zdaniuk & Levine, 1996.

ties may lead members of the majority to consider ideas they would otherwise have ignored. For instance, would large numbers of people have paid any attention to the hole in the ozone layer or the possibility of the greenhouse effect during the 1980s and 1990s if vocal minorities had not called these problems vigorously to their attention? It seems unlikely. In sum, even if minorities fail to sway majorities initially, they may initiate processes, such as more careful consideration of opposing ideas, that lead to eventual social change (e.g, Alvaro & Crano, 1996). In this respect, at least, there is much truth to the phrase "Long live the loyal opposition!"

KEY POINTS

● Although pressures toward conformity are strong many persons resist them, at least part of the time. This resistance seems to stem from two strong motives: the desire to retain one's individuality, or *individuation*, and the desire to exert *control* over one's own life.

● Under some conditions, minorities can induce even large majorities to change their attitudes or behaviour. Recent evidence suggests that this may occur, in part, because minorities induce majorities to think more systematically about the issues they raise, and also because minorities themselves engage in such systematic processing; as a result, they formulate strong and persuasive arguments for their views.

COMPLIANCE: TO ASK—SOMETIMES—IS TO RECEIVE

Suppose that you wanted someone to do something for you, how would you go about getting them to do it? If you think about this question for a moment, you'll quickly realize that you have quite a few tricks up your sleeve for gaining **compliance**—for getting others to say yes to your requests. What are these techniques like? Which ones work best? These are among the questions studied by social psychologists in their efforts to understand this, the most frequent form of social influence. In the discussion that follows, we'll examine many tactics for gaining compliance. Before turning to these however, we'll introduce a basic framework for understanding the nature of all of these procedures and why they often work.

Compliance A form of social influence in which one or more persons attempt to influence one or more others through direct requests.

Compliance: The Underlying Principles

Some years ago, the well-known social psychologist Robert Cialdini decided that the best way to find out about compliance was to study what he termed compliance professionals—people whose success (financial or otherwise) depends on their ability to get others to say yes. Who are such persons? They include salespeople, advertisers, political lobbyists, fund-raisers, politicians, con artists, professional negotiators, and many others. Cialdini's technique for learning from these people was simple: he temporarily concealed his true identity and took jobs in various settings where gaining compliance is a way of life. In other words, he worked in advertising, direct (door-to-door) sales, fund-raising, and other compliance-focused fields. On the basis of these firsthand experiences, he concluded that although techniques for gaining take many different forms, they all rest to some degree on six basic principles (Cialdini, 1994):

1. *Liking/friendship*: In general, we are more willing to comply with requests from people we like or from friends than with requests from strangers or people we don't like.

2. *Commitment/consistency*: Once we have committed ourselves to a position or action, we are more willing to comply with requests for behaviours that are consistent with this position or action than to accede to requests that are inconsistent with it.

3. *Scarcity*: In general, we value, and try to secure, outcomes or objects that are scarce or decreasing in their availability. As a result, we are more likely to comply with requests that focus on scarcity than with ones that make no reference to this issue.

4. *Reciprocity*: We are generally more willing to comply with a request from someone who has previously provided a favour or concession to us than to oblige someone who has not. In other words, we feel impelled to pay people back in some way for what they have done for us.

5. *Social validation*: We are generally more willing to comply with a request for some action if this action is consistent with what we believe persons similar to ourselves are doing (or thinking). We want to be correct, and one way to be so is to act and think like others.

6. *Authority*: In general, we are more willing to comply with requests from someone who holds legitimate authority—or who simply appears to do so.

According to Cialdini (1994), these six basic principles underlie many techniques that professionals—and we ourselves—use for gaining compliance from others. We'll now examine specific techniques based on some of these principles.

Tactics Based on Liking: Using Impression Management

The desire to make a favourable impression on others is strong. Most of us engage in active efforts to regulate how we appear to others in order to appear in the best or most favourable light possible. This process is known as **impression management** (or **self-presentation**), and considerable evidence indicates that persons who can perform it successfully gain important advantages in many social settings (e.g., Schlenker, 1980; Wayne & Liden, 1995). Our aim when we do this is to achieve **ingratiation**—make others like us in order that we can influence them (Liden & Mitchell, 1988; Wortman & Linsenmeier, 1977). But what tactics do individuals use to create favourable impressions on others and appear likeable? And which of these are most successful? These are the issues we'll consider next.

As your own experience probably suggests, impression management takes many different forms and involves a wide range of specific tactics. Most of these, however, seem to fall into two major categories: *other-enhancement*—efforts to make a target person feel good in our presence, and *self-enhancement*—efforts to boost our own image.

Other-Enhancement: Aren't You Wonderful?

The first type of impression management tactis involves what are sometimes described as **other-enhancement techniques**—efforts to induce favourable reactions in target persons by specific actions toward them. Among the most important of these tactics are *flattery*—making statements that praise the target person, his or her traits or accomplishments, or the organizations with which the target person is associated (Kilduff & Day, 1994). Such tactics are often highly successful, provided they are not overdone. Additional tactics of other-enhancement involve expressing agreement with target persons' views, showing a high degree of interest in them as people, doing small favours for them, asking for their advice and feedback in some manner (Morrison & Bies, 1991), or expressing liking for them nonverbally (e.g., through high levels of eye contact, nodding in agreement, and smiling; Wayne & Ferris, 1990).

Self-Enhancement: Aren't I Wonderful?

Among **self-enhancement techniques**, perhaps the most obvious is altering our own appearance in specific ways. For example, we dress in ways that we believe will be evaluated favourably by others. Such tactics appear to succeed. It has been found, for example, that when women dress in a professional manner (business suit or dress, subdued jewelry), they are evaluated more favourably for management positions than when they dress in a more traditionally feminine manner (dresses with patterns, large jewelry; Forsythe, Drake, & Cox, 1985). Many other aspects of personal appearance, too, are involved in efforts at impression management, including hair styles, cosmetics, and even eyeglasses (e.g., Baron, 1989; Terry & Krantz, 1993). Additional tactics include *self-deprecation*—providing negative information about oneself as a means of promoting the image of modesty—and *self-disclosure*, or offering personal information about oneself even if it is not requested. This tactic fosters the information that the ingratiator is honest and likes the target person (Tedeschi & Melburg, 1984).

That individuals often employ such tactics is obvious: you can probably recall many instances in which you either used or were the target of such strategies. A key question, however, is this: Do impression management tactics work? Research findings

Impression Management (self-presentation) Efforts by individuals to produce favourable first impressions on others.

Ingratiation A technique for gaining compliance in which requesters first induce target persons to like them, then attempt to change their behaviour in some desired manner.

Other-enhancement Techniques of impression management in which the individual attempts to make the target person feel good about him or herself

Self-enhancement Techniques of impression management in which the individual attempts to increase his or her own appeal to others.

from a growing body of literature indicate that all of these tactics can be successful and increase the likelihood of *ingratiation*—that target persons will be influenced and agree to various requests (e.g., Kacmar, Delery, & Ferris, 1992; Paulhus, Bruce, & Trapnell, 1995; Wayne & Liden, 1995). However, recent research also suggests that there may be limitations on their effects.

When Impression Management Fails

First of all, if *other-enhancement* is overused, or used ineffectively, it can backfire and produce negative rather than positive reactions from others. For instance, in ingenious recent research, Vonk (1998) found strong evidence for what he terms the "slime effect"—a tendency to form very negative impressions of persons who "lick upward but kick downward"; that is, persons in a work setting who play up to their superiors but treat subordinates with disdain and contempt. Specifically, Vonk (1998) asked students at a university in the Netherlands to read descriptions of an individual who showed one of several patterns of behaviour: (1) *slimy behaviour*—likable actions toward superiors (e.g., getting coffee for them) but dislikable actions toward subordinates (e.g., refusing to help them); (2) *nonslimy behaviour*—dislikable behaviour toward superiors but likable behaviour toward subordinates; (3) *mixed behaviour*—a mixed pattern of likable and dislikable behaviours toward both superiors and subordinates; (4) *negative behaviours*—only dislikable behaviours toward everyone; or (5) *positive behaviours*—only likable behaviours toward everyone. After reading these descriptions, participants rated this person in terms of how slimy he was and how likable he was. As you can see from Figure 7.8, results offered clear evidence for the dangers of unsubtle impression management: the stranger was rated as least likable when he engaged in slimy behaviour.

A second line of research suggests that constant use of *self-enhancement* techniques may backfire in the long-run, as described in the following section, Canadian Research: On the Cutting Edge.

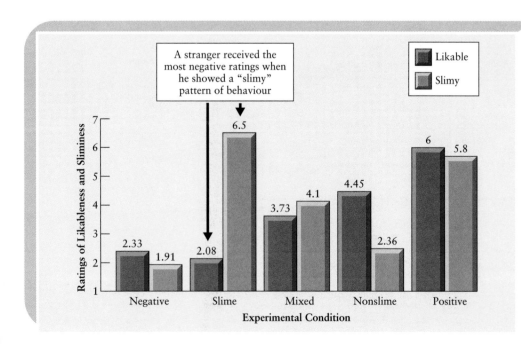

■ The "slime effect": When impression management fails

FIGURE 7.8 An individual who showed a pattern of "licking upward but kicking downward" (directing likable behaviours toward superiors but dislikable behaviours toward subordinates) was perceived in very negative terms by research participants. In fact, they viewed him as even more negative than someone who showed only dislikable behaviours.

Source: Based on data from Vonk, 1998.

The Long-Term Social Impact of Self-Enhancement

While studies have shown that self-enhancement can be an effective technique of impression management, a few questions remain. If boosting your own image is effective in the short-term, will the use of prolonged or extreme trait self-enhancement be as effective? If exposed to such trait self-enhancement in the long-term will others continue to evaluate the enhancer positively? Del Paulhus of the University of British Columbia addressed these questions by examining **trait self-enhancers** (1998). These individuals show an enduring tendency to exaggerate their achievements, talents and abilities. In contrast to people who use

> **Trait Self-enhancement** Those who show an enduring tendency to exaggerate their own achievements, talents, and abilities. The underlying trait involves narcissistic self-importance and a self-deceptive lack of insight.

self-enhancement as a deliberate part of ingratiation attempts, trait self-enhancers are not consciously attempting to mislead their audience—they honestly believe in their own superiority (Paulhus, 1998). Thus as well as being extremely self-important, or *narcissistic*, such individuals are also strongly *self-deceiving* in their lack of insight, and inability to respond to feed back about themselves.

Subjects in Paulhus' study were students in an undergraduate class who were randomly assigned to discussion groups as part of their class attendance. Before their first meeting each group member completed a series of questionnaires including measures of narcissism and self-deceptive enhancement. These two latter scales were combined to give a measure of *trait self-enhancement*. The groups, consisting of four or five members,

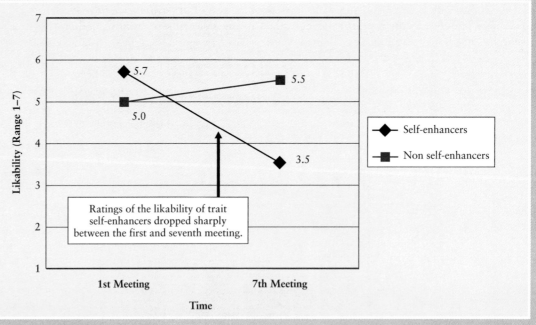

The effectiveness of self-enhancement in the long run

FIGURE 7.9 At a first meeting, those who showed trait self-enhancement were liked more by others in their group than were non self-enhancers. However, this positive social effect was short-lived—by the seventh meeting, liking had dropped sharply. In contrast, liking of non self-enhancers did not drop and showed a tendency to increase as other group members became more familiar with them.

discussed issues relevant to class topics. In addition, they filled out two sets of questionnaires estimating other group members' performance (whether they were "effective," "contributed to group goals" and "performed well") and personality characteristics (including their warmth and agreeableness). The first set of questionnaires was completed after the first group discussion and the second set after the seventh group meeting.

In line with previous studies, results showed that self-enhancement had a positive social impact at the first meeting: Trait self-enhancers were liked (a measure combing warmth and agreeableness) by other group members more than non self-enhancers. However, as shown in Figure 7.9, this positive impact was short-lived. By the seventh meeting liking for trait self-enhancers had deteriorated drastically, whereas non self-enhancers had maintained their position and even made some inroads. A similar pattern was found for ratings of performance: an initial positive response to trait self-enhancers' performance had disappeared by the seventh meeting. Left unanswered was the question of whether their fellow group members caught on to their self-enhancement.

Nevertheless, these findings challenge the assumption sometimes made that self-enhancement is always adaptive for the individual (e.g., Taylor & Armor, 1996; Taylor & Brown, 1994)—something we discussed in Chapter 4. In the long term, the extreme and prolonged self-promotion shown by trait self-enhancers was not at all *socially* adaptive and was the opposite of ingratiating. But as Paulhus put it, trait self-enhancement appears to be a "mixed blessing." Although this type of self-enhancement was ineffective with others in the long-run, it certainly seems to work for the enhancers themselves—compared to non self-enhancers, the trait self-enhancers showed much higher self-esteem.

KEY POINTS

- Individuals use many different tactics for gaining *compliance*—getting others to say *yes* to various requests. Many of these tactics rest on basic principles well known to social psychologists.

- The use of *impression management* techniques—techniques to regulate how we appear to others—such as *other-enhancement* and *self-enhancement* can help to achieve *ingratiation*, or compliance through increased liking. Many of these techniques work if not used ineffectively as occurs with the *slime effect*, or overused as occurs with *trait self-enhancers*.

Tactics Based on Commitment or Consistency

Have you ever been approached at your local supermarket or food court by one or more persons who offered you free samples of various foods? The reason behind these actions is obvious: The persons offering the free samples hope that once you have accepted these gifts, you'll like the taste of the food and will be more willing to buy your lunch at their business. This is the basic idea behind an approach for gaining compliance known as the **foot-in-the-door technique**. In operation, this tactic involves inducing target persons to agree to a small initial request ("Accept this free sample") and then hitting them with a larger request—the one desired all along. The results of many studies indicate that this tactic works: it succeeds in inducing increased compliance (e.g., Beaman et al., 1983; Freedman & Fraser, 1966). Why is this the case? Because the foot-in-the-door technique rests on the principle of *consistency*: once we have said yes to the small request, we are more likely to say yes to subsequent and larger ones, too, because refusing these would be inconsistent with our previous behaviour (e.g., DeJong & Musilli, 1982).

Foot-in-the-door A procedure for gaining compliance in which requesters begin with a small request and then, when this is granted, escalate to a larger one (the one they actually desired all along).

The foot-in-the-door technique is not the only tactic based on the consistency/commitment principle, however. Another is the **lowball** procedure. In this technique, which is often used by automobile salespersons, a very good deal is offered to a customer. After the customer accepts, however, something happens that makes it necessary for the salesperson to change the deal and make it less advantageous for the customer—for example, the sales manager rejects the deal. The totally rational reaction for customers, of course, would be to walk away. Yet often, they agree to the changes and accept the less desirable arrangement.

These informal observations have been confirmed by careful research. In one investigation of the lowball procedure, for example, students first agreed to participate in a psychology experiment. Only after making this commitment did they learn that it started at 7:00 a.m. (Cialdini et al., 1978). Despite the inconvenience of this early hour, however, almost all students in this lowball condition appeared for their appointments. In contrast, a much smaller proportion of students who learned about the 7:00 a.m. starting time *before* deciding whether to participate agreed to take part in the study. In instances such as this, an initial commitment seems to make it more difficult for individuals to say no, even though the conditions under which they said yes are now changed.

Tactics Based on Reciprocity

Reciprocity is a basic rule of social life: we usually do unto others as they have done unto us. If they have done a favour for us, therefore, we feel that we should be willing to do one for them in return. While this convention is viewed by most persons as being fair and just, the principle of reciprocity also serves as the basis for several techniques for gaining compliance. One of these is, on the face of it, the opposite of the foot-in-the-door technique. Instead of beginning with a small request and then escalating to a larger one, persons seeking compliance sometimes start with a very large request and then, after this is rejected, shift to a smaller request—the one they wanted all along. This tactic is known as the **door-in-the-face** technique (because the first refusal seems to slam the door in the face of the requester), and several studies indicate that it can be quite effective. For example, in one well-known experiment, Cialdini and his colleagues (1975) stopped college students on the street and presented a huge request: Would the students serve as unpaid counselors for juvenile delinquents two hours a week for the next *two years*? As you can guess, none agreed. When the experimenters then scaled down their request to a much smaller one—would the same students take a group of delinquents on a two-hour trip to the zoo—fully 50 percent agreed. In contrast, fewer than 17 percent of those in a control group agreed to this smaller request when it was presented cold rather than after the larger request.

The same tactic is often used by negotiators, who may begin with a position that is extremely advantageous to themselves but then retreat to a position much closer to the one they really hope to obtain. Similarly, sellers often begin with a price they know buyers will reject, then lower the price to a more reasonable one—but one that is still quite favourable to themselves, and close to what they wanted all along.

Another procedure explained as based on reciprocity is known as the **"that's-not-all"** technique. Here, an initial request is followed, *before the target person can say yes or no*, by something that sweetens the deal—a small extra incentive from the persons using this tactic (e.g., a reduction in price, "throwing in" something additional for the same price). For example, as suggested by Figure 7.10, television commercials for various products frequently offer something extra to induce viewers to pick up the phone and place an order. Several studies confirm informal observations suggesting that the

FIGURE 7.10 Would you be influenced by this type of commercial? Research evidence indicates that throwing in some small extra before people make up their minds about a request or a product can often tip the balance in favour of a yes.

"How much would you pay for all the secrets of the universe? Wait, don't answer yet. You also get this six-quart covered combination spaghetti pot and clam steamer. Now how much would you pay?"

"that's-not-all" technique really works (Burger, 1986). These studies also suggest that it is based on the principle of reciprocity: persons on the receiving end of this technique view the "extra" thrown in by the other side as an added concession, and so feel obligated to make a concession themselves. The result: The probability that they will say yes is increased.

Another possible explanation is that compliance in this case is based on the use of heuristics or simple *mindless* processing of information (e.g., Langer, 1989). You may not be thinking deeply about the influencer's tactics, particularly if an item is not going to stretch your budget. All that you are aware of is "This is a bargain," and in accordance with this heuristic thinking, become more likely to say yes than if they were thinking more systematically. Evidence for this suggestion has recently been reported by Pollock et al., (1998). They found that a small price reduction produced the "that's not all" effect for a low-cost item (a $1.25 box of chocolates reduced to $1.00), but did not produce this effect for a more expensive item (a $6.25 box reduced to $5.00). Apparently, individuals thought more carefully about spending $5.00, and this countered their tendency to respond automatically. Whatever its precise basis, the "that's-not-all" technique can often be an effective means for increasing the likelihood that others will say yes to various requests.

A more subtle use of the notion of reciprocity underlies what social psychologists term the **foot-in-the-mouth** technique (e.g., Howard, 1990). Briefly, this involves a requester establishing some kind of relationship, no matter how trivial, with the target person, and so increasing the target's feelings of an obligation to comply with reasonable requests. By admitting the existence of this relationship (for example, "We're all human beings, right?")—which may be a very tenuous one—the target person gives the requester an important edge. In a sense, then, the target person "puts his or her foot in his or her mouth" by agreeing that the relationship exists. A clear demonstration of the power of this tactic is provided by research conducted recently by Aune and Basil (1994).

These researchers had female accomplices stop students on a university campus and ask them to contribute to a well-known charitable organization. In the foot-in-the-mouth

Foot-in-the-mouth A procedure for gaining compliance in which the requester establishes some kind of relationship, no matter how trivial, with the target person, thereby increasing this person's feeling of obligation to comply.

condition, they asked passersby if they were students, and then commented, "Oh, that's great, so am I." Then they made their request for funds. Results indicated that a much larger percentage of the persons approached made a donation in the foot-in-the-mouth condition (25.5 percent) than in a control condition where no relationship was established (9.8 percent). These findings, and those of a follow-up study by the same authors, suggest that the reciprocity principle can be stretched even to such tenuous relationships as "We're both students, right? And students help students, right? So how about a donation?"

Tactics Based on Scarcity

It's a general rule of life that things that are scarce, rare, or difficult to obtain are viewed as being more valuable than those that are plentiful or easy to obtain. Thus, we are often willing to expend more effort or go to greater expense to obtain items or outcomes that are scarce than to obtain ones that are in large supply. This principle serves as the foundation for several techniques for gaining compliance. One of the most common of these is **playing hard to get**.

> **Playing Hard to Get** A technique that can be used for increasing compliance by suggesting that a person, object, or outcome is scarce and hard to obtain.

Many people know that playing hard to get can be effective in the area of romance: by suggesting that it is difficult to win their affection or that there are many rivals for their love, individuals can greatly increase their desirability (e.g., Walster, et al., 1973). This tactic is not restricted to interpersonal attraction, however; research findings indicate that it is also sometimes used by job candidates to increase their attractiveness to potential employers, and hence to increase the likelihood that these employers will offer them a job. For example, consider a study by Williams and her colleagues (1993).

These researchers arranged for corporate recruiters who were interviewing students at large universities to review information about potential job candidates. This information, which was presented in folders, indicated either that the job candidate already had either two job offers (a hard-to-get candidate) or no other job offers (easy-to-get candidate), and was either highly qualified (very high grades) or less well qualified (low average grades). After reviewing this information, the recruiters then rated the candidates in terms of their qualifications and desirability, the company's likelihood of inviting them for an on-site interview, and the company's likelihood of considering them for a job. Results were clear: The hard-to-get candidates were rated more favourably than the easy-to-get candidates, regardless of their grades. However, hard-to-get candidates who were also highly qualified received by far the highest ratings. As it is persons who receive high ratings who usually get the jobs, these findings indicate that creating the impression of being a scarce and valuable resource (being hard to get) can be another effective means for gaining compliance.

■ The deadline technique in action

FIGURE 7.11 Advertisers often use the deadline technique to convince customers to buy now—before it's too late!

A related technique based on the same "what's-scarce-is-valuable" principle is one frequently used by retailers. Ads using this **deadline** technique state a specific time limit during which an item can be purchased for a specific price. After the deadline runs out, the ads suggest, the price will go up. Of course, in many cases the sale is not a real one, and the time limit is bogus. Yet many people reading ads like the ones in Figure 7.11 believe them and hurry to the store in order to avoid missing a great opportunity. So when you encounter an offer that suggests that the "clock is ticking," be cautious: it may be based more on good sales techniques than on reality.

Deadline A technique for increasing compliance in which target persons are told that they have only limited time to take advantage of some offer or to obtain some item.

KEY POINTS

- Two widely used tactics, the *foot-in-the-door technique* and the *lowball procedure*, rest on the principle of commitment/consistency.
- In contrast, the *door-in-the-face*, the *"that's-not-all,"* and the *foot-in-the-mouth* techniques all rest on the principle of reciprocity.
- *Playing hard to get* and the *deadline technique* are based on the principle of scarcity— the idea that what is scarce or hard to obtain is valuable.

Putting Others In a Good Mood: The Basis of Many Compliance Techniques

Many of the tactics for gaining compliance involve putting others in a good mood. Flattery and other tactics of ingratiation, as we noted earlier, are often used for this purpose and can be quite successful if not overdone (Gordon, 1996). As mentioned in Chapter 6, we tend to like people who put us in a good mood and, as a result, we are more willing to allow them to influence us. People also feel happy about snagging a real bargain or being the one lucky enough to get the last one left. But many other techniques can—and apparently do—accomplish the same end (e.g., Rind, 1996). For example, Rind and Bordia (1996) found that female servers who put smiley faces on their bills had tips almost 19 percent greater than when there was no smiling face. This effect was not observed for male servers, probably because drawing smiley faces is not considered gender appropriate. These results, and those of many other studies conducted both in the lab and in the field (e.g., Baron, 1997; Rind, 1996), suggest that almost anything that puts people in a better mood (i.e., that induces positive affect) can increase their tendency to say *yes* to various requests.

But why, precisely, does being in a good mood increase our tendency to comply? One interesting possibility is suggested by the *affect infusion model* (AIM) that we discussed in Chapter 2. As you may recall, this model is designed to explain the effects of our current moods (affective states) on our judgments and decisions. Research related to this model (e.g, Forgas, 1998) indicates that putting people into a good mood may increase their willingness to say yes to a request. This is particularly true if it causes them to think systematically about the request and its potential effects in *positive ways*: "That's a reasonable thing to ask" or "If I agree, good things will follow." These are the kind of thoughts people in a good mood may have, and such thoughts may increase their tendency to comply.

For an overview of various tactics for gaining compliance, please see the Ideas to Take with You feature at the end of the chapter.

Individual Differences in the Use of Social Influence

Group pressure, the foot in the door, the door in the face, playing hard to get, flattery—the list of tactics people use to influence one another seems almost endless. We're sure you have encountered most, if not all, of these approaches in your own life, and we're also certain you have used some of them yourself. But which do you prefer? Part of the answer to this question, it appears, may involve your own personality. In other words, different persons, possessing different patterns of traits, may well prefer certain tactics over others. Evidence for just such differences has recently been reported by Caldwell and Burger (1997).

These researchers reasoned that several of the important "Big Five" dimensions of personality (Costa & McCrae, 1992), as well as degree of self-monitoring (Lennox & Wolfe, 1984) and level of desire for personal control (Burger & Cooper, 1979), would be related to preferences for various tactics of social influence. (These aspects of personality are described in Table 7.1.) To test this general hypothesis, Caldwell and Burger asked several hundred business students to complete a survey indicating the extent to which they used a wide range of influence tactics: rational argument and persuasion, pressure tactics, ingratiation, inspirational appeals designed to engage others' enthusiasm, and reciprocity—offering them something in return. Measures of various aspects of the students' personality were also obtained. Then the researchers analyzed these two sets of data (preferences for social influence tactics and aspects of personality) to see if any links between them existed. Major results are shown in Table 7.1.

So it appears that depending on their own personality traits, different individuals do tend to prefer different tactics for influencing others. Further, individuals differ in

As shown here, individuals with contrasting personality profiles tend to prefer different techniques for exerting social influence. In other words, the specific tactics we choose seem to reflect our own traits and characteristics.

TABLE 7.1 Personality and tactics of social influence

Aspects of Personality	Preferred Tactics of Influence	Nonpreferred Tactics of Influence
High agreeableness (trust, cooperativeness)	Rational persuasion Inspirational appeals	Pressure tactics
High conscientiousness (neatness, orderliness, responsibleness)		
High extraversion (friendliness, sociability)	Almost all tactics	Rational persuasion
High self-monitoring (sensitivity to reactions of others; willingness to change behaviour across situations)		
High desire for control (control over events in one's life)	Rational persuasion Pressure tactic	Ingratiation

Source: Based on data from Caldwell & Burger, 1997.

terms of how successful they are in gaining compliance (e.g., Shestowsky, Wegener, & Fabrigar, 1998). Those who enjoy effortful cognitive activities (are high in the *need for cognition*) tend to be more successful because their efforts are more vigorous and their arguments stronger. In other words, we all want to get our way and have others do what we would like them to do; but, depending on our own traits, we tend to choose different paths to this goal with different levels of success.

KEY POINTS

- Putting others in a good mood before making a request is a common feature of many compliance techniques. The affect infusion model suggest that it may be especially likely to succeed if the request induces target persons to think systematically and positively about it.

- While everyone engages in efforts to exert social influence on others, research findings indicate that the specific tactics individuals choose are related to their own traits and characteristics.

OBEDIENCE: SOCIAL INFLUENCE BY DEMAND

What is the most direct technique one person can use to change the behaviour of another? In one sense, the answer is as follows: He or she can order the target to do something. This approach is less common than either conformity pressure or tactics for gaining compliance, but it is far from rare. Business executives issue orders to their subordinates; military officers bark commands that they expect to be followed at once; and parents, police officers, and sports coaches, to name just a few, seek to influence others in the same manner. **Obedience** to the commands of sources of authority is far from surprising; such sources usually possess some means of enforcing their directives (e.g., they can reward obedience and punish resistance). More surprising, though, is the fact that even persons lacking in such power can sometimes induce high levels of submission from others. The clearest and most dramatic evidence for the occurrence of such effects has been reported by Stanley Milgram in a series of famous—and controversial—investigations (Milgram, 1963, 1974).

Obedience A form of social influence in which one person simply orders one or more others to perform some action(s).

Destructive Obedience: Some Basic Findings

In his research Milgram wished to learn whether individuals would obey commands from a relatively powerless stranger requiring them to inflict what appeared to be considerable pain on another person—a totally innocent stranger. Milgram's interest in this topic derived from the occurrence of tragic real-life events in which seemingly normal, law-abiding persons actually obeyed such directives. For example, during World War II, troops in the German army obeyed commands to torture and murder unarmed civilians—millions of them—in infamous death camps set up specifically for this grisly purpose. Similar appalling events have occurred in many other cases and at many other points in history (e.g., the My Lai massacre during the Vietnam war; or the murder of unarmed civilians in Kosovo). To try to gain insights into the nature of such events, Milgram designed an ingenious, if disturbing, laboratory simulation. The experimenter informed participants in his studies (all males) that they were partici-

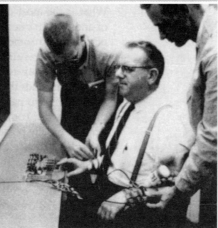

■ Studying obedience in
the laboratory

FIGURE 7.12 Left: Stanley
Milgram with the apparatus he used
in his famous experiments on obedience. (It has recently been displayed
in a special exhibit at the Smithsonian
Institution in Washington, D.C.) Right:
The experimenter (right front) and a
participant (rear) attaching electrodes
to the learner's (accomplice's) wrists.

Source: From the film *Obedience*, distributed by the New York University Film
Library, copyright © 1965 by Stanley
Milgram. Reprinted by permission of the
copyright holder.

pating in an investigation of the effects of punishment on learning. Their task was to
deliver electric shocks to another person (actually an accomplice) each time he made
an error in a simple learning task. These shocks were to be delivered by means of 30
switches on the equipment shown in Figure 7.12. Participants were told to move to the
next higher switch each time the learner made an error. Since the first switch supposedly delivered a shock of 15 volts, it was clear that if the learner made many errors,

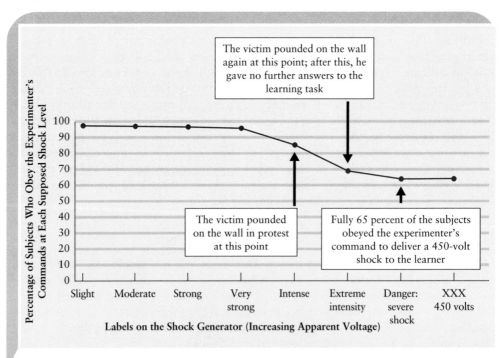

■ Obedience to the commands of a powerless authority

FIGURE 7.13 A surprisingly large proportion of the male participants in Milgram's research obeyed the experimenter's
orders to deliver electric shocks of increasing strength to an innocent victim. Fully 65 percent demonstrated total obedience to these commands.

Source: Based on data from Milgram, 1963.

he would soon be receiving powerful jolts. Indeed, according to the labels on the equipment, the final shock would be 450 volts! In reality, of course, the accomplice (the learner) *never received any shocks during the experiment.* The only real shock ever used was a mild demonstration pulse from one button (number three) to convince subjects that the equipment was real.

During the session the "learner" (following prearranged instructions) made many errors. Thus, subjects soon found themselves facing a dilemma: Should they continue punishing this person with what seemed to be increasingly painful shocks? Or should they refuse to go on? The experimenter pressured them to continue; whenever they hesitated or protested, he made one of a series of graded remarks. These began with "Please go on," escalated to "It is absolutely essential that you continue," and finally shifted to "You have no other choice; you *must* go on."

Since subjects were all volunteers and were paid in advance, you might predict that they would quickly refuse the experimenter's orders. Yet, in reality, fully *65 percent showed total obedience* to the experimenter's commands, proceeding through the entire series to the final 450-volt level (see Figure 7.13). In contrast, subjects in a control group who were not given such commands generally used only very mild shocks during the session. Many persons, of course, protested and asked that the session be ended. When ordered to proceed, however, a majority yielded to the experimenter's social influence and continued to obey. Indeed, they continued to do so even when the victim pounded on the wall as if in protest against the painful treatment he was receiving.

In further experiments (1965a, 1974), female subjects showed the same degree of obedience as males and Milgram also found that similar results could be obtained even under conditions that might be expected to reduce such obedience. When the study was moved from its original location on the campus of Yale University to a run-down office building in a nearby city, subjects' level of obedience remained virtually unchanged. Similarly, a large proportion continued to obey even when the accomplice complained about the painfulness of the shocks and begged to be released. Most surprising of all, many (about 30 percent) continued to obey even when they were required to grasp the victim's hand and force it down upon the "shock" plate! That these chilling results were not due to special conditions present in Milgram's laboratory is indicated by the fact that similar findings were soon reported in studies conducted in other countries.

Cultural Differences in Obedience

Researchers in at least eight other countries have attempted to replicate Milgram's studies. Generally, the findings indicate that levels of obedience were similar to those found with American subjects (Smith & Bond, 1993). The Australian and the British subjects were slightly less obedient than the Americans whereas the Jordanians were comparable to U.S. levels and the Spanish, Austrians, Germans, and Italians were slightly higher (see Figure 7.14). Although the exact procedures of the non-American studies may have differed slightly from Milgram's original studies, the general pattern of consistent results suggests that substantial numbers of people in a variety of countries (though mostly industrialized Western countries) will carry out orders from authority, even when this compliance will harm others. However, it is important to remember that obedience to authority is not absolute and certain strategies can be utilized to reduce this tendency to obey. These will be discussed in a later section.

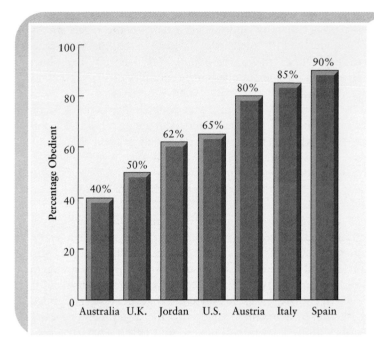

■ Cultural differences in destructive obedience

FIGURE 7.14 Destructive obedience to authority figures is a common response among people all over the world. However, some cultural variation is evident—notably, studies from Australia and the United Kingdom show lowest levels, while those from Italy and Spain show the highest.

Source: Based on data from Smith and Bond, 1993.

KEY POINTS

- *Obedience* is a form of social influence in which one or more persons are ordered to do something, and they do it. It is, in a sense, the most direct form of social influence.
- Research by Stanley Milgram indicates that many persons readily obey commands from a relatively powerless source of authority, even if these commands require them to harm an innocent stranger.
- When cultures are compared some variation is found although considerable levels of destructive obedience are found in all cultures studied.

Destructive Obedience: Its Social Psychological Basis

As we noted earlier, one reason why Milgram's results are so disturbing is that they seem to parallel many real-life events involving atrocities against innocent victims. Why does such destructive obedience occur? Why were participants in these experiments—and why are many persons in tragic situations outside the laboratory—so willing to yield to this powerful form of social influence? Social psychologists have identified several factors that seem to play a role.

First, in many situations, the persons in authority relieve those who obey of the responsibility for their own actions. "I was only carrying out orders," is the defense many offer after obeying harsh or cruel directives. In life situations, this transfer of responsibility may be implicit. In Milgram's experiments, in contrast, it was quite explicit. Subjects were told at the start that the experimenter (the authority figure), not they, would be responsible for the victim's well-being. Given this fact, it is not surprising that many tended to obey.

Second, persons in authority often possess visible badges or signs of their status and power. These consist of special uniforms or insignia, have special titles, and similar factors (see Figure 7.15). Faced with such obvious reminders of who is in charge,

■ Symbols of authority: Often they are hard to resist

FIGURE 7.15 Few of us would choose to ignore someone in an official uniform. Uniforms are outward signs of authority that are designed, in many cases, to tell us who is in charge; we disobey people who wear them at our own risk.

most people find it difficult to resist. The powerful impact of such cues has been demonstrated by Bushman (1984, 1988) in several similar experiments. For example, in one of these investigations, a female accomplice of the researcher ordered pedestrians to give a nickel to a young man who needed it for a parking meter. In one condition the accomplice was dressed in a uniform (although its precise nature was ambiguous). In a second condition she was dressed as a business executive, and in a third she was dressed as a panhandler. Not surprisingly, a higher percentage of subjects obeyed in the first condition (72 percent) than in the others (48 and 52 percent respectively). Other data, which the researcher collected by asking subjects who obeyed why they did so, indicated that the uniform had the expected effect: Subjects in this condition reported that they obeyed simply because they had been ordered to do so by someone with authority. These findings, and those in related studies, suggest that the possession of outward signs of authority, even if they are largely irrelevant to the present situation, play an important role in the ability of authority figures to induce high levels of obedience to their commands.

A third reason for obedience in many situations where the targets of such influence might resist involves its *gradual* nature. Initial commands are often relatively small and innocuous. Only later do they increase in scope and come to require behaviour that is dangerous or objectionable. For example, police or military personnel may at first be ordered to question, arrest, or threaten potential victims. Gradually, demands are increased to the point where they are commanded to beat, torture, or even kill unarmed civilians. In a similar manner, subjects in the laboratory research on obedience were first required to deliver only mild and harmless shocks to the victim. Only as this person continued to make errors on the learning task did the intensity of these "punishments" rise to supposedly harmful levels.

In sum, several factors contribute to the high levels of obedience witnessed in laboratory studies and in a wide range of real-life contexts. Together these merge into a powerful force—one that most persons find difficult to resist. Unfortunately, the consequences of this compelling form of social influence can be disastrous for many innocent and largely defenseless victims.

Destructive Obedience: Resisting Its Effects

Now that we have considered some of the factors responsible for the strong tendency to obey sources of authority, we will turn to a related question: How can this type of social influence be resisted? Several strategies seem to be effective in helping to reduce the tendency to obey.

First, individuals exposed to commands from authority figures can be reminded that they—not the authorities—are responsible for any harm produced. Under these conditions, sharp reductions in the tendency to obey have been observed in American, Australian, German, and Dutch subjects (e.g., Hamilton, 1978; Kilham & Mann, 1974; Mantell, 1971; Meeus & Raaijmakers, 1986).

Second, individuals can be provided with an indication that, beyond some point, unquestioning submission to destructive commands is inappropriate. For example, they can be exposed to the actions of *disobedient models*—people who refuse to obey an authority figure's commands. Research findings suggest that this strategy, too, is quite effective in reducing obedience (Milgram, 1965b; Powers & Geen, 1972). Again, this strategy was also effective in reducing obedience in Dutch and German participants.

Third, individuals may find it easier to resist influence from authority figures if they question the expertise and motives of the authority figures. Are such persons really in a better position to judge what is appropriate and what is inappropriate? What motives lie behind their commands—socially beneficial goals or selfish gain? By asking such questions, persons who might otherwise obey may find support for independence rather than submission.

Finally, simply knowing about the power of authority figures to command blind obedience may be helpful in itself. Growing evidence (e.g., Sherman, 1980) suggests that when individuals learn about the findings of social psychological research, they may change their behaviour to take account of this knowledge. With respect to destructive obedience, there is some hope that knowing about this process can enhance individuals' ability to resist. To the extent this is the case, then even exposure to findings as disturbing as those reported by Milgram can have positive social value. As they become widely known, they may produce desirable shifts within society.

To conclude: The power of authority figures to command obedience is certainly great, but it is definitely *not* irresistible. Under appropriate conditions it can be countered and reduced. As in many other spheres of life, there is a choice. Deciding to resist the dictates of authority can, of course, be dangerous. Those holding power wield tremendous advantages in terms of weapons and technology. Yet, as events in Eastern Europe, the former Soviet Union, and elsewhere have demonstrated, the outcome is by no means certain when committed groups of citizens choose to resist. Ultimately, victory may go to those on the side of freedom and decency rather than to those who possess the guns, tanks, and planes. The human spirit, in short, is not so easily controlled or extinguished as many dictators would like to believe.

> **KEY** POINTS
>
> ● Destructive obedience, which plays a role in many real-life atrocities, stems from several factors. These include shifting of responsibility to the authority figure, outward signs of authority on the part of this person, a gradual escalation of the scope of the commands given, and the rapid pace with which such situations proceed.

- Several strategies can help reduce the occurrence of destructive obedience. These include reminding individuals that they share in the responsibility for any harm produced, reminding them that beyond some point obedience is inappropriate, calling into question the motives of authority figures, and informing people of the findings of social psychological research on this topic.

Ideas to Take with You

Tactics for Gaining Compliance

How can we get other persons to say yes to our requests? This is an eternal puzzle of social life. Research by social psychologists indicates that all of the techniques described here can be useful—and that they are widely used. So, whether or not you use these approaches yourself, you are likely to be on the receiving end of many of them during your lifetime. Here are tactics that are especially common.

Ingratiation.
Getting others to like us so that they will be more willing to agree to our requests. We can ingratiate ourselves through flattery, by making ourselves attractive, and by showing liking for and interest in the target person. But be careful not to go too far.

The Foot-in-the-Door Technique.
Starting with a small request and, after it is accepted, escalating to a larger one.

The Door-in-the-Face Technique.
Starting with a large request and then, when this is refused, backing down to a smaller one.

Playing Hard to Get.
Making it appear as though we are much in demand, thereby making it more likely that others will value us and agree to our requests—implicit or explicit.

Putting Others in a Good Mood.
Using any of countless tactics to make other people feel more cheerful—and thus more likely to say yes to our requests.

Summary and Review of Key Points

Conformity: Group Influence in Action

- *Social influence*—efforts by one or more persons to change the attitudes or behaviour of one or more others—is a common part of life.

Most people behave in accordance with *social norms* most of the time; in other words, they show strong tendencies towards *conformity*.

Conformity was first systematically studied by Solomon Asch, whose classic research indicated that many persons will yield to social pressure from a unanimous group.

Many factors determine whether, and to what extent, conformity occurs. These include *cohesiveness*, or the degree of attraction felt by an individual toward some group; *group size* and *unanimity*; and type of social norm—*descriptive* or *injunctive*—operating in that situation.

Some cultures place greater emphasis on the need for conformity among members and this appears to derive from the need for cooperation in order to survive. Generally, there is more pressure to conform in collective cultures to those in an individual's ingroup.

Early investigations suggested that females are more susceptible to conformity pressures than males. It now appears that it is not gender *per se*, but unfamiliarity with a situation and low status that can increase conformity. When these factors are controlled in research there appear to be no overall gender differences.

Two important motives seem to underlie our tendency to conform: the desire to be liked by those we like or respect and the desire to be right or accurate. These two motives are reflected in two distinct types of social influence, *normative social influence* and *informational social influence*.

Once we show conformity in a given situation, we tend to view our conforming as justified, even if it has required us to behave in ways contrary to our true beliefs.

Although pressures toward conformity are strong many persons resist them, at least part of the time. This resistance seems to stem from two strong motives: the desire to retain one's individuality or *individuation*, and the desire to exert control over one's own life.

Under some conditions, minorities can induce even large majorities to change their attitudes or behaviour. Recent evidence suggests that this may occur, in part, because minorities induce majorities to think more systematically about the issues they raise, and also because minorities themselves engage in such systematic processing; as a result, they formulate strong and persuasive arguments for their views.

Compliance: To Ask—Sometimes—Is to Receive

● Individuals use many different tactics for gaining *compliance*—getting others to say *yes* to various requests. Many of these tactics rest on basic principles well known to social psychologists.

The use of *impression management* techniques—techniques to regulate how we appear to others—such as *other-enhancement* and *self-enhancement* can help to achieve *ingratiation*, or compliance through increased liking. Many of these techniques work if not used ineffectively as occurs with the *slime effect*, or overused as occurs with *trait self-enhancers*.

Two widely used tactics, the *foot-in-the-door technique* and the *lowball procedure*, rest on the principle of commitment/consistency.

In contrast, the *door-in-the-face*, the *"that's-not-all"* and the *foot-in-the-mouth* techniques all rest on the principle of reciprocity.

Playing hard to get and the *deadline technique* are based on the principle of scarcity—the idea that what is scarce or hard to obtain is valuable.

Putting others in a good mood before making a request is a common feature of many compliance techniques. The affect infusion model suggest that it may be especially likely to succeed if the request induces target persons to think systematically and positively about it.

While everyone engages in efforts to exert social influence on others, research findings indicate that the specific tactics individuals choose are related to their own traits and characteristics.

Obedience: Social Influence by Demand

● *Obedience* is a form of social influence in which one or more persons are ordered to do something, and they do it. It is, in a sense, the most direct form of social influence.

Research by Stanley Milgram indicates that many persons readily obey commands from a relatively powerless source of authority, even if these commands require them to harm an innocent stranger.

When cultures are compared some variation is found although considerable levels of destructive obedience are found in all cultures studied.

Destructive obedience, which plays a role in many real-life atrocities, stems from several factors. These include shifting of responsibility to the authority figure, outward signs of authority on the part of this person, a gradual escalation of the scope of the commands given, and the rapid pace with which such situations proceed.

Several strategies can help reduce the occurrence of destructive obedience. These include reminding individuals that they share in the responsibility for any harm produced, reminding them that beyond some point obedience is inappropriate, calling into question the motives of authority figures, and informing people of the findings of social psychological research on this topic.

For More Information

Cialdini, R. B. (1993). *Influence: Science and practice* (3rd ed.). New York: HarperCollins.

An insightful account of the major techniques people use to influence others. The book draws both on the findings of systematic research and on informal observations made by the author in a wide range of practical settings (e.g., sales, public relations, fund-raising agencies, organizations). This is the most readable and informative account of knowledge about influence currently available.

Milgram, S. (1974). *Obedience to authority.* New York: Harper & Row.

More than 25 years after it was written, this book remains the definitive work on obedience as a social psychological process. The untimely death of its author at age 51 only adds to its value as a lasting contribution to our field.

Weblinks

www.envmed.rochester.edu/wwwrap/behavior/ jaba/jabahome.htm
Journal of Applied Behavior Analysis

www.csj.org
Resources about psychological manipulation, cult groups, sects, and new religious movements

www.aabt.org
Association for Advancement of Behavior Therapy

www.wmich.edu/aba
Association for Behavior Analysis

www.eahb.org
Experimental Analysis of Human Behavior Bulletin

Helping and Harming:
Prosocial Behaviour and Aggression

SPECIAL SECTIONS

■ Some people need a lot of help

FIGURE 8.1 Prosocial behaviour takes many forms—from risking one's life in order to save the life of a stranger to providing information to tourists who can't read a map. However different prosocial acts may be, they each require some amount of time and effort and have an outcome that is beneficial to the one who receives help but of no obvious benefit to the one who helps.

"O.K., this is the West Coast, O.K.? What you want is the East Coast, so turn around and go back twenty-four, twenty-five hundred miles, and that's the East Coast. You can't miss it."

Even if you live a sheltered life, there are few of us who aren't aware that human behaviour can vary tremendously. Just a brief exposure to any newspaper can bring that clearly to consciousness. One page may feature a story of domestic violence or the report of atrocities inflicted by one national group on another. Yet an adjacent column may give details of heroism—an incident where someone took considerable risks to rescue a stranger. Social psychologists have focused a great deal of attention on both topics—the factors that influence whether we *help* or *harm* others.

In this chapter we will examine some of what is known about the variables that predict who does and does not engage in prosocial behaviour when emergency situations arise. By **prosocial behaviour**, we mean actions that provide benefit to others rather than the person who carries them out. A related term, **altruistic behaviour**, refers to acts that suggest an unselfish concern for the welfare of others, in which there are costs for the actor. In this chapter we begin with the story of how an important program of research into helping behaviour started back in 1964, stimulated by a real-life case where there was failure to help—what we now term the *bystander effect*. We then examine some of the specific variables that increase or decrease the likelihood that helping behaviour will occur, as well as its effect on the recipient.

The second part of this chapter examines **aggression**—the intentional infliction of some form of harm on others. In view of its destructive impact on society and its prevalence (Geen, 1990), it is hardly surprising that aggression has been an important topic of research in social psychology for several decades (Baron & Richardson, 1994). First, we'll describe several different theoretical perspectives on aggression—contrasting views about the nature and origins of such behaviour. Next, we'll review important determinants of aggression—aspects of others' behaviour (or our interpretations of their actions) and of the situations that play a role in the initiation of aggressive outbursts. Finally, we'll end on an optimistic note by examining various techniques for the prevention and control of human aggression. As will soon become apparent, a degree of optimism really is justified in this respect, for several effective techniques for reducing overt aggression do indeed exist.

Prosocial Behaviour Acts that benefit others rather than the person who carries them out.

Altruistic Behaviour Acts that suggest an unselfish concern for the welfare of others, are costly for the individual who behaves altruistically, and sometimes involve risk.

Aggression Behaviour directed toward the goal of harming or injuring another living being who is motivated to avoid such treatment.

BYSTANDER RESPONSE TO AN EMERGENCY

At a minimum, providing help requires that you stop whatever you are doing and spend some amount of time dealing with the needs of others, as in Figure 8.1. Even when the problem is only one of stupidity or ignorance, the need is real. And the factors that determine bystanders' readiness to help remain the same, whether bystander behaviour involves providing information to map-challenged tourists, bringing a stranger into your warm home after an automobile accident, driving angrily past an injured woman lying on a busy highway (*Washington Post*, April 22, 1998), walking away and taking no action after discovering that your teenage friend is molesting and murdering a seven-year-old child (Booth, 1998), returning a bag containing $70 000 to its owner (Hurewitz, 1998), or risking death by diving 40 metres off of a bridge in order to save a woman intent on suicide (Fitzgerald, 1996).

Back in 1964, another actual emergency took place. Help was badly needed, many bystanders were present, but not one of them responded. As a result, a young woman was murdered. This instance of seemingly indifferent bystanders motivated two social psychologists to try to understand why no one had helped, as described in the following Cornerstones section.

Cornerstones

Darley and Latané: Why Bystanders Don't Respond

The event involving the absence of prosocial behaviour became a matter of widespread concern. It took place in the early morning hours of March 13, 1964. In New York City, Catherine (Kitty) Genovese was returning home from her job as manager of a bar. As she crossed the street from her car to the apartment building where she lived, a man armed with a knife approached her. She began running in an effort to avoid him, but he ran in pursuit, caught up to her, and then stabbed her. She screamed for help, and numerous people apparently heard her, because lights quickly came on in several of the apartment windows that overlooked the street. The attacker retreated briefly, but when no one came to help his bleeding victim, he returned to finish the job. She screamed again, but he stabbed her repeatedly until she lay dead. It was later determined that this horrifying forty-five-minute interaction was seen and heard by thirty-eight witnesses, but no one took direct action or even bothered to call the police (Rosenthal, 1964).

On the basis of the many news stories about this incident, the general response was one of shock and disappointment about the failure of the bystanders to come to the victim's aid. Why didn't they help? Possibly people in general had become apathetic, cold, and indifferent to the problems of others. Perhaps living in a big city made people callous. Perhaps violence on TV and in the movies had desensitized viewers to the horror of real violence and real suffering. Maybe modern American society, which had recently experienced the assassination of a president, was no longer able to empathize with the plight of a stranger in need of help.

As we now know, there are psychological explanations for the failure of those bystanders to respond—explanations that do not involve apathy, indifference, callousness, or a general absence of empathy. A novel idea began to take shape shortly after the murder as Professors John Darley and Bibb Latané ate lunch and discussed what had happened in their city. They believed that the problem was not that the bystanders didn't care about the crime victim, but that something about the situation must have made them hesitate to act. As these psychologists speculated, they began to outline proposed experiments on their tablecloth (Krupat, 1975).

The initial hypothesis (Darley & Latané, 1968) was that the inaction of the bystanders in the Genovese murder resulted from the fact that many people were present at the scene and that no one person felt responsible for taking action. Thus, there was **diffusion of responsibility.** Darley and Latané tested the hypothesis that as the number of bystanders increases, the diffused responsibility results in a decrease in prosocial behaviour. Each subject in their initial experiment was exposed to a bogus medical emergency and believed himself or herself to be either the only one who knew about the problem, one of two bystanders, or

Diffusion of Responsibility The presence of multiple bystanders at the scene of an emergency, resulting in the responsibility for taking action being shared among all members of the group. As a result of diffusion of responsibility, each individual feels less responsible and is less likely to act than if he or she were alone.

one of five bystanders. The basic question was whether helpfulness would decrease as the number of bystanders increased.

When undergraduate subjects arrived at the laboratory to participate in a psychological experiment, the instructions indicated that they would discuss with fellow students some of the problems involved in attending college in a high-pressure urban setting. The participants were told that each of them would be assigned to a separate room and could communicate only by an intercom system; they could hear each other, but the experimenter would not be listening. This arrangement was supposedly designed to avoid any embarrassment about discussing personal matters.

Some subjects were told that they were one of two discussants, others that they were part of a group of three, and still others that six students were participating. Each participant was supposed to talk for two minutes, after which the listener or listeners would comment on what the others had said. In reality, only one subject took part in each session, and the other participant or participants were simply tape recordings. Thus, the stage was set for a controlled emergency apparently overheard by varying numbers of bystanders.

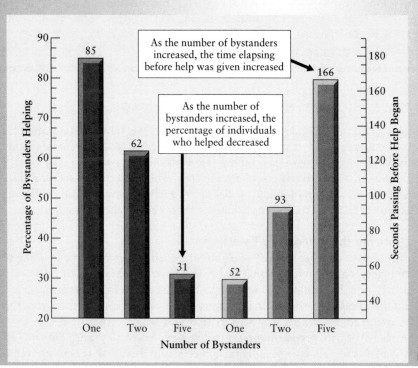

■ The bystander effect: more bystanders = less help

FIGURE 8.2 In the initial experiment designed to explore the bystander effect, students heard what seemed to be a fellow student having a seizure. The research participant was supposedly either the only bystander to this emergency, one of two bystanders, or one of five. As the number of bystanders increased, the percentage of individuals who tried to help the "victim" decreased. In addition, among those who did help, as the number of bystanders increased, the more time passed before help began. This effect was initially explained on the basis of diffusion of responsibility.

Source: Based on data from Darley & Latané, 1968.

In each session the first person to speak was the tape-recorded individual who was to be the "victim." He said, sounding embarrassed, that he sometimes had seizures, especially when facing a stressful situation such as exams. After the participant (and, in two of the conditions, other "participants") had given a two-minute talk about college problems, the victim spoke again:

> I er I think I need er if if could er er somebody er er help because I er I'm er h-h-having a a a real problem er right now and I er if somebody could help me out it would er er s-s-sure be good because er there er er a thing's coming on and and I could really er use some help so if somebody here er help er uh uh uh (choking sounds) I'm gonna die er er I'm gonna die er help er er seizure (chokes, then is quiet). (Darley & Latané, 1968, p. 379.)

Two aspects of bystander responsiveness were measured, and the results are shown in Figure 8.2. A helpful response consisted of leaving the experimental room to look for the imaginary victim. As the number of apparent bystanders increased, the percentage of subjects attempting to help decreased. Further, among those who did respond, an increase in the number of bystanders led to increased delay in taking action. Such findings are consistent with Darley and Latané's hypothesis that the presence of others leads to diffused responsibility and makes helpfulness less probable.

It is well worth noting that the student bystanders who hesitated or failed to respond were not apathetic or uncaring. Compared to the 85 percent of lone bystanders who helped in the first sixty seconds, far fewer participants tried to help in the conditions in which fellow bystanders were believed to be present; but even the totally unhelpful individuals appeared to be concerned, upset, and confused.

The conclusion is that the prosocial tendencies of a single witness to an emergency are inhibited by the presence of additional witnesses, a phenomenon that became known as the **bystander effect**. Darley (1991) has indicated that neither he nor his colleague could have foreseen the flood of research that their experiment initiated. As you will see in the remainder of this section, this one experiment was just the first of a great many investigations that have made prosocial behaviour much more understandable and predictable. The initial insight about diffusion of responsibility was only the beginning.

Bystander Effect The finding that as the number of bystanders witnessing an emergency increases, the likelihood of each bystander's responding, and the speed of responding, decrease.

Providing Help: Five Essential Cognitive Steps

Following the initial experiment on diffusion of responsibility, Latané and Darley (1970)—as well as others—carried out numerous interrelated experiments, and they eventually formulated a theoretical model (see Figure 8.3) to explain why bystanders sometimes do and sometimes do not help a victim. They described a helping response as the end point of a series of cognitive decisions. Help is provided only if the appropriate decision is made at each step. What are these crucial choice-points?

Step 1: Noticing the Emergency Event

The first decision is whether to shift one's attention from whatever one is doing to the unexpected emergency—to notice that something is wrong. Many factors can prevent this. You may not be facing the emergency situation, so seeing or hearing it may be impaired. Other people or sounds in your immediate vicinity may distract you. Or you may be so involved in your present activity that you notice very little else.

The role of such preoccupation was studied by Darley and Batson (1973). Seminary students served as experimental subjects, and their task was to go to a near-

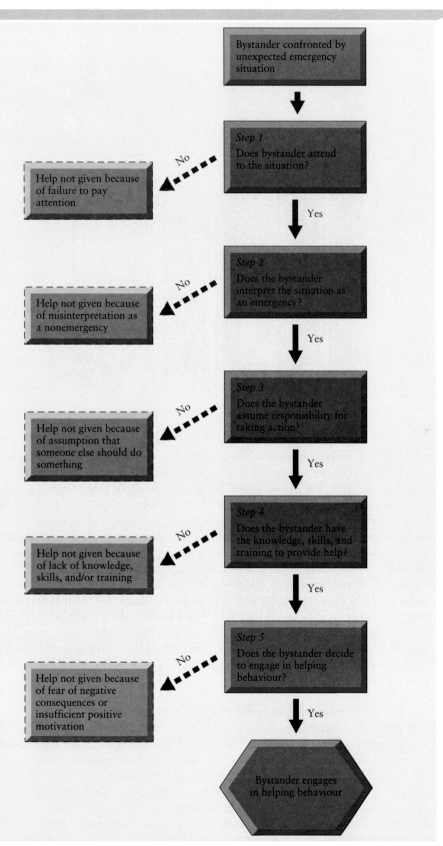

FIGURE 8.3 Latané and Darley conceptualized prosocial behaviour as the end point of a series of five cognitive steps, representing choice points. At each step in the process, the choices (whether conscious or unconscious) result in either (1) no help being given or (2) movement to the following step in a progression toward possible helping.

Bystander confronted by unexpected emergency situation

Step 1
Does bystander attend to the situation?

No → Help not given because of failure to pay attention

Yes

Step 2
Does the bystander interpret the situation as an emergency?

No → Help not given because of misinterpretation as a nonemergency

Yes

Step 3
Does the bystander assume responsibility for taking action?

No → Help not given because of assumption that someone else should do something

Yes

Step 4
Does the bystander have the knowledge, skills, and training to provide help?

No → Help not given because of lack of knowledge, skills, and/or training

Yes

Step 5
Does the bystander decide to engage in helping behaviour?

No → Help not given because of fear of negative consequences or insufficient positive motivation

Yes

Bystander engages in helping behaviour

FIGURE 8.4 When potential helpers are preoccupied with other concerns, they are much less likely to help a person in need. Among other factors, they are too busy to pay attention to the victim. Research participants who believed they had plenty of time to reach the room in which they were giving a talk were most likely to stop and help a stranger who was slumped, coughing and groaning, in a doorway. Those who believed they were running behind schedule were least likely to help.

Source: Based on data from Darley & Batson, 1973.

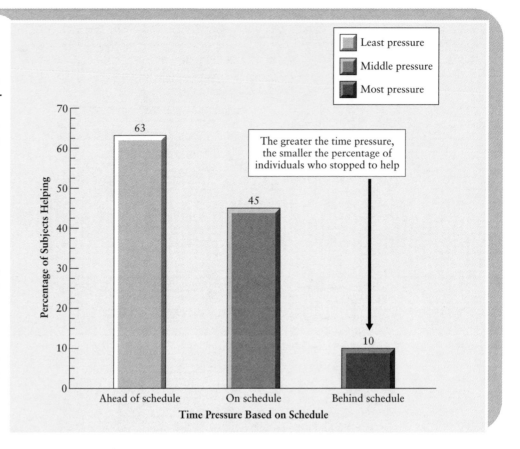

by building to present a talk. In an attempt to prime a helping response, the researchers specified that the talk was to be either about providing help to a stranger in need (Luke's parable of the Good Samaritan) or about jobs. To manipulate preoccupation, the investigators told the subjects that they were (1) ahead of schedule, with plenty of time; (2) right on schedule; or (3) late for the speaking engagement. It was assumed that the third group would be the least attentive to an emergency situation.

On their way to give the talk, the subjects each encountered an experimental assistant who was slumped in a doorway, coughing and groaning. Would they notice this individual and offer help? The topic of the upcoming speech had no effect on their response, but the time pressure did. As shown in Figure 8.4, help was offered by 63 percent of those who believed they had time to spare, 45 percent of those who were on schedule, and only 10 percent of those who were told they were late. The preoccupied subjects were in such a hurry that even when they were going to talk about the Good Samaritan, some simply stepped over the victim and rushed along to keep the speaking appointment.

Step 2: Interpreting an Emergency as an Emergency

Once the situation gets a bystander's attention, the second step is to interpret the situation correctly. What is going on? In general, it is easier to imagine a routine, everyday explanation of events than a highly unusual and unlikely one (Macrae & Milne, 1992). And a problem with interpreting an everyday situation as an emergency is that you can end up looking foolish. To avoid being embarrassed about being incorrect and behaving in an inappropriate way, most people fail to engage in any drastic action until the evidence is clear and convincing that an emergency is actually occurring.

Often there is some degree of ambiguity in emergency situations, so potential helpers hold back and wait for additional information in order to be sure about what is going on. The more ambiguous the situation, the less likely people are to offer help (Bickman, 1972). Because it is easier not to help than to take an active helping role, and because we tend to give more weight to negative than to positive information (see Chapter 2), people are especially attentive to any information that suggests there is no reason to be concerned (Wilson & Petruska, 1984).

When more than one bystander witnesses an emergency, each interprets the event in part on the basis of what the others do or say—each relies on social comparison (see Chapter 6). If fellow witnesses fail to react, helping behaviour is strongly inhibited. A special problem is that in our culture we are taught to remain calm in an emergency; it isn't socially acceptable to begin screaming when we see a stranger slip on an icy path, for example. As a result, most bystanders pretend to be calm, and this cool response is perceived by other bystanders as evidence that nothing serious is occurring. In an actual emergency, therefore, multiple bystanders can inadvertently and incorrectly inform one another that everything is all right.

This phenomenon is known as **pluralistic ignorance**, and an experiment by Latané and Darley (1968) demonstrates how it operates. The investigators asked subjects to fill out questionnaires in a room either alone or in groups of three. Shortly after they began, smoke was pumped into the room through a vent. The experimenters waited for the subjects to respond (but terminated the experimental session after six minutes if the subjects remained in their seats and failed to act). When subjects were in the room alone, 75 percent went out to report the smoke, and half of those who responded did so within two minutes. When three people were in the room, only one person reacted in the first four minutes—the majority (62 percent) did nothing for the entire six minutes even though the smoke became thick enough to make it difficult to see.

Ambiguity and social acceptability also inhibit the tendency to help when a man is hurting a woman. Suppose you heard an argument in a neighboring apartment, and the woman yelled, "I hate you! I don't ever want to see you again!" Would you do anything? Most people would decide that it was simply a lovers' quarrel and none of their business. Bystanders would probably be likely to respond, however, if the woman shouted, "Whoever you are, just get out of my apartment!" In an experimental version of such interactions, Shotland and Strau (1976) found that three times as many interventions took place when an argument was between a man and woman who were strangers than when it involved a married couple.

Ambiguity sometimes includes indecision as to whether a victim wants to be helped. That is one reason why people are hesitant to respond to a domestic quarrel; sometimes the victim of domestic aggression resents an outsider's interference as much as the aggressor does.

Step 3: Assuming That Helpfulness Is Your Responsibility

Once an individual pays attention to some external event and interprets it correctly as an emergency, a prosocial act will follow only if the person takes responsibility for providing help. In many instances the responsibility is clear. Firefighters are the ones to do something about a burning house; police officers are the ones to do something about a crime; medical personnel deal with injuries and illnesses. When responsibility is not as clear as in those examples, people tend to assume that anyone in a leadership role must be responsible (Baumeister et al., 1988). For example, professors should be responsible for dealing with classroom emergencies and bus drivers for emergencies involving their vehicles. When there is one adult and several children, the adult is expected to take charge.

Pluralistic Ignorance
A phenomenon that can occur when multiple bystanders witness an emergency: Each interprets the event in part on the basis of what the others do or say, but when none of them is sure about what is happening, all hold back and pretend that everything is all right. Each then uses this "information" to justify not responding.

One of the reasons that a lone bystander is more likely to act than a bystander in a group is that there is no one else present who could take responsibility. With a group, as we have discussed, the responsibility is diffuse and much less clear.

Step 4: Knowing What to Do

Even if a bystander reaches the point of assumed responsibility, nothing useful can be done unless that person knows how to be helpful. Some emergencies are sufficiently simple that almost everyone has the necessary skills. If you see someone slip on an icy sidewalk, you help that person up. If you see two suspicious strangers trying to break into a parked car, you find a phone and dial 911. Even in the latter instance, though, a child or a recent immigrant might not possess the necessary information. In Figure 8.5, for example, Snoopy is quite willing to act, but he can't because he doesn't know how to identify the number 9.

Some emergencies require special knowledge and skills that are not possessed by most bystanders. For example, you can help someone who is drowning only if you know how to swim and how to handle a drowning person. With bystanders at an accident, a registered nurse is more likely to assume responsibility and more likely to help than someone not employed in a medical profession (Cramer et al., 1988).

Step 5: Deciding to Help

Even if a bystander's response at each of the first four steps is yes, help will not occur unless he or she makes the final decision to act. Helping at this point can be inhibited by fears (often realistic) about potential negative consequences. For example, if you try to help a person who slipped on the ice, you might fall yourself. A sick person who has collapsed in a doorway may throw up on your shoes when you try to provide assistance. The person who seems to be in need may be a crook who is only pretending.

An especially unpleasant consequence may arise when there is family violence: The well-meaning outsider often arouses only anger. For this reason, bystanders rarely offer help when they believe that a woman is being attacked by her husband or boyfriend (Shotland & Strau, 1976) or that a child is being physically abused by a parent (Christy & Voigt, 1994). And police have learned that even when they have been called to an angry domestic scene by someone involved in the situation, intervention in this kind of family violence is more dangerous than interference in a hostile interaction between two strangers.

■ Even Snoopy can't provide help when he lacks the necessary knowledge

FIGURE 8.5 Among bystanders who are aware of a problem, who correctly interpret the situation as an emergency, and who assume responsibility to take action, prosocial behaviour may nevertheless be inhibited because of the absence of necessary skills.

Source: United Feature Syndicate, Inc., March 8, 1998.

For some very good reasons, then, bystanders may decide to hold back and avoid the risks that are sometimes associated with performing prosocial acts. While the five steps are still fresh in your mind, you might want to review them by taking a close look at the Ideas to Take with You section at the end of the chapter.

FURTHER DETERMINANTS OF HELPING BEHAVIOUR: INTERNAL AND EXTERNAL INFLUENCES

Prosocial behaviour can occur beyond the emergency situation. We help each other out when we give money to charity, arrange to help a friend move house, lend notes to a classmate and so on. In none of these situation is there the time pressures or the intensity that an emergency involves. In this section we will examine both internal and external influences on general prosocial behaviour. Internal influences considered are our *genes*, our *emotions and cognitions*, and *dispositional* or personality factors. External determinants are the immediate influence of others as *role models*, *characteristics of the victim*, and the long-term influence of our *culture*—whether this is rural versus urban, regional, or national culture.

The Genetic Contribution: Have We Evolved to be Prosocial?

Evolutionary theories assume that we have evolved to be prosocial or altruistic, though we are not indiscriminate in this tendency. For example, the **genetic determinism model** is based on a more general theory of human behaviour (Pinker, 1998). Rushton (1989) stresses that we are not conscious of responding to genetic influences but that we simply do so because we are built that way. In effect, humans are programmed to help just as they are programmed with respect to prejudice (Chapter 5), and attraction on mate selection (Chapter 6).

Evolutionary theories assume that genetic similarity is important in prosocial behaviour. Studies on nonhuman animal species indicate that the greater the genetic similarity between two individual organisms, the more likely it is that one will help the other when such help is needed (Ridley & Dawkins, 1981). Such behaviour has been

Genetic Determinism Model The proposal that prosocial behaviour is driven by genetic attributes that evolved because they enhanced reproductive success and thus the probability that individuals would be able to transmit their genes to subsequent generations.

described as the result of the "selfish gene" (Dawkins, 1976). That is, the more similar individual A is to individual B, the more genes they presumably have in common, and if A helps B, A's genes will be represented in future generations even if A dies in the process (Rushton, Russell, & Walls, 1984). Thus, instinctively each individual organism is fundamentally motivated to live long enough to reproduce or to enhance the reproductive odds of another individual whose genetic makeup is similar to his or her own (Browne, 1992).

Much the same conclusion was reached by Burnstein, Crandall, and Kitayama (1994). They reasoned that natural selection would favour those who help others who specifically are most closely related to themselves and even more specifically are *young enough to be able to reproduce*. Burnstein and colleagues conducted a series of studies based on hypothetical decisions to help. As predicted, research participants were more likely to help someone closely related than to help either a distant relative or someone totally unrelated. The importance of reproductive ability was indicated by the fact that more help was offered to young relatives than to old ones, and that more help was offered to women young enough to bear children than to women past menopause.

In a review of the altruism literature, Buck and Ginsburg (1991) concluded that, at least as yet, there is no evidence of a gene that determines prosocial behaviour. Among humans, and among other animals as well (de Waal, 1996), there are genetically based capacities to communicate emotions and to form social bonds. Such inherited behaviours make it likely that we will help one another when problems arise. In effect, people are inherently sociable and capable of empathy. When they interact in social relationships, "they are always prosocial, usually helpful, and often altruistic" (Fiske, 1991, p. 209).

Emotional Influences on Prosocial Behaviour

Offhand, it might seem that being in a good mood would make people more likely to help, while a bad mood would interfere with helping; and there is evidence that supports such assumptions (Forgas, 1998a). Nevertheless, research indicates that the effects of emotional state on helping are someone more complicated than one might guess, because several additional factors must be taken into account (Salovey, Mayer, & Rosenhan, 1991).

Positive Emotions and Their Effect on Prosocial Behaviour

Children sometimes wait for the magic moment when their parents are in a good mood before they make a special request. From a very early age, boys and girls assume that a happy parent is more likely to do something nice for them than is an unhappy parent. This is an accurate theory, at least under the right circumstances. For example, experimenters have put research participants in a positive mood by playing a comedy album (Wilson, 1981), arranging for them to find money in the coin return slot of a public phone (Isen & Levin, 1972), asking them to spend time outdoors on a pleasant sunny day (Cunningham, 1979), or by introducing a pleasant fragrance (e.g., Baron & Thomley, 1994; Baron, 1997). In each instance, the resulting positive feelings led to prosocial behaviour toward a stranger. You can see that many quite different investigations consistently indicate the positive effect of positive emotions on prosocial behaviour.

Additional factors complicate the relationship, however. Consider a somewhat different situation. What if a bystander is in a very positive mood when he or she encounters an ambiguous emergency situation? In unclear situations, a common reaction seems to be: Why spoil your happy feelings by assuming that someone needs help when you can just as easily assume that no real emergency exists? In effect, failure to

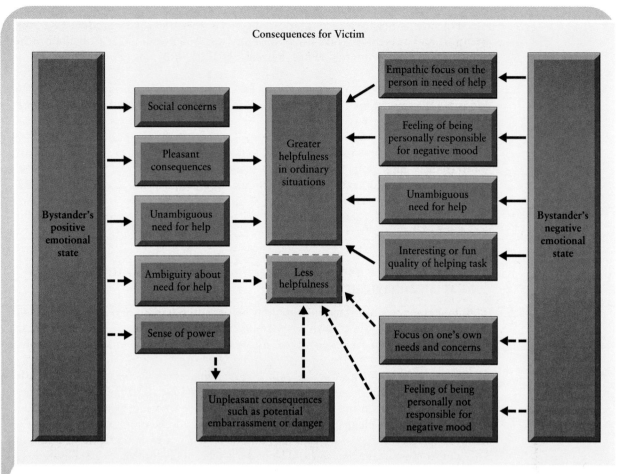

Consequences for Victim

■ Positive and negative emotions: Sometimes enhancing, sometimes hindering prosocial behaviour

FIGURE 8.6 Depending on several specific factors, a positive emotional state can either increase or decrease the likelihood of a prosocial response— and the same is true of a negative emotional state. This diagram summarizes the factors that influence these quite different effects based on emotions.

interpret the event as a problem allows you to remain in a good mood. Further, what if the emergency is unmistakable, but helping would require you to do something unpleasant or even dangerous (Rosenhan, Salovey, & Hargis, 1981)? Research evidence indicates that you would prefer simply to say no and walk away from the problem. The fact that you feel good actually gives you a sense of power, including the power to refuse to be helpful. The general point is that whenever being helpful might spoil a person's good mood, a positive emotional state actually tends to result in *less* helpfulness (Isen, 1984).

In summary, if the need for help is very clear and does not involve negative consequences for the helper, positive emotions increase the probability of a prosocial response. If, however, the need for help is ambiguous or possible negative consequences are involved, positive emotions decrease the probability of a prosocial response.

Negative Emotions and Their Effects on Prosocial Behaviour

Again, a common belief is that someone in a negative mood is less likely to be helpful; and again this effect has been confirmed by empirical research. When your affective state is negative through no fault of your own and you are focusing your attention on yourself and on how bad things are, you are unlikely to be helpful to someone in need (Amato, 1986; Rogers et al., 1982; Thompson, Cowan, & Rosenhan, 1980).

As you may have guessed, however, negative emotions can also have the opposite effect under specific conditions. For example, if the act of helping is something that seems likely to make you feel better, negative emotions tend to increase the occurrence of prosocial acts (Cialdini, Kenrick, & Bauman, 1982). This positive effect of negative emotions is most likely to occur if your negative emotions are not extremely intense, if the emergency is clear, and if the act of helping is interesting and satisfying rather than difficult and unpleasant (Berkowitz, 1987; Cunningham et al., 1990).

These mixed effects for positive and negative emotional states are summarized in Figure 8.6.

Attributions of Responsibility: The Cognitive Contribution to Prosocial Behaviour

In non-emergency situations the potential helper often has time to assess the object of their behaviour—the person in need of help. These cognitive evaluations can interact with, or sometimes produce, an emotional response which will, in turn, determine helping.

If you were taking a walk and came across a man lying unconscious by the curb, your tendency to help or not help would be influenced by all of the factors we have discussed earlier—from the presence of other bystanders to interpersonal attraction. But let's add another element to this situation. Would you be more willing to help the man if his clothes were stained and torn and he clutched a wine bottle in his hand, or if his clothes were neat and clean and he had a bruise on his forehead? (See Figure 8.7.) The odds are that you would be less strongly motivated to help the badly dressed man with the wine. Why? Despite the fact that both of these strangers seem to need assistance, you would be more likely to act if you did not make the attribution that the man was *personally responsible for his difficulty*. In general, if the victim is perceived to be the cause of the problem, people are less motivated to help; in fact, they are likely to respond with the emotion of disgust and be unwilling to help, because, after all, "the victim is to blame" (Weiner, 1980). Help is much more likely if the problem is believed to be caused by *circumstances beyond the victim's control*. As shown in Figure 8.8, a model formulated by Weiner (1980) proposes that we respond with disgust to a victim who is responsible for the problem, and that this reaction does not motivate helping. When the victim is not responsible for the problem, we respond with empathy, which motivates a helpful response.

Attributing blame to the victim is not always totally objective, however. If you are prejudiced against a particular group your attributions may be more negative, as well as your emotional response and decrease the likelihood of helping. For example, Shaw, Borough, and Fink (1994) found that a homosexual stranger in need received less help than a heterosexual stranger, although the two were in exactly the same position and for the same reason. In a method called the "wrong number technique," a male research assistant dialed random telephone numbers from a pay phone. When the call was answered he pretended he had called the wrong number and just used up his last quarter. He explained that he had a flat tire and asked if the person who answered could call his boyfriend (in the homosexual condition) or girlfriend (in the heterosexual condition) to say that he would be late for the celebration of their first anniver-

■ Would you help this stranger? Why not?

FIGURE 8.7 One possible explanation is that you are making negative attributions as to the reason for his lying unconscious beside the curb. Do you believe that this man might be responsible for his difficulty?

sary. Most people (over 70 percent) called the "girlfriend" of the man in distress but few (less than 35 percent) called the "boyfriend" of the man in distress.

Most religious belief-systems encourage selflessness and helpfulness. On this basis you might expect that those with strong religious beliefs would be particularly prosocial or altruistic. In general, research has not supported that expectation (e.g. Batson Schoenrade & Ventis, 1993): religious individuals are often as vulnerable as others to the many barriers that can prevent helping. The following On the Applied Side section also indicates that occasionally religious beliefs can themselves act as a barrier to positive attributions about the person in need.

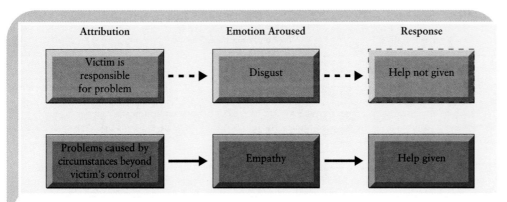

■ Who is responsible for the victim's plight?

FIGURE 8.8 Weiner's (1980) attributional analysis of helping behaviour suggests that perceptions of the cause of the victim's problems have different effects on the emotions aroused by the situation. If the victim is believed to be responsible for the problem, disgust is aroused and help is not given. If, in contrast, the problem is attributed to external circumstances, empathy is aroused and help is given.

Religious Fundamentalism and Helping the "Undeserving" Poor

Though you might assume that prosocial acts would be especially characteristic of religious individuals (Campbell, 1975), even religious individuals often refrain from helping because of attributions of victim responsibility. The crucial factor seems to be whether the victim poses a threat to the values of one's religion (Jackson & Esses, 1997). If an individual threatens your values, there is a strong tendency to make attributions of personal responsibility for his or her problems. If it's the victim's fault, there is no reason to provide help. The victim should engage in self-help or seek solutions elsewhere.

These ideas were tested by Lynne Jackson and Victoria Esses who carried out two studies at the University of Western Ontario (1997). Their focus

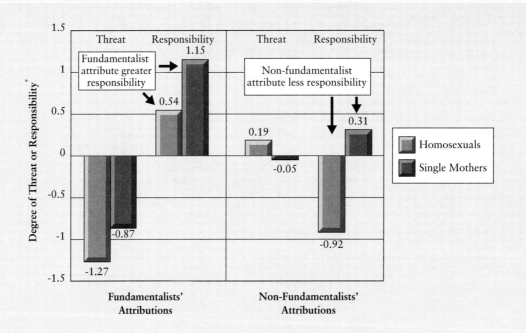

*Scales:

    1) Degree of Threat scale ranges from +3 to -3. The plus side of the scale indicates that the target group is seen as promoting the subject's values. The minus side of the scale indicates that they are seen as threatening the subject's values.

    2) Degree of Responsibility scale ranges from +3 to -3. The plus side of the scale indicates that the target group is seen as "responsible for their unemployment." The minus side of the scale indicates the responsibility for their unemployment is "due to forces beyond their control."

■ Attributions of threat and responsibility

FIGURE 8.9 Fundamentalists saw both homosexuals and single mothers as threatening their values and as responsible for their unemployment problems. In contrast, non-fundamentalists did not see these groups as a threat and attributed less responsibility to them for their unemployment situation.

was on religious fundamentalism—belief in the absolute and literal truth of the teachings of a specific religion. Subjects were university students who had a variety of religious affiliations including Christian (Protestant, Catholic), Jewish, Hindu, and Islam, as well as some who were atheist or agnostic. Fundamentalism was measured using the Altemeyer and Hunsberger *Religious Fundamentalism Scale* (1992). It measures the extent to which subjects endorse a number of statements such as "To lead the best, most meaningful life, one must belong to the one true religion" or "No single book of religious writings contains all the important truths about life." Those classified as fundamentalist would tend to agree with the first statement and disagree with the second. Those classified as non-fundamentalist would show the reverse pattern. Subjects were asked to evaluate certain target groups: homosexuals or Native Canadians (in the first study) and single mothers or students (in the second study). These groups were also described as having disproportionately high levels of unemployment. Evaluative measures were (1) the *degree of threat* to subjects' values posed by the target group and (2) the *degree of responsibility* that target groups had for their unemployment. In addition, subjects were asked to indicate the type of help each group should be given.

Results showed that the values of those high in religious fundamentalism were threatened by two particular target groups—homosexuals and single mothers. As predicted, they also attributed greater responsibility to these two groups for their employment difficulties. These findings are shown in Figure 8.9, contrasting the attributions of fundamentalists and non-fundamentalists. When it came to the kind of help that should be offered, fundamentalists went on to recommend that such persons change their lifestyles rather than relying on other people to provide help.

But when fundamentalists were given unemployment information about individuals who did not threaten their values (Native Canadians and students), these victims were not perceived to be responsible for their predicament, and were seen as deserving help. They assumed these groups to be much more similar in values to themselves than were homosexuals or single mothers.

This research indicates the importance of understanding the role of attributions of responsibility in prosocial behaviour, or the lack of it in this case. It appears that if a group presents a challenge to your own values then you will be less willing to offer them help. And this can then be justified by your view that somehow they are more responsible for their predicament.

KEY POINTS

- The *genetic determinism* model traces prosocial behaviour to the general effects of natural selection, which favours any attribute that increases the odds that one's genes will be transmitted to future generations.

- Positive and negative *emotional states* can either enhance or inhibit prosocial behaviour, depending on specific factors in the situation, in the individual, and in the nature of the required assistance.

- Attributions of *responsibility* can determine emotion and prosocial behaviour. We are more likely to help if we attribute the problem to circumstances beyond the victim's control and if our values are not threatened by the victim.

Dispositional Differences in Prosocial Behaviour

While changing emotions and cognitions may have a temporary impact on prosocial behaviour, researchers have long sought to discover the enduring characteristics that comprise the prosocial or **altruistic personality**. Table 8.1 shows some of the major variables that have been considered and we will describe related research below.

Altruistic Personality
The combination of dispositional variables that make an individual more likely to engage in altruistic behaviour. Included are an empathic self-concept, belief in a just world, feelings of social responsibility, internal locus of control, and low egocentrism.

In an attempt to identify the factors that make up the altruistic personality, investigators compared citizens who witnessed a traffic accident and provided first aid to the victim with citizens who witnessed such an accident and did not provide first aid. As indicated here, five personality characteristics were found to differentiate the two groups. Together these characteristics identify altruistic individuals.

TABLE 8.1 Aspects of the altruistic personality

Personality Characteristics of those who offered assistance	Description
Higher empathy	*Empathy* is the ability to take another person's perspective and to feel or imagine the other's emotions and cognitions.
Were higher in internal locus of control	The belief that one can control own outcomes: That is, choose to behave in ways that maximize good outcomes and minimize bad ones. Those with an *external locus of control* believe that they are at the mercy of external and uncontrollable factors and that their own chosen behaviour has little effect on outcomes.
Strong belief in a just world	Perceive the world as a fair and predictable place in which people get what they deserve. This belief leads to the conclusion that not only is helping those in need the right thing to do, but the person who helps will actually benefit from doing so.
Felt more socially responsible	Are interested in public matters and involved in the community; feel a sense of duty. Believe each person is responsible for helping those in need.
Showed relatively low egocentrism	Were not self-absorbed and competitive.

Source: Based on data in Bierhoff, Klein, & Kramp, 1991.

Research on the Altruistic Personality

An attempt to identify the altruistic personality was undertaken by Bierhoff, Klein, and Kramp (1991). These investigators selected several personality variables identified in previous prosocial research and administered measures to assess their levels in two groups of German citizens. The first group consisted of men and women who had been at the scene of an accident and administered first aid before an ambulance arrived. The second group consisted of the control subjects who reported witnessing an automobile accident but provided no help to the victims. These two groups were matched with respect to sex, age, and social status. This work demonstrated the importance of the five factors in Table 8.1. These factors distinguished the first, prosocial group from the less helpful accident witnesses.

These five characteristics of the altruistic personality were confirmed in another study of people who helped a quite different kind of victim. Oliner and Oliner (1988) obtained personality data on people throughout Europe who were actively involved in rescuing Jews from the Nazis during World War II. Those who bravely defied the authorities and protected Jews were found to be remarkably similar to those who provided first aid to accident victims.

Altogether, people with an altruistic personality have a strong sense of internal control, a high belief in a just world, a sense of duty, a self-concept involving empathy, and a concern for others rather than an egocentric concern for self. How would you rate yourself on these five dimensions?

Empathy: Putting Myself in Your Shoes

Much of the interest in individual differences in helpfulness has concentrated on what appear to be the altruistic motives of bystanders based on **empathy** (Clary & Orenstein, 1991; Grusec, 1991). Empathy has been defined in several different ways, but two aspects are common to most definitions. There is an *affective* component: an empathetic person feels what another person is feeling (Darley, 1993). And there is a *cognitive* component: an empathetic person understands what another person is feeling and why (Azar, 1997). Human beings differ dramatically in empathy, ranging from people who are deeply concerned about any distress experienced by others to psychopathic individuals who are totally indifferent to and unaffected by the emotional state of those around them (Hare, 1995).

Empathy Vicariously experiencing the emotions and cognitions of another through perspective taking—imagining how they feel in the situation or how you would feel in it.

The *affective* component seems to be the essential component of empathy, and children as young as twelve months react in ways that indicate their tendency to feel distress in response to the distress of others (Brothers, 1990). This same characteristic is also observed in monkeys and apes (Ungerer et al., 1990) and perhaps among dogs and dolphins as well (Azar, 1997a). Evolutionary psychologists interpret such findings as indications of the biological underpinnings of prosocial behaviour, probably stemming from its utility in the survival of various species. A second aspect of the affective component of empathy is feeling sympathetic—not only feeling another's pain but also expressing concern and attempting to do something to relieve the pain.

While the affective component of empathy is characteristic of adult and infant humans and a few other mammals, the *cognitive component* seems to be a uniquely human quality that develops only as we progress beyond infancy. Central to this cognitive component is the ability to consider the viewpoint of another person, sometimes referred to as *perspective taking*—being able "to put oneself in someone else's shoes." To further expand the picture, social psychologists have identified three different types of perspective taking (Batson, Early, & Salvarani, 1997; Stotland, 1969): (1) an "imagine other" perspective—imagining how the other person perceives an event and feels as a result; (2) an "imagine self" perspective—imagining how you would feel as a result; (3) a fantasy perspective—taking the form of empathy for a fictional character, as when someone reacts emotionally to the joys and sorrows of an imaginary person or animal. For example, when children cry as Bambi discovers that his mother has died, or people of various ages cry when Jack dies in the movie *Titanic*. The emotional response is not exactly the same for these perspectives, however. Those who take the "imagine other" perspective experience relatively pure empathy that motivates altruistic behaviour. The "imagine self" perspective also produces empathy, but it is accompanied by feelings of distress that arouse egoistic motives that can actually interfere with altruism.

Why do people differ so widely? Genetic differences in empathy were investigated by Davis, Luce, and Kraus (1994). They examined more than 800 sets of identical and nonidentical twins and found that inherited factors underlie the two affective aspects of empathy (personal distress and sympathetic concern). Genes account for about a third of the differences among people in affective empathy. Presumably, learning accounts for the remaining affective differences as well as for differences in the cognitive aspects of empathy, and children as young as two begin to show observable differences in empathy. Canadian psychologist Janet Strayer (quoted in Azar, 1997) suggests that we are all born with the biological and cognitive capacity for empathy. Depending on our experience—and our parents seem particularly important here as teachers (e.g., Azar, 1997a)—this capacity can become a vital part of our self, or its development can be totally blocked.

Either because of genetic differences or because of different socialization experiences, women generally react with higher levels of empathy than men (Trobst, Collins, & Embree, 1994). Consistent with this finding are studies of non-Jewish Germans who helped rescue Jews from the Nazis in World War II. Gender differences in helping were common among these brave individuals, with a two-to-one ratio of female to male rescuers (Anderson, 1993).

We will now turn from internal influences on prosocial behaviour (our genes, emotions and cognitions) to external influences such as whether other people provide us with *role models* of prosocial behaviour, the nature of the person in need of help—*the victim*, and *cultural influences*.

Role Models: Providing Helpful Cues

If you are out shopping and pass someone collecting money to help the homeless, provide warm coats for needy children, buy food for those in poverty, or whatever, do you reach in your pocket or purse to make a contribution? One determinant of your behaviour is whether you see someone else contribute. People are much more likely to donate money if they observe others doing so (Macauley, 1970). Even the presence of paper money and coins in the collection box acts as an encouragement to a charitable response.

The presence of fellow bystanders who fail to respond to an emergency inhibits helpfulness, as we have seen. In an analogous way, the presence of a helpful bystander provides a *role model* and encourages helpfulness. This modeling effect was shown in a field experiment in which a female confederate was parked by the side of a road with a flat tire. Male motorists were much more likely to stop and help if (several minutes earlier) they had observed another woman with car trouble receiving help (Bryan & Test, 1967).

The positive effect of models is not limited to real-life encounters. Television is found to influence viewers in various ways, and altruism is one of them. In a study of the effects of TV, investigators showed six-year-olds an episode of *Lassie* that con-

■ The impact of a prosocial model

FIGURE 8.10
Investigators have found that when preschool children are exposed to prosocial programs such as *Mister Dressup*, they are more likely to behave in an altruistic way than children who have not watched such shows.

tained a rescue scene, an episode of the same program unrelated to prosocial behaviour, or a humorous segment of *The Brady Bunch* (Sprafkin, Liebert, & Poulous, 1975). Children exposed to the rescue were more likely to help in a subsequent play session. Other investigators have found that when preschool children are exposed to prosocial programs such as *Mister Dressup* or *Sesame Street* (see Figure 8.10), they are more likely to behave in an altruistic way than children who have not watched such shows (Forge & Phemister, 1987). These studies consistently indicate that television can exert a very positive influence on the development of prosocial responses.

Of course, for most children their first prosocial models are their parents. As research on the altruistic personality has found, those with the strongest prosocial tendencies often have parents who were altruistic and involved in the community (e.g., Oliner & Oliner, 1988).

KEY POINTS

- The *altruistic personality* consists of empathy, internal locus of control, belief in a just world, high social responsibility and low egocentricity.

- Individual differences in altruistic behaviour are based in large part on *empathy*—vicariously experiencing the emotions and cognitions of another through perspective taking. The extent to which a person is able to respond with empathy depends on both genetic and environmental factors.

- Exposure to prosocial models in real life and in the media has a positive effect on prosocial acts.

Who Needs Help? Characteristics of the Victim

Research consistently shows that a similar victim is more likely to receive help than a dissimilar one (Clark et al., 1987; Dovidio & Morris, 1975; Hayden, Jackson & Guydish, 1984). You will recall that similarity almost always has a positive influence on attraction (see Chapter 6) and research also indicates that we are more likely to help those that we like or are attracted to. So a physically attractive victim receives more help that an unattractive one (Benson, Karabenick, & Lerner, 1976).

Though it sounds like a sexist stereotype, research has consistently shown that men are very likely to provide help to women (Latané & Dabbs, 1975; Piliavin & Unger, 1985). How can such findings be explained? Helpful men are puzzling, because adult women are higher in empathy than men, and the same is true for young girls versus young boys (Shigetomi, Hartmann, & Gelfand, 1981).

One possibility lies in Step 4 of the decision-making model. Many emergency situations require certain skills and knowledge (for example, changing a flat tire or determining what is wrong with an automobile engine) or a level of strength and special training (for example, overpowering an attacker or ripping a seat belt out of a car) that have traditionally been associated with men rather than women. Perhaps it is for this reason that a female motorist in distress by the side of the road (see Figure 8.11) receives more offers of assistance than a male or a male-female couple in the same predicament (Pomazal & Clore, 1973; Snyder, Grether, & Keller, 1974). Also, the motorists who stop to provide help are most often young males who are driving alone.

The motivation for providing such help may not be entirely prosocial or altruistic, however. For one thing, men stop to help an attractive woman more frequently

■ Helping a lady in distress: What motivates males?

FIGURE 8.11 In many situations, women are more likely to receive help than either men or couples, and men are more likely to provide help than woman. Because attractive women receive more help than unattractive ones, and because men exposed to erotic stimuli are more helpful to women than men not exposed to such stimuli, it seems reasonable to suggest that the motivation for male helpfulness in these instances is sometimes based on sexual attraction rather than on altruism.

than to help an unattractive one (West & Brown, 1975). It seems possible, then, that the motivation is primarily romantic or sexual. Przybyla (1985) found that men who had just seen an erotic tape were more helpful to female laboratory assistant than to a male assistant who had the same problem with dropped papers. Note also that viewing or not viewing an erotic tape had no effect on the helping behaviour of women in response to representatives of either gender.

However, more recent research among the police officers suggests that both genders may show a prosocial bias towards the opposite sex. Koehler and Willis (1994) investigated whether police officers in two-dozen municipal police departments reacted more helpfully to members of the opposite sex. They suggest that issuing a warning is a more prosocial response than issuing a traffic ticket. Their overall finding was that both male and female officers were more likely to issue traffic tickets to drivers of the same gender than to drivers of the opposite gender.

Cultural Context: Regional and Societal Differences in Prosocial Behaviour

People are often quite convinced that those who live in one region of a country are more helpful than those in another, or that country-folk are more kind and considerate than city-folk. And if you were raised in one of these contexts you probably support this belief. The source of, for example, a rural-urban discrepancy is often thought to be differences in cultural values. Similarly, it is also true that some nationalities have more prosocial reputations than others. Social psychology has investigated these questions, and an answer can be provided, at least to the rural-urban issue though not to the issues of societal or national differences.

Rural Versus Urban Helping

Although social diversity is most often studied with respect to racial, ethnic, or national differences, place of residence can also be an important determinant of human behaviour. If you have ever spent much time in a large city and/or in a small town, do you believe that interpersonal interactions and interpersonal behaviour may be affected by such settings?

Milgram (1970) suggested that the external demands of an urban environment involve *stimulus overload* for city dwellers. For example, crowded cities are noisier than small towns—filled with the sounds of traffic, sirens, and squealing brakes both day and night (Cooke, 1992). And, by definition, people in a city come into contact with more people (including more strangers) each day than people in a less crowded community. The best way to survive in such an environment is to screen out nonessential stimuli and go on about one's own business. For example, as population increases, the environment becomes more fast-paced (Sadalla, Sheets, & McCreath, 1990). The larger the city, the faster pedestrians walk (Walmsley & Lewis, 1989)—much like the seminary students rushing between campus buildings. Even those who commute from suburbia to city behave differently in the two locations.

An expected consequence of stimulus overload, fast pace, and concentrating on oneself is a general disregard for others, especially strangers. As a result, as Levine and colleagues (1994) predicted, helpfulness should decrease. These researchers obtained relevant data on prosocial behaviour in 36 small, medium, and large cities across the United States. They measured several different forms of helping, which included informing a stranger that he or she had dropped a pen, assisting a person in a leg brace pick up magazines when they slipped to the sidewalk, making change for a quarter, helping a blind person cross the street, picking up and mailing a stamped letter that apparently had been lost, and per capita charitable contributions to the United Way. A strong negative relationship was found between these combined indicators of prosocial acts and population density (Levine et al., 1994). That is, the greater the number of people living in a given locality, the less helpful the residents.

Earlier research also supported the generalization that city dwellers are less friendly and less helpful to strangers than are small-town residents (Korte, 1980, 1981; Krupat & Guild, 1980). And the relationship between population and helpfulness exists not only in Canada (e.g. Rushton, 1978) but all over the world (e.g., Amato, 1983; Yousif & Korte 1995). Clearly, our surroundings can influence the decisions that are essential to prosocial actions.

Cross-Cultural Comparisons

A (nonscientific) test of helping behaviour conducted by *Reader's Digest* provides some interesting comparisons for Canadians (reported in the *Globe and Mail*, February 19, 1997). Ten wallets, each containing $50 cash, were dropped in 12 Canadian cities and the number returned intact to their owners was tracked. Toronto, Canada's largest city, had the lowest return rate. Only 4 of the 10 wallets were returned. Moncton had the greatest honesty rate of 100 percent. Charlottetown ranked second with eight wallets returned. Seven wallets were returned in Vancouver and Winnipeg, six in Montreal, Calgary, Saskatoon, Whitehorse, Val D'Or, Quebec, and St. John's, and five in Halifax. Women were more likely to return the wallets (73 percent) than men (56 percent). In comparison to previous tests conducted in other countries, Canada's return rate of 64 percent was slightly lower than Britain (65 percent) and the United States (67 percent) and higher than Asia (57 percent) and Europe (58 percent).

The focus of cross-cultural comparisons of prosocial behaviour has been on societies that differ in individualism versus collectivism (see Smith and Bond, 1999). At the individualistic extreme of the spectrum, values stress that each person strives to be a self-contained unit and seeks success and recognition on the basis of individual achievement. It's every man for himself, every woman for herself. In contrast, collectivistic societies stress interlocking family-like connections in which individuals depend on one another, sharing both hardship and success. It's one for all and all for one. Given such differences in outlook, differences in help-seeking behaviour might well be expected.

However, the picture that emerges is somewhat more complex. In general, the demand to be prosocial to those in the ingroup may be greater in collective cultures, but this may not be true where helping strangers is concerned (see Smith & Bond, 1999). It appear that helping a stranger depends upon the culture's evaluation of the person in need of help and the local social norms: for example, whether the stranger is seen as threatening in that particular culture, or of high or low status, and so on. Though one recent study, comparing large cities in 18 countries, found that those in the large cities of wealthy countries were less likely to give help to strangers than those in similar sized cities in poorer countries (Norenzayan & Levine, 1994).

Taking a different perspective, Nadler (1986) examined the effect of both individualistic and collectivistic cultures on *help-seeking* behaviour in the citizens of a single nation—Israel. He points out that this country provides a unique opportunity for such comparisons because there are both urban dwellers whose environment stresses typical Western values such as self-reliance and individual achievement and *kibbutz* dwellers whose environment stresses egalitarian-communal ideology—that is, more collectivistic values.

Based on these cultural differences, Nadler predicted that those living in a kibbutz would expect to be dependent on one another and thus should be willing to seek help when it is needed. This should be an expected and normative way to cope with problems. Those living in a city, however, should view self-reliance as all-important and thus should be reluctant to turn to others for help. He asked study participants from *kibbutzim* and urban settings to imagine a series of everyday situations in which they faced a problem and a potential helper was available; for each situation the participants were to indicate the likelihood that they would actually seek help from the other person. As predicted, *kibbutz* dwellers indicated more help-seeking than did city dwellers.

KEY POINTS

- Help is more likely to be given to those who are similar to oneself and by men to women more often than vice versa.
- The culture context can influence prosocial behaviour. Research shows higher levels of helping in rural than urban settings. Pressure to be helpful to others in your ingroup may be greater in collectivistic cultures but this does not necessarily extend to helping a stranger. Help-seeking is more likely among individuals familiar with a communal experience than among those with an individualistic background.

SOURCES OF AGGRESSION: THEORIES ABOUT ITS NATURE AND CAUSES

Why do human beings aggress against others? What makes them turn, with brutality unmatched by even the fiercest of predators, against their fellow human beings? Scholars and scientists have pondered such questions for centuries, with the result that many contrasting explanations for the paradox of human violence have been proposed. Here, we'll examine several that have been especially influential.

The Evolution of Aggression: A Part of Human Nature?

Is aggression a part of human nature? Are wars and violence an inevitable part of human behaviour because we have evolved that way—is aggression instinctive? This is the suggestion of the oldest and probably best-known explanation for human aggression. It suggests that we are "programmed" for violence by our biological nature. Interestingly, in a different form, that is the focus of the most recent social psychological trend—that of *evolutionary social psychology*.

Early Instinct Theories

The most famous early supporter of the **instinct theory** perspective was Sigmund Freud, who held that aggression stems mainly from a powerful *death wish* or instinct (that he termed *thanatos*) possessed by all persons (Freud, 1930). According to Freud, this instinct is initially aimed at self-destruction but is soon redirected outward, toward others. Freud believed that the hostile impulses it generates increase over time and, if not released periodically, soon reach high levels capable of generating dangerous acts of violence. Freud also suggested that directly opposed to this death wish is another instinct, that he termed *eros*, which is focused on pleasure, love, and procreation. The complex relationship between these two powerful forces fascinated Freud, and is reflected in modern research on the potential links between sex and aggression discussed later in this chapter.

Another view, much more closely related to today's evolutionary approach, was proposed by Konrad Lorenz, a Nobel Prize-winning scientist. Lorenz (1966, 1974), a zoologist, proposed that aggression springs mainly from an inherited *fighting instinct* that human beings share with many other species. This instinct developed during the course of evolution because it yielded important benefits for the species. For example, fighting serves to disperse populations over a wide area, thus ensuring maximum use of available natural resources. Further, because it is often closely related to mating, fighting helps to ensure that only the strongest and most vigorous individuals will pass on their genes to the next generation.

> **Instinct Theory** A view suggesting that specific forms of behaviour (e.g., aggression) stem from innate tendencies that are universal among members of a given species.

Modern Evolutionary Approaches

Originating in the 1970s with the field of sociobiology (e.g., Dawkins, 1976; Wilson, 1975), the modern *evolutionary social psychology* approach (see Chapter 1) suggests that many aspects of social behaviour, including aggression, can be understood in terms of evolution. Briefly, behaviours that help individuals get their genes into the next generation will become increasingly prevalent in the species' population. For example, since aggression aids the males of many species in obtaining mates, principles of natural selection will, over time, favour increasing levels of aggression, at least among males. While sociobiologists initiated this view as applied to many animal species, modern evolutionary social psychology focuses on human beings, suggesting that we too have evolved in the context of natural selection. Similarly, our strong tendencies toward aggressive behaviour can be understood in this context. Thus, they are now part of our inherited biological nature. The following Canadian Research: On the Cutting Edge section features an evolutionary explanation for the existence of violent insurrections in society.

Canadian Research: On the Cutting Edge

Evolution and Collective Aggression: The Young Male Syndrome?

The modern evolutionary approach to aggression has often focused on extreme manifestations of aggression, in particular interpersonal violence. For example, two long-term proponents of evolutionary psychology, Martin Daly and Margo Wilson at McMaster University, have examined patterns of homicide and demonstrated that victim-killer relations follow evolutionary predictions: homicide is much less likely to occur between those who share genetic material than those who don't (e.g., Daly & Wilson, 1982, 1988, 1999). They also coined the term "young male syndrome" to refer to the fact that young males are more likely to be involved in violence and risk-taking generally than older males or females (Wilson & Daly, 1985). From the evolutionary perspective, the preponderance of young males involved in violence is explained as stemming ultimately from competition for reproductive success. It has been suggested that compared to males, females have a greater physical investment in reproduction (they bear and feed the infant) and are more limited in the number of offspring they can produce. Because of this high investment/low return ratio, evolution would favour females who have a mate with resources. This could ensure the survival of their offspring and the passing on of their genes to the next generation. It follows from this that females will have evolved to find resource-rich males attractive, and that males will have evolved to compete with each other for the resources necessary to attract a mate. Thus, young males are more likely to be in conflict and to perpetrate violence upon other young males, their major source of competition.

Christian Mesquida and Neil Wiener (1996) of York University have taken this idea and extended it to apply to the ultimate manifestation of our aggression—warfare. However, their emphasis is not so much on inter-male violence as on male collective violence. They suggest that "the relative number of young males in a given population... is likely to influence political affairs and lead to collective violence" (Mesquida & Wiener, 1996, p. 249). In support of this hypothesis, they examined the relationship between the proportion of 15-29 year old males in a population and the severity of collective violence in that society (as indicated by the number of fatalities sustained in violent collective conflicts). In one such comparison they collected information about 88 countries from United Nations data for the 14 year period from 1980 to 1993. A significant and positive relationship was found—the greater the proportion of young males in a population, the greater the severity of collective violence. Further analyses of this kind included looking at the 15 republics of the former Soviet Union between 1989 and 1993. Results were very similar.

Why should this relationship exist? These researchers suggest that with a large proportion of young males there will be a larger number who fail to acquire substantial resources and successfully mate. These young men can perhaps achieve their evolutionary goals if they participate in collective aggression: they band together to attain the resources. This could occur within a country in the form of uprisings or revolution, which could result in a redistribution of resources from older to younger generations. Alternatively, the collective violence could be cross-border warfare, which might result in a widening of the resource-base for the society. Although it is not typically the young who make the decision to send a nation into war, they may provide the political pressure and perhaps internal instability that will force the hand of their leaders.

Please note that the data of Mesquida and Wiener are correlational and therefore do not definitively establish a *causal* relationship between proportion of young males and collective violence. As the authors discuss, other factors could also explain the variations in severity of collective violence—particularly poverty and political instability. Those nations that had a higher proportion of young males, were by and large developing countries that also had fewer resources and were more politically unstable. These factors could themselves be independent causes or could contribute to lethal collective violence. Modern evolutionary theorists and researchers seldom suggest that instinctive tendencies are the sole cause of

aggression in human beings, rather they tend to see such evolved tendencies as *interacting* with other factors, both environmental and internal, that can facilitate or inhibit them (e.g., Daly & Wilson, 1999).

Nonetheless, the findings of Mesquida and Wiener fit with those of Daly and Wilson and other researchers who show a connection between the level of young males in society and other kinds of violent behaviour (e.g., Cohen & Land, 1987; Moller, 1967/68). For example, it has been pointed out that as the Baby-Boom generation ages and the proportion of young males in North American society becomes smaller, so the violent crime rate declines (Foot, 1998)—we will discuss this again in Chapter 10. Internationally, commentators have remarked on the high number of male adolescents who are involved in warfare particularly in developing countries, as shown in Figure 8.12. This evolutionary approach suggests that in part their involvement may stem from their own instinctive, and evolved, tendencies.

■ The Young Male Syndrome in collective violence

FIGURE 8.12 The evolutionary perspective has suggested that the Young Male Syndrome (the greater involvement of young males in violence) occurs because of instinctive tendencies in males to compete with each other for the resources needed to attract a mate. Taking this idea further, Mesquida and Wiener (1996) have suggested that the likelihood of collective unrest in a society will increase as the proportion of young males in the population increases. This photograph shows adolescent males taking part in a political uprising in Liberia. Could their involvement stem, at least in part, from evolved tendencies?

The early, and more simple, instinct theories of aggression have generally been rejected by social psychologists for the following reasons. First, as we'll see in later sections of this chapter, human aggression stems from a very large number of different factors; thus, emphasizing innate tendencies as a primary cause of such behaviour seems inappropriate. Second, in most animal species, the kind of fighting behaviour described by Lorenz does not lead to serious injury or death of the combatants. In contrast, human aggression is far more deadly: each year, millions of persons are killed and tens of millions seriously injured in assaults by other human beings. Innate tendencies to engage in such lethal behaviour make little sense from an evolutionary perspective. Third, human aggression takes a tremendous range of forms—from ignoring another person or spreading false rumors about her to destroying the target's property or attacking this person directly, either verbally or physically. It is hard to imagine how all these forms of behaviour could be the direct result of innate urges or tendencies. Finally, there are wide cultural variations in aggression as we will discuss later. Clearly, such facts are inconsistent with the idea that human beings are genetically programmed for aggression.

While social psychologists generally reject the view that human aggression stems largely from innate factors, they do however accept the possibility that genetic factors play some role in human aggression. In addition, they recognize the potentially important role of *biological factors* in such behaviour. Indeed, research findings point to the conclusion that the inability to restrain aggressive urges may stem, at least in part, from disturbances in the nervous system—for instance, from low levels of certain neurotransmitters such as serotonin (Marazzitti et al., 1993). Similarly, there is growing evidence that certain sex hormones may also play a role in aggression (e.g., Van Goozen, Frijda, & de Poll, 1994). In one recent study on this topic, for example, participants completed questionnaires designed to measure both their tendencies to behave aggressively and their tendencies to behave in a helpful, nurturant manner (e.g., "I often take people under my wing"; "I like helping other people") in a wide range of situations (Harris et al., 1996). The researchers also obtained two measures of participants' level of testosterone, an important male sex hormone. Results indicated that for both genders, the higher the testosterone levels, the higher the tendency to engage in aggression and the lower the tendency to engage in helpful, nurturant behaviours as reported by participants. Although these findings were based on correlations, further analyses indicated that the relationship between testosterone and aggression was a direct one: increments in testosterone appeared to cause increased tendencies to aggress.

While these results are far from conclusive—they are based on self-reports of aggression and helping rather than on actual observations of these behaviours—they agree with the results of other studies (e.g., Patrick, Bradley, & Lang, 1993) in suggesting that biological factors do indeed play a role in aggressive behaviour. For this reason, it is important that biological aspects be included in our overall picture of the nature of human aggression.

KEY POINTS

- Aggression is the intentional infliction of harm on others.
- *Instinct theories* suggest that aggression stems largely from innate urges or tendencies. The modern form of this approach stems from evolutionary social psychology. The *young male syndrome*—the preponderance of young males involved in violence—is seen as derived from evolved competition between males for reproductive success. While social psychologists have not endorsed a simple instinct theory, they do recognize the potential role of evolution and biological factors in human aggression.

Drive Theories
Theories suggesting that aggression stems from external conditions that arouse the motive to harm or injure others. The most famous of these theories is the frustration-aggression hypothesis.

Aggression As An Elicited Drive: The Motive to Harm or Injure Others

An alternative view concerning the nature of aggression, and one that continues to enjoy more support among psychologists, suggests that such behaviour stems mainly from an externally elicited drive to harm or injure others. This approach is reflected in several different **drive theories** of aggression (e.g., Berkowitz, 1988, 1989; Feshbach, 1984). Such theories propose that external conditions (e.g., frustration, loss of face) arouse a strong motive to engage in harm-producing behaviours. This aggressive drive, in turn, leads to the performance of overt assaults against others. The first truly social psychological theory of aggression took this approach—the famous **frustration-aggression hypothesis**, first proposed by Dollard and his colleagues more than 50 years ago (Dollard et al., 1939). In its original form, this hypothesis made the following sweeping assertions: (1) Frustration always leads to some form of aggression, and (2) aggression always stems from frustration (Dollard et al., 1939). In short, the theory held that frustrated persons always engage in some type of aggression and that all acts of aggression, in turn, result from frustration. Bold statements like these are always appealing—they are intellectually stimulating if nothing else. But evidence suggests that both portions are also far too sweeping in scope to be accurate.

Frustration-aggression Hypothesis The suggestion that frustration is a very powerful determinant of aggression.

Berkowitz (1989) has recently proposed a revised version of the frustration-aggression hypothesis that seems consistent with a large amount of existing evidence. According to this view, frustration is an aversive, unpleasant experience, and frustration leads to aggression because of this fact. In short, frustration sometimes produces aggression because of the basic relationship between negative feelings and aggressive behaviour we described earlier in this chapter.

These suggestions seem to be quite straightforward, and they contribute much to our understanding of the role of frustration in aggression. In particular, they help explain why unexpected frustration and frustration that is viewed as illegitimate (e.g., the result of someone's whims or hostile motives) produce stronger aggression than frustration that is expected or viewed as legitimate. Presumably this is so because unexpected and illegitimate frustration generates stronger negative feelings than that which is expected or legitimate.

Because they suggest that external conditions rather than innate tendencies are crucial in the occurrence of aggression, drive theories seem somewhat more optimistic about the possibility of preventing such behaviour than instinct theories. Since being frustrated or thwarted in various ways is a common aspect of everyday life, however, drive theories, too, seem to leave us facing continuous—and often unavoidable—sources of aggressive impulses.

Aggression As Learned Social Behaviour

Yet another important perspective on aggression, the **social learning view**, is more of a general framework than a fully developed theory. This approach (Bandura, 1973; Baron & Richardson, 1994) emphasizes the fact that aggression, like other complex forms of social behaviour, is largely learned. Human beings, this perspective contends, are not born with a large array of aggressive responses at their disposal. Rather, they must acquire these in much the same way that they acquire other complex forms of social behaviour: through direct experience or by observing the behaviour of others (i.e., social models; Bandura, 1973). Thus, depending on their past experience, people in different cultures learn to attack others in contrasting ways—by means of kung fu, blowguns, machetes, or revolvers. But this is not all that is learned where aggression is concerned. Through direct and vicarious experience, individuals also learn (1) which persons or groups are appropriate targets for aggression, (2) what actions by others either justify or actually require aggressive retaliation, and (3) what situations or contexts are ones in which aggression is either appropriate or inappropriate.

Social Learning View A perspective suggesting that aggression is a complex form of learned behaviour.

In short, the social learning perspective suggests that whether a specific person will aggress in a given situation depends on a vast array of factors, including that person's past experience, the current reinforcements associated with aggression, and many variables that shape the person's thoughts and perceptions concerning the appropriateness and potential effects of such behaviour (refer to Figure 8.13). Consideration of these factors may offer some understanding of a particularly abhorrent type of aggression—spousal abuse. Furthermore, since most, if not all, of these factors are open to change, the social

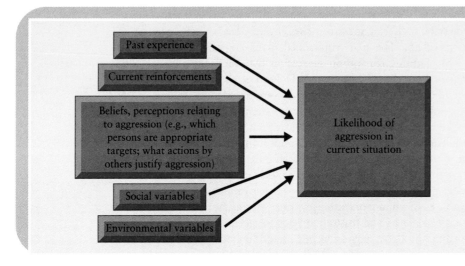

FIGURE 8.13 According to the
social learning view, aggression is a
learned form of social behaviour.
Whether it occurs in a given situation depends on such factors as the
past experience of potential aggressors, current reinforcements for
aggression, and many social and
cognitive factors that determine
perceptions regarding the appropriateness of such behaviour.

Source: **Based on suggestions by
Bandura, 1986, and others.**

learning approach offers some possibilities for preventing or controlling spousal abuse
and other forms of aggression. Indeed, it is more encouraging in this respect than any of
the other views we have considered.

Modern Theories of Aggression: Taking Account of Learning, Cognitions, Mood, and Arousal

Unlike earlier views, modern theories of aggression (e.g., Anderson, 1997; Berkowitz,
1993; Zillmann, 1994) do not focus on a single factor as the primary cause of aggression. Rather, they draw on advances in many fields of psychology in order to gain added
insight into such behaviour. While no single theory includes all the elements that social
psychologists now view as important, one approach—the **general affective aggression
model (GAAM)**, proposed by Anderson (Anderson, 1997; Anderson et al., 1996)—provides a good illustration of the breadth and sophistication of these new perspectives.

The GAAM suggests that aggression is triggered or elicited by a wide range of
input variables—aspects of the current situation and/or tendencies individuals bring with
them to a given situation. Variables falling into the first category (the current situation)
include frustration, some kind of attack from another person (e.g., an insult), exposure
to *aggressive models* (other persons behaving aggressively), the presence of cues associated with aggression (e.g., guns or other weapons), and virtually anything that causes
individuals to experience discomfort—from excessively high temperatures to a dentist's
drill to an extremely dull lecture. Variables in the second category (*individual differences*), include traits that predispose individuals toward aggression (e.g., high irritability), certain attitudes and beliefs about violence (e.g., believing that it is acceptable and
appropriate), values about violence (e.g., the view that it is a "good" thing—perhaps that
it shows an individual's worth or masculinity), and specific skills related to aggression
(e.g., knowing how to fight, knowing how to use various weapons).

According to the GAAM, these situational and individual difference variables
can then lead to overt aggression through their impact on three basic processes:
arousal—they may increase physiological arousal or excitement; *affective states*—
they can arouse hostile feelings and outward signs of these (e.g., angry facial expressions); and *cognitions*—they can induce individuals to think hostile thoughts or bring
hostile memories to mind. Depending on individuals' *appraisals* (interpretations) of
the current situation and on possible restraining factors (e.g., the presence of police
or the threatening nature of the intended target person), aggression either occurs or
does not occur. See Figure 8.14 for an overview of the GAAM.

**General Affective
Aggression Model
(GAAM)** A modern
theory of aggression
suggesting that aggres-
sion is triggered by a
wide range of input
variables; these influ-
ence arousal, affective
stages, and cognitions.

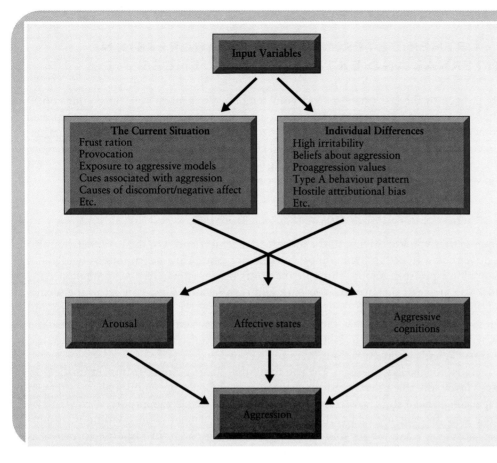

■ The GAAM: One modern theory of human aggression

FIGURE 8.14 As shown here, the general affective aggression model suggests that human aggression stems from many different factors. A wide range of input variables influence cognitions, affect, and arousal, and these internal states plus other factors determine whether, and in what form, aggression occurs.

Source: Based on suggestions by Anderson, 1997.

Modern theories like the GAAM are, admittedly, much more complex than the early ones offered by Freud and Lorenz, or even the famous frustration-aggression hypothesis (Dollard et al., 1939). But, they are also supported by a growing body of evidence (e.g., Lieberman & Greenberg, 1999), and are much more likely to provide an accurate and complete picture of the origins of human aggression—and that, of course, is what science is all about.

KEY POINTS

- *Drive theories* suggest that aggression stems from externally elicited drives to harm or injure others. The *frustration-aggression hypothesis* is the most famous example of such theories.

- Contrary to the famous *frustration-aggression hypothesis*, not all aggression stems from frustration, and frustration does not always lead to aggression. Frustration is a strong elicitor of aggression only under certain limited conditions.

- The *social learning view* of aggression suggests that aggression is acquired through past and current learning experiences, as well as influenced by cognitive, social and environmental variables.

- Modern theories of aggression such as the *general affective aggression model* (GAAM) recognize the importance in aggression of learning, various eliciting input variables, cognitions, individual tendencies, and affective states.

FURTHER DETERMINANTS OF AGGRESSION: INTERNAL AND EXTERNAL INFLUENCES

Think back to the last time you lost your temper. What made you "lose your cool?" Chances are quite good that your anger, and any subsequent aggression, stemmed from the actions of another person together with difficulties of the situation. Aggression often stems from various social conditions that either initiate its occurrence or increase its intensity, as the GAAM suggests. Many factors play a role in this regard and we will examine several of these in more detail below.

Heightened Arousal: Emotion, Cognition, and Aggression

Suppose that you are driving to the airport to meet a friend. On the way there, another driver cuts you off and you almost have an accident. Your heart pounds wildly and your blood pressure shoots through the roof; but, fortunately, no accident occurs. Now you arrive at the airport. You park and rush inside. When you get to the security check, an elderly man in front of you sets off the buzzer. He becomes confused and can't seem to understand that the security guard wants him to empty his pockets. You are irritated by this delay. In fact, you begin to lose your temper and mutter—not too softly—"What's wrong with him? Can't he get it?"

Now for the key question: Do you think that your recent near miss in traffic may have played any role in your sudden surge of anger? Could the emotional arousal from that incident have somehow transferred to the scene inside the airport? Growing evidence suggests that it could (Zillmann, 1988, 1994). Under some conditions, heightened arousal—whatever its source—can enhance aggression in response to provocation, frustration, or other factors. In fact, in various experiments, arousal stemming from such varied sources as participation in competitive games (Christy, Gelfand, & Hartmann, 1971), vigorous exercise (Zillmann, 1979), and even some types of music (Rogers & Ketcher, 1979) has been found to increase subsequent aggression. Why is this the case? A compelling explanation is offered by **excitation transfer theory** (Zillmann, 1983, 1988).

Excitation Transfer Theory A theory suggesting that arousal produced in one situation can persist and intensify emotional reactions occurring in subsequent situations.

This theory suggests that because physiological arousal tends to dissipate slowly over time, a portion of such arousal may persist as a person moves from one situation to another. In the example above, some portion of the arousal you experienced because of the near miss in traffic may still be present as you approach the security gate in the airport. When you encounter minor annoyance at the gate, that arousal intensifies your emotional reactions to the annoyance. The result: You become enraged rather than just mildly irritated. Excitation transfer theory further suggests that such effects are most likely to occur when the persons involved are relatively unaware of the presence of *residual arousal*—a common occurrence, as small elevations in arousal are difficult to notice (Zillmann, 1994). Excitation transfer theory also suggests that such effects are likely to occur when the persons involved recognize their residual arousal but attribute it to events occurring in the present situation (Taylor et al., 1991). In the airport incident, for instance, your anger would be intensified if you recognized your feelings of arousal but attributed them to the elderly man's actions (see Figure 8.15).

Sexual Arousal and Aggression: Are Love and Hate Really Two Sides of the Same Behavioural Coin?

Love and hate, it is often contended, are closely linked. Consider the following quotation: *"The more one loves a mistress, the more one is ready to hate her"* (de La

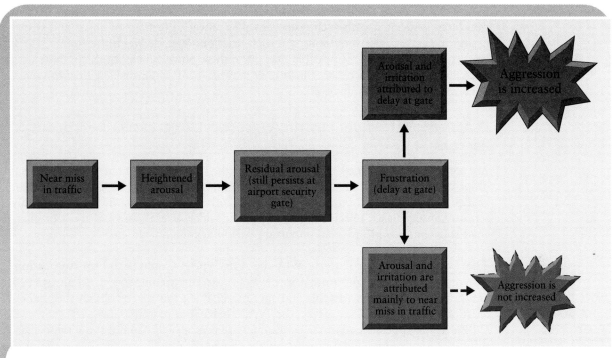

■ Excitation transfer theory

FIGURE 8.15 Excitation transfer theory suggests that arousal occurring in one situation can persist and intensify emotional reactions in later, unrelated situations. Thus the arousal produced by a near miss in traffic can intensify feelings of annoyance stemming from delays at an airport security gate.

Source: Based on suggestions by Zillmann, 1988, 1994.

Rochefoucauld, 1678). Are such observations accurate? If love is taken to mean primarily sexual arousal or excitement, research by social psychologists offers some support for this age-old idea.

Extensive research findings suggest that the relationship between sexual arousal and aggression is *curvilinear* in nature. Mild sexual arousal reduces aggression to a level below that shown in the absence of such arousal, while higher levels of arousal actually increase aggression above this level. Why is this so? One explanation is provided by the following *two-component model* (Zillmann, 1984).

According to this theory, exposure to erotic stimuli produces two effects: It increases *arousal* and it influences current *affective states*—negative or positive moods or feelings. Whether sexual arousal will increase or reduce aggression, then, depends on the overall pattern of such effects. Mild erotic materials generate weak levels of arousal but high levels of positive affect—most people enjoy looking at them. As a result, aggression is reduced. In contrast, explicit sexual materials generate stronger levels of arousal, but also higher levels of negative affect—many people find some of the acts shown to be unpleasant or even repulsive. As a result, such materials may increase aggression. The findings of several studies support this two-factor theory (e.g., Ramirez, Bryant, & Zillmann, 1983), so it appears to provide a useful explanation for the curvilinear relationship between sexual arousal and aggression.

One important topic to which these findings seem relevant is *crimes of passion*—instances in which one lover or spouse attacks or even kills another. Do intense feelings of sexual arousal play a role in such events? No direct evidence currently exists on this issue. However, research findings indicate that *sexual jealousy*, another emotion often associated with such crimes, evokes powerful feelings of anger and strong desires to aggress against the source of such reactions (e.g., de Weerth & Kalma, 1993; Paul et al., 1993). It seems possible that when these powerful emotions combine with high levels of sexual arousal, the results may be truly explosive—with dire consequences for the persons involved.

Dispositional Influences on Aggression: Aggressive Personality Factors

Are some persons "primed" for aggression by their personal characteristics? Informal observation suggests that this is so. Some individuals rarely lose their tempers or engage in aggressive actions; but others seem to be forever losing it, with potentially serious consequences. In this section we will consider several personal traits or characteristics that seem to play an important role in aggression.

The Type A Behaviour Pattern: Why the *A* in Type A Could Stand for Aggression

Do you know anyone you could describe as (1) extremely competitive, (2) always in a hurry, and (3) especially irritable and aggressive? If so, this person shows the characteristics of what psychologists term the **Type A behaviour pattern** (Glass, 1977; Strube, 1989). At the opposite end of the continuum are persons who do not show these characteristics—individuals who are *not* highly competitive, who are not always fighting the clock, and who do *not* readily lose their temper; such persons are described as showing the **Type B behaviour pattern**.

Given the characteristics mentioned above, it seems only reasonable to expect that Type A's would tend to be more aggressive than Type B's in many situations. And in fact, the results of several experiments indicate that this is actually the case (Baron, Russell, & Arms, 1985; Carver & Glass, 1978). For example, consider a study by Berman, Gladue, and Taylor (1993). These researchers exposed young men known to be Type A or Type B to increasing provocation from a stranger. As part of the experimental procedure subjects were required to choose a level of electric shock to be delivered to this person. Another feature of the study involved measurement of participants' testosterone level; as we pointed out before, testosterone is an important sex hormone, found in much higher levels in males than in females. Results indicated that during the competitive task, Type A's who also had a high level of testosterone set the highest level of shocks for their opponent. In addition, Type A's with high testosterone levels were much more likely than other participants to use the highest shock setting available. These findings indicate that two different personal characteristics—the Type A behaviour pattern and testosterone level—both play a role in determining aggressive behaviour.

Additional findings indicate that Type A's are truly hostile people: they don't merely aggress against others because this is a useful means for reaching other goals, such as winning athletic contests or furthering their own careers. Rather, they are more likely than Type B's to engage in what is known as **hostile aggression**—aggression in which the prime objective is inflicting harm on the victim (Strube et al., 1984). In view of this fact, it is not surprising to learn that Type A's are more likely than Type B's to engage in such actions as child abuse or spouse abuse (Strube et al., 1984). In contrast, Type A's are not more likely to engage in **instrumental aggression**—aggression performed primarily to attain other goals aside from harming the victim, goals such as control of valued resources or praise from others for behaving in a "tough" manner.

Type A Behaviour Pattern A pattern consisting primarily of high levels of competitiveness, time urgency, and hostility.

Type B Behaviour Pattern A pattern consisting of the absence of characteristics associated with the Type A behsaviour pattern.

Hostile Aggression Aggression in which the prime objective is to harm the victim, as opposed to aggression whose prime objective is some other purpose.

Instrumental Aggression Aggression in which the primary objective is not harm to the victim but attainment of some other goal, such as access to valued resources.

Narcissism, Ego-Threat, and Aggression: On the Dangers of Wanting to Be Superior

Do you know the story of Narcissus? He was a character in Greek mythology who fell in love with his own reflection in the water and drowned trying to reach it. His name has now become a synonym for excessive self-love; for holding an over-inflated view of one's own virtues or accomplishments. Research findings indicate that this trait may be linked to aggression in important ways. Specifically, studies by Bushman and Baumeister (1998) suggest that persons high in narcissism (ones who agree with such items as "If I ruled the world it would be a much better place" and "I am more capable than other people") react with exceptionally high levels of aggression to slights from others—feedback that threatens their inflated self-image. Why? Because such persons have nagging doubts about the accuracy of their inflated egos and so react with intense anger toward anyone who threatens to undermine them. This tendency to be aggressive may be one reason why their attempts at impression management ultimately fail, as we saw in Chapter 7.

KEY POINTS

- *Excitation transfer theory* and research shows that heightened arousal can increase aggression if it persists beyond the situation in which it was induced and is falsely interpreted as anger.
- Mild levels of sexual arousal reduce aggression, while higher levels increase such behaviour.
- Persons showing the *Type A* behaviour pattern are more irritable and more aggressive than persons with the *Type B* behaviour pattern.
- Persons high in *narcissism* (ones who hold an over-inflated view of their own worth) react with exceptionally high levels of aggression to feedback from others that poses a threat to their egos.

Evaluating Others' Behaviour: Provocation and Attribution

Suppose that one day, another shopper in a supermarket bumped you with her cart. Suppose she then remarked: "Out of my way, stupid!" How would you react? Probably with anger, and perhaps with some kind of retaliation. You might make a biting remark such as "What's wrong with you—are you nuts?" Alternatively, you might, if you were angry enough, push *your* cart into hers, or even into her!

This incident illustrates an important point about aggression: Often, it is the result of physical or verbal **provocation** from others. When we are on the receiving end of some form of aggression from others, we rarely turn the other cheek. Instead, we tend to reciprocate, returning as much aggression as we have received—or perhaps even slightly more, especially if we are certain that the other person *meant* to harm us (Dengerink, Schnedler, & Covey, 1978; Ohbuchi & Kambara, 1985). Such effects are demonstrated very clearly by a study conducted by Chermack, Berman, and Taylor (1997).

In this study, participants competed with an opponent on a competitive reaction-time task devised by Stuart Taylor. On each trial, the participant and his opponent (who was not really there) set a level of shock the loser—the person slower to respond—would receive after that trial. The shocks were set by means of ten buttons on the equipment and could range in intensity from ones that could not be felt to ones that participants found painful. Prior to each reaction-time trial, participants learned what level of shock had been set for them by their opponent. In one condition (low

Provocation Actions by others that are perceived as acts of aggression deriving from hostile intentions.

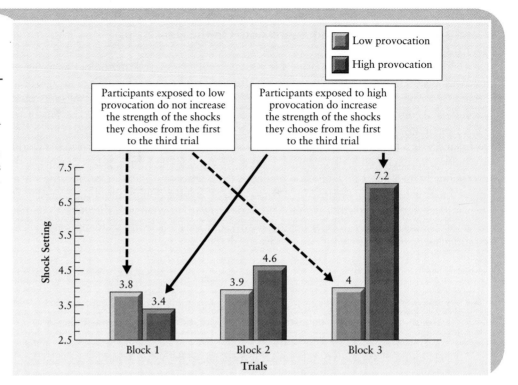

■ Effects of provocation on aggression

FIGURE 8.16 Research participants who were strongly provoked by another person directed much more aggression against this person than did participants who were not strongly provoked, and also increased their aggression over time from Block 1 to Block 3 of the trials. Those who were weakly provoked did not increase aggression in this way.

Source: Based on data from Berman, Chermack, & Taylor, 1997.

provocation), the opponent chose button two on all occasions. In another condition (high provocation), he gradually raised the level of shocks he set for the participant from two to nine. (Needless to say, participants were warned about the possibility of receiving actual shocks during the informed consent procedures.)

As you can see from Figure 8.16, participants' aggression was strongly influenced by the level of provocation they received. In the low-provocation condition, they set relatively low shocks for their opponent and did not increase these over time. In the high-provocation condition, they set higher shocks (except in the first block of trials), and they raised these dramatically over time. The findings also illustrate the "and then some" effect mentioned above: even in the low-provocation condition, participants set a slightly higher level of shocks for their opponent than they received.

A related tendency may potentially play an important role in the interpretation of other's behaviour: the tendency to perceive hostile intent in others even when it is totally lacking. Presumably, the stronger this tendency—known as **hostile attributional bias**—the greater individuals' likelihood of engaging in reactive aggression in response to provocation from others.

Evidence that this is actually the case has been provided by several studies (Dodge, Murphy, & Buchsbaum, 1984). For example, in one of these studies, Dodge et al. (1990) examined the relationship between hostile attributional bias and aggression among a group of male adolescents confined to a maximum security prison for juvenile offenders. These young men had been convicted of a wide range of violent crimes, including murder, sexual assault, kidnapping, and armed robbery. The researchers found that hostile attributional bias among these men was related to the number of interpersonally violent crimes they had committed and to trained observers' ratings of the prisoners' tendencies to engage in reactive aggression in response to provocation.

In short, the tendency to perceive malevolence or malice in the actions of others, even when it doesn't really exist, is an important trait—one that can exacerbate the effect of others' provocation.

Hostile Attributional Bias The tendency to perceive others' actions as stemming from hostile intent when these actions are ambiguous.

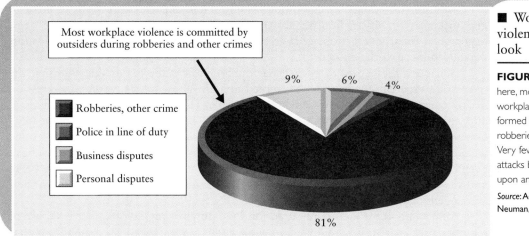

Most workplace violence is committed by outsiders during robberies and other crimes

9%   6%   4%

Robberies, other crime

Police in line of duty

Business disputes

Personal disputes

81%

■ Workplace violence: A closer look

FIGURE 8.17 As shown here, most instances of workplace violence are performed by outsiders during robberies and other crimes. Very few instances involve attacks by one employee upon another.

Source: Adapted from Baron & Neuman, 1996.

Workplace Aggression

We mentioned the occurrence of extreme workplace violence in Chapter 1. In particular the distressing incident in which an angry ex-employee of the Ottawa bus service shot and killed four of his fellow workers, and then himself. Reports of incidents such as these have appeared with alarming frequency in recent years, and appear to reflect a rising tide of violence in workplaces. These reports might seem to suggest that workplaces are becoming truly dangerous locations where disgruntled employees frequently attack or even shoot one another, but two facts should be carefully noted: (1) A large majority of violence occurring in work settings is performed by outsiders—people who do not work there but who enter a workplace to commit robbery or other crimes (see Figure 8.17); and (2) careful surveys indicate that threats of physical harm or actual harm in work settings are quite rare. In fact, the chances of being killed at work—by outsiders or coworkers combined—are something like 1 in 450 000 overall (although this is considerably higher in some high-risk occupations such as taxi driving or police work; Sloboda, 1996).

Growing evidence suggests that workplace violence, although certainly an important topic worthy of careful study, is relatively rare and is actually only the dramatic tip of the much larger problem of workplace aggression—all forms of behaviour through which individuals seek to harm others in their workplace (Baron & Neuman, 1996; Neuman & Baron, 1998).

What specific forms of aggression do individuals actually use in workplaces? A recent study by Baron, Neuman, and Geddes (1999) provides information on this issue. These researchers asked almost 500 employed persons to rate the frequency with which they had personally experienced a wide range of aggressive behaviours on the job. Careful analysis of their responses indicated that most aggression occurring in workplaces falls into three major categories:

1. *Expressions of hostility*: Behaviours that are primarily verbal or symbolic in nature (e.g., belittling others' opinions, talking behind their backs).

2. *Obstructionism*: Behaviours designed to obstruct or impede the target's performance (e.g., failure to return phone calls or respond to memos, failure to transmit needed information, interference with activities important to the target).

3. *Overt aggression*: Behaviours that have typically been included under the heading "workplace violence" (e.g., physical assault, theft or destruction of property, threats of physical violence).

Additional findings indicated that, as you might expect, expressions of hostility and instances of obstructionism are much more frequent than instances of overt aggression. Thus, covert forms of aggression do seem to be strongly preferred by most persons in most work settings.

What are the causes of such behaviour? This was the major question that the inquest into the Ottawa incident attempted to address. Again, as is true of aggression in any context, many factors seem to play a role. However, one that emerged again and again in research on this topic is *perceived unfairness* in the workplace (e.g., Greenberg & Alge, 1997; Skarlicki & Folger, 1997; Neuman & Baron, 1997)—a topic we will address more fully in Chapter 9. The persons involved believe that they have been fired, passed over for promotion, or mistreated in some other way, and this belief and the accompanying intense feelings of unfairness plays an important role in their subsequent aggression (Folger et al., 1998).

Other important factors relate to job loss: downsizing, layoffs, increased use of temporary and part-time employees, to name a few. Several recent studies indicate that the greater the extent to which these changes have occurred, the greater the aggression (e.g., Baron & Neuman, 1996; Neuman & Baron, 1998).

In sum, media attention to dramatic instances of workplace violence may be somewhat misleading; while such actions do indeed occur, they are far less frequent than more subtle but still harmful instances of workplace aggression. And such behaviour, in turn, appears to be influenced by many of the same factors that influence aggression in other contexts. Our conclusion: Workplace aggression is not a new or unique form of behaviour; rather, it is simply aggression occurring in one kind of setting. Thus, efforts to understand it—and to reduce it—should be linked as closely as possible to the large body of research on human aggression summarized in this chapter and in other sources.

KEY POINTS

- *Provocation* from others is a powerful elicitor of aggression. We rarely turn the other cheek; rather, we match—or slightly exceed—the level of aggression we receive from others.
- A tendency to exhibit the *hostile attributional bias* leads people to attribute others' actions to hostile intent even when this is not so. As a result, they are more aggressive than persons low in this characteristic.
- Workplace aggression takes many different forms but is usually covert in nature. A wide range of factors influence workplace aggression, including perceptions of unfairness and changes relating to job loss.

Exposure to Media Violence: The Effects of Witnessing Aggression

List several films you have seen in recent months. Now answer the following question: How much aggression or violence did each movie contain? How often did the characters hit, shoot at, or otherwise attempt to harm others (see Figure 8.18)? Unless you chose very carefully, many of the films probably contained a great deal of violence—much more than you are ever likely to see in real life (Reiss & Roth, 1993; Waters et al., 1993).

This fact raises an important question that social psychologists have studied for decades: Does exposure to such materials increase aggression among children and/or

FIGURE 8.18 Many films and television shows currently contain large amounts of violence. Does exposure to such materials increase aggression among viewers? A large body of research evidence suggests that it does.

adults? Literally hundreds of studies have been performed to test this possibility, and the results seem clear: *Exposure to media violence may indeed be one factor contributing to high levels of violence in countries where such materials are viewed by large numbers of persons* (e.g., Anderson, 1997; Berkowitz, 1993; Paik & Comstock, 1994; Wood et al., 1991).

Many kinds of evidence lend support to this conclusion. For example, in *short-term laboratory experiments*, children or adults have viewed either violent films and television programs or nonviolent ones; then the participants' tendency to aggress against others has been measured. In general, the results of such experiments have revealed higher levels of aggression among participants who viewed the violent films or programs (e.g., Bandura, Ross, & Ross, 1963; Geen, 1991b).

Other and perhaps even more convincing research has employed *longitudinal procedures*, in which the same participants are studied for many years (e.g, Huesmann & Eron, 1984, 1986). One interesting longitudinal study was a natural experiment carried out by Tannis Williams and her colleagues (Williams, 1986). These researchers were able to take advantage of the fact that a small logging town in British Columbia was about to have television (one channel of the CBC) introduced into its community for the first time. Children's level of physical and verbal aggression in the school playground was measured before the introduction of television and nearly two years after the introduction. At that time, when the children of the town had been exposed to TV for two years, they were significantly more aggressive both physically and verbally than they had been before its introduction. And perhaps more interestingly, they were more aggressive than comparable logging towns where children had been exposed television long-term.

In general, results of this kind of research are clear: The more violent films or television programs participants watch as children, the higher their levels of aggression as teenagers or adults; for instance, the higher the likelihood that they will be arrested for violent crimes. Such findings have been replicated in many different countries—Australia, Finland, Israel, Poland, and South Africa (Botha, 1990). Thus, they appear to hold across different cultures. While these longitudinal studies have been carefully conducted, it's important to remember that they are still only correlational in nature. As we noted in Chapter 1, the fact that two variables are correlated does *not* imply that one necessarily causes the other. However, when the results of these studies are combined with the findings of short-term laboratory experiments, a strong case does seem to emerge for the suggestion that exposure to media violence is one potential cause of human aggression.

But why, you may be wondering, do these media effects occur? Several possibilities exist. First, individuals may simply *learn* new ways of aggressing from watching television programs and films—ways they would not have imagined before. "Copycat crimes," in which a real or fictional violent crime depicted in the media is then copied by different persons in distant locations, suggest that such effects are real. For instance, this has been suggested as one factor in the recent spate of high school student shootings.

Another effect of watching media violence involves what are known as *desensitization effects*. After viewing many vivid scenes of violence, individuals become hardened to the pain and suffering of other persons; they experience less emotional reaction to such cues than they did before (e.g., Baron, 1974a). This may lessen their own restraints against engaging in aggression.

Recent research indicates that a third effect may occur as well: watching scenes of violence may serve to *prime* hostile thoughts, so that these come to mind more readily—they become more accessible to conscious thought. This, in turn, can increase the likelihood that a person will engage in overt aggression (Anderson, 1997). Because repeated exposure to media violence may strengthen such *priming effects* over time, the impact of watching violence may be cumulative—and even more important than was previously assumed.

Since exposure to media violence may have harmful effects on society, why, you may be wondering, is there so much of it on television and in films? One answer is that the advertisers who pay for these programs believe that "violence sells"—it is one way to increase audience size. While this may be true, findings reported by Bushman (1998) suggest that media violence may actually backfire from the point of view of increasing the sales of products advertised on such shows. He found that audiences who watch violent programs are significantly *less* likely to remember the content of commercials shown during these programs than audiences who watch nonviolent programs. Apparently violent images on the television screen trigger memories of other violent scenes, and such thoughts distract viewers from paying attention to commercials. These findings suggest that sponsoring violent television programs is not just questionable from a moral point of view; it may also make little economic sense for sponsors!

The importance of factors other than media in contributing to levels of violence in society is underlined when you consider that Canada and the United States have virtually the same media but very different levels of violence. The issue of the cultural impact on aggressive behaviour will be discussed in a later section.

Gender and Aggression: Are There Real Differences?

Are males more aggressive than females? Folklore suggests that they are, and research findings suggest that in this case such informal observation is correct: when asked whether they have ever engaged in any of a wide range of aggressive actions, males report a higher incidence of many aggressive behaviours than do females (Harris, 1994, 1997). On close examination, however, the picture regarding gender differences in aggression becomes more complex. On the one hand, males are generally more likely than females both to perform aggressive actions and to be the targets of such behaviour (Bogard, 1990; Harris, 1992, 1994). Further, this difference seems to persist throughout the lifespan, occurring even among people in their 70s and 80s (Walker,

Richardson, & Green, 1999). On the other hand, however, the magnitude of these gender differences appears to vary greatly across situations.

First, gender differences in aggression are much larger in the absence of provocation than in its presence. In other words, males are significantly more likely than females to aggress against others when these persons have not provoked them in any manner (Bettencourt & Miller, 1996). But in situations where provocation is present, and especially when it is intense, females may be just as aggressive as males.

Second, the size—and even the direction—of gender differences in aggression seem to vary greatly with the *type* of aggression in question. Research findings indicate that males are more likely than females to engage in various forms of *direct* aggression—actions that are aimed directly at the target and which clearly stem from the aggressor (e.g., physical assaults, pushing, shoving, throwing something at another person, shouting, making insulting remarks) (Bjorkqvist et al., 1994). However, females are more likely to engage in various forms of *indirect* aggression—actions that allow the aggressor to conceal his or her identity from the victim. Such actions include spreading vicious rumors about the target person, gossiping behind this person's back, telling others not to associate with the intended victim, making up stories to get the victim in trouble, and so on. Research findings indicate that females' greater tendencies to engage in indirect aggression are present among children as young as eight and increase through age fifteen (Bjorkqvist et al., 1992; Osterman et al., 1998), and they seem to persist into adulthood as well (Bjorkqvist, Osterman, & Hjelt-Back, 1994; Green, Richardson, & Lago, 1996). Further, these tendencies have been observed in several different countries—Finland, Sweden, Poland, and Italy (Osterman et al., 1998)—and so appear to be quite general in scope. In sum, gender differences with respect to aggression exist, but they are smaller and more complex in nature than common sense might suggest.

Culture and Aggression: The Social Context of Violence

Earlier we called attention to the existence of variations in the levels of aggression around the world. A recent study comparing violent crime across 11 Western nations provides ample evidence of such differences. For example, the reports of criminal victimization due to violent offences (robbery, assault and sexual assault) vary from eight percent of the population in England and Wales, to seven percent in the United States, six percent in Canada, Finland, Netherlands and Sweden, to the lowest level of three percent in Northern Ireland. Homicide rates also vary, though they show a different pattern—see Figure 8.19. Moreover, the rate of violence within a given culture can change drastically over time as social conditions change (e.g., Robarchek & Robarchek, 1997).

Many cultural values include the abhorrence of violence. Given that, what accounts for the massive differences we can see in the levels of aggression, violent crime and homicide? Cultural norms about the appropriateness of aggression do vary, as we will discuss below, and that will have an impact. But in order to explain violent crime, a web of economic, political and socio-historical factors need to be taken into account. We will discuss psychological evidence related to one political issue—gun control—in Chapter 10.

One cultural consideration has been the existence of *microcultures*—cultural differences between groups within a larger culture. For example, in the Mexican state of Oaxaca, there are two Zapotec villages located less than seven kilometres apart. The two villages have existed in their present locations for at least 450 years, and in terms of language, religion, economics, and virtually every other aspect, they are identical. Yet the murder rate in one is more than six times higher than in the other. Thus, while residents of the nonviolent village might expect to witness one murder every 14 years, those in the violent village could expect to see one every 18 months to 2 years (Fry, 1990).

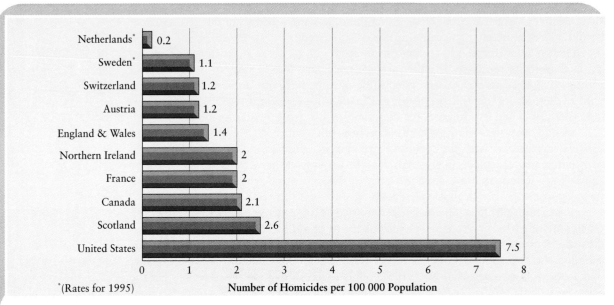

■ International comparison of homicide rates 1996

FIGURE 8.19 This figure illustrates that levels of violence, as indicated by homicide rates, can vary tremendously between different cultures. In the context of Western nations, as shown here, the United States stands out with a rate of 7.5 homicides per 100 000 of the population. In the context of the world as a whole the United States is not one of the highest—Colombia at 70.9 in 1995 takes that honour. However, what is really remarkable worldwide is the tremendous variation in homicide rates between even geographically adjacent nations: Note that Canadian rates are less than a third of those in the United States.

Source: Statistics Canada 1998 Juristat, Catalogue No. 85-002, Vol. 18, No. 6.

In short, culture does seem to play an important role in aggression. Growing evidence suggests that it determines not only the rate of violence but also the forms violence generally takes and the targets selected. A group of researchers (Ostermann et al., 1994) recently investigated cultural differences in aggression in eight-year-old children in several different cultural and ethnic groups. They found that African-American children were more aggressive (both in self-ratings and ratings by peers) than Caucasian-American, Polish, and Finnish children. Such findings have been attributed to differences in childrearing practices (Kumagai, 1983; Osterwell and Nagano-Nakamura, 1992). These studies emphasize the importance of cultural values and beliefs in determining aggression in society. Contrasting beliefs about aggression influence childrearing practices in various cultures, and these, in turn, help to explain why cultural differences in the rate and intensity of many forms of aggression tend to persist over time (Fraczek & Kirwil, 1992).

KEY POINTS

● Exposure to media violence has been found to increase aggression among viewers. This occurs because of several factors, such as the priming of aggressive thoughts and a weakening of restraints against aggression.

- Males are more aggressive overall than females, but this difference tends to disappear in the face of strong provocation. Males are more likely to use direct forms of aggression, but females are more likely to use indirect forms of aggression.

- Research indicates wide cultural variation in the levels of violence and aggression. Cultural norms about aggression vary and may be related to childrearing practices.

THE PREVENTION AND CONTROL OF AGGRESSION: SOME USEFUL TECHNIQUES

If there is one idea in this chapter we hope you'll remember in the years ahead, it is this: Aggression is not an inevitable or unchangeable form of behaviour. On the contrary, because it stems from a complex interplay of external events, cognitions, and personal characteristics, it can be prevented or reduced. In this final section we'll consider several procedures that, when used appropriately, can be effective in this regard.

Punishment: An Effective Deterrent to Violence?

Throughout history, most societies have used **punishment** as a means of deterring human violence. Nations have established harsh punishment for such crimes as murder, sexual assault, and assault. Are such tactics effective? Will the threat of severe punishment actually prevent individuals from engaging in aggressive acts in the first place? The pendulum of scientific opinion on this issue has swung back and forth for decades. At present, however, the weight of existing evidence seems to suggest that if used in an appropriate manner, punishment can be an effective deterrent to violence. In order for it to succeed, however, several conditions must be met (Baron & Richardson, 1994; Bower & Hilgard, 1981).

What conditions must be met for punishment to succeed? Four are most important: (1) It must be *prompt*—it must follow aggressive actions as quickly as possible. (2) It must be *certain*—the probability that it will follow aggression must be very high. (3) It must be *strong*—strong enough to be highly unpleasant to potential recipients. And (4) it must be perceived by recipients as *justified* or deserved. Unfortunately, of course, these conditions are often the ones lacking from the criminal justice systems of many nations. The delivery of punishment for aggressive actions is often delayed for months or even years; the magnitude of punishment itself is variable from one locale to another; and it is well known that many violent crimes go unpunished—no one is ever apprehended, tried, or convicted of them. In view of these facts, it is hardly surprising that punishment has often seemed to fail as a deterrent to violent crime. The dice, so to speak, are heavily loaded against the possibility of its succeeding. However, if these conditions were changed, the potential impact of punishment might well be enhanced.

Learning Not to be Aggressive

Interventions based on social learning theory suggest that if we learn aggressive behaviour, it can be unlearned, or perhaps, not taught at all.

One approach is to use modeling to a constructive end by exposure to nonaggressive models. If exposure to aggressive actions by others in the media or in person can increase aggression, it seems possible that exposure to *non*-aggressive behaviour might produce opposite effects. In fact, the results of several studies indicate that this is

Punishment
Procedures in which aversive consequences are delivered to individuals each time they engage in specific actions. Under appropriate conditions, punishment can serve as an effective deterrent to human aggression.

so (e.g., Baron, 1972b; Donnerstein & Donnerstein, 1976). When individuals who have been provoked are exposed to others who either demonstrate or urge restraint, the tendency of potential aggressors to lash out is reduced. These findings suggest that it may be useful to place restrained, non-aggressive models in tense and potentially dangerous situations. Their presence may well tip the balance against overt violence.

Techniques of *social skills training* can also be useful in decreasing aggression. Many people don't know how to respond to provocations from others in a way that will soothe these persons rather than annoy them. They don't know how to make requests, or how to say no to requests from others, without making people angry. Persons lacking in basic social skills seem to account for a high proportion of violence in many societies (Toch, 1985), so equipping such persons with improved social skills may go a long way toward reducing aggression. This can be done by watching other persons (social models) demonstrate both effective and ineffective behaviours (Schneider, 1991). Such gains can be obtained through just a few hours of treatment (Bienert & Schneider, 1993), so this approach is practical and cost-effective as well as successful.

Catharsis: Does Getting It Out of Your System Really Help?

Does somehow blowing off steam really help individuals get rid of—or at least control—their aggressive impulses? The belief that such activities are effective in this respect is very widespread. Many persons accept some version of what psychologists describe as the **catharsis hypothesis** (Dollard et al., 1939)—the idea that participation in activities that allow individuals to vent their anger and hostility in some relatively safe way will actually reduce later aggression. Presumably, such activities yield two important benefits: (1) They help to reduce emotional tension; and (2) since they help to eliminate anger, they reduce the likelihood of more dangerous forms of aggression.

Is this hypothesis valid? Contrary to what the cartoon in Figure 8.20 suggests, existing evidence offers a mixed picture (Feshbach, 1984; Geen, 1991b). On the one hand, participation in various activities that are not harmful to others (e.g., vigorous physical activity, shouting obscenities into an empty room) can reduce emotional arousal stemming from frustration or provocation (Zillmann, 1979). On the other hand, such effects appear to be temporary. Arousal stemming from provocation may reappear as soon as individuals remember the incidents that made them angry (Caprara et al., 1994).

Catharsis Hypothesis The view that providing angry persons with an opportunity to engage in vigorous but noninjurious activities will reduce their level of emotional arousal and lower their tendencies to aggress against others.

■ Catharsis: Is it really effective?

FIGURE 8.20 Contrary to what this cartoon suggests, there is little evidence that releasing one's anger or hostility can reduce subsequent aggression.

What about the idea that performing "safe" aggressive actions reduces the likelihood of more harmful forms of aggression? The results of research on this issue are even less encouraging. Overt physical aggression, it appears, is not reduced by (1) watching scenes of media violence (Geen, 1978), (2) attacking inanimate objects (Bushman, Baumeister, & Stack, 1999; Mallick & McCandless, 1966), or (3) aggressing verbally against others. Indeed, some findings suggest that aggression may actually be increased by these activities. For instance, Bushman, Baumeister, and Stack (1999) recently found that hitting a punching bag increased rather than reduced aggression.

In short, contrary to popular belief, catharsis does not appear to be a very effective means for reducing aggression. Participating in "safe" forms of aggression or merely in vigorous, energy-draining activities may produce temporary reductions in arousal; but feelings of anger may quickly return when individuals meet, or merely think about, the persons who previously annoyed them. For this reason, catharsis may be less effective in producing lasting reductions in aggression than is widely believed.

Cognitive Interventions: Apologies and Overcoming Cognitive Deficits

Suppose that you are standing at the counter in a store, waiting your turn. Suddenly, another customer walks up and starts to place an order. You are beginning to get angry when this person turns toward you, notices you, and quickly apologizes. "I'm so sorry," he says. "I didn't see you. You were here first." How do you react? Probably, your anger will dissipate; you may even smile at this person in appreciation for his courtesy. This incident suggests that **apologies**—admissions of wrongdoing that include expressions of regret and requests for forgiveness—often go a long way toward defusing aggression. Research findings support this conclusion: apologies (e.g., Ohbuchi, Kameda, & Agarie, 1989) and excuses that make reference to factors beyond the excuse-giver's control, are quite effective in reducing aggression by persons who have been provoked in some manner (e.g., Baron, 1989b; Weiner et al., 1987). So if you feel that you are making another person angry, apologize without delay. The trouble you will save makes it quite worthwhile to say "I'm sorry."

Apologies Admissions of wrongdoing that include expressions of regret and requests for forgiveness.

Other cognitive mechanisms for reducing aggression relate to the fact that when we are very angry, our ability to think clearly—for instance, to evaluate the consequences of our own actions—may be sharply reduced. In addition, as noted recently by Lieberman and Greenberg (1999), we may adopt modes of thought in which we process information in a quick and impetuous manner, thus increasing the chances that we will "lash out against" someone else—including other persons who are not the cause of our annoyance or irritation. This phenomenon is known as *displaced aggression*—aggression is directed against innocent victims rather than the persons who provoked us or caused our discomfort (Lieberman & Greenberg, 1999; Tedeschi & Norman, 1985). Any procedures that serve to overcome such cognitive deficits, therefore, may help reduce overt aggression (Zillmann, 1993). One such technique involves *preattribution*—attributing annoying actions by others to unintentional causes before the provocation actually occurs. For example, before meeting with someone you know can be irritating, you could remind yourself that she or he doesn't mean to make you angry—it's just the result of an unfortunate personal style. Another technique involves preventing yourself (or others) from dwelling on real or imagined wrongs. You can accomplish this by distracting yourself in some way—for instance, by watching an absorbing movie or television program or working on complex puzzles. Such activities allow for a cooling-off period during which anger can dissipate. They also help to reestablish cognitive controls over behaviour—controls that help to hold aggression in check.

Ideas to Take with You

Being a Responsive Bystander

In this chapter you have read examples of real and staged emergencies. In your own life you undoubtedly have in the past and will in the future come across numerous unexpected situations in which your help is badly needed. How you decide to respond is obviously up to you, but at least consider the following suggestions that might be useful in assisting you to make an informed decision.

Pay Attention to What is Going On Around You.
In our everyday lives we often think more about ourselves (our plans, worries, expectancies, etc.) than about our surroundings. For many reasons, we would do well not only to stop and smell the roses, but also to stop and pay attention. Remember the seminary students who were behind schedule and in such a hurry that they ignored a man who appeared to have collapsed in a doorway? There are often other things worth thinking about and observing beyond yourself.

If You See Something Unusual, Consider More Than One Alternative.
The crying child might be unhappy about not getting a second piece of candy, but she also might be the target of abuse. The man who is running down the street might be a jogger, but he might also be a thief. The smoke you smell might be burnt toast, but it might indicate that the building is on fire. The idea is not to panic or jump to conclusions, but rather to consider various possibilities. Seek additional evidence. Is someone hitting the child? Is the running man carrying a large bag? Is there smoke coming out of the basement? Most unexpected events of this sort are probably easily explained and of little importance, but you need to be alert to the possibility that in rare instances there may really be an emergency.

Consider Yourself to Be as Responsible as Anyone Else for Responding.
No, it's not really your special responsibility, but think of it as everyone's responsibility. I (Donn Byrne) was once in a multiplex movie theatre in a mall, and when it was time for the film to begin, nothing happened. A roomful of people sat in their seats and stared at a blank screen. This seemed ridiculous to me, so I left my seat, went to the refreshment counter, and asked the person selling the popcorn to inform someone that the movie had not begun on screen 12. She told the manager, someone pushed the right button, and the movie began. This was a very mild emergency, and I didn't expect a medal; but the same general principle applies to serious situations as well as to trivial ones. If you let the unresponsiveness of others be your guide, you are acting as foolishly as they are.

Be Willing to Act.
It is not reasonable simply to react to what others do and never to act on your own. If you are afraid of what other people might think of you and of being evaluated negatively, just remember that others are as uncertain and confused as you may be. It may feel cool to stand back and do nothing, but it often is actually the stupid choice. What if the worst possible thing occurs—that is, what if you make an honest mistake and look foolish? It's not the end of the world, and you will probably never see these people again anyway. Do what you think is the right thing to do.

Summary and Review of Key Points

Bystander Response to an Emergency

● The purest form of *prosocial behaviour* is *altruism*—selfless actions that benefit another and are costly to the actor. Such behaviour contrasts with *aggression*—behaviour that intends harm to others.

In part because of *diffusion of responsibility*, the more bystanders present as witnesses to an emergency, the less likely is help to be given and the greater the delay before the help occurs: this is termed the *bystander effect*.

When faced with an emergency, a bystander must go through five crucial steps involving decisions that either inhibit or enhance the likelihood of a prosocial response. First, he or she must notice the emergency; second, correctly interpret what is occurring, and this process can be blocked by *pluralistic ignorance*; third, assume responsibility for providing help; fourth, have the necessary skills knowledge to help; fifth, actually decide to provide assistance.

Further Determinants of Helping Behaviour: Internal and External Influences

● The *genetic determinism* model traces prosocial behaviour to the general effects of natural selection, which favours any attribute that increases the odds that one's genes will be transmitted to future generations.

Positive and negative *emotional states* can either enhance or inhibit prosocial behaviour, depending on specific factors in the situation, in the individual, and in the nature of the required assistance.

Attributions of *responsibility* can determine emotion and prosocial behaviour. We are more likely to help if we attribute the problem to circumstances beyond the victim's control and if our values are not threatened by the victim.

The *altruistic personality* consists of empathy, internal locus of control, belief in a just world, high social responsibility and low egocentricity.

Individual differences in altruistic behaviour are based in large part on *empathy*—vicariously experiencing the emotions and cognitions of another through perspective taking. The extent to which a person is able to respond with empathy depends on both genetic and environmental factors.

Exposure to prosocial models in real life and in the media has a positive effect on prosocial acts.

Help is more likely to be given to those who are similar to oneself and by men to women more often than vice versa.

The cultural context can influence prosocial behaviour. Research shows higher levels of helping in rural than urban settings. Pressure to be helpful to others in your in-group may be greater in collectivistic cultures but this does not necessarily extend to helping a stranger. Help-seeking is more likely among individuals familiar with a communal experience than among those with an individualistic background.

Sources of Aggression: Theories About its Nature and Causes

● *Aggression* is the intentional infliction of harm on others.

Instinct theories suggest that aggression stems largely from innate urges or tendencies. The modern form of this approach stems from evolutionary social psychology. The *young male syndrome*—the preponderance of young males involved in violence—is seen as derived from evolved competition between males for reproductive success. While social psychologists have not endorsed a simple instinct theory, they do recognize the potential role of evolution and biological factors in human aggression.

Drive theories suggest that aggression stems from externally elicited drives to harm or injure others. The *frustration-aggression hypothesis* is the most famous example of such theories.

Contrary to the famous frustration-aggression hypothesis, not all aggression stems from frustration, and frustration does not always lead to aggression. Frustration is a strong elicitor of aggression only under certain limited conditions.

The *social learning view* of aggression suggests that aggression is acquired through past and current learning experiences, as well as influenced by cognitive, social and environmental variables.

Modern theories of aggression such as the *general affective aggression model* (GAAM) recognize the importance in aggression of learning, various eliciting input variables, cognitions, individual tendencies, and affective states.

Further Determinants of Human Aggression: Internal and External Influences

● *Excitation transfer theory* and research shows that heightened arousal can increase aggression if it persists beyond the situation in which it was induced and is falsely interpreted as anger.

Mild levels of sexual arousal reduce aggression, while higher levels increase such behaviour.

Persons showing the *Type A* behaviour pattern are more irritable and more aggressive than persons with the *Type B* behaviour pattern.

Persons high in *narcissism* (ones who hold an over-inflated view of their own worth) react with exceptionally high levels of aggression to feedback from others that poses a threat to their egos.

Provocation from others is a powerful elicitor of aggression. We rarely turn the other cheek; rather, we match—or slightly exceed—the level of aggression we receive from others.

A tendency to exhibit the *hostile attributional bias* leads people to attribute others' actions to hostile intent even when this is not so. As a result, they are more aggressive than persons low in this characteristic.

Workplace aggression takes many different forms but is usually covert in nature. A wide range of factors influence workplace aggression, including perceptions of unfairness and changes relating to job loss.

Exposure to media violence has been found to increase aggression among viewers. This occurs because of several factors, such as the priming of aggressive thoughts and a weakening of restraints against aggression.

Males are more aggressive overall than females, but this difference tends to disappear in the face of strong provocation. Males are more likely to use direct forms of aggression, but females are more likely to use indirect forms of aggression.

Research indicates wide cultural variation in the levels of violence and aggression. Cultural norms about aggression vary and may be related to childrearing practices.

The Prevention and Control of Aggression: Some Useful Techniques

● *Punishment* can be effective in reducing aggression, but only when it is delivered in accordance with specific principles.

The *catharsis hypothesis* appears to be mainly false. Engaging in vigorous activities may produce reductions in arousal, but these are only temporary. Similarly, engaging in apparently "safe" forms of aggression does not reduce aggressive tendencies.

Aggression can also be not learned or unlearned through reduced by exposure to nonaggressive models and training in social skills

Aggression can be reduced by *apologies*—admissions of wrongdoing that include requests for forgiveness—and by engaging in activities that distract attention away from causes of anger.

For More Information

Clark, M. S. (Ed.). (1991). *Prosocial behavior.* Newbury Park, CA: Sage.

A review of the current status of research on prosocial behaviour, with individual chapters written by those most active in this field of inquiry. Included are such topics as empathy, volunteerism, mood, and help-seeking.

Eisenberg, N. (1985). *Altruistic emotion, cognition, and behavior.* Hillsdale, NJ: Erlbaum.

Two of the crucial factors determining altruism—emotions and cognitions—are the central focus of this book. Specific topics include sympathy, conceptions of altruism, and moral decision making.

Baenninger, R. (Ed.). (1991). *Targets of violence and aggression*. Amsterdam: Elsevier/North-Holland.

This book deals with aggression toward targets that are either helpless or unable to retaliate. Separate chapters (each written by a different expert) examine such important and timely topics as human aggression toward other species, children, athletes, homosexuals, as well as aggression on roads. A comprehensive overview of what we currently know about several especially distressing forms of violence.

Baron, R. A., & Richardson, D. R. (1994). *Human aggression* (2nd ed.). New York: Plenum.

A broad introduction to current knowledge about human aggression. Separate chapters examine the biological, social, environmental, and personal determinants of aggression. Additional chapters examine the development of aggression and the occurrence of aggression in many natural settings.

Weblinks

www.bfskinner.org
B.F. Skinner Foundation

home.att.net/~angerk/BTS.html
Behavioral Toxicology Society

www.trauma-pages.com/index.phtml
David Baldwin's Trauma Information Pages

ccp.uchicago.edu/~jyin/evolution.html
Evolution and Behavior

www.lafayette.edu/allanr/behavior.html
International Behaviorology Association

CHAPTER NINE

Groups and Individuals:
The Consequences of Belonging

SPECIAL SECTIONS

■ What makes a group a group?

FIGURE 9.1 In order for two or more persons to be termed a group, several criteria must be met. The left photo shows an actual social group; the right photo shows a mere collection of individuals who are not part of a group.

All of us belong to many different groups some we choose and others that are chosen for us. For example, membership in cultural, gender, or family groups is seldom voluntary: We are born into such groups and raised within them. However, later in life we often choose to join various groups: clubs, political parties, groups of friends or work groups. Once people belong to a number of groups, whether involuntarily or by choice, they are subject to a wide variety of forces and processes and, as we'll soon see, the effects of such membership can be profound.

To provide you with an overview of the scope and magnitude of *group influence*—the effects of group membership on individual behaviour—we'll focus on five topics. First, we'll consider the basic *nature of groups*: what they are and how they influence their members. Second, we'll examine the impact of groups on individual *task performance*—how our performance on various tasks can be affected by our working with others or, in some cases, merely by others' presence on the scene. Third, we'll consider *decision making* in groups, focusing on the potential benefits and costs of this process. Fourth, we'll turn to the question of what might be termed *coordination* within groups—the extent to which individuals pool their efforts and work together toward goals (i.e., cooperate with one another) or, instead, choose to work against one another in what is known as conflict. Finally, we'll examine the question of *fairness* in groups—the extent to which individuals believe that they are being treated fairly or unfairly, and the impact of such beliefs on their behaviour. Another important topic closely related to group functioning, *leadership*, is discussed in Chapter 10.

GROUPS: THEIR NATURE AND FUNCTION

Group Two or more persons who interact with one another, share common goals, are somehow interdependent, and recognize that they belong to a group.

Look at the photos in Figure 9.1. Which show social groups? In order to answer, we must first define the term **group** in concrete terms. According to most social psychologists, a *group* consists of two or more interacting persons who share common goals, have a stable relationship, are somehow interdependent, and perceive that they are in fact part of a group (Paulus, 1989). In other words, the term group does not apply to mere collections of individuals who happen to be in the same place at the same time but who have no lasting relationship to one another. Rather, this term is restricted to collections of persons that meet certain criteria.

First, such persons must *interact* with each other, either directly or indirectly. In the age of the Internet, of course, such interaction does not necessarily involve face-to-face contact; tens of millions of persons around the world now belong to "virtual groups"—such as news groups—with which they often strongly identify (e.g., McKenna & Bargh, 1998). Second, they must be *interdependent* in some manner—what happens to one must affect what happens to the others. Third, their relationship must be relatively *stable*: it must persist over appreciable periods of time (e.g., weeks, months, or even years). Fourth, the individuals involved must have some *shared goals*—goals that all members seek to attain. Finally, the persons involved must *perceive themselves as members of a group*—they must recognize the existence of a lasting relationship among them.

Applying this definition to the photos in Figure 9.1, it is easy to see that the people in the left picture are members of a group. In contrast, those in the right photo are not; they are simply persons who happen to be in the same place at the same time but who have no real relationship to one another.

But, are all these conditions really necessary before it makes sense to describe several persons as belonging to a group? Opinion is divided (e.g., Taylor & Moghaddam, 1994; Turner, 1985), but if there is a key issue, it is whether the persons involved perceive themselves as being part of a group. Focusing on membership in involuntary groups, some theorists have emphasized that even if individuals *do not* perceive themselves as members of a social group, nonetheless, sometimes the group may still exist, and those individuals may be members of it. This can occur when *other people* perceive individuals as forming a group and treat them accordingly (Taylor & Moghaddam, 1994). For example, you may not regard the cultural heritage from which your ancestors came as an important part of yourself, and you may not feel that you and people with a similar background form a group (i.e., you don't have interdependence and shared goals). However, if other people continue to label and group you in that way, or the laws of the land treat you differently on that basis, then a group can be said to exist and you are a member—whether you like it or not. In contrast when it comes to voluntary membership then individual perceptions become crucial. Such groups emerge out of a continuous process of social integration in which bonds between potential members strengthen gradually, as people develop shared feelings, beliefs, and behaviours. People belong to a particular group when they perceive that they belong to it and only to the extent that they do does it make sense to describe them as constituting a social group (Moreland, 1987; Witte & Davis, 1996).

Group Formation: Why Do People Join?

At present you probably belong voluntarily to several different groups. Why did you join them in the first place? Existing evidence on this question suggests that individuals generally enter groups for several major reasons (Greenberg & Baron, 1993). First, group membership has a *social-psychological function*—while interacting in groups, important psychological or social needs can be satisfied such as those for belonging and receiving attention and affection. Second, group membership has an *instrumental function*, in that it can help us achieve secondary goals that we could not attain as individuals. By working within groups we can perform tasks we could not perform alone, gain knowledge and information that would otherwise not be available to us, and increase our sense of security and protection against common, external enemies. Finally, group membership has a *social identity function*, contributing to establishment of a positive social identity—it becomes part of the self-concept (refer to Chapter 4). As you might imagine, the greater the number of prestigious groups to which an individual is admitted, the more her or his self-concept is bolstered.

In sum, there are many important reasons for joining groups, so it is not at all surprising that most persons seek entry to numerous groups over the course of their lives. Many of the factors that encourage us to join a group also play a role in our continued sense of loyalty and attachment—this *organizational commitment* will be considered in the following Canadian Research: On the Cutting Edge section.

Canadian Research: On the Cutting Edge

Commitment to the Group:
Continued Loyalty in Times of Change

An individual's sense of commitment to the group and its aims is one of the factors that determines his or her willingness to work and contribute towards group goals, as we will discuss in a later section. Natalie Allen and John Meyer (1991; Meyer, Allen & Topolnytsky, 1998) of the University of Western Ontario have developed a model to describe what they term **organizational commitment**—the extent to which individual members of an organization feel emotional attachment, continued dependence, and moral obligation towards their group or organization. This *three component model* (shown in Figure 9.2) comes from the area of industrial and organizational psychology, a topic on which we will expand in the next chapter.

According to Allen and Meyer, organizational commitment consists of three components which singly or together can contribute to an individual's level of commitment. *Affective commitment* is the emotional attachment, identification and involvement with the organization. The more the group contributes to the individual's sense of worth, social enjoyment and personal fulfillment,

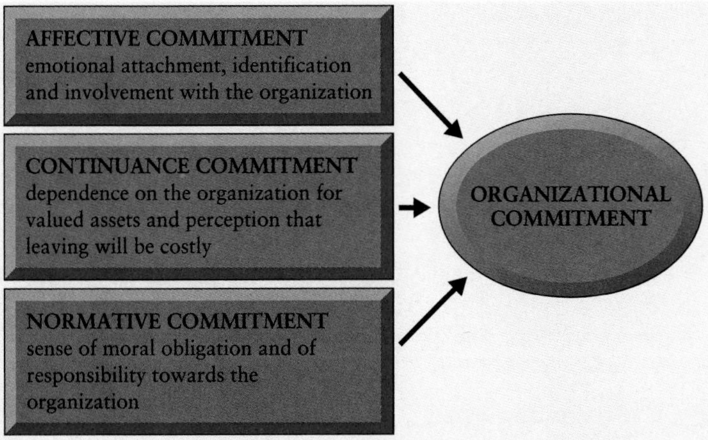

> **Organizational Commitment** The extent to which individual members of an organization feel emotional attachment, continued dependence and moral obligation towards their group or organization.

■ A model of organizational commitment

FIGURE 9.2 The three-component model of organizational commitment suggests that *affective commitment, continuance commitment* and *normative commitment* all contribute towards an individual's continued sense of loyalty and willingness to work for an organization, as well as lessening the likelihood that the individual will try to leave.

AFFECTIVE COMMITMENT
emotional attachment, identification and involvement with the organization

CONTINUANCE COMMITMENT
dependence on the organization for valued assets and perception that leaving will be costly

NORMATIVE COMMITMENT
sense of moral obligation and of responsibility towards the organization

ORGANIZATIONAL COMMITMENT

the greater the feeling of affective commitment. This component is parallel to the social-psychological need which draws individuals to join the group, as mentioned above. *Continuance commitment* is an individual's dependence on the organization for valued assets such as money or status in the community. The more the retention of valued assets is contingent upon belonging to the organization, the greater the perceived costs of discontinued membership. This component parallels the instrumental function of a group, mentioned above. Finally, *normative commitment* is an individual's sense of moral obligation to remain in the group. The strength of this component will be influenced by cultural and social experiences that emphasize the importance of responsibility to the group or organization, as well as any sense of obligation to reciprocate benefits received from membership.

This description of commitment in a group context also has many parallels with the model of interpersonal commitment mentioned in Chapter 6—the *investment model of commitment*. This speaks to the importance of group membership in our lives. In a way very similar to an interpersonal relationship, the stronger the organizational commitment the more an individual will work for the group and the less likely he or she is to leave. Further, the loss of membership in a group can sometimes be as devastating as the loss of a close relationship. For example, being laid off from a job or profession to which one is strongly committed can lead to depression and a loss of identity.

When individuals join a work organization, or any other group, there is an implicit two-way commitment termed a *psychological contract*—the members' perceptions of reciprocal obligations between themselves and the group (Morrison & Robinson, Rousseau, 1995). That is, the member commits to contribute to the organization and the organization commits to provide its benefits to the member. But what happens to commitment when rapid change in organizations occurs? This kind of change has been frequent in the world of work in the last two decades with

many mergers and downsizing of corporations. Allen and Meyer (1998) point out the difficulty of maintaining organizational commitment in times of change because very often the basis of the relationship between member and organization, or between employee and employer is fundamentally changed. For instance, if the nature of a person's job is changed—more work is put on their desk, their work relationships are disrupted due to downsizing—this may alter his or her *affective commitment*. If the perceived benefits of employment lessen as job security decreases, then *continuance commitment* may alter. In fact, if individuals have marketable skills they may realize that they should not depend on this organization alone and look elsewhere. Finally, the sense of moral obligation may be damaged, lessening *normative commitment*. This is particularly likely to occur if the person feels that the organization has violated the *psychological contract*—not held up its end of the bargain.

Meyer and colleagues comment that due to a rapidly changing employment sphere, the traditional basis for commitment in the world of work—the offering of secure and long-term employment—is becoming increasingly difficult for employers to guarantee. Many young people can expect to change occupations, even a number of times, throughout their work career. What appears to be crucial to both affective and normative commitment to an employer is a sense that the organization has treated its members with fairness and support during the process of change (Meyer & Allen, 1997). In such situations where an employer has, for example, kept employees informed about pending changes, explained why jobs are being restructured, offered retraining to those who will lose their jobs, included employees in the decision-making process and so on, then a higher level of commitment is maintained despite the insecurity (DeNisi, 1991; Meyer, et al, 1998). As we will see in the last section of this chapter, such behaviour is characteristic of attempts to maintain *interpersonal justice*.

How Groups Function: Roles, Status, Norms, and Cohesiveness

That groups often exert powerful effects upon their members is obvious and will be a basic theme of this chapter. Before turning to group influence, however, we should address a basic issue: How, precisely, do groups affect their members? A complete answer to this question involves many processes we have already examined in this book, including conformity, persuasion, and attraction. In addition, four aspects of groups themselves play a key role in this regard: *roles*, *status*, *norms*, and *cohesiveness*.

Roles: Differentiation of Functions Within Groups

Think of a group to which you belong or have belonged—anything from the Scouts to a professional association. Now consider this question: Did everyone in the group act in the same way or perform the same functions? Your answer is probably *no*. Different persons performed different tasks and were expected to accomplish different things for the group. In short, they played different **roles**. Sometimes roles are assigned; for instance, a group may select different individuals to serve as its leader, treasurer, or bouncer. In other cases individuals gradually acquire certain roles without being formally assigned to them. Regardless of how roles are acquired, people often *internalize* them; they link their roles to key aspects of their self-perceptions and self-concept (see Chapters 2 and 4). When this happens, a role may exert profound effects on a person's behaviour, even when she or he is not in the group. For instance, a professor, used to lecturing to students, may lecture his or her family when at home—something the authors have each been accused of doing!

Roles The set of behaviours that individuals occupying specific positions within a group are expected to perform.

Roles help to clarify the responsibilities and obligations of group members, so in this respect they are very useful. They do have a downside, though. Group members sometimes experience *role conflict*—stress stemming from the fact that roles they play within different groups are somehow at odds with each other. For instance, the parents of young children often experience conflict between their role as *parent* and their role as *student* or *employee*, and this can be highly stressful for them (Williams et al., 1991).

Status: The Prestige of Various Roles

Compare the two offices shown in Figure 9.3. Do they tell you anything about the people who occupy them? Clearly, the one on the right belongs to someone who

■ The outward signs of status

FIGURE 9.3 As you can readily tell, the woman who occupies the office on the right probably has much higher status in her organization (group) than the woman who occupies the office on the left.

Status Social standing or rank.

has high standing or status, while the one on the left probably belongs to someone who is lower on this dimension. **Status** refers to social standing or rank within a group; and even today, a time when there is a strong tendency to downplay such differences in many settings, status distinctions continue to exist and to influence individual behaviour. Different roles or positions in a group are often associated with different levels of status, and people are often extremely sensitive to this fact. Why? Because status is linked to a wide range of desirable outcomes—everything from salary and "perks" to first choice among potential romantic partners (Buss, 1993). For this reason, groups often use status as a means of influencing the behaviour of their members: only "good" members—ones who follow the group's rules—receive high status.

Norms: The Rules of the Game

Norms Rules within a group indicating how its members should (or should not) behave.

We just alluded to a third factor responsible for the powerful impact of groups on their members: rules, or **norms**, established by groups to tell their members how they are supposed to behave. We discussed social norms in detail in Chapter 7; here, we simply want to note again that norms often exert powerful effects on behaviour. Moreover, as mentioned above, adherence to norms is often a necessary condition for gaining status and other rewards controlled by groups.

Cohesiveness: The Force That Binds

Cohesiveness All forces acting on group members to cause them to remain part of a group; including mutual attraction, interdependence, shared goals, and so on.

Consider two groups. In the first, members like one another very much, strongly desire the goals their group is seeking, and feel that they could not possibly find another group that would better satisfy their needs. In the second, the opposite is true: members don't like one another very much, don't share common goals, and are actively seeking other groups that might offer them a better deal. Which group will exert stronger effects on the behaviour of its members? The answer is obvious: the first. The reason for this difference involves what social psychologists describe as **cohesiveness**—all the forces that cause members to remain in the group, including factors such as liking for the other members and the desire to maintain or increase one's status by belonging to the "right" groups (Festinger et al., 1950). At first glance, it might seem that cohesiveness would involve primarily liking between individual group members. However, recent evidence suggests that it involves *depersonalized attraction*—liking for other group members stemming from the fact that they belong to the group and embody or represent its key features, quite apart from their traits as individuals (Hogg & Haines, 1996).

Several factors influence cohesiveness, including: (1) status within the group (Cota et al., 1995)—cohesiveness is often higher for high- than for low-status members; (2) the effort required to gain entry into the group—the greater these costs, the higher the cohesiveness (see our discussion of *dissonance theory* in Chapter 4); (3) the existence of external threats or severe competition—such threats increase members' attraction and commitment to the group; and (4) size—small groups tend to be more cohesive than large ones.

In sum, several aspects of groups—roles, status, norms, and cohesiveness—determine the extent to which the groups can, and do, influence their members' behaviour. We'll have reason to refer to these factors at later points in this chapter, as we discuss specific ways in which groups influence their members.

HOW GROUPS AFFECT INDIVIDUAL PERFORMANCE: FACILITATION OR SOCIAL LOAFING?

Sometimes, when we perform a task, we work totally alone—for instance, studying alone in your room. In many other cases, even if we are working on a task by ourselves, other people are present—for instance, studying in a crowded library. In still other cases, we work on tasks together with other persons, as part of a task-performing group. What are the effects of other persons on our performance in these various settings? The answer seems to vary as a function of our relationship with these other persons. If others are simply present but not working with us, one set of effects occurs. If, instead, they are working with us as part of a group or team, another set occurs. Let's take a closer look at both situations.

Social Facilitation: Performance in the Presence of Others

Imagine that you are a young athlete—an ice-skater, for example—and that you are preparing for your first important competition. You practise your routines alone for several hours each day, month after month. Finally, the big day arrives and you skate out onto the ice in a huge arena filled with the biggest crowd you've ever seen. How will you do? Better or worse than when you practised alone? This was one of the first topics ever studied in social psychology, so before we turn to modern findings concerning this issue, let's consider some very early research on it by Floyd Allport (1920), whose early and influential work is described in the Cornerstones section below.

Performance in the Presence of Others: The Simplest Group Effect?

Social psychology was literally struggling for its existence as an independent field when Floyd Allport decided to study what, in his opinion, was a very basic question: What are the effects of working on a task in the presence of other persons who are working on the same, or even a different, task—persons who are not competing with each other? Allport felt that this was an important question and—more to the point—one that would allow the new field to replace speculation with scientific data. To study the effects of the presence of others on task performance, he used several different, but related, methods.

In one study, for example, he asked participants to write down as many associations as they could think of for words printed at the top of an otherwise blank sheet of paper (e.g., "building," "laboratory"). The participants were allowed to work for three one-minute periods, and they performed this task both alone and in the presence of two other persons. Results were clear: 93 percent of the participants produced more associations when working in the presence of others than when working alone.

Allport was encouraged by these findings but realized that in many cases, participants could think of more words than they could actually list. This, he reasoned, might be affecting the results. To eliminate this problem, he asked participants to write down every third or every

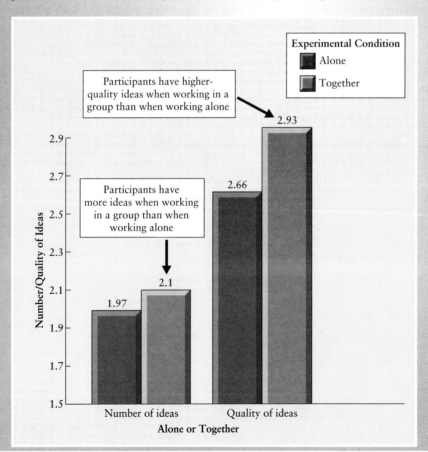

■ Effects of coactors on cognitive performance

FIGURE 9.4 Not only did participants in Allport's (1920) research think of more arguments when they worked in the presence of others; the quality of these arguments was better, too. On the basis of such findings social psychologists concluded—in error, as it turned out—that the presence of other persons usually facilitates task performance.

Source: Based on data from Allport, 1920.

fourth word they thought of—not all of them. Again results indicated that performance was increased in the presence of others. But still Allport was not satisfied: he wondered whether the same effect would be found with a more complex task—one requiring high levels of thought. To find out, he asked participants to read short passages from ancient Roman authors, then to write down all the arguments they could think of that would tend to *disprove* the points made in these passages. Again, they performed this task while alone and while in the presence of several other persons; and once more, results indicated that performance was increased when individuals worked in groups. Not only did participants come up with more arguments—the quality of these ideas was better, too (see Figure 9.4).

Allport's research paved the way for the study of what soon came to be known in social psychol-

Social Facilitation Effects upon performance resulting from the presence of others.

ogy as **social facilitation**. Early researchers defined this term as improvements in performance produced by the mere presence of others, either as audience or as coactors—persons performing the same task but independently (for example, students taking an exam in the same room). As we'll soon see, the concept of social facilitation turned out to be premature: the presence of others does not always enhance performance, and social psychologists now understand why this is so. There can be little doubt, however, that although some of his conclusions were later modified, Allport's early studies were, in many ways, a model for the young field of social psychology—a model still reflected in its scientific orientation today.

The Presence of Others: Is It Always Facilitating?

Allport's research and that conducted by other early social psychologists (e.g., Triplett, 1989) seemed to indicate that the presence of others is a definite plus—it improves performance on many different tasks. As the volume of research on this topic increased, however, puzzling findings began to appear: sometimes the presence of others facilitated performance, but sometimes it produced the opposite effect (Pessin, 1933). So social facilitation did not always facilitate. Why? Why did the presence of others sometimes enhance but sometimes reduce performance? This question remained largely unanswered until the mid-1960s, when a famous researcher, Robert Zajonc, offered an insightful answer. Let's take a look at his ideas.

The Drive Theory of Social Facilitation: Other Persons as a Source of Arousal.

Imagine that you are performing some task alone. Then several other people arrive on the scene and begin to watch you intently. Will your pulse beat quicker because of this audience? Informal experience suggests that it may—that the presence of other persons in the form of an interested audience can increase our activation or arousal. Zajonc suggested that this fact might provide the solution to the social facilitation puzzle. Here's why.

When arousal increases, our tendency to perform *dominant responses*—the ones we are most likely to perform in a given situation—also rises. Such dominant responses, in turn, can be correct or incorrect for that situation. If this is so, then it follows logically that if the presence of an audience increases arousal, this factor will *improve* performance when our dominant responses are correct ones, but may *impair* performance when such responses are incorrect (please see Figure 9.5).

Another implication of Zajonc's reasoning, which is known as the **drive theory of social facilitation** because it focuses on arousal or drive, is this: The presence of others will improve individuals' performance when they are highly skilled at the task in question (because in this case their dominant responses will tend to be correct) but will

Drive Theory of Social Facilitation A theory suggesting that the mere presence of others is arousing and increases the tendency to perform dominant responses.

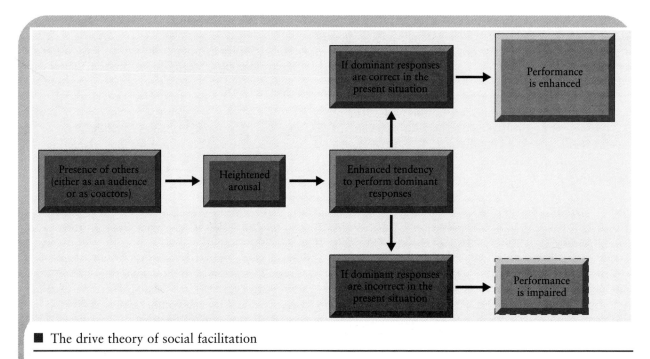

■ The drive theory of social facilitation

FIGURE 9.5 According to the drive theory of social facilitation (Zajonc, 1965), the presence of others increases arousal, and this in turn increases the tendency to perform dominant responses. If dominant responses are correct, performance is enhanced; if they are incorrect, performance is impaired.

interfere with individuals' performance when they are not highly skilled—for instance, when they are learning to perform a task. (Under these conditions, their dominant responses will probably *not* be correct.)

Many studies soon provided support for Zajonc's theory. Individuals were more likely to perform dominant responses in the presence of others than when alone, and their performance on various tasks was either enhanced or impaired depending on whether these responses were correct or incorrect in each situation (e.g., Geen, 1989; Zajonc & Sales, 1966).

Additional research raised an important question, however: Does social facilitation stem from the *mere physical presence of others*? Or do other factors, such as concern over others' evaluations of us, also play a role? Support for the latter conclusion was provided by the findings of several ingenious studies indicating that social facilitation effects occurred only when individuals believed that their performance could be observed and evaluated by others (e.g., Bond, 1982). For instance, such effects did not occur if the audience was blindfolded or showed no interest in watching (Cottrell et al., 1968). Such findings led some researchers to suggest that social facilitation actually stems either from **evaluation apprehension**—concern over being judged by others (which is often arousing)—or from concerns over *self-presentation*—making a good impression on others, a topic we discussed in Chapter 7.

Reasonable as these suggestions seem, they don't apply in all cases. For example, animals—even cockroaches!—perform simple tasks such as running through a maze better when in the presence of an audience than when alone (Zajonc, Heingartner, & Herman, 1969). It would seem weird to suggest that insects are concerned about the impressions they make on others, so these findings are not compatible with the suggestion that social facilitation stems solely from evaluation apprehension or self-presentation concerns. What's the final answer? Read on for one possibility.

Evaluation Apprehension
Concern over being evaluated by others. Such concern can increase arousal and so contribute to social facilitation.

Distraction-Conflict Theory: A Possible Resolution.

The apparent answer is provided by a theory known as **distraction-conflict theory**, proposed by Robert S. Baron and his colleagues (yes, a different Robert Baron from the one who is writing these words). This theory, like Zajonc's view, assumes that audiences and coactors both increase arousal. It also suggests, however, that such arousal stems from conflict between two competing tendencies: (1) the tendency to pay attention to the task being performed, and (2) the tendency to direct attention to the audience or coactors. Such conflict is arousing; and this, in turn, increases the tendency to perform dominant responses (see Figure 9.6). If these responses are correct, performance is enhanced; if they are incorrect, performance is impaired (e.g., Baron, 1986; Sanders, 1983).

Several findings offer support for this view. For example, audiences produce social facilitation effects only when directing attention to them conflicts in some way with task demands (Groff, Baron, & Moore, 1983). When paying attention to an audience does not conflict with task performance, social facilitation fails to occur. Similarly, individuals experience greater distraction when they perform various tasks in front of an audience than when they perform them alone (Baron, Moore, & Sanders, 1978). Finally, when individuals have little reason to pay attention to others present on the scene—for instance, when these persons are performing a different task—social facilitation fails to occur; but when they have strong reasons for paying attention to others, social facilitation occurs (Sanders, 1983).

One major advantage of distraction-conflict theory is that it can explain why animals, as well as people, are affected by the presence of an audience. Because animals, too, can experience conflicting tendencies to work on a task *and* pay attention to an audience, they should also be susceptible to social facilitation. A theory that can explain similar patterns of behaviour among organisms ranging from cockroaches

Distraction-conflict Theory A theory suggesting that social facilitation stems from the conflict produced when individuals attempt simultaneously to pay attention to other persons and to the task being performed.

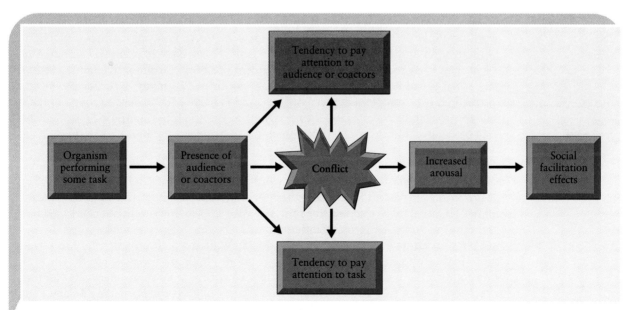

■ The distraction-conflict theory

FIGURE 9.6 According to this theory, the presence of an audience or coactors increases arousal by inducing conflicting tendencies to (1) pay attention to the audience and (2) pay attention to the task being performed. This arousal, in turn, increases the tendency to perform dominant responses. This theory helps explain why animals as well as human beings show social facilitation effects.

through human beings is powerful indeed, and worthy of very careful attention. So distraction-conflict theory, although it may not provide a complete or final answer to the question "Why does social facilitation occur?" clearly represents a major step toward this goal and remains social psychology's best answer to the persistent puzzle of social facilitation.

Social Loafing: Letting Others in the Group Do the Work

Suppose that you and several other people are helping a friend to move. In order to lift the heaviest pieces of furniture, you join forces, with each person lending a hand. Will all of the people helping exert equal effort? Probably not. Some will take as much of the load as possible, while others will simply hang on, appearing to help without really doing much.

This pattern is quite common in situations where groups of person perform what are known as **additive tasks**—tasks in which the contributions of each member are combined into a single group product. On such tasks, some persons work hard while others goof off, doing less than their share, and less than they might do if they were working alone. Social psychologists refer to such effects as **social loafing**—reductions in motivation and effort when individuals work collectively in a group compared to when they work individually or as independent coactors (Karau & Williams, 1993).

That social loafing occurs has been demonstrated in many experiments. In one of the first, for example, Latané, Williams, and Harkins (1979) asked groups of male students to clap or cheer as loudly as possible at specific times, supposedly so that the experimenter could determine how much noise people make in social settings. They performed these tasks in groups of two, four, or six persons. Results were clear: Although the total amount of noise rose as group size increased, the amount produced *by each participant* dropped. In other words, each person put out less and less effort as group size increased. Such effects are not restricted to simple and seemingly meaningless situations like this; on the contrary, they appear to be quite general in scope and occur with respect to many different tasks—cognitive ones as well as ones involving physical effort (Weldon & Mustari, 1988; Williams & Karau, 1991). Moreover, social loafing appears in both genders, and among children as well as adults. The only exception to the generality of such effects seems to be a cultural one: social loafing effects don't seem to occur in *collectivistic cultures*, such as those in many Asian countries—cultures where the collective good is more highly valued than individual accomplishment or achievement (Earley, 1993). In such cultures, in fact, people seem to work *harder* when in groups than they do when alone—sometimes termed *social striving* to contrast with social loafing. So, as we've noted repeatedly, cultural factors sometimes play a very important role in social behaviour.

Additive Tasks Tasks in which the group product is the sum or combination of the efforts of individual members.

Social Loafing Reductions in motivation and effort when people work collectively in a group, compared to when they work individually or as independent co-actors.

Aside from this important exception, however, social loafing appears to be a pervasive fact of social life. If this is indeed true, then two important questions arise: *Why* do such effects occur? And what steps can be taken to reduce their occurrence?

The Collective Effort Model: An Expectancy Theory of Social Loafing

Many different explanations for the occurrence of social loafing have been proposed. For example, one view—*social impact theory*—related social loafing to a topic we examined in Chapter 8, *diffusion of responsibility* (Latané, 1981). According to social impact theory, as group size increases each member feels less and less responsible for the task being performed. The result: Each person exerts decreasing effort on it. In contrast, other theories have focused on the fact that in groups, members' motivation decreases because they realize that their contributions can't be evaluated individually—so why work hard? (Harkins & Szymanski, 1989). Perhaps the most comprehensive explanation of social loafing offered to date, however, is the **collective effort model (CEM)** proposed by Karau and Williams (1993).

These researchers suggest that we can understand social loafing by extending a basic theory of individual motivation—*expectancy-valence theory*—to situations involving group performance. Expectancy-valence theory suggests that individuals will work hard on a given task only to the extent that the following conditions exist: (1) They believe that working hard will lead to better performance (*expectancy*); (2) they believe that better performance will be recognized and rewarded (*instrumentality*); and (3) the rewards available are ones they value and desire (*valence*). In other words, individuals working alone will exert effort only to the extent that they perceive direct links between hard work and the outcomes they want.

According to Karau and Williams (1993), these links often appear weaker when individuals work together in groups than when they work alone. First, consider *expectancy*—the belief that increased effort will lead to better performance. This may be high when individuals work alone, but lower when they work together in groups, because people realize that other factors aside from their own effort will determine the group's performance; for instance, the amount of effort exerted by other members. Similarly, *instrumentality*—the belief that good performance will be recognized and rewarded—may also be weaker when people work together in groups. They realize that valued outcomes are divided among all group members, and that as a result they may not get their fair share given their level of effort. Because there is more uncertainty about the links between how hard people work and the rewards they receive, social loafing occurs; and within the framework of the collective effort model, this is not surprising. After all, when individuals work together with others, the relationship between their own performance and rewards is more uncertain than when working alone.

Is the collective effort model accurate? To find out, Karau and Williams performed a meta-analysis of dozens of studies of social loafing. The CEM makes several predictions concerning the conditions under which social loafing should be most and least likely to occur. For example, it predicts that social loafing will be weakest (1) when individuals work in small rather than large groups; (2) when they work on tasks that are intrinsically interesting or important to them; (3) when they work with respected others (friends, teammates, etc.); (4) when they perceive that their contributions to the group product are unique or important; (5) when they expect their coworkers to perform poorly; and (6) when they come from cultures that emphasize group effort and outcomes rather than individual outcomes (Asian cultures versus Western ones, for instance). The results of the meta-analysis offered support for all these predictions. In other words, social loafing was weakest (and strongest) under conditions predicted by the theory (see Figure 9.7). In addition, it was found that social loafing was a very reli-

Collective Effort Model (CEM) An explanation of social loafing suggesting that perceived links between individuals' efforts and their outcomes are weaker when they work together with others in a group.

■ Social loafing:
When it is least
likely to occur

FIGURE 9.7 Research
findings indicate that the
social loafing effect is weakest under the conditions
shown here.

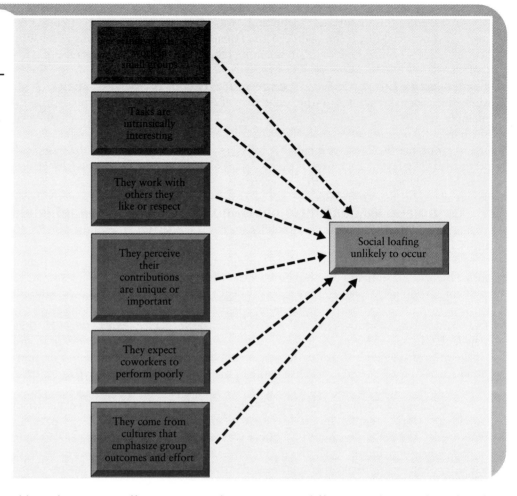

Individuals work in small groups

Tasks are intrinsically interesting

They work with others they like or respect

They perceive their contributions are unique or important

They expect coworkers to perform poorly

They come from cultures that emphasize group outcomes and effort

Social loafing unlikely to occur

able and pervasive effect: it occurred across many different studies conducted with
many different kinds of participants and many different kinds of tasks.

Reducing Social Loafing: Some Useful Techniques

Unfortunately, the conditions for social loafing exist in many settings where groups of persons work together—for instance, in many manufacturing plants, government offices and
even student groups. Social loafing has the effect of disrupting group morale, because
some members, at least, will feel that they are being taken advantage of by others. If social
loafing poses a threat to performance in many settings, the next question is obvious: What
steps can be taken to reduce it? Research findings offer some useful suggestions.

First, and most obvious, groups can devise ways to make the output or effort of
each participant readily identifiable (e.g., Williams, Harkins, & Latané, 1981). Under
these conditions, people can't sit back and let others do their work, so social loafing
is in fact reduced. Second, groups can reduce social loafing by increasing members'
commitment to successful task performance (Brickner et al., 1986). Pressures toward
working hard will then serve to offset temptations to engage in social loafing. Third,
groups can diminish social loafing by increasing the apparent importance or value of
a task (Karau & Williams, 1993). Fourth, social loafing declines when individuals
view their contributions to the task as unique rather than merely duplicating those of
others (Weldon & Mustari, 1988). And finally, social loafing can be reduced through
the strengthening of group cohesiveness—a factor we discussed earlier.

Together, these steps *can* sharply reduce the magnitude of social loafing in many situations. Social loafing, it appears, can be reduced if appropriate safeguards are built into the situation. When they are, individuals will perceive strong links between their effort, the group's performance, and their own outcomes. Then the tendency to goof off at the expense of others may be greatly reduced.

See the Ideas to Take with You feature at the end of the chapter for some practical suggestions on how you can both benefit from social facilitation and protect yourself against social loafing by others.

KEY POINTS

- When individuals work together on a task, *social loafing*—reduced output by each group member—sometimes occurs.
- According to the *collective effort model* (CEM), such effects occur because when working together with others as compared to working alone, individuals experience weaker links between their effort and outcomes.
- Groups can reduce social loafing in several ways: by making outputs individually identifiable, by increasing commitment to the task and sense of task importance, and by building group cohesiveness.

DECISION MAKING BY GROUPS: HOW IT OCCURS AND THE PITFALLS IT FACES

Groups are called upon to perform many tasks—everything from conducting surgical operations through harvesting the world's crops. One of the most important activities they perform, however, is **decision making**—combining and integrating available information in order to choose one out of several possible courses of action. Governments, large corporations, military units, sports teams—virtually all social entities entrust key decisions to groups. Why? While many factors play a role, the most important seems to be this: Most people believe that groups usually reach better decisions than individuals. After all, it is reasoned, they can pool the expertise of their members and avoid extreme courses of action.

Decision Making The process of combining and integrating available information in order to choose one out of several possible courses of action.

Are such beliefs accurate? Do groups really make better or more accurate decisions than individuals? In their efforts to answer this question, social psychologists have focused on three major topics: (1) How do groups actually make decisions and reach consensus? (2) Do decisions reached by groups differ from those reached by individuals? (3) What accounts for the fact that groups sometimes make truly disastrous decisions—ones so bad it is hard to believe they were actually reached?

The Decision-Making Process: How Groups Attain Consensus

When a group first begins to discuss an issue, its members rarely voice unanimous agreement. Rather, the members come to the decision-making task with different information and so support a wide range of views (e.g., Larson, Foster-Fishman, & Franz, 1998; Gigone & Hastie, 1997). After some period of discussion, however, they usually reach a decision. This is not always the case—for example, juries become "hung," and other decision-making groups, too, may deadlock. In most cases, though, some decision is reached. Is there any way of predicting this final outcome? In short, can we predict the decision a group is likely to reach from information about the views initially held by its members? Growing evidence suggests that we can (e.g., Kerr & MacCoun, 1985; Kaplan & Miller, 1987).

Social Decision Schemes: Blueprints for Decision

Social Decision Schemes Rules relating the initial distribution of member views to final group decisions.

To summarize some very complex findings in simple terms, it appears that the final decisions reached by groups can often be predicted quite accurately by relatively simple rules known as **social decision schemes**. These rules relate the initial distribution of member views or preferences to the group's final decisions. For example, one scheme—the *majority-wins rule*—suggests that in many cases the group will opt for whatever position is initially supported by a majority of its members. According to this rule, discussion serves mainly to confirm or strengthen the most popular view. In contrast, a second decision scheme—the *truth-wins rule*—indicates that the correct solution or decision will ultimately come to the fore as its correctness is recognized by a growing number of members. A third decision scheme, adopted by many juries, is the *two-thirds majority rule*. Here, juries tend to convict defendants if two-thirds of the jurors initially favour this decision (Davis et al., 1984). Finally, some groups seem to follow a *first-shift rule*. They tend, ultimately, to adopt a decision consistent with the direction of the first shift in opinion shown by any member.

Surprising as it may seem, the results of many studies indicate that these straightforward rules are quite successful in predicting even complex group decisions. Indeed, they have been found to be accurate in this regard up to 80 percent of the time (e.g., Stasser, Taylor, & Hanna, 1989). Thus, they seem to provide important insights into how groups move toward consensus: apparently, it seems, in accordance with straightforward decision rules that can predict the final outcome with surprising accuracy.

Influence From Other Group Members: Normative and Informational Influence

Do you recall the distinction between *normative social influence* and *informational social influence* that we made in Chapter 7? If so, you remember that the former refers to influence attempts that focus on our desire to be liked or accepted, while the latter focuses on our desire to be right—to have accurate information about various issues or topics. It seems reasonable that group members may attempt to influence each through these distinct kinds of social influence; and, in fact, existing evidence suggests that they do (e.g., Kaplan, 1989). It also seems possible, though, that people may tend to prefer one or the other of these two kinds of influence under different conditions. Specifically, when a decision involves reaching a factually correct solution—what social psychologists term an *intellective task*—group members may tend to rely more on informational influence. In contrast, when a decision does not have any single "right" answer, members may tend to rely more heavily on normative influence. *Time pressures*, too, may make a difference. If a group is in a hurry and must make a decision quickly, there is little time to rely on information; under these conditions, most influence may be *normative* in nature. In contrast, when the group has more time for its discussions, influence may be primarily *informational* in nature. Evidence for the accuracy of these predictions has been reported recently by Kelly and her colleagues (1997).

In this study, groups of three college students worked on tasks requiring them to rank order various topics. One task involved rank-ordering the topics people dream about most frequently; the other involved rank-ordering the leading causes of death. Both tasks had a "right" answer; but, as you can probably guess, the one concerning causes of death seemed more factual (intellective) than the one concerning dreams.

Half of the groups worked under high time pressure: they were told that their perform-ance would depend on the speed with which they completed the task. The other half worked under low time pressure: they were told to take as much time as they wished. Kelly and her colleagues (1997) predicted that group members would tend to utilize informational influence for the causes-of-death task and under low time pressure, but would employ normative influence for the dream task and when time pressure was high. This is precisely what was found.

These findings underscore an important point about how groups reach decisions. During group discussions, members try to influence one another in various ways, and whether these attempts are mainly normative or mainly informational depends on sev-eral factors. In other words, groups reach agreement through a complex process of reciprocal influence among members, but the specifics of this process vary with the task faced by the group.

The Nature of Group Decisions: Moderation or Polarization?

Truly important decisions are rarely left to individuals. Instead, they are usually assigned to groups—and highly qualified groups at that. Even total dictators usually consult with groups of skilled advisers before taking major actions. As we noted earl-ier, the major reason behind this strategy is the belief that groups are far less likely than individuals to make serious errors—to rush blindly over the edge. Is this really true?

Research on this issue has yielded surprising findings. Contrary to popular belief, a large body of evidence indicates that groups are actually more likely to adopt extreme positions than individuals making decisions alone. In fact, across many different kinds of decisions and in many different contexts, groups show a pronounced tendency to shift toward views more extreme than the ones with which they initially began (Burnstein, 1983; Lamm & Myers, 1978). This phenomenon is known as **group polarization**, and its major effects can be summarized as follows: Whatever the initial leaning or preference of a group prior to its discussions, it is strengthened during the group's deliberations. The result: Not only does *the group* shift toward more extreme views—individual members, too, often show such a shift. (The term *group polarization* does not refer to a tendency of groups to split apart into two opposing camps or poles; on the contrary, it refers to a strengthening of the group's initial preferences.)

Group Polarization
The tendency of group members to shift toward more extreme positions than those they initially held as a result of group discussion.

Why does this effect occur? Research findings have helped provide an answer. Apparently, two major factors are involved. First, it appears that *social comparison*, a process we examined in Chapters 3 and 6, plays an important role. Everyone, it seems, wants to be "above average." Where opinions are concerned, this implies holding views that are "better" than those of most other persons—and, especially, better than those of other members of one's group. What does "better" mean? This depends on the specific group: Among a group of liberals, "better" would mean "more liberal." Among a group of conservatives, it would mean "more conservative." Among a group of racists, it would mean "even more bigoted." In any case, during group discussions, at least some members discover—to their shock!—that their views are *not* "better" than those of most other members. The result: After comparing themselves with these persons, they shift to even more extreme views, and the group polarization effect is off and running (Goethals & Zanna, 1979).

A second factor involves the fact that during group discussion, most arguments presented are ones favouring the group's initial leaning or preference. As a result of hear-ing such arguments, persuasion occurs (presumably through the *central route* described in Chapter 3), and members shift increasingly toward the majority view. This, of course, increases the proportion of arguments favouring this view, and ultimately members con-

FIGURE 9.8 Did group polarization play a role in the decision of Communist hard-liners in the former Soviet Union to stage a coup in 1991—a decision that ultimately led to their total loss of power? We can't tell for sure, but it seems very possible that this and other disastrous group decisions were influenced by this important process.

vince themselves that this is the "right" view and shift toward it with increasing strength. The result: Group polarization occurs (Vinokur & Burnstein, 1974).

While both of these factors seem to play a role in group polarization, research evidence (Zuber, Crott, & Werner, 1992) suggests that social comparison may be somewhat more important, at least in some contexts, or that group polarization can best be understood in terms of a social decision scheme comparable to the ones we described earlier. Specifically, it appears that the view supported by the typical group member is often the best predictor of the final group decision.

Regardless of the precise mechanisms of group polarization, this process definitely has important implications. The occurrence of polarization may lead many decision-making groups to adopt positions that are increasingly extreme, and therefore increasingly dangerous. In this context, it is chilling to speculate about the potential role of such shifts in disastrous decisions that have actually been made by political, military, and business groups that should, by all accounts, have known better—for example, the decision by the hard-liners in the now vanished Soviet Union to stage a coup to restore firm Communist rule (see Figure 9.8), or the decision by Apple computer not to license its software to other manufacturers, a decision that ultimately cost Apple most of its market. Did group polarization influence these and other disastrous decisions? It is impossible to say for sure, but research findings suggest that this is a real possibility.

Decision Making By Groups: Some Potential Pitfalls

The tendency of many decision-making groups to drift toward polarization is a serious factor that can interfere with their ability to make accurate decisions. Unfortunately, this is not the only process that can exert such negative effects. Several others, too, seem to emerge out of group discussions and can lead groups into disastrous courses of action (Hinsz, 1995). Among the most important of these are (1) *groupthink* and (2) groups' seeming inability to share and use information held by some but not all of their members.

Groupthink: When Too Much Cohesiveness is a Dangerous Thing

Earlier, we suggested that tendencies toward group polarization may be one reason why decision-making groups sometimes go off the deep end, with catastrophic results. However, another and even more disturbing factor may also contribute to such outcomes. This is a process known as **groupthink,** a mode of thinking by group members in which concern with maintaining group consensus—or *concurrence seeking*—overrides the motivation to evaluate all potential courses of action as accurately and realistically as possible (Janis, 1982). A decision-making group will close ranks, cognitively, around a decision, assume that the group can't be wrong, that all members must support the decision strongly, and that any information contrary to it should be rejected. Historically a number of high-powered group decisions, from the decision to launch the ill-fated space shuttle *Challenger* in the United States to the devising of the Meech Lake Accord in Canada can be seen as influenced by the process of groupthink (Baron, Byrne & Watson, 1997; Janis, 1982).

Once a decision-making group develops this collective state of mind, it appears, it becomes unwilling—even, perhaps, *unable*—to change its course of action, even if external events suggest very strongly that the original decision was a poor one. In fact, according to Janis (1982), the social psychologist who originated the concept of groupthink, norms soon emerge in the group that actively prevent its members from considering alternative courses of action. The group is viewed as being incapable of making an error, and anyone with lingering doubts is quickly silenced, both by group pressure and by his or her own desire to conform.

Why does groupthink occur? Research findings (e.g., Kameda & Sugimori, 1993; Tetlock et al., 1992) suggest that two factors may be crucial. The first is a very high level of *cohesiveness* among group members who are similar in background, interests, and values and so tend to like each other very much. The second is the kind of emergent group norms mentioned above—norms suggesting that the group is both infallible and morally superior, and that because of these factors there should be no further discussion of the issue at hand; the decision has been made, and the only task now is to support it as strongly as possible. According to Janis this process is most likely to occur when decision makers are under pressure and isolated from outside input (Janis, 1982). The result: The group shifts from focusing on making the best decision possible to focusing on maintaining a high level of consensus and achieving a decision at all costs, with truly disastrous effects.

The Failure to Share Information

As we noted earlier, one reason why many key decisions are entrusted to groups is the belief that members will pool their resources—share ideas and knowledge unique to each individual. In this way, the decisions they reach will be better informed, and presumably more accurate, than those that would be reached by individuals working in isolation. Is this actually the case? Do groups really share the knowledge and expertise brought to them by individual members? Many studies suggests that in fact such pooling of resources may be the exception rather than the rule (Gigone & Hastie, 1993, 1997; Stasser, 1992; Stasser & Titus, 1985, 1987; Stasser, Taylor, & Hanna, 1989).

These studies were undertaken to test the validity of a model of group discussion known as the **information sampling model** (Stasser & Titus, 1985). This model suggests decision-making groups are more likely to discuss—and discuss again—information shared by most members than information known to only a single member (unshared information). More specifically, the model predicts that the larger the group, the greater the tendency to ignore unshared information in preference for shared. When this failure to discuss unshared information leads to the wrong decision, such situations are said to possess a hidden profile. This is because information pointing to the best choice is present but is hidden from the group's view because it is held by only a few members and is not discussed.

Why do the decisions reached by groups tend to favour information most members share at the beginning? Two possibilities exist: (1) Group decisions simply reflect the views members hold before group discussion begins—members start with certain views, and these are further strengthened during the discussion; (2) group decisions reflect the information exchanged during the discussion, and because most of this is shared information, it is such information that shapes the decision. If this latter view is correct, then to the extent that groups *do* manage to bring to the surface unshared information, their decisions, too, may change. The results of several recent studies (e.g., Larson et al., 1998; Winquist & Larson, 1998) offer support for this idea. In these studies, the greater the tendency of groups to discuss information known to only some of the members—information pointing to the correct decision—the more accurate were the groups' final choices. This was true even in such important contexts as medical diagnosis; despite the potentially life-and-death nature of this activity, teams of interns and medical students were found to pool more shared than *unshared* information during group discussions. However, the more they pooled unshared information (information known, initially, to only some members), the more accurate were the groups' diagnoses.

In short, hidden profiles may be discovered and improved decisions made. The trick, of course, is to encourage groups to discover and discuss such information. What strategies can produce this result? One is to convince groups that there is a correct solution or decision and that their task is to find it (Stasser & Stewart, 1992). Another is to allow group members ample opportunity to work together; as they do, they may come to recognize what information most members share and what information is unique. Then the likelihood of a pooling-of-resources effect may tend to increase (Stasser & Hinkle, 1994). Taken as a whole, however, existing evidence indicates that decision-making groups do not automatically benefit from their members' unique knowledge and skills; often, they don't realize that these assets exist and so can't profit from them.

KEY POINTS

- It is widely believed that groups make better decisions than individuals. However, research findings indicate that groups are often subject to *group polarization effects*, which lead them to make more extreme decisions than individuals.

- In addition, groups often suffer from *groupthink*—when a desire to achieve concensus takes precedence over reaching the right decision.

- Groups often fail to pool information known only to some members. As the *information sampling model* suggests, their decisions tend to reflect only the information most members already share.

COORDINATION IN GROUPS: COOPERATION OR CONFLICT?

In Chapter 8 we explored the subject of *prosocial behaviour*—actions that benefit others but have no obvious or immediate benefits for the persons who perform them. Although prosocial behaviour is far from rare, another pattern—one in which helping is mutual and both sides benefit—is even more common. This pattern is known as cooperation and involves situations in which group members work together to attain shared goals. Cooperation can be highly beneficial; indeed, through this process, groups can attain goals that their individual members could never hope to reach by themselves. Surprisingly, though, cooperation does not always develop. Frequently, persons belonging to a group try to coordinate their efforts but somehow fail in this attempt (see Figure 9.9).

Even worse, group members may perceive their respective personal interests as incompatible, with the result that instead of working together and coordinating their efforts, they work *against* each other—often producing negative results for both sides. This state of affairs, known as **conflict**, can be defined as a process in which individuals or groups perceive that others have taken or will soon take actions incompatible with their own interests. Conflict is indeed a process; for, as you probably know from your own experience, it has a nasty way of escalating—starting, perhaps, with simple mistrust, and quickly moving through a spiral of anger, resentment, and actions designed to harm the other side. When conflict is carried to extremes, the ultimate effects can be very harmful to both sides.

In one sense, cooperation and conflict can be viewed as falling on opposite ends of a continuum relating to *coordination*—the extent to which individuals in groups work together or against one another. We'll now take a closer look at the nature of both of these processes as well as at some of the factors that influence their occurrence.

Cooperation
Behaviour in which group members work together to attain shared goals.

Conflict A process in which individuals or groups perceive that others have taken or will soon take actions incompatible with their own interests.

Cooperation: Working With Others to Achieve Shared Goals

That cooperation can be highly beneficial is obvious. So why, you may be wondering, don't group members always coordinate their activities so that all can benefit? One answer is straightforward: Some goals that people seek simply can't be shared. Several people seeking the same job, promotion, or romantic partner can't combine forces to attain their goals: the desired outcome is available to only one person in each case, so cooperation is not possible. In such cases conflict may quickly develop, as each person attempts to optimize his or her own outcomes (Tjosvold, 1993).

In many other situations, however, cooperation *could* develop but does not. Why? The answer seems to involve a number of different factors that together serve to tip the balance either toward or away from the kind of coordination that cooperation requires.

■ Cooperation: Why it sometimes fails

FIGURE 9.9 Even when individuals attempt to cooperate—to coordinate their efforts in order to reach a shared goal—they may fail to do so.
Source: King Features Syndicate, 1986.

The Nature of Cooperation: Dealing with Social Dilemmas

Many situations in which cooperation could potentially develop but does not can be described as ones involving **social dilemmas**; they are situations in which each person can increase his or her individual gains by acting in a certain way, but if all (or most) persons act that same way, the outcomes experienced by all are reduced (Komorita & Parks, 1994). As a result, the persons in such situations must deal with *mixed motives*; there are reasons to cooperate (to avoid negative outcomes for all), but also reasons to *defect*—to do what is best for oneself. Many situations in everyday life qualify as social dilemmas (e.g., Baron, Kerr, & Miller, 1992). For instance, many communities are now involved in recycling schemes requiring citizens to separate glass, plastic, cans, and paper from regular garbage. From a purely selfish point of view, the easiest thing for an individual to do would be to ignore the rule and mix all their garbage together. After all, the authorities don't check what's in an individual's garbage bag! If everyone did this, however, we would all lose: our landfill would become full very quickly, and we would have to pay much higher taxes to cope with the overflow.

The problem is that individuals often reason that if they are the *only* ones who are "defecting" and violating the rules, they will personally gain, while their actions will have little impact on the community as a whole. However, you can be sure that if one person thinks this way, their neighbors will too, with obvious results. As demonstrated in Figure 9.10, the same principles apply to many other aspects of life—from paying taxes to observing fishing regulations—and individual short-term gain is too often at the long-term expense of the community.

■ The nature of social dilemmas

FIGURE 9.10 In social dilemmas, each person can enhance her or his outcomes by acting in a selfish manner. However, when many of the persons involved behave this way, outcomes for all are reduced. In the situation shown here, the person driving the small, fuel-efficient car is behaving in a cooperative manner: such vehicles conserve natural resources and pollute the atmosphere to a relatively small degree. The person driving the large minivan can be viewed as acting in a more selfish manner; such vehicles waste fuel and pollute to a much greater extent.

In such situations, the key question becomes one of *trust* versus *defection*. Will everyone do what's good for the group, or will each person pursue his or her selfish interests? What factors tip the balance one way or the other? That question has been the subject of much research by social psychologists.

Factors Influencing Cooperation: Reciprocity, Personal Orientations, and Communication

Among the many different factors that determine whether individuals will choose to cooperate with others in situations involving the mixed motives generated by social dilemmas, three appear to be most important: tendencies toward *reciprocity*, *personal orientations* concerning cooperation, and *communication*.

Reciprocity is probably the most obvious of these factors. Throughout life, we are urged to follow the Golden Rule and to do unto others as we would like them to do unto us. Despite such appeals, however, we often behave in a different manner. Most people tend to react to others not as they would prefer to be treated themselves, but rather as they have *actually* been treated by these people in the past. In short, people generally follow the principle of **reciprocity** much of the time: they return the kind of treatment they have previously received from others (e.g., Pruitt & Carnevale, 1993). The choice between cooperation and competition is no exception to this powerful rule. When others cooperate with us and put their selfish interests aside, we usually respond in kind. In contrast, if they defect and pursue their own interests, we generally do the same (Kerr & Kaufman-Gilliland, 1994).

Now let's consider the role of *personal orientation* in cooperation. Think about the many people you have known during your life. Can you remember ones who strongly preferred cooperation—people who could be counted on to try to work together with other group members in almost every situation? In contrast, can you remember others who usually preferred to pursue their own selfish interests and could *not* be relied on to cooperate? You probably have little difficulty in bringing examples of both types to mind, for large individual differences in tendencies to cooperate exist. Such differences, in turn, seem to reflect contrasting perspectives toward working with others—perspectives that individuals carry with them from situation to situation, even over relatively long periods of time (e.g., Knight & Dubro, 1984). Research carried out by DeDreu and McCusker (1997) provided clear evidence for the existence and impact of such differences in personal orientation or social motivation.

On the basis of previous research, DeDreu and McCusker (1997) reasoned that individuals can actually possess three distinct orientations toward situations involving social dilemmas: (1) a *cooperative orientation*, in which they prefer to maximize the joint outcomes received by all the persons involved; (2) an *individualistic orientation*, in which they focus primarily on maximizing their own outcomes; or (3) a *competitive orientation*, in which they focus primarily on defeating others—on obtaining better outcomes than other persons do (Van Lange & Kuhlman, 1994). Further, DeDreu and McCusker reasoned that the effects of these orientations on behaviour in a situation in which people could choose to cooperate or defect would be maximized by a *negative frame*—by information that caused individuals to think about the situation in terms of potential losses rather than potential gains. Why? Because thinking about outcomes as losses increases the apparent difference in utility or value for these two strategies. Thus, negative framing would increase the tendency for persons with a competitive or individualistic orientation to defect, but would increase the tendency for persons with a cooperative orientation to cooperate.

To test these predictions, DeDreu and McCusker had students at a university in the Netherlands play a game in which they could choose either to cooperate with

Reciprocity A basic rule of social life suggesting that individuals tend to treat others as these persons have treated them.

another person, thus maximizing joint gains, or defect, thus maximizing their own gains while reducing the outcomes of the other person. Before participants played the game, the researchers had them complete a measure that revealed their personal orientation—cooperative, individualistic, or competitive. (For instance, if individuals indicated that they preferred equal outcomes for all members of a group, they were classified as being cooperative in orientation; if they indicated that they preferred to maximize their own outcomes and reduce those of others, they were identified as being competitive.) To vary the presence of a negative frame, the researchers gave participants information at the start designed to make them think about the game they would play in terms of either gains (a positive frame) or losses (a negative frame). To induce a positive frame, they told them they would start with 0 points but could win points by making certain decisions; to induce a negative frame, they told them they would start with 22 points but would lose points if they made certain decisions. It was predicted that the negative frame would increase the tendency of persons with a cooperative orientation to make cooperative choices, but would increase the tendency of persons with an individualistic or competitive orientation to defect. As you can see from Figure 9.11, these predictions were confirmed for the cooperative and individualistic orientations. However, persons with a competitive orientation cooperated less regardless of the frame they received. This latter finding was confirmed in another study; so it appears that persons with a competitive orientation have a strong tendency to defect and pursue their own interests—and even getting them to think about a situation in terms of losses can't alter this tendency. They compete no matter what! So personal orientations do play an important role in determining whether individuals will choose to cooperate with others.

Finally, let's consider the role of *communication* in the development of cooperation. Common sense suggests that if individuals can discuss a situation with others, they may soon conclude that the best option is for everyone to cooperate; after all, this will result in gains for all. Surprisingly, though, early research on this commonsense assumption produced mixed results. In many situations the opportunity for group

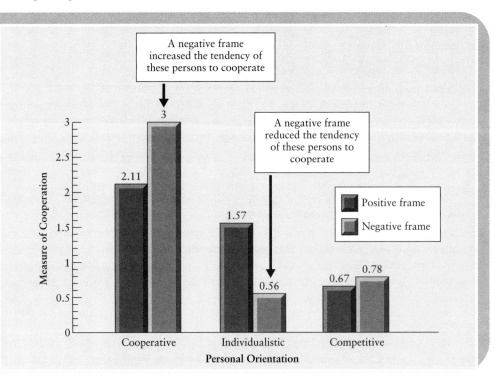

■ Effects of personal orientation on cooperation

FIGURE 9.11 As shown here, a negative frame (describing a situation in terms of potential losses) increased the tendency of persons with a cooperative orientation to cooperate, but reduced the tendency of persons with an individualistic orientation to cooperate. Framing did not significantly change the behaviour of persons with a competitive orientation.

Source: Based on data from DeDreu & McCusker, 1997.

members to communicate with one another about what they should do did *not* increase cooperation. On the contrary, group members seemed to use this opportunity primarily to *threaten* one another, with the result that cooperation did not occur (e.g., Deutsch & Kraus, 1960). Is this always the case? Fortunately, recent findings point to more optimistic conclusions: apparently, communication between group members can lead to increased cooperation, provided certain conditions are met (e.g., Kerr & Kaufman-Gilliland, 1994; Sally, 1998). Specifically, beneficial effects can and do occur if group members make personal commitments to cooperate with one another and if these commitments are backed up by a strong sense of obligation to honor them (e.g. Braver, 1995; Kerr & Kaufman-Gilliland, 1994; Kerr, et al., 1997). In short, cooperation based on communication in social dilemma situations appear to depend more on the effects of personal conscience than on public or group norms.

In sum, several factors, including tendencies toward reciprocity, personal orientations toward cooperation, and communication coupled with personal conscience and commitments, strongly determine what individuals do in situations where they can choose between cooperation and defection. The choice, in short, is neither simple nor automatic; rather, it is the result of a complex interaction between social and personal factors.

KEY POINTS

- *Cooperation*—working together with others to obtain shared goals—is a common aspect of social life.
- However, cooperation does not develop in many situations in which it is possible. One reason is that such situations often involve *social dilemmas*, in which overall joint gains can be increased by cooperation but individuals can increase their own gains by defection.
- Several factors influence whether cooperation occurs in social dilemma situations. These include individuals' tendencies toward *reciprocity*, *personal orientation* toward cooperation, and communication.

Conflict: Its Nature, Causes, and Effects

If prosocial behaviour and cooperation constitute one end of the coordination dimension—a dimension describing how individuals and groups work together—then *conflict* lies at or near the other end. As we noted earlier, conflict is a process in which one individual or group perceives that others have taken or will soon take actions incompatible with that individual's or group's own interests. The key elements in conflict, then, seem to include (1) opposing interests between individuals or groups, (2) recognition of such opposition, (3) the belief by each side that the other will act to interfere with its interests, and (4) actions that in fact produce such interference.

Conflict is, unfortunately, an all-too-common part of social life, and it can be extremely costly to both sides. What factors cause individuals and groups to enter into this seemingly irrational process? And, perhaps even more important, what can be done to reduce such behaviour? These are the questions that social psychologists have addressed in their research.

Major Causes of Conflict

Our definition of conflict emphasizes the existence—and recognition—of incompatible interests. And indeed, incompatible interests constitute the defining feature of conflicts. Interestingly, though, conflicts sometimes fail to develop even though both sides have incompatible interests; and in other cases, conflicts occur even though the two sides don't really have opposing interests—they may simply *believe* that these exist (e.g., DeDreu & Van Lang, 1995; Tjosvold & DeDreu, 1997). Clearly, then, conflict involves much more than opposing interests. In fact, a growing body of evidence suggests that *social* factors may play a role as strong as or even stronger than incompatible interests in initiating conflicts.

One social factor that plays a role in this respect consists of what have been termed *faulty attributions*—errors concerning the causes behind others' behaviour (e.g., Baron, 1989b). When individuals find that their interests have been thwarted, they generally try to determine why this occurred. Was it bad luck? A lack of planning on their part? A lack of needed resources? Or was it due to intentional interference by another person or group? If they conclude that the latter is true, then the seeds for an intense conflict may be planted—*even if other persons actually had nothing to do with the situation*. In other words, erroneous attributions concerning the causes of negative outcomes can and often do play an important role in conflicts, and sometimes cause conflicts to occur when they could readily have been avoided. (See Chapter 8 for a related discussion of the effects of the *hostile attributional bias*.)

Another social factor that seems to play an important role in conflict is what might be termed *faulty communication*—the fact that individuals sometimes communicate with others in a way that angers or annoys them, even though it is not their intention to do so. Have you ever been on the receiving end of harsh criticism—criticism you felt was unfair, insensitive, and not in the least helpful? The results of several studies indicate that feedback of this type, known as *destructive criticism*, can leave the recipient hungry for revenge—and so set the stage for conflicts that, again, do not necessarily stem from incompatible interests (e.g., Baron, 1990a; Cropanzano, 1993).

A third social cause of conflict involves our tendency to perceive our own views as objective and as reflecting reality, but to see those of others as biased by their ideology (e.g., Robinson et al., 1995). As a result of this tendency, which is known as *naive realism*, we may tend to magnify differences between our views and those of others, and so also exaggerate conflicts of interest between us. Interestingly, recent findings indicate that this tendency may be stronger for groups or individuals who currently hold dominant or powerful positions: such persons tend to exaggerate differences between their own positions and those of potential opponents to an even greater degree than is true for individuals or groups who do not hold dominant positions (Keltner & Robinson, 1997).

Finally, personal traits or characteristics, too, seem to play a role in conflict. For example, as mentioned in Chapter 8, *Type A* individuals—ones who are highly competitive, always in a hurry, and relatively irritable—tend to become involved in conflicts more often than calmer and less irritable *Type B* persons (Baron, 1989a).

So where does all this leave us? With the conclusion that conflict does *not* stem solely from opposing interests. On the contrary, it often derives from social factors—long-standing grudges or resentment, the desire for revenge, inaccurate social perceptions, poor communication, and similar factors. In short, conflict, like cooperation, has many different roots. While the most central of these may indeed be incompatible interests, this is far from the entire story, and the social and cognitive causes of this process should definitely not be overlooked.

Resolving Conflicts: Some Useful Techniques

Because conflicts are often very costly, the persons involved usually want to resolve them as quickly as possible. What steps are most useful for reaching this goal?

While many strategies may succeed, two seem especially useful—bargaining and superordinate goals.

Bargaining: The Universal Process

By far the most common strategy for resolving conflicts is **bargaining** or negotiation (e.g., Pruitt & Carnevale, 1993). In this process, opposing sides exchange offers, counteroffers, and concessions, either directly or though representatives. If the bargaining process is successful, a solution acceptable to both sides is attained and the conflict is resolved. If, instead, bargaining is unsuccessful, costly deadlock may result and the conflict may intensify. What factors determine which of these outcomes occurs? As you can probably guess, many play a role.

Bargaining A negotiating process in which opposing sides exchange offers, counteroffers, and concessions, either directly or though representatives.

First, and perhaps most obviously, the outcome of bargaining is determined, in part, by the specific *tactics* adopted by the bargainers. Many of these are designed to accomplish a key goal: to reduce the opponent's aspirations so that this person or group becomes convinced that it cannot get what it wants and should, instead, settle for something more favourable to the other side. Tactics for reducing opponents' aspirations include (1) beginning with an extreme initial offer—one that is very favourable to the side proposing it; (2) the "big lie" technique—convincing the other side that one's break-even point is much higher than it is so that they offer more than would otherwise be the case; for example, a used car salesperson may claim that she will lose money on the deal if she lowers the price, when in fact this is false; and (3) convincing the other side that you have an "out"—that if they won't make a deal with you, you can go elsewhere and get even better terms (Thompson, 1998). Perhaps even more unsettling than these tactics, however, is one involving misrepresentation concerning what are known as *common-value issues*.

Common-value issues are ones on which the opposing sides actually want the same thing, although one or both sides may not realize it. If one side is unaware of a common-value issue, this leaves lots of room for the other side to misrepresent its real position and so gain a key advantage. For instance, imagine a case of divorce in which there are two major issues: custody of the couple's children and alimony for the wife. Suppose that in fact, both husband and wife want the wife to have custody of the children. The husband quickly realizes this, but the wife continues to believe that he wants custody of them. As a result, the husband can suggest that he'll make a concession on this issue, allowing his wife to keep the children, but that in return he expects to pay lower alimony. If she accepts, the husband has used misrepresentation of his real position on the common-value issue—an issue on which the two sides actually agreed—to wring a concession from his wife on another issue. Evidence suggesting that this tactic is actually widely used is provided by a study conducted by O'Connor and Carnevale (1997).

These researchers had students play the role of union and management representatives, who then bargained on five contract issues: salary, vacation, start date of the contract, annual raises, and medical benefits. The two sides actually agreed on the start-date issue (this was the common-value issue); but in one condition (the asymmetric-information condition), one side knew this was so whereas the other did not. In two other conditions, either both sides (complete information) or neither side (incomplete information) had such knowledge. Another aspect of the study involved the motivation given to the bargainers before they started. Half were told to be cooperative—to focus on maximizing joint gains; the others were told to be individualistic—to focus on maximizing their own gains.

O'Connor and Carnevale (1997) predicted that misrepresentation with respect to the common-value issue would occur, and that this would be especially likely in the asymmetric-information condition. As shown in Figure 9.12, these predictions were confirmed. The researchers also predicted that individuals who used this tactic would

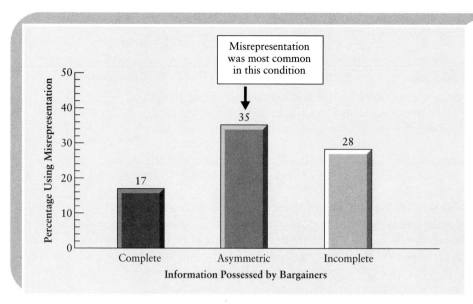

Misrepresentation was most common in this condition

■ Misrepresentation about a common-value issue: An unethical but successful tactic in bargaining

FIGURE 9.12 As shown here, when only one person in a bargaining situation knew that both he or she and the opponent held the same position on an important issue (the asymmetric information condition), this person often took advantage of this knowledge, misrepresenting his or her actual position in order to obtain concessions from the opponent on other issues.

Source: Based on data from O.Connor & Carnevale, 1997.

obtain better outcomes in the bargaining; findings supported this hypothesis too. What kind of misrepresentation did the bargainers who knew about the common-value issue use? There were both *commissions*, involving overt efforts to mislead the other side (e.g., "Okay...I'll go along with that; but since we're missing a couple of weeks, you should grant us a larger raise"), and *omissions*—simple failure to mention the fact that the two sides agreed on one issue. In sum, bargainers use many different tactics to lower the hopes of their opponents; and if used with skill, these tactics can succeed very well.

A second, and very important, determinant of the outcome of bargaining involves the bargainers' overall *orientations* toward the process (Pruitt & Carnevale, 1993). People taking part in negotiations can approach such discussions from either of two distinct perspectives. They can view the negotiations as "win-lose" situations, in which gains by one side are necessarily linked with losses for the other. Or they can approach negotiations as potential "win-win" situations, in which the interests of the two sides are not necessarily incompatible and in which the potential gains of both sides can be maximized.

Not all situations offer the potential for win-win agreements; but, as our discussion of common-value issues suggests, many conflicts that at first glance seem to involve head-on clashes do in fact provide such possibilities. If participants are willing to explore all options carefully, they can sometimes attain what are known as *integrative agreements*—ones that offer greater joint benefits than simple compromise (in which all differences are split down the middle). An example: Suppose that two cooks are preparing recipes that call for an entire orange, and they have only one orange between them. What should they do? One possibility is to divide the orange in half. That leaves both with less than they need. Suppose, however, that one cook needs all the juice and the other needs all the peel. Here, a much better solution is possible: they can share the orange, each using the part she or he needs. Many techniques for attaining such integrative solutions exist; a few of these are summarized in Table 9.1.

Finally, the outcomes of bargaining are strongly influenced by the perceptions of the two sides—especially by errors in perception bargainers may make. One such error is known as the **incompatibility error**—the tendency for both sides to assume that their interests are entirely incompatible. This error overlooks the fact that the sides agree, or at least are largely in agreement, on some issues (e.g., Thompson & Hastie, 1990). Another error is known as the **fixed-sum error**—the tendency to assume that each side places the same importance or priority as the other on every issue (e.g., Thompson, 1998). Again, this assumption may be wrong. For instance, suppose three friends are discussing

Incompatibility Error The tendency for both sides in a negotiation to assume that their interests are entirely incompatible.

Fixed-sum Error The tendency for bargainers to assume that each side places the same importance or priority as the other on every issue.

Many different strategies can be useful in attaining integrative agreements—ones that offer better outcomes than simple compromise. A few of these are summarized here.

TABLE 9.1 Tactics for reaching integrative agreements

Tactic	Description
Broadening the pie	Available resources are increased so that both sides can obtain their major goals.
Nonspecific compensation	One side gets what it wants; the other is compensated on an unrelated issue.
Logrolling	Each party makes concessions on low-priority issues in exchange for concessions on issues it values more highly.
Bridging	Neither party gets its initial demands, but a new option that satisfies the major interests of both sides is developed.
Cost cutting	One party gets what it desires, and the costs to the other party are reduced in some manner.

what apartment to rent for the coming year. They disagree on this overall issue, but it turns out that they place different weights on (1) rent, (2) location, and (3) number of bathrooms. For one friend, rent is the most important factor; for another, location is key; and for the third, number of bathrooms is most important. The friends may be able to find an apartment on which they all agree by juggling these different priorities so that all get what they want, or close to it, on their top issue. Finally, recent findings indicate that bargainers often suffer from another error known as *transparency overestimation*—the belief that their goals and motives are more clearly recognized by their opponents than is actually true (Vorauer & Claude, 1998). This overestimation can lead to serious problems. For instance, bargainer A may believe that she has clearly signaled to the other side her intention to compromise, but her opponent, bargainer B, may continue to act in a "tough" manner. In fact, bargainer B may have failed to notice A's compromise signal, but bargainer A may nonetheless become angry with her opponent for not responding.

Many other factors too, determine the outcome of bargaining, but the ones we've discussed are among the most important. Thus, all are worth considering the next time you must bargain with others over one or more issues.

Superordinate Goals: "We're All in This Together"
As we saw in Chapter 5, individuals often divide the world into two opposing camps— "us" and "them." They perceive members of their own group (us) as quite different from, and usually better than, people belonging to other groups (them). These tendencies to magnify differences between one's own group and others and to disparage outsiders are very powerful and often play a role in the occurrence and persistence of conflicts. Fortunately, they can be countered through the induction of **superordinate goals**—goals that both sides seek and that tie their interests together rather than driving them apart (e.g., Sherif et al., 1961; Tjosvold, 1993). Mediators in a dispute will often look for such goals in order to overcome such tactics as misrepresentation of common value issues. If a mediator

Superordinate Goals
Goals that both sides to a conflict seek and that tie their interests together rather than driving them apart.

had pointed out, in the example used earlier, that *both* parents put their children's welfare first and that must be the primary consideration, the discussion might have begun on a better footing.

In sum, resolution of conflicts can be achieved through bargaining and the introduction of superordinate goals, though there are many potential pitfalls along the way. As the next On the Applied Side section discusses, there are sometimes added barriers to resolution introduced when conflict occurs across ethnic boundaries.

On the **Applied Side**

Conflict Across Ethnic and Cultural Boundaries

When individuals engage in conflict, the outcomes they receive are important to them. But, as noted by Tyler and Lind (1992) and other social psychologists (e.g., Ohbuchi, Chiba, & Fukushima, 1994), this is far from the entire story. In addition, because conflicts often involve individuals who know each other well—for instance, people who work together—the persons involved are often also interested in the *quality* of their relationships. Have they been treated with respect and dignity? Does the other side behave in a way suggesting that it can be trusted? According to a perspective known as the *relational model*, these are the kinds of questions individuals consider (e.g., Huo et al., 1996).

At this point another interesting issue arises. In recent decades the world's economy has become increasingly globalized. In addition, migration has risen to unprecedented heights. This means that ever-increasing numbers of people from different cultural and ethnic backgrounds now come into contact with one another and, inevitably, experience conflict. Will relational concerns be stronger or weaker in these cross-cultural contexts? Interestingly, the relational model suggests that they may be weaker, for two important reasons. First, the way we are treated by members of our own group may tell us more about how they view us than the way we are treated by people outside our own group. Second, we are less confident of our ability to "read" people from other cultures accurately, so we may be less likely to rely on their treatment of us as a source of useful information. Thus, when interacting with people from other groups, we may focus more on the outcomes we experience than on relational concerns.

Support for this reasoning has been reported in recent research by Tyler and his colleagues (1998). In the first of these studies, employees of a large university were asked to describe recent conflicts with their supervisor and to rate both the *outcomes* they received (e.g., "How favourable was the outcome to you?") and their *treatment* by this person (e.g., "How politely were you treated?" "How much concern was shown for your rights?"). In addition, participants also rated their willingness to accept the supervisor's decision in this dispute. Because participants and their supervisors varied in ethnic background, it was possible to compare employees' concern with how they were treated with their concern over outcomes in cases where these individuals were of the same ethnic background as their supervisor and in cases where they were of different backgrounds. Results were clear: For within-group conflicts, relational factors were more important in determining acceptance of the supervisor's decision; for between-group conflicts, outcomes were more important.

These findings were replicated in another study, which was conducted in Japan and examined disputes between Japanese and Western teachers of English. Again, participants rated the kind of treatment they received from a third party who mediated such disputes, the outcomes they received, and the extent to which they accepted these decisions. Results again indicated that relational concerns were more important for disputes between persons belonging to the same culture, while outcomes were more important for disputes involving persons from the two cultures.

These findings have important implications for efforts to resolve conflicts. In many conflicts, one or even both sides to a dispute may find the outcomes they receive disappointing. Yet individuals may still accept such results if they feel that they were treated with dignity and respect (e.g., Tyler & Smith, 1997). Unfortunately, however, such "relational adjustments" seem less likely to occur in conflicts between persons from different cultures—because in such situations, each sides focuses primarily on the outcomes it receives. In short, relational factors may combine with stereotyping, the "us" versus "them" division, and several other factors to make cross-cultural conflicts especially difficult to resolve. In a world where such conflicts seem likely to be increasingly common, this finding suggests the need for vigorous steps to develop new strategies for resolving them effectively and achieving a just outcome—something we'll consider in the next section.

PERCEIVED FAIRNESS IN GROUPS: GETTING WHAT WE DESERVE—OR ELSE!

Group membership, we have already noted, is a two-way street. On the one hand, groups demand—and generally receive—contributions from their members: adherence to the group's norms, effort on group tasks, support of the group and its goals. On the other hand, individuals expect to get something back for these investments: satisfaction of their basic needs, information, boosts to their self-concept. In addition, they usually want something else: *fair treatment* by the group and other group members. In other words, individuals want to feel that what they receive from any group to which they belong is a fair reflection of what they have contributed to the group (Greenberg, 1993a; Tyler, 1994). How important is this desire for fairness? If you've ever been in a situation where you felt that you were being shortchanged by others, you already know the answer: very strong indeed. In situations where we feel that we are being treated unfairly, we often experience anger, resentment, and a strong desire to even the score (Croponazno, 1993; Scher, 1997).

Judgments of Fairness: Outcomes, Procedures, and Courtesy

One major circumstance that leads individuals to perceive that they are being treated unfairly is an imbalance between the *contributions*, or inputs, individuals make to a relationship or group and the *outcomes* they receive in return—their share of available rewards (Adams, 1965). In general, we expect these to be *proportional* to those of others in the group: the more a person contributes, the larger the share of available reward that person should receive. Thus if someone who makes a large contribution to a group receives a lion's share of the rewards, while someone who makes a small contribution receives a much smaller share, everything is fine: contributions and outcomes are in balance, and we perceive that fairness or *equity* exists. However, when there is a perceived imbalance in contributions and subsequent rewards—for example, when someone's contributions are perceived to be large and yet the rewards are small—an experience of *inequity* or unfairness results. A large body of research findings indicate that in fact, we do base many of our judgments of fairness on this kind of cognitive equation (see Figure 9.13). We compare the ratio of our inputs and outcomes to those of other persons to determine whether we are being treated fairly. Social psychologists refer to this as **distributive justice**—whether individuals feel they are receiving a fair share of available rewards proportionate to their contributions to the group or any social relationship.

Two more points are worth carefully noting. First, judgments about distributive justice are very much in the eye of the beholder; *we* do the comparing and *we* decide whether our share of available rewards is fair relative to that of other group members (Greenberg, 1990). Second, we are much more sensitive about receiving *less* than we feel we deserve than about receiving *more* than we feel we deserve. In other words, the *self-serving bias* we described in Chapter 2 operates strongly in this context (Greenberg, 1996). This is especially likely to occur when individuals consider the division of available rewards between themselves and others (see Figure 9.14); in such cases, they tend to view "splits" favouring themselves as fair even if these would appear unfair or unjustified to an outside observer (e.g., Diekman et al., 1997).

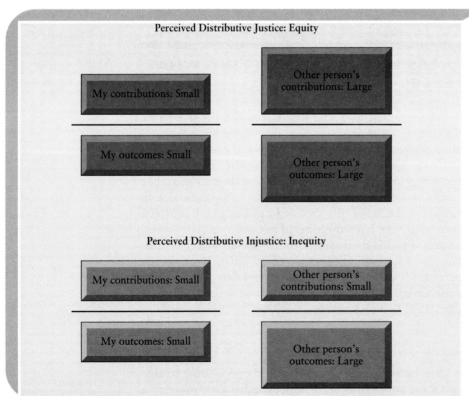

Perceived Distributive Justice: Equity

My contributions: Small

My outcomes: Small

Other person's contributions: Large

Other person's outcomes: Large

Perceived Distributive Injustice: Inequity

My contributions: Small

My outcomes: Small

Other person's contributions: Small

Other person's outcomes: Large

■ Distributive justice: Deciding whether we have received our fair share

FIGURE 9.13 In order to determine whether they have received a fair share of available rewards, individuals compare the ratio of their own contributions and outcomes with other persons' ratios. If these are roughly in balance, then they perceive that *equity*—fairness— exists (top panel). If they are out of balance, then they perceive that *inequity*—unfairness—exists.

■ The self-serving bias: Its role in perceived fairness

FIGURE 9.14 Research findings indicate that we are extremely sensitive to receiving less than we feel we deserve. As shown here, even very small departures from our perceived fair share can cause us to experience strong emotional reactions. In other words, the self-serving bias seems to play a role in our judgments of fairness.

Source: King Features Syndicate, 1996.

In addition to concern over how much we receive relative to others, we are also interested in (1) the procedures followed in the allocation of available rewards—**procedural justice**; and (2) the considerateness and courtesy shown to us by the parties responsible for dividing the available rewards—**interpersonal justice** (Folger & Bies, 1989; Shapiro, Buttner, & Barry, 1995).

What factors influence judgments concerning procedural justice? Ones such as these: (1) the *consistency* of procedures—the extent to which they are applied in the same manner to all persons; (2) *accuracy*—the extent to which procedures are based on accurate information about the relative contributions of all group members; and (3) *opportunity for corrections*—the extent to which any errors in distributions can be adjusted (e.g., Brockner et al., 1994; Leventhal, Karuza, & Fry, 1980).

What about *interpersonal justice*—what factors play a role with respect to this type of fairness? Research on this topic is quite recent, but already two important factors have been identified. The first is the extent to which individuals feel they were given clear and rational reasons for why they received what they did. Individuals will perceive they have been treated fairly to the extent that such information is provided. A second factor involves the courtesy and sensitivity with which reward allocations are presented. Have we been treated with the respect that we deserve? Or have the people in charge of distributing rewards acted in a high-handed, insensitive manner? These are the kind of questions we ask ourselves in deciding whether we have been treated in an interpersonally fair manner.

Are any of these types of justice more important than the others? Although you might guess that we would pay more attention to the rewards we receive (i.e., distributive justice) than to procedures or courtesy, a growing body of evidence suggests that this is not necessarily so—we also care quite strongly about both procedures and courtesy (e.g., Brockner & Wiesenfeld, 1996; Greenberg & Alge, 1997). In addition, we seem to be most strongly influenced by the information we receive first. In other words, if we learn first about the *outcomes* we will receive and only later about *procedures*, our judgments of fairness are more strongly influenced by outcome information. If, instead, we learn first about procedures and only then about outcomes, our judgments are more strongly affected by procedure-related information (Van den Bos, Vermunt, & Wilke, 1997). Why is this the case?

Procedural Justice
The fairness of the procedures used to allocate available rewards among group members.

Interpersonal Justice
Courtesy and consideration shown to group members by those responsible for distributing rewards; an important factor in perceived fairness.

Apparently because the information we receive first plays a key role in shaping what are known as *fairness heuristics*—rules we use for evaluating the overall fairness of a situation (e.g., Lind, 1994). As we saw in Chapter 2, we often rely on heuristics in making judgments about other persons and social situations, and fairness is no exception to this general rule.

Reactions to Perceived Unfairness: Tactics for Dealing with Injustice

If *dissonance* is unpleasant (see Chapter 3), then *inequity*—the perception that one has been cheated or shortchanged by others—is downright obnoxious. As we noted earlier, most people react quite strongly to such treatment. But what, precisely, do they do? What steps do they take to restore fairness, or at least to reduce perceptions of unfairness? Here are some of the most important strategies that people adopt.

Individuals who perceive their situation as one of *distributive injustice* often attempt to restore fairness through a number of tactics. Most important are attempts at *changing the balance of contributions and outcomes* for themselves or others. For example, they may reduce contributions or demand larger rewards. If this does not work, they may take more drastic actions, such as leaving the group altogether. All these reactions are readily visible in workplaces—settings where judgments concerning fairness play a key role. Employees who feel that they are being underpaid may come in late, leave early, do less on the job. And/or they may request more benefits—higher pay, more vacation, and so on. If these tactics fail, they may protest; join a union and go out on strike; or, ultimately, quit and look for another job.

If, in contrast, unfairness relates primarily to procedures (*procedural justice*) or a lack of courtesy on the part of the persons who announce or deliver reward divisions (*interpersonal justice*), individuals may adopt different tactics. Procedures are often harder to change than specific outcomes, because they frequently go on behind closed doors and may depart from announced policies in many ways. Similarly, changing the negative attitudes or personality traits that lie behind inconsiderate treatment by bosses, professors, or other reward allocators is a difficult if not impossible task. The result? Individuals who feel that they have been treated unfairly in these ways often turn to more *covert techniques* to even the score. For instance, a growing body of evidence suggests that feelings of procedural or interpersonal unfairness lie behind many instances of employee theft and sabotage (e.g., Greenberg & Scott, 1996). And, as we noted in Chapter 8, feelings of unfairness also play a major role in many forms of workplace aggression—especially in subtle, hidden actions individuals perform to get even with others who they believe have treated them unfairly.

Finally, individuals who feel that they have been treated unfairly but conclude that there is little they can do about it may cope with the situation simply by *changing their perceptions*. They may conclude, in short, that they are being treated fairly—because, for instance, other persons who receive larger rewards somehow *deserve* this special treatment by virtue of possessing something "special": extra talent, greater experience, a bigger reputation, or some other special qualities (see Figure 9.15). In such cases, individuals who feel that they cannot eliminate unfairness can at least cope with it and reduce the discomfort it produces, even though they may continue to be treated unfairly by others.

■ Changing perceptions of injustice

FIGURE 9.15 For centuries monarchs and their nobles, as shown here in the British parliament, were considered to *deserve* their privileged position of power because of their right of birth. It is only as we move into the twenty-first century that Britons have changed their perceptions of justice and decided to abolish the House of Lords, where hereditary Peers had the automatic right to sit.

KEY POINTS

● Individuals wish to be treated fairly by the groups to which they belong. Fairness can be judged in terms of outcomes (*distributive justice*), in terms of procedures (*procedural justice*), or in terms of courteous treatment (*interpersonal justice*).

● When individuals feel that they have been treated unfairly, they often take steps to restore fairness.

● These steps include moderating their contributions, demanding greater rewards, protesting, engaging in covert actions such as employee theft or sabotage, and/or changing their own perceptions about fairness.

Ideas to Take with You

Maximizing Your Own Performance

Social facilitation effects seem to occur because the presence of others is arousing. Arousal increases our tendency to perform dominant responses. If these are correct for the situation, our performance is improved; if they are incorrect, our performance is impaired. This analysis leads to several practical suggestions.

Study Alone, But Take Tests In The Presence of Others.
If you study alone, you'll avoid the distraction caused by other persons and so will learn new material more efficiently. If you have studied hard, your dominant responses will probably be correct ones; so when you take a test, the increased arousal generated by other persons will improve your performance.

Work on simple tasks in front of an audience.
The presence of an audience will increase your arousal and thus enhance your ability to exert physical effort on tasks requiring pure physical effort.

Minimizing Social Loafing By Others

Social loafing occurs when persons working together put out less effort than they would if they were working alone. This can be costly to you if you work hard but others goof off. Here are some ways you can avoid such outcomes.

Don't Let Social Loafers Hide!
Make sure that the contribution of each member of the group can be assessed individually.

Make Sure That Each Person's Contribution Is Unique.
Every group member's contribution should be unique—not identical to that of others. In this way, each person can be held personally responsible for what he or she produces, and assessment of individual contribution is easier.

Increase Commitment.
Try to work only with people who are committed to the group's goals. If you cannot choose your group members, use other means of increasing commitment. These can be informal, such as ensuring that each member contributes to group plans and agrees in front of other group members to accomplish certain tasks; or formal, such as drawing up a "group contract" clearly outlining expectations of each person in the group and getting all group members to sign it.

Summary and Review of Key Points

Groups: Their Nature and Function

● A *group* consists of two or more interacting persons who share common goals, have a stable (i.e., lasting) relationship, are somehow interdependent, and perceive that they are in fact part of a group.

People join groups to satisfy important needs, reach goals they can't achieve alone, boost their self-identity, and/or gain safety.

Commitment to groups—termed *organizational commitment*—consists of affective, continuance and normative components.

Groups influence their members in many ways, but such effects are often produced through *roles*, *status*, *norms*, and *cohesiveness*.

How Groups Affect Individual Performance: Facilitation or Social Loafing?

● The mere presence of other persons either as an audience or as coactors can influence our performance on many tasks. Such effects are known as *social facilitation*.

The *drive theory of social facilitation* suggests that the presence of others is arousing and can either increase or reduce performance, depending on whether dominant responses in a given situation are correct or incorrect.

The *distraction-conflict theory* suggests that the presence of others is arousing because it induces conflicting tendencies to focus on the task being performed and on an audience or coactors. This theory helps explain why social facilitation occurs for animals as well as people.

When individuals work together on a task, *social loafing*—reduced output by each group member—sometimes occurs.

According to the *collective effort model* (CEM), such effects occur because when working together with others as compared to working alone, individuals experience weaker links between their effort and outcomes.

Groups can reduce social loafing in several ways: by making outputs individually identifiable, by increasing commitment to the task and sense of task importance, and by building group cohesiveness.

Decision Making by Groups: How it Occurs and the Pitfalls it Faces

● It is widely believed that groups make better decisions than individuals. However, research findings indicate that groups are often subject to *group polarization effects*, which lead them to make more extreme decisions than individuals.

In addition, groups often suffer from *groupthink*—when a desire to achieve consensus takes precedence over reaching the right decision.

Groups often fail to pool information known only to some members. As the *information sampling model* suggests, their decisions tend to reflect only the information most members already share.

Coordination in Groups: Cooperation or Conflict?

● *Cooperation*—working together with others to obtain shared goals—is a common aspect of social life.

However, cooperation does not develop in many situations in which it is possible. One reason is that such situations often involve *social dilemmas*, in which overall joint gains can be increased by cooperation but individuals can increase their own gains by defection.

Several factors influence whether cooperation occurs in social dilemma situations. These include individuals' tendencies toward *reciprocity*, *personal orientation* toward cooperation, and communication.

Conflict is a process that begins when individuals or groups perceive that others' interests are incompatible with their own.

Conflict can also stem from social factors such as faulty attributions, poor communication, the tendency to perceive our own views as objective, and personal traits.

Conflict can be reduced in many ways, but bargaining and the induction of *superordinate goals* seem to be most effective.

When individuals experience conflicts with members of their own cultural or ethnic groups, they often focus on *relational* concerns. In conflicts with persons from other groups, however, they tend to focus on *outcome* concerns.

Perceived Fairness in Groups: Getting What We Deserve—or Else!

● Individuals wish to be treated fairly by the groups to which they belong. Fairness can be judged in terms of outcomes (*distributive justice*), in terms of procedures (*procedural justice*), or in terms of courteous treatment (*interpersonal justice*).

When individuals feel that they have been treated unfairly, they often take steps to restore fairness.

These steps include moderating their contributions, demanding greater rewards, protesting, engaging in covert actions such as employee theft or sabotage, and/or changing their own perceptions about fairness.

For More Information

Baron, R. S., Kerr, N. L., & Miller, N. (1992). *Group process, group decision, group action.* Pacific Grove, CA: Brooks/Cole.

This book covers many of the topics examined in this chapter, including effects of groups on task performance, social facilitation, and decision making. Written in a clear and straightforward style, it provides an excellent overview of research on these important topics.

Thompson, L. (1998). *The mind and heart of the negotiator.* Upper Saddle River, NJ: Prentice Hall.

In this well-written and relatively brief book, a noted researcher describes the nature of negotiation from the perspective of modern social psychology. The roles of various cognitive processes and biases, perceived fairness, past experience, and group processes are all described. An excellent source to consult if you'd like to know more about bargaining.

Witte, E., & Davis, J. H. (Eds.). (1996). *Understanding group behavior: Consensual action by small groups.* Hillsdale, NJ: Erlbaum.

Noted experts summarize existing knowledge about many aspects of group behaviour. The sections on decision making are especially interesting, and expand greatly upon the information on this topic presented in this chapter.

Weblinks

www.trinity.edu/~mkearl/socpsy-8.html
Collective Behavior and the Social Psychologies of Social Institutions

www.u.arizona.edu/~jearl/cbsm.html
American Sociological Association—Collective Behavior and Social Movements

www.communitypsychology.net/
Community Psychology Net

home.sol.no/~hmelberg/papers/980522.htm
"Is Ethnic Conflict the Outcome of Individual Choices?" by Hans O. Melberg, University of Oslo

www.spiraldynamics.com/documents/hotspots/ Kosovo/Kosovo_Balkans_Bloom.htm
"The Balkans" by Harold Bloom

CHAPTER TEN

Applied Social Psychology:

Health, Work and Legal Applications

We began this book by emphasizing how useful social psychology can be when applied to social problems. We end the book by reiterating that point in this applied chapter. By **applied social psychology** we mean the use of social psychological principles and research methods in real-world settings in efforts to solve a variety of individual and societal problems (Weyant, 1986). Applications of social psychology have expanded tremendously in recent years. You will recall that this was one of the trends mentioned in Chapter 1. The fact that social psychology can be applied to so many diverse areas, is a mark of the strength and relevance of its accumulated theory and research. We also mentioned in Chapter 1 that the origins of psychology in Canada were very much based in applied research and this tradition has continued to the present. Many of the Canadian social psychologists mentioned in this book are involved in applying their ideas and research to Canadian social problems. Perhaps the most famous of the early applied contributions comes from the work of Wallace Lambert at McGill University. The following Cornerstones section describes his examination of second language learning that provided a model.

Applied Social Psychology
Psychological research and practice in real-world settings, directed toward the understanding of human social behaviour and the attempted solution of social problems.

Cornerstones

Second Language Learning and Bilingualism: The Contribution of Wallace Lambert

Second language learning and bilingualism has been a particularly important issue in Canada's bilingual society. It is not surprising, therefore, that Canadian researchers were pioneers in this area and remain on the forefront of research today. The most notable of these researchers is Wallace Lambert of McGill University, whose work has extended over 30 years.

Canada became an officially bilingual country in 1969 when the *Official Languages Act* was endorsed by Parliament, giving equal status to the English and French languages. Currently, 83 percent of the population can speak English, 32 percent can speak French, and 16 percent are English-French bilingual. This latter figure represents a 33 percent increase since the 1950s in the proportion of the population who are bilingual (Harrison & Marmen, 1994).

One reason for this increase may be the growth of French immersion programs for non-Francophone children. These programs were initiated in Quebec in 1965, when the Protestant School Board of Montreal launched the "St.

Lambert Project" for children of Anglophone and immigrant parents. Wallace Lambert and his colleagues investigated the children's progress, and the results of their research have guided the introduction of French immersion programs since that time (Genesee, 1984; Lambert & Tucker, 1972). Children in the project were taught entirely in French from kindergarten to grade two. English language was introduced for half-hour periods during grade two and the proportion of the curriculum taught in English was gradually increased until by grade seven this included about half of the classes. The progress of these mostly Anglophone children was compared with that of Anglophone children taught in English and Francophone children taught in French.

Parents at that time, as now, had many questions about the effects of French immersion. For example, does being initially taught exclusively in French create deficits in English language proficiency? Would problems arise if children were taught a particular subject (e.g., history or mathematics) in French originally and then had to switch to English? Results of Lambert's research were encouraging. Children in the St. Lambert project achieved a level of spoken French far superior to that of Anglophone children in conventional French-as-a-second-language programs, though they did not quite achieve the proficiency of native French speakers. Further, their written and oral skills in English were as good as those of the children taught in English (Lambert, 1974). There was also no deficit shown if children were tested in English on a subject that they had studied in French. In fact, the overall results of the St. Lambert project, and subsequent research into similar programs, tend to confirm that early French immersion produces no detrimental effects on English language development or progress of other academic subjects, while French language progress is much enhanced (Genesee, 1984).

Beyond the academic effects of acquiring a second language, Lambert has been interested in the *social* implications of such bilingualism for the individual and for group relations. For example, the St. Lambert project found that the children involved had a more positive attitude to Francophones than conventionally educated Anglophone children. However, later research suggested that this more positive attitude may not last into adulthood (Genesee, 1984).

Lambert has also suggested (1978; Lambert & Taylor, 1984) that acquiring a second language may have different implications for a majority individual and a minority individual. The acquisition of a second language may be entirely beneficial for persons who belong to the majority group in a particular society, enhancing their academic, employment, and social opportunities. Lambert termed this *additive bilingualism*. However, there may be some personal and social loss involved in second language acquisition (usually the language of the majority) for the minority individual. For example, there may be a danger of loss of one's own identity and of the strength of one's native language in the community. Lambert termed this *subtractive bilingualism*. The bilingual minority individual may find him- or herself drawn increasingly to participate in the majority culture and communicate in that language, with consequent losses of own culture and sense of social identity. For example, Bourhis's (1990) research examined communication in the bilingual New Brunswick civil service. Anglophones are a majority in that context and tend to be of higher status. He found that Francophones were more likely to switch to English (even if not fluent) when addressed in that language by an Anglophone colleague than a fully bilingual Anglophone was to switch to French when addressed in that language.

Lambert's body of work has combined theoretical and applied research in addressing social problems: a true example of Lewin's *action research*. As Lewin suggested (1948), social psychologists can also be agents of social change. Building on the pioneering research described above, many researchers in Quebec continue to investigate the social psychology of language, studying, for example, its importance to intergroup relations and cross-cultural communication (Bourhis, 1979, 1984; Genesee & Bourhis, 1988) or to individual social identity and acculturation (Clément, 1987; Young & Gardner, 1990).

Because of the tremendous expansion of *applied social psychology* in the years since Wallace Lambert carried out his classic research, no one chapter can possibly represent the breadth of this exciting work. What we do provide, however, is selections from three major applied areas. The first two of these sections (applications related to *health* and to *work* issues) are well established disciplines with extensive literatures; the last section (applications to the *legal system*) provides a sample of a more recent, but rapidly developing, applied topic. These three topics will give you an idea of the exciting work being carried out in today's "action research."

APPLYING SOCIAL PSYCHOLOGY TO HEALTH ISSUES

Though you may think of health and illness in terms of physical processes and the field of medicine, we now know that psychological factors affect all aspects of our physical well-being (Rodin & Salovey, 1989). **Health psychology** is the specialty that studies the psychological processes affecting the development, prevention, and treatment of physical illness (Glass, 1989). Let's consider a number of ways in which social psychological research has been applied to health.

Health Psychology
The study of the effects of psychological factors in the origins, prevention, and treatment of physical illness.

Processing Health-Related Information

If headlines were our main source of knowledge, we would live in constant fear of AIDS, Lyme disease, mad cow disease, flesh-eating bacteria, and new viruses from African monkeys that turn our insides into spaghetti. In contrast to the headlines, the latest Health Canada report on the health of Canadians paints a positive picture (Health Canada, 2000). Life expectancy in Canada has reached an all-time high of 81.4 years for women and 75.7 years for men; ranking in the top three in the world. There has also been a decline in the infant mortality rate. Further improvements relevant to health include the first-ever decline in the incidence of cancer, as well as decreased use of drugs and cigarettes; even the accidental death rate is declining (Easterbrook, 1999). We tend to overestimate the threat of disease because of the workings of the *availability heuristic* (discussed in Chapters 2). How can we make sensible use of information on health and disease?

The first step in attempting to maintain good health and prevent illness is the requirement that we process the very large amount of health information that bombards us daily (Thompson, 1992). We are told which foods to eat and which to avoid, which vitamins and minerals are especially important, the vital importance of exercise, the effects of a multitude of supplements from St. John's Wort to grapefruit seed extract, and on and on (Greenwald, 1998). Then, as suggested in Figure 10.1, later on we may very well be told that new research findings indicate something different. One of the more pleasant examples of health-related news is one recent finding that people who eat candy

■ When health information is inconsistent, do what you want?

FIGURE 10.1 Though it is frustrating to try to take account of health-related information that changes on the basis of new data, Sarge's solution is probably not the wisest alternative.

regularly live about one year longer than those who completely avoid candy (Bowman, 1998). While waiting for scientific research to sort out inconsistencies, we must continue to make decisions about drinking alcohol, adding beta carotene supplements to our diets, avoiding specific kinds of fat, smoking cigars, and so forth.

When health information is unclear, people tend to accept some of the findings and reject others. Even when the information is very clear, some people change their behaviour radically but others are reluctant to modify what they do. What do we know about why people react in such divergent ways?

One factor is the affective nature of health warnings. Experts often present data about disease prevention in an emotion-arousing manner in the hope that fear will motivate us to do the right thing. One difficulty with this approach is that people often reject as "untrue" a health message that arouses anxiety. The rejection acts to reduce our anxiety and thus makes it unnecessary for us to change our behaviour (Liberman & Chaiken, 1992). Information about something as frightening as breast cancer, for example, can activate defence mechanisms that interfere with women's attending to, remembering, and/or acting on relevant information about the importance of early detection (Millar, 1997).

One common way to deal with threatening information actually increases the odds that the person will engage in behaviour involving health risks. Consider a situation in which unmarried individuals are contemplating sexual intercourse. Among many factors to consider are the threat of disease and the threat of unwanted pregnancy. Such considerations create anxiety. One "remedy" for anxiety is alcohol. Whenever people drink alcohol, anxiety is decreased—but so is cognitive capacity. The resulting *alcohol myopia* (Steele & Josephs, 1990) causes people to focus on the perceived benefits of having intercourse rather than on the potential negative consequences of failure to use condoms (MacDonald, Zanna, & Fong, 1996). Thus, drinking can lead to unsafe sex, and can also lead to unsafe driving and unsafe dining.

Altogether, the findings concerning the effects of health-related messages involving fear and threat are complex. Rothman and his colleagues (1993) were able to show, however, that a *positively framed* message is best for motivating *preventive* behaviour ("Eat high-fibre food to promote good health and prevent disease"), whereas a *negatively framed* message is best for motivating *detection* behaviour ("Get a Pap smear annually to avoid the pain and suffering associated with uterine cancer").

Stress and Health

Stress Any physical or psychological event perceived as being able to cause us harm or distress.

Coping Responding to stress in a way that reduces the threat and its effects; includes what a person does, feels, or thinks in order to master, tolerate, or decrease the negative effects of a stressful situation.

At least since World War II, psychologists have been interested in **stress** and its effects on human behaviour (Lazarus, 1993). For the present purposes, this term is defined as any physical or psychological event perceived as being able to cause us harm or distress. The original focus on the physical aspects of stress (Selye, 1956) was soon broadened to include the psychological (Lazarus, 1966). In response to perceived physical or psychological danger, the individual feels threatened and engages in **coping** behaviour in an attempt to deal with stressful situations and their emotional reactions to them (Taylor, Buunk, & Aspinwall, 1990). Of special importance is the effect of stress on physical illness.

The Relationship Between Stress and Illness

Research consistently indicates that as stress increases, depression and illness become more likely. And we encounter a great many sources of stress. Most common sources are occupational stresses such as work overload, lack of control in the work environment, confusion about one's role, and the worst work-related stress—unemployment (Marshall & Barnett, 1993; Revicki et al., 1993; Shaefer & Moos, 1993; Schwarzer,

Jerusalem, & Hahn, 1994). For college students, common sources of stress include low grades, the divorce of parents, or problems revolving around romance and sexuality (Brody, 1989).

For each of us, everyday hassles such as arguing with loved ones (Chapman, Hobfoll, & Ritter, 1997) or living under crowded conditions (Evans, Lepore, & Schroeder, 1996), commuting in heavy traffic (Weinberger, Hiner, & Tierney, 1987), and dealing with environmental noise (Evans, Bullinger, & Hygge, 1998; Staples, 1996) is associated with an increased probability of developing a cold or flu. With a more serious problem such as the death of a loved one or facing active warfare the likelihood of becoming ill is even greater (King et al., 1998; Schleifer, et al., 1983). When several negative events occur in the same general time period, they appear to have a cumulative effect (Seta, Seta, & Wong, 1991); that is, as the total number of stressful experiences increases, the probability of illness increases (Cohen, Tyrrell, & Smith, 1993).

How, exactly, could stress result in illness? In general, those who are stressed report a negative affective state, aches and pains, and more physical symptoms of illness (Affleck et al., 1994; Brown & Moskowitz, 1997); but the effects of stress go

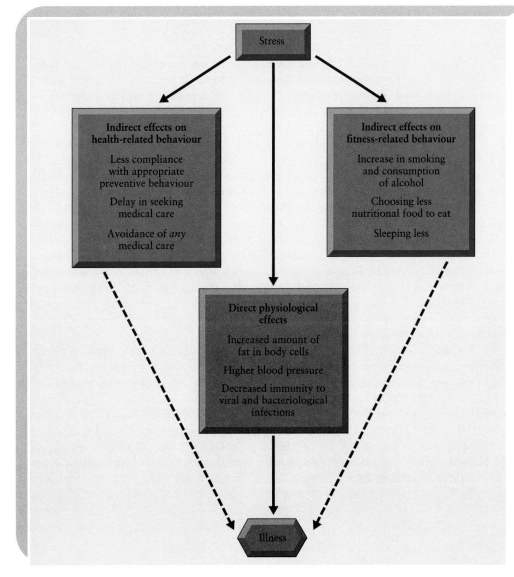

■ Stress and illness: Direct and indirect effects

FIGURE 10.2 It has long been known that as stress increases, the likelihood of illness also increases. The mechanisms underlying this relationship are gradually beginning to be understood. It appears that stress has indirect effects (it leads to behavioural changes) as well as direct physiological effects.

Source: Based on material in Baum, 1994.

beyond that. As outlined in Figure 10.2, Baum (1994) proposes both direct and indirect effects of stress. There are indirect effects when the emotional turmoil (depression and worry) caused by stress interferes with health-related behaviours such as seeking medical care or eating a balanced diet (Whisman & Kwon, 1993; Wiebe & McCallum, 1986). There are also direct physiological effects in that stress delays the healing process in wounds, has adverse effects on the endocrine system, and causes the body's immune system to function less well (Kiecolt-Glaser et al., 1998; Stone et al., 1987).

Findings of a direct link between psychological responses and the body's defence against disease has led to the development of the field of **psychoneuroimmunology**. This interdisciplinary approach studies stress, emotional and behavioural reactions, and the immune system simultaneously (Ader & Cohen, 1993). For example, Jemmott and Magloire (1988) obtained samples of students' saliva, which contains *secretory immunoglobulin A*, the body's primary defence against such infections. The level of this substance was found to drop during final exams and then to rise again when exams were over. Thus, the psychological stress of finals was related to a change in body chemistry that facilitated the development of disease.

Individual Differences in Vulnerability to Stress

Given the same objectively stressful conditions, some people experience more negative emotional reactions than others and are thus more likely to get sick. For example, men who are perfectionists ("I feel that I must do things perfectly, or not do them at all") are more depressed than nonperfectionists when stress is high (Joiner & Schmidt, 1995).

Though genetic factors explain some of the differences in the effects of stress (Kessler et al., 1992), Friedman, Hawley, and Tucker (1994) present evidence from a large number of studies indicating a difference between **disease-prone personalities** and **self-healing personalities**. Those who are disease-prone respond to stressful situations with negative emotions and unhealthy behaviour patterns, and the result is illness and a shorter life span. Self-healing individuals are at the opposite extreme—tending to be enthusiastic about life, emotionally balanced, alert, responsive to others, energetic, curious, secure, and constructive. Self-healing people can be described as people one likes to be around. Research has confirmed that similar responses are related to subjective feelings of well-being and optimism (Myers & Diener, 1995; Segerstrom et al., 1998). Table 10.1 provides an overview of many of the personality differences between those who are disease-prone and those who are self-healing.

A specific personality characteristic that is associated with a specific health problem was introduced in Chapter 8. The *Type A* behaviour pattern, described as a personal determinant of aggression, is also associated with an increased risk of heart disease. Type A individuals, compared to the more placid *Type B* individuals, are more hostile, have higher blood pressure (Contrada, 1989), produce less HDL—the "good cholesterol" (*Albany Times Union*, November 18, 1992, p. A-5), and are twice as likely to develop heart disease (Weidner, Istvan, & McKnight, 1989). Anger seems to be the critical component that leads to coronary disease (Smith & Pope, 1990).

Psychoneuro immunology The study of the way responses to external events affect the internal physiological states that are crucial to the immune system in defending the body against disease.

Disease-prone Personalities Personality characterized by negative emotional reactions to stress, ineffective coping strategies, and unhealthy behaviour patterns; often associated with illness and a shortened life span.

Self-healing Personalities Personality characterized by effective coping with stress; self-healing individuals are balanced, energetic, responsive to others, and positive about life.

In general, stress often leads to illness, but some individuals are far more vulnerable than others. The difference in vulnerability is associated with a variety of personality differences.

TABLE 10.1 Personality differences of those most and least vulnerable to stress

	Self-Healing Personality	Disease-Prone Personality
Behavioural Tendencies	nonperfectionist	perfectionist
	extraverted	introverted
	completes school assignments on time	procrastinates
	internal locus of control	external locus of control
Expectancies and Beliefs	believes in a just world	does not believe in a just world
	high self-efficacy	low self-efficacy
	optimistic	pessimistic
	approaches goals focusing on positive outcomes toward which to strive	avoidance goals focusing on negative outcomes from which to stay away
	not neurotic	neurotic
Personal Characteristics	well adjusted	maladjusted
	high self-esteem	low self-esteem
	accessible attitudes: knows own likes and dislikes	inaccessible attitudes: unsure of own likes and dislikes
	independent	dependent

Sources, in order of listing in the table: Joiner & Schmidt, 1995; Amirkhan, Risinger, & Swickert, 1995; Tice & Baumeister, 1997; Birkimer, Lucas, & Birkimer, 1991; Tomaka & Blascovich, 1994; Bandura, 1993; Dykema, Bergbower, & Peterson, 1995; Elliot & Sheldon, 1998; Booth-Kewley & Vickers, 1994; Bernard & Belinsky, 1993; Campbell, Chew, & Scratchley, 1991; Fazio & Powell, 1997; Bornstein, 1995.

Coping with Stress

Because stress is essentially inevitable in our lives and because not everyone is fortunate enough to have a self-healing personality, we need strategies for dealing with stress. What strategies are helpful? A sensible first step is to be in the best possible physical condition.

Increasing Physical Fitness to Ward Off the Effects of Stress.

A healthful pattern of eating nutritious foods, getting enough sleep, and engaging in regular physical exercise results in increased *fitness* (being in good physical condition as indicated by one's endurance and strength). Even 15 to 20 minutes of aerobic exercise (jogging, biking, swimming, dancing, etc.) daily or every other day is an effective way to increase fitness, a sense of well-being, and feelings of self-efficacy as well as to decrease feelings of distress (Jessor, Turbin, & Costa, 1998; Lox & Rudolph, 1994; Mihalko, McAuley, & Bane, 1996). In a study of Korean undergraduates, Rudolph and Kim (1996) found positive emotional effects from aerobic activities as diverse as dancing and soccer, but not from less aerobic activities such as tennis and bowling. While some bodily exertion is better than none, the most beneficial exercise program is one that involves high intensity (Winett, 1998).

Though the positive effects of fitness are clear, the biggest barrier to becoming fit is the fact that changing from a sedentary lifestyle to one that includes regular exercise requires strong motivation, continuing commitment, and the ability to regulate one's own behaviour (Mullan & Markland, 1997).

Coping Strategies.

Compas and his colleagues (1991) proposed that *coping*, or responding effectively to stress, involves a two-level process. As outlined in Figure 10.3, at the first level emotional distress is ordinarily the initial response to a threatening event, and *emotion-focused coping* occurs as a way to deal with one's feelings by reducing the negative arousal. People most often reduce negative feelings by trying to increase positive affect or by seeking social support. If, for example, you received a very low grade in your social psychology midterm exam, you might attempt to relieve your depression by watching a funny television show or by attending an enjoyable social event. At the second level, *problem-focused coping* represents an attempt to deal with the threat and gain control of the situation. Ideally, this leads not only to reduced negative emotions but also to reduced threat. With your imaginary low course grade, for example, you might study harder, hire a tutor, or find out what questions you missed on the exam so that you could try to figure out why.

Creating Positive Affect.

A useful emotion-focused strategy for coping with stress is to discover how to create positive affect for oneself. People who are able to regulate their emotions seek ways to experience positive, happy feelings and an optimistic outlook despite negative events (Chang, 1998; Mayer & Salovey, 1995). As stress increases, those who seldom laugh respond with increasingly negative affect, but those who laugh the most do not (Kuiper & Martin, 1998). Stone and his colleagues (1994) reported that positive events (such as a family gathering or spending time with friends) actually enhance the immune system for a longer time period than negative events (such as getting a low grade or being the target of criticism) weaken it. Further, a *decrease* in positive events has a negative effect on health similar to that of an *increase* in negative events (Goleman, 1994b). Other effective aids to positive feelings range from enjoyable work (Csikszentmihalyi, 1993) to humour (Lefcourt et al., 1995) to pleasant fragrances (Baron & Bronfen, 1994). Any activity that helps improve one's mood seems able to counteract the negative effects of stress.

Seeking Social Support.

Social Support The physical and psychological comfort provided by a person's friends and family members.

A very important coping strategy is to seek **social support**—the physical and psychological comfort provided by other people (Sarason, Sarason, & Pierce, 1994). In part, just being with those you like seems helpful. Monkeys show an increase in affiliative behaviour in response to stressful situations (Cohen et al., 1992), and you may remember the discussion of a similar pattern of human affiliation in Chapter 6. As you might also guess on the basis of attraction research, people who desire social support tend to turn to others who are similar to themselves (Morgan, Carder, & Neal, 1997).

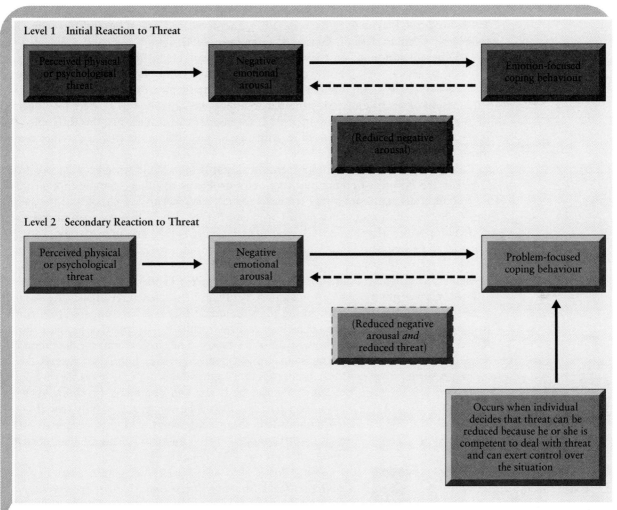

Level 1   Initial Reaction to Threat

Perceived physical or psychological threat → Negative emotional arousal → Emotion-focused coping behaviour

(Reduced negative arousal)

Level 2   Secondary Reaction to Threat

Perceived physical or psychological threat → Negative emotional arousal → Problem-focused coping behaviour

(Reduced negative arousal *and* reduced threat)

Occurs when individual decides that threat can be reduced because he or she is competent to deal with threat and can exert control over the situation

■ Responding to threat: Focus on emotions, then focus on problem

FIGURE 10.3 We respond to threat in two ways. The initial reaction is an emotional one (Level 1), and we must cope with our feelings of distress—emotion-focused coping. If the threat cannot be reduced in any way, emotional coping is all that can be done. If the threat can be modified or removed, however, it is possible to cope with the problem itself (Level 2)—problem-focused coping.

Source: Based on information in Compas et al., 1991.

People are better able to avoid illness in response to threat (and to recover from any illness that develops) if they interact with others rather than remaining isolated (Roy, Steptoe, & Kirschbaum, 1998). The negative effects of workplace stress can be lessened when an employee is given support by coworkers or by the organization (Shinn et al., 1993). During the Gulf War, Israeli military personnel and civilians who exhibited a *secure attachment style* (see Chapter 6) were best able to seek and to receive the benefits of social support (Mikulincer & Florian, 1995). Students whose attachment style is secure report the most social support, and those who are fearful and avoidant report the least (Davis, Morris, & Kraus, 1998). The positive effects of social support noted in research include fewer sports injuries among youngsters (Smith, Smoll, & Ptacek, 1990), feelings of well-being during pregnancy (Zachariah, 1996), lower stress and less postpartum depression among new mothers (Collins et al.,

1993; Logsdon, Birkimer, & Barbee, 1997), and decreased risk of heart disease among the elderly (Uchino, Kiecolt-Glaser, & Cacioppo, 1992).

Different amounts of social support are available in different ethnic groups (Gamble & Dalla, 1997). For example, Mexican-American families report larger support networks than Anglophone families. The importance of social support is one explanation of the finding that people who attend weekly religious services live longer than people who do not (Crumm, 1998). Among African-Americans, this difference is remarkable in that those involved in religious activity live about 14 years longer than those who are not involved.

What is it about social support that makes it helpful? One reason for the positive effects is the benefit of communicating one's problems to others. Simple though this may sound, talking about stress tends to reduce one's negative feelings and the incidence of both major and minor health problems (Clark, 1993). In one experimental test of this proposition (Lepore, 1997), students scheduled to take graduate entrance exams were asked to write either about their feelings or about a trivial topic; only those who wrote about their feelings experienced decreased depression (also see Greenberg & Stone, 1992; Hughes, Uhlmann, & Pennebaker, 1994; Pennebaker, 1997). Strangely enough, even writing about an imaginary traumatic experience resulted in fewer illnesses in research participants during the subsequent four weeks, compared to a control group that didn't write about such an event (Greenberg, Wortman, & Stone, 1996). When people suppress their thoughts in order to avoid negative emotions, the immune system is adversely affected (Petrie, Booth, & Pennebaker, 1998). It appears that confession is not only good for the soul, but good for the body as well (Emmons & Colby, 1995; Larson & Chastain, 1990). However, this is only true if you are unambivalent about being emotionally expressive to others (Katz & Campbell, 1994) and can be sure of a supportive response from others (Holahan et al., 1997).

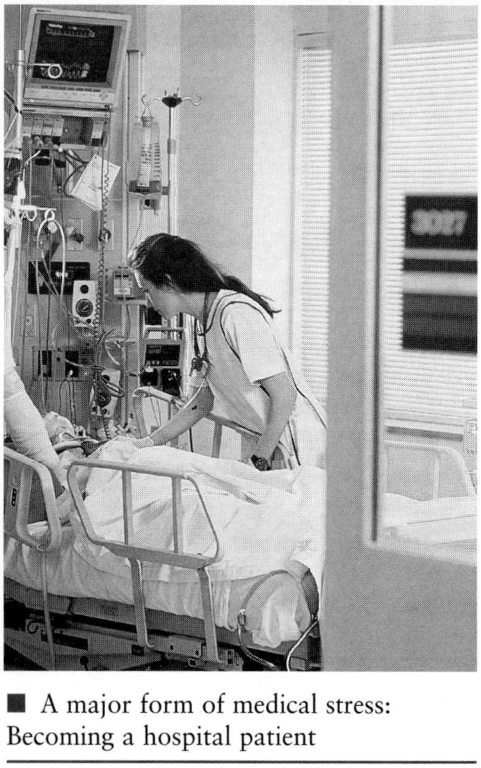

Coping with the Stress of Illness and Medical Treatment.

Not only does stress lead to illness, but the illness itself and its treatment often constitute new kinds of stress. Even the possibility of illness is stressful—it can be very upsetting to worry about contracting Lyme disease, herpes, mumps, coronary trouble, cancer, or anything else. If a medical problem does develop, it is stressful to experience bodily discomfort, notice something different about your skin, have an acute pain, or feel overly tired—and to realize that you may be sick, with all that that entails.

Beyond the various aspects of coping already discussed, coping with illness and medical care raises additional considerations. Deciding to seek medical help usually represents an active coping strategy (Wills & DePaulo, 1991), but the prospects of examination and diagnosis can then become new stressors. How do you react when you awaken one morning and realize that your doctor's appointment is later that day? If you must be hospitalized for surgery or other treatment (see Figure 10.4), this is usually an extremely stressful experience.

One of the more important steps is to learn as much as is possible, because fear of the unknown makes illness and treatment especially unpleasant. Read about your condition,

■ A major form of medical stress: Becoming a hospital patient

FIGURE 10.4 Experiencing physical symptoms, visiting a doctor for diagnosis and treatment, and being hospitalized for surgery or other medical procedures are all stressful. Among the major sources of threat in a hospital are fear of the unknown and the loss of perceived control.

ask your doctor questions, and seek out others who have undergone similar medical experiences (Rall, Peskoff, & Byrne, 1994). One of the reasons that knowledge is important is that accurate information about what is happening to you now and what will happen next gives you a sense of control. Even knowledge about painful procedures is less stressful than ignorance and fear of the unknown (Suls & Wan, 1989).

Earlier, we described denial as a maladaptive way to cope; but during medical or dental treatment, it can actually be very helpful to think about something else and deny what is being done to you (Suls & Fletcher, 1985). You are better off if your thoughts are elsewhere while you are having blood drawn for a laboratory test or having a dental technician scraping away at your gumline. Pain can also be reduced by anything that induces a positive mood (Stalling, 1992), including humorous videotapes (Zillmann et al., 1993).

As we have noted more than once in this chapter, *perceived control* is extremely important in the coping process (Thompson, Nanni, & Levine, 1994). For example, it is much less stressful and much less painful to remove a splinter from your own finger than to have someone else do it. Most stressors seem beyond our control, and that fact exacerbates our response to the stress. One way to reduce the impact of any kind of stress is to identify your possible options and then choose among them (Paterson & Neufeld, 1995). Once the options are in front of you, you are able to take charge and (ideally) select the most sensible one.

Even patients who simply believe they can control their symptoms, health care, and treatment handle medical stress much better than patients who believe that what happens is totally beyond their control (Thompson et al., 1993). In fact, people often have unrealistic beliefs about their ability to control illness, and such false beliefs actually help them to adapt to a disease as devastating as AIDS (Griffin & Rabkin, 1998). Perceived lack of control is found to be associated with relatively low income and education levels. Individuals in these circumstances often feel they are under the control of others, and this leads to negative affect, dissatisfaction with life, and poor health (Lachman & Weaver, 1998).

KEY POINTS

- Health-related information comes to us daily, and new research findings often modify or reverse earlier findings. Consumers of health information need to remain informed, open-minded, and cautious.

- *Stress* is defined as any event that is perceived as a potential source of physical or emotional harm. *Psychoneuroimmunology* studies the way in which stress can lead to physical illness both indirectly, by affecting health-related behaviour, and directly, through its effect on physiological functioning.

- A wide variety of dispositional differences are associated with the ability to resist the negative effects of stress (the *self-healing personality*) as opposed to the tendency to be badly affected by stress (the *disease-prone personality*).

- Effective strategies for *coping* with stress include increasing one's physical fitness; *regulatory control* of emotion and cognitions; encouraging *positive affect*; and establishing networks of *social support*.

- Coping with the stress of illness and medical treatment requires all of these same coping strategies as well as (1) acquiring as much knowledge as possible about each aspect of one's condition and the treatment procedures and (2) gaining as much control as possible of every step of the process.

APPLYING SOCIAL PSYCHOLOGY TO THE WORLD OF WORK: JOB SATISFACTION, HELPING, AND LEADERSHIP

What single activity fills more of most persons' time than any other? For most people the answer is provided by a single word: work. And we don't work alone; on the contrary, most of us work together with other persons in what, from the point of view of social psychology, are social situations. It's not surprising, then, that the principles and findings of social psychology have often been applied to the task of understanding what goes on in work settings. These findings have been put to use in work settings by social psychologists themselves, and by **industrial/organizational psychologists**—psychologists who specialize in studying all aspects of behaviour in work settings, including work settings in many different cultures (e.g., Johns & Xie, 1998; Murnighan, 1993). Similarly, many findings of social psychology have been adapted and put to practical use by persons in management, especially in a field known as *organizational behaviour*—which, as its name suggests, studies human behaviour in organizations (e.g., Greenberg & Baron, 1997).

In this section we'll consider some of the contributions made by social psychology in this respect. Specifically, we'll examine three major topics: *job satisfaction*—employees' attitudes toward their jobs; *organizational citizenship behaviour*—prosocial behaviour (e.g., helping) at work; and *leadership*—the process through which one member of a group, its leader, influences other members to work toward attaining shared group goals (e.g., Yukl, 1994).

> **Industrial/ organizational psychologists**
> Psychologists who study all aspects of behaviour in work settings.

Job Satisfaction: Attitudes About Work

As we saw in Chapter 3, we are rarely neutral in response to the social world. On the contrary, we hold strong attitudes about many aspects of it. Jobs are no exception to this rule. If asked, most persons can readily report their attitudes toward their jobs, and also toward the organizations that employ them. Attitudes concerning one's own job or work are generally referred to by the term **job satisfaction** (e.g., Wanous, Reichers, & Hudy, 1997), while attitudes toward one's company are known as *organizational commitment* (e.g. Allen & Meyer, 1991; Meyer et al., 1998)—see our discussion of that topic in Chapter 9.

> **Job Satisfaction**
> Attitudes concerning one's job or work.

Factors Affecting Job Satisfaction

Despite the fact that many jobs are repetitive and boring in nature, surveys involving literally hundreds of thousands of employees conducted over the course of several decades point to a surprising finding: Most people indicate that they are quite satisfied with their jobs (e.g., Page & Wiseman, 1993), though wide range of job satisfaction levels do exist. A key question, then, is: What factors influence such attitudes? Research on this issue indicates that two major groups of factors are important: *organizational factors* related to a company's practices or the working conditions provided, and *personal factors* related to the traits of individual employees.

The organizational factors that influence job satisfaction contain few surprises: people report higher satisfaction when they feel that the reward systems in their companies are fair (when raises, promotions, and other rewards are distributed fairly—see Chapter 9); when they like and respect their bosses and believe these persons have their best interests at heart (see Figure 10.5); when they can participate in the decisions that affect them; when the work they perform is interesting rather than boring and repetitive; and when they are neither *overloaded* with too much to do in a given amount of time nor *underloaded* with too little to do (e.g., Callan, 1993; Melamed et al., 1993; Miceli & Lane, 1991). Physical working conditions also play a role: when they are comfortable, employees report higher job satisfaction than when they are uncomfortable (e.g., too hot, too noisy, too crowded; Baron, 1994).

Turning to personal factors, some findings are, perhaps, more unexpected. First, and probably least surprising, job satisfaction is positively related to both seniority and status: the longer people have been in a given job and the higher their status, the greater their satisfaction (Zeitz, 1990). Similarly, the greater the extent to which jobs are closely matched to individuals' personal interests, the greater their satisfaction (Fricko & Beehr, 1992). A bit more surprising, perhaps, is the finding that certain personal traits are closely related to job satisfaction. For instance, Type A persons tend to be *more* satisfied than Type B's, despite their greater overall irritability (see Chapter 8). Perhaps this is so because jobs allow people to stay busy, and Type A's, of course, *like* to be busy all the time!

At first glance, the really surprising results in this area are those indicating that job satisfaction may actually have an important genetic component—and that as a result, individuals have a tendency to express either relatively high or relatively low levels of job satisfaction *no matter where they work*. The first research pointing to such conclusions was conducted by Arvey and his colleagues (1989) more than ten years ago. They found that the level of job satisfaction reported by identical twins who had been raised apart correlated significantly, and that these correlations were higher than was true for unrelated pairs of individuals. Remember that identical twins share the same genetic make-up, which unrelated individuals, of course, do not. Further, additional findings indicated that as much as 30 percent of variation in job satisfaction from one person to another may stem from genetic factors! While these findings remain somewhat controversial (e.g., Cropanzano & James, 1990), they have been replicated in other studies (e.g., Keller et al., 1992). As we discussed in Chapter 3, it may be that basic tendencies to experience positive or negative affect are inherited and such tendencies would influence feelings about our work. Thus, it appears that job satisfaction may stem, at least in part, from genetic factors.

■ Job satisfaction: How to destroy it

FIGURE 10.5 When employees believe that their bosses do not care about them—do not have their best interests at heart—job satisfaction can drop to dismal levels.

Even if genetic factors do not play the important role suggested by these results, additional studies indicate that attitudes toward work are highly stable over time, even when individuals change jobs. Persons who express high levels of satisfaction in one job at a given time are likely to express high levels of satisfaction in a different job at a later time, and so on. Clear evidence for such effects has been reported recently by Steel and Rentsch (1997). These researchers obtained measures of job satisfaction and job involvement (the extent to which individuals feel personally involved in their jobs) from almost 200 persons who worked in a large government agency; these measures were obtained at two different times, ten years apart. In addition, Steel and Rentsch (1997) also obtained information on the extent to which the persons in the study were performing the same or a very different job the second time they were surveyed. As you can see from Figure 10.6, job satisfaction and job involvement showed considerable stability over a ten-year period, both for individuals who reported performing much the same job and for those who reported performing different work. However, stability was greater for those performing the same job.

These findings, and those of related research (e.g., Gerhart, 1987), suggest that personal factors—genetic or otherwise—play an important role in job satisfaction. While working conditions, the nature of the jobs people perform, and many organizational factors combine to shape job satisfaction (Steel and Rentsch also found evidence for the importance of such factors in their study), job satisfaction is also, to an important degree, very much in the eye of the beholder. Some persons express a high level of satisfaction no matter where they work, while others express a low level no matter where they work. It is clear that most of us would usually prefer to work with people who fall into the first category than with the kind of chronic complainers who fall into the second.

The Effects of Job Satisfaction on Task Performance: Weaker Than You Might Guess

Are happy workers—people who like their jobs—productive workers? Common sense seems to suggest that they would be, but it's important to remember that job satisfaction is a kind of attitude. And, as we noted in Chapter 3, attitudes are not always strong predictors of overt behaviour. Thus, you should not be surprised to learn that although job satisfaction is related to performance in many jobs, this relationship is

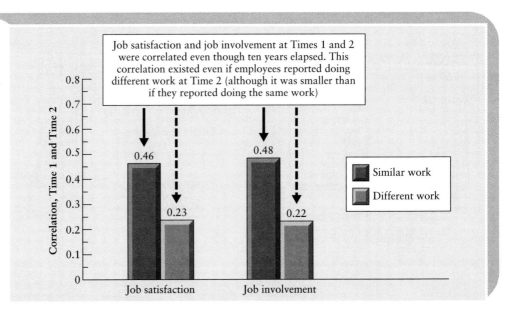

■ Job satisfaction: Evidence that it is stable

FIGURE 10.6 As shown here, the job satisfaction expressed by a group of employees at one point in time correlated significantly with job satisfaction expressed by the same group of persons ten years later. This was true even if the participants' jobs had changed significantly during this period.

Source: Based on data from Steel & Rentsch, 1997.

relatively weak—correlations in the range of 0.15 to 0.20 (e.g., Judge, 1993; Tett & Meyer, 1993).

Why isn't this relationship stronger? Because several factors may tend to weaken or moderate the impact of job satisfaction on performance. First, if the job is very rigidly structured and absolutely the same level of performance is demanded of the worker (as in assembly-line work), then there is little room for changes in job performance and, therefore, job satisfaction cannot have any influence. Second, there are many additional factors (other than job satisfaction) that can also determine performance: working conditions, the availability of required materials and tools, the extent to which the task is structured, and so on. In many cases, the effects of these factors may be more important than job satisfaction in determining performance. For instance, even employees who love their jobs can't do their best work if the environment in which they work is too hot, too cold, or too noisy. Finally, it is possible that positive attitudes toward one's job—or toward coworkers or the entire organization—may be reflected primarily in forms of behaviour unrelated to performance (e.g., Keller, 1997), for instance, through praising the company to people outside it, conserving its resources, or helping other coworkers. Such actions can have very beneficial effects on an organization, so let's take a closer look at them now.

Organizational Citizenship Behaviour: Prosocial Behaviour At Work

In Chapter 8, we examined many aspects of *prosocial behaviour*—helpful actions that benefit others but have no obvious benefits for the persons who perform them. As we saw in that chapter, prosocial behaviour stems from many different factors and can yield a wide range of effects. Do such actions also occur in work settings, between persons who work together in an organization? And if so, what forms do they take, and what effects do they produce? These are the questions that have been investigated recently by industrial/organizational psychologists and others, and as you can see, they are directly related to basic research in the field of social psychology. Let's take a brief look at what research on these issues has revealed.

The Nature of Prosocial Behaviour at Work: Some Basic Forms

While various terms have been used to describe prosocial behaviour in work settings (e.g., Van Dyne & LePine, 1998), most researchers refer to such behaviour as **organizational citizenship behaviour (OCB)**—defined as prosocial behaviour occurring within an organization that may or may not be rewarded by the organization (e.g., Organ, 1997). The fact that such behaviour is not automatically or necessarily rewarded (e.g., through a bonus or a raise in pay) is important, because it suggests that OCB is performed voluntarily, often without any thought of external reward for doing so. Thus, it does indeed qualify as prosocial behaviour according to the definition noted above. How do individuals working in an organization seek to help one another? Research findings suggest that they do so in many different ways. However, most helpful actions at work appear to take one of five different forms:

Organizational Citizenship Behaviour (OCB) Prosocial behaviour occurring within an organization that may or may not be rewarded by the organization.

1. *Altruism*: Helping others to perform their jobs—see Figure 10.7

2. *Conscientiousness*: Going beyond the minimum requirements of a job, doing more than is required. For instance, an employee who prides himself on never missing a day of work or on taking short breaks is showing conscientiousness.

3. *Civic virtue*: Participating in and showing concern for the "life" of the organization. One example: attending voluntary meetings. Another example: reading memos rather than throwing them in the trash!

4. *Sportsmanship*: Showing willingness to tolerate unfavourable conditions without complaining. If an employee decides to grin and bear it rather than complain, she or he is showing this form of OCB.

5. *Courtesy*: Making efforts to prevent interpersonal problems with others. Examples include "turning the other cheek" when annoyed by another person at work or behaving courteously toward others even when they are rude.

The results of several studies (e.g., Podsakoff & MacKenzie, 1994) suggest that a large proportion of prosocial behaviour at work falls into one or more of these categories, so they seem to provide a useful framework for studying helpful actions in organizations. As you might expect, OCB appears to have a positive influence in the workplace. For example, recent studies indicate that the greater the incidence of OCB in an organization, the higher the level of performance (Podsakoff, Ahearne, & MacKenzie, 1997). In addition, it appears that individuals who engage in prosocial behaviour are often recognized, both formally and informally, receiving higher performance evaluations from their bosses and greater liking from their coworkers (Allen & Rush, 1998).

OCB: Its Causes and Effects

What factors lead individuals to engage in various forms of organizational citizenship behaviour? One of the most important of these appears to be *trust*—employees' belief that they will be treated fairly by their organizations and, more specifically, by their immediate bosses. The more that employees believe their bosses will treat them fairly, the greater their trust in these persons and thus the greater their willingness to engage in prosocial behaviour (e.g., Konovsky & Pugh, 1994).

Another noted factor is employees' perceptions of the *breadth of their jobs*—what behaviours are required and which are voluntary. The more broadly employees define their jobs, the more likely they are to engage in instances of OCB (Morrison, 1994; Van Dyne & LePine, 1998). This is because the individual with a broader definition will be more willing to take on extra tasks to help another person.

Finally, you may not be surprised to hear that the frequency of OCB seems to be influenced by employees' *organizational commitment*, as described in Chapter 9 (Randall, Fedor, & Longenecker, 1990). The stronger their commitment, the higher the frequency of OCB. In sum, as is true of prosocial behaviour in other settings, individuals' tendency to engage in such actions at work is influenced by several different factors.

■ Organizational citizenship in action: Prosocial behaviour at work

FIGURE 10.7 Organizational citizenship behaviour (OCB) takes many different forms, but most of these involve one or more of what have been termed altruism, conscientiousness, civic virtue, sportsmanship, and courtesy.

Leadership: Patterns of Influence Within Groups

Research on leadership has long been part of social psychology, but it is also an applied topic studied by other fields as well (e.g., Bass, 1998). We could easily devote an entire chapter to this topic, so to hold the length of this discussion within bounds, we'll focus on the following topics: (1) why some individuals, but not others, become leaders; (2) contrasting *styles* of leadership; and (3) the nature of *charismatic* and *transformational* leadership.

But what is **leadership**? To a degree, it's like love: easy to recognize, but hard to define (see Chapter 6). However, psychologists generally use this term to mean the process through which one member of a group (its leader) influences other group members toward attainment of shared group goals (Yukl, 1994). In other words, being a leader involves influence—a **leader** is the group member who exerts most influence within the group.

Who Becomes a Leader? The Role of Traits and Situations

Are some people born to lead? Common sense suggests that this is so. Famous leaders such as Alexander the Great, Queen Elizabeth I, and more recently, Pierre Trudeau

Leadership The process through which one member of a group (its leader) influences other group members toward attainment of shared group goals.

Leader The group member who exerts the greatest influence within the group.

■ The great person theory of leadership

FIGURE 10.8 According to the great person theory, all great leaders share certain traits that set them apart from other persons, and they possess these traits no matter where or when they lived. Research findings offer little support for this view, but research does suggest that leaders differ from other persons with respect to certain traits.

seem to differ from ordinary people in several respects. Such observations led early researchers to formulate the **great person theory** of leadership—the view that great leaders possess certain traits that set them apart from most human beings, traits that are possessed by all such leaders, no matter when or where they lived (see Figure 10.8).

Currently, leadership is seen as a product of many factors. However recent research has shown that leaders often possess special qualities (Kirkpatrick & Locke, 1991). They rate higher than most people on the following traits: *drive*—the desire for achievement coupled with high energy and resolution; *self-confidence*; *creativity*; and *leadership motivation*—the desire to be in charge and exercise authority over others. Perhaps the most important single characteristic of leaders, however, is a high level of *flexibility*—the ability to recognize what actions or approaches are required in a given situation and then to act accordingly (Zaccaro, Foti, & Kenny, 1991).

While certain traits do seem to be related to leadership, however, it is also clear that leaders do not operate in a social vacuum. On the contrary, different groups, facing different tasks and problems, seem to require different types of leaders—or at least leaders who demonstrate different styles (House & Podsakoff, 1994; Locke, 1991). So yes, traits do matter where leadership is concerned, but they are definitely only part of the total picture. With this thought in mind, let's take a closer look at precisely *how* leaders lead—the contrasting styles they can adopt.

How Leaders Operate: Contrasting Styles and Approaches

All leaders are definitely not alike. They may share certain traits to a degree, but they differ greatly in terms of personal style or approach to leadership (e.g., George, 1995; Peterson, 1997). While there are probably as many different *styles* of leadership as there are leaders, research has focused on the extent to which leaders encourage participation of their followers in decisions. This was the focus for some of the first research on leadership ever performed, by Kurt Lewin and colleagues (Lewin, Lippitt & White, 1939). They distinguished between two styles of leadership: *autocratic* (controlling and making all decisions) and *democratic* (allowing participation and decision-making by members).

Modern research is still refining elements of these styles. For example, research has examined the extent to which leaders try to run the show by closely directing the activities of all group members, a *directive-permissive* dimension (Muczyk & Reimann, 1987). Further, recent findings suggest that this latter dimension itself can be divided into two separate components that exert sharply contrasting effects on a group's success.

The clearest evidence pointing to such conclusions is provided by an ingenious series of studies conducted by Peterson (1997). He distinguished between two types of directive leader. One type would show *process directiveness*, directing the group's discussion in such a way as to insist that all possible views and perspectives be heard. A second type would state his or her own position and try to ram it down the throats of the group—a high level of *outcome directiveness*. Peterson (1997) further reasoned that these different approaches to being directive would have contrasting effects on group performance. Process directiveness, he suggested, would have mostly positive effects. In contrast, outcome directiveness might actually prove counterproductive. To test these predictions, Peterson (1997) arranged for groups of students to play the role of an elite decision-making group facing an international crisis. The leaders of the groups were instructed to behave with either high or low *process directiveness* (insisting on member participation and the discussion of all possible views) and high or low *outcome directiveness* (stating their personal view and advocating it strongly).

Several different measures of group performance were collected: the quality of the group process, the extent to which groups made the correct decisions (the same decisions recommended by experts in international affairs), and member satisfaction with the group and the leader. On all these measures, results indicated that high process directiveness was beneficial. In contrast, high outcome directiveness was not (see Figure 10.9). In short, when leaders played a directive role by insisting that all views be discussed and that all members have a chance to participate, the groups' effectiveness was enhanced.

These findings suggest that leader directiveness is not, in and of itself, necessarily a bad thing. On the contrary, it can be seen as a neutral force that can produce positive or negative effects, depending on whether it is used to insist that all views be considered and all members get a chance to participate. What becomes evident after decades of research is that no single style of leadership is always best; rather, which style succeeds best depends on the specific circumstances in which a group operates.

Charismatic Leaders: Leaders Who Change the World

Have you ever seen films of Pierre Trudeau? John F. Kennedy? Nelson Mandela? Martin Luther King, Jr.? If so, you may have noticed that there seemed to be something special about these leaders. As you listened to their speeches, you may have found yourself being moved by their words and stirred by the vigour of their presentations. You are definitely not alone in such reactions: these leaders exerted powerful effects on many millions of persons and, by doing so, changed their societies. Leaders who accomplish such feats are termed **charismatic leaders** (or, sometimes, *transformational* leaders; House & Howell, 1992; Kohl, Steers, & Terborg, 1995).

What characteristics make certain leaders charismatic? And how do these leaders exert such dramatic influence on their followers? There is a growing consensus among researchers who have studied this topic that it makes sense to try to understand such leadership in terms of a *special type of relationship* between leaders and their followers (House, 1977) and in terms of the actions taken by these leaders that seem to magnify their impact on followers (Pillai et al., 1997).

With respect to their relationship with followers, charismatic leaders seem to generate (1) high levels of devotion and loyalty, (2) high levels of enthusiasm for the

Charismatic Leaders Leaders who exert exceptionally powerful effects on large numbers of followers or on entire societies; also known as *transformational* leaders.

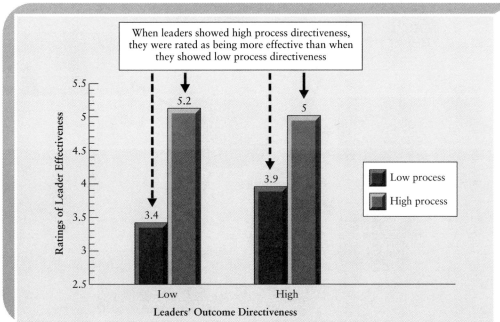

■ Leaders' directiveness: Some of the effects are positive

FIGURE 10.9 When an appointed leader showed a high level of process directiveness, insisting that all views be discussed and that all group members be given a chance to participate, many beneficial effects were obtained. One of these effects—high ratings of the leaders' effectiveness by group members—is shown here. In contrast a high level of outcome directiveness did not produce similar benefits.

Source: Based on data from Peterson, 1997.

leader and her or his ideas, (3) willingness by followers to sacrifice their own interests for the sake of the group's goals, and (4) levels of performance beyond those that would normally be expected. As one expert in this area puts it, charismatic leaders somehow "make ordinary people do extraordinary things" (Conger, 1991). Of course, this may not always be toward positive ends, as the influence of Adolf Hitler or some cult leaders attests.

But what, precisely, do charismatic leaders do to produce such effects? Research findings emphasize the importance of the following factors. First, such leaders usually propose a *vision* (Howell & Frost, 1989). They describe in vivid, emotion-provoking terms an image of what their nation or group can—and should—become. To the extent that followers accept this vision, their level of commitment to the leader and the leader's goals can become intense.

Second, charismatic leaders go beyond stating a dream or vision: they also offer a *route* for reaching it. They tell their followers, in straightforward terms, how to get from here to there. This too seems crucial, for a vision that appears to be out of reach is unlikely to motivate people to work to attain it. Third, charismatic leaders engage in *framing* (Conger, 1991): they define the goals for their group in a way that gives extra meaning and purpose both to the goals and to the actions needed to attain them.

Other facets of charismatic leadership include a high level of self-confidence, a high degree of concern for followers' needs, an excellent communication style, and a stirring personal style (House, Spangler, & Woycke, 1991). Finally, transformational leaders are often masters of *impression management*, a process we described in Chapter 7. When this skill is added to the various traits and behaviours, the vision, and the gift for framing described above, the ability of charismatic leaders to influence large numbers of followers loses some of its mystery. (See Figure 10.10 for a summary of these factors.) In fact, it appears that charisma rests firmly on principles and processes well understood by social psychologists.

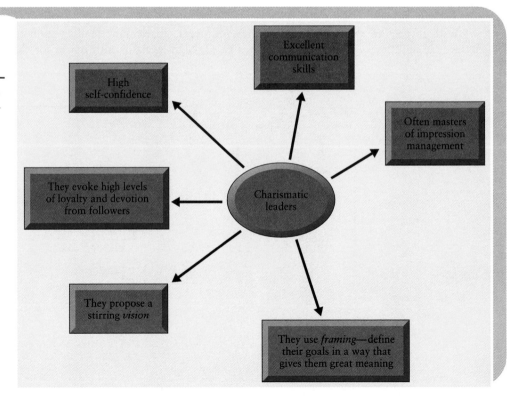

■ Charismatic leaders: How they exert their effects

FIGURE 10.10 Research findings indicate that charismatic leaders exert their powerful effects on followers because of the factors shown here.

Excellent communication skills

High self-confidence

Often masters of impression management

They evoke high levels of loyalty and devotion from followers

Charismatic leaders

They propose a stirring *vision*

They use *framing*—define their goals in a way that gives them great meaning

Cultural Differences in Leadership: North American and Asian CEOs

Are the kind of leadership processes we have described above universal—present in all cultures? Or does leadership operate differently in different cultures? In the twenty-first century, it seems more and more evident that in economic terms we are globally interdependent: an economic down-turn in of one part of the world will have a negative impact on other parts of the world. With such interdependence it becomes increasingly important that the leaders of business understand each other. However, significant differences have been noted in the style of such leaders in different countries (Bhagat, Kedia, Crawford, & Kaplan, 1990; Kotter, 1982).

When comparing leadership in Asian and North American corporations, researchers point to *cultural values* as the source of leadership differences (see Chapter 3 for a discussion of cultural values). For example, Doktor (1990) notes that business leaders in Japan and Korea perceive that what affects one part of society may well affect other parts as well—in line with the collectivism of the culture, they emphasize the *interdependence* of different segments of society. Thus, they view their corporate decisions in a broad context that takes account of the decisions' consequences for other segments of society outside the business community. In North America, in contrast, decisions tend to be viewed in a somewhat narrower context, which focuses on a company and its goals. How do these contrasting cultural values influence the leadership style of Asian and American CEOs? Doktor contends that because Japanese and Korean managers consider the broader context of their actions and decisions, they feel more strongly than American CEOs that these should not be rushed.

In support of these contentions, Doktor carried out a comparative study of the heads of major companies in the United States, Japan, Korea, and Hong Kong (1990). He found that while CEOs in each country spent about the same proportions of their days working alone (25 percent) and working in groups (75 percent), the duration of each task they performed varied greatly. In the United States, almost 50 percent of all tasks were of short duration (completed in only nine minutes or less). In contrast, the percentage of short tasks in Japan and Korea was much lower (10 percent and 14 percent, respectively). The percentage for Hong Kong, where cultural values are a mix between the traditional Chinese values and Western individualism, was in between these two.

A second cultural value that has been considered important is *power distance*, referring to the extent of hierarchical status-differences in a society—see Chapter 3. Those nations that score highly on Hofstede's measure of power distance also tend to be high in collectivism (Hofstede, 1983). In such cultures, there tends to be a strictly maintained hierarchy which limits communication between those at different levels of a society or organization. For example, Smith and colleagues (1999) found that leaders in high power distance cultures did not refer to subordinates when making decisions or resolving group problems. Similarly in a survey of the attitudes of pilots and flight attendants from eight nations, Merrit and Helmreich (1996) found that subjects from Asian nations endorsed autocratic leadership styles, with *top-down* communication and decision making (communication and decisions come from the leaders to the followers rather than the reverse). However, in many collective cultures there are also mechanisms whereby members can contribute to the leader's decisions through participating in collective consultations (Smith & Bond, 1998).

One study of attitudes to leadership styles in electronic plants in the United states, Mexico, Japan, Taiwan and Korea (Howell, et al., 1997) found that subjects from all five nations rated positively leaders who were supportive and made rewards contingent on performance. However, directive leadership was more positively rated in Mexico, Korea and Taiwan than in the United States and Japan, and participative leadership was endorsed only by those in the United States. This and similar studies (see Smith & Bond, 1999) suggest that the relationship between leaders and their groups will vary in subtle ways among nations that we consider collectivistic. We cannot assume a uniform leadership style.

These findings suggest that even today, when modern technology dictates the form of many business practices, cultural differences can and do play a key role in shaping the actions and perceptions of business leaders. As T. Fujisawa, the cofounder of Honda Corporation, once put it, "Japanese and American management are 95 percent the same—and differ in all important respects." We might add: "And those differences can be traced, to an important degree, to specific cultural factors."

KEY POINTS

- Work is often our most time-consuming activity and one usually carried out in a social setting. Thus, the findings and principles of social psychology help to explain behaviour in work settings.

- *Job satisfaction* is an individual's attitude toward her or his job. It is influenced by organizational factors such as working conditions and the fairness of reward systems, and by personal factors. Recent findings suggest that job satisfaction is often highly stable over time and may be influenced by genetic factors.

- The relationship between job satisfaction and task performance is relatively weak, partly because many factors other than work-related attitudes influence performance.

- Individuals often engage in prosocial behaviour at work, known as *organizational citizenship behaviour* (OCB). OCB is influenced by several factors, including employees' trust in their boss and the organization, the extent to which employees define their job responsibilities broadly, and organizational commitment.

- *Leadership* refers to the process through which one member of a group (its leader) influences other group members toward the attainment of shared group goals.

- Although the *great person theory* of leadership is no longer supported, research findings suggest that leaders do indeed have special traits.

- Leadership styles studied by early researchers were the *democratic* and *autocratic* styles of leadership. More recent research has focused on a *directiveness-permissiveness* dimension of leadership.

- Leaders high in *process directiveness* direct the group process so as to ensure that all views are heard and all members participate. Leaders high in *outcome directiveness* try to induce the group to accept their views. Research shows process directiveness is more beneficial for group functioning.

- *Charismatic leaders* exert profound effects on their followers and often change their societies, using such behaviours as stating a clear vision, framing the group's goals in ways that magnify their importance, and using a stirring personal style.

- Cross-cultural research suggests that major differences between leaders in Asian and North American corporations stem from differences in cultural values such as the extent to which *interdependence* of corporation and society is recognized and *power-distance*.

SOCIAL PSYCHOLOGY AND THE LEGAL SYSTEM

If the real world matched our ideals, the judicial process would provide an elaborate and totally fair set of procedures that ensured objective, unbiased, and consistent decisions about violations of criminal and civil laws. Our legal and judicial system ordinarily strives to live up to that ideal—not to leave justice to the arbitrary whims of legal professionals or to chance: see Figure 10.11. Yet research in **forensic psychology** (psychology specifically concerned with legal issues) repeatedly indicates that the human participants in the process do not always function according to rational guidelines (Davis, 1989). Social psychologists have provided a considerable body of evidence indicating that when people interact, their behaviour and their judgments are affected by attitudes, cognitions, and emotions that may be biased, irrational, and unfair. And those same factors are equally relevant when people evaluate and interact in the justice system. Research in the area of forensic psychology has expanded tremendously in the past decade (e.g., Gudjonsson & Haward, 1998; Loftus, 1992). We will concentrate on examining four of the major figures in the justice system: (1) The media and public opinion; (2) police procedures; (3) eyewitnesses; (4) the defendant.

> **Forensic Psychology**
> Psychological research and theory that deals with the effects of cognitive, affective, and behavioural factors on legal proceedings and the law.

Social Perceptions of Justice: The Role of Media and Public Opinion

Public perceptions of the justice system and how it functions can have an important impact on changes that are made in legal process and ultimately on the legislation a nation enacts. Unfortunately, social perceptions of justice are not always objective and can become biased by the kinds of information available to us.

Media publicity

On a regular basis, daily newspapers, radio and television news programs, and sometimes magazines and books devote a lot of space to information about crimes, accidents, and lawsuits, especially if they are dramatic or unusual or involve famous people (Barnes, 1989; Henry, 1991). One of the potentially negative aspects of a free press in this instance is that public opinion (including the opinion of individuals who might later be jurors) can be affected by how such news is presented. In Canada, the details of cases or evidence are sometimes suppressed by the courts if their publication might detract from a fair trial. An example is the ban on reporting of evidence during the trial for manslaughter of Karla

"That's the law for you; you never know what the outcome of a trial is going to be. In this case, it's tails, and you're guilty."

■ What if judicial decisions were based entirely on chance?

FIGURE 10.11 The judicial process suggested in this cartoon would be a frightening prospect. Though such factors as chance, misperception, and emotions are important in the courtroom, we are fortunate that the outcome rests much more heavily on factual evidence, reason, and legal precedents.

Homolka to prevent biasing a future jury during the subsequent murder trial of her husband, Paul Bernardo. There were objections by Canadian media to those restrictions. It has been said, only half jokingly, that the United States sequesters a jury after the trial begins, but Canada "sequesters" the public beforehand (Farnsworth, 1995). The United States does allow media publicity before and during trials, even sometimes allowing cameras in the courtroom. In some notable cases, the mass of publicity and evidence disclosed by the media has caused many people to question the possibility of an unbiased trial. When should the rights of the accused to a fair trial supersede the rights of the press or of the public to see that justice is being done? The answer to this question obviously differs somewhat in Canada and the United States.

In research on two highly publicized cases involving defendants accused of distributing marijuana and a defendant charged with murdering a police officer, Moran and Cutler (1991) surveyed potential jurors. They found in each instance that the more knowledge people had about the details of the case, the more blame they placed on those arrested for the crimes. The investigators also found that knowledge of the crimes was unrelated to whether the respondents believed they could make impartial judgments. Given people's mistaken faith in their own lack of bias, Judge O'Connell (1988) suggests that asking potential jurors whether they can be fair and impartial is as useless as asking a person who is a practising alcoholic if he or she has the drinking under control.

Not only does media publicity affect people's judgment about a specific case, but media information also has more general effects. For example, when people are exposed to descriptions of very serious crimes, they then view other crimes and other offenders more harshly than if they have not had such exposure (Roberts & Edwards, 1989)—this would appear to be a *priming effect* (see Chapter 2). Presumably, they interpret all crime more negatively because of exposure to a few serious cases.

Media reportage of crime also appears to influence the public's perception of the *prevalence* of crime. Anthony Doob of the University of Toronto's Centre of Criminology has been investigating such issues for many years (e.g., Doob & Macdonald, 1979; Roberts & Doob, 1990). Statistics for 1998 show that crime rates in Canada, including those for violent crime, have been falling for over six years since 1992, with the homicide rate at its lowest since 1968 (Statistics Canada, 1999). Despite this good news, Canadians feel more unsafe than ever in their neighbourhoods. An international survey of criminal victimization in 11 industrialized countries (Besserer, 1998) asked individuals how safe they felt "walking alone in your area after dark." Canada was one of the three countries with the lowest ratings—27 percent did *not* feel safe in their neighbourhood after dark and, in a period when crime was declining, feeling unsafe increased by 5 percent from 1992 to 1998. Further, a Canadian victimization survey reported that 46 percent of Canadians believe the level of crime has increased in the past five years (Gartner & Doob, 1994).

Why should our perceptions be so at odds with reality? Doob's research indicates that media publicity may be at fault insofar as it tends to over represent violent crime, as well as report it inadequately (Doob, 1985; Roberts & Doob, 1990). For example, Doob found that over 50 percent of newspaper crime reporting in Canada concerned violent crime (1985), though it is in fact a small percentage of all crime. Further, 95 percent of the public cite the news media as the principle source of information about criminal cases (Roberts & Doob, 1990). The *availability heuristic* clearly applies here (see Chapter 2)— when we make assumptions about the crime rate and its dangers we are relying on the biased information that is available to us.

One place where media publicity has certainly played a role is in the issue of gun control. We will examine this controversial subject in the following On the Applied Side section.

The Weapons Effects: A Social Psychological Perspective on the Impact of Firearms

In February 2000, a boy in first grade took a gun to school and shot a six-year-old classmate. This was perhaps the most shocking in a long series of incidents of students arming themselves and killing others at school in recent years. The majority of the incidents we have heard about took place in the United States. But in Taber, Alberta a 14-year-old boy shot and killed another student in school and might have gone on to kill more if not disarmed. One of the major questions raised by these incidents is whether the widespread availability of firearms contributes to such violence. When this is suggested, it is sometime countered with the National Rifle Association slogan: "Guns don't kill people, people kill people." What does research suggest?

The first source of information comes from social psychological experiments examining what has been termed the weapons effect (the stimulating effect of the mere presence of a gun or other weapon on aggressive impulses).

A noted authority on aggression research, Leonard Berkowitz, conducted the original experiment demonstrating the weapons effect (Berkowitz & Lepage, 1967). Subjects were initially angered by both a series of mild but annoying electric shocks and a negative evaluation delivered by another subject (actually an experimenter). They were then given the opportunity to reciprocate and were taken into a laboratory where the shocking apparatus was located. Researchers varied whether or not subjects were simultaneously exposed to violent weapons. In one condition, there were a shotgun and a revolver on the table beside the apparatus, in a second condition there were sports racquets and in the control condition there was nothing at all. The experimenter appeared surprised to see the objects on the table and pushed them aside in a matter-of-fact way explaining that another experimenter must have left them there. Berkowitz predicted that the presence of the weapons, even though they were not relevant to the subjects'

task, would facilitate aggression. Results supported this hypothesis: subjects exposed to the firearms delivered significantly more shocks than those in the other two conditions. The weapons effect has been replicated many times and in a number or countries including Sweden, Belgium and Italy (see Berkowitz, 1993).

A second body of research consists of correlational studies from a wide variety of disciplines examining the relationship between firearms availability and violence of various kinds. This research relates crime statistics to levels of gun ownership or the restrictiveness of gun laws. A number of reviews of this complex literature exist (Cukier, 1998; Gabor, 1994; Lester, 1984). To summarize from these, the strongest relationship appears to be between firearms availability and homicide rates in general, and with rates of homicide using firearms in particular. Many studies have shown that the greater the availability of firearms, the higher the homicide rate (e.g., Cook, 1979, 1987; Killias, 1993; Lester, 1991). Figure 10.12 shows an example of this relationship for four English-speaking countries taken from a recent international study of firearms regulation (United Nations,1998).

There is heated debate about interpretation of this correlational research (e.g., Kleck, 1991; Lott, 1998; Mundt, 1990, 1993) and some studies do not find the relationships mentioned above and suggest that gun control will have little impact on crime (e.g., Kleck, 1991; Mauser, 1996, cited in Cukier, 1998). Further, some research demonstrates a deterrent effect of gun availability (Kleck, 1991, 1988). For example, John Lott (1998), in his book More Guns, Less Crime provides data suggesting that as gun laws become less restrictive (and guns become more available), violent crimes decrease, particularly robbery and homicide. This and most studies showing a deterrent effect come from the United States and use data from within that country only (Gabor, 1994).

Among methodological problems raised by critics of the deterrent effect research (e.g., Hemenway, 1998; Gabor, 1994; Webster, Vernick, Ludwig, & Lester, 1997), a major limitation is a lack of variation in levels of firearms availability. Since firearms are so widely available in the United State, there is insufficient opportunity to examine whether the absence of firearms is associated with lower levels of violence. For this we need to turn to international data such as that shown in Figure 10.12. Firearms are much less prevalent in other Western countries and so is violent crime, and homicide in particular (United Nations, 1998). Also, deterrent effects appear to be temporary and disappear when long-term trends are examined (McDowall, et al., 1989, 1991).

In summary, there is substantial research supporting the view that increased firearms availability can contribute to rates of homicide—though this research is not without its detractors. A final question that these data raise is: If greater firearms availability contributes to higher homicide rates, what are the mechanisms through which this could occur?

Beyond the obvious fact that guns are by nature more lethal than knives or clubs (Cook, 1987), two important social psychological processes may be at work (Berkowitz, 1993).

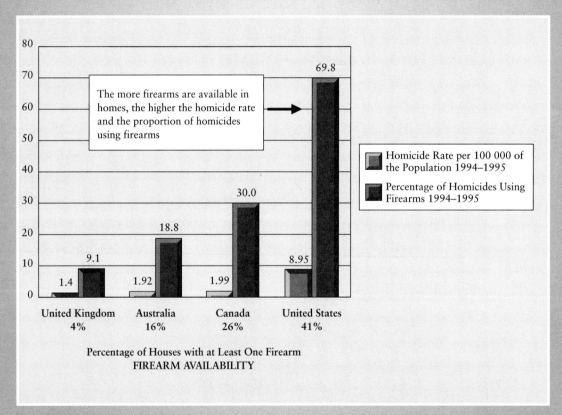

■ The relationship between firearm availability and homicide in four English-speaking countries

FIGURE 10.12 Correlational research relating firearms and violence finds the strongest relationship between homicide rates and availability of firearms. As shown, firearms are available in only 4 percent of the homes in the United Kingdom but in 41 percent of homes in the United States. The homicide rate in 1994 was six times higher in the U.S. than in the U.K., and the proportion of firearms used in homicides was almost eight times higher.

Source: Adapted from United Nations International Study on Firearm Regulation, 1998.

First, the social learning view might suggest that the more firearms available, the greater the opportunity for modeling their use. For example, the string of school student shootings may be what are termed "copycat" crimes—that is modeled on each other. The incident in Taber, Alberta occurred not long after a highly publicized case at Columbine High School in Colorado where 12 students and a teacher were killed. Modeling from films or video games has been suggested as a factor influencing the two teenaged boys who committed those murders. And parental modeling may have contributed to the actions of the first grade boy who killed the six-year old—his father had been prosecuted for gun-related offences (Globe & Mail, March 1, 2000, p. A 8).

Second, the existence of a weapons effect undermines the assertion that "Guns don't kill people, people kill people." This phenomenon suggests that the greater the availability of guns,

Aggressive Cue
An environmental cue that has become associated with violence and has the effect of intensifying or activating impulsive aggression.

the more violence will be triggered. Berkowitz (1993) has explained the weapons effect as occurring because a gun acts as an **aggressive cue**—a stimulus that past experience has taught us is associated with aggression. Such cues work to increase the likelihood of impulsive aggression (rather than premeditated or deliberate) by raising emotional arousal and increasing cognitive priming related to aggression. These notions are incorporated in the GAAM theory of aggression (see Chapter 8). Many aggressive cues exist in our environments but guns are particularly associated with extreme aggression—killing. As Berkowitz put it: "Guns not only permit violence, they can stimulate it as well. The finger pulls the trigger, but the trigger may also be pulling the finger"(1968, p.22).

Police Procedures

Long before a case reaches a courtroom, it is the job of the police to investigate and accumulate evidence that will be presented during a trial. Social psychological factors can influence the success of this process, as police interact with and question the suspects and eyewitnesses.

Questioning Suspects and Witnesses: The Effects of Police Procedures

Social psychological research indicates that most people are very likely to obey the law and to accept the outcomes of legal procedures so long as they believe that the laws and the procedures are fair and just (Miller & Ratner, 1996; Tyler et al., 1997). Each individual's beliefs are based in part on personal experiences with the legal system, and such experiences begin with the police.

In both the United Kingdom and North America, most citizens agree that police investigators should stress an *inquisitorial approach*—a search for the truth—rather than an *adversarial approach*—an attempt to prove guilt (Williamson, 1993). In the United Kingdom legislation was passed to provide training for police officers in an effort to persuade them to conduct interviews in a cooperative way—simply investigating the facts. One reason for such legislation is that court rulings on both sides of the Atlantic consistently agree that confessions obtained by means of coercive confrontation are unreliable and inadmissible (Gudjonsson, 1993).

Does police behaviour actually conform to the guidelines preferred by the public and mandated by the courts? In a Scotland Yard study designed to determine what detectives actually do, Williamson (1993) found that many officers had in fact adopted the desired investigative approach. Nevertheless, about half remained oriented toward obtaining a confession. The questioning of suspects can be viewed as falling along two dimensions. One dimension involves the goal of the interrogation: getting the suspect to confess (adver-

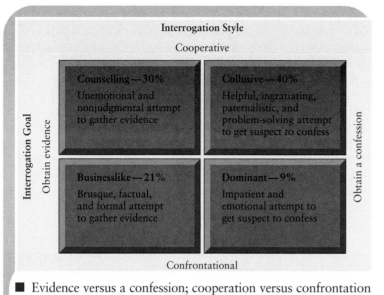

Interrogation Style

Cooperative

Counselling—30%	**Collusive—40%**
Unemotional and nonjudgmental attempt to gather evidence	Helpful, ingratiating, paternalistic, and problem-solving attempt to get suspect to confess
Businesslike—21%	**Dominant—9%**
Brusque, factual, and formal attempt to gather evidence	Impatient and emotional attempt to get suspect to confess

Interrogation Goal — Obtain evidence / Obtain a confession

Confrontational

■ Evidence versus a confession; cooperation versus confrontation

FIGURE 10.13 Police interrogations can be classified according to the goal of the questioning (to obtain evidence or to obtain a confession) and the style of the person asking the questions (cooperative or confrontational). About half of the detectives in a British study remained oriented toward obtaining a confession, despite official policy that stresses the importance of evidence.

Source: Based on data from Williamson, 1993

sarial) versus gathering evidence to determine the truth (inquisitorial). The other dimension deals with the way the interrogator seeks to achieve either goal: a friendly, cooperative style versus an angry, confrontational style.

When both dimensions are considered simultaneously, there are four possible styles of interrogation, as shown in Figure 10.13. Of the British detectives who were studied, 40 percent were classified as *collusive*; that is, they used a helpful, ingratiating, and fatherly approach as a way to obtain a confession. A *counselling* style was used by 30 percent; they made a friendly, unemotional, and nonjudgmental effort to obtain accurate evidence. The *businesslike* style was characteristic of 21 percent of the detectives; they were brusque, factual, and formal in the attempt to gather evidence. Only 9 percent were classified as *dominant*—behaving impatiently and emotionally as a way to get the suspect to confess.

Even though about half of the British detectives were observed seeking evidence rather than a confession, Moston and Stephenson (1993) raise doubts as to whether police in general are genuinely behaving in this fashion. They suggest that many officers still seek confessions but have learned to limit accusatory, persuasive questioning to times when outside observers and recording equipment are absent. Suspects, witnesses, or even victims may be especially vulnerable; for example, they may be mentally ill, extremely anxious, or highly suggestible. Given these vulnerabilities, dominant interrogators can and do take unfair advantage (Pearse, 1995).

Whatever the style of interrogation, its impact on the person being questioned is increased by the physical setting of the questioning (Schooler & Loftus, 1986; Smith & Ellsworth, 1987). It is not surprising that investigators much prefer to conduct a formal investigation in an intimidating location such as police headquarters rather than in nonthreatening surroundings such as the suspect's home or place of work. Both the setting and the authority of the questioner (a government representative) reinforce the ordinary citizen's belief that whoever is asking the questions is an expert possessing detailed knowledge of the case (Gudjonsson & Clark, 1986) and should not be opposed. In effect, the individual finds himself or herself as the target of social influence procedures designed to obtain compliance or even obedience, as described in Chapter 7.

Under these circumstances, three factors operate to encourage compliant and obedient responding. The witness usually feels (1) some *uncertainty* about the "right" answers, (2) some degree of *trust* in the officer asking the questions, and (3) an unspoken *expectation* that he or she is supposed to know the answer. As a result, rather than saying "I don't know" or "I don't remember" or "I'm not sure," most people tend to provide answers, at least tentative ones. Such answers are often provided by the use of **leading questions**. This type of questioning *leads* the witness

Leading Questions
Questions that are worded so as to suggest and elicit answers that the interrogator expects.

towards a particular answer—one that the interrogator implies that he or she expects (e.g., Smith & Ellsworth, 1987). And once a person provides an answer, he or she is inclined to accept its accuracy, especially if the interrogator provides immediate reinforcement with a nod or by saying "good," or the like. One result is that the person being questioned can honestly believe and even "remember" the details of something that never happened.

Interrogators need not resort to heavy-handed methods to elicit testimony or confession (Kassin & McNall, 1991). A "soft-sell" technique can produce the same ends. For example, in interacting with a suspect, an interrogator can *minimize* the strength of the evidence and the seriousness of the charge, implying that punishment will be mild or seeming to blame the victim for what happened. Kassin and McNall (1991) point out, however, that although this soft-sell technique may seem to be noncoercive, it is simply a less obvious way to elicit compliance. In effect, the suspect confesses after being lulled into a false sense of security.

The use of social influence techniques to elicit confessions sometimes goes a step beyond the soft sell; for example, deceit, such as lying to a suspect about evidence, can be used. Kassin examined the power of *deceit* in obtaining a false confession (e.g., Kassin & Kiechel,1996). From his review of such techniques, Kassin (1997) concludes that the criminal justice system currently does not provide adequate protection to the innocent person who becomes a suspect and that confessions obtained by means of manipulative procedures should not be considered credible.

The Eyewitness

Eyewitness Accuracy and Memory

Each year in courtrooms, witnesses present crucial evidence concerning many suspects (Goldstein, Chance, & Schneller, 1989). This testimony has a major impact on jurors—even though eyewitnesses are frequently wrong (Wolf & Bugaj, 1990). Altogether, jurors are most convinced by such characteristics as speaking style (speaking without hesitation in long elaborate sentences and without contradictions), inclusion of many details, and age (children are believed less than adults; Bell & Loftus, 1988; Leippe, Manion, & Romanczyk, 1992; Whitley & Greenberg, 1986). The more nervous the witness appears, the less accurate he or she is perceived to be (Bothwell & Jalil, 1992).

Because the events that are witnessed are almost always totally unexpected, of brief duration, and stressful (Hosch & Bothwell, 1990), even the most honest, intelligent, and well-meaning citizen may be inaccurate when asked to recall the details of a past event or to identify a suspect. Studies of mistakes (wrongful convictions) indicate that inaccurate eyewitness identification is the single most important reason that innocent defendants are convicted (Wells, 1993; Wells, Luus, & Windschitl, 1994).

Many factors have been found to affect the accuracy of witnesses in laboratory studies (Wells & Luus, 1990). For example, accuracy decreases if there is a weapon in the suspect's hand (Tooley et al., 1987), or if the suspect and the witness belong to different racial or ethnic groups (Platz & Hosch, 1988). Yuille and Tollestrup of the University of British Columbia found that eyewitnesses who had been drinking alcohol were less accurate than sober eyewitnesses in recalling the details of a staged theft, but they were equally able to recognize the thief's picture (Yuille & Tollestrup, 1990). Other research has shown that real life witnesses have a higher level of accuracy than is usually found in laboratory studies or simulations, perhaps because the real-life events of a crime are more important to witnesses (Yuille, 1983; Yuille & Cutshall, 1986). A witness's certainty is found to be unrelated to his or her accuracy

(Bothwell, Deffenbacher, & Brigham, 1987). In fact, one study demonstrated that the confidence of eyewitnesses can be manipulated (Luus & Wells, 1994). For instance, an eyewitness who falsely identifies a suspect can become highly confident if positive feedback is given by the investigating detective—"Another witness picked out the same one you did." This confidence remains high (a *perseverance effect*) even if the choice is later discredited.

Recovering Forgotten Memories of Past Events

You may have heard of "recovered memories": instances in which an adult, often during therapy, suddenly remembers a traumatic past event, most often centring on having been the victim of sexual abuse. More women than men report such memories, possibly because more young girls than young boys are sexually abused in childhood. Several recent celebrity autobiographies contain such accounts. However some commentators have emphasized that such memories can be innacurate (Humphreys, 1998).

At present, debate over **repressed memory** (totally forgetting a traumatic incident or incidents) has generated polarized opinions and strong emotions (Dineen, 1998; Pope, 1996). There is a conflict between (1) those who believe that victims accurately recall previously forgotten traumatic events, and that these events often involve child molesters who deserve punishment (Brown, 1997); and (2) those who believe that false recovered memories are subtly encouraged by well-meaning therapists and others. They inadvertently engage in "memory-recovery" practices, leading suggestible clients to remember events that did not actually occur (Frank, 1996; Lindsay, 1998; Loftus, 1998).

Considering how easy it is to encourage false confessions and false memories about a very recent event, false memories of events in the distant past should be at least as easy to create and perhaps more so. Indeed, a number of researchers have demonstrated that it is not difficult to create false childhood memories among adult subjects (Loftus, 1997; Loftus, Coan, & Pickrell, 1996; Loftus & Pickrell, 1995; Pezdek, Finger, & Hodge, 1997).

Studies of other types of traumatic experiences that result in memory loss (e.g., automobile accidents, natural disasters, combat, attempted suicide and the death of a parent are some examples) can be informative (Arrigo & Pezdek, 1997). This research indicates that sometimes memory of trauma is quite accurate and sometimes quite false. These findings suggest that recovered memories of childhood sexual abuse are also sometimes true and sometimes not, and that it would be extremely useful to develop ways to differentiate accurate memories from inaccurate ones (Poole & Lindsay, 1998).

Increasing the Accuracy of Witnesses

Despite the possibility for errors, you should not conclude that eyewitnesses are always wrong; often they are extremely accurate (Yuille & Cutshall, 1986). In addition, many attempts have been made to find ways of increasing the accuracy of witnesses. In Munsterberg's (1907) early research, he turned to hypnosis as a possible solution, but gave it up when he discovered the ease with which false memories can be suggested.

One target for improvement has been the police lineup in which witnesses examine several individuals (the suspect plus several nonsuspects) and try to identify the one who is guilty. Wells and Luus (1990) suggest that a lineup is analogous to a social psychological experiment. The officer conducting the lineup is the experimenter, the eyewitnesses are the research participants, the suspect is the primary stimulus, a witness's positive identification constitutes the behavioural data, and the presence of nonsuspects and the arrangement of the lineup constitute the research design. Also, the police have a hypoth-

Represessed Memory A form of psychogenic amnesia: forgetting the details of a traumatic event in order to protect against the anxiety and fear associated with that event.

There are many parallels between police lineups and social psychological experiments, according to Wells and Luus (1990). Based on this analogy, it follows that police officers can improve the accuracy of lineups by following well-established experimental procedures that provide safeguards against contaminated data. In lineups as well as in experiments, it is crucial to avoid biasing the data, demanding characteristics, and so forth.

TABLE 10.2 Lineups and experiments: How to obtain reliable and objective information

Recommended Procedures for Police Lineups and Photo Lineups	Analogous Procedures in Psychological Experiments
Witnesses should be separated and not permitted to interact.	Participants cannot communicate with one another before responding; otherwise, their data are not independent.
A witness should not be told or led to believe that the actual perpetrator is in the lineup.	Experimental instructions should be worded so as not to create demands that the participants respond in a given way.
The officer conducting the lineup should not know the identity of the suspected perpetrator.	The experimental assistants who interact with the participants should be kept "blind" as to both the hypothesis and the experimental condition to which the participant is assigned.
If there is more than one witness, the position of the suspect in the lineup should be different for each witness.	The order in which stimuli are presented should be randomized or counterbalanced across participants.
Not until the lineup procedure is totally concluded should cues of any kind be given to a witness with respect to whether or not the person he or she identified is actually the suspect in the case.	Not until the experiment is concluded and all dependent measures collected should a participant be debriefed and told the experimenter's hypothesis.

esis that the suspect is guilty. Finally, for either experiments or testimony, the data are stated in terms of probability, because neither experiments nor lineups can provide absolute certainty.

In Chapter 1 you read about factors that can interfere with obtaining accurate experimental results—for example, demand characteristics, experimenter bias, and the absence of a control group. The same factors can interfere with witness accuracy in police lineups. Based on this analogy, police can improve the accuracy of lineups by using common experimental procedures such a control group. For example, with a **blank-lineup control** procedure, a witness is first shown a lineup containing only innocent nonsuspects (Wells, 1984). If the witness fails to identify any of them, there is increased confidence in his or her accuracy. If an innocent person is identified, the witness is informed and then cautioned about the danger of making a false identification; this improves witness accuracy when actual lineups are presented. Table 10.2 summarizes parallels between lineups and experiments and indicates possible ways to improve the accuracy of eyewitnesses.

Other procedures that improve accuracy include presenting pictures of the crime scene and of the victim to the witness before an identification is made (Cutler, Penrod, & Martens, 1987), showing the lineup one member at a time rather than as a group (Leary, 1988), and encouraging witnesses to give their first impressions (Dunning & Stern, 1994).

Blank-lineup Control A procedure in which a witness is shown a police lineup that does not include a suspect; this helps police to determine the accuracy of the witness and to emphasize the importance of being cautious in making a positive identification.

FIGURE 10.14 Research shows that more attractive individuals tend to be treated more leniently in the legal system, especially if they are female. However, this advantage tends to decrease when fatality is involved in the crime. Given that often we believe that "what is beautiful is also good," would the attractiveness of this person influence your judgment of her during a trial?

The Defendant

Characteristics of Defendants

If you think of a defendant as a stranger at a party and a juror as someone who encounters and evaluates this stranger, you should be able to think of many social psychological factors that might determine how the juror would react to the defendant. Especially important are nonverbal communication and attribution (Chapter 2); prejudice and discrimination (Chapter 5); impression formation and impression management (Chapters 6 and 7), and interpersonal attraction (Chapter 6). Such matters should, of course, be irrelevant when we judge the guilt or innocence of someone accused of committing a crime; but they nevertheless do influence the outcomes of both real and simulated trials (Dane, 1992).

Research consistently indicates that attractive defendants are treated better than unattractive ones in gaining acquittals, receiving light sentencing, eliciting sympathy of the jury, and being considered not dangerous, according to studies conducted in Canada (Esses & Webster, 1988) and in the United States (Stevens, 1980; Wuensch, Castellow, & Moore, 1991; Castellow, Wuensch, & Moore, 1990). This *attractiveness effect* is stronger with serious but nonfatal crimes such as burglary, and with female defendants (Quigley, Johnson, & Byrne, 1995)—see Figure 10.14. Some investigators conclude that attractiveness has such effects because of the stereotype that "what is beautiful is good." If this stereotype is operative, judicial decisions may be based primarily on inferences about character that are based on appearance (Egbert et al., 1992; Moore et al., 1994). Because lawyers are aware of this attractiveness bias, they advise their clients to do everything possible to improve their appearance before entering the courtroom.

The defendant's gender and socio-economic status can sometimes affect judicial decisions (Mazella & Feingold, 1994): being female and of high socio-economic status is usually an advantage. However, in mock trial, Cruse and Leigh (1987) presented jurors with testimony in an assault case in which either a male or a female defendant was alleged to have cut a victim with a kitchen knife. In this case, the woman was judged guilty more often. The researchers suggest that stabbing someone with a knife was a masculine behaviour—a woman "shouldn't act that way." In other words, she violated expectancies based on gender roles, making her behaviour seem more heinous.

The defendant's ethnicity and race also influence the outcome. Defendants whose testimony is in another language that must be translated are judged more guilty than when the same testimony is originally given in English (Stephan & Stephan, 1986). The police forces of a number of major Canadian cities have had internal inquiries into charges of biased treatment or brutality towards Asian, African or Native Canadians. The Royal Commission of Inquiry into the wrongful conviction for murder of Donald Marshall, a Micmac Indian, identified racist attitudes of the police and other officials as one of the causes of this injustice. Further, Aboriginal people are disproportionately represented in the Canadian prison population, accounting for less than 3 percent of the population as a whole, but for 20 percent of provincial prison admissions and 12 percent of federal admissions (Menzies, 1999). After reviewing their treatment at many levels of the judicial process, Pontin and Kiely suggest that "Aboriginal people are victims of a discriminatory criminal justice system" (Pontin & Kiely, p. 155, 1997). In the United States, African-American defendants are more likely to be convicted than white defendants, and are more likely to receive a prison sentence (Stewart, 1980) or the death penalty (Sniffen, 1991). A study of American trials also indicated that 11.1 percent of criminals (regardless of race) who kill a white victim receive a death sentence, while only 4.5 percent of those who kill a black victim are sentenced to die (Henderson & Taylor, 1985). Research into the O. J. Simpson case showed that public opinion was split along racial lines: white Americans believed overwhelmingly in his guilt, while black Americans were equally sure of his innocence (Graham, Weiner & Zucker, 1997; Toobin, 1995).

KEY POINTS

- *Forensic psychology* studies psychological factors that influence the legal system.
- Extensive media coverage of crime leads to misperceptions about its frequency, but the coverage occurs because people find it interesting.
- Social psychology has studied the importance of *aggressive cues*, such as guns, as contributors to the level of violence. These findings have implications for the issue of gun or firearms control.
- Most people would prefer police to search for the truth rather than attempt to prove guilt, but both interrogation approaches are common.
- For a variety of reasons, it is not uncommon for an innocent person to confess to a crime and even to believe himself or herself to be guilty.
- A serious and controversial legal problem is the recovery of *repressed memories* of past criminal events that sometimes turn out to be false memories.
- Eyewitnesses to a crime often make mistakes, but a variety of procedures have been developed to help ensure greater accuracy.
- Defendants' physical and social characteristics can influence legal outcomes. One example is that racial similarity or dissimilarity of defendants and jurors can have a major impact on the final verdict in a trial.

Ideas to Take with You

Don't Rush to Judgment

Whether as a potential juror or as an official member of a jury, you will be exposed to a great deal of information, many arguments, and diverse facts about any given crime and about the suspected criminal. Even if you are simply a member of the general public with no formal role to play, it is still important that you keep in mind some of the issues involved in reaching valid conclusions about legal matters. If you are actually a member of the jury, your open-mindedness can have a huge impact on the defendant's life.

Remember: When a Suspect is Arrested, This Does Not Automatically Indicate Guilt.

When you hear the details of a brutal crime and then learn on TV or in the newspapers that a suspect has been arrested, don't assume that the crime is necessarily solved or that the arrested individual had been found guilty. Before guilt or innocence is determined, there must be an indictment, a trial, the presentation of evidence for and against the defendant, a consideration of precise legal issues, and an attempt by the jury to reach consensus. The most reasonable position to take is that either the prosecution or the defence might be correct, so you would be wise to construct two alternative schemas for yourself—one in which you store all of the information indicating guilt and one in which you store all of the information indicating innocence. Wait until all the facts are in before deciding which schema makes more sense.

Separate Attraction from Judgments Based on Evidence.

It is probably not possible to enter any situation with a totally objective, open mind. Remember, research findings suggest that we automatically respond to stimuli with relatively positive or relatively negative attitudes. The best we can do is to separate how much we like the defendant from what we know on the basis of testimony and physical evidence. No matter how you feel about the individual's appearance, ethnic background, political views, sexual orientation, or whatever else, the question is not how much you like him or her but whether or not the bulk of the evidence indicates guilt beyond a reasonable doubt. In everyday life, we often blur the distinction between attraction toward someone and factual knowledge about that person. In the courtroom, it is crucial that such distinctions be made.

Don't Let Your Opinion be Swayed by Emotional Appeals.

We all know that the prosecutor and the defence lawyer have very specific and quite different scenarios to "sell." Each side wants to convince the onlookers that there is only one version of the truth; and each side will try to appeal to your feelings, your prejudices, your patriotism, or whatever else might be effective in convincing you. Again, your task is not to deny the disgust you may feel about a brutal crime or the sympathy you may feel toward an innocent citizen who has been dragged into court and accused unfairly of committing a criminal act. Both feelings are reasonable. The question, however, is once again a matter of what is indicated by the evidence and what is prescribed as legally relevant. The courtroom is clearly a place where it is important to separate emotional processes from cognitive ones; indeed, our system of law is based on the assumption that regular citizens have the ability to do this.

Summary and Review of Key Points

Applying Social Psychology to Health Issues

● Health-related information comes to us daily, and new research findings often modify or reverse earlier findings. Consumers of health information need to remain informed, open-minded, and cautious.

Stress is defined as any event that is perceived as a potential source of physical or emotional harm. *Psychoneuroimmunology* studies the way in which stress can lead to physical illness both indirectly, by affecting health-related behaviour, and directly, through its effect on physiological functioning.

A wide variety of dispositional differences are associated with the ability to resist the negative effects of stress (the *self-healing personality*) as opposed to the tendency to be badly affected by stress (the *disease-prone personality*).

Effective strategies for *coping* with stress include increasing one's physical fitness; *regulatory control* of emotion and cognition; encouraging *positive affect*; and establishing networks of *social support*.

Coping with the stress of illness and medical treatment requires all of these same coping strategies as well as (1) acquiring as much knowledge as possible about each aspect of one's condition and the treatment procedures and (2) gaining as much control as possible of every step of the process.

Applying Social Psychology to the World of Work: Job Satisfaction, Helping, and Leadership

● Work is often our most time-consuming activity and one usually carried out in a social setting. Thus, the findings and principles of social psychology help to explain behaviour in work settings.

Job satisfaction is an individual's attitude toward her or his job. It is influenced by organizational factors such as working conditions and the fairness of reward systems, and by personal factors. Recent findings suggest that job satisfaction is often highly stable over time and may be influenced by genetic factors.

The relationship between job satisfaction and task performance is relatively weak, partly because many factors other than work-related attitudes influence performance.

Individuals often engage in prosocial behaviour at work, known as *organizational citizenship behaviour* (OCB). OCB is influenced by several factors, including employees' trust in their boss and the organization, the extent to which employees define their job responsibilities broadly, and organizational commitment.

Leadership refers to the process through which one member of a group (its leader) influences other group members toward the attainment of shared group goals.

Although the *great person theory* of leadership is no longer supported, research findings suggest that leaders do indeed have special traits.

Leadership styles studied by early researchers were the *democratic* and *autocratic* styles of leadership. More recent research has focussed on a *directiveness-permissiveness* dimension of leadership.

Leaders high in *process directiveness* direct the group process so as to ensure that all views are heard and all members participate. Leaders high in *outcome directiveness* try to induce the group to accept their views. Research shows process directiveness is more beneficial for group functioning.

Charismatic leaders exert profound effects on their followers and often change their societies, using such behaviours as stating a clear vision, framing the group's goals in ways that magnify their importance, and using a stirring personal style.

Cross-cultural research suggests that major differences between leaders in Asian and North American corporations stem from differences in cultural values such as the extent to which *interdependence* of corporation and society is recognized and *power-distance*.

Social Psychology and the Legal System

● *Forensic psychology* studies psychological factors that influence the legal system.

Extensive media coverage of crime leads to misperceptions about its frequency, but the coverage occurs because people find it interesting.

Social psychology has studied the importance of *aggressive cues*, such as guns, as contributors to the level of violence. These findings have implication for the issue of gun or firearms control.

Most people would prefer police to search for the truth rather than attempt to prove guilt, but both interrogation approaches are common.

For a variety of reasons, it is not uncommon for an innocent person to confess to a crime and even to believe himself or herself to be guilty.

A serious and controversial legal problem is the recovery of *repressed memories* of past criminal events that turn out to be false memories.

Eyewitnesses to a crime often make mistakes, but a variety of procedures have been developed to help ensure greater accuracy.

Defendant physical and social characteristics can influence legal outcomes. One example is that racial similarity or dissimilarity of defendants and jurors can have a major impact on the final verdict in a trial.

For More Information

Bass, B. M. (1998). *Transformational leadership: Industrial, military, and educational impact.* Mahwah, NJ: Erlbaum.

An expert researcher who has studied leadership for several decades reviews existing evidence concerning the nature and effects of transformational leadership. A stimulating, thought-provoking book.

Loftus, E. F. (1992). *Witness for the defense.* New York: St. Martin's Press.

A comprehensive summary of research in the area of forensic psychology by one of the leading investigators in this field.

Pope, K. S., & Brown, L. S. (1996). *Recovered memories of abuse: Assessment, therapy, forensics.* Washington, DC: American Psychological Association.

This guide presents an overview of the problem of recovered memories, dealing with both legal and psychological issues. The authors cover such issues as the study of memory, the effects of trauma, the ways in which people are questioned, and the issues that face therapists and expert witnesses.

Radley, A. (1994). *Making sense of illness: The social psychology of health and disease.* Thousand Oaks, CA: Sage.

The author cuts across the fields of health psychology, sociology, and medicine to clarify the importance of psychological factors in health issues. The book discusses responding to stress, coping with acute and chronic health problems, and behaving in ways that promote good health and prevent disease.

Weblinks

www.ncbe.gwu.edu/ncbepubs/symposia/first/issues-dis.htm
"Issues in Foreign Language and Second Language Education" by Wallace Lambert (Proceedings of the First Research Symposium on Limited English Proficient Student Issues, 1990)

www.carleton.ca/~rthibode/activism.html
Activism and Psychology home page, Carleton University

www.law.emory.edu/ELJ/volumes/fall97/brown.html
"Some Thoughts About Social Perception and Employment Discrimination Law" by Brown, Subrin, Baumann, Northeastern University School of Law

www.ntu.ac.uk/soc/psych/miller/objects.htm
"The Social Psychology of Objects" by Hugh Miller, Nottingham Trent University, England

miavx1.muohio.edu/~shermarc/p324opt.htmlx
"Optimistic Bias in Perceiving Physical and Mental Health Risks" by Berger, Magnuson, Maxwell, Tubbs, Miami University, Ohio

References

Abrams, D., Wetherell, M., Cochrane, S., Hogg, M. A., & Turner, J. C. (1990). Knowing what to think by knowing who you are: Self-categorization and the nature of norm information, conformity, and group polarization. *British Journal of Social Psychology, 29,* 97–119.

Adair, J. G. (1992). Empirical study of indigenization and development of the discipline in developing countries. In Saburo Iwawaki et al., *Innovations in Cross-cultural Psychology* (pp. 62–74). Amsterdam: Swets and Zeitlinger.

Adair, J. G. (1996). The indigenous psychology bandwagon: Cautions and considerations. In J. Pandey, D. Sinha, & D. P. S. Bhawuk (Eds.), *Asian contribution to cross-cultural psychology* (pp. 50–58). Thousand Oaks, CA: Sage.

Adams, J. M., & Jones, W. H. (1997). The conceptualization of marital commitment: An integrative analysis. *Journal of Personality and Social Psychology, 72,* 1177–1196.

Adams, J. S. (1965). Inequity in social exchange. In L. Berkowitz (Ed.), *Advances in experimental social psychology* (Vol. 2, pp. 267–299). New York: Academic Press.

Adams, M. (1997). *Sex in the snow: Canadian social values at the end of the millennium.* Toronto: Viking Penguin.

Adams, R. G., & Blieszner, R. (1994). An integrative conceptual framework for friendship research. *Journal of Social and Personal Relationships, 11,* 163–184.

Ader, R., & Cohen, N. (1993). Psychoneuroimmunology: Conditioning and stress. In L. W. Porter & M. R. Rosenzweig (Eds.), *Annual review of psychology* (Vol. 44, pp. 53–85). Palo Alto, CA: Annual Reviews, Inc.

Adorno, T. W., Frenkel-Brunswick, E., Levinson, D. J., & Sanford, R. H. (1950). *The authoritarian personality.* New York: Harper & Row.

Affleck, G., Tennen, H., Urrows, S., & Higgins, P. (1994). Person and contextual features of daily stress reactivity: Individual differences in relations of undesirable daily events with mood disturbance and chronic pain intensity. *Journal of Personality and Social Psychology, 66,* 329–340.

Agnew, C. R., & Thompson, V. D. (1994). Causal inferences and responsibility attributions concerning as HIV-positive target: The double-edged sword of physical attractiveness. *Journal of Social Behavior and Personality, 9,* 181–190.

Ajzen, I. (1987). Attitudes, traits, and actions: Dispositional prediction of behavior in personality and social psychology. In L. Berkowitz (Ed.), *Advances in experimental social psychology* (Vol. 20). San Diego, CA: Academic Press.

Ajzen, I. (1991). The theory of planned behavior: Special issue: Theories of cognitive self-regulation. *Organizational Behavior and Human Decision Processes, 50,* 179–211.

Ajzen, I., & Fishbein, M. (1980). *Understanding attitudes and predicting social behavior.* Englewood Cliffs, NJ: Prentice-Hall.

Alagna, F. J., Whitcher, S. J., & Fisher, J. D. (1979). Evaluative reactions to interpersonal touch in a counseling interview. *Journal of Counseling Psychology, 26,* 465–472.

Albright, L., Malloy, T.E., Qi, D. & Kenny, D.A. (1997). Cross-cultural consensus in personality judgments. *Journal of Personality and Social Psychology, 73,* 270–280.

Alexander, M. J., & Higgins, E. T. (1993). Emotional trade-offs of becoming a parent: How social roles influence self-discrepancy effects. *Journal of Personality and Social Psychology, 65,* 1259–1269.

Alicke, M. D., & Largo, E. (1995). The role of the self in the false consensus effect. *Journal of Experimental Social Psychology, 31,* 28–47.

Allen, N.J., & Meyer, J.P. (1990). The measurement and antecedents of affective, continuance, and normative commitment to the organization. *Journal of Occupational Psychology, 63,* 1–18.

Allen, V. L., & Levine, J. M. (1971). Social support and conformity: The role of independent assessment of reality. *Journal of Experimental Social Psychology, 4,* 48–58.

Alliger, G. M., & Williams, K. J. (1991). Affective congruence and the employment interview. *Advances in Information Processing in Organizations, 4,* 31–43.

Allison, S. T., Worth, L. T,m & King, M. C. (1990). Group decisions as social inference heuristics. *Journal of Personality and Social Psychology, 58,* 801–811.

Allport, F. H. (1920). The influence of the group upon association and thought. *Journal of Experimental Psychology, 3,* 159–182.

Allport, F. H. (1924). *Social psychology.* Boston: Houghton Mifflin.

Allport, G.W. (1954). *The nature of prejudice.* Reading, MA: Addison-Wesley.

Allyn, J., & Festinger, L. (1961). The effectiveness of unanticipated persuasive communications. *Journal of Abnormal and Social Psychology, 62,* 35–40.

Allyn, J., & Festinger, L. (1961). The effectiveness of unanticipated persuasive communication. *Journal of Abnormal and Social Psychology, 62,* 35–40.

Altemeyer, B. (1981). *Right-wing authoritarianism.* Winnipeg: University of Manitoba Press.

Altemeyer, B. (1988). *Enemies of freedom.* San Fancisco: Jossey-Bass.

Altman, I & Taylor, D.A. (1973). *Social penetration: The development of interpersonal relationships.* New York: Holt, Rinehart & Winston.

Alvaro, E. M., & Crano, W. D. (1996). Cognitive responses to minority- or majority-based communications: Factors that underlie minority influence. *British Journal of Social Psychology, 34,* 105–121.

Amato, P. R. (1986). Emotional arousal and helping behavior in a real-life emergency. *Journal of Applied Social Psychology, 16,* 633–641.

Amato, P.R. (1983). Helping behavior in urban and rural settings: Field studies based on a taxonomic organization of helping episodes. *Journal of Personality and Social Psychology, 45,* 571–586.

Ambady, N., & Rosenthal, R. (1992). Thin slices of expressive behavior as predictors of interpersonal consequences: A meta-analysis. *Psychological Bulletin, 111,* 256–274.

Ambiguity. *Journal of Personality and Social Psychology, 64,*

Amirkhan, J. H., Risinger, R. T., & Swickert, R. J. (1995). Extraversion: A "hidden" personality factor in coping? *Journal of Personality, 63,* 189–212.

Andersen, S. M., & Baum, A. (1994). Transference in interpersonal relations: Inferences and affect based on significant-other representations. *Journal of Personality, 62,* 459–497.

Anderson, C. A. (1989). Temperature and aggression: The ubiquitous effects of heat on the occurrence of human violence. *Psychological Bulletin, 106,* 74–96.

Anderson, C. A. (1997). Effects of violent movies and trait hostility on hostile feelings and aggressive thoughts. *Aggressive Behavior, 23,* 161–178.

Anderson, C. A., Anderson, K. B., & Deuser, W. E. (1996). A general framework for the study of affective aggression: Tests of effects of extreme temperatures and of viewing weapons on hostility. *Personality and Social Psychology Bulletin, 22* 366–376.

Anderson, C. A., Anderson, K. B., & Deuser, W. E. (1996). Examining an affective aggression framework: Weapon and temperature effects on aggressive thoughts, affect, and attitudes. *Personality and Social Psychology Bulletin, 22,* 366–376.

Anderson, C. A., Bushman, B. J., & Groom, R. W. (1997). Hot years and serious and deadly assault: Empirical tests of the heat hypothesis. *Journal of Personality and Social Psychology, 73,* 1213–1223.

Anderson, N. H. (1981). *Foundations of information interaction theory.* New York: Academic Press.

Anderson, V. L. (1993). Gender differences in altruism among holocaust rescuers. *Journal of Social Behavior and Personality, 8,* 43–58.

Anthony, T., Cooper, C., & Mullen, B. (1992). Cross-racial identification: A social cognitive integration. *Personality and Social Psychology Bulletin, 18,* 296–301.

Argyle, M. (1988). *Bodily communication.* New York: Methuen

Armstrong, P. (1996). From caring and sharing to greedy and mean? In A. Lapierre, P. Savard.& P. Smart (Eds.), *Language, culture and values in Canada at the dawn of the twenty-first century.* Ottawa: Carleton University Press.

Aron, A., & Henkemeyer, L. (1995). Marital satisfaction and passionate love. *Journal of Social and Personal Relationships, 12,* 139–146.

Aron, A., & Westbay, L. (1996). Dimensions of the prototype of love. *Journal of Personality and Social Psychology, 70,* 535–551.

Aron, A., Aron, E. N., & Allen, J. (1998). Motivations for unreciprocated love. *Personality and Social Psychology Bulletin, 24,* 787–796.

Aron, A., Dutton, D. G., Aron, E. N., & Iverson, A. (1989). Experiences of falling in love. *Journal of Social and Personal Relationships, 6,* 243–257.

Aronoff, J., Woike, B. A., & Hyman, L. M. (1992). Which are the stimuli in facial displays of anger and happiness? Configurational bases of emotion recognition. *Journal of Personality and Social Psychology, 62,* 1050–1066.

Aronson, E. (1999). *The social animal.* (8th ed.). New York: Worth.

Aronson, E., Bridgeman, D. L., & Oeffner, R. (1978). Interdependent interactions and prosocial behavior. *Journal of Research and Development in Education, 12,* 16–27.

Aronson, E., Fried, C., & Stone, J. (1991). Overcoming denial: Increasing the intention to use condoms through the induction of hypocrisy. *American Journal of Public Health, 18,* 1636–1640.

Arriaga, X. B., & Rusbult, C. E. (1998). Standing in my partner's shoes: Partner perspective taking and reactions to accommodative dilemmas. *Personality and Social Psychology Bulletin, 24,* 927–948.

Arrigo, J. M., & Pezdek, K. (1997). Lessons from the study of psychogenic amnesia. *Current Directions in Psychological Science, 6,* 148–152.

Arvey, R. D., Bouchard, T. J., Jr., Segal, N. L., & Abraham, L. M. (1989). Job satisfaction: Genetic and environmental components. *Journal of Applied Psychology, 74,* 187–192.

Asante, M. K. (1980). *Afrocentricity: The theory of social change.* Buffalo, NY: Amulefi Publishing Company.

Asch, S. E. (1946). Forming impressions of personality. *Journal of Abnormal and Social Psychology, 41,* 258–290.

Asch, S. E. (1951). Effects of group pressure upon the modification and distortion of judgment. In H. Guetzkow (Ed.), *Groups, leadership, and men.* Pittsburgh, PA: Carnegie.

Asch, S. E. (1955). Opinions and social pressure. *Scientific American, 193*(5), 31–35.

Asch, S. E. (1956). Studies of independence and conformity: A minority of one against unanimous majority. *Psychological Monographs, 70* (Whole no. 416).

Aspinwall, L. G. (1998). Rethinking the role of positive affect in self-regulation. *Motivation and Emotion, 22,* 1–32.

Atwood, M. (1984). *Second words: Selected critical prose.* Boston: Beacon Press.

Azar, B. (1997a, November). Defining the trait that makes us human. *APA Monitor, 1,* 15.

Azar, B. (1997b, November). Forgiveness helps keep relationships steadfast. *APA Monitor,* 14.

Baer, D. (1999). Educational credentials and the changing occupational structure. In J. Curtis, E. Grabb, & N. Guppy (Eds.), *Social inequality in Canada: Patterns, problems, and policies* (2nd ed., pp. 92–106). Scarborough, Ont.: Prentice Hall.

Baize, H. R., Jr., & Schroeder, J. E. (1995). Personality and mate selection in personal ads: Evolutionary preferences in a public mate selection process. *Journal of Social Behavior and Personality, 10,* 517–536.

Bandura, A. (1973). *Aggression: A social learning analysis.* Englewood Cliffs, NJ: Prentice-Hall.

Bandura, A. (1993). Self-efficacy mechanisms in psychobiological functioning. *Stanford University Psychologist*, 1, 5–6.

Bandura, A., Ross, D., & Ross, S. (1963). Imitation of film-mediated aggressive models. *Journal of Abnormal and Social Psychology*, 66, 3–11.

Banner, L.W. (1983). *American beauty.* Chicago: The University Press.

Bargh, J. A. (1997). The automaticity of everyday life. In R. S. Wyer Jr. (Ed.), *Advances in social cognition* (Vol. 10). Mahwah, NJ: Erlbaum.

Barnes, F. (1989). Fearless leader. *New Republic*, 201(22), 11–13.

Barnlund, D.C. (1989). *Communicative styles of Japanese and Americans.* Belmont, CA: Wadsworth Publishing.

Baron, R. A. (1972a). Aggression as a function of ambient temperature and prior anger arousal. *Journal of Personality and Social Psychology*, 21, 183–189.

Baron, R. A. (1972b). Reducing the influence of an aggressive model: The restraining effects of peer censure. *Journal of Experimental Social Psychology*, 8, 266–275.

Baron, R. A. (1974a). Aggression as a function of victim's pain cues, level of prior anger arousal, and exposure to an aggressive model. *Journal of Personality and Social Psychology*, 29, 117–124.

Baron, R. A. (1987). Interviewer's moods and reactions to job applicants: The influence of affective states on applied social judgments. *Journal of Applied Social Psychology*, 16, 16–28.

Baron, R. A. (1989a). Applicant strategies during job interviews. In G. R. Ferris & R. W. Eder (Eds.), *The employment interview: Theory, research, and practice* (pp. 204–216). Newbury Park, CA: Sage.

Baron, R. A. (1989b). Personality and organizational conflict: The Type A behavior pattern and self-monitoring. *Organizational Behavior and Human Decision Processes*, 44, 281–297.

Baron, R. A. (1990). Attributions and organizational conflict. In S. Graham & V. Folkes (Eds.), *Attribution theory: Applications to achievement, mental health, and interpersonal conflict* (pp. 185–204). Hillsdale, NJ: Erlbaum.

Baron, R. A. (1993). Effects of interviewers' moods and applicant qualifications on ratings of job applicants. Manuscript submitted for publication.

Baron, R. A. (1994). The physical environment of work settings: Effects of task performance, interpersonal relations, and job satisfaction. In M. Staw & L. L. Cummings (Eds.), *Research in organizational behavior* (Vol. 16, pp. 1–46). Greenwich, CT: JAI Press.

Baron, R. A. (1995). The sweet smell of . . . helping: Effects of pleasant ambient odors on prosocial behavior in shopping malls. Manuscript submitted for publication.

Baron, R. A. (1997a). The sweet smell of helping: Effects of pleasant ambient fragrance on prosocial behavior in shopping malls. *Personality and Social Psychology Bulletin*, 23, 498–503.

Baron, R. A., & Bronfen, M. I. (1994). A whiff of reality: Empirical evidence concerning the effects of pleasant fragrances on work-related behavior. *Journal of Applied Social Psychology*, 23, 1179–1203.

Baron, R. A., & Neuman, J. H. (1996). Workplace violence and workplace aggression: Evidence on their relative frequency and potential causes. *Aggressive Behavior*, 22, 161–173.

Baron, R. A., & Richardson, D. R. (1994). *Human aggression* (2nd ed.). New York: Plenum.

Baron, R. A., & Thomley, J. (1994). A whiff of reality: Positive affect as a potential mediator of the effects of pleasant fragrances on task performance and helping. *Environment and Behavior*, 26, 766–784.

Baron, R. A., Neuman, J. H., & Geddes, D. (1999). Social and personal determinants of workplace aggression: Evidence for the impact of perceived injustice and the Type A behavior pattern. *Aggressive Behavior*, 25.

Baron, R. A., Rea, M. S., & Daniels, S. G. (1992). Lighting as a source of environmentally-generated positive affect in work settings: Impact on cognitive tasks and interpersonal behaviors. *Motivation and Emotion*, 14, 1–34.

Baron, R. A., Russell, G. W., & Arms, R. L. (1985). Negative ions and behavior: Impact on mood, memory, and aggression among Type A and Type B persons. *Journal of Personality and Social Psychology*, 48, 746–754.

Baron, R. S. (1986). Distraction-conflict theory: Progress and problems. In L. Berkowitz (Ed.), *Advances in experimental social psychology*, Vol. 20. New York: Academic Press.

Baron, R. S., Kerr, N. L., & Miller, N. (1992). *Group process, group decision, group action. Pacific Grove, CA:* Brooks/Cole.

Baron, R. S., Moore, D., & Sanders, G. S. (1978). Distraction as a source of drive in social facilitation research. *Journal of Personality and Social Psychology*, 36, 816–824.

Baron, R. S., Vandello, U. A., & Brunsman, B. (1996). The forgotten variable in conformity research: Impact of task importance on social influence. *Journal of Personality and Social Psychology*, 71, 915–927.

Barrett, L. F., & Russell, J. A. (1998). Independence and bipolarity in the structure of current affect. *Journal of Personality and Social Psychology*, 74, 967–984.

Barrett, S.R. (1987). *Is God a racist? The right wing in Canada.* Toronto: University of Toronto Press.

Barry, H., Child, I., & Bacon, M. (1959).Relation of child training to subsistence economy. *American Anthropologist*, 61, 51–63.

Bartholomew, K. (1990). Avoidance of intimacy: An attachment perspective. *Journal of Social and Personal Relationships*, 7, 147–178.

Bartholomew, K. (1993). From childhood to adult relationships: Attachment theory and research. In S.W. Duck (Ed.), *Understanding relationship processes 2: Learning about relationships* (pp. 30–32). London: Sage.

Bartholomew, K., & Horowitz, L.M. (1991) Attachment styles among young adults: A test of a four-category model. *Journal of Personality and Social Psychology*, 61, 226–244.

Bass, B. I. (1998). *Leadership* (2nd ed.). New York: Free Press.

Batson, C. D., Early, S., & Salvarani, G. (1997). Perspective taking: Imagining how another feels versus imagining how you would feel. *Personality and Social Psychology Bulletin*, 23, 751–758.

Batson, C.D., Schoenrade, P., & Ventis, W.L. (1993). *Religion and the individual: A social-psychological perspective.* New York: Oxford University Press.

Baum, A. (1994). Behavioral, biological, and environmental interactions in disease processes. In S. Blumenthal, K. Matthews, & S. Weiss (Eds.), *New research frontiers in behavioral medicine: Proceedings of the national conference* (p. 62). Washington, DC: NIH Publications.

Baumeister, R. F., Chesner, S. P., Sanders, P. S., & Tice, D. M. (1988). Who's in charge here? Group leaders do lend help in emergencies. *Personality and Social Psychology Bulletin, 14,* 17–22.

Baumeister, R. F., Wotman, S. R., & Stillwell, A. M. (1993). Unrequited love: On heartbreak, anger, guilt, scriptlessness, and humiliation. *Journal of Personality and Social Psychology, 64,* 377–394.

Baumrind, D. (1985). Research using intentional deception: Ethical issues revisited. *American Psychologist, 40,* 165–174.

Beaton, A., Tougas, F., & Joly, S. (1996). Neosexism among male managers: Is it a matter of numbers? *Journal of Applied Social Psychology, 26,* 2189–2203.

Beckwith, J. B. (1994). Terminology and social relevance in psychological research on gender. *Social Behavior and Personality, 22,* 329–336.

Bednar, R.L., Wells, M.G., & Peterson, S.R. (1989). *Self-esteem: Paradoxes and innovations in clinical theory and practice.* Washington, DC: American Psychological Association.

Bell, B. E., & Loftus, E. F. (1988). Degree of detail of eyewitness testimony and mock juror judgments. *Journal of Applied Social Psychology, 18,* 1171–1192.

Bell, P. A. (1992). In defense of the negative affect escape model of heat and aggression. *Psychological Bulletin, 111,* 342–346.

Bell, S. T., Kuriloff, P. J., & Lottes, I. (1994). Understanding attributions of blame in stranger rape and date rape situations: An examination of gender, race, identification, and students' social perceptions of rape victims. *Journal of Applied Social Psychology, 24,* 1719–1734.

Bem, S. L. (1974). The measurement of psychological androgyny. *Journal of Consulting and Clinical Psychology, 42,* 155–162.

Bem, S. L. (1981). Gender schema theory: A cognitive account of sex typing. *Psychological Review, 88,* 354–364.

Bem, S. L. (1983). Gender schema theory and its implications for child development: Raising gender-aschematic children in a gender schematic society. Science: *Journal of Women in Culture and Society, 8,* 598–616.

Bem, S. L. (1984). Androgyny and gender-schema theory: A conceptual and empirical integration. In *Nebraska symposium on motivation*: Psychology and gender (pp. 179–226). Lincoln: University of Nebraska Press.

Bem, S. L. (1995). Dismantling gender polarization and compulsory heterosexuality: Should we turn the volume down or up? *Journal of Sex Research, 32,* 329–334.

Beninger, J.R. (1987). Personalization of mass media and the growth of pseudo-community. *Communications Research, 14,* 352–371.

Benjamin, E. (1998, January 14). Storm brings out good, bad and greedy. *Albany Times Union,* pp. A1, A6.

Benson, P. L., Karabenick, S. A., & Lerner, R. M. (1976). Pretty pleases: The effects of physical attractiveness, race, and sex on receiving help. *Journal of Experimental Social Psychology, 12,* 409–415.

Berk, R. A. (Ed.). (1982). *Handbook of methods for detecting item bias. Baltimore,* MD: The Johns Hopkins University Press.

Berkowitz, L. (1968). Impulse, aggression and the gun. *Psychology Today, 2 (4),* 18–22.

Berkowitz, L. (1987). Mood, self-awareness, and willingness to help. *Journal of Personality and Social Psychology, 52,* 721–724.

Berkowitz, L. (1988). Frustrations, appraisals, and aversively stimulated aggression. *Aggressive Behavior, 14,* 3–11.

Berkowitz, L. (1989). Frustration-aggression hypothesis: Examination and reformulation. *Psychological Bulletin, 106,* 59–73.

Berkowitz, L. (1993). *Aggression: Its causes, consequences, and control.* Philadelphia: Temple University Press.

Berkowitz, L., & LePage, A. (1967). Weapons as aggression-eliciting stimuli. *Journal of Personality and Social Psychology, 7,* 202–207.

Berman, M., Gladue, B., & Taylor, S. (1993). The effects of hormones, Type A behavior pattern and provocation on aggression in men. *Motivation and Emotion, 17,* 125–138, 182–199.

Bernard, L. C., & Belinsky, D. (1993). Hardiness, stress, and maladjustment: Effects on self-reported retrospective health problems and prospective health center visits. *Journal of Social Behavior and Personality, 8,* 97–110.

Berry J.W. (1999). Intercultural relations in plural societies. *Canadian Psychology, 40,* 12–21.

Berry, J. W., & Kalin, R. (1995). Multicultural and ethnic attitudes in Canada: An overview of the 1991 national survey. *Canadian Journal of Behavioural Science, 27,* 301–320.

Berry, D. S. (1991). Accuracy in social perception: Contributions of facial and vocal information. *Journal of Personality and Social Psychology, 68,* 291–307.

Berry, D. S., & Hansen, J. S. (1996). Positive affect, negative affect, and social interaction. *Journal of Personality and Social Psychology, 71,* 796–809.

Berry, J.W. (1967). Independence and conformity in subsistence-level societies. *Journal of Personality and Social Psychology, 7,* 415–418.

Berry, J.W. (1969). On cross-cultural comparability. *International Journal of Psychology, 4,* 119–28.

Berry, J.W. (1976). *Human ecology and cognitive style: Comparative studies in cultural and psychological adaptation.* New York: Sage/Halsted.

Berry, J.W. (1978). Social psychology: Comparative, societal and universal. *Canadian Psychogical Review, 19,* 93–104.

Berry, J.W. (1989). Imposed etics–emics–derived etics: the operationalisation of a compelling idea. *International Journal of Psychology, 24,* 721–735.

Berry, J.W., & Annis, R.C. (1974) Ecology, culture and psychological differentiation. *International Journal of Psychology*, 9, 173–193.

Berry, J.W., Kalin, R., & Taylor, D.M. (1977). *Multiculturalism and ethnic attitudes in Canada*. Ottawa: Supply and Services Canada.

Berry, J.W., Kim, U., Minde, T., & Mok, D. (1987). Comparative studies of acculturative stress. *International Migration Review*, 21, 491–551.

Berry, J.W., Poortinga, Y.H., & Pandey, J. (Eds.). (1997). *Handbook of cross-cultural psychology: Volume 1*. (2nd ed.) Needham Heights, MA: Allyn & Bacon.

Berry, J.W., Poortinga, Y.P., Segal, M.H., & Dasen, P.R. (1992). *Cross-cultural psychology: Research and applications*. New York: Cambridge University Press.

Berry, W. (1993). *Sex, economy, freedom, and community*. New York: Pantheon.

Berscheid, E., Dion, K. K., Walster, E., & Walster, G. W. (1971). Physical attractiveness and dating choice: A test of the matching hypothesis. *Journal of Experimental Social Psychology*, 7, 173–189.

Berscheid, E., Snyder, M., & Omoto, A. M. (1989). The Relationship Closeness Inventory: Assessing the closeness of interpersonal relationships. *Journal of Personality and Social Psychology*, 57, 792–807.

Besserer, S. (1998). Criminal victimization: An international perspective. *Juristat*, 18 (6). Ottawa: Statistics Canada

Betancourt, B. A., & Miller, N. (1996). Gender differences in aggression as a function of provocation: A meta-analyis. *Psychological Bulletin*, 119, 422–447.

Bettencourt, B. N., & Miller, N. (in press) Sex differences in aggression as a function of provocation: A meta-analysis. *Psychological Bulletin*.

Bibby, R. W. (1990). *Mosaic Madness*. Toronto: Stoddart.

Bibby, R. W. (1995). *The Bibby report: Social trends Canadian style*. Toronto: Stoddart.

Bickman, L. D. (1975). Personality constructs of senior women planning to marry or to live independently after college. Unpublished doctoral dissertation, University of Pennsylvania.

Bienert, H., & Schneider, B. H. (1993). Diagnosis-specific social skills training with peer-nominated aggressive-disruptive and sensitive-isolated preadolescents. *Journal of Applied Developmental Psychology*, 26 182–199.

Bierhoff, H. W., Klein, R., & Kramp, P. (1991). Evidence for the altruistic personality from data on accident research. *Journal of Personality*, 59, 263–280.

Birkimer, J. C., Lucas, M., & Birkimer, S. J. (1991). Health locus of control and status of cardiac rehabilitation graduates. *Journal of Social Behavior and Personality*, 6, 629–640.

Birnbaum, G. E., Orr, I., Mikulincer, M., & Florian, V. (1997). When marriage breaks up—does attachment style contribute to coping and mental health? *Journal of Social and Personal Relationships*, 14, 643–654.

Bissoondath, N. (1994). Selling Illusions. Toronto: Penguin.

Bjorkqvist, K., Lagerspetz, K. M. J., & Kaukiainen, A. (1992). Do girls manipulate and boys fight? Developmental trends in regard to direct and indirect aggression. *Aggressive Behavior*, 18, 117–127.

Bjorkqvist, K., Osterman, K., & Hjelt-Back, M. (1994). Aggression among university employees. *Aggressive Behavior*, 20, 173–184.

Blanck, P.D., & Rosenthal, R. (1992). Nonverbal behavior in the courtroom. In R.S. Feldman (Ed.) et al., *Applications of nonverbal behavioral theories and research*. (pp.89–115). Hillsdale, NJ: Lawrence Erlbaum.

Blascovich, J., Wyer, N. A., Swart, L. A., & Kibler, J. L. (1997). Racism and racial categorization. *Journal of Personality and Social Psychology*, 72, 1364–1372.

Blazer, D. G., Kessler, R. C., McGonagle, K. A., & Swartz, M. S. (1994). The prevalence and distribution of major depression in a national community sample: The National Comorbidity Survey. *American Journal of Psychiatry*, 151, 979–986.

Bobo, L. (1983). Whites' opposition to busing: Symbolic racism or realistic group conflict? *Journal of Personality and Social Psychology*, 45, 1196–1210.

Bochner, A. P. (1991). On the paradigm that would not die. In J. A. Anderson (Ed.), *Communication yearbook 14* (pp. 44–491). Newbury Park, CA: Sage.

Bodenhausen, G. V. (1988). Stereotypic biases in social decision making and memory: Testing process models of stereotype use. *Journal of Personality and Social Psychology*, 55, 726–737.

Bodenhausen, G. V., Kramer, G. P., & Susser, K. (1994). Happiness and stereotypic thinking in social judgment. *Journal of Personality and Social Psychology*, 66, 621–632.

Bogard, M. (1990). Why we need gender to understand human violence. *Journal of Interpersonal Violence*, 5, 132–135.

Bond, C. F. (1982). Social facilitation: A self-presentational view. *Journal of Personality and Social Psychology*, 42, 1042–1050.

Bond, M.H. (1993). Emotions and their expression in Chinese culture. *Journal of Nonverbal Behavior*, 17, 245–62.

Bond, M.H. Leung, K., & Wan, K.C. (1982). The social impact of self effacing attributions: The Chinese case. *Journal of Social Psychology*, 118, 157–166.

Bond, R., & Smith, P. B. (1996). Culture and conformity: A meta-analysis of studies using Asch's (1952b, 1956) line judgment task. *Psychological Bulletin*, 119, 111–137.

Bookwala, J., Frieze, I. H., & Grote, N. K. (1994). Love, aggression and satisfaction in dating relationships. *Journal of Social and Personal Relationships*, 11, 625–632.

Booth-Kewley, S., & Vickers, R. R. Jr. (1994). Associations between major domains of personality and health behavior. *Journal of Personality*, 62, 281–298.

Bornstein, R. F. (1995). Interpersonal dependency and physical illness: The mediating roles of stress and social support. *Journal of Social and Clinical Psychology*, 14, 225–243.

Botha, M. (1990). Television exposure and aggression among adolescents: A follow-up study over 5 years. *Aggressive Behavior*, 16, 361–380.

Bothwell, R. K., & Jalil, M. (1992). The credibility of nervous witnesses. *Journal of Social Behavior and Personality*, 7, 581–586.

Bothwell, R. K., Brigham, J. C., & Malpass, R. S. (1989). Cross-racial identification. *Personality and Social Psychology Bulletin*, 15, 19–25.

Bothwell, R. K., Deffenbacher, K. A., & Brigham, J. C. (1987). Correlation of eyewitness accuracy and confidence: Optimality hypothesis revisited. *Journal of Applied Psychology*, 72, 691–695.

Bouchard, T. J., Arvey, R. D., Keller, L. M., & Segal, N. L. (1992). Genetic influences on job satisfaction: A reply to Cropanzano and Hames. *Journal of Applied Psychology*, 77, 89–93.

Bourhis, R.Y. (1979) Language in ethnic interaction: A social psychological approach. In H. Giles & B. Saint-Jacques (Eds.), *Language and ethnic relations*. Oxford: Pergamon.

Bourhis, R.Y. (1984). Cross-cultural communication in Montreal: Two field studies since Bill 101. *International Journal of the Sociology of Language*, 46, 33–47.

Bourhis, R.Y. (1990). Organization communication in bilingual settings: The linguistic work environment survey. In H. Giles, N. Coupland, & J. Coupland (Eds.), *Contexts of accommodation: Developments in applied psycholinguistics*. Cambridge: Cambridge University Press.

Bower, G. H. (1991). Mood congruity of social judgments. In J. P. Forgas (Ed.), *Emotion and social judgments* (pp. 31–55). Oxford: Pergamon Press.

Bower, G. H., & Hilgard, E. R. (1981). *Theories of learning* (5th ed.). Englewood Cliffs, NJ: Prentice-Hall.

Bowlby, J. (1973). *Attachment and loss: Vol. 2 Separation: Anxiety and anger*. New York: Basic Books.

Bowman, L. (1998, December 18). Sweet life longer for candy lovers, research study concludes. *Scripps Howard*.

Branscombe, N. R., & Wann, D. L. (1993). Collective self-esteem consequences of outgroup derogation under identity-threatening and identity-bolstering conditions. *European Journal of Social Psychology*, in press.

Braver, S. L. (1995). Social contracts and the provision of public goods. In D. Schroeder (Ed.), *Social dilemmas: Perspectives on individuals and groups* (pp. 69–86). Westport, CT: Praeger.

Brehm, J. W. (1966). *A theory of psychological reactance*. New York: Academic Press.

Brewer, B. W. (1993). Self-identity and specific vulnerability to depressed mood. *Journal of Personality*, 61, 343–386.

Brewer, M. B., Ho, H., Lee, J., & Miller, M. (1987). Social identity and social distance among Hong Kong school children. *Personality and Social Psychology Bulletin*, 13, 156–165.

Brewer, M.B. (1986). The role of ethnocentrism in intergroup conflict. In S. Worchel & W.G. Austin (Eds.), *Psychology of intergroup relations* (2nd ed.) (pp. 88–102). Chicago: Nelson-Hall.

Brickner, M., Harkins, S., & Ostrom, T. (1986). Personal involvement: Thought-provoking implications for social loafing. *Journal of Personality and Social Psychology*, 51, 763–769.

Bringle, R. G., & Bagby, G. J. (1992). Self-esteem and perceived quality of romantic and family relationships in young adults. *Journal of Research in Personality*, 26, 340–356.

Bringle, R. G., & Winnick, T. A. (1992, October). The nature of unrequited love. Paper presented at the first Asian Conference in Psychology, Singapore.

Brockner, J. M., & Wiesenfeld, B. M. (1996). An integrative framework for explaining reactions to decisions: Interactive effects of outcomes and procedures. *Psychological Bulletin*, 120, 189–208.

Brockner, J., Konovsky, M., Cooper-Schneider, R., Folger, R., Martin, C., & Bies, R. J. (1994). Interactive effects of procedural justice and outcome negativity on victims and survivors of job loss. *Academy of Management Journal*, 37, 397–409.

Brody, J. E. (1989, August 24). Boning up on possible mental and physical health needs of children who are bound for college. *New York Times*, p. 912.

Brooks-Gunn, J., & Lewis, M. (1981). Infant social perception: Responses to pictures of parents and strangers. *Developmental Psychology*, 647–649.

Brothers, L. (1990). The neural basis of primate social communication. *Motivation and Emotion*, 14, 81–91.

Brown, J. D., & Rogers, R. J. (1991). Self-serving attributions: The role of physiological arousal. *Personality and Social Psychology Bulletin*, 17, 501–506.

Brown, J. D., Novick, N. J., Lord, K. A., & Richards, J. M. (1992). When Gulliver travels: Social context, psychological closeness, and self-appraisals. *Journal of Personality and Social Psychology*, 62, 717–727.

Brown, K. W., & Moskowitz, D. S. (1997). Does unhappiness make you sick? The role of affect and neuroticism in the experience of common physical symptoms. *Journal of Personality and Social Psychology*, 72, 907–917.

Brown, L. S. (1997). The private practice of subversion: Psychology as tikkun olam. *American Psychologist*, 52, 449–462.

Brown, S. L. (1998). Associations between peer drink driving, peer attitudes toward drink, driving, and personal drink driving. *Journal of Applied Social Psychology*, 28, 423–436.

Bruder, G. E., Stewart, M. M., Mercier, M. A., Agosti, V., Leite, P., Donovan, S., & Quitkin, F. M. (1997). Outcome of cognitive-behavioral therapy for depression: Relation to hemispheric dominance for verbal processing. *Journal of Abnormal Psychology*, 106, 138–144.

Bryan, J. H., & Test, M. A. (1967). Models and helping: Naturalistic studies in aiding behavior. *Journal of Personality and Social Psychology*, 6, 400–407.

Buck, R., & Ginsburg, B. (1991). Spontaneous communication and altruism: The communicative gene hypothesis. In M. S. Clark (Ed.), *Prosocial behavior* (pp. 149–175). Newbury Park, CA: Sage.

Budesheim, T. L., & Bonnelle, K. (1998). The use of abstract trait knowledge and behavioral exemplars in causal explanations of behavior. *Personality and Social Psychology Bulletin*, 24, 575–587.

Buehler, R., & Griffin, D. (1994). Change-of-meaning effects in conformity and dissent: Observing contrual processes over time. *Journal of Personality and Social Psychology*, 67, 984–996.

Buehler, R., Griffin, D., & MacDonald, H. (1997). The role of motivated reasoning in optimistic time predictions. *Personality and Social Psychology Bulletin*, 23, 238–247.

Buehler, R., Griffin, D., & Ross, M. (1994). Exploring the "planning fallacy": Why people underestimate their task completion times. *Journal of Personality and Social Psychology*, 67, 366–381.

Burger, J. M. (1991). Changes in attributions over time: The ephemeral fundamental attribution error. *Social Cognition*, 9, 182–193.

Burger, J. M. (1992). *Desire for control: Personality, social, and clinical perspectives*. New York: Plenum.

Burger, J. M., & Cooper, H. N. (1979). The desirability of control. *Motivation and Emotion*, 3, 381–393.

Burger, J. M., & Pavelich, J. L. (1993). Attributions for presidential elections: The situational shift over time. Unpublished manuscript, Santa Clara University.

Burke, J. P., Hunt, J. P., & Bickford, R. L. (1985). Causal internalization of academic performance as a function of self-esteem and performance satisfaction. *Journal of Research in Personality*, 19, 321–329.

Burns-Glover, A. L., & Veith, D. J. (1995). Revisiting gender and teaching evaluations: Sex still makes a difference. *Journal of Social Behavior and Personality*, 10, 69–80.

Burnstein, E. (1983). Persuasion as argument processing. In M. Brandstatter, J. H. Davis, & G. Stocker-Kriechgauer (Eds.), *Human decision processes*. London: Academic Press.

Burnstein, E., Crandall, C., & Kitayama, S. (1994). Some neo-Darwinian rules for altruism: Weighing cues for inclusive fitness as a function of the biological importance of the decision. *Journal of Personality and Social Psychology*, 67, 773–789.

Bushman, B. J. (1984). Perceived symbols of authority and their influence on compliance. *Journal of Applied Social Psychology*, 14, 501–508.

Bushman, B. J. (1988). The effects of apparel on compliance: A field experiment with a female authority figure. *Personality and Social Psychology Bulletin*, 14, 459–467.

Bushman, B. J. (1998). Effects of television violence on memory for commercial messages. *Journal of Experimental Psychology: Applied*, 4, 1–17.

Bushman, B. J., & Baumeister, R. F. (1998). Threatened egotism, narcissism, self-esteem, and direct and displaced aggression: Does self-love or self-hate lead to violence? *Journal of Personality and Social Psychology*, 75, 219–229.

Bushman, B. J., Baumeister, R. F., & Stack, A. D. (1999). Catharsis messages and anger-reducing activities. *Journal of Personality and Social Psychology*, 76, 367–376.

Buss, D. M. (1989). Conflict between the sexes: Strategic interference and the evocation of anger and upset. *Journal of Personality and Social Psychology*, 56, 735–747.

Buss, D. M. (1994). The strategies of human mating. *American Scientist*, 82, 238–249.

Buss, D. M. (1995). Evolutionary psychology: A new paradigm for psychological science. *Psychological Inquiry*, 6, 1–30.

Buss, D. M. (1998). *Evolutionary psychology*. Boston: Allyn and Bacon.

Buss, D. M., & Schmitt, D. P. (1993). Sexual strategies theory: An evolutionary perspective on human mating. *Psychological Review*, 100, 204–232.

Buss, D. M., & Shackelford, T. K. (1997). From vigilance to violence: Mate retention tactics in married couples. *Journal of Personality and Social Psychology*, 72, 346–361.

Buss, D.M. (1999). Human nature and individual differences: The evolution of human personality. In L.A. Pervin, O.P. John, et al. (Eds.), *Handbook of personality theory and research. Second edition*. New York: Guilford Press.

Butler & Geis, D., & Geis, F. L. (1990). Nonverbal affect responses to male and female leaders: Implications for leadership evaluations. *Journal of Personality and Social Psychology*, 58, 48–59.

Butler, A. C., Hokanson, J. E., & Flynn, H. A. (1994). A comparison of self-esteem lability and low trait self-esteem as vulnerability factors for depression. *Journal of Personality and Social Psychology*, 66, 166–177.

Buunk, B. P. (1995). Sex, self-esteem, dependency and extradyadic sexual experience as related to jealousy responses. *Journal of Social and Personal Relationships*, 12, 147–153.

Buunk, B. P., & van der Eijnden, R. J. J. M. (1997). Perceived prevalence, perceived superiority, and relationship satisfaction: Most relationships are good, but ours is the best. *Personality and Social Psychology Bulletin*, 23, 219–228.

Byrne D. (1991). Perspectives on research classics: This ugly duckling has yet to become a swan. *Contemporary Social Psychology*, 15, 84–85.

Byrne, B. M., & Shavelson, R. J. (1996). On the structure of social self-concept for pre-, early, and late adolescents: A test of the Shavelson, Hubner, and Stanton (1976) model. *Journal of Personality and Social Psychology*, 70, 599–613.

Byrne, D. (1961). The influence of propinquity and opportunities for interaction on classroom relationships. *Human Relations*, 4, 63–69.

Byrne, D. (1961a). The influence of propinquity and opportunities for interaction on classroom relationships. *Human Relations*, 14, 63–69.

Byrne, D. (1992). The transition from controlled laboratory experimentation to less controlled settings: Surprise! Additional variables are operative. *Communication Monographs*, 190–198.

Byrne, D., & Blaylock, B. (1963). Similarity and assumed similarity of attitudes among husbands and wives. *Journal of Abnormal and Social Psychology*, 67, 636–640.

Byrne, D., & Buehler, R. A. (1955). A note on the influence of propinquity upon acquaintanceships. *Journal of Abnormal and Social Psychology*, 51, 147–148.

Byrne, D., & Clore, G. L. (1970). A reinforcement-affect model of evaluative responses. *Personality: An International Journal*, 1, 103–128.

Byrne, D., & Kelley, K. (1981). *An introduction to personality* (3rd ed.). Englewood Cliffs, NJ: Prentice-Hall.

Byrne, D., & Murnen, S. K. (1988). Maintaining loving relationships. In R. J. Sternberg & M. L. Barnes (Eds.), *The psychology of love* (pp. 293–310). New Haven, CT: Yale University Press.

Byrne, D., & Nelson, D. (1965). Attraction as a linear function of proportion of positive reinforcements. *Journal of Personality and Social Psychology, 1,* 659–663.

Byrne, D., & Smeaton, G. (1998). The Feelings Scale: Positive and negative affective responses. In C. M. Davis, W. L. Yarber, R. Bauserman, G. Scheer, & S. L. Davis (Eds.), *Handbook of sexuality-related measures* (pp. 50–52). Thousand Oaks, CA: Sage.

Byrne, D., Gouaux, C., Griffitt, W., Lamberth, J., Murakawa, N., Prasad, M. B., Prasad A., & Ramirez, M., III. (1971). The ubiquitous relationship: Attitude similarity and attraction: A cross-cultural study. *Human Relations, 24,* 201–207.

Caldwell, D. F., & Burger, J. M. (1997). Personality and social influence strategies in the workplace. *Personality and Social Psychology Bulletin, 23,* 1003–1012.

Caldwell, M.A. & Peplau, L.A. (1982). Sex differences in same-sex friendship. *Sex Roles, 8,* 721–732.

Callan, V. J. (1993). Subordinate manager communication in different sex-dyads: Consequences for job satisfaction. *Journal of Occupational and Organizational Psychology, 66,* 13–27.

Cameron, C. (1977). Sex-role attitudes. In S. Oskamp (Ed.), *Attitudes and opinions* (pp, 339–359). Englewood Cliffs, NJ: Prentice Hall.

Campbell, J. D., Chew, B., & Scratchley, L. S. (1991). *Cognitive and emotional reactions to daily events: The effects of self-esteem and self-complexity.*

Caprara, G. V., Barbaranelli, C., Pastorelli, C., & Perugini, M. (1994). Individual differences in the study of human aggression. *Aggressive Behavior, 20,* 291–303.

Carey, M. P., Morrison-Beedy, D., & Johnson, B. T. (1997). The HIV-Knowledge Questionnaire: Development and evaluation of a reliable, valid, and practical self-administered questionnaire. AIDS and Behavior, 1, 61–74.

Carli, L. L., Ganley, R., & Pierce-Otay, A. (1991). Similarity and satisfaction in roommate relationships. *Personality and Social Psychology Bulletin, 17,* 419–426.

Carnelley, K. B., Pietromonaco, P. R., & Jaffe, K. (1996). Attachment, caregiving, and relationship functioning in couples: Effects of self and partner. *Personal Relationships, 3,* 257–278.

Carroll, J. M., & Russell, J. A. (1996). Do facial expressions signal specific emotions? Judging emotion from the face in context. *Journal of Personality and Social Psychology, 70,* 205–218.

Carter, D. B. & McCloskey, L. A. (1984). Peers and the maintenance of sex-typed behavior: The development of children's conceptions of cross-gender behavior in their peers. *Social Cognition, 2,* 294–314.

cartoons on preschool children. *Child Development Journal, 17,* 83–88.

Carver, C. S., & Glass, D. C. (1978). Coronary-prone behavior pattern and interpersonal aggression. *Journal of Personality and Social Psychology, 376,* 361–366.

Carver, C. S., Reynolds, S. L., & Scheier, M. F. (1994). The possible selves of optimists and pessimists. *Journal of Research in Personality, 28,* 133–141.

Cash, T. F., & Derlega, V. J. (1978). The matching hypothesis: Physical attractiveness among same-sexed friends. *Personality and Social Psychology Bulletin, 4,* 240–243.

Cash, T. F., & Duncan, N. C. (1984). Physical attractiveness stereotyping among black American college students. *Journal of Social Psychology, 122,* 71–77.

Cash, T. F., & Jacobi, L. (1992). Looks aren't everything (to everybody): The strength of ideals of physical appearance. *Journal of Social Behavior and Personality, 7,* 621–630.

Cash, T. F., & Trimer, C. A. (1984). *Sexism and beautyism in women's evaluation of peer performance. Sex Roles,* 10, 87–98.

Caspi, A., Herbener, E. S., & Ozer, D. J. (1992). Shared experiences and the similarity of personalities: A longitudinal study of married couples. *Journal of Personality and Social Psychology, 62,* 281–291.

Castellow, W. A., Wuensch, K. L., & Moore, C. H. (1990). Effects of physical attractiveness of the plaintiff and defendant in sexual harassment judgments. *Journal of Social Behavior and Personality, 5,* 547–562.

Chaiken, A.L. , & Derlega, V.J. (1974). Liking for the norm-breaker in self-disclosure. *Journal of Personality, 42,* 117–129.

Chandra, S. (1973). The effects of group pressure in perception: A cross-cultural conformity study. *International Journal of Psychology, 8,* 37–39.

Chang, E. C. (1998). Dispositional optimism and secondary appraisal of a stressor: Controlling for confounding influences and relations to coping and psychological and physical adjustment. *Journal of Personality and Social Psychology, 74,* 1109–1120.

Chapman, B. (1992). The Byrne-Nelson formula revisited: The additional impact of number of dissimilar attitudes on attraction. Unpublished masters thesis, University at Albany, State University of New York.

Chapman, B. (1992). The Byrne-Nelson formula revisited: The additional impact of number of dissimilar attitudes on attraction. Unpublished masters thesis, University at Albany, State University of New York.

Chappell, K. D., & Davis, K. E. (1998). Attachment, partner choice, and perception of romantic partners: An experimental test of the attachment-security hypothesis. *Personal Relationships, 5,* 327–342.

Che-Alford, J., Allan, C., & Butlin, G. (1994). *Families in Canada* (Focus on Canada series). Scarborough, Ont.: Statistics Canada and Prentice Hall Canada.

Cheney, D. L., & Seyfarth, R. M. (1992). Précis of how monkeys see the world. *Behavioral and Brain Sciences, 15,* 135–182.

Chermack, S. T., Berman, M., & Taylor, S. P. (1997). Effects of provocation on emotions and aggression in males. *Aggressive Behavior, 23,* 1–10.

Choi, I., & Nisbett, R. E. (1998). Situational salience and cultural differences in the correspondence bias and actor-observer bias. *Personality and Social Psychology Bulletin, 24,* 949–960.

Christy, C. A., & Voigt, H. (1994). Bystander responses to public episodes of child abuse. *Journal of Applied Social Psychology, 24,* 824–847.

Christy, P. R., Gelfand, D. N., & Hartmann, D. P. (1971). Effects of competition-induced frustration on two classes of modeled behavior. *Developmental Psychology, 5,* 104–111.

Church, E. (2000). Women still shut out of many top posts. *Globe and Mail*, February 10, pp. B15.

Cialdini, R. B. (1988). *Influence: Science and practice*, (2nd ed.). Glenview, IL: Scott, Foresman.

Cialdini, R. B. (1994). Interpersonal influence. In S. Shavitt & T. C. Brock (Eds.), *Persuasion* (pp. 195–218). Boston: Allyn & Bacon.

Cialdini, R. B., & Petty, R. (1979). Anticipatory opinion effects. In R. B. Petty, T. Ostrom, & T. Brock (Eds.), *Cognitive responses in persuasion*. Hillsdale, NJ: Erlbaum.

Cialdini, R. B., Cacioppo, J. T., Bassett, R., & Miller J. A. (1978). A low-ball procedure for producing compliance: Commitment then cost. *Journal of Personality and Social Psychology*, 36, 463–476.

Cialdini, R. B., Kallgren, C. A., & Reno, R. R. (1991). A focus theory of normative conduct. *Advances in Experimental Social Psychology*, 24, 201–234.

Cialdini, R. B., Kenrick, D. T., & Bauman, D. J. (1982). Effects of mood on prosocial behavior in children and adults. In N. Eisenberg-Berg (Ed.), *Development of prosocial behavior*. New York: Academic Press.

Cialdini, R. B., Vincent, J. E., Lewis, S. K., Catalan, J., Wheeler, D., & Darby, B. L. (1975). Reciprocal concessions procedure for inducing compliance: The door-in-the-face technique. *Journal of Personality and Social Psychology*, 31, 206–215.

Civin, M.A. (1999). On the vicissitudes of cyberspace as potential-space. *Human Relations,52*, 485–506.

Clark, K., & Clark, M. (1947). Racial identification and racial preferences in Negro children. In T. M. Newcomb & E. L. Hartley, *Readings in social psychology* (pp.169–178). New York: Holt.

Clark, L. A., & Watson, D. (1988). Mood and the mundane: Relations between daily life events and self-reported mood. *Journal of Personality and Social Psychology*, 54, 296–308.

Clark, L. F. (1993). Stress and the cognitive-conversational benefits of social interaction. *Journal of Social and Clinical Psychology*, 12, 25–55.

Clark, M. S., Ouellette, R., Powel, M. C., & Milberg, S. (1987). Recipient's mood, relationship type, and helping. *Journal of Personality and Social Psychology*, 53, 94–103.

Clary, E. G., & Orenstein, L. (1991). The amount and effectiveness of help: The relationship of motives and abilities to helping behavior. *Personality and Social Psychology Bulletin*, 17, 58–64.

Clore, G. L., Schwarz, N., & Conway, M. (1993). Affective causes and consequences of social information processing. In R. S. Wyer & T. K. Srull (Eds.), *Handbook of social congition* (2nd ed.). Hillsdale, NJ: Erlbaum.

Cl_ment, R. (1987). Second language proficiency and acculturation: an investigation of the effects of language status and individual characteristics. *Journal of Language and Social Psychology*, 5, 271–290.

Cohen, L.E., & Land, K.C. (1987). Age structure and crime: Symmetry versus asymmetry and the projection of crime rates through the 1990's. *American Sociological Review*, 52, 170–183.

Cohen, S., Tyrrell, D. A. J., & Smith, A. P. (1993). Negative life events, perceived stress, negative affect, and susceptibility to the common cold. *Journal of Personality and Social Psychology*, 64, 131–140.

Cohn, E. G., & Rotton, J. (1997). Assault as a function of time and temperature: A moderator-variable time-series analysis. *Journal of Personality and Social Psychology*, 72, 1322–1334.

Cole, T., & Bradac, J. J. (1996). A lay theory of relational satisfaction with best friends. *Journal of Social and Personal Relationships*, 13, 57–83.

Coleman, L. M., Jussim, L., & Abraham, J. (1987). Students' reactions to teachers' evaluations: The unique impact of negative feedback. *Journal of Applied Social Psychology*, 1051–1070.

Collins, M. A., & Zebrowitz, L. A. (1995). The contributions of appearance to occupational outcomes in civilian and military settings. *Journal of Applied Social Psychology*, 25, 129–163.

Collins, N. L. (1996). Working models of attachment: Implications for explanation, emotion, and behavior. *Journal of Personality and Social Psychology*, 71, 810–832.

Collins, N. L., Dunkel-Schetter, C., Lobel, M., & Scrimshaw, S. C. M. (1993). Social support in pregnancy: Psychosocial correlates of Birth outcomes and postpartum depression. *Journal of Personality and Social Psychology*, 65, 1243–1258.

Collins, N.L., & Miller, L.C. (1994). Self-disclosure and liking: A meta-analytic review. *Psychological Bulletin, 116*, 457–475.

Colvin, C. R., Block, J., & Funder, D. C. (1995). Overly positive self-evaluations and personality: Negative implications for mental health. *Journal of Personality and Social Psychology*, 68, 1152–1162.

Compas, B. E., Banez, G. A., Malcarne, V., & Worsham, N. (1991). Perceived control and coping with stress: A developmental perspective. *Journal of Social Issues*, 47(4), 23–34.

Condon, J. W., & Crano, W. D. (1988). Inferred evaluation and the relation between attitude similarity and interpersonal attraction. *Journal of Personality and Social Psychology*, 54, 789–797.

Conger, J. A. (1991). Inspiring others: The language of leadership. Academy of Management Executives 5(1), 31–45.

Connolly, J. A., & Johnson, A. M. (1996). Adolescents' romantic relationships and the structure and quality of their close interpersonal ties. *Personal Relationships*, 3, 185–195.

Constantian, C. (1981). Solitude, attitudes, beliefs, and behavior in regard to spending time alone. Unpublished doctoral dissertation, Harvard University.

Contrada, R. J. (1989). Type A behavior, personality hardiness, and cardiovascular responses to stress. *Journal of Personality and Social Psychology*, 57, 895–903.

Conway, M., & Ross, M. (1984). Getting what you want by revising what you had. Journal of Personality and Social Psychology, 47, 738–748.

Conway, M., Giannopoulos, C., Csank, P., & Mendelson, M. (1993). Dysphoria and specificity in self-focused attention. *Personality and Social Psychology Bulletin*, 19, 265–268.

Cook, P.J. (1981). The effect of gun availability on violent crime patterns. *Annals of the American Academy for Political and Social Sciences*, 455, 63–79.

Cook, P.J. (1987). Robbery violence. *Journal of criminal Law and Criminology*, 78, 357–376.

Cook, S. W. (1985). Experimenting on social issues: The case of school desegregation. *American Psychologist*, 40, 452–460.

Cooke, P. (1992). *Noises out: What it's doing to you*. New York, 25(4), 28–33.

Cooley, C.H. (1902/1964) *Human nature and the social order*. New York: Schocken Books.

Cooper, J., & Scher, S. J. (1992). Actions and attitudes: The role of responsibility and aversive consequences in persuasion. In T. Brock & S. Shavitt (Eds.), *The psychology of persuasion*. San Francisco: Freeman.

Cooper, J., Fazio, R. H., & Rhodewalt, F. (1978). Dissonance and humor: Evidence for the undifferentiated nature of dissonance arousal. *Journal of Personality and Social Psychology*, 36, 280–285.

Cooper, M. L., Shaver, P. R., & Collins, N. L. (1998). Attachment styles, emotion regulation, and adjustment in adolescence. *Journal of Personality and Social Psychology*, 74, 1380–1397.

Costa, P. T., Jr., & McCrae, R. R. (1992). Professional manual for the Revised NEO Personality Inventory and NEO Five-Factor Inventory. Odessa, FL: Psychological Assessment Resources.

Cota, A. A., Evans, C. R., Dion, K. L., Kilik, L., & Longman, R. S. (1995). The structure of group cohesion. *Personality and Social Psychology Bulletin*, 21, 572–580.

Cottrell, H. B., Wack, K. L., Sekerak, G. J., & Rittle, R. (1968). Social facilitation of dominant responses by the presence of an audience and the mere presence of others. *Journal of Personality and Social Psychology*, 51, 245–250.

Cousins, S. D. (1989). Culture and self-perception in Japan and the United States. *Journal of Personality and Social Psychology*, 56, 124–131.

Cowan, G., & Curtis, S. R. (1994). Predictors of rape occurrence and victim blame in the William Kennedy Smith case. *Journal of Applied Social Psychology*, 24, 12–20.

Cramer, R. E., McMaster, M. R., Bartell, P. A., & Dragna, M. (1988). Subject competence and minimization of the bystander effect. *Journal of Applied Social Psychology*, 18, 1133–1148.

Crandall, C. S. (1995). Do parents discriminate against their heavyweight daughters? *Personality and Social Psychology Bulletin*, 21, 724–735.

Crano, W. D. (1995). Attitude strength and vested interest. In R. E. Petty & J. A. Krosnick (Eds.), *Attitude strength: Antecedents and consequences* (Vol. 4, pp. 131–157). Hillsdale, NJ: Erlbaum.

Crano, W. D. (1997). Vested interest, symbolic politics, and attitude-behavior consistency. *Journal of Personality and Social Psychology*, 72, 485–491.

Crano, W. D., & Prislin, R. (1995). Components of vested interest and attitude-behavior consistency. *Basic and Applied Social Psychology*, 17, 1–21.

Crealia, R., & Tesser, A. (1996). Attitude heritability and attitude reinforcement: A replication. Personality and Individual Differences, 21, 803–808.

Creese, G., & Beagan, B. (1999). Gender at work: Seeking solutions for women's equality. In J. Curtis, E. Grabb, & N. Guppy (Eds.), *Social inequality in Canada: Patterns, problems, and policies* (2nd ed., pp. 199–211). Scarborough, Ont.: Prentice Hall.

Crittenden, K. S. (1991). Asian self-effacement or feminine modesty? Attributional patterns of women university students in Taiwan. *Gender and Society*, 5, 98–117.

Crittenden, K. S. (1996). Causal attribution Processes among the Chinese. In M.H. Bond (Ed.), *Handbook of Chinese Psychology*. Oxford: Oxford University Press.

Crocker, J. (1993). Memory for information about others: Effects of self-esteem and performance feedback. *Journal of Research in Personality*, 27, 35–48.

Crocker, J., & Major, B. (1993). When bad things happen to bad people: The perceived justifiability of negative outcomes based on stigma. Unpublished Manuscript.

Crocker, J., Cornwell, B., & Major, B. (1993). *The stigma of being overweight: Affective consequences of attributional*

Crocker, J., Luhtanen, R., Blaine, B., & Broadnax, S. (1994). Collective self-esteem and psychological well-being among white, black, and Asian college students. *Personality and Social Psychology Bulletin*, 20, 503–513.

Croizet, J. C., & Claire, T. (1998). Extending the concept of stereotype threat to social class: The intellectual underperformance of students from low socioeconomic backgrounds. *Personality and Social Psychology Bulletin*, 24, 588–594.

Cropanzano, R. (Ed.). (1993). *Justice in the workplace* (pp. 79–103). Hillsdale, NJ: Erlbaum.

Cropanzano, R., & James, K. (1990). Some methodological considerations for the behavioral-genetic analysis of work attitudes. *Journal of Applied Psychology*, 71, 433–439.

Crosby, F. J. (1982). Relative deprivation and working women. Oxford: Oxford University Press.

Crumm, D. (1998, December 11). Keeping the faith may keep mind, body going. Knight Ridder.

Crusco, A. H., & Wetzel, C. G. (1984). The Midas touch: The effects of interpersonal touch on restaurant tipping. *Personality and Social Psychology Bulletin*, 10, 512–517.

Cruse, D., & Leigh, B. S. (1987). "Adam's Rib" revisited: Legal and non-legal influences on the processing of trial testimony. *Social Behavior*, 2, 221–230.

Crutchfield, R. A. (1955). Conformity and character. *American Psychologist*, 10, 191–198.

Csikszentmihalyi, M. (1993). *Relax? Relax and do what?* New York Times, P. A25.

Cukier, W. (1998). Firearms regulation: Canada in the international context. *Health Canada - Chronic Diseases in Canada*, 19 (1).

Culnan, M.J., & Markus, M.L. (1987). Information technologies. In F. Jablin, L.L. Putnam, K. Roberts, & L. Porter (Eds.), *Handbook of organizational communication* (pp. 420–443). Newbury Park: Sage.

Cunningham, D. R. (1989). Reactions to heterosexual opening gambits: Female selectivity and male responsiveness. *Personality and Social Psychology Bulletin*, 15, 27–41.

Cunningham, M. R. (1979). Weather, mood, and helping behavior: Quasi-experiments with the sunshine samaritan. *Journal of Personality and Social Psychology*, 37, 1947–1956.

Cunningham, M. R. (1986). Measuring the physical in physical attractiveness: Quasi-experiments on the sociobiology of female facial beauty. *Journal of Personality and Social Psychology*, 50,

Cunningham, M. R. (1988). Does happiness mean friendliness? Induced mood and heterosexual self-disclosure. *Personality and Social Psychology Bulletin*, 14, 283–297.

Cunningham, M. R., Roberts, A. R., Wu, C.-H., Barbee, A. P., & Druen, P. B. (1995). "Their ideas of beauty are, on the whole, the same as ours": Consistency and variability in the cross-cultural perception of female physical attractiveness. *Journal of Personality and Social Psychology*, 68, 261–279.

Cunningham, M. R., Shaffer, D. R., Barbee, A. P., Wolff, P. L., & Kelley, D. J. (1990). Separate processes in the relation of elation and depression to helping: Social versus personal concerns. *Journal of Experimental Social Psychology*, 26, 13–33.

Cutler, B. L., Penrod, S. D., & Martens, T. K. (1987). Improving the reliability of eyewitness identification: Putting content into context. *Journal of Applied Psychology*, 72, 629–637.

Daly, M., & Wilson, M. I. (1999). Human evolutionary psychology and animal behavior. *Animal behavior, 57*, 509–519.

Daly, M., & Wilson, M.I. (1988*). Homicide*. Hawthorne, NY: Aldine de Gruyter.

Damasio, A. R. (1994). *Descartes' error: Emotion, reason and the human brain*. New York: Putnam.

Dana, E. R., Lalwani, N., & Duval, S. (1997). Objective self-awareness and focus of attention following awareness of self-standard discrepancies: Changing self or changing standards of correctness. *Journal of Social and Clinical Psychology*, 16, 359–380.

Darley, J. M. (1991). Altruism and prosocial behavior research: Reflections and prospects. In M. S. Clark (Ed.), *Prosocial Behavior* (pp. 312–327). Newbury Park, CA: Sage.

Darley, J. M. (1993). Research on morality: Possible approaches, actual approaches. *Psychological Science*, 4, 353–357.

Darley, J. M., & Batson, C. D. (1973). From Jerusalem to Jericho: A study of sitautional and dispositional variables in helping behavior. *Journal of Personality and Social Psychology*, 27, 100–108.

Darley, J. M., & Latan_, B. (1968). Bystander intervention in emergencies: Diffusion of responsibility. *Journal of Personality and Social Psychology*, 8, 377–383.

Darwin, C. (1872). *The expression of emotion in man and animals*. London: Murray.

Daubman, K. A. (1993). The self-threat of receiving help: A comparison of the threat-to-self-esteem model and the theat-to-interpersonal-power model. Unpublished manuscript, Gettysburg College, Gettysburg, PA.

Davie, M. R., & Reeves, R. J. (1939). Propinquity of residence before marriage. *American Journal of Sociology*, 44, 510–517.

Davis, C., Brewer, H., & Weinstein, M. (1993). A study of appearance anxiety in young men. *Social Behavior and Personality*, 21, 63–74.

Davis, C.G., Lehman, D.R., Wortman, C.B., Silver, R.C., & Thompson, S.C. (1994) Undoing of traumatic life events. *Personality and Social Psychology Bulletin*.

Davis, J. H. (1989). Psychology and the law: The last 15 years. *Journal of Applied Social Psychology*, 19, 119–230.

Davis, J. H., Tindale, R. S., Naggao, D. H., Hinsz, V. B., & Robertson, B. (1984). Order effects in multiple decisions by gruops: A demonstration with mock juries and trial procedures. *Journal of Personality and Social Psychology*, 47, 1003–1012.

Davis, M. H., Luce, C., & Kraus, S. J. (1994). The heritability of characteristics associated with dispositional empathy. *Journal of Personality*, 62, 369–391.

Davis, M. H., Morris, M. M., & Kraus, L. A. (1998). Relationship-specific and global perceptions of social support: Associations with well-being and attachment. *Journal of Personality and Social Psychology*, 74, 468–481.

Dawkins, R. (1976). *The selfish gene*. Oxford: Oxford University Press.

de Waal, F. (1996). *Good natured: The origins of right and wrong in humans and other animals*. Cambridge, MA: Harvard University Press.

de Weerth, C., & Kalma, A. P. (1993). Female aggression as a response to sexual jealousy: A sex role reversal? *Aggressive Behavior*, 19, 265–279.

Dean-Church, L., & Gilroy, F. D. (1993). Relation of sex-role orientation to life satisfaction in a healthy elderly sample. *Journal of Social Behavior and Personality*, 8, 133–140.

Deaux, K. (1993). Commentary: Sorry, wrong number—a reply to Gentile's call. *Psychological Science*, 4, 125–126.

Deaux, K., & Hanna, R. (1984). Courtship in the personals column: The influence of gender and sexual orientation. *Sex Roles*, 11, 363–375.

Deaux, K., Reid, A., Mizrahi, K., & Ethier, K. A. (1995). Parameters of social identity. *Journal of Personality and Social Psychology*, 68, 280–291.

DeBono, K. G., & Packer, M. (1991). The effects of advertising appeal on perceptions of product quality. *Personality and Social Psychology Bulletin*, 17, 194–200.

DeBono, K. G., & Snyder, M. (1995). Acting on one's attitudes: The role of a history of choosing situations. *Personality and Social Psychology Bulletin*, 21, 629–636.

DeDreu, C. K. W., & McCusker, C. (1997). Gain-loss frames and cooperation in two-person social dilemmas: A transformational analysis. *Journal of Personality and Social Psychology*, 72, 1093–1106.

DeDreu, C. K. W., & Van Lange, P. A. M. (1995). Impact of social value orientation on negotiator cognition and behavior. *Personality and Social Psychology Bulletin*, 21, 1178–1188.

DeJong, W., & Musilli, L. (1982). External pressure to comply: Handicapped versus nonhandicapped requesters and the foot-in-the-door phenomenon. *Personality and Social Psychology Bulletin*, 8, 522–527.

DeKeseredy, W.S., & Kelly, K. (1995). Sexual abuse in Canadian university and college dating relationship: The contribution of male peer support. *Journal of Family Violence, 10*, 41–53.

Denes-Raj, V., & Epstein, S. (1994). Conflict between intuitive and rational processing: When people behave against their better judgment. *Personality and Social Psychology Bulletin*, 66, 819–829.

Dengerink, H. A., Schnedler, R. W., & Covey, M. X. (1978). Role of avoidance in aggressive responses to attack and no attack. *Journal of Personality and Social Psychology*, 36, 1044–1053.

DePaulo, B. M. (1992). Nonverbal behavior and self-presentation. *Psychological Bulletin*, 111, 230–243.

DePaulo, B. M., & Kashy, D. A. (1998). Everyday lies in close and casual relationships. *Journal of Personality and Social Psychology*, 74, 63–79.

Derlega, V.J. & Grzelak, A.L. (1979). Appropriate self-disclosure. In G.J. Chelune (Ed.) *Self-disclosure: Origins, patterns, and implications of openness in interpersonal relationships.* San Francisco: Jossey-Bass.

Desmarais, S., & Curtis, J. (1997). Gender and perceived pay entitlement: Testing for effects of experience with income. *Journal of Personality and Social Psychology*, 72, 141–150.

Deutsch, F. M., Zalenski, C. M., & Clark, M. E. (1986). Is there a double standard of aging? *Journal of Applied Social Psychology*, 16, 771–785.

Deutsch, M., & Gerard, H. B. (1955). A study of normative and informational social influences upon individual judgment. *Journal of Abnormal and Social Psychology*, 51, 629–636.

Deutsch, M., & Krauss, R. M. (1960). The effect of threat upon interpersonal bargaining. *Journal of Abnormal and Social Psychology*, 61, 181–189.

Dickinson, P. & Ellison, J. (1999). Plugged into the Internet. *In Canadian Social Trends, Winter1999*. Ottawa, Ont.: Statistics Canada, Catalogue No. 11–008.

Diehl, M., Elnick, A. B., Bourbeau, L. S., & Labouvie-Vief, G. (1998). Adult attachment styles: Their relations to family context and personality. *Journal of Personality and Social Psychology*, 74, 1656–1669.

Diekmann, K. A., Samuels, S. M., Ross, L., & Bazerman, M. H. (1997). Self-interest and fairness in problems of response allocation: Allocators versus recipients. *Journal of Personality and Social Psychology*, 72, 1061–1074.

Diener, E., Wolsic, B., & Fujita, F. (1995). Physical attractiveness and subjective well-being. *Journal of Personality and Social Psychology*, 69, 120–129.

Dijkstra, P., & Buunk, B. P. (1998). Jealousy as a function of rival characteristics: An evolutionary perspective. *Personality and Social Psychology Bulletin*, 24, 1158–1166.

Dindia, K., & Allen, M. (1992). Sex differences in self-disclosure: A meta-analysis. *Psychological Bulletin, 112*, 106–124.

Dion, K. K., & Dion, K. L. (1991). Psychological individualism and romantic love. *Journal of Social Behavior and Personality*, 6, 17–33.

Dion, K. K., & Dion, K. L. (1993). Individualistic and collectivistic perspectives on gender and the cultural context of love and intimacy. *Journal of Social Issues*, 49, 53–69.

Dion, K. K., & Dion, K. L. (1996). Cultural perspectives on romantic love. *Personal Relationships*, 3, 5–17.

Dion, K. K., Berscheid, E., & Walster, E. (1972). What is beautiful is good. *Journal of Personality and Social Psychology*, 24, 285–290.

Dion, K. K., Pak, A. W.-P., & Dion, K. I. (1990). Stereotyping physical attractiveness: A sociocultural perspective. *Journal of Cross-Cultural Psychology*, 21, 158–179.

Dion, K. L., & Dion, K. K. (1987). Belief in a just world and physical attractiveness stereotyping. *Journal of Personality and Social Psychology*, 52, 775–780.

Dion, K. L., & Dion, K. K. (1988). Romantic love: Individual and cultural perspectives. In R. J. Sternberg & M. L. Barnes (Eds.), *The psychology of love* (pp. 264–289). New Haven, CT: Yale University press.

Dion, K. L., Dion, K. K., & Keelan, J. P. (1990). Appearance anxiety as a dimension of social-evaluative anxiety: Exploring the ugly duckling syndrome. *Contemporary Social Psychology*, 14, 220–224.

Dion, K.L. (1975).Women's reactions to discrimination from members of the same or opposite sex. *Journal of Research in Personality*, 9, 294–306.

Dion, K.L., & Earn, B.M. (1975). The phenomenology of being a target of prejudice. *Journal of Personality and Social Psychology*, 32, 944–950.

Directions in Psychological Science, 1, 121–123.

Ditto, P. H., & Griffin, J. (1993). The value of uniqueness: Self-evaluation and the perceived prevalence of valenced characteristics. *Journal of Social Behavior and Personality*, 8, 221–240.

Dixon, T. M., & Baumeister, R. F. (1991). Escaping the self: The moderating effect of self-complexity. *Personality and Social Psychology Bulletin*, 17, 363–368.

Dodge, K. A., Murphy, R. R., & Buchsbaum, K. (1984). The assessment of intention-cue detection skills in children: Implications for developmental psychopathology. *Child Development*, 55, 163–173.

Dodge, K. A., Price, J. N., Bachorowski, J. A., & Newman, J. P. (1990). Hostile attributional biases in severely aggressive adolescents. *Journal of Abnormal Psychology*, 99, 385–392.

Doktor, R. H. (1990). *Asian and American CEOs: A comparative study. Organizational Dynamics*. 18(3), 46–56.

Dollard, J., Doob, L., Miller, N., Mowrer, O. H., & Sears, R. R. (1939). *Frustration and aggression*. New Haven: Yale University Press.

Dona, G. (1991). Acculturation and ethnic identity of Central American refugees in Canada. *Hispanic Journal of Behavioral Sciences*, 13, 230–231.

Dona, G., & Berry, J. W. (1994). Acculturation attitudes and acculturative stress of Central American refugees. *International Journal of Psychology, 29,* 57–70.

Donnerstein, E., & Donnerstein, M. (1976). Research in the control of interracial aggression. In R. G. Geen & E. C. O'Neal (Eds.), *Perspectives on aggression.* New York: Academic Press.

Doob, A.N. (1976). Evidence, procedure and psychological research. In G. Bermant, C Nemeth & N Vidmar (Eds.), *Psychology and the law.* Lexington, MA: Lexington Books.

Doob, A.N. (1985). The many realities of crime. In A.N. Doob, & E.L. Greenspan (Eds.), *Perspectives in criminal law.* Aurora, Ont.: Canada Law Book.

Doob, A.N., & Roberts, J.V. (1983). *An analysis of the public's view of sentencing.* Ottawa: Department of Justice, Canada.

Dovidio, J. F., & Gaertner, S. L. (1993). Steretoypes and evaluative intergroup bias. In D. M. Mackie & D. L. Hamilton (Eds.), *Affect, cognition, and stereotyping: Interactive processes in perception.* Orlando, FL: Academic Press.

Dovidio, J. F., & Morris, W. N. (1975). Effects of stress and commonality of fate on helping behavior. *Journal of Personality and Social Psychology, 31,* 145–149.

Dovidio, J. F., Brigham, J., Johnson, B. & Garerner, S. (1996). Stereotyping, prejudice, and discrimination: Another look. In N. Macrae, C. Stangor, & M. Hwestone (Eds.), *Stereotypes and stereotyping* (pp. 1276–1319). New York: Guilford.

Dovidio, J. F., Evans, N., & Tyler, R. B. (1986). Racial stereotypes: The contents of their cognitive representations. *Journal of Experimental Social Psychology, 22,* 22–37.

Dovidio, J. F., Gaertner, S. L., Isen, A. M., & Lowrance, R. (1995). Group representations and intergroup bias: Politive affect, similarity, and group size. *Personality and Social Psychology Bulletin, 21,* 856–865.

Downey, J. L., & Damhave, K. W. (1991). The effects of place, type of comment, and effort expended on the perception of flirtation. *Journal of Social Behavior and Personality, 6,* 35–43.

Drigotas, S. M., & Rusbult, C. E. (1992). Should I stay or should I go? A dependence model of breakups. *Journal of Personality and Social Psychology, 62,* 62–87.

Driscoll, R., Davis, H. E., & Lipetz, M. E. (1972). Parental interference and romantic love: The Romeo and Juliet effect. *Journal of Personality and Social Psychology, 24,* 1–10.

Duck, J. M., Terry, D. J., & Hogg, M. A. (1998). Perceptions of a media campaign: The role of social identity and the changing intergroup context. *Personality and Social Psychology Bulletin, 24,* 3–16.

Duck, S., & Barnes, M. H. (1992). Disagreeing about agreement: Reconciling differences about similarity. Communication Monographs, 59, 199–208.

Duffy, S.M., & Rusbult, C.E. (1986). Satisfaction and commitment in homosexual and heterosexual relationships. *Journal of Homosexuality, 12,* 1–23.

Dunning, D. (1995). Trait importance and modifiability as factors influencing self-assessment and self-enhancement motives. *Personality and Social Psychology Bulletin, 21,* 1297–1306.

Dunning, D., & Sherman, D. A. (1997). Stereotypes and tacit inference. *Journal of Personality and Social Psychology, 73,* 459–471.

Dunning, D., & Stern, L. B. (1994). Distinguishing accurate from inaccurate eyewitness identification via inquiries about decision processes. *Journal of Personality and Social Psychology, 67,* 818–835.

Dutton, D. G., & Aron, A. P. (1974). Some evidence for heightened sexual attraction under conditions of high anxiety. *Journal of Personality and Social Psychology, 30,* 510–517.

Dutton, D. G., Sauders, K., Starzomski, A., & Bartholomew, D. (1994). Intimacy-anger and insecure attachment as precursors of abuse in intimate relationships. *Journal of Applied Social Psychology, 24,* 1367–1386.

Dutton, D.G. (1992). Theoretical and empirical perpectives on the etiology and prevention of wife assault. In R.D. Peters, R.J. McMahon, & V.L. Quinsey (Eds.). *Aggression and violence throughout the life span.* Newbury Park: Sage.

Dutton, K. A., & Brown, J. D. (1997). Global self-esteem and specific self-views as determinants of people's reactions to success and failure. *Journal of Personality and Social Psychology, 73,* 139–148.

Dykema, J., Bergbower, K., & Peterson, C. (1995). Pessimistic explanatory style, stress, and illness. *Journal of Social and Clinical Psychology, 14,* 357–371.

Eagly, A. H. (1995). The science and politics of comparing women and men. *American Psychologist, 50,* 145–158.

Eagly, A. H., & Carli, L. (1981). Sex of researchers and sex-typed communications as determinants of sex differences in influence-ability: A meta-analysis of social influence studies. *Psychological Bulletin, 90,* 1–20.

Eagly, A. H., & Chaiken, S. (1998). Attitude structure and function. In G. Lindsey, S. T., Fiske, & D. T. Gilbert (Eds.), *Handbook of social psychology* (4th ed.). New York: Oxford University Press and McGraw-Hill.

Eagly, A. H., & Steffen, V. J. (1986). Gender and aggressive behavior: A meta-analytic review of the social psychological literature. *Psychological Bulletin, 100,* 309–330.

Eagly, A. H., & Wood, W. (1982). Inferred sex differences in status as a determinant of gender stereotypes about social influence. *Journal of Personality and Social Psychology, 43,* 915–928.

Eagly, A. H., Makhijani, M. G., & Klonsky, B. G. (1992). Gender and the evaluation of leaders: A meta-analysis. *Psychological Bulletin, 111,* 3–22.

Earley, P. C. (1993). East meets West meets Mideast: Further explorations of collectivistic and individualistic work groups. *Academy of Management Journal, 36,* 319–348.

Earn, B., & Towson, S. (Eds.) (1986). *Readings in social psychology: Classic and Canadian contributions.* Peterborough, Ont.: Broadview Press.

Easterbrook, G. (1999, January 4 and 11). America the O.K. *The New Republic,* pp. 19–25.

Edwards, K., & Bryan, T. S. (1997). Judgmental biases produced by instructions to disregard: The (paradoxical) case of emotional information. *Personality and Social Psychology Bulletin, 23,* 849–864.

Egbert, J. M. Jr., Moore, F. H., Wuensch, K. L., & Castellow, W. A. (1992). The effect of litigant social desirability on judgements regarding a sexual harassment case. *Journal of Social Behavior and Personality, 7,* 569–579.

Eisenberg, N., Cialdini, R. B., McCreath, H., & Shell, R. (1987). Consistency based compliance: When and why do children become vulnerable? *Journal of Personality and Social Psychology, 52,* 1174–1181.

Eisenman, R. (1985). Marijuana use and attraction: Support for Byrne's similarity-attraction concept. *Perceptual and Motor Skills, 61,* 582.

Eisenstadt, D., & Leipe, M. R. (1994). The self-comparison process and self-discrepant feedback: Consequences of learning you are what you thought you were not. *Journal of Personality and Social Psychology, 67,* 611–626.

Ekman, P. (1972). Universals and cultural differences in facial expressions of emotion. In J. Cole (Ed.), *Science, 164,* 86–88.

Ekman, P. (1973). Cross-cultural studies of facial expression. In P. Ekman (Ed.), *Darwin and facial expression.* New York: Academic Press.

Ekman, P. (1989). The argument and evidence about universals in facial expressions of emotion. In H. Wagner & A. Manstead (Eds.), *Handbook of psychophysiology: Emotion and social behavior* (pp. 143–164). New York: Wiley.

Ekman, P., & Friesen, W. V. (1975). *Unmasking the face.* Englewood Cliffs, NJ: Prentice-Hall.

Elliot, A. J., & Devine, P. G. (1994). On the motivational nature of cognitive dissonance: Dissonance as psychological discomfort. *Journal of Personality and Social Psychology, 67,* 382–394.

Elliot, A. J., & Sheldon, K. M. (1998). Avoidance personal goals and the personality-illness relationship. *Journal of Personality and Social Psychology, 75,* 1282–1299.

Ellsworth, P. C., & Carlsmith, J. M. (1973). Eye contact and gaze aversion in aggressive encounter. *Journal of Personality and Social Psychology, 33,* 117–122.

Emmons, R. A., & Colby, P. M. (1995). Emotional conflict and well-being: Relation to perceived availability, daily utilization, and observer reports of social support. *Journal of Personality and Social Psychology, 68,* 947–959.

Epley, N., & Huff, C. (1998). Suspicion, affective response, and educational benefit as a result of deception in psychology research. *Personality and Social Psychology Bulletin, 24,* 759–768.

Erber, R. (1991). Affective and semantic priming: Effects of mood on category accessibility and inference. *Journal of Experimental Social Psychology, 27,* 480–498.

Erber, R. (1991). Affective and semantic priming: Effects of mood on category accessibility and inference. *Journal of Experimental Social Psychology, 27,* 480–498.

Esses, V. M. (1989). Mood as a moderator of acceptance of interpersonal feedback. *Journal of Personality and Social Psychology, 57,* 769–781.

Esses, V. M., & Webster, C. D. (1988). Physical attractiveness, dangerousness, and the Canadian criminal code. *Journal of Applied Social Psychology, 18,* 1017–1031.

Esses, V.M., & Gardner, R.C. (1966). Multiculturalism in Canada: Context and current status. *Canadian Journal of Behavioural Science, 28,* 145–152.

Esteem and self-complexity. *Journal of Personality, 59,* 473–505.

Estrada, C. A., Isen, A. M., & Young, M. J. (1995). Positive affect improves creative problem solving and influences reported source of practice satisfaction in physicians. *Motivation and Emotion, 18,* 285–300.

Ethier, K. A., & Deaux, K. (1994). Negotiating social identity when contexts change: Maintaining identification and responding to threat. *Journal of Personality and Social Psychology, 67,* 243–251.

Evans, G. W., Bullinger, M., & Hygge, S. (1998). Chronic noise exposure and physiological response: A prospective study of children living under environmental stress. *Psychological Science, 9,* 75–77.

Evans, G. W., Lepore, S. J., & Schroeder, A. (1996). The role of interior design elements in human responses to crowding. *Journal of Personality and Social Psychology, 70,* 41–46.

Evans, M. C., & Wilson, M. (1949). Friendship choices of university women students. *Educational and Psychological Measurement, 9,* 307–312.

Exline, R. (1962). Need affiliation and initial communication behavior in problem-solving groups characterized by low interpersonal visibility. *Psychological Reports, 10,* 79–89.

Fabrigar, L. R., & Krosnick, J. A. (1995). Attitude importance and the false consensus effect. *Personality and Social Psychology Bulletin, 21,* 468–479.

Farnsworth, C. H. (1995, June 4). Canada puts different spin on sensational murder trial. *Albany Times Union,* pp. E-8.

Fazio, R. H. (1989). On the power and functionality of attitudes: The role of attitude accessibility. In A. R. Pratkanis, S. J. Breckler, & A. G. Greenwald (Eds.), *Attitude structure and function* (pp. 153–179). Hillsdale, NJ: Erlbaum.

Fazio, R. H., & Roskos-Ewoldsen, D. R. (1994). Acting as we feel: When and how attitudes guide behavior. In S. Shavitt & T. C. Brock (Eds.), *Persuasion* (pp. 71–93). Boston: Allyn & Bacon.

Federal Bureau of Investigation (1999). *Homicide Statistics.* Web site.

Fein, S., & Spencer, S. J. (1997). Prejudice as self-image maintenance: Affirming the self through derogating others. *Journal of Personality and Social Psychology, 73,* 31–44.

Feingold, A. (1990). Gender differences in the effects of physical attractiveness on romantic attraction: A comparison across five research paradigms. *Journal of Personality and Social Psychology, 59,* 981–993.

Feingold, A. (1992a). Good-looking people are not what we think. *Psychological Bulletin, 111,* 304–341.

Feingold, A. (1992b). Gender differences in mate selection preferences: A test of the parental investment model. *Psychological Bulletin, 112,* 125–139.

Feingold, A. (1994). Gender differences in personality: A meta-analysis. *Psychological Bulletin, 116,* 412–428.

Feldman, S. S., & Nash, S. C. (1984). The transition from expectancy to parenthood: Impact of the firstborn child on men and women. *Sex Roles*, 11, 61–78.

Felmlee, D. H. (1995). Fatal attractions: Affection and disaffection in intimate relationships. *Journal of Social and Personal Relationships*, 12, 295–311.

Felmlee, D. H. (1998). "Be careful what you wish for . . ." : A quantitative and qualitative investigation of "fatal attractions." *Personal Relationships*, 5, 235–253.

Fenigstein, A., & Abrams, D. (1993). Self-attention and the egocentric assumption of shared perspectives. *Journal of Experimental Social Psychology*, 29, 287–303.

Feshbach, S. (1984). The catharsis hypothesis, aggressive drive, and the reduction of aggression. *Aggressive Behavior*, 10, 91–101.

Festinger, L. (1950). Informal social communication. *Psychological Review*, 57, 271–282.

Festinger, L. (1954). A theory of social comparison processes. *Human Relations*, 7, 117–140.

Festinger, L. (1957). *A theory of cognitive dissonance.* Evanston, IL: Row, Peterson.

Festinger, L. (1964). *Conflict, decision and dissonance.* Stanford, CA: Stanford University Press.

Festinger, L., & Carlsmith, J. M. (1959). Cognitive consequences of forced compliance. *Journal of Abnormal and Social Psychology*, 38, 203–210.

Festinger, L., Schachter, S., & Back, K. (1950). *Social pressures in informal groups: A study of a housing community.* New York: Harper.

Finn, J. (1986). The relationship between sex-role attitudes and attitudes supporting marital violence. *Sex Roles*, 14,

Fischer, G. J. (1986). College student attitudes toward forcible date rape: I. Cognitive predictors. *Archives of Sexual Behavior*, 15, 457–466.

Fisher, H. (1992). *Anatomy of love.* New York: Norton.

Fiske, A. P. (1991). The cultural relativity of selfish individualism: Anthropological evidence that humans are inherently sociable. In M. S. Clark (Ed.), *Prosocial behavior* (pp. 176–214), Newbury Park, CA: Sage.

Fiske, S. T. (1993). Social cognition and social perception. In L. W. Porter & M. R. Rosenzweig (Eds.), *Annual Review of Psychology*, 44, 155–194.

Fiske, S. T., & Taylor, S. E. (1991). *Social cognition* (2nd ed.). New York: Random House.

Fitzgerald, J. (1996, September 11). A hero leaps from bridge into breach. *Albany Times Union*, p. B2.

Folger, R., & Baron, R. A. (1996). Violence and hostility at work: A model of reactions to perceived injustice. In G. R. VandenBos and E. Q. Bulato (Eds.), *Violence on the job: Identifying risks and developing solutions* (pp. 51–85). Washington, DC: American Psychological Association.

Folger, R., & Bies, R. J. (1989). Managerial responsibilities and procedural justice. *Employee Responsibilities and Rights Journal*, 2, 79–90.

Foot, D.K. (1996). *Boom, bust and echo: How to profit from the coming demographic shift.* Toronto: Macfarlane, Walter & Ross.

Foot, D.K. (1998). *Boom, bust and echo 2000: Profiting from the demographic shift in the new millennium.* Toronto: Macfarlane, Walter & Ross.

Forgas, J. P. (1993c). On making sense of odd couples: Mood effects on the perception of mismatched relationships. *Personality and Social Psychology Bulletin*, 19, 59–70.

Forgas, J. P. (1994). The role of emotion in social judgments: An introductory review and an affect infusion model (AIM). *European Journal of Social Psychology*.

Forgas, J. P. (1995). Mood and judgment: The affect infusion model (AIM). *Psychological Bulletin*, 117, 39–66.

Forgas, J. P. (1998a). Asking nicely? The effects of mood on responding to more or less polite requests. *Personality and Social Psychology Bulletin*, 24, 173–185.

Forgas, J. P. (1998b). On feeling good and getting your way: Mood effects on negotiator cognition and bargaining strategies. *Journal of Personality and Social Psychology*, 74, 565–577.

Forgas, J. P. (l993b,). Mood and the perception of unusual people: Affective asymmetry in memory and social judgments. *European Journal of Social Psychology, in press.*

Forgas, J. P., & Fiedler, K. (1996). Us and them: Mood effects on intergroup discrimination. *Journal of Personality and Social Psychology*, 70, 28–40.

Forge, K. L., & Phemister, S. (1987). The effect of prosocial

Forston, M. T., & Stanton, A. L. (1992). Self-discrepancy theory as framework for understanding bulimic syptomatology and associated distress. *Journal of Social and Clinical Psychology*, 11, 103–118.

Forsyth, D. R. (1992). *An introduction to group dynamics*, (2nd ed.). Monterey, CA: Brooks/Cole.

Forsythe, S., Drake, M. F., & Cox, C. E. (1985). Influence of applicant's dress on interviewer's selection decisions. *Journal of Applied Psychology*, 70, 374–378.

Fraczek, A., & Kirwil, L. (1992). Living in the family and child aggression: Studies on some socialization conditions of development of aggression. In A. Fraczek & H. Zumkey (Eds.), *Socialization and aggression.* Berlin: Springer-Verlag.

Frank, M. G., & Gilovich, T. (1989). Effect of memory perspective on retrospective causal attributions. *Journal of Personality and Social Psychology*, 57, 399–403.

Frank, R. A. (1996). Tainted therapy and mistaken memory: Avoiding malpractice and preserving evidence with possible adult victims of childhood sexual abuse. *Applied & Preventive Psychology*, 5, 135–164.

Fredrickson, B. L. (1995). Socioemotional behavior at the end of college life. *Journal of Social and Personal Relationships*, 12, 261–276.

Freedman, J. L., & Fraser, S. C. (1966). Compliance without pressure: The foot-in-the-door technique. *Journal of Personality and Social Psychology*, 4, 195–202.

Freud, S. (1930/1963). *Civilization and Its Discontents.* London: Hogarth Press.

Freudenheim, M. (1992, October 14). Software helps patients make crucial choices. *New York Times*, p. D6.

Friedman, H. S., Hawley, P. H., & Tucker, J. S. (1994). *Personality, health, and longevity. Current Directions in Psychological Science*, 3, 37–41.

Fry, D. P. (1990). Aggressive interaction among Zapotec children in two different microcultural environments. Proceedings of the Ninth World Meeting of the International Society for Research on Aggression, Banff, Canada.

Fry, P.S., & Ghosh, R. (1980). Attributions of success and failure: comparison of cultural differences between Asian and Caucasian children. *Journal of Cross-Cultural Psychology*, 11, 343–363.

Gabor, T. (1994). *The impact of the availability of firearms on violent crime, suicide and accidental death: A review of the literature with special reference to the Canadian situation.* Ottawa: Department of Justice, WD1994–15e.

Gabriel, M. T., Critelli, J. W., & Ee, J. S. (1994). Narcissistic illusions in self-evaluations of intelligence and attractiveness. *Journal of Personality*, 62, 143–155.

Gaertner, S. L., Mann, J. A., Dovidio, J. F., Marrell, A. J., & Pomare, M. (1990). How does cooperation reduce intergroup bias? *Journal of Personality and Social Psychology*, 59, 692–704.

Gaertner, S. L., Mann, J., Murrell, A., & Dovidio, J. F. (1989). Reducing intergroup bias: The benefits of recategorization. *Journal of Personality and Social Psychology*, 57, 239–249.

Gaertner, S. L., Rust, M. C., Dovidio, J. F., Bachman, B. A., & Anastasio, P. A. (1993). The contact hypothesis: The role of a common ingroup identity on reducing intergroup bias. Small Business Research, in press.

Gaines, S. O. Jr. (1994). Exchange of respect-denying behaviors among male-female friendships. *Journal of Social and Personal Relationships*, 11, 5–24.

Galt, V. (1999). Schools short-change the poor, study says: Low teacher expectations hurt pupil's prospects. *Globe and Mail*, September. pp. A1.

Gamble, W. C., & Dalla, R. L. (1997). Young children's perceptions of their social worlds in single- and two-parent, Euro- and Mexican-American families. *Journal of Social and Personal Relationships*, 14, 357–372.

Gangestad, S. W., & Simpson, J. A. (1993). Development of a scale measuring genetic variation related to expressive control. *Journal of Personality*, 61, 133–158.

Gangestad, S., & Snyder, M. (1985). On the nature of self-monitoring: An examination of latent causal structure. In P. Shaver (Ed.), *Review of Personality and Social Psychology* (Vol. 6, pp. 65–85). Beverly Hills, CA: Sage.

Garcia, L. T. (1982). Sex role orientation and stereotypes about male-female sexuality. *Sex Roles*, 8, 863–876.

Geen, R. G. (1978). Some effects of observing violence upon the behavior of the observer. In B. A. Maher (Ed.), *Progress in experimental personality research*, (Vol. 8). New York: Academic Press.

Geen, R. G. (1989). Alternative conceptions of social facilitation. In P. B. Paulus (Ed.), *Psychology of group influence* (2nd ed., pp. 1–37). New York: Academic Press.

Geen, R. G. (1991b). Behavioral and physiological reactions to observed violence: Effects of prior exposure to aggressive stimuli. *Journal of Personality and Social Psychology*, 40, 868–875.

Geen, R., & Donnerstein, E. (Eds.). (1998). *Human aggression: Theories, research and implications for policy.* Pacific Grove, CA: Brooks/Cole.

Geertz, C. (1974). "From the native's point of view:" On the nature of anthropological understanding. In R.A.Shweder & R.A.LeVine (Eds.), *Culture theory: Essays on mind, self and emotion.* Cambridge: Cambridge University Press.

Genesee, F. (1984). Beyond bilingualism: Social psychological studies of French immersion programs in Canada. *Canadian Journal of Behavioral Science*, 16, 338–352.

Genesee, F., & Bourhis, R.Y. (1988). *Evaluative reactions to language choice strategies:The role of sociostructural factors.* Language and Communication, 8, 229–250.

Gentile, D. A. (1993). Just what are sex and gender, anyway? A call for a new terminological standard. *Psychological Science*, 4, 120–122.

George, J. M. (1990). Personality, affect, and behavior in groups. *Journal of Applied Psychology*, 75, 107–116.

George, J. M. (1991). State or trait: Effects of positive mood on prosocial behaviors at work. *Journal of Applied Psychology*, 76, 299–307.

George, J. M. (1995). Leader positive mood and group performance: The case of customer service. *Journal of Applied Social Psychology*, 25, 778–794.

George, M. S., Ketter, T. A., Parekh-Priti, I., Horwitz, B., et al. (1995). Brain activity during transient sadness and happiness in healthy women. *American Journal of Psychiatry*, 152, 341–351.

Gerard, H. B., Wilhelmy, R. A., & Conolley, E. S. (1968). Conformity and group size. *Journal of Personality and Social Psychology*, 8, 79–82.

Gerhart, B. (1987). How important are dispositional factors as determinants of job satisfaction? Implications for job design and other personnel programs. *Journal of Personality and Social Psychology*, 72, 366–377.

Gibbons, F. X., Eggleston, T. J., & Benthin, A. C. (1997). Cognitive reactions to smoking relapse: The reciprocal relation between dissonance and self-esteem. *Journal of Personality and Social Psychology*, 72, 184–195.

Gifford, R. (1994). A lens-mapping framework for understanding the encoding and decoding of interpersonal dispositions in nonverbal behavior. *Journal of Personality and Social Psychology*, 66, 398–412.

Gigone, D., & Hastie, R. (1993). The common knowledge effect: Information sharing and group judgment. *Journal of Personality and Social Psychology*, 65, 959–974.

Gigone, D., & Hastie, R. (1997). The impact of information on small group choice. *Journal of Personality and Social Psychology*, 72, 132–140.

Gilbert, D. T., & Malone, P. S. (1995). The correspondence bias. *Psychological Bulletin*, 117, 21–38.

Gilbert, D. T., Pelham, B. W., & Srull, D. S. (1988). On cognitive busyness: When person perceivers meet persons perceived. *Journal of Personality and Social Psychology*, 54, 733–740.

Gilbert, D., & Jones, E. E. (1986). Perceiver-induced constraint: Interpretations of self-generated reality. *Journal of Personality and Social Psychology, 50,* 269–280.

Gilbert, L. A. (1993). *Two careers/One family.* Newbury Park, CA: Sage.

Giles, H., Mulac, A., Bradac, J., & Johnson, P. (1986). Speech accommodation theory: The first decade and beyond. *Communication Yearbook, 10,* 8–34.

Gillen, B. (1981). Physical attractiveness: A determinant of two types of goodness. *Personality and Social Psychology Bulletin, 7,* 277–281.

Giner-Sorolla, R., & Chaiken, S. (1994). The causes of hostile media effects. *Journal of Experimental Social Psychology, 30,* 165–180.

Glass Ceiling Commission. (1995). *Good for business: Making full use of the nation's human capital.* Washington, DC: Glass Ceiling Commission.

Glass, D. C. (1977). *Behavior patterns, stress, and coronary disease.* Hillsdale, NJ: Erlbaum.

Glass, D. C. (1989). Psychology and health: Obstacles and opportunities. *Journal of Applied Social Psycholoqy, 19,* 1145–1163.

Gleicher, F., Boninger, D., Strathman, A., Armor, D., Hetts, J., & Ahn, M. (1995). With an eye toward the future: Impact of counterfactual thinking on affect, attitudes, and behavior. In N. J. Roses & J. M. Olson (Eds.), *What might have been: the social psychology of counterfactual thinking.* (pp. 283–304). Mahwah, NJ: Erlbaum.

Globe and Mail. (1999). Civil servants win on pay equity. *Globe and Mail,* October 20, pp. A1.

Gold, J. A., Ryckman, R. M., & Mosley, N. R. (1984). Romantic mood induction and attraction to a dissimilar other: Is love blind? *Personality and Social Psychology Bulletin, 10,* 358–368.

Goldstein, A. G., Chance, J. E., & Schneller, G. R. (1989). Frequency of eyewitness identification in criminal cases: A survey of prosecutors. *Bulletin of the Psychonomic Society, 27,* 71–74.

Goldstein, M. D., & Strube, M. J. (1994). Independence revisited: The relation between positive and negative affect in a naturalistic setting. *Personality and Social Psychology Bulletin, 20,* 57–64.

Goleman, D. (1994, May 11). Seeking out small pleasures keeps immune system strong. *New York Times,* pp. C1, C15.

Goodwin, R., & Findlay, C. (1997). "We were just fated together" . . . Chinese love and the concept of yuan in England and Hong Kong. *Personal Relationships, 4,* 85–92.

Goodwin, R., & Lee, I.(1994). Taboo topics among Chinese and English friends. *Journal of Cross-Cultural Psychology, 25,* 325–338.

Gordin, F. M., Willoughby, A. D., Levine, L. A., Ourel, L., & Neill, K. M. (1987). Knowledge of AIDS among hospital workers: Behavioral correlates and consequences. *AIDS, 1,* 183–188.

Gordon, R. A. (1996). Impact of ingratiation in judgments and evaluations: A meta-analytic investigation. *Journal of Personality and Social Psychology, 71,* 54–70.

Graham, B., & Folkes, V. (Eds.).(1990). *Attribution theory: Applications to achievement, mental health, and interpersonal conflict.* Hillsdale, NJ: Erlbaum.

Graham, J. L. (1985). The influence of culture on the process of business negotiations: an exploratory study. *Journal of International Business Studies, 16,* 81–96.

Graham, S., Weiner, B., & Zucker, G. S. (1997). An attributional analysis of punishment goals and public reactions to O. J. Simpson. *Personality and Social Psychology Bulletin, 23,* 331–346.

Gray, P. (1993). What is love? *Time, 141*(7), 46–49.

Graziano, W. G., & Bryant, W. H. M. (1998). Self-monitoring and the self-attribution of positive emotions. *Journal of Personality and Social Psychology, 74,* 250–261.

Graziano, W. G., Jensen-Campbell, L. A., & Hair, E. C. (1996). Perceiving interpersonal conflict and reacting to it: The case for agreeableness. *Journal of Personality and Social Psychology, 70,* 820–835.

Green, L. R., Richardson, D. R., & Lago, T. (1996). How do friendship, indirect, and direct aggression relate? *Aggressive Behavior, 22,* 81–86.

Greenbaum, P., & Rosenfield, H. W. (1978). Patterns of avoidance in responses to interpersonal staring and proximity: Effects of bystanders on drivers at a traffic intersection. *Journal of Personality and Social Psychology, 36,* 575–587.

Greenberg, J. (1990). Employee theft as a reaction to underpayment inequity: The hidden cost of pay cuts. *Journal of Applied Psychology, 75,* 561–568.

Greenberg, J. (1993a). The social side of fairness: Interpersonal and informational classes of organizational justice. In R. Cropanzano (Ed.), *Justice in the workplace* (pp. 79–103). Hillsdale, NJ: Erlbaum.

Greenberg, J. (1996). *The quest for justice: Essays and experiments.* Thousand Oaks, CA: Sage Publications.

Greenberg, J., & Alge, B. J. (1997). Aggressive reactions to workplace injustice. In R. W. Griffin, A. O'Leary-Kelly, & J. Collins (Eds.), *Dysfunctional behavior in organizations: Vol. 1. Violent behaviors in organizations.* Greenwich, CT: JAI Press.

Greenberg, J., & Baron, R. A. (1997). *Behavior in organizations* (6th ed.). Upper Saddle River, NJ: Prentice-Hall.

Greenberg, J., & Scott, K. S. (1996). Why do workers bite the hands that feed them? Employee theft as social exchange process. In B. M. Staw & L. L. Cummings (Eds.), *Research in organizational behavior* (Vol. 18, pp. 111–156). Greenwich, CT: JAI Press.

Greenberg, J., Pyszcynski, T., & Solomon, S. (1982). The self-serving attributional bias: Beyond self-presentation. *Journal of Experimental Social Psychology, 18,* 56–67.

Greenberg, J., Solomon, S., Pyszczynski, T., Rosenblatt, A., Burling, J., Lyon, D., Simon, L., & Pinel, E. (1992). Why do people need self-esteem? Converging evidence that self-esteem serves an anxiety-buffering function. *Journal of Personality and Social Psychology, 63,* 913–922.

Greenberg, M. A., & Stone, A. A. (1992). Emotional disclosure about traumas and its relation to health: Effects of previous disclosure and trauma severity. *Journal of Personality and Social Psychology, 63,* 75–84.

Greenberg, M. A., Wortman, C. B., & Stone, A. A. (1996). Emotional expression and physical health: Revising traumatic memories or fostering self-regulation? *Journal of Personality and Social Psychology, 71,* 588–602.

Greenwald, J. (1998, November 23). Herbal healing. *Time*, pp. 58–67.

Griffin, D. W., & Buehler, R. (1993). Role of construal process in conformity and dissent. *Journal of Personality and Social psychology, 65*, 657–669.

Griffin, D.W., & Bartholomew, K. (1994). The metaphysics of measurement: The case of adult attachment. In D. Perlman & K. Bartholomew (Eds.), *Advances in Personal Relationships*, 5,

Griffin, K. W., & Rabkin, J. G. (1998). Perceived control over illness, realistic acceptance, and psychological adjustment in people with AIDS. *Journal of Social and Clinical Psychology*, 17, 407–424.

Groff, D. B., Baron, R. S., & Moore, D. L. (1983). Distraction, attentional conflict, and drive like behavior. *Journal of Experimental Social Psychology*, 19, 359–380.

Grossman, M., & Wood, W. (1993). Sex differences in intensity of emotional experience: A social role interpretation. *Journal of Personality and Social Psychology*, 65, 1010–1022.

Grote, N. K., Frieze, I. H., & Stone, C. A. (1996). Children, traditionalism in the division of family work, and marital satisfaction: "What's love got to do with it?" *Personal Relationships*, 3, 211–228.

Grusec, J. E. (1991). The socialization of altruism. In M. S. Clark (Ed.), *Prosocial behavior* (pp. 9–33). Newbury Park, CA: Sage.

Gudjonsson, G. H. (1993). Confession evidence, psychological vulnerability and expert testimony. *Journal of Community and Applied Social Psychology*, 3, 117–129.

Gudjonsson, G. H., & Clark, N. K. (1986). Suggestibility in police interrogation: A social psychological model. *Social Behaviour*, 1, 83–104.

Gudykunst, W.B., Gao, G., Schmidt, K.L., et al. (1992). The influence of individualism-collectivism, self-monitoring and predicted-outcome value on communication in in-group and out-group relationships. *Journal of Cross-Cultural Psychology*, 23, 196–213.

Guerrero, L. K. (1998). Attachment-style differences in the experience and expression of romantic jealousy. *Personal Relationships*, 5, 273–291.

Guimond, S., & Dubé-Simard, L. (1983). Relative deprivation theory and the Quebec nationalist movement: The cognitive-emotion distinction and the personal-group deprivation issue. *Journal of Personality and Social Psychology*, 44, 526–535.

Guimond, S., & Palmer, D. L. (1990). Type of academic training and causal attributions for social problems. *European Journal of Social Psychology*, 20, 61–75.

Guimond, S., & Palmer, D. L. (1996). The political socialization of commerce and social science students: Epistemic authority and attitude change. *Journal of Applied Social Psychology*, 26,

Guimond, S., B_gin, G., & Palmer, D.L. (1989). Education and causal attributions: The development of "person-blame and system-blame" ideology. *Social Psychology Quarterly*, 52, 126–140.

Gur, R. C., Mozley, L. H., Mozley, P. D., Resnick, S. M., Karp, J. S., Alavi, A., Arnold, S. E., & Gur, R. E. (1995). Sex differences in regional glucose metabolism during a resting state. *Science*, 267, 528–531.

Hackel, L. S., & Ruble, D. N. (1992). Changes in the marital relationship after the first baby is born: Predicting the impact of expectancy disconfirmation. *Journal of Personality and Social Psychology*, 62, 944–957.

Hagborg, W. J. (1993). Gender differences on Harter's Self-Perception Profile for Adolescents. *Journal of Social Behavior and Personality*, 8, 141–148.

Hamilton, D. L., & Sherman, S. J. (1989). Illusory correlations: Implications for stereotype theory and research. In D. Bar-Tal, C. F. Graumann, A. W. Kruglanski, & W. Stroebe (Eds.), *Stereotyping and prejudice: Changing conceptions* (pp. 59–82). New York: Springer-Verlag.

Hamilton, G. V. (1978). Obedience and responsibility: A jury simulation. *Journal of Personality and Social Psychology*, 36, 126–146.

Hamilton, J. C., Falconer, J. J., & Greenberg, M. D. (1992). The relationship between self-consciousness and dietary restraint. *Journal of Social and Clinical Psychology*, 11, 158–166

Hamilton, V. L., & Sanders, J. (1995). Crimes of obedience and conformity in the workplace: Surveys of Americans, Russians, and Japanese. *Journal of Social Issues*, 51, 67–88.

Han, S-P., & Shavitt, S. (1994). Persuasion and culture: Advertising appeals in individualistic and collectivistic societies. *Journal of Experimental Social Psychology*, 30, 326–350.

Hansen, C. H, & Hansen, R. D. (1988). Finding the face in the crowd: An anger superiority effect. *Journal of Personality and Social Psychology*, 54, 917–924.

Hansen, R. D. (1980). Common sense attribution. *Journal of Personality and Social Psychology*, 17, 398–411.

Hare, R, (1994). *Without conscience: The disturbing world of the psychopaths among us*. New York: Pocket Books.

Harkins, S., & Szymanski, K. (1989). Social loafing and group evaluation. *Journal of Personality and Social Psychology*, 56, 934–941.

Harrigan, J. A., Lucic, K. S., Kay, D., McLaney, A., & Rosenthal, R. (1991). Effect of expresser role and type of self-touching on observers' perceptions. *Journal of Applied Social Psychology*, 21, 585–609.

Harris, M. B. (1994). Gender of subject and target as mediators of aggression. *Journal of Applied Social Psychology*, 24, 453–471.

Harris, M. B. (1996). Aggressive experiences and aggressiveness: Relationship to gender, ethnicity, and age. *Journal of Applied Social Psychology*, 26, 843–870.

Harris, M. B., (1992). Sex, race, and experiences of aggression. *Aggressive Behavior*, 18, 201–217.

Harris, M. B., Harris, R. J., & Bochner, S. (1982). Fat, four-eyed, and female: Stereotypes of obesity, glasses, and gender. Journal of Applied Social Psychology, 12, 503–516.

Harris, M. J., Milich, R., Corbitt, E. M., Hoover, D. W., & Brady, M. (1992). Self-fulfilling effects of stigmatizing information on children's social interactions. *Journal of Personality and Social Psychology*, 63, 41–50.

Harrison, A. A., & Saeed, L. (1977). Let's make a deal: An analysis of revelations and stipulations in lonely hearts advertisements. *Journal of Personality and Social Psychology*, 35, 257–264.

Harrison, B., & Marmen, L. (1994). *Languages in Canada* (Focus on Canada series). Scarborough Ont.: Statistics Canada and Prentice Hall Canada.

Harr_, R., & Secord, P.F. (1972). *The explanation of social behaviour*. Oxford: Blackwell.

Harvey, J. H., & Omarzu, J. (1997). Minding the close relationship. *Personality and Social Psychology Review*, 1, 224–240.

Harvey, J. H., & Weary, G. (Eds.). (1989). *Attribution: Basic issues and applications*. San Diego: Academic Press.

Hastie, R., Penrod, S., & Pennington, N. (1983). *Inside the jury*. Cambridge, MA: Harvard University Press.

Hatfield, E. (1988). Passionate and companionate love. In R. L. Sternberg & M. I. Barnes (Eds.), *The psychology of love* (pp. 191–217). New Haven, CT: Yale University Press.

Hatfield, E., & Rapson, R. L. (1992a). Similarity and attraction in close relationships. Communication Monographs, 59, 209–212.

Hatfield, E., & Rapson, R. L. (1993). *Love, sex, and intimacy: Their psychology, biology, and history*. New York: Harper Collins.

Hatfield, E., & Rapson, R.L. (1996). *Love and sex: Cross-cultural perspectives*. Needham Heights, MA: Allyn & Bacon.

Hatfield, E., & Sprecher, S. (1986a). Measuring passionate love in intimate relations. *Journal of Adolescence*, 9, 383–410.

Hatfield, E., & Walster, G. W. (1981). A new look at love. Reading, MA: Addison-Wesley.

Hayden, S. R., Jackson, T. T., & Guydish, J. N. (1984). Helping behavior of females: Effects of stress and commonality of fate. *Journal of Psychology*, 117, 233–237.

Hazan, C., & Shaver, P. R. (1990). Love and work: An attachment-theoretical perspective. *Journal of Personality and Social Psychology*, 59, 270–280.

Hebl, M. R., & Heatherton, T. E. (1998). The stigma of obesity in women: The difference is black and white. *Personality and Social Psychology Bulletin*, 24, 417–426.

Heider, F. (1958). *The psychology of interpersonal relations*. New York: Wiley.

Heilman, D. E., Block, C. J., & Lucas, J. A. (1992). Presumed incompetent? Stigmatization and affirmative action efforts. *Journal of Applied Psychology*, 77, 536–544.

Heinberg, L. J., & Thompson, J. K. (1992). Social comparison: Gender, target importance ratings, and relation to body image disturbance. *Journal of Social Behavior and Personality*, 7, 335–344.

Heine, S. J., & Lehman, D. R. (1995). Cultural variation in unrealistic optimism: Does the West feel more invulnerable than the East. *Journal of Personality and Social Psychology*, 68, 595–607.

Heine, S. J., & Lehman, D. R. (1996). Culture and group-serving biases. Manuscript submitted for publication.

Heine, S. J., & Lehman, D. R. (1997a). Culture, dissonance, and self-affirmation. *Personality and Social Psychology Bulletin*, 23, 389–400.

Heine, S. J., & Lehman, D. R. (1997b). The cultural construction of self-enhancement: An examination of group-serving bias. *Journal of Personality and Social Psychology*, 72, 1268–1283.

Helson, R., & Roberts, B. (1992). The personality of young adult couples and wives' work patterns. *Journal of Personality*, 60, 575–597.

Hemenway, D. (1998). Survey research and self-defense gun use: An exploration of extreme over estimates. *Journal of Law Criminology*.

Henderson, J., & Taylor, J. (1985, November 17). Study finds bias in death sentence: Killers of whites risk execution. *Albany Times Union*, p. A–19.

Henderson-King, E., Henderson-King, D., Zhermer, N., Posokhova, S., & Chiker, V. (1997). In-group favoritism and perceived similarity: A look at Russians' perceptions in the post-Soviet era. *Personality and Social Psychology Bulletin*, 23, 1013–1021.

Hendrick, C., & Hendrick, S. S. (1986). A theory and method of love. *Journal of Personality and Social Psychology*, 50, 392–402.

Hendrick, C., Hendrick, S. S., Foote, F. H., & Slapion-Foote, M. J. (1984). Do men and women love differently? *Journal of Social and Personal Relationships*, 1, 177–195.

Hendrick, S. S., & Hendrick, C. (1987). Love and sex attitudes and religious beliefs. *Journal of Social and Clinical Psychology*, 5, 391–398.

Hendrick, S. S., Hendrick, C., & Adler, N. L. (1988). Romantic relationships: Love, satisfaction, and staying together. *Journal of Personality and Social Psychology*, 54, 980–988.

Henry, F. & Ginzberg, E. (1985). *Who gets the work: A test of racial discrimination in employment in Toronto*. Toronto: The Urban Alliance on Race Relations and the Social Planning Council of Metropolitan Toronto.

Henry, F. (1978). *The dynamics of racism in Toronto*. Unpublished research report. York University.

Henry, F. (1999). Two studies of racial discrimination in employment. In J. Curtis, E. Grabb, & N. Guppy (Eds.), *Social inequality in Canada: Patterns, problems, and policies* (2nd ed., pp. 226–235). Scarborough, Ont.: Prentice Hall.

Henry, F., Tator, C., Mattis, W., & Rees, T. (1995). *The colour of democracy: Racism in Canadian society*. Toronto: Harcourt Brace.

Henry, W. A., III. (1991). The journalist and the murder. *Time*, 138(15), 86.

Hensley, W. E. (1996). The effect of a ludus love style on sexual experience. *Social Behavior and Personality*, 24, 205–212.

Hepworth, J. T., & West, S. G. (1988). Lynchings and the economy: A time-series reanalysis of Hovland and Sears (1940). *Journal of Personality and Social Psychology*, 55, 239–247.

Hershberger, S. L., Lichtenstein, P., & Knox, S. S. (1994). Genetic and environmental influences on perceptions of organizational climate. *Journal of Applied Psychology*, 79, 24–33.

Hewstone, M. (1990). The 'ultimate attribution error'? A review of the literature on intergroup causal attribution. *European Journal of Social Psychology, 20*, 311–335.

Higgins, E. T. (1987). Self-discrepancy: A theory relating self and affect. *Psychological Review*, 94, 319–340.

Higgins, E. T. (1989). Self-discrepancy theory:What patterns of self-beliefs cause people to suffer? In L. Berkowitz (Ed.), *Advances in experimental social psychology* (Vol. 22, pp. 93–136). San Diego, CA: Academic Press.

Higgins, E. T. (1990). Personality, social psychology, and

Higgins, E. T., & Bargh, J. A. (1987). Social cognition and social perception. In M. R. Rosenszweig & L. W. Porter (Eds.), *Annual review of psychology* (Vol. 38, pp. 369–425). Palo Alto, CA: Annual Reviews Inc.

Hill, C. A. (1987). Affiliation motivation: People who need people but in different ways. *Journal of Personality and Social Psychology*, 52, 1008–1018.

Hill, C. A., Blakemore, J. E. O., & Drumm, P. (1997). Mutual and unrequited love in adolescence and young adulthood. *Personal Relationships*, 4, 15–23.

Hilliard, A. (1985). Parameters affecting the African-American child. Paper presented at the Black Psychology Seminar, Duke Unviersity, Durham, NC.

Hinkley, K., & Andersen, S. M. (1996). The working self-concept in transference: Significant-other activation and self change. *Journal of Personality and Social Psychology*, 71, 1279–1295.

Hinsz, V. B. (1995). Goal setting by groups performing an additive task: A comparison with individual goal setting. *Journal of Applied Social Psychology*, 25, 965–990.

Hirt, E. R., Zillmann, D., Erickson, G. A., & Kennedy, C. (1992). Costs and benefits of allegiance: Changes in fans' self-ascribed competencies after team victory versus defeat. *Journal of Personality and Social Psychology*, 61, 724–738.

Hixon, J. G., & Swann, W. B., Jr. (1993). When does introspection bear fruit? Self-reflection, self-insight, and interpersonal choices. *Journal of Personality and Social Psychology*, 64, 35–43.

Hofstede, G. (1980). *Culture's consequences: International differences in work-related values*. Beverly Hills, CA: Sage.

Hofstede, G. (1983). Dimensions of national cultures in fifty countries and three regions. In J. Deregowski, S. Dzuirawiec & R. Annis (Eds.), *Expiscations in cross-cultural psychology*. Lisse, Netherlands: Swets & Zeitlinger.

Hogg, M. A., & Hains, S. C. (1996). Intergroup relations and group solidarity: Effects of group identification and social beliefs on depersonalized attraction. *Journal of Personality and Social Psychology*, 70, 25–309.

Hogg, M. A., Cooper-Shaw, L., & Hozworth, D. W. (1993). Group prototypicality and depersonalized attraction in small interactive groups. *Personality and Social Psychology Bulletin*, 19, 425–465.

Holahan, C. J., Moos, R. H., Holahan, C. K., & Brennan, P. L. (1997). Social context, coping strategies, and depressive symptoms: An expanded model with cardiac patients. *Journal of Personality and Social Psychology*, 72, 918–928.

Holtgraves, T. (1997). Styles of language use: Individual and cultural variability in conversational indirectness. *Journal of Personality and Social Psychology, 73*, 624–637.

Holtgraves, T.M., & Yang, J.N. (1990). Politeness as universal: Cross-cultural perceptions of request strategies and inferences based on their use. *Journal of Personality and Social Psychology, 59*, 149–160.

Homer, P.M., & Kahle, L. (1988). A structural equation test of the value-attitude-behavior heirarchy. *Journal of Personality and Social Psychology*, 54, 638–646.

Hosch, H. M., & Bothwell, R. K. (1990). Arousal, description and identification accuracy of victims and bystanders. *Journal of Social Behavior and Personality*, 5, 481–488.

House, R. J. (1977). A theory of charismatic leadership. In J. G. Hunt & L. L. Larson (Eds.), *Leadership: The cutting edge* (pp. 189–207). Carbondale, IL: Southern Illinois University Press.

House, R. J., & Podsakoff, P. M. (1994). Leadership effectiveness: Past perspectives and future directions for research. In J. Greenberg (Ed.), *Organizational behavior: The state of the science* (pp. 45–82). Hillsdale, NJ: Erlbaum.

House, R. J., Spangler, W. D., & Woycke, J. (1991). Personality and charisma in the U. S. presidency: A psychological theory of leader effectiveness. *Administrative Science Quarterly*, 36, 364–396.

Hovland, C. I., & Sears, R. R. (1940). Minor studies in aggression: VI. Correlation of lynchings with economic indices. *Journal of Psychology*, 9, 301–310.

Hovland, C. I., & Weiss, W. (1951). The influence of source credibility on communication effectiveness. *Public Opinion Quarterly*, 1, 635–650.

Hovland, C. I., Janis, I. L., & Kelley, H. H. (1953). *Communication and persuasion: Psychological studies of one on one*. New Haven, CT: Yale University Press.

Howard, G. S. (1985). The role of values in the science of psychology. *American Psychologist*, 40, 255–265.

Howell, J. M., & Frost, P. J. (1989). A laboratory study of charismatic leadership. Organizational Behavior and Human Decision Processes, 43, 243–269.

Howells, G. N. (1993). Self-monitoring and personality: Would the real high self-monitor please stand up? *Journal of Social Behavior and Personality*, 8, 59–72.

Hoyle, R. H., & Sowards, B. A. (1993). Self-monitoring and the regulation of social experience: A control-process model. *Journal of Social and Clinical Psychology*, 12, 280–306.

Huang, I.-C. (1998). Self-esteem, reaction to uncertainty, and physician practice variation: A study of resident physicians. *Social Behavior and Personality*, 26, 181–194.

Huesmann (Ed.), *Aggressive behavior*, pp. 153–186. New York: Plenum.

Huesmann, L. R. (1982). Television violence and aggressive behavior. In D. Pearl, L. Bouthilet, & J. Lazar (Eds.), *Television and behavior: Vol., 2. Technical reviews* (pp. 220–256). Washington, DC: National Institute of Mental Health.

Huesmann, L. R., & Eron, L. D. (1984). Cognitive processes and the persistence of aggressive behavior. *Aggressive Behavior*, 10, 243–251.

Huesmann, L. R., & Eron, L. D. (1986). *Television and the aggressive child: A cross-national comparison*. Hillsdale, NJ: Erlbaum.

Hughes, C. F., Uhlmann, C., & Pennebaker, J. W. (1994). The body's response to processing emotional trauma: Linking verbal text with autonomic activity. *Journal of Personality*, 62, 565–585.

Humphreys, L. G. (1998). A little noticed consequence of the repressed memory epidemic. *American Psychologist*, 53, 485–486.

Humphriss, N. (1989, November 20). Letters. *Time*, p. 12.

Hunter, C. E., & Ross, M. W. (1991). Determinants of health-care workers' attitudes toward people with AIDS. *Journal of Applied Social Psychology*, 21, 947–956.

Huo, Y. J., Smith, H. J., Tyler, T. R., & Lind, E. A. (1996). Superordinate identification subgroup identification and justice concerns: Is separation the problem, is assimilation the answer? *Psychological Science*, 7, 40–45.

Hurewitz, M. (1998, March 26). Young man finds honesty has its rewards. *Albany Times Union*, pp. B1, B7.

Hyde, J. S., & Plant, E. A. (1995). Magnitude of psychological gender differences: Another side to the story. *American Psychologist*, 50, 159–161.

Ickes, W., Reidhead, S., & Patterson, M. (1986). Machiavellianism and self-monitoring: As different as "me" and "you." *Social Cognition*, 4, 58–74.

Insel, T. R., & Carter, C. S. (1995, August). The monogamous brain. *Natural History*, 12–14.

Insko, C. A. (1985). Balance theory, the Jordan paradigm, and the West tetrahedron. In L. Berkowitz (Ed.), *Advances in experimental social psychology*. New York: Academic Press.

Isen, A. M. (1984). Toward understanding the role of affect in cognition. In S. R. Wyer & T. K. Srull (Eds.), *Handbook of social cognition* (Vol. 3, pp. 179–236). Hillsdale, NJ: Erlbaum.

Isen, A. M., & Baron, R. A. (1991). Affect and organizational behavior. In B. M. Staw & L. L. Cummings (Eds.), *Research in organizational behavior* (vol. 15, pp. 1–53). Greenwich CT: JAI Press.

Isen, A. M., & Levin, P. A. (1972). Effect of feeling good on helping: Cookies and kindness. *Journal of Personality and Social Psychology*, 21, 384–388.

Israel, J., & Tajfel, H. (Eds.) (1972). *The context of social psycholgy: A critical assessment*. London: Academic Press.

Istvan, J., Griffitt, W., & Weidner, G. (1983). Sexual arousal and the polarization of perceived sexual attractiveness. *Basic and Applied Social Psychology*, 4, 307–318.

Ito, T. A., & Cacioppo, J. T. (1999). The psychopysiology of utility appraisals. In D. Kahneman, E. Diener, & N. Schwartz (Eds.), *Understanding quality of life: Scientific perspectives on enjoyment and suffering*. New York: Russell Sage Foundation.

Ito, T. A., Larsen, J. T., Smith, N. K., & Cacioppo, J. T. (1998). Negative information weighs more heavily on the brain: The negativity bias in evaluative categorizations. *Journal of Personality and Social Psychology*, 75, 887–900.

Izard, C. (1991). *Human emotions* (2nd ed.). New York: Plenum.

Jackson, L. A., Gardner, P., & Sullivan, L. (1992). Explaining gender differences in self-pay expectations: Social comparison standards and perceptions of fair pay. *Journal of Applied Psychology*, 77, 651–663.

Jackson, L. M., & Esses, V. M. (1997). Of scripture and ascription: The relation between religious fundamentalism and intergroup helping. *Personality and Social Psychology Bulletin*, 23, 893–906.

James, W. (1890). *The principles of psychology* (Vols. 1 and 2). New York: Holt.

Janis, I. L. (1954). Personality correlates of susceptablity to persuasion. *Journal of Personality*, 22, 504–518.

Janis, I. L. (1982). Victims of groupthink (2nd ed.). Boston: Houghton Mifflin.

Janoff-Bulman, R., & Wade, M. B. (1996). The dilemma of self-advocacy for women: Another case of blaming the victim? *Journal of Social and Clinical Psychology*, 15, 143–152.

Jemmott, J. B., III, & Magloire, K. (1988). Academic stress, social support, and secretory immunoglobulin. *Journal of Personality and Social Psychology*, 55, 803–810.

Jemmott, J. B., III, Ashby, K. L., & Lindenfield, K. (1989). Romantic commitment and the perceived availability of opposite-sex persons: On loving the one you're with. *Journal of Applied Social Psychology*, 19, 1198–1211.

Jessor, R., Turbin, M. S., & Costa, F. M. (1998). Protective factors in adolescent health behavior. *Journal of Personality and Social Psychology*, 75, 788–800.

Jex, S. M., Cvetanovski, J., & Allen, S. J. (1994). Self-esteem as a moderator of the impact of unemployment. *Journal of Social Behavior and Personality*, 9, 69–80.

Johns, G., & Jia Lin Xie (1998). Perceptions of absence from work: People's Republic of China versus Canada. *Journal of Applied Psychology*, 83, 515–530.

Johnson, A. B., & Byrne, D. (1996, March). Effects of proximity in familiarity and preferences for places of work. Paper presented at the meeting of the Eastern Psychological Association, Philadelphia.

Johnson, B. T. (1994). Effects of outcome-relevant involvement and prior information on persuasion. *Journal of Experimental Social Psychology*, 30, 556–579.

Johnson, M. K., & Sherman, S. J. (1990). Constructing and reconstructing the past and the future in the present. In E. T. Higgins & R. M. Sorrentino (Eds.), *Handbook of motivation and social cognition: Foundations of social behavior* (pp. 482–526). New York: Guilford.

Johnston, C., T., & Short, K. H. (1993). Depressive symptoms and perceptions of child behavior. *Journal of Social and Clinical Psychology*, 12, 164–181.

Johnston, V. S., & Franklin, M. (1993). Is beauty in the eye of the beholder? *Ethology and Sociobiology*, 14, 183–199.

Johnston, V. S., & Oliver-Rodriguez, J. C. (1997). Facial beauty and the late positive component of event-related potentials. *Journal of Sex Research*, 34, 188–198.

Johnstone, B., Frame, C. L., & Bouman, D. (1992). Physical attractiveness and athletic and academic ability in controversial-aggressive and rejected-aggressive children. *Journal of Social and Clinical Psychology, 11*, 71–79.

Joiner, T. E. Jr., & Schmidt, N. B. (1995). Dimensions of perfectionism, life stress, and depressed and anxious symptoms: Prospective support for diathesis-stress but not specific vulnerability among male undergraduates. *Journal of Social and Clinical Psychology, 14*, 165–183.

Joiner, T. E., Jr. (1994). The interplay of similarity and self-verification in relationship formation. *Social Behavior and Personality, 22*, 195–200.

Jones, E. E. (1990). *Interpersonal perception.* New York: W. H. Freeman.

Jones, E. E., & Davis, K. E. (1965). From acts to disposition: The attribution process in person perception. In L. Berkowitz (Ed.), *Advances in experimental social psychology* (Vol. 2, pp. 219–266). New York: Academic Press.

Jones, E. E., & Davis, K. E. (1965). From acts to disposition: The attribution process in person perception. In L. Berkowitz (Ed.), *Advances in experimental social psychology.* (Vol. 2, pp. 219–266). New York: Academic Press.

Jones, E. E., & McGillis, D. (1976). Corresponding inferences and the attribution cube: A comparative reappraisal. In J. H. Harvey, W. J. Ickes, & R. F. Kidd (Eds.), *New directions in attribution research* (Vol. 1). Morristown, NJ: Erlbaum.

Jones, E. E., & Nisbett, R. E. (1971). *The actor and the observer: Divergent perceptions of the causes of behavior.* Morristown, NJ: General Learning Press.

Jones, M. (1993). Influence of self-monitoring on dating motivations. *Journal of Research in Personality, 27*, 197–206.

Jourard, S.M. (1971). *Self-disclosure.* New York: Wiley

Judd, C. M., Ryan, C. N., & Parke, B. (1991). Accuracy in the judgment of in-group and out-group variability. Journal of Personality and Social Psychology, 61, 366–379.

Judge, T. A. (1993). Does affective disposition moderate the relationships between job satisfaction and voluntary turnover? *Journal of Applied Psychology, 78*, 395–401.

Jussim, L. (1991). Interpersonal expectations and social reality: A reflection-construction model and reinterpretation of evidence. *Psychological Review, 98*, 54–73.

Kacmar, K. M., Delery, J. E., & Ferris, G. R. (1992). Differential effectiveness of applicant impression management tactics on employment interview decisions. *Journal of Applied Social Psychology, 22*, 1250–1272.

Kagitcibasi, C. (1970). Social norms and authoritarianism: a Turkish-American comparison. *Journal of Cross-Cultural Psychology, 4*, 157–174.

Kahn, W., & Crosby, F. (1985). Change and stasis: Discriminating between attitudes and discriminating behavior. *Women and Work: An Annual Review, 1*, 215–238.

Kahneman, D., & Miller, D. T. (1986). Norm theory: comparing reality to its alternatives. *Psychological Review, 93*, 136–153.

Kahneman, D., & Tversky, A. (1982). The simulation heuristic. In D. Kahneman, P. Slovic, & Tversky, A. (Eds.), *Judgments under uncertainty: Heuristics and biases* (pp. 201–208). New York: Cambridge University Press.

Kalichman, S. C., Sarwer, D. B., Johnson, J. R., Ali, S. A., Early, J., & Tuten, J. T. (1993). Sexually coercive behavior and love styles: A replication and extension. *Journal of Psychology & Human Sexuality, 6*, 93–106.

Kalick, S. M. (1988). Physical attractiveness as a status cue. *Journal of Experimental Social Psychology, 24*, 469–489.

Kalick, S. M., Zebrowitz, L. A., Langlois, J. H., & Johnson, R. M. (1998). Does human facial attractiveness honestly advertise health? Longitudinal data on an evolutionary question. *Psychological Science, 9*, 8–13.

Kalin, R., & Berry, J. W. (1996). Interethnic attitudes in Canada: Ethnocentrism, consensual heirarchy and reciprocity. *Canadian Journal of Behavioural Science, 28*, 253–261.

Kalin, R., & Berry, J.W. (1982). The social ecology of ethnic attitudes in Canada. *Canadian Journal of Behavioral Science, 14*, 97–109.

Kallen, E. (1995). *Ethnicity and Human Rights in Canada*, 2nd ed. Toronto: Oxford University Press Canada.

Kameda, T., & Sugimori, S. (1993). Psychological entrapment in group decision making: An assigned decision rule and a groupthink phenomenon. *Journal of Personality and Social Psychology, 65*, 282–292.

Kandel, D. B. (1978). Similarity in real-life adolescent friendship pairs. *Journal of Personality and Social Psychology, 36*, 306–312.

Kaplan, M. F. (1981). State dispositions in social judgment. *Bulletin of the Psychonomic Society, 18*, 27–29.

Kaplan, M. F. (1989). Task, situational and perceived determinants of influence processes in group decision making. In E. Lawler & B. Markovsky (Eds.), *Advances in group processes* (Vol. 6, pp. 87–1050). Greenwich, CT: JAI.

Karau, S. J., & Williams, K. D. (1993). Social loafing: A meta-analytic review and theoretical integration. *Journal of Personality and Social Psychology, 65*, 681–706.

Kashima, Y., & Triandis, H.C. (1986). The self-serving bias in attributions as a coping strategy: a cross-cultural study. *Journal of Cross-Cultural Psychology, 17*, 83–97.

Kassin, S. M. (1997). The psychology of confession evidence. *American Psychologist, 52*, 221–233.

Kassin, S. M., & Kiechel, K. L. (1996). The social psychology of false confessions: Compliance, internalization, and confabulation. *Psychological Science, 7*, 125–128.

Kassin, S. M., & McNall, K. (1991). Police interrogations and confessions: Communicating promises and threats by pragmatic implication. *Law and Human Behavior, 15*, 233–251.

Kassin., S. M., & Kiechel, K. L. (1996). The social psychology of false confessions: Compliance, internalization, and confabulation. *Psychological Science.* In press.

Katz, I.M., & Campbell, J.D. (1994). Ambivalence over emotional expression and well-being: Nomothetic and Idiographic tests of the stress-buffering hypothesis. *Journal of Personality and Social Psychology, 67*, 513–524.

Kawakami, K., Dion, K. L., & Dovidio, J. F. (1998). Racial prejudice and stereotype activation. *Personality and Social Psychology Bulletin, 24*, 407–416.

Keinan, G. (1994). Effects of stress and tolerance of ambiguity on magical thinking. *Journal of Personality and Social Psychology*, 67, 48–55.

Keller, L. M., Bouchard, T. J., Jr., Arvey, R. D., Segal, N. L., & Dawis, R. V. (1992). Work values: Genetic and environmental influences. *Journal of Applied Psychology*, 77, 79–88.

Keller, L. M., Bouchard, T. J., Jr., Arvey, R. D., Segal, N. L., & Dawis, R. V. (1992). Work values: Genetic and environmental influences. *Journal of Applied Psychology*, 77, 79–88.

Keller, R. T. (1997). Job involvement and organizational commitment as longitudinal predictors of job performance: A study of scientists and engineers. *Journal of Applied Psychology*, 82, 539–545.

Kellerman, J., Lewis, J., & Laird, J. D. (1989). Looking and loving: The effects of mutual gaze on feelings of romantic love. *Journal of Research in Personality*, 23, 145–161.

Kelley, H. H. (1972). Attribution in social interaction. In E. E. Jones et al. (Eds.), *Attribution: Perceiving the causes of behavior*. Morristown, NJ: General Learning Press.

Kelley, H. H., & Michela, J. L. (1980). Attribution theory and research. *Annual Review of Psychology*, 31, 457–501.

Kelly, A. E., & Nauta, M. M. (1997). Reactance and thought suppression. *Personality and Social Psychology Bulletin*, 23, 1123–1132.

Kelly, J. R., Jackson, J. W., & Hutson-Comeaux, S. L. (1997). The effects of time pressure and task differences on influence modes and accuracy in decision-making groups. *Personality and Social Psychology Bulletin*, 23, 10–22.

Kelman, H. C. (1967). Human use of human subjects: The problem of deception in social psychological experiments. *Psychological Bulletin*, 67, 1–11.

Keltner, D., & Robinson, R. J. (1997). Defending the status quo: Power and bias in social conflict. *Personality and Social Psychology Bulletin*, 23, 1066–1077.

Kendzierski, D., & Whitaker, D. J. (1997). The role of self-schema in linking intentions with behavior. *Personality and Social Psychology Bulletin*, 23, 139–147.

Kenealy, P., Gleeson, K., Frude, N., & Shaw, W. (1991). The importance of the individual in the "causal" relationship between attractiveness and self-esteem. *Journal of Community and Applied Social Psychology*, 1, 45–56.

Kenney, D. A., & Kashy, D. A. (1994). Enhanced co-orientation in the perception of friends: A social relations analysis. *Journal of Personality and Social Psychology*, 67, 1024–1033.

Kenney, D. A., Albright, L., Malloy, T. E., & Kashy, D. A. (1994). Consensus in interpersonal perception: Acquaintance and the big five. *Journal of Personality and Social Psychology*, 116, 245–258.

Kenrick, D. T., Montello, D. R., Gutierres, S. E., & Trost, M. R. (1993). Effects of physical attractiveness on affect and perceptual judgments: When social comparison overrides social reinforcement. *Personality and Social Psychology Bulletin*, 19, 195–199.

Kenrick, D. T., Neuberg, S. L., Zierk, K. L., & Krones, J. M. (1994). Evolution and social cognition: Contrast effects as a function of sex, dominance, and physical attractiveness. *Personality and Social Psychology Bulletin*, 20, 210–217.

Kent, G. G., Davis, J. D., & Shapiro, D. A. (1981). Effect of mutual acquaintance on the construction of conversation. *Journal of Experimental Social Psychology*, 17, 197–209.

Kernis, M. H., Whisenhunt, C. R., Waschull, S. B., Greenier, K. D., Berry, A. J., Herlocker, C. E., & Anderson, C. A. (1998). Multiple facets of self-esteem and their relations to depressive symptoms. *Personality and Social Psychology Bulletin*, 24, 657–668.

Kerr, D. & Ram, B. (1994). *Population dynamics in Canada (Focus on Canada series)*. Scarborough, Ont: Statistics Canada and Prentice Hall Canada

Kerr, H. L., & MacCoun, R. J. (1985). The effects of jury size and polling method on the process and product of jury deliberations. *Journal of Personality and Social Psychology*, 48, 349–363.

Kerr, N. L., & Kaufman-Gilliland, C. M. (1994). Communication, commitment, and cooperation in social dilemmas. *Journal of Personality and Social Psychology*, 66, 513–529.

Kerr, N. L., Garst, J., Lewandowski, D. A., & Harris, S. E. (1997). That still, small voice: Commitment to cooperate as an internalized versus a social norm. *Personality and Social Psychology Bulletin*, 23, 1300–1311.

Kessler, R. C., Kendler, K. S., Heath, A., Neale, M. C., & Eaves, L. J. (1992). Social support, depressed mood, and adjustment to stress: A genetic epidemiologic investigation. *Journal of Personality and Social Psychology*, 62, 257–272.

Kiecolt-Glaser, J. K., Page, G. G., Marucha, P. T., MacCallum, R. C., & Glaser, R. (1998). Psychological influences on surgical recovery: Perspectives from psychoneuroimmunology. *American Psychologist*, 53, 1209–1218.

Kiesler, S.B., Siegal, J., & McGuire, T.W. (1984). Social psychological aspects of computer-mediated communication. *American Psychologist, 39*, 1123–1134.

Kiesler, S., & Kraut, R. (1999). Internet use and the ties that bink. *American Psychologist, 54*, 783–784,

Kilduff, M., & Day, D. V. (1994). Do chameleons get ahead? The effects of self-monitoring on managerial careers. *Academy of Management Journal*, 37, 1047–1060.

Kilham, W., & Mann, L. (1974). Level of destructive obedience as a function of transmitter and executant roles in the Milgram obedience paradigm. *Journal of Personality and Social Psychology*, 29, 696–702.

Killeya, L. A., & Johnson, B. T. (1998). Experimental induction of biased systematic processing: The directed through technique. *Personality and Social Psychology Bulletin*, 24, 17–33.

Killias, M. (1993). International correlation between gun ownership and rates of homicide and suicide. *Canadian Medical Association Journal, 148*, 1721–1725.

Kim, U. (1990). Indigenous psychology: Science and application. In R. Brislin (Ed.), *Applied cross-cultural psychology*. Newbury Park, CA: Sage.

Kim, U. , Triandis, H. C., Kagitcibasi, C., Choi, S., & Yoon, G. (Eds.). (1994). *Individualism and collectivism: Theory, method and applications*. Thousand Oaks, CA: Sage.

Kinsella, W. (1994). *Web of hate: Inside Canada's far right network*. Toronto: HarperCollins.

Kirkpatrick, L. A., & Epstein, S. (1992). Cognitive-experiential self theory and subjective probability: Further evidence for two conceptual systems. *Journal of Personality and Social Psychology*, 63, 534–544.

Kirkpatrick, S. A., & Locke, E. A. (1991). Leadership: Do traits matter? Academy of Management Executive, 5(2), 48–60.

Kitayama, S., & Karasawa, M. (1997). Implicit self-esteem in Japan: Name letters and birthday numbers. *Personality and Social Psychology Bulletin*, 23, 736–742.

Kitayama, S., Markus, H. R., Matsumoto, H., & Norasakkunkit, V. (1997). Individual and collective processes in the construction of the self: Self-enhancement in the United States and self-criticism in Japan. *Journal of Personality and Social Psychology*, 72, 1245–1267.

Klagsbrun, F. (1992). *Mixed feelings: Love, hate, rivalry, and reconciliation in brothers and sisters.* New York: Bantam.

Kleck, G. (1988). Crime control through the private use of armed force. *Social problems, 35,* 1–21.

Kleck, G. (1991). *Point blank: Guns and violence in America.* Hawthorne, NY: Aldine de Gruyter.

Klein, S. B., & Loftus, J. (1988). The nature of self-referent encoding: The contributions of elaborative and organizational processes. *Journal of Personality and Social Psychology*, 55, 5–11.

Klein, S. B., & Loftus, J. (1993). Behavioral experience and trait judgments about the self. *Personality and Social Psychology Bulletin*, 16, 740–745.

Klein, S. B., Loftus, J., & Burton, H. A. (1989). Two self-reference effects: The importance of distinguishing between self-descriptiveness judgments and autobiographical retrieval in self-referent encoding. *Journal of Personality and Social Psychology*, 56, 853–865.

Klein, S. B., Loftus, J., & Plog, A. E. (1992). Trait judgments about the self: Evidence from the encoding specificity paradigm. *Personality and Social Psychology Bulletin*, 18, 730–735.

Kleinke, C. L. (1986). Gaze and eye contact: A research review. *Psychological Bulletin*, 100, 78–lOO.

Kleinke, C. L., & Dean, G. O. (1990). Evaluation of men and women receiving positive and negative responses with various acquaintance strategies. *Journal of Social Behavior and Personality*, 5, 369–377.

Kleinke, C. L., Meeker, G. B., & Staneske, R. A. (1986). Preference for opening lines: Comparing ratings by men and women. *Sex Roles*, 15, 585–600.

Klohnen, E. C., & Mendelsohn, G. A. (1998). Partner selection for personality characteristics: A couple-centered approach. *Personality and Social Psychology Bulletin*, 24, 268–278.

Knee, C. R. (1998). Implicit theories of relationships: Assessment and prediction of romantic relationship initiation, coping, and longevity. *Journal of Personality and Social Psychology*, 74, 360–370.

Knight, G. P., & Dubro, A. (1984). Cooperative, competitive, and individualistic social values: An individualized regression and clustering approach. *Journal of Personality and Social Psychology*, 46, 98–105.

Koehler, S. P., & Willis, F. N. (1994). Traffic citations in relation to gender. *Journal of Applied Social Psychology*, 24, 1919–1926.

Koestner, R., Bernieri, F., & Zuckerman, M. (1992). Self-regulation and consistency between attitudes, traits, and behaviors. *Personality and Social Psychology Bulletin*, 18, 52–59.

Kolata, G. (1995, February 28). Man's world, woman's world? Brain studies point to differences. *New York Times*, C1, C7.

Komorita, M., & Parks, G. (1994). Interpersonal relations: Mixed-motive interaction. *Annual Review of Psychology*, 46, 183–207.

Konovsky, M. A., & Pugh, S. D. (1994). Citizenship behavior and social exchange. *Academy of Management Journal*, 37, 656–669.

Korte, C. (1980). Urban-nonurban differences in social behavior and social psychological models of urban impact. *Journal of Social Issues*, 36, 29–51.

Korte, C. (1981). Constraints on helping in an urban environment. In J. P. Rushton & R. M. Sorrentino (Eds.), *Altruism and helping behavior.* Hillsdale, NJ: Erlbaum.

Kotter, J. (1982). *The general managers.* New York: Free Press.

Kraus, S. J. (1995). Attitudes and the prediction of behavior: A meta-analysis of the empirical literature. *Personality and Social Psychology Bulletin*, 21, 58–75.

Kraut, R., Patterson, M., Lundmark, V., Kiesler, S., Mukopadhyay, T., & Scherlis, W. (1998). Internet paradox: A social technology that reduces social involvement and psychological well-being? *American Psychologist, 53.* 1017–1031.

Krosnick, J. A. (1988). The role of attitude importance in social evaluation: A study of political preferences, presidential candidate evaluations, and voting behavior. *Journal of Personality and Social Psychology*, 55, 196–210.

Krosnick, J. A. (1989). Attitude importance and attitude accessibility. *Personality and Social Psychology Bulletin*, 15, 297–308.

Krosnick, J. A., Betz, A. L., Jussim, L. J., & Lynn, A. R. (1992). Subliminal conditioning of attitudes. *Personality and Social Psychology Bulletin*, 18, 152–162.

Krosnick, J. A., Boninger, D. S., Chuang, Y. C., Berent, M. K., & Carnot, C. G. (1993). Attitude strength: One construct or many related constructs? *Journal of Personality and Social Psychology*, 65, 1132–1151.

Krueger, J., & Clement, R. W. (1994). The truly false consensus effect: An ineradicable and egocentric bias in social perception. *Journal of Personality and Social Psychology*, 67, 596–610.

Krupat, E. (1975). *Psychology is social.* Glenview, IL: Scott, Foresman.

Krupat, E., & Guild, W. (1980). Defining the city: The use of objective and subjective measures of community description. *Journal of Social Issues*, 36, 9–28.

Kuiper, N. A., & Martin, R. A. (1998). Laughter and stress in daily life: Relation to positive and negative affect. *Motivation and Emotion*, 22, 133–153.

Kulik, J. A., Mahler, H. I. M., & Moore, P. J. (1996). Social comparison and affiliation under threat: Effects on recovery from major surgery. *Journal of Personality and Social Psychology*, 71, 967–979.

Kunda, Z., & Oleson, K. C. (1995). Maintaining stereotypes in the face of disconfirmation: Constructing grounds for subtyping deviants. *Journal of Personality and Social Psychology*, 68,

Kunda, Z., & Sherman-Williams, B. (1993). Stereotypes and the construal of individuating information. Personality and *Social Psychology Bulletin*, 19, 90–99.

Kurdek, L. A. (1993). Predicting marital dissolution: A 5-year longitudinal study of newlywed couples. *Journal of Personality and Social Psychology*, 64, 221–242.

Kurdek, L. A. (1996). The deterioration of relationships quality for gay and lesbian cohabiting couples: A five-year prospective longitudinal study. *Personal Relationships*, 3, 417–442.

Kurdek, L.A. (1998). Relationship outcomes and their predictors: Longitudinal evidence from heterosexual married, gay cohabiting and lesbian cohabiting couples. *Journal of Marriage and the Family*, 60, 553–568.

Kwan, L. K. (1998). Attitudes and attraction: A new view on how to diagnose the moderating effects of personality. Unpublished master's thesis, National University of Singapore.

Kwan, V. S. Y., Bond, M. H., & Singelis, T. M. (1997). Pancultural explanations for life satisfaction: Adding relationship harmony to self-esteem. *Journal of Personality and Social Psychology*, 73, 1038–1051.

Kwon, Y.-H. (1994). Feeling toward one's clothing and self-perception of emotion, sociability, and work competency. *Journal of Social Behavior and Personality*, 9, 129–139.

Lachman, M. E., & Weaver, S. L. (1998). The sense of control as a moderator of social class differences in health and well-being. *Journal of Personality and Social Psychology*, 74, 763–773.

LaFromboise, T., Coleman, H. L. K., & Gerton, J. (1993). Psychological impact of biculturalism: Evidence and theory. *Psychological Bulletin*, 114, 395–412.

Lakoff, R. (1977). Women's language. *Language and Style*, 10, 222–296.

Lalonde, R.N., & Cameron, J.E. (1994). Behavioral responses to discrimination: A focus on action. In M.P. Zanna & J.M. Olson (Eds.), *The psychology of prejudice: The Ontario symposium, Vol. 7* (pp. 257–288). Hilldale, NJ: Lawrence Erlbaum.

Lalone, R.N., & Majumder, S., & Parris, R.D. (1995). Preferred responses to situations of housing and employment discrimination. *Journal of Applied Social Psychology, 25*, 1105–1119.

Lambert, A. J. (1995). Stereotypes and social judgment: The consequences of group variability. *Journal of Personality and Social Psychology*, 68, 388–403.

Lambert, W.E. (1967). A social psychology of bilingualism. *Journal of Social Issues*, 23, 91–109.

Lambert, W.E. (1974). The St. Lambert project. In S.T. Carey (Ed.), Bilingualism, biculturalism and education. Edmonton: University of Alberta.

Lambert, W.E. (1978). Some cognitive and sociocultural aspects of being bilingual. In J.P. Alatis (Ed.), International dimensions of bilingual education. Washington, DC: Georgetown University Press.

Lambert, W.E., & Taylor, D. M. (1984). Language and the education of ethnic minority children in Canada. In R.J. Samuda, J.W. Berry, & M. Laferriere (Eds.), *Multiculturalism in Canada*. Toronto: Allyn & Bacon.

Lambert, W.E., & Tucker, G.R. (1972). *Bilingual education in children: The St. Lambert experiment*. Rowley, MA: Newbury House.

Lambert, W.E., Gardner, R.C., Barik, H.C., & Tunstall, K. (1963). Attitudinal and cognitive aspects of intensive study of a second language. *Journal of Abnormal and Social Psychology*, 66, 358–368.

Lambert, W.E., Mermigis, L., & Taylor, D.M. (1986). Greek Canadians' attitudes toward own group and other Canadian ethnic groups: A test of the multiculturalism hypothesis. *Canadian Journal of Behavioral Science*, 18, 35–51.

Lamm, H. & Myers, D. G. (1978). Group-induced polarization of attitudes and behavior. In L. Berkowitz (Ed.), *Advances in experimental social psychology*. New York: Academic Press.

Lamm, H., & Wiesmann, U. (1997). Subjective attributes of attraction: How people characterize their liking, their love, and their being in love. *Personal Relationships*, 4, 271–284.

Lander, M. (1992, June 8). Corporate women. Business Week, 74, 76–78.

Langlois, F. H., & Roggman, L. A. (1990). Attractive faces are only average. *Psychological Science*, 1, 115–112.

Langlois, J. H., Roggman, L. A., & Musselman, L. (1994). What is average and what is not average about attractive faces? *Psychological Science*, 5, 214–220.

LaPiere, R. T. (1934). Attitude and actions. *Social Forces*, 13, 230–237.

LaPrelle, J., Hoyle, R. H., Insko, C. A., & Bernthal, P. (1990). Interpersonal attraction and descriptions of the traits of others: Ideal similarity, self similarity, and liking. *Journal of Research in Personality*, 24, 216–240.

Larson, D. G., & Chastain, R. L. (1990). Self-concealment: Conceptualization, measurement, and health implications. *Journal of Social and Clinical Psychology*, 9, 439–455.

Larson, J. H., & Bell, N. J. (1988). Need for privacy and its effects upon interpersonal attraction and interaction. *Journal of Social and Clinical Psychology*, 6, 1–10.

Larson, J. R., Jr., Foster-Fishman, P. G., & Franz, T. M. (1998). Leadership style and the discussion of shared and unshared information in decision-making groups. *Personality and Social Psychology Bulletin*, 24, 482–495.

Latane, B., & Darley, J. M. (1968). Group inhibition of bystander intervention in emergencies. *Journal of Personality and Social Psychology*, 10, 215–221.

Latane, B., & Darley, J. M. (1970). *The unresponsive bystander: Why doesn't he help?* New York: Appleton-Century-Crofts.

Latane, B., Williams, K., & Harkins, S. (1979). Many hands make light the work: The causes and consequences of social loafing. *Journal of Personality and Social Psychology*, 37, 822–832.

Latan_, B. (1981). The psychology of social impacts. *American Psychologist, 36*, 343–356.

Latan_, B., & Dabbs, J. M., Jr. (1975). Sex, group size, and helping in three cities. *Sociometry, 38*, 180–194.

Latan_, B., & Darley, J. M. (1968). Group inhibition of bystander intervention in emergencies. *Journal of Personality and Social Psychology, 10*, 215–221.

Latty-Mann, H., & Davis, K. E. (1996). Attachment theory and partner choice: Preference and actuality. *Journal of Social and Personal Relationships, 13*, 5–23.

Lau, S. (1989). Sex role orientation and domains of self esteem. *Sex Roles, 21*, 415–422.

Lauer, J., & Lauer, R. (1985, June). Marriages made to last. *Psychology Today*, pp. 22–26.

Laumann, E. O., Gagnon, J. H., Michael, R. T., & Michaels, S. (1994). *The social organization of sexuality: Sexual practices in the United States*. Chicago: University of Chicago Press.

Laurenceau, J.-P., Barrett, L. F., & Pietromonaco, P. R. (1998). Intimacy as an interpersonal process: The importance of self-disclosure, partner disclosure, and perceived partner responsiveness in interpersonal exchanges. *Journal of Personality and Social Psychology, 74*, 1238–1251.

Lazarus, R. S. (1966). *Psychological stress and the coping process*. New York: McGraw-Hill.

Lazarus, R. S. (1993). From psychological stress to the emotions: A history of changing outlooks. In L. W. Porter & M. R. Rosenzweig (Eds.), *Annual review of psychology* (Vol. 44, pp. 1–21). Palo Alto, CA: Annual Reviews, Inc.

Leary, M. R., Schreindorfer, L. S., & Haupt, A. L. (1995). The role of low self-esteem in emotional and behavioral problems: Why is low self-esteem dysfunctional? *Journal of Social and Clinical Psychology, 14*, 297–314.

Leary, M. R., Spinger, C., Negel, L., Ansell, E., & Evans, K. (1998). The causes, phenomenology, and consequences of hurt feelings. *Journal of Personality and Social Psychology, 74*, 1225–1237.

Leary, W. E. (1988, November 15). Novel methods unlock witnesses' memories. *New York Times*, pp. C1, C15.

Lee, M. E., Matsumoto, D., Koyayashi, M., Krupp, D., Maniatis, E. F., & Roberts, W. (1992). Cultural influences on nonverbal behavior in applied settings. In R. S. Feldman (Ed.), *Applications of nonverbal behavioral theories and research*. Hillsdale, NJ: Erlbaum.

Lee, Y. T., & Ottati, V. (1993). Determinannts of ingroup and out-group perceptions of heterogeneity: An investigation of Sino-American differences. *Journal of Cross-cultural Psychology, 25*, 146–158.

Lee, Y. T., & Seligman, M. E. P. (1997). Are Americans more optimistic than the Chinese? *Personality and Social Psychology Bulletin, 23*, 32–40.

Lefcourt, H. M., Davidson, K., Shepherd, R., Phillips, M., Prkachin, K., & Mills, D. (1995). Perspective-taking humor: Accounting for stress moderation. *Journal of Social and Clinical Psychology, 14*, 373–391.

Leippe, M. R., Manion, A. P., & Romanczyk, A. (1992). Eyewitness persuasion: How and how well do fact finders judge the accuracy of adults' and children's memory reports? *Journal of Personality and Social Psychology, 63*, 181–197.

Lemonick, M. D. (1992). The ozone vanishes. *Time, 139*(7), 60–63.

Lennox, R. D., & Wolfe, R. N. (1984). Revision of the self-monitoring scale. *Journal of Personality and Social Psychology, 46*, 1349–1364.

Leonard, M. (1998, February 15). Making a mark on the culture. *Boston Sunday Globe*, pp. C1, C2, C11, C12.

Lepore, L., & Brown, R. (1997). Category and stereotype activation: Is prejudice inevitable? *Journal of Personality and Social Psychology, 72*, 275–287.

Lepore, S. J. (1997). Expressive writing moderates the relation between intrusive thoughts and depressive symptoms. *Journal of Personality and Social Psychology, 73*, 1030–1037.

Lerner, M. J. (1980). *The belief in a just world: A fundamental delusion*. New York: Plenum Press.

Lester, D. (1984). *Gun control: Issues and answers*. Springfield, IL: Charles Thomas.

Lester, D. (1988). Firearm availability and the incidence of suicide and homicide. *Acta Psychiatrica Belgium, 88*, 387–393.

Levenson, R. W., Carstensen, L. L., & Gottman, J. M. (1994). The influence of age and gender on affect, physiology, and their interrelations: A study of long-term marriages. *Journal of Personality and Social Psychology, 67*, 56–68.

Levenson, R. W., Ekman, P., & Friesen, W. V. (1990). Voluntary facial action generates emotion-specific autonomic nervous system activity. *Psychophysiology, 27*, 363–384.

Levenson, R. W., Ekman, P., Heider, K., & Friesen, W. V. (1992). Emotion and autonomic nervous system activity in the Minangkabau of West Sumatra. *Journal of Personality and Social Psychology, 62*, 972–988.

Leventhal, G. S., Karuza, J., & Fry, W. R. (1980). Beyond fairness: A theory of allocation preferences. In G. Mikula (Ed.), *Justice and social interaction* (pp. 167–218). New York: Springer-Verlag.

Leventhal, H., Singer, R., & Jones, S. (1965). The effects of fear and specificity of recommendation upon attitudes and behavior. *Journal of Personality and Social Psychology, 2*, 20–29.

Levin, J.R., Reinhold, A., & Levine-Young, M. (1999) *The internet for dummies: Quick reference*. (5th ed.). Foster City, CA: IDG Books.

Levine, R. V., Martinez, T. S., Brase, G., & Sorenson, K. (1994). Helping in 36 U.S. cities. *Journal of Personality and Social Psychology, 67*, 69–82.

Levine, R.V., Sato, S., Hashimoto, T., & Verma, J. (1995). Love and marriage in eleven cultures. *Journal of Cross-Cultural Psychology, 26*, 554–571.

Levy, K. N., Blatt, S. J., & Shaver, P. R. (1998). Attachment styles and parental representations. *Journal of Personality and Social Psychology, 74*, 407–419.

Lewin, K. (1948). *Resolving social conflicts: Selected papers on group dynamics.* New York: Harper & Row.

Lewin, K., Lippitt, R., & White, R. R. (1939). Patterns of aggressive behavior in experimentally created "social climates." *Journal of Social Psychology,* 10, 271–299.

Lewis, M. (1992). Will the real self or selves please stand up? *Psychological Inquiry,* 3, 123–124.

Liberman, A., & Chaiken, S. (1992). Defensive processing of personally relevant health messages. *Personality and Social Psychology Bulletin,* 18, 669–679.

Liden, R. C., & Mitchell, T. R. (1988). Ingratiatory behaviors in organizational settings. *Academy of Management Review,* 13, 572–587.

Lieberman, J. D., & Greenberg, J. (1999). Cognitive-experiential self-theory and displaced aggression. *Journal of Personality and Social Psychology,* in press.

Lind, E. A. (1994). Procedural justice and culture: Evidence for ubiquitous process concerns. *Zeitschrift fur Rechtssoziologie,* 15, 24–36.

Linden, E. (1992a). Chimpanzees with a difference: Bonobos. *National Geographic,* 18(3), 46–53.

Lindsay, D. S. (1998). Recovered memories and social justice. *American Psychologist,* 53, 486–487.

Linville, P. W., & Fischer, G. W. (1993). Exemplar and abstraction models of perceived group variability and stereotypicality. *Social Cognition,* 11, 92–125.

Linville, P. W., Fischer, G. W., & Salovey, P. (1989). Perceived distributions of the characteristics of in-group and out-group members: Empirical evidence and a computer simulation. *Journal of Personality and Social Psychology,* 57, 165–188.

Linville, P. W., Fischer, O. W., & Salovey, P. (1989). Perceived distributions of the characteristics of in-group and out-group members: Empirical evidence and a computer simulation. *Journal of Personality and Social Psychology,* 57, 165–188.

Lipset, S.M. (1990a). *Continental divide: The values and institutions of the United States and Canada.* New York: Routledge.

Lipset, S.M. (1990b). *North American cultures: Values and institutions in Canada and the United States.* Orona, ME: Borderlands.

Little, B. (2000). New jobs: 1990s belonged to women. *Globe and Mail,* February 21. pp. A2.

Lobel, T. E. (1994). Sex typing and the social perception of gender stereotypic and nonstereotypic behavior: The uniqueness of feminine males. *Journal of Personality and Social Psychology,* 66, 379–385.

Locke, E. A. (1991). *The essence of leadership.* New York: Lexington Books.

Locke, M. (1995, May 25). Love better with age, study says. *Albany Times Union,* p. C-5.

Loftus, E. F. (1992a). *Witness for the defense.* New York: St. Martin's Press.

Loftus, E. F. (1997). Memory for a past that never was. *Current Directions in Psychological Science,* 6, 60–65.

Loftus, E. F. (1998). The private practice of misleading direction. *American Psychologist,* 53, 484–485.

Loftus, E. F., & Pickrell, J. E. (1995). The formation of false memories. *Psychiatric Annals,* 25, 720–725.

Loftus, E. F., Coan, J. A., & Pickrell, J. E. (1996). Manufacturing false memories using bits of reality. In L. Reder (Ed.), *Implicit memory and metacognition* (pp. 195–220). Mahwah, NJ: Erlbaum.

Logsdon, M. C., Birkimer, J. C., & Barbee, A. P. (1997). Social support providers for postpartum women. *Journal of Social Behavior and Personality,* 12, 89–102.

Lopez, F. G., Gover, M. R., Leskela, J., Sauer, E. M., Schirmer, L., & Wyssmann, J. (1997). Attachment styles, shame, guilt, and collaborative problem-solving orientations. *Personal Relationships,* 4, 187–199.

Lord, C. G., Ross, L., & Lepper, M. R. (1979). Biased assimilation and attitude polarization: The effects of prior theories on subsequently considered evidence. *Journal of Personality and Social Psychology,* 37, 2098–2109.

Lorenz, K. (1966). *On aggression.* New York: Harcourt, Brace, & World.

Lorenz, K. (1974). *Civilized man's eight deadly sins.* New York: Harcourt, Brace, Jovanovich.

Lott, J.R. (1998). *More guns, less crime.* Chicago: University of Chicago Press.

Louis, W., & Taylor, D.M. (1999). From passive acceptance to social disruption: Towards an understanding of behavioural responses to discrimination. *Canadian Journal of Behaviousal Science,* 31, 19–28.

Lox, C. L., & Rudolph, D. L. (1994). The Subjective Exercise Experiences Scale (SEES): Factorial validity and effects of acute exercise. *Journal of Social Behavior and Personality,* 9, 837–844.

Lumsdaine, A., & Janis, I. (1953). Resistance to counter-propaganda produced by a one-sided versus a two-sided propaganda presentation. *Public Opinion Quarterly,* 17, 311–318.

Lupfer, M. B., Clark, L. F., & Hutcherson, H. W. (1990). Impact of context on spontaneous trait and situational attributions. *Journal of Personality and Social Psychology,* 58, 239–249.

Luus, C. A., & Wells, G. L. (1994). The malleability of eyewitness confidence: Co-witness and perseverance effects. *Journal of Applied Psychology,* 79, 714–723.

Lydon, J. E., Jamieson, D. W., & Holmes, J. G. (1997). The meaning of social interactions in the transition from acquaintanceship to friendship. *Journal of Personality and Social Psychology,* 73, 536–548.

Lyness, K. S., & Thompson, D. E. (1997). Above the glass ceiling? A comparison of matched samples of female and male executives. *Journal of Applied Psychology,* 82, 359–375.

Lynn, M., & Mynier, K. (1993). Effects of server posture on restaurant tipping. *Journal of Applied Social Psychology,* 23,

Lyubomirsky, S., & Nolen-Hoeksema, S. (1995). Effects of self-focused rumination on negative thinking and interpersonal problem solving. *Journal of Personality and Social Psychology,* 69, 176–190.

Maas, A., & Clark, R. D. III. (1984). Hidden impact of minorities: Fifteen years of minority influence research. *Psychological Bulletin,* 95, 233–243.

Macaulay, J. (1970). A shill for charity. In J. Macaulay & L. Berkowitz (Eds.), *Altruism and helping behavior* (pp. 43–59). New York: Academic Press.

MacDonald, G., & Waldie, P. (1999). In or out of hockey, Gretzky can score big. *Globe and Mail*, April 14, pp. B1.

MacDonald, T. K., Zanna, M. P., & Fong, G. T. (1995). Decision making in altered states: Effects of alcohol on attitudes toward drinking and driving. *Journal of Personality and Social Psychology*, 68, 973–985.

Mackie, D. M., & Worth, L. T. (1989). Processing deficits and the mediation of positive affect in persuasion. *Journal of Personality and Social Psychology*, 57, 27–40.

Mackie, D. M., Allison, S. T., Worth, L. T., & Asuncion, A. G. (1992). The impact of outcome biases on counterstereotypic inferences about groups. *Personality and Social Psychology Bulletin*, 18, 44–51.

MacKinnon, M. (1999). Women gaining ground in work force. *Globe and Mail*, April 19, pp. B1

Macrae, C. N. (1992). A tale of two curries: Counterfactual thinking and accident-related judgments. *Personality and Social Psychology Bulletin*, 18, 84–87.

Macrae, C. N., & Milne, A. B. (1992). A curry for your thoughts: Empathic effects on counterfactual thinking. *Personality and Social Psychology Bulletin*, 18, 625–630.

Madon, S., Jussim, L., Keiper, S., Eccles, J., Smith, A., & Palumbo, P. (1998). The accuracy and power of sex, social class, and ethnic stereotypes: A naturalistic study in person perception. *Personality and Social Psychology Bulletin*, 24, 1304–1318.

Maheswaran, D., & Chaiken, S. (1991). Promoting systematic processing in low-motivation settings: Effect of incongruent information on processing and judgment. *Journal of Personality and Social Psychology*, 61, 13–25.

Maio, G. R., Esses, V M., & Bell, D. W. (1994). The formation of attitudes toward new immigrant groups. *Journal of Applied Social Psychology*, 24, 1762–1776.

Maisonneuve, J., Palmade, G., & Fourment, C. (1952). Selective choices and propinquity. *Sociometry*, 15, 135–140.

Major, B., Carnevale, P. J. D., & Deaux, K. (1981). A different perspective on androgyny: Evaluations of masuline and feminine personality characteristics. *Journal of Personality and Social Psychology*, 41, 988–1001.

Major, B., Carrington, P. I., & Carnevale, P. J. D. (1984). Physical attractiveness and self-esteem: Attributions for praise from an other-sex evaluator. *Personality and Social Psychology Bulletin*, 10, 43–50.

Major, B., Sciacchitano, A. M., & Crocker, J. (1993). Ingroup versus out-group comparisons and self-esteem. *Personality and Social Psychology Bulletin*, 19, 711–721.

Mallick, S. K., & McCandless, B. R. (1966). A study of catharsis of aggression. *Journal of Personality and Social Psychology*, 4, 591–596.

Marazziti, D., Rotondo, A., Presta, S., Pancioloi-Guadagnucci, M. L., Palego, L., & Conti, L. (1993). Role of serotonin in human aggressive behavior. *Aggressive Behavior*, 19,

Markus, H., & Nurius, P. (1986). Possible selves. *American Psychologist*, 41, 954–969.

Markus, H.R., & Kitayama, S. (1991a). Culture and the self: Implication for cognition, emotion, and motivation. *Psychological Review*, 98, 224–253.

Marsh, H. W. (1993). Relations between global and specific domains of self: The importance of individual importance, certainty, and ideal. *Journal of Personality and Social Psychology*, 65, 975–992.

Marsh, H. W. (1995). A Jamesian model of self-investment and self-esteem: Comment on Pelham (1995). *Journal of Personality and Social Psychology*, 69, 1151–1160.

Marshall, N. L., & Barnett, R. C. (1993). Variations in job strain across nursing and social work specialties. *Journal of Community and Applied Social Psychology*, 3, 261–271.

Martin, C. L., & Parker, S. (1995). Folk theories about sex and race differences. *Personality and Social Psychology Bulletin*, 21, 45–57.

Martin, R. (1997). "Girls don't talk about garages!": Perceptions of conversation in same- and cross-sex friendships. *Personal Relationships*, 4, 115–130.

Martz, J. M., Verette, J., Arriaga, X. B., Slovik, L. F., Cox, C. L., & Rusbult, C. E. (1998). Positive illusion in close relationships. *Personal Relationships*, 5, 159–181.

Maslach, C., Santee, R. T., & Wade, C. (1987). Individuation, gender role, and dissent: Personality mediators of situational forces. *Journal of Personality and Social Psychology*, 53, 1088–1094.

Mathes, E. W., Adams, H. E., & Davies, R. M. (1985). Jealousy: Loss of relationship rewards, loss of self-esteem, depression, anxiety, and anger. *Journal of Personality and Social Psychology*, 48, 1552–1561.

Matsumoto, D. & Kudoh, T. (1993). American-Japanese cultural differences in attributions of personality based on smiles. *Journal of Nonverbal Behavior*, 17, 231–244.

Matsumoto, D. (1994). *People: Psychology from a cultural perspective*. Pacific Grove, CA: Brooks/Cole.

Matsumoto, D., & Kudoh, T. (1990). *Cultural differences in social judgments of facial expressions of emotions: What's in a smile?*

Matthews, S. H. (1986). *Friendship through the life course*. Newbury Park, CA: Sage.

Matthews, S. H. (1986). *Friendship through the life course*. Newbury Park, CA: Sage.

Maugh, T. H., II. (1998, February 21). To keep marriage going, try giving in to your wife. *Los Angeles Times*.

May, J. L., & Hamilton, P. A. (1980). Effects of musically evoked affect on women's interpersonal attraction and perceptual judgments of physical attractiveness of men. *Motivation and Emotion*, 4, 217–228.

Mayer, J. D., & Hanson, E. (1995). Mood-congruent judgment over time. *Personality and Social Psychology Bulletin*, 21, 237–244.

Mayer, J. D., & Salovey, P. (1995). Emotional intelligence and the construction and regulation of feelings. *Applied & Preventive Psychology*, 4, 197–208.

Mazzella, R., & Feingold, A. (1994). The effects of physical attractiveness, race, socioeconomic status, and gender of defendants and victims on judgments of mock jurors: A meta-analysis. *Journal of Applied Social Psychology*, 24, 1315–1344.

McArthur, L. A. (1972). The how and what of why: Some determinants and consequences of causal attribution. *Journal of Personality and Social Psychology*, 22, 171–193.

McCall, M. E., & Struthers, N. J. (1994). Sex, sex-role orientation and self-esteem as predictors of coping style. *Journal of Social Behavior and Personality*, 9, 801–810.

McConnell, A. R., & Fazio, R. H. (1996). Women as men and people: Effects of gender-marked language. *Personality and Social Psychology Bulletin*, 22, 1004–1013.

McConnell, A. R., Sherman, S. J., & Hamilton, D. L. (1994). Illusory correlation in the perception of groups: An extension of the distinctiveness-based account. *Journal of Personality and Social Psychology*, 67, 414–429.

McCullough, M. E., Worthington, E. L., Jr., & Rachal, K. C. (1997). Interpersonal forgiving in close relationships. *Journal of Personality and Social Psychology*, 73, 321–336.

McDowall, D. (1991). Firearm availability and homicide rates in Detroit, 1951–86. *Social Forces, 69*, 1085–1101.

McDowall, D., Wiersema, B., & Loftin, C. (1989). Did mandatory firearm ownership in Kennesaw really prevent burglaries? *Sociology and Sociological Research, 74*, 48–51.

McFarland, C., & Buehler, R. (1995). Collective self-esteem as a moderator of the frog-pond effect in reactions to performance feedback. *Journal of Personality and Social Psychology*, 68, 1055–1070.

McGonagle, K. A., Kessler, R. C., & Schilling, E. A. (1992). The frequency and determinants of marital disagreements in a community sample. *Journal of Social and Personal Relationships*, 9, 507–524.

McGowan, S., Daniels, L. K., & Byrne, D. (1999b). The Albany Measure of Attachment Style: A multi-item measure of Bartholomew's four-factor model. Manuscript submitted for publication.

McGuire, W. J., & McGuire, C. V. (1996). Enhancing self-esteem by directed-thinking tasks: Cognitive and affective positivity asymmetries. *Journal of Personality and Social Psychology*, 70, 1117–1125.

McKenna, K. Y. A., & Bargh, J. A. (1998). Coming out in the age of the internet: Identity "demarginalization" through virtual group participation. *Journal of Personality and Social Psychology*, 75, 681–694.

McKillip, J., & Reidel, S. L. (1983). External validity of matching on physical attractiveness for same and opposite sex couples. *Journal of Applied Social Psychology*, 13, 328–337.

McMullen, M. N., Markman, K. D., & Gavanski, I. (1995). Living in neither the best nor the worst of all possible worlds: Antecedents and consequences of upward and downward counterfactual thinking. In N. J. Roese & J. M. Olson (Eds.), *What might have been: The social psychology of counterfactual thinking* (pp. 133–167). Mahwah, NJ: Erlbaum.

McNulty, S. E., & Swann, W. B., Jr. (1994). Identity negotiation in roommate relationships: The self as architect and consequence of social reality. *Journal of Personality and Social Psychology*, 67, 1012–1023.

McQuillan, K., & Belle, M. (1999). Who does what? Gender and the division of labour in Canadian households. In J. Curtis, E. Grabb, & N. Guppy (Eds.), *Social inequality in Canada: Patterns, problems, and policies* (2nd ed., pp. 186–198). Scarborough, Ont.: Prentice Hall.

McWhirter, B. T. (1997). A pilot study of loneliness in ethnic minority college students. *Social Behavior and Personality*, 25, 295–304.

Mead, G.H. (1934). *Mind, self and society*. (C.W. Morris, Ed.). Chicago: University of Chicago Press.

Medvec, V. H., & Savitsky, K. (1997). When doing better means feeling worse: The effects of categorical cutoff points on counterfactual thinking and satisfaction. *Journal of Personality and Social Psychology*, 72, 1284–1296.

Medvec, V. H., Madey, S. F., & Gilovich, T. (1995). When less is more: Counterfactual thinking and satisfaction among Olympic athletes. *Journal of Personality and Social Psychology*, 69, 603–610.

Mehrabian, A., & Weiner, M. (1967). Decoding of inconsistent communications. *Journal of Personality and Social Psychology*, 6, 109–114.

Meindl, J. R., & Lerner, M. J. (1985). Exacerlation of extreme responses to an out-group. *Journal of Personality and Social Psychology*, 47, 71–84.

Melamed, S., Ben-Avi, I., Luz, J., & Green, M. S. (1995). Objective and subjective work monotony: Effects on job satisfaction, psychological distress, and absenteeism in blue-collar workers. *Journal of Applied Psychology*, 80, 29–42.

Mellers, B. A., Richards, V., & Birnbaum, M. H. (1992). Distributional theories of impression formation. *Organizational Behavior and Human Decision Processes*, 51, 313–343.

Mesquida, C.G., & Wiener, N.I. (1996). Human collective aggression: A behavioral ecology perspective. *Ethology and Sociobiology*, 17, 247–262.

Meyer, J.P., & Allen, N.J. (1997). *Commitment in the workplace: Theory, research, and application*. Thousand Oaks, CA: Sage.

Meyer, J.P., Allen, N.J., & Topolnytsky, L. (1998). Commitment in a changing world of work. *Canadian Psychology. 39*, 83–93.

Meyers, S. A., & Berscheid, E. (1997). The language of love: The difference a preposition makes. *Personality and Social Psychology Bulletin*, 23, 347–362.

Miceli, M. P., & Lane, M. C. (1991). Antecedents of pay satisfaction: A review and extension. In K. Rowland & O. R. Ferris (Eds.), *Research in personnel and human resources management* (Vol. 9, pp. 235–309). Greenwich, CT: JAI Press.

Michael, R. T., Gagnon, J. H., Laumann, E. O., & Kolata, G. (1994). *Sex in America: A definitive survey*. Boston: Little, Brown.

Mihalko, S. L., McAuley, E., & Bane, S. M. (1996). Self-efficacy and affective responses to acute exercise in middle-aged adults. *Journal of Social Behavior and Personality*, 11, 375–385.

Mikulincer, M. (1995). Attachment style and the mental representation of the self. *Journal of Personality and Social Psychology*, 69, 1203–1215.

Mikulincer, M. (1998a). Adult attachment style and individual differences in functional versus dysfunctional experiences of anger. *Journal of Personality and Social Psychology*, 74, 513–524.

Mikulincer, M. (1998b). Attachment working models and the sense of trust: An exploration of interaction goals and affect regulation. *Journal of Personality and Social Psychology*, 74, 1209–1224.

Mikulincer, M., & Florian, V. (1995). Appraisal of and coping with a real-life stressful situation: The contribution of attachment styles. *Personality and Social Psychology Bulletin*, 21, 406–414.

Mikulincer, M., Orbach, I., & Iavnieli, D. (1998). Adult attachment style and affect regulation: Strategic variations in subjective self-other similarity. *Journal of Personality and Social Psychology*, 75, 436–448.

Miles, S. M., & Carey, G. (1997). Genetic and environmental architecture of human aggression. *Journal of Personality and Social Psychology*, 72, 207–217.

Milestones. (1989, September 18). *Time*, p. 75.

Milgram, S. (1963). Behavioral study of obedience. *Journal of Abnormal and Social Psychology*, 67, 371–378.

Milgram, S. (1965a). Liberating effects of group pressure. *Journal of Personality and Social Psychology*, 1, 127–134.

Milgram, S. (1965b). Some conditions of obedience and disobedience to authority. *Human Relations*, 18, 57–76.

Milgram, S. (1970). The experience of living in cities. *Science*, 13, 1461–1468.

Milgram, S. (1974). Obedience to authority. New York: Harper.

Millar, M. G. (1997). The effects of emotion on breast self-examination: Another look at the health belief model. *Social Behavior and Personality*, 25, 223–232.

Miller, A. G., McHoskey, J. W., Bane, C. M., & Dowd, T. G. (1993). The attitude polarization phenomenon: Role of response measure, attitude extremity, and behavioral consequences of reported attitude change. *Journal of Personality and Social Psychology*, 64, 516–574.

Miller, D. T., & McFarland, C. (1986). Counterfactual thinking and victim compensation: A test of norm theory. *Personality and Social Psychology Bulletin*, 12, 513–519.

Miller, D. T., & Ratner, R. K. (1996). The power of the myth of self-interest. In L. Montada & M. Lerner (Eds.), *Current societal concerns about justice*. New York: Plenum.

Miller, D. T., & Ross, M. (1975). Self-serving biases in attribution of causality: Fact or fiction? Psychological Bulletin, 82, 313–325.

Miller, D. T., Turnbull, W., & McFarland, C. (1990). Counterfactual thinking and social perception: Thinking about what might have been. In M. P. Zanna (Ed.), *Advances in experimental social psychology* (Vol. 23, pp. 305–331). Orlando FL: Academic Press.

Miller, J. (1984). Culture and the development of everyday social explanation. *Journal of Personality and Social Psychology*, 46, 961–978.

Miller, L. C. (1990). Intimacy and liking: Mutual influence and the role of unique relationships. *Journal of Personality and Social Psychology*, 58, 33–47.

Miller, L.C. (1990). Intimacy and liking: Mutual influence and the role of unique relationships. *Journal of Personality and Social Psychology*, 59, 50–60.

Miller, M. L., & Thayer, J. F. (1989). On the existence of discrete classes in personality: Is self-monitoring the correct joint to carve? *Journal of Personality and Social Psychology*, 57, 143–155.

Miller, N., Maruyama, G., Beaber, R. J., & Valone, K. (1976). Speed of speech and persuasion. *Journal of Personality and Social Psychology*, 34, 615–624.

Miller, R. S. (1991). On decorum in close relationships: Why aren't we polite to those we love? *Contemporary Social Psychology*, 15, 63–65.

Miyake, K., & Zuckerman, M. (1993). Beyond personality impressions: effects of physical and vocal attractiveness on false consensus, social comparison, affiliation, and assumed and perceived similarity. *Journal of Personality*, 61, 411–437.

Mizokawa, D. T., & Ryckman, D.B. (1990). Attributions of academic success and failure: A comparison of six Asian-American ethnic groups. *Journal of Cross-Cultural Psychology*, 21, 434–51.

Moghaddam, F.M. (1987). Psychology in the three worlds: As reflected by the crisis in social psychology and the move toward indigenous Third World psychology. *American Psychologist*, 42, 912–920.

Moghaddam, F.M. (1990). Modulative and generative orientations in psychology: Implications for Psychology in the three worlds. *Journal of Social Issues*, 46, 21–41.

Moghaddam, F.M., Taylor, D.M., & Wright, S.C. (1993). *Social psychology in cross-cultural perspective*. NewYork: W.H. Freeman.

Moller, H. (1967/68). Youth as a force in the modern world. *Comparative Studies in Society and History*, 10, 237–260.

Monsour, M., Betty, S., & Kurzweil, N. (1993). Levels of perspectives and the perception of intimacy in cross-sex friendships: A balance theory explanation of shared perceptual reality. *Journal of Social and Personal Relationships*, 10, 529–550.

Monteith, M.J. (1993). Self-regulation of prejudiced responses: Implications for progress in prejudice-reduction efforts. *Journal of Personality and Social Psychology*, 65, 469–485.

Moore, C. H., Wuensch, K. L., Hedges, R. M., & Castellow, W. A. (1994). The effects o f physical attractiveness and social desirability on judgments regarding a sexual harassment case. *Journal of Social Behavior and Personality*, 9, 715–730.

Moore, J. S., Graziano, W. G., Miller, M. G. (1987). Physical attractiveness, sex role orientation, and the evaluation of adults and children. *Personality and Social Psychology Bulletin*, 13, 95–102.

Moran, G., & Cutler, B. L. (1991). The prejudicial impact of pretrial publicity. *Journal of Applied Social Psychology, 21,* 345–367.

Moreland, R. L. (1987). The formation of small groups. In C. Hendrick (Ed.), *Review of personality and social psychology,* (Vol. 8, pp. 80–110). Newbury Park, CA: Sage.

Moreland, R. L., & Beach, S. R. (1992). Exposure effects in the classroom: The development of affinity among students. *Journal of Experimental Social Psychology, 28,* 255–276.

Moreland, R. L., & Zajonc, R. B. (1982). Exposure effects in person perception: Familiarity, similarity, and attraction. *Journal of Experimental Social Psychology, 18,* 395–415.

Morgan, D. L., & White, R. L. (1993). The structure of the field of personal relationships: Part I. Disciplines. *Personal Relationships Issues, 1,* 2–5.

Morgan, D., Carder, P., & Neal, M. (1997). Are some relationships more useful than others? The value of similar others in the networks of recent widows. *Journal of Social and Personal Relationships, 14,* 745–759.

Morgan, H. J., & Janoff-Bulman, R. (1994). Positive and negative self-complexity: Patterns of adjustment following traumatic versus non-traumatic life experiences. *Journal of Social and Clinical Psychology, 13,* 63–85.

Mori, D. L., & Morey, L. (1991). The vulnerable body image of females with feelings of depression. *Journal of Research in Personality, 25,* 343–354.

Morris, M. W., & Peng, K. (1994). Culture and cause: American and Chinese attributions for social and physical events. *Journal of Personality and Social Psychology, 67,* 949–971.

Morrison, E. W. (1994). Role definitions and organizational citizenship behavior: The importance of employees' perspective. *Academy of Management Journal, 37,* 1543–1567.

Morrison, E.W., & Robinson, S.L. (1997). When employees feel betrayed: A model of how psychological contract violation develops. *Academy of Management Review, 22,* 226–256.

Morrison, H. W. (1954). The validity and behavioral manifestations of female need for affiliation. Unpublished master's thesis, Wesleyan University.

Morrow, G. D., Clark, E. M., & Brock, K. F. (1995). Individual and partner love styles: Implications for the quality of romantic involvements. *Journal of Social and Personal Relationships, 12,* 363–387.

Moscovici, S. (1972). Society and theory in social psychology. In J. Israel & H. Tajfel (Eds.), *The context of social psychology.* London: Academic Press.

Moscovici, S. (1985). Social influence and conformity. In G. Lindzey & E. Aronson (Eds.), *Handbook of social psychology.* 3rd ed. New York: Random House.

Moston, S., & Stephenson, G. M. (1993). The changing face of police interrogation. *Journal of Community and Applied Social Psychology, 3,* 101–115.

Muczyk, J. P., & Reimann, B. C. (1987). The case for directive leadership. *Academy of Management Review, 12,* 637–647.

Mugny, G. (1975). Negotiations, image of the other and the process of minority influence. *European Journal of Social Psychology, 5,* 209–229.

Mullan, E., & Markland, D. (1997). Variations in self-determination across the stages of change for exercise in adults. *Motivation and Emotion, 21,* 349–362.

Mullen, B., & Johnson, C. (1990). Distinctiveness-based illusory correlations and stereotyping: A meta-analytic integration. *British Journal of Social Psychology, 29,* 11–28.

Mullen, B., Brown, R. & Smith, C. (1992). Ingroup bias as a function of salience, relevance, and status: An integration. *European Journal of Social Psychology, 22,* 103–122.

Mundt, R.J. (1990). Gun control and rates of firearms violence in Canada and the United States. *Canadian Journal of Criminology, 35,* 42–47.

Mundt, R.J. (1993). Rejoinder to comments on 'Gun control and rates of firearms violence in Canada and the United States. *Canadian Journal of Criminology, 35,* 42–47.

Munro, G. D., & Ditto, P. H. (1997). Biased assimilation, attitude polarization, and affect in reactions to stereotype-relevant scientific information. *Personality and Social Psychology Bulletin, 23,* 636–653.

Munsterberg, H. (1907). *On the witness stand: Essays in psychology and crime.* New York: McClure.

Murnighan, K. (Ed.). (1993). *Handbook of social psychology in organizations.* Englewood Cliffs, N.J.

Murray, H. A. (1938/1962). *Explorations in personality.* New York: Science Editions.

Murray, S. L., & Holmes, J. G. (1997). A leap of faith? Positive illusions in romantic relationships. *Personality and Social Psychology Bulletin, 23,* 586–604.

Murray, S. L., Holmes, J. G., & Griffin, D. W. (1996). The benefits of positive illusions: Idealization and the construction of satisfaction in close relationships. *Journal of Personality and Social Psychology, 70,* 79–98.

Myers, D. G., & Diener, E. (1995). Who is happy? *Psychological Science, 6,* 10–19.

Nardi, P. M., & Sherrod, D. (1994). Friendship in the lives of gay men and lesbians. *Journal of Social and Personal Relationships, 11,* 185–199.

Nemeth, C. J. (1995). Dissent as driving cognition, attitudes, and judgments. *Social Cognition, 13,* 273–291.

Neuberg, S. L. (1989). The goal of forming accurate impressions during social interactions: Attenuating the impact of negative expectancies. *Journal of Personality and Social Psychology, 56,* 374–386.

Neuman, J. H., & Baron, R. A. (1997). Aggression in the workplace. In Giacalone, R. A., & Greenberg, J. (Eds.), *Antisocial behavior in organizations.* Thousand Oaks, CA: Sage.

Neuman, J. H., & Baron, R. A. (1998). Workplace violence and workplace aggression: Evidence concerning specific forms, potential causes, and preferred targets. *Journal of Management, 24,* 391–420.

Newcomb, T. M. (1961). *The acquaintance process.* New York: Holt, Rinehart, & Winston.

Niedenthal, P. M., Setterlund, M. B., & Wherry, M. B. (1992). Possible self-complexity and affective reactions to goal–relevant evaluation. *Journal of Personality and Social Psychology, 63,* 5-16

Nisbett, R. E. (1990). Evolutionary psychology, biology, and cultural evolution. *Motivation and Emotion*, 14, 255–264.

Nisbett, R.E., & Kunda, Z. (1985). Perception of social distributions. *Journal of Personality and Social Psychology*, 48, 297–311.

Nix, G., Watson, C., Pyszczynski, T., & Greenberg, J. (1995). Reducing depressive affect through external focus of attention. *Journal of Social and Clinical Psychology*, 14, 36–52.

Norenzayan, A, & Levine, R. V. (1994). Helping in 18 international cities. Paper presented at the annual meeting of the Western Psychological Association, Kona Hawaii.

O'Connell, P. D. (1988). Pretrial publicity, change of venue, public opinion polls—A theory of procedural justice. *University of Detroit Law Review*, 65, 169–197.

O'Connor, K., & Carnevale, P. J. (1997). A nasty but effective negotiation strategy: Misrepresentation of a common-value issue. *Personality and Social Psychology Bulletin*, 23, 504–515.

O'Connor, S. C., & Rosenblood, L. K. (1996). Affiliation motivation in everyday experience: A theoretical comparison. *Journal of Personality and Social Psychology*, 70, 513–522.

O'Grady, K. E. (1989). Physical attractiveness, need for approval, social self-esteem, and maladjustment. *Journal of Social and Clinical Psychology*, 8, 62–69.

O'Neil, J. (1998, December 8). That sly 'don't-come-hither' stare. *New York Times*, p. F7.

O'Sullivan, C. S., & Durso, F. T. (1984). Effects of schema-incongruent information on memory for stereotypical attributes. *Journal of Personality and Social Psychology*, 47, 55–70.

of personality: Theory and research (pp. 301–338). New York: Guilford.

Ohbuchi, K., & Kambara, T. (1985). Attacker's intent and awareness of outcome, impression management, and retaliation. *Journal of Experimental Social Psychology*, 21, 321–330.

Ohbuchi, K., Chiba, S., & Fikushima, O. (1994). Mitigation of interpersonal conflict: Politeness and time pressure. Unpublished manuscript, Tohoku University.

Ohbuchi, K., Kameda, M., & Agarie, N. (1989). Apology as aggression control: Its role in mediating appraisal of and response to harm. *Journal of Personality and Social Psychology*, 56, 219–227.

Ohlott, P. J., Ruderman, M. N., & McCauley, C. D. (1994). Gender differences in managers' developmental job experiences. *Academy of Management Journal*, 37, 46–67.

Oliner, S. P., & Oliner, P. M. (1988). *The altruistic personality: Rescuers of Jews in Nazi Europe*. New York: Free Press.

Olivenstein, L. (1992). Cold comfort. *Discover*, 13(8), 18, 20–21.

Oliver, M. B., & Hyde, J. S. (1993). Gender differences in sexuality: A meta-analysis. *Psychological Bulletin*, 114, 29–51.

Olmstead, R. E., Guy, S. M., O'Malley, P. M., & Bentler, P. M. (1991). Longitudinal assessment of the relationship between self-esteem, fatalism, loneliness, and substance use. *Journal of Social Behavior and Personality*, 6, 749–770.

Organ, D. W. (1997). Organizational citizenship behavior: It's construct clean-up time. *Human Performance*, 10, 85–98.

Orive, R. (1988). Social projection and social comparison of opinions. *Journal of Personality and Social Psychology*, 54, 953–964.

Orlofsky, J. L., & O'Heron, C. A. (1987). Stereotypic and nonstereotypic sex role trait and behavior orientations: Implications for personal adjustment. *Journal of Personality and Social Psychology*, 52, 1034–1042.

Osborne, J. W. (1995). Academics, self-esteem, and race: A look at the underlying assumptions of the disidentification hypothesis. *Personality and Social Psychology Bulletin*, 21, 449–455.

Osterman, K., Bjorkqvist, K., Lagerspetz, K. M. J., Kaukiainen, A., Landua, S. F., Fraczek, A., & Caprara, G. V. (1998). Cross-cultural evidence of female indirect aggression. *Aggressive Behavior*, 24, 1–8.

Osterman, K., Bjorkqvist, K., Lagerspetz, K. M. J., Kaukianainen, A., Huesmann, L. W., & Fraczek, A. (1994). Peer and self-estimated aggression and victimization in 8-year-old children from five ethnic groups. *Aggressive Behavior*, 20, 411–428.

Osterwell, Z., & Nagano-Hakamura, K. (1992). Maternal views on aggression: Japan and Israel. *Aggressive Behavior*, 18, 263–270.

Ottati, V., Terkildsen, N., & Hubbard, C. (1997). Happy faces elicit heuristic processing in a televised impression formation task: A cognitive tuning account. *Personality and Social Psychology Bulletin*, 23, 1144–1156.

Page, N. R., & Wiseman, R. L. (1993). Supervisory behavior and worker satisfaction in the United States, Mexico, and Spain. *Journal of Business Communication*, 30, 161–180.

Paik, H., & Comstock, G. (1994). The effects of television violence on antisocial behavior: A meta-analysis. *Communication Research*, 21, 516–546.

Pandey, J., Sinha, D., Bhawuk, D. P. S. (Eds.). (1996). *Asian contributions to cross-cultural psychology*. Thousand Oaks, CA: Sage.

Parks, M. R., & Floyd, K. (1996). Meanings for closeness and intimacy in friendship. *Journal of Social and Personal Relationships*, 13, 85–107.

Parks, M.R., & Floyd, K. (1996). Making friends in cyberspace. *Journal of Communications, 46*, 80–97.

Parks, M.R., & Roberts, L.D. (1998). 'Making MOOsic': The development of personal relationships on line and a comparison to their off-line counterparts. *Journal of Social and Personal Relationships., 15*, 517–537.

Paterson, R. J., & Neufeld, R. W. J. (1995). What are my options? Influences of choice availability on stress and the perception of control. *Journal of Research in Personality*, 29, 145–167.

Patrick, C. J., Bradley, M. M., & Lang, P. J. (1993). Emotion in the criminal psychopath: Startle reflex modulation. *Journal of Abnormal Psychology*, 102, 83–92.

Paul, L., Foss, M. A., & Galloway, J. (1993). Sexual jealousy in young women and men: Aggressive responsiveness to partner and rival. *Aggressive Behavior*, 19, 401–420.

Paulhus, D. L., & Bruce, M. N. (1992). The effect of acquaintanceship on the validity of personality impressions: A longitudinal study. *Journal of Personality and Social Psychology, 63*, 816–824.

Paulhus, D. L., Bruce, M. N., & Trapnell, P.D. (1995). Effects of self-presentation strategies on personality profiles and their structure. *Personality and Social Psychology Bulletin, 21*, 100–108.

Paulhus, D.L. (1998). Interpersonal and intrapsychic adaptiveness of trait self-enhancement: A mixed blessing? *Journal of Personality and Social Psychology, 74*, 1197–1208.

Paulus, P. B. (ed.) (1989). *Psychology of influence* (2nd ed.). Hillsdale, NJ: Erlbaum.

Pear, R. (1993, January 15). Poverty erodes family, study finds. *Albany Times Union*, pp. A–I, A–8.

Pearse, J. (1995). Police interviewing: The identification of vulnerabilities. *Journal of Community and Applied Social Psychology, 5*, 147–159.

Pearson, K., & Lee, A. (1903). On the laws of inheritance in man: I. Inheritance of physical characters. *Biometrika, 2*, 357–462.

Pedersen, D. M. (1994). Privacy preferences and classroom seat selection. *Social Behavior and Personality, 22*, 393–398.

Pelham, B. W. (1995a). Self-investment and self-esteem: Evidence for a Jamesian model of self-worth. *Journal of Personality and Social Psychology, 69*, 1141–1150.

Pelham, B. W. (1995b). Further evidence for a Jamesian model of self-worth: Reply to Marsh (1995). *Journal of Personality and Social Psychology, 69*, 1161–1165.

Pelham, B. W., & Wachsmuth, J. O. (1995). The waxing and waning of the social self: Assimilation and contrast in social comparison. *Journal of Personality and Social Psychology, 69*, 825–838.

Peplau, L.A., Veniegas, R.C. & Campbell, S.M. (1996). Gay and lesbian relationships. In R.C. Savin-Williams & K.M. Cohen (Eds.), *The lives of lesbians, gays, and bisexuals* (pp.250–273). New York: Harcourt Brace.

Perloff, L. S. (1983). Perceptions of vulnerability to victimization. *Journal of Social Issues, 39*, 41–61.

Perloff, L. S., & Fetzer, B. K. (1986). Self-other judgments and perceived vulnerability to victimization. *Journal of Personality and Social Psychology, 50*, 502–510.

Perrin, S., & Spencer, C. P. (1981). Independence or conformity in the Asch experiment as a reflection of cultural and situational factors. *British Journal of Social Psychology, 20*, 205–210.

Personality and Social Psychology, 65, 494–511.

Pessin, J. (1933). The comparative effects of social and mechanical stimulation on memorizing. *American Journal of Psychology, 45*, 263–270.

Peterson, R. S. (1997). A directive leadership style in group decision making can be both a virtue and vice: Evidence from elite and experimental groups. *Journal of Personality and Social Psychology, 72*, 1107–1121.

Peterson, R.A., & Jolibert, A.J.P. (1995). A meta-analysis of country-of-origin effects. *Journal of International Business Studies, 26*, 883–900.

Petkova, K. G., Ajzen, I., & Driver, B. L. (1995). Salience of anti-abortion beliefs and commitment to an attitudinal position: On the strength, structure, and predictive validity of anti-abortion attitudes. *Journal of Applied Social Psychology, 25*, 463–483.

Petrie, K. J., Booth, R. J., & Pennebaker, J. W. (1998). The immunological effects of thought suppression. Journal of *Personality and Social Psychology, 75*, 1264–1272.

Pettigrew, T. F. (1969). Racially separate or together? *Journal of Social Issues, 25*, 43–69.

Pettigrew, T. F. (1981). Extending the stereotype concept. In D. L. Hamilton (Ed.), *Cognitive processes in stereotyping and intergroup behavior* (pp. 303–331). Hillsdale, NJ: Erlbaum.

Pettigrew, T. F. (1997). Generalized intergroup contact effects on prejudice. *Personality and Social Psychology Bulletin, 23*, 173–185.

Petty, R. E., & Cacioppo, J. T. (1986). The elaboration likelihood model of persuasion. In L. Berkowitz (Ed.), *Advances in experimental social psychology* (Vol. 19, pp. 123–205). New York: Academic Press.

Petty, R. E., & Cacioppo, J. T. (1990). Involvement and persuasion: Tradition versus integration. *Psychological Bulletin, 107*, 367–374.

Petty, R. E., Cacioppo, J. T., Strathman, A. J., & Priester, J. R. (1994). To think or not to think: Exploring two routes to persuasion. In S. Shavitt & T. C. Brock (Eds.), *Persuasion* (pp. 113–147). Boston: Allyn and Bacon.

Petty, R. E., Cacioppo, J. T., Strathman, A. J., & Priester, J. R. (1994). To think or not to think: Exploring two routes to persuasion. In S. Shavitt & T. C. Brock (Eds.), *Persuasion* (pp. 113–147). Boston: Allyn & Bacon.

Petty, R. J., & Krosnick, J. A. (Eds.). (1995). *Attitude strength: Antecedents and consequences* (Vol. 4). Hillsdale, NJ: Erlbaum.

Pezdek, K., Finger, K., & Hodge, D. (1997). Planting false childhood memories: The role of event plausibility. *Psychological Science, 8*, 437–441.

Philbrick, J. L. (1987). Sex differences in romantic attitudes tward love in engineering studens. Psychological Reports, 61, 482.

Philbrick, J. L., & Opolot, J. A. (1980). Love style: comparison of African and American attitudes. Psychological Reports, 46, 286.

Phinney, J. S. (1990). Ethnic identity in adolescents and adults: Review of research. *Psychological Bulletin, 108*, 499–514.

Phinney, J. S. (1991). Ethnic identity and self-esteem: A review and integration. *Hispanic Journal of Behavioral Sciences, 13*, 193–208.

Pierce, C. A. (1992). The effects of physical attractiveness and height on dating choice: A meta-analysis. Unpublished masters thesis, University at Albany, State University of New York.

Pietromonaco, P. R., & Barrett, L. F. (1997). Working models of attachment and daily social interactions. *Journal of Personality and Social Psychology, 73*, 1409–1423.

Piliavin, J. A., & Unger, R. K. (1985). The helpful but helpless female: Myth or reality? In V. E. O'Leary, R. K. Unger, & B.

S. Wallston (Eds.), *Women, gender, and social psychology* (pp. 149–189). Hillsdale, NJ: Erlbaum.

Pillai, R., Sittes-Doe, S., Grewal, D., & Meindl, J. R. (1997). Winning charisma and losing the presidential election. *Journal of Applied Social Psychology*, 27, 1716–1726.

Pines, A. (1997). Fatal attractions or wise unconscious choices: The relationship between causes for entering and breaking intimate relationships. *Personal Relationship Issues*, 4, 1–6.

Pines, A., & Aronson, E. (1983). Antecedents, correlates, and consequences of sexual jealousy. *Journal of Personality*, 51, 108–136.

Pinker, S. (1998). *How the mind works*. New York: Norton.

Platz, S. G., & Hosch, H. M. (1988). Cross-racial/ethnic eyewitness identification: A field study. *Journal of Applied Social Psychology*, 13, 972–984.

Pleck, J. H., Sonenstein, F. L., & Ku, L. C. (1993). Masculinity ideology: Its impact on adolescent males' heterosexual relationships. *Journal of Social Issues*, 49(3), 11–29.

Pliner, P., Chaiken, S., & Flett, G. L. (1990). Eating, social motives and self-presentation in women and men. *Journal of Experimental Social Psychology*, 26, 240–254.

Podsakoff, P. M., & MacKenzie, S. B. (1994). Organizational citizenship behaviors and sales unit effectiveness. *Journal of Marketing Research*, 31, 351–363.

Podsakoff, P. M., Ahearne, M., & MacKenzie, S. B. (1997). Organizational citizenship behavior and the quantity and quality of work group performance. *Journal of Applied Psychology*, 82, 262–270.

Pollock, C. L., Smith, S. D., Knowles, E. S., & Bruce, H. J. (1998). Mindfulness limits compliance with the that's-not-all technique. Personality and Social Psychology *Bulletin*, 24, 1153–1157.

Pomazal, R. J., & Clore, G. L. (1973). Helping on the highway: The effects of dependency and sex. *Journal of Applied Social Psychology*, 3, 150–164.

Pomerantz, E. M., Chaioken, S., & Tordesilla, S. (1995). Attitude strength and resistance processes. *Journal of Personality and Social Psychology*, 69, 408–419.

Poole, D. A., & Lindsay, D. S. (1998). Assessing the accuracy of young children's reports: Lessons from the investigation of child sexual abuse. *Applied & Preventive Psychology*, 7, 1–26.

Poortinga, Y. H. (1971). Cross-cultural comparison of maximum performance tests: Some methodological aspects and some experiments. Psychologia Africana, Monograph Supplement, 6.

Poortinga, Y. H., & Foden, B. I. M. (1995). A comparative study of curiosity in black and white South African students. Psycholgia Africana, Monograph Supplement, 8.

Pope, K. S. (1996). Memory, abuse, and science: Questioning claims about the false memory syndrome epidemic. *American Psychologist*, 51, 957–974.

Powell, G. N., & Butterfield, D. A. (1994). Investigating the "glass ceiling" phenomenon: An empirical study of actual promotions to top management. *Academy of Management Journal*, 37, 68–86.

Powers, P. C., & Geen, R. G. (1972). Effects of the behavior and perceived arousal of a model on instrumental aggression. *Journal of Personality and Social Psychology*, 23, 175–184.

Prager, K. J., & Bailey, J. M. (1985). Androgyny, ego develpment , and psychosocial crisis. *Sex Roles*, 13, 525–536.

Pratkanis, A. R., Breckler S. J., & Greenwald, A. G. (Eds.). (1989). *Attitude structure and function*. Hillsdale, NJ: Erlbaum.

Pratto, F., Stallworth, L. M., Sidanius, J., & Siers, B. (1997). The gender gap in occupational role attainment: A social dominance approach. *Journal of Personality and Social Psychology*, 72, 37–53.

Pruitt, D. G., & Carnevale, P. J. (1993). *Negotiation in social conflict*. Pacific Grove, CA: Brooks/Cole.

Przybyla, D. P. J. (1985). The facilitating effect of exposure to erotica on male prosocial behavior. Unpublished doctoral dissertation, University at Albany, State University of New York.

Radecki-Bush, C., Farrell, A. D., & Bush, J. P. (1993). Predicting jealous responses: The influence of adult attachment and depression on threat appraisal. *Journal of Social and Personal Relationships*, 10, 569–588.

Rall, M. L., Peskoff, F. S., & Byrne, J. J. (1994). The effects of information-giving behavior and gender on the perceptions of physicians: An experimental analysis. *Social Behavior and Personality*, 22, 1–16.

Ramirez, J., Bryant, J., & Zillmann, D. (1983). Effects of erotica on retaliatory behavior as a function of level of prior provocation. *Journal of Personality and Social Psychology*, 43, 971–978.

Randall, D. M., Fedor, D. P., & Longenecker, C. O. (1990). The behavioral expression of organizational commitment. *Journal of Vocational Behavior*, 36, 210–224.

Rands, M., & Levinger, G. (1979). Implicit theories of relationship: An intergenerational study. *Journal of Personality and Social Psychology*, 37, 649–661.

Regan, P. C., Snyder, M., & Kassin, S. M. (1995). Unrealistic optimism: Self-enhancement or person positivity? *Personality and Social Psychology Bulletin*, 21, 1073–1082.

Reis, H. T., Nezlek, J., & Wheeler, L. (1980). Physical attractiveness in social interaction. *Journal of Personality and Social Psychology*, 38, 604–617.

Reis, H.T., & Wheeler, L. (1990). Studying social interaction with the Rochester Interaction Record. In M.P.Zanna (Ed.), *Advances in experimental social psychology* (pp.269–318). New York: Academic Press.

Reis, T. J., Gerrard, M. & Gibbons, F. X. (1993). Social comparison and the pill: Reactions to upward and downward comparison of contraceptive behavior. *Personality and Social Psychology Bulletin*, 19, 13–20.

Reiss, A. J., & Roth, J. A. (Eds.). (1993). *Understanding and preventing violence*. Washington, DC: National Academy Press.

Reno, R. R., Cialdini, R. B, & Kalgren, C. A (1993). The transsitutional influence of social norms. *Journal of Personality and Social Psychology*, 64, 104–112.

Reno, R. R., Cildini, R. B., & Kallgren, C. A. (1993). The transsitutional influence of social norms. *Journal of Personality and Social Psychology*, 64, 104–112.

Rensberger, B. (1993, November 9). Certain chemistry between vole pairs. *Albany Times Union*, pp. C–1, C–3.

Rentsch, J. R., & Heffner, T. S. (1994). Assessing self-concept: Analysis of Gordon's coding scheme using "Who am I?" responses. *Journal of Social Behavior and Personality, 9,* 283–300.

Revicki, D. A., Whitley, T. W., Gallery, M. E., & Allison, E. J. Jr. (1993). Impact of work environment characteristics on work-related stress and depression in emergency medicine residents: A longitudinal study. *Journal of Community & Applied Social Psychology, 3,* 273–284.

Rheingold, H. (1993). *The virtual community: Homesteading on the electronic frontier.* Reading, MA: Addison-Wesley.

Rhodes, N., & Wood, W. (1992). Self-esteem and intelligence affect influenceability: The mediating role of message reception. *Psychological Bulletin, 111,* 156–171.

Rhodewalt, F. R., Madrian, J. C., & Cheney, S. (1998). Narcissism, self-knowledge organization, and emotional reactivity: The effect of daily experience on self-esteem and affect. *Personality and Social Psychology Bulletin, 24,* 75–87.

Rhodewalt, F., & Davison, J., Jr. (1983). Reactance and the coronary-prone behavior pattern: The role of self-attribution in response to reduced behavioral freedom. *Journal of Personality and Social Psychology, 44,* 220–228.

Rice, R.E., & Love, G. (1987). Electronic emotion: Socioemotional content in a computer mediated communication network. *Communications Research, 14,* 85–108.

Ridley, M., & Dawkins, R. (1981). The natural selection of altruism. In J. P. Rushton & R. M. Sorrentino (Eds.), *Altruism and helping behavior.* Hillsdale, NJ: Erlbaum.

Rierdan, J. (1999). Internet-Depression Link? *American Psychologist, 54,* 781–782.

Riess, M., & Schlenker, B. R. (1977). Attitude change and responsibility avoidance as modes of dilemma resolution in forced-compliance situations. *Journal of Personality and Social Psychology, 35,* 21–30.

Rind, B. (1996). Effect of beliefs about weather conditions on tipping. *Journal of Applied Social Psychology, 26,* 137–147.

Rind, B., & Bordia, P. (1996). Effect on restaurant tipping of male and female servers drawing a happy, smiling face on the backs of customers' checks. *Journal of Applied Social Psychology, 26,* 218–225.

Riordan, C. A. (1978). Equal-status interracial contact: A review and revision of a concept. *International Journal of Intercultural Relations, 2,* 161–185.

Robarchek, C. A., & Robarchek, C. J. (1997). Waging peace: The psychological and sociocultural dynamics of positive peace. In A. W. Wolfe, & H. Yang (Eds.), *Anthropological contributions to conflict resolution* (pp. 64–80). Athens, GA: University of Georgia Press.

Roberts, B. W., & Donahue, E. M. (1994). One personality, multiple selves: Integrating personality and social roles. *Journal of Personality, 62,* 199–218.

Roberts, J. E., & Monroe, S. M. (1992). Vulnerable self-esteem and depressive symptoms: Prospective findings comparing three alternative conceptualizations. *Journal of Personality and Social Psychology, 62,* 804–812.

Roberts, J. V., & Edwards, D. (1989). Contextual effects in judgments of crimes, criminals, and the purposes of sentencing. *Journal of Applied Social Psychology, 19,* 902–917.

Roberts, J.V., & Doob, A.N. (1990). News media influences on public views of sentencing. *Law and Human Behavior, 14,* 451–468.

Robinson, L. A., Berman, J. S., & Neimeyer, R. A. (1990). Psychotherapy for the treatment of depression: A comprehensive review of controlled outcome research. *Psychological Bulletin, 108,* 30–49.

Robinson, R., Keltner, D., Ward, A., & Ross, L. (1995). Actual versus assumed differences in construal: "Naïve realism" in intergroup perception and conflict. *Journal of Personality and Social Psychology, 68,* 404–417.

Rodgers, J. L., Billy, J. O. B., & Udry, J. R. (1984). A model of friendship similarity in mildly deviant behaviors. *Journal of Applied Social Psychology, 14,* 413–425.

Rodgers, K. (1994). Wife assault in Canada. *Canadian Social Trends,* Autumn, 3–8.

Rodin, J., & Salovey, P. (1989). Health psychology. In M. R. Rosenzweig & L. W. Porter (Eds.), *Annual review of psychology* (Vol. 40, pp. 533–579). Palo Alto, CA: Annual Reviews.

Roese, N. J. (1997). Counterfactual thinking. *Psychological Bulletin, 121,* 133–148.

Roese, N.J., & Maniar, S.D. (1997). Perceptions of purple: Counterfactual hindsight judgments at Northwestern Wildcats football games. *Personality and Social Psychology Bulletin, 23,* 1245–1253.

Rogers, C. R. (1951). *Client-centered therapy.* Boston: Houghton Mifflin.

Rogers, C. R., & Dymond, R. F. (Eds.). (1954). *Psychotherapy and personality change.* Boston: Houghton Mifflin.

Rogers, M., Miller, N., Mayer, F. S., & Duvall, S. (1982). Personal responsibility and salience of the request for help: Determinants of the relations between negative affect and helping behavior. *Journal of Personality and Social Psychology, 43,* 956–970.

Rogers, R. W. (1980). Subjects' reactions to experimental deception. Unpublished manuscript, University of Alabama, Tuscaloosa.

Rogers, R. W., & Ketcher, C. M. (1979). Effects of anonymity and arousal on aggression. *Journal of Psychology, 102,* 13–19.

Rose, S. M. (1984). How friendships end: Patterns among young adults. *Journal of Social and Personal Relationships, 1,* 267–277.

Rosenbaum, M. E. (1986). The repulsion hypothesis: On the nondevelopment of relationships. *Journal of Personality and Social Psychology, 51,* 1156–1166.

Rosenbaum, M. E., & Levin, I. P. (1969). Impression formation as a function of source credibility and the polarity of information. *Journal of Personality and Social Psychology, 12,* 34–37.

Rosenberg, E. L., & Ekman, P. (1995). Conceptual and methodological issues in the judgment of facial expressions of emotion. *Motivation and Emotion*, 19, 111–138.

Rosenhan, D. L., Salovey, P., & Hargis, K. (1981). The joys of helping: Focus of attention mediates the impact of positive affect on altruism. *Journal of Personality and Social Psychology*, 40, 899–905.

Rosenthal, A. M. (1964). *Thirty-eight witnesses*. New York: McGraw-Hill.

Rosenthal, R., & Jacobson, L. (1968). *Pygmalion in the classroom: Teacher expectation and student intellectual development*. New York: Holt, Rinehart, & Winston.

Rosenzweig, J. M., & Daley, D. M. (1989). Dyadic adjustment/sexual satisfaction in women and men as a function of psychological sex role self-perception. *Journal of Sex and Marital Therapy*, 15, 42–56.

Ross, L. D. (1977). Problems in the interpretation of 'self-serving' assymetries in causal attribution: Comments on the Stephan et al. paper. *Sociometry*, 40, 112–114.

Ross, L., Lepper, M. R., & Hubbard, M. (1975). Perseverance in self-perception and social perception: Biased attributional processes in the debriefing paradigm. *Journal of Personality and Social Psychology*, 32, 880–892.

Rotenberg, K. J., & Korol, S. (1995). The role of loneliness and gender in individuals' love styles. *Journal of Social Behavior and Personality*, 10, 537–546.

Rothgerber, H. (1997). External intergroup threat as an antecedent to perceptions of in-group and out-group homogeneity. *Journal of Personality and Social Psychology*, 73, 1206–1212.

Rothman, A. J., & Hardin, C. D. (1997). Differential use of the availability heuristic in social judgment. *Personality and Social Psychology Bulletin*, 23, 123–138.

Rousseau, D.M. (1995). *Psychological contracts in organizations*. Thousand Oaks, CA: Sage.

Rowe, P. M. (1996, September). On the neurobiological basis of affiliation. *APS Observer*, 17–18.

Roy, M. P., Steptoe, A., & Kirschbaum, C. (1998). Life events and social support as moderators of individual differences in cardiovascular and cortisol reactivity. *Journal of Personality and Social Psychology*, 75, 1273–1281.

Rozin, P. & Nemeroff, C. (1990). The laws of sympathetic magic: A psychological analysis of similarity and contagion. In W. Stigler, R. A. Shweder, & G. Herdt (Eds.), *Cultural psychology: Essays in comparative human development* (pp. 205–232). Cambridge, England: Cambridge University Press.

Rozin, P., Lowery, L., & Ebert, R. (1994). Varieties of disgust faces and the structure of disgust. *Journal of Personality and Social Psychology*, 66, 870–881.

Rozin, P., Millman, L., & Nemeroff, C. (1986). Operation of the laws of sympathetic magic in disgust and other domains. *Journal of Personality and Social Psychology*, 50, 703–712.

Rubin, J. Z. (1985). Deceiving ourselves about deception: Comment on Smith and Richardson's "Amelioration of deception and harm in psychological research." *Journal of Personality and Social Psychology*, 48, 252–253.

Rubin, Z., Hill, C.T., Peplau, L.A., & Dunkel-Schetter, C. (1980). Self-disclosure in dating couples: Sex roles and the ethic of openness. *Journal of Marriage and the Family*, 42, 305–317.

Rudolph, D. L., & Kim, J. G. (1996). Mood responses to recreational sport and exercise in a Korean sample. *Journal of Social Behavior and Personality*, 11, 841–849.

Rule, B.G., & Ferguson, T.J. (1986). The effects of media violence on attitudes, emotions and cognitions. *Journal of Social Issues*, 2, 29–50.

Rule, B.G., & Nesdale, A.R. (1976). Emotional arousal and aggressive behavior. *Psychological Bulletin*, 83, 851–863.

Rule, B.G., & Well, G. L. (1981). Experimental social psychology in Canada: A look at the seventies. *Canadian Psychology*, 22, 69–84.

Rusbult, C. E. (1983). A longitudinal test of the investment model: The development (and deterioration) of satisfaction and commitment in heterosexual involvements. *Journal of Personality and Social Psychology*, 45, 101–117.

Rusbult, C. E. (1983). A longitudinal test of the investment model: The development (and deterioration) of satisfaction and commitment in heterosexual involvements. *Journal of Personality and Social Psychology*, 45, 101–117.

Rusbult, C. E., & Martz, J. M. (1995). Remaining in an abusive relationship: An investment model analysis of nonvoluntary dependence. *Personality and Social Psychology Bulletin*, 21, 558–571.

Rusbult, C. E., & Zembrodt, I. M. (1983). Responses to dissatisfaction in romantic involvements: A multidimensional scaling analysis. *Journal of Experimental Social Psychology*, 19, 274–293.

Rusbult, C. E., Martz, J. M., & Agnew, C. R. (1998). The Investment Model Scale: Measuring commitment level, satisfaction level, quality of alternatives, and investment size. *Personal Relationships*, 5, 467–484.

Rushton, J. P. (1989a). Genetic similarity, human altruism, and group selection. *Behavioral and Brain Sciences*, 12, 503–559.

Rushton, J. P. (1989b). Genetic similarity in male friendships. *Ethology and Sociobiology*, 10, 361–373

Rushton, J. P. (1990). Sir Francis Galton, epigenetic rules, genetic similarity theory, and human life-history analysis. *Journal of Personality*, 58, 117–140.

Rushton, J. P., Russell, R. J. H., & Wells, P. A. (1984). Genetic similarity theory: Beyond kin selection. *Behavior Genetics*, 14, 179–193.

Rushton, J.P. (1978). Urban density and altruism: Helping strangers in a Canadian city, suburb, and small town. *Psychological Reports*, 43, 987–990.

Russell, J. A. (1994). Is there universal recognition of emotionfrom facial expression? A review of the cross-cultural studies. *Psychological Bulletin*, 115, 102–141.

Sadalla, E. K., Sheets, V., & McCreath, H. (1990). The cognition of urban tempo. *Environment and Behavior*, 22, 230–254.

Sadker, M., & Sadker, D. (1994). *Failing at fairness: How America's schools cheat girls*. New York: Charles Scribners Sons.

Safir, M. P., Peres, Y., Lichtenstein, M., Hoch, Z., & Shepher, J. (1982). Psychological androgyny and sexual adequacy. *Journal of Sex and Marital Therapy*, 8, 228–240.

Sally, D. (1998). Conversation and cooperation in social dilemmas: A meta-analysis of experiments from 1958–1992. *Rationality and Society*.

Salovey, P. (1992). Mood-induced self-focused attention. *Journal of Personality and Social Psychology*, 62, 699–707.

Salovey, P., & Rodin, J. (1991). Provoking jealousy and envy: Domain relevance and self-esteem threat. *Journal of Social and Clinical Psychology*, 10, 395–413.

Salovey, P., Mayer, J. D., & Rosenhan, D. L. (1991). Mood and helping: Mood as a motivator of helping and helping as a regulator of mood. In M. S. Clark (Ed.), *Prosocial behavior* (pp. 215–237). Newbury Park, CA: Sage.

Sampson, E. E. (1991). *Social worlds, personal lives*. New York: Harcourt Brace Jovanovich.

Sanchez, J. I., & Fernandez, D. M. (1993). Acculturative stress among Hispanics: a bidimensional model of ethnic identification. *Journal of Applied Social Psychology*, 23, 654–668.

Sanders Thompson, V. L. (1988). A multi-faceted approach to racial identification. Unpublished doctoral dissert at ion, Duke University, Durham, NC.

Sanders Thompson, V. L. (1990). Factors affecting the level of African American identification. *Journal of Black Psychology*, 17, 14–23.

Sanders, G. S. (1983). An attentional process model of social facilitation. In A. Hare, H. Blumberg, V. Kent, and M. Davies (Eds.), *Small groups*. London: Wiley.

Sanna, L. J. (1997). Self-efficacy and counterfactual thinking: Up a creek with and without a paddle. *Personality and Social Psychology Bulletin*, 23, 654–666.

Sarason, I. G., Sarason, B. R., & Pierce, G. R. (1994). Social Support: Global and relationship-based levels of analysis. *Journal of Social and Personal Relationships*, 11, 295–312.

Sauvé, R. (1994). Borderlines: *What Canadians and Americans should—but don't—know about each other... a witty, punchy and personal look*. Toronto: McGraw-Hill.

Schachter, S. (1959). *The psychology of affiliation*. Stanford, CA: Stanford University Press.

Scher, S. J. (1997). Measuring the consequences of injustice. *Personality and Social Psychology Bulletin*, 23, 482–497.

Scherer, K. R. (1997). The role of culture in emotion-antecedent appraisal. *Journal of Personality and Social Psychology*, 73, 902–922.

Schleifer, S. J., Keller, S. E., Camerino, M., Thornton, J. C., & Stein, M. (1983). Suppression of lymphocyte function following bereavement. *Journal of the American Medical Association*, 250, 374–377.

Schlenker, B. R. (1980). *Impression management: The self-concept, social identity, and interpersonal relations*. Belmont, CA: Brooks/Cole.

Schlenker, B. R., Britt, T., Pennington, J., Murphy, R., & Doherty, K. (1994). The triangle model of responsibility. *Psychological Bulletin*, 101, 632–653.

Schneider, B. H. (1991). A comparison of skill-building and desensitization strategies for intervention with aggressive children. *Aggressive Behavior*, 17, 301–311.

Schooler, J. W., & Loftus, E. F. (1986). Individual differences and experimentation: Complementary approaches to interrogative suggestibility. *Social Behaviour*, 1, 105–112.

Schuster, E., & Elderton, E. M. (1906). The inheritance of psychical characters. *Biometrika*, 5, 460–469.

Schwartz, A. E. (1994, December 20). Americans on line seldom fond of disagreement. Albany Times Union, p. A–11.

Schwartz, S.H. (1992). The universal content and structure of values: Theoretical advances and empirical tests in 20 countries. In M. Zanna (Ed.), *Advances in experimental social psychology* (Vol. 25, pp. 1–65). New York: Academic Press.

Schwarz, N., Bless, H., Strack, F., Klumpp, G., Rittenauer-Schatka, G., & Simons, A. (1991b). Ease of retrieval as information: Another look at the availability heuristic. *Journal of Personality and Social Psychology*, 61, 195–202.

Schwarzer, R., Jerusalem, M., & Hahn, A. (1994). Unemployment, social support and health complaints: A longitudinal study of stress in East German refugees. *Journal of Community and Applied Social Psychology*, 4, 31–45.

Schwarzwald, J., Amir, Y,., & Crain, R. L. (1992). Long-term effects of school desegregation experiences on interpersonal relations in the Israeli defense forces. *Personality and Social Psychology Bulletin*, 18, 357–368.

Sears, D. O.(1988). Symbolic racism. In P. A. Katz and D. A. Taylor (Eds.), *Eliminating racism: Profiles in controversy* (pp. 53–84). New York: Plenum.

Sears, D.O. (1981). Life stage effects on attitude change, especially among the elederly. In S.B. Kiesler, J.N. Morgan & V.K. Oppenheimer (Eds.), *Aging: Social change* (pp.183–204). New York: Academic Press.

Sears, D.O. (1986). College sophomores in the laboratory: Influences of a narrow data base on social psychology's view of human nature. *Journal of Personality and Social Psychology*, 51, 515–530.

Sedikides, C. (1993). Assessment, enhancement, and verification determinants of the self-evaluation process. *Journal of Personality and Social Psychology*, 65, 317–338.

Sedikides, C. (1995). Central and peripheral self-conceptions are differentially influenced by mood: Test of the differential sensitivity hypothesis. *Journal of Personality and Social Psychology*, 69, 759–777.

Sedikides, C., & Skowronski, J. J. (1997). The symbolic self in evolutionary context. *Personality and Social Psychology Review*, 1, 80–102.

Segal, M. M. (1974). Alphabet and attraction: An unobtrusive measure of the effect of propinquity in a field setting. *Journal of Personality and Social Psychology*, 30, 654–657.

Segall, M.H., Dasen, P..R., Berry, J.W., & Poortinga, Y.H. (1999*). Human behavior in global perspective: An introduction to cross-cultural psychology*. Needham Heights, MA: Allyn & Bacon.

Segerstrom, S. C., Taylor, S. E., Kemeny, M. E., & Fahey, J. L. (1998). Optimism is associated with mood, coping, and immune change in response to stress. *Journal of Personality and Social Psychology*, 74, 1646–1655.

Selye, H. (1956). *The stress of life*. New York: McGraw-Hill.

Seta, C. E., Hayes, N. S., & Seta, J. J. (1994). Mood, memory and vigilance: The influence of distraction on recall and impression formation. *Personality and Social Psychology Bulletin*, 20, 170–177.

Seta, J. J., Seta, C. E., & Wong, M. A. (1991). Feelings of negativity and stress: An averaging summation analysis of impressions of negative life experiences. *Personality and Social Psychology Bulletin*, 17, 376–384.

Shapiro, D. L., Buttner, E. H., & Barry, B. (1995). Explanations: What factors enhance their perceived adequacy? Organizational Behavior and Human Decision *Processes*, 58, 346–358.

Shapiro, J. P., Baumeister, R. F., & Kessler, J. W. (1991). A three-component model of children's teasing: Aggression, humor, and ambiguity. *Journal of Social and Clinical Psychology*, 10, 459–472.

Sharpe, D., Adair, J. G., & Roese, N. J. (1992). Twenty years of deception research: A decline in subjects' trust? *Personality and Social Psychology Bulletin*, 18, 585–590.

Sharpsteen, D. J. (1995). The effects of relationship and self-esteem threats on the likelihood of romantic jealousy. *Journal of Social and Personal Relationships*, 12, 89–101.

Sharpsteen, D. J., & Kirkpatrick, L. A. (1997). Romantic jealousy and adult romantic attachment. *Journal of Personality and Social Psychology*, 72, 627–640.

Shaver, J. (1993, August). America's legal immigrants: Who they are and where they go. *Newsweek*, pp. 20–21.

Shaver, P. R., & Brennan, K. A. (1992). Attachment styles and the "big five" personality traits: Their connections with each other and with romantic relationship outcomes. *Personality and Social Psychology Bulletin*, 18, 536–545.

Shaver, P. R., Papalia, D., Clark, C. L., Koski, L. R., Tidwell, M. C., & Nalbone, D. (1996). Androgyny and attachment security: Two related models of optimal personality. *Personality and Social Psychology Bulletin*, 22, 582–597.

Shaw, J. I., Borough, H. W., & Fink, M. I. (1994). Perceived sexual orientation and helping behavior by males and females: The wrong number technique. *Journal of Psychology and Human Sexuality*, 6, 73–81.

Sheeran, P., & Abraham, C. (1994). Unemployment and self-conception: A symbolic interactionist analysis. *Journal of Community & Applied Social Psychology*, 4, 115–129.

Sher, J. (1983). *White hoods: Canada's Ku Klux Klan*. Vancouver: New Star Books.

Sherif, M. (1935). A study of some social factors in perception. *Archives of Psychology*, No. 187.

Sherif, M., Harvey, O. J., White, B. J., Hood, W. E., & Sherif, C. W. (1961). *Intergroup conflict and cooperation: The Robbers Cave experiment*. Norman, OK: Institute of Group Relations.

Sherman, J. W., & Klein, S. B. (1994). Development and representation of personality impressions. *Journal of Personality and Social Psychology*, 67, 972–983.

Sherman, M. D., & Thelen, M. H. (1996). Fear of intimacy scale: Validation and extension with adolescents. *Journal of Social and*

Sherman, S. J., Presson, C. C., & Chassin, L. (1984). Mechanisms underlying the false consensus effect: The special role of threats to the self. *Personality and Social Psychology Bulletin*, 10, 127–138.

Shestowsky, D., Wegener, D. T., & Fabrigar, L. R. (1998). Need for cognition and interpersonal influence: Individual differences in impact on dyadic decisions. *Journal of Personality and Social Psychology*, 74, 1317–1328.

Shigetomi, C. C., Hartmann, D. P., & Gelfand, D. M. (1981). Sex differences in children's altruistic behavior and reputations for helpfulness. *Developmental Psychology*, 17, 434–437.

Shinn, M., Morch, H., Robinson, P. E., & Neuner, R. A. (1993). Individual, group and agency strategies for coping with job stressors in residential child care programmes. *Journal of Community and Applied Social Psychology*, 3, 313–324.

Shotland, R. I., & Strau, M. K. (1976). Bystander response to an assault: When a man attacks a woman. *Journal of Personality and Social Psychology*, 34, 990–999.

Shotland, R. L., & Goodstein, L. (1983). Just because she doesn't want to doesn't mean its rape: An experimentally causal model of the perception of rape in a dating situation. *Social Psychology Quarterly*, 46, 220–232.

Shulman, S., Elicker, J., & Sroufe, L. A. (1994). Stages of friendship growth in preadolescence as related to attachment history. *Journal of Social and Personal Relationships*, 11, 341–361.

Shweder, R. A. (1990). Cultural psychology: What is it? In J. W. Stigler, R. A. Shweder, & G. Herdt (Eds.), *Cultural psychology: Essays on comparative development* (pp. 1–43). Cambridge: Cambridge University Press.

Shweder, R. A., & Sullivan, M. A. (1993). Cultural psychology: Who needs it? *Annual Review of Psychology*, 44, 497–523.

Sigall, H. (1997). Ethical considerations in social psychological research: Is the bogus pipeline a special case? *Journal of Applied Social Psychology*, 27, 574–581.

Sigelman, C. K., Thomas, D. B., Sigelman, L., & Ribich, F. D. (1986). Gender, physical attractiveness, and electability: An experimental invesigation of voter biases. *Journal of Applied Social Psychology*, 16, 229–248.

Sillars, A. L., Folwell, A. L., Hill, K. C., Maki, B. K., Hurst, A. P., & Casano, R. A. (1994). *Journal of Social and Personal Relationships*, 11, 611–617.

Silverman, T. (1999). The Internet and relational theory. *American Psychologist*, 54, 780–781.

Silverstein, R. (1994). Chronic identity diffusion in traumatized combat veterans. *Social Behavior and Personality*, 22, 69–80.

Simmons, C.H., von Kolke, A. & Shimizu, H. (1986). Attitudes toward romantic love among American, German and Japanese students. *Journal of Social Psychology*, 126, 327–336.

Simon, L., Greenberg, J., & Brehm, J. (1995). Trivialization: The forgotten mode of dissonance reduction. *Journal of Personality and Social Psychology*, 68, 247–260.

Simpson, J. A. (1987). The dissolution of romantic relationships: Factors involved in relationship stability and emotional stress. *Journal of Personality and Social Psychology*, 53, 683–692.

Simpson, J. A., & Gangestad, S. W. (1992). Sociosexuality and romantic partner choice. *Journal of Personality, 60,* 31–51.

Simpson, J. A., Ickes, W., & Blackstone, T. (1995). When the head protects the heart: Empathic accuracy in dating relationships. *Journal of Personality and Social Psychology, 69,* 629–641.

Singh, D. (1993). Adaptive significance of female physical attractiveness: Role of waist-to-hip ratio. *Journal of Personality and Social Psychology, 65,* 293–307.

Singh, D. (1995). Female judgment of male attractiveness and desirability for relationships: Role of waist-to-hip ratio and financial status. *Journal of Personality and Social Psychology, 69,* 1089–1101.

Singh, R., & Tan, L. S. C. (1992). Attitudes and attraction: A test of the similarity-attraction and dissimilarity-repulsion hypotheses. *British Journal of Social Psychology, 31,* 227–238.

Sinha, D. (1984). Community as the target: a new perspective to research on prosocial behavior. In E. Staub, D. Bar-Tal, J. Karlowski, & J. Reykowski (Eds.), *Development and maintenance of prosocial behavior.* New York: Plenum Press.

Sinha, D. (1988). Indigenisation of psychology in India and its relevance. *The Indian Journal of Social Science, 1,* 77–91.

Sinha, D. (1996). Cross-cultural psychology: The Asian scenario. In J. Pandey, D. Sinha, & D. P. S. Bhawuk (Eds.), *Asian contribution to cross-cultural psychology* (pp. 20–41). Thousand Oaks, CA: Sage.

Sivacek, J., & Crano, W. D. (1982). Vested interest as a moderator of attitude-behavior consistency. *Journal of Personality and Social Psychology, 43,* 210–221.

Skarlicki, D. P., & Folger, R. (1997). Retaliation in the workplace: The roles of distributive, procedural, and interactional justice. *Journal of Applied Psychology, 821,* 434–443.

Smeaton, G. (1998). STD risk in the eye of the beholder: The effects of physical attractiveness, body piercing, and social perceptions on judgments of STD risk. Unpublished manuscript, University of Wisconsin-Stout.

Smeaton, G., Byrne, D., & Murnen, S. K. (1989). The repulsion hypothesis revisited: Similarity irrelevance or dissimilarity bias? *Journal of Personality and Social Psychology, 56,* 54–59.

Smeaton, G., Rupp, D., Vig, C., & Byrne, D. (1995). The mediating role of similarity assumptions on the effects of attitude similarity and dissimilarity on attraction and repulsion. Unpublished manuscript, University of Wisconsin–Stout, Menomonie.

Smith, C. M., Tindale, R. S., & Dugoni, B. L. (1996). Minority and majority influence in freely interacting groups: Qualitative versus quantitative differences. *British Journal of Social Psychology, 35,* 137–149.

Smith, D. E., Gier, J. A., & Willis, F. N. (1982). Interpersonal touch and compliance with a marketing request. *Basic and Applied Social Psychology, 3,* 35–38.

Smith, E. R., & Zarate, M. A. (1992). Exemplar-based model of social judgment. *Psychological Review, 99,* 3–21.

Smith, E. R., Byrne, D., & Fielding, P. J. (1995). Interpersonal attraction as a function of extreme gender role adherence. *Personal Relationships, 2,* 161–172.

Smith, E. R., Byrne, D., Becker, M. A., & Przybyla, D. P. J. (1993). Sexual attitudes of males and females as predictors of interpersonal attraction and marital compatibility. *Journal of Applied Social Psychology, 23,* 1011–1034.

Smith, P. B., & Bond, N. H. (1998). *Social psychology across cultures,* 2nd ed. Boston: Allyn & Bacon.

Smith, R. E., Smoll, F. L., & Ptacek, J. T. (1990). Conjunctive moderator variables in vulnerability and resiliency research: Life stress, social support and coping skills, and adolescent sport injuries. *Journal of Personality and Social Psychology, 58,* 360–370.

Smith, R. H., Kim, S. H., & Parrott, W. G. (1988). Envy and jealousy: Semantic problems and experiential distinctions. *Personality and Social Psychology Bulletin, 14,* 401–409.

Smith, S. S., & Richardson, D. (1985). On deceiving ourselves about deception: Reply to Rubin. *Journal of Personality and Social Psychology, 48,* 254–255.

Smith, T. W., & Pope, M. K. (1990). Cynical hostility as a health risk: Current status and future directions. *Journal of Social Behavior and Personality, 5,* 77–88.

Smith, V. I., & Ellsworth, P. C. (1987). The social psychology of eyewitness accuracy: Misleading questions and communicator expertise. *Journal of Applied Psychology, 72,* 294–300.

Snell, W. E., Jr. (1998). The Relationship Awareness Scale: Measuring relational-consciousness, relational-monitoring, and relational-anxiety. *Contemporary Social Psychology, 18,* 23–49.

Sniffen, M. J. (1991, September 30). Blacks make up 40% of death row. *Albany Times Union,* p. A–3.

Snyder, C. R., & Endelman, J. R. (1979). Effects of degree of interpersonal similarity on physical distance and self-reported attraction: A comparison of uniqueness and reinforcement theory predictions. *Journal of Personality, 47,* 492–505.

Snyder, C. R., & Fromkin, H. L. (1980). *Uniqueness: The human pursuit of difference.* New York: Plenum.

Snyder, M. (1974). Self-monitoring of expressive behavior. *Journal of Personality and Social Psychology, 30,* 526–537.

Snyder, M., & Ickes, W. (1985). Personality and social behavior. In G. Lindzey & E. Aronson (Eds.), *The handbook of social psychology* (Vol. 1, 3rd ed., pp. 883–947). New York: Random House.

Snyder, M., & Simpson, J. A. (1984). Self-monitoring and dating relationships. *Journal of Personality and Social Psychology, 47,* 1281–1291.

Snyder, M., Gangestad, S., & Simpson, J. A. (1983). Choosing friends as activity partners: The role of self-monitoring. *Journal of Personality and Social Psychology, 45,* 1061–1072.

Snyder, M., Grether, J., & Keller, K. (1974). Staring and compliance: A field experiment on hitchhiking. *Journal of Applied Social Psychology, 4,* 165–170.

Solomon, R. C. (1981, October). The love lost in cliches. *Psychology Today,* pp. 83–85, 87–88.

Sorenson, K. A., Russell, S. M., Harkness, D. J., & Harvey, J. H. (1993). Account-making, confiding, and coping with the ending of a close relationship. *Journal of Social Behavior and Personality, 8,* 73–86.

Spencer, M. B., & Markstrom-Adams, C. (1990). Identity processes among racial and ethnic minority children in America. *Child Development*, 61, 290–310.

Sprafkin, J. N., Liebert, R. M., & Poulous, R. W. (1975). Effects of a prosocial televised example on children's helping. *Journal of Personality and Social Psychology*, 48, 35–46.

Stalling, R. (1992). Mood and pain: The influence of positive and negative affect on reported body aches. *Journal of Social Behavior and Personality*, 7, 323–334.

Stangor, C., & Ruble, D. N. (1989). Strength of expectancies and memory for social information: What we remember depends on how much we know. *Journal of Experimental Social Psychology*, 25, 18–35.

Staples, S. L. (1996). Human response to environmental noise: Psychological research and public policy. *American Psychologist*, 51, 143–150.

Stasser, G. (1992). Pooling of unshared information during group discussion. In S. Worchel, W. Wood, & J. H. Simpson (Eds.), *Process and productivity* (pp. 48–67). Newbury Park, CA: Sage.

Stasser, G., & Hinkle, S. (1994). *Research in progress*, Miami University, Oxford, Ohio.

Stasser, G., & Stewart, D. (1992). Discovery of hidden profiles by decision-making groups: Solving a problem versus making a judgment. *Journal of Personality and Social Psychology*, 63, 426–434.

Stasser, G., & Titus, W. (1985). Pooling of unshared information in group decision making: Biased information sampling during discussion. *Journal of Personality and Social Psychology*, 48, 1467–1478.

Stasser, G., & Titus, W. (1987). Effects of information load and percentage of shared information on the dissemination of unshared information during group discussion. *Journal of Personality and Social Psychology*, 55, 81–93.

Stasser, G., Taylor, L. A., & Hanna, C. (1989). Information sampling in structured and unstructured discussions of three- and six-person groups. *Journal of Personality and Social Psychology*, 57, 67–78.

Statistics Canada (1996). Earnings of men and women in 1995: Tables 1 & 5. In *The Labour force: Annual averages*. Ottawa, Ont.: Statistics Canada

Statistics Canada (1998). Criminal victimization: An international perspective. *Juristat*, 18 (6).

Statistics Canada (1999). *Annual demographic statistics, 1998*. Ottawa: Statistics Canada Catologue no. 91–213.

Statistics Canada (1999). *CANSIM Matrix 2*. Statistics Canada Web site:

Statistics Canada (1999). *Census families in private households by family structure, 1991 and 1996 Censuses*. Statistics Canada Web site:

Statistics Canada. (1999). *1996 Census Nation tables*. Statistics Canada Web site:

Steel, R. P., & Rentsch, J. R. (1997). The dispositional model of job attitudes revisited: Findings of a 10-year study. *Journal of Applied Psychology*, 82, 873–879.

Steele, C. M. (1988). The psychology of self-affirmation: Sustaining the integrity of the self. In L. Berkowitz (Ed.), *Advances in experimental social psychology* (pp. 261–302). Hillsdale, NJ: Erlbaum.

Steele, C. M. (1992, April). Race and the schooling of Black Americans. *The Atlantic Monthly*, 269(4), 68–78.

Steele, C. M. (1997). A threat in the air: How stereotypes shape the intellectual identities and performance of women and African-Americans. *American Psychologist*, 52, 613–629.

Steele, C. M., & Josephs, R. A. (1990). Alcohol myopia: Its prized and dangerous effects. *American Psychologist*, 45, 921–933.

Steele, C. M., & Lui, T. J. (1983). Dissonance processes as self-affirmation. *Journal of Personality and Social Psychology*, 45, 5–19.

Steele, C. M., Southwick, L., & Critchlow, B. (1981). Dissonance and alcohol: Drinking your troubles away. *Journal of Personality and Social Psychology*, 41, 831–846.

Steele, C. M., Spencer, S. J., & Lynch, M. (1993). Self-image resilience and dissonance: The role of affirmational resources. *Journal of Personality and Social Psychology*, 64, 885–896.

Steiner, I.D. (1974). Whatever happened to the group in social psychology? *Journal of Experimental Social Psychology*, 10, 94–108.

Stephan, W. G. (1985). Intergroup relations. In G. Lindzey & E. Aronson (Eds.), *Handbook of social psychology* (Vol. 2, pp. 599–658). New York: Random House.

Stephan, W. G., & Stephan, C. W. (1988). Emotional reactions to interracial achievement outcomes. *Journal of Applied Social Psychology*, 19, 608–621.

Sternberg, R. J. (1986). A triangular theory of love. *Psychological Review*, 93, 119–135.

Sternberg, R. J. (1988). Triangulating love. In R. J. Sternberg & M. L. Barnes (Eds.), *The psychology of love* (pp. 119–138). New Haven, CT: Yale University Press.

Sternberg, R. J. (1988a). *The triangle of love*. New York: Basic Books.

Stewart, J. E. (1980). Defendant's attractiveness as a factor in the outcome of criminal trials: An observational study. *Journal of Applied Social Psychology*, 10, 348–361.

Stice, E., & Shaw, H. E. (1994). Adverse effects of the media portrayed thin-ideal on women and linkages to bulimic symptomatology. *Journal of Social and Clinical Psychology*, 13, 288–308.

Stone, A. A., Cox, D., Valdimarsdotti, H., Jandorf, L., & Neale, J. M. (1987). Evidence that secretory IGA antibody is associated with daily mood. *Journal of Personality and Social Psychology*, 52, 988–993.

Stone, A. A., Neale, J. M., Cox, D. S., Napoli, A., Valdimarsdottir, H., & Kennedy-Moore, E. (1994). Daily events are associated with a secretory immune response to an oral antigen in men. *Health Psychology*, 13, 440–446.

Stone, J., Aronson, E., Crain, A. L., Winslow, M. P., T Fried, C. B. (1994). Inducing hypocrisy as a means of encouraging young adults to use condoms. *Personality and Social Psychology Bulletin*, 20, 116–128.

Stone, J., Wiegand, A. W., Cooper, J., & Aronson, E. (1997). When exemplification fails: Hypocrisy and the motives for self-integrity. *Journal of Personality and Social Psychology, 72,* 54–65.

Stotland, E. (1969). Exploratory investigations of empathy. *Advances in Experimental Social Psychology, 4,* 271–313.

Stradling, S. G., Crowe, G., & Tuohy, A. P. (1993). Changes in self-concept during occupational socialization of new recruits to the police. *Journal of Community & Applied Social Psychology, 3,* 131–147.

Strauman, T. J., Lemieux, A. M., & Coe, C. L. (1993). Self-discrepancy and natural killer cell activity: Immunological consequences of negative self-evaluation. *Journal of Personality and Social Psychology, 64,* 1042–1052.

Strauman, T.J. (1996). Stability within the self: A longitudinal study of the structural implications of self-discrepancy theory. *Journal of Personality and Social Psychology, 71,* 1142–1153.

Street, R. L., & Buller, D. B. (1987). Nonverbal response patterns in physician-patient interactions: A functional analysis. *Journal of Nonverbal Behavior, 11,* 234–253.

Street, R. L., Jr., & Buller, D. G. (1987). Nonverbal response patterns in physician-patient interactions: A functional analysis. *Journal of Nonverbal Behavior, 11,* 234–253.

Strickland, B. R. (1992). Women and depression. *Current Directions in Psychological Science, 1,* 132–135.

Strickland, L.H., Aboud, F.E., & Gergen, K.J. (Eds.). (1974). *Social psychology in transition.* New York: Plenum Press.

Stroessner, S. J., Hamilton, D. L., & Mackie, D. M. (1992). Affect and stereotyping: The effect of induced mood on distinctiveness-based illusory correlations. *Journal of Personality and Social Psychology, 62,* 564–576.

Strube, M. J. (1989). Evidence for the Type in Type A behavior: A taxonometric analysis. *Journal of Personality and Social Pychology, 56,* 972–987.

Strube, M., Turner, C. W., Cerro, D., Stevens, J., & Hinchey, F. (1984). Interpersonal aggression and the Type A coronary-prone behavior pattern: A theoretical distinction and practical implications. *Journal of Personality and Social Psychology, 47,* 839–847.

Suls, J., & Fletcher, B. (1985). The relative efficacy of avoidant and nonavoidant coping strategies: A meta-analysis. *Health Psychology, 4,* 249–288.

Suls, J., & Rosnow, J. (1988). Concerns about artifacts in behavioral research. In M. Morawski (Ed.), *The rise of experimentation in American psychology* (pp. 163–187). New Haven, CT: Yale University Press.

Suls, J., & Wan, C. K. (1989). The effects of sensory and procedural information on coping with stressful medical procedures and pain: A meta-analysis. *Journal of Consulting and Clinical Psychology, 57,* 372–379.

Suls, J., Wan, C. K., & Sanders, G. S. (1988). False consensus and false uniqueness in estimating the prevalence of health-protective behaviors. *Journal of Applied Social Psychology, 19,* 66–79.

Sunnafrank, M. (1992). On debunking the attitude similarity myth. *Communication Monographs, 59,* 165–179.

Sutton, C.D., & Moore, K.K. (1985). Probing opinions: Executive women 20 years later. *Harvard Business Review, 63* (5), 43–66.

Swann, W. B., Jr., & Gill, M. J. (1997). Confidence and accuracy in person perception: Do we know what we think we know about our relationship partners? *Journal of Personality and Social Psychology, 73,* 747–757.

Swann, W. B., Jr., Griffin, J. J., Jr., Predmore, S. C., & Gaines, B. (1987). Cognitive-affective crossfire: When self-consistency meets self-enhancement. *Journal of Personality and Social Psychology, 52,* 881–889.

Swap, W. C. (1977). Interpersonal attraction and repeated exposure to rewarders and punishers. *Personality and Social Psychology Bulletin, 3,* 248–251.

Swim, J. K., Aikin, K. J., Hall, W. S., & Hunter, B. A. (1995). Sexism and racism: Old-fashioned and modern prejudices. *Journal of Personality and Social Psychology, 68,* 199–214.

Tafarodi, R. W. (1998). Paradoxical self-esteem and selectivity in the processing of social information. *Journal of Personality and Social Psychology, 74,* 1181–1196.

Tafarodi, R. W., & Vu, C. (1997). Two-dimensional self-esteem and reactions to success and failure. *Personality and Social Psychology Bulletin, 23,* 626–635.

Tajfel, H. (1970). Experiments in intergroup discrimination. *Scientific American, 223* (5), 96–102.

Tajfel, H. (1978). *Differentiation between social groups: Studies in the social psychology of intergroup relations.* London: Academic Press.

Tajfel, H. (1982). *Social identity and intergroup relations.* Cambridge: Cambridge University Press.

Tajfel, H., & Turner, J.C. (1979). An integrative theory of intergroup conflict. In W.G. Austin & S. Worchel (Eds.), *The social psychology of intergroup relations* (pp. 33–47). Monterey, CA: Brooks/Cole.

Takata, T., & Hashimoto, H. (1973). Effects of insufficient justification upon the arousal of cognitive dissonance: Timing of justification and evaluation of task. *Japanese Journal of Experimental Social Psychology, 13,* 77–85.

Tan, D. T. Y., & Singh, R. (1995). Attitudes and attraction: A developmental study of the similarity-attraction and dissimilarity-repulsion hypotheses. *Personality and Social Psychology Bulletin, 21,* 975–986.

Tanaka-Matsumi, J., & Draguns, J. (1997). Culture and Psychopathy. In J.W. Berry, M.H. Segall, & C. Kagitcibasi (Eds.), *Handbook of cross-cultural psychology: Volume 3* (2nd ed.). Needham Heights, MA: Allyn & Bacon.

Tannen, D. (1994). *Talking from 9 to 5.* New York: William Morrow.

Tannen, D. (1995, January 9–15). And rarely the twain shall meet. *Washington Post National Weekly Edition 25.*

Tassinary, L. G., & Hansen, K. A. (1998). A critical test of the waist-to-hip ratio hypothesis of female physical attractiveness. *Psychological Science, 9,* 150–155.

Taylor, D.M., & Brown, R.J. (1979). Towards a more social social psychology? *British Journal of Social and Clinical Psychology*, 18, 173–180.

Taylor, D.M., & Gardner, R.C. (1969). Ethnic stereotypes: Their effects on the perception of communicators of varying credibility. *Canadian Journal of Psychology*, 23, 161–173.

Taylor, D.M., & McKirnan, D.J. (1984). A five-stage model of intergroup relations. *British Journal of Social Psychology*, 23, 291–300.

Taylor, D.M., & Moghaddam, F.M. (1994). *Theories of intergroup relations: International social psychological perspectives.* Second Edition.New York: Praeger.

Taylor, D.M., Wong-Rieger, D., McKirnan, D.J., & Bercusson, T. (1982). Social comparison in a group context. *Journal of Social Psychology*, 117, 257–259.

Taylor, D.M., Wright, S.C., Moghaddam, F.M., & Lalonde, R.N. (1990). *Personality and Social Psychology Bulletin*, 16, 254–262.

Taylor, S. E., & Brown, J. D. (1988). Illusion and well-being: A social psychological perspective on mental health. *Psychological Bulletin*, 103, 193–210.

Taylor, S. E., & Brown, J. D. (1994). "Illusion" of mental health does not explain positive illusions. *American Psychologist*, 49, 972–973.

Taylor, S. E., Buunk, B. P., & Aspinwall, L. G. (1990). Social comparison, stress, and coping. *Personality and Social Psychology Bulletin*, 16, 74–89.

Taylor, S. E., Helgeson, V. S., Reed, G. M., & Skokan, L. A. (1991). Self-generated feelings of control and adjustment to physical illness. *Journal of Social Issues*, 47, 91–109.

Taylor, S. E., Pham, L. B., Rivkin, I. D., & Armor, D. A. (1998). Harnessing the imagination: Mental stimulation, self-regulation, and coping. *American Psychologist*, 53, 429–439.

Taylor, S.E., & Armor, D.A. (1996). Positive illusions and coping with adversity. Journal of Personality, 64, 873–898.

Tedeschi, J. T., & Melburg, V. (1984). Impression management and influence in organizations. In S. B. Bacharach & E. J. Lawler (Eds.), *Research in the sociology of organizations* (Vol 3., pp. 31–58). Greenwich, CT: JAI Press.

Tedeschi, J. T., & Norman, N. M. (1985). A social psychological interpretation of displaced aggression. *Advances in Group Processes*, 2, 29–56.

Terry, R. L., & Krantz, J. H. (1993). Dimensions of trait attributions associated with eyeglasses, men's facial hair, and women's hair length. *Journal of Applied Social Psychology*, 23, 1757–1769.

Tesser, A. (1988). Toward a self-evaluation maintenance model of social behavior. In L. Berkowitz (Ed.), *Advances in experimental social psychology* (Vol. 21, pp.181–227). New York: Academic Press.

Tesser, A. (1993). On the importance of heritability in psychological research: The case of attitudes. *Psychological Review*, 100, 129–142.

Tesser, A., & Martin, L. (1996). The psychology of evaluation. In E. T. Higgins & A. W. Kruglanski (Eds.), *Social psychology: Handbook of basic principles* (pp. 400–423). New York: Guilford Press.

Tesser, A., Martin, L. L., & Cornell, D. P. (1996). On the substitutability of the self-protecting mechanisms. In P. Gollwitzer & J. Bargh (Eds.), *The psychology of action* (pp. 48–68). New York: Guilford.

Tetlock, P. E., Peterson, R. S., McGuire, C., Change, S., & Feld, P. (1992). Assessing political group dynamics: A test of the groupthink model. *Journal of Personality and Social Psychology*, 63, 403–425.

Tett, R. P., & Meyer, J. P. (1993). Job satisfaction, organizational commitment, turnover intention, and turnover: Path analyses based on meta-analytic findings. *Personnel Psychology*, 46, 259–293.

Thompson, D. (1992). The danger in doomsaying. *Time*, 139 (10), 61.

Thompson, J. K., & Tantleff, S. (1992). Female and male ratings of upper torso: Actual, ideal, and sterotypical conceptions. *Journal of Social Behavior and Personality*, 7, 345–354.

Thompson, L. (1998). *The mind and heart of the negotiator.* Upper Saddle River, NJ: Prentice-Hall.

Thompson, L., & Hastie, R. (1990). Social perception in negotiation. *Organizational Behavior and Human Decision Processes*, 47, 98–123.

Thompson, S. C., Nanni, C., & Levine, A. (1994). Primary versus secondary and central versus consequence-related control in HIV-positive men. *Journal of Personality and Social Psychology*, 67, 540–547.

Thompson, S. C., Sobolew-Shubin, A., Galbraith, M. E., Schwankovsky, L., & Cruzen, D. (1993). Maintaining perceptions of control: Finding perceived control in low-control circumstances. *Journal of Personality and Social Psychology*, 64, 293–304.

Thompson, W. C., Cowan, C. L., & Rosenhan, D. L. (1980). Focus of attention mediates the impact of negative affect on altruism. *Journal of Personality and Social Psychology*, 38, 291–300.

Tice, D. M., & Baumeister, R. F. (1997). Longitudinal study of procrastination, performance, stress, and health: The costs and benefits of dawdling. *Psychological Science*, 8, 454–458.

Tice, D. M., Butler, J. L., Muraven, M. B., & Stillwell, A. M. (1995). When modesty prevails: Differential favorability of self-presentation to friends and strangers. *Journal of Personality and Social Psychology*, 69, 1120–1138.

Tidwell, M.-C. O., Reis, H. T., & Shaver, P. R. (1996). Attachment, attractiveness, and social interaction: A diary study. *Journal of Personality and Social Psychology*, 71, 729–745.

Ting-Toomey, S. (1988). A face-negotiation theory. In Y Kim and W.B. Gudykunst (Eds.), *Theory in intercultural communication.* Newbury Park, CA: Sage.

Tjosvold, D. (1993). *Learning to manage conflict: Getting people to work together productively.* New York: Lexington.

Tjosvold, D., & De Dreu, C. (1997). Managing conflict in Dutch organizations: A test of the relevance of Deutsch's cooperation theory. *Journal of Applied Social Psychology*, 27, 2213–2227.

Toch, H. (1985). *Violent men* (rev. ed.). Cambridge, MA: Schenkman.

Tomaka, J., & Blascovich, J. (1994). Effects of justice beliefs on cognitive appraisal of and subjective, physiological, and behavioral responses to potential stress. *Journal of Personality and Social Psychology, 67*, 732–740.

Toobin, J. (1995b, July 17). *Putting it in black and white.* New Yorker, 31–34.

Tooley, V., Brigham, J. C., Maass, A., & Bothwell, R. K. (1987). Facial recognition: Weapon effect and attentional focus. *Journal of Applied Social Psychology, 17*, 845–859.

Tougas, F., Brown, R., Beaton, A.M., & Joly, S. (1995). Neo-sexism: Plus ca change, plus c'est pareil. *Personality and Social Psychology Bulletin, 21*, 842–849.

Tremblay, S. (1999*). Crime statistics in Canada, 1998.* Statistics Canada — Catalogue no. 85–002–XIE Vol. 19 no. 9

Triandis, H. C. (1990). Cross-cultural studies of individualism and collectivism. In J. Berman (Ed.), *Nebraska Symposium on Motivation*. Lincoln, NB: University of Nebraska Press.

Triandis, H. C. (1995). *Individualism and collectivism.* Boulder, CO: Westview Press.

Triandis, H.C. (1980). Introduction. In. H.C. Triandis & W.W. Lambert (Eds.) *Handbook of cross-cultural psychology, 1,* Perspectives. Boston: Allyn & Bacon.

Triandis, H.C. (1988). Cross-cultural contributions to theory in social psychology. In M.H. Bond (Ed.), *The cross-cultural challenge to social psychology.* Newbury Park, CA: Sage.

Triandis, H.C. (1989) The self and social behavior in different cultural contexts. *Psychological Review, 96,* 506–20.

Trinke, S. J., & Bartholomew, K. (1997). Hierarchies of attachment relationships in young adulthood. *Journal of Social and Personal Relationships, 14,* 603–625.

Trobst, K. K., Collins, R. L., & Embree, J. M. (1994). The role of emotion in social support provision: Gender, empathy, and expressions of distress. *Journal of Social and Personal Relationships, 11,* 45–62.

Trope, Y. (1986). Identification and inferential processes in dispositional attribution. *Psychological Review, 93,* 239–257.

Tucker, P., & Aron, A. (1993). Passionate love and marital satisfaction at key transition points in the family life cycle. *Journal of Social and Clinical Psychology, 12,* 135–147.

Turner, J. C., Hogg, M. A., Oakes, P. J., Reicher, S. D., & Wetherell, M. S. (1987). *Rediscovering the social group: A self-categorization theory.* Oxford, England: Blackwell.

Tversky, A., & Kahneman, D. (1973). Availability: A heuristic for judging frequency and probability. *Cognitive Psychology, 5,* 207–232.

Tversky, A., & Kahneman, D. (1982). Judgment under uncertainty: Heuristics and biases. In D. Kahnamen, P. Slovic, & A. Tversky (Eds.), *Judgment under uncertainty* (pp. 3–20). New York: Cambridge University Press.

Tyler, T. R. (1994). Psychological models of the justice motive: Antecedents of distributive and procedural justice. *Journal of Personality and Social Psychology, 67,* 850–863.

Tyler, T. R., & Lind, E. A. (1992). A relational model of authority in groups. In M. Zanna (Ed.), *Advances in experimental social psychology* (Vol. 27, 115–191). New York: Academic Press.

Tyler, T. R., & Smith, H. J. (1997). Social justice and social movements. In D. Gilbert, S. T. Firks, & G. Lindzey (Eds.), *Handbook of social psychology* (Vol. 2, 2nd edition, pp. 595–629. New York: McGraw-Hill.

Tyler, T. R., Boeckmann, R. J., Smith, H. J., & Huo, Y. J. (1997). *Social justice in a diverse society.* Boulder, CO: Westview.

U.S. Department of Labor. (1992). *Employment and earnings* (Vol. 39, No. 5: Table A–22). Washington, DC: U.S. Department of Labor.

Uchino, G. N., Kiecolt-Glaser, J. K., & Cacioppo, J. T. (1992). Age-related changes in cardiovascular response as a function of a chronic stressor and social support. *Journal of Personality and Social Psychology, 63,* 839–846.

Udry, J. R. (1980). Changes in the frequency of marital intercourse from panel data. *Archives of Sexual Behavior, 9,* 319–325.

Ullman, C. (1987). From sincerity to authenticity: Adolescents' view of the "true self." *Journal of Personality, 55,* 583–595.

Unger, R. K., & Crawford, M. (1993). Commentary: Sex and gender—The troubled relationship between terms and concepts. *Psychological Science, 4,* 122–124.

Ungerer, J. A., Dolby, R., Waters, B., Barnett, B., Kelk, N., & Lewin, V. (1990). The early development of empathy: Self-regulation and individual differences in the first year. *Motivation and Emotion, 14,* 93–106.

United Nations (1998). *International study on firearm regulation.* New York :United Nations.

Urbanski, L. (1992, May 21). Study uncovers traits people seek in friends. *The Evangelist,* p. 41

Vallone, R., Ross, L., & Lepper, M. (1985). Social status, cognitive alternatives, and intergroup relations. In H. Tajfel (Ed.), *Differentiation between social groups* (pp. 201–226). London: Academic Press.

Van den Bos, K., Vermunt, R., & Wilke, H. A. M. (1997). Procedural and distributive justice: What is fair depends more on what comes first than on what comes next. *Journal of Personality and Social Psychology, 72,* 94–104.

Van Dyne, L., & LePine, J. A. (1998). Helping and voice extra-role behaviors: Evidence of construct and predictive validity. *Academy of Management Journal, 41,* 108–119.

Van Goozen, S., Frijda, N., & de Poll, N. V. (1994). Anger and aggression in women: Influence of sports choice and testosterone administration. *Aggressive Behavior, 20,* 213–222.

Van Hook, E., & Higgins, E. T. (1988). Self-related problems beyond the self-concept: Motivational consequences of discrepant self-guides. *Journal of Personality and Social Psychology, 55,* 625–633.

Van Lange, P. A. M., & Kuhlman, M. D. (1994). Social value orientation and impressions of partner's honesty and intelligence: A test of the might versus morality effect. *Journal of Personality and Social Psychology, 67,* 126–141.

Van Lange, P. A. M., & Rusbult, C. E. (1995). My relationship is better than—and not as bad as—yours is: The perception of superiority in close relationships. *Personality and Social Psychology Bulletin, 21,* 32–44.

Vanman, E. J., Paul, B. Y., Ito, T. A., & Miller, N. (1997). The modern face of prejudice and structure features that moderate the effect of cooperation on affect. *Journal of Personality and Social Psychology*, 73, 941–959.

Vinokur, A., & Burnstein, E. (1974). Effects of partially shared persuasive arguments on group-induced shifts: A group problem-solving approach. *Journal of Personality and Social Psychology*, 29, 305–315.

Vogel, D. A., Lake, M. A., Evans, S., & Karraker, K. H. (1991). *Children's and adults' sex-stereotyped perceptions of infants*. Sex Roles, 24, 605–616.

Vonk, R. (1998). The slime effect: Suspicion and dislike of likeable behavior toward superiors. *Journal of Personality and Social Psychology*, 74, 849–864.

Vonk, R., & van Knippenberg, A. (1995). Processing attitude statements from in-group and out-group members: Effects of within-group and within-person inconsistencies on reading times. Journal of *Personality and Social Psychology*, 68, 215–227.

Vorauer, J. D., & Claude, S. D. (1998). Perceived versus actual transparency of goals in negotiation. *Personality and Social Psychology Bulletin*, 24, 371–385.

Vorauer, J.D., Main, K.J., & O'Connell, G.B. (1998). How do individuals expect to be viewed by members of lower status groups? Content and implications of meta-stereotypes. *Journal of Personality and Social Psychology*, 75, 917–937.

Waller, N. G., Koietin, B. A., Bouchard, T. J., Jr., Lykken, D. T., & Tellegen, A. (1990). Genetic and environmental influences on religious interests, attitudes, and values: A study of twins reared apart and together. *Psychological Science*, 1, 138–142.

Walmsley, D. J., & Lewis, G. J. (1989). The pace of pedestrian flows in cities. *Environment and Behavior*, 21, 123–150.

Walster, E., & Festinger, L. (1962). The effectiveness of "overheard" persuasive communication. *Journal of Abnormal and Social Psychology*, 65, 395–402.

Walster, E., Walster, G. W., Piliavin, J., & Schmidt, L. (1973). "Playing hard-to-get": Understanding an elusive phenomenon. *Journal of Personality and Social Psychology*, 26, 113–121.

Wan, K.C., & Bond, M.H. (1982). Chinese attributions for success and fialure under public and anonymous conditions of rating. *Acta Psychologica Taiwanica*, 24, 23–31.

Wanous, J. P., Reiches, A. E., & Hudy, M. J. (1997). Overall job satisfaction: How good are single-item measures? *Journal of Applied Psychology*, 82, 247–252.

Wardle, J., Bindra, R., Fairclough, B., & Westcombe, A. (1993). Culture and body image: Body perception and weight concern in young Asian and Caucasian British women. *Journal of Community & Applied Social Psychology*, 3, 173–181.

Waters, H. F., Block, D., Friday, C., & Gordon, J. (1993, July 12). Networks under the gun. *Newsweek*, 64–66.

Watts, B. L. (1982). Individual differences in circadian activity rhythms and their effects on roommate relationships. *Journal of Personality*, 50, 374–384.

Wayment, H. A., & Taylor, S. E. (1995). Self-evaluation processes: Motives, information use, and self-esteem. *Journal of Personality*, 63, 729–757.

Wayne, S. J., & Liden, R. C. (1995). Effects of impression management on performance ratings: a longitudinal study. *Academy of Managment Journal*, 38, 232–260.

Webbink, P. (1986). *The power of the eyes*. New York: Springer.

Webster, D.W., Vernick, J.S., Ludwig, J., & Lester, K.J. (1997). Flawed gun policy research could endanger public safety. *American Public Health*, 87, 918–921.

Wegner, D. M. (1992a). The premature demise of the solo experiment. *Personality and Social Psychology Bulletin*, 18, 504–508.

Wegner, D. M. (1992b). You can't always think what you want: Problems in the suppression of unwanted thoughts. In M. Zanna (Ed.), *Advances in experimental social psychology* (Vol. 25, pp. 193–225). San Diego, CA: Academic Press.

Wegner, D. M. (1994). Ironic processes of mental control. *Psychological Review*, 101, 34–54.

Wegner, D. M., & Gold, D. B. (1995). Fanning old flames: Emotional and cognitive effects of suppressing thoughts of a past relationship. *Journal of Personality and Social Psychology*, 68, 782–792.

Wegner, D. M., & Zanakos, S. (1994). Chronic thought suppression. *Journal of Personality*, 62, 615–640.

Weidner, G., Istvan, J., & McKnight, J. D. (1989). Clusters of behavioral coronary risk factors in employed women and men. *Journal of Applied Social Psychology*, 19, 468–480.

Weigel, F. H., Kim, E. L., & Frost, J. L. (1995). Race relations on prime time television reconsidered: Patterns of continuity and change. *Journal of Applied Social Psychology*, 25, 223–236.

Weigel, R. H., Loomis, J. S., & Soja, M. J. (1980). Race relations on prime time television. *Journal of Personality and Social Psychology*, 39, 884–893.

Weinberger, M., Hiner, S. L., & Tierney, W. M. (1987). In support of hassles as a measure of stress in predicting health outcomes. *Journal of Behavioral Medicine*, 16, 19–32.

Weiner, B. (1980). A cognitive (attribution) emotion-action model of motivated behavior: An analysis of judgments of help-giving. *Journal of Personality and Social Psychology*, 39, 186–200.

Weiner, B. (1985). An attributional theory of achievement motivation and emotion. *Psychological Review*, 92, 548–573.

Weiner, B. (1993). On sin versus sickness: A theory of perceived responsibility and social motivation. *American Psychologist*, 48, 957–965.

Weiner, B. (1995). *Judgments of responsibility: A foundation for a theory of social conduct*. New York: Guilford.

Weiner, B., Amirkhan, J., Folkes, V. S., & Verette, J. A. (1987). An attributional analysis of excuse giving: Studies of a naive theory of emotion. *Journal of Personality and Social Psychology*, 52, 316–324.

Weinstein, N. D. (1982). Unrealistic optimism about susceptibility to health problems. *Journal of Behavioral Medicine*, 5,

Weinstein, N. D. (1984), Why it won't happen to me: Perceptions of risk factors and susceptibility. *Health Psychology*, 3, 431–457.

Weldon, E., & Mustari, L. (1988). Felt dispensability in groups of coactors: The effects of shared responsibility and explicit anonymity on cognitive effort. *Organizational Behavior and Human Decision Processes*, 41, 330–351.

Wells, G. L. (1984). The psychology of lineup identification. *Journal of Applied Social Psychology*, 14, 89–103.

Wells, G. L. (1993). What do we know about eyewitness identification? *American Psychologist*, 48, 553–571.

Wells, G. L., & Luus C. A. E. (1990). Police lineups as experiments: Social methodology as a framework for properly conducted lineups. *Personality and Social Psychology Bulletin*, 16, 106–117.

Wells, G. L., Luus, C. A. E., & Windschitl, P. D. (1994). Maximizing the utility of eyewitness identification evidence. *Current Directions in Psychological Science*, 3, 194–197.

Wells, G. L., Wrightsman, L. S., & Miene, P. K. (1985). The timing of the defense opening statement: Don't wait until the evidence is in. *Journal of Applied Social Psychology*, 15, 758–772.

Wells, J. (1997). Stuck on the ladder: Not only is the glass ceiling still in place, but men and women have very different views of the problem. *Maclean's*, October 20, p. 60.

Werner, C. M., Altman, I., & Brown, B. B. (1992). A transactional approach to interpersonal relations: Physical environment, social context, and temporal qualities. *Journal of Social and Personal Relationships*, 9, 297–323.

West, S. G., & Brown, T. J. (1975). Physical attractiveness, the severity of the emergency, and helping: A field experiment and interpersonal simulation. *Journal of Experimental Social Psychology*, 11, 531–538.

Whaley, K. L., & Rubenstein, T. S. (1994). How toddlers "do" friendship: A descriptive analysis of naturally occurring friendships in a group child care setting. *Journal of Social and Personal Relationships*, 11, 383–400.

Wheeler, L. Reis, H. T. & Bond, M. H. (1989). Collectivism-individualism in everyday social life: The middle kingdom and the melting pot. *Journal of Personality and Social Psychology*, 57, 79–86.

Wheeler, L., & Kim, Y. (1997). What is beautiful is culturally good: The physical attractiveness stereotype has different content in collectivistic cultures. *Personality and Social Psychology Bulletin*, 23, 795–800.

Whisman, M. A., & Kwon, P. (1993). Life stress and dysphoria: The role of self-esteem and hopelessness. *Journal of Personality and Social Psychology*, 65, 1054–1060.

White, G. L., & Mullen, P. E. (1990). *Jealousy: Theory, research, and clinical strategies*. New York: Guilford.

White, R. K. (1977). Misperception in the Arab-Israeli conflict. *Journal of Social Issues*, 33, 190–221.

Whitley, B. E. Jr. (1993). Reliability and aspects of the construct validity of Sternberg's triangular love scale. *Journal of Social and Personal Relationships*, 10, 475–480.

Whitley, G. E., & Greenberg, M. S. (1986). The role of eyewitness confidence in juror perceptions of credibility. *Journal of Applied Social Psychology*, 16, 387–409.

Wicker, A. W. (1969). Attitudes versus actions: The relationship of verbal and overt behavioral responses to attitude objects. *Journal of Social Issues*, 25, 41–78.

Wiebe, D. J., & McCallum, D. M. (1986). Health practices and hardiness as mediators in the stress-illness relationship. *Health Psychology*, 5, 425–438.

Wiederman, M. W., & Allgeier, E. R. (1996). Expectations and attributions regarding extramarital sex among young married individuals. *Journal of Psychology & Human Sexuality*, 8, 21–35.

Wiener, Y., Muczyk, J. P., & Martin, H. J. (1992). Self-esteem and job involvement as moderators of the relationship between work satisfaction and well-being. *Journal of Social Behavior and Personality*, 7, 539–554.

Williams, D. E., & D'Alessandro, J. D. (1994). A comparison of three measures of androgyny and their relationship to psychological adjustment. *Journal of Social Behavior and Personality*, 9, 469–480.

Williams, K. B., Radefeld, P. A., Binning, J. F., & Suadk, J. R. (1993). When job candidates are "hard–" versus "easy-to-get": Effects of candidate availability on employment decisions. *Journal of Applied Social Psychology*, 23, 169–198.

Williams, K. D., & Karau, S. J. (1991). Social loafing and social compensation: The effects of expectations of co-worker performance. *Journal of Personality and Social Psychology*, 61, 570–581.

Williams, K., Harkins, S., & Latane, B. (1981). Identifiability as a deterrent to social loafing: Two cheering experiments. *Journal of Personality and Social Psychology*, 40, 303–311.

Williams, R. L. (1976). *Manual of directions for Williams awareness sentence completion*. St. Louis, MO: Robert L. Williams & Associates, Inc.

Williams, T. P., & & Sogon, S. (1984). Group composition and conforming behavior in Japanese students'. *Japanese Psychological Research*, 26, 231–4.

Williams, T.M. (Ed.) (1986). *The impact of television: a natural experiment in three communities*. New York: Academic Press.

Williamson, T. M. (1993). From interrogation to investigative interviewing: Strategic trends in police questioning. *Journal of Community and Applied Social Psychology*, 3, 89–99.

Wills, T. A., & DePaulo, B. M. (1991). Interpersonal analysis of the help-seeking process. In C. R. Snyder & D. R. Forsyth (Eds.), *Handbook of social and clinical psychology* (pp. 357–375). Elmsford, NY: Pergamon.

Wilson, D. W. (1981). Is helping a laughing matter? *Psychology*, 18, 6–9.

Wilson, E. O. (1975). *Sociobiology: The new synthesis*. Cambridge, MA: Harvard University Press.

Wilson, J. P., & Petruska, R. (1984). Motivation, model attributes, and prosocial behavior. *Journal of Personality and Social Psychology*, 46, 458–468.

Wilson, M.I., & Daly, M. (1985). Competitiveness, risk taking, and violence: The young male syndrome. *Ethology and Sociobiology*, 6, 59–73.

Wilson, T. D., & Klaaren, K. J. (1992). Effects of affective expectation on willingness to relive pleasant and unpleasant events. Unpublished data. Cited in Wilson, T. D., & Klaaren, K. J., "expectation whirl me round": The role of affective expectations in affective experience. In M. S. Clark (Ed.), *Emotion and social behavior* (pp. 1–31). Newbury Park, CA: Sage.

Wilson, T. D., & Kraft, D. (1993). Why do I love thee?: Effects of repeated introspections about a dating relationship on attitudes toward the relationship. *Personality and Social Psychology Bulletin*, 19, 409–418.

Wilson, T. D., & Schooler, J. (1991). Thinking too much: Introspection can reduce the quality of preferences and decisions. *Journal of Personality and Social Psychology*, 60, 181–192.

Wilson, T. D., Lisle, D. J., Kraft, D., & Wetzel, C G. (1989). Preferences as expectation-driven inferences: Effects of affective expectations on affective experience. *Journal of Personality and Social Psychology*, 56, 519–530.

Winett, R. A. (1998). Developing more effective health-behavior programs: Analyzing the epidemiological and biological bases for activity and exercise programs. *Applied & Preventive Psychology*, 7, 209–224.

Winquist, J. R., & Larson, J. R., Jr. (1998). Information pooling: When it impacts group decision making. *Journal of Personality and Social Psychology*, 74, 317–377.

Winstead, B. A., Derlega, V. J., Montgomery, M. J., & Pilkington, C. (1995). The quality of friendships at work and job satisfaction. *Journal of Social and Personal Relationships*, 12, 199–215.

Witte, E., & Davis, J. H. (Eds.). (1996). *Understanding group behavior: Consensual action by small groups*. Hillsdale, NJ: Erlbaum.

Wolf, S., & Bugaj, A. M. (1990). The social impact of courtroom witnesses. *Social Behaviour*, 5, 1–13.

Wolfe, S. (1985). Manifest and latent influence of majorities and minorities. *Journal of Personality and Social Psychology*, 48, 899–908.

Wolfgang, A. (1979). The teacher and nonverbal behavior in the multicultural classroom. In A. Wolfang (Ed.), *Nonverbal behavior: Applications and cultural implications*. New York: Academic Press.

Won-Doornink, M. (1985). Self-disclosure and reciprocity in conversation: A cross-national study. *Social Psychology Quarterly*, 48, 97–107.

Wood, W. (1982). Retrieval of attitude-relevant information from memory: Effects on susceptibility to persuasion on intrinsic motivation. *Journal of Personality and Social Psychology*, 42, 798–810.

Wood, W., Pool, G. J., Leck, K., & Purvis, D. (1996). Self-definition, defensive processing, and influence: The normative impact of majority and minority groups. *Journal of Personality and Social Psychology*, 71, 1181–1193.

Wood, W., Wong, F. Y., & Chachere, J. G. (1991). Effects of media violence on viewers' aggression in unconstrained social interaction. *Psychological Bulletin*, 109, 371–383.

Wortman, C. B., & Linsenmeier, J. A. W. (1977). Interpersonal attraction and techniques of ingratiation in organizational settings. In B. N. Staw & G. R. Salancik (Eds.), *New directions in organizational behavior* (pp. 133–178). Chicago: St. Clair Press.

Wright, M.J., & Myers, C.R. (Eds.) (1982). *History of academic psychology in Canada*. Toronto: Hogrefe.

Wright, P. H. (1984). Selfreferent motivation and the intrinsic quality of friendship. *Journal of Social and Personal Relationships*, 1, 115–130.

Wright, S. C., Aron, A., McLaughlin-Volpe, T., & Ropp, S. A. (1997). The extended contact effect: Knowledge of cross-group friendships and prejudice. *Journal of Personality and Social Psychology*, 73, 73–90.

Wright, S.C., Taylor, D.M., & Moghaddam, F.M. (1990). Responding to membership in a disadvantaged group: From acceptance to collective protest. *Journal of Personality and Social Psychology*, 58, 994–1003.

Wuensch, K. L., Castellow, W. A., & Moore, C. H. (1991). Effects of defendant attractiveness and type of crime on juridic judgment. *Journal of Social Behavior and Personality*, 6, 713–724.

Wyer, R. S. Jr., & Srull, T. K. (Eds.). (1994). *Handbook of social cognition* (2nd ed.) (Vol. 1). Hillsdale, NJ: Erlbaum.

Wyer, R. S., Jr., & Budesheim, T. L., Lambert, A. J., & Swan, S. (1994). Person memory judgment: Pragmatic influences on impressions formed in a social context. *Journal of Personality and Social Psychology*, 66, 254–267.

Yang, K.S. (1996). Psychological transformation of the Chinese people as a result of societal modernization. In M.H. Bond (Ed.), *The handbook of Chinese psychology*. Hong-Kong: Oxford University Press.

Yik, M. S. M., Bond, M. H., & Paulhus, D. L. (1998). Do Chinese self-enhance or self-efface? It's a matter of domain. *Personality and Social Psychology Bulletin*, 24, 399–406.

Yoshida, T. (1977). Effects of cognitive dissonance on task evaluation and task performance. *Japanese Journal of Psychology*, 48, 216–223.

Young, M.Y., & Gardner, R.C. (1990). Modes of acculturation and second language proficiency. *Canadian Journal of Behavioral Science*, 22, 59–71.

Yousif, Y., & Korte, C. (1995). Urbanization, culture, and helpfulness: Cross-cultural studies in England and the Sudan. *Journal of Cross-Cultural Psychology*, 26, 474–489.

Yovetich, N. A., & Rusbult, C. E. (1994). Accommodative behavior in close relationships: Exploring transformation of motivation. *Journal of Experimental Social Psychology*, 30, 138–164.

Yuille, J. C., & Cutshall, J. L. (1986). A case study of eyewitness memory of a crime. *Journal of Applied Psychology*, 71, 291–301.

Yuille, J. C., & Tollestrup, P. A. (1990). Some effects of alcohol on eyewitness memory. *Journal of Applied Psychology*, 75, 268–273.

Yukl, G. (1994). *Leadership in organizations*. Englewood Cliffs, NJ: Prentice-Hall.

Zaccaro, S. J., Foti, R. J., & Kenny, D. A. (1991). Self-monitoring and trait-based variance in leadership: An investigation of leader flexibility across multiple group situations. *Journal of Applied Psychology*, 76, 308–315.

Zachariah, R. (1996). Predictors of psychological well-being of women during pregnancy: Replication and extension. *Journal of Social Behavior and Personality*, 11, 127–140.

Zajonc, R. B. (1965). Social facilitation. *Science*, 149, 269–274.

Zajonc, R. B. (1968). Attitudinal effects of mere exposure. *Journal of Personality and Social Psychology Monograph Supplement*, 9, 1–27.

Zajonc, R. B., & McIntosh, D. N. (1992). Emotions research: Some promising questions and some questionable promises. *Psychological Science*, 3, 70–74.

Zajonc, R. B., & Sales, S. H. (1966). Social facilitation of dominant and subordinate responses. *Journal of Experimental Social Psychology*, 2, 160–168.

Zajonc, R. B., Adelmann, P. K., Murphy, S. T., & Niedenthal, P. M. (1987). Convergence in the physical appearance of spouses. *Motivation and Emotion*, 11, 335–346.

Zajonc, R. B., Heingartner, A., & Herman, E. M. (1969). Social enhancement and impairment of performance in the cockroach. *Journal of Personality and Social Psychology*, 13, 83–92.

Zammichieli, M. E., Gilroy, F. D., & Sherman, M. F. (1988). Relation between sex-role orientation and marital satisfaction. *Personality and Social Psychology Bulletin*, 14, 747–754.

Zanna, M. P., & Aziza, C. (1976). On the interaction of repression-sensitization and attention in resolving cognitive dissonance. *Journal of Personality and Social Psychology*, 44, 577–593.

Zdaniuk, B., & Levine, J. M. (1996). Anticipated interaction and thought generation: The role of faction size. *British Journal of Social Psychology*, 35, 201–218.

Zebrowitz, L. A. (1997). *Reading faces*. Boulder, CO: Westview Press.

Zebrowitz, L. A., & Collins, M. A. (1997). Accurate social perception at zero acquaintance: The affordances of a Gibsonian approach. *Personality and Social Psychology Review*, 1, 204–223.

Zeitz, G. (1990). Age and work satisfaction in a government agency: A situational perspective. *Human Relations*, 43, 419–438.

Ziller, R. C. (1990). *Photographing the self: Methods for observing personal orientations*. Newbury Park, CA: Sage.

Zillmann, D. (1979). *Hostility and aggression*. Hillsdale, NJ: Erlbaum.

Zillmann, D. (1983). Transfer of excitation in emotional behavior. In J. T. Cacioppo & R. E. Petty (Eds.), *Social psychophysiology: A sourcebook* (pp. 215–240). New York: Guilford Press.

Zillmann, D. (1984). *Connections between sex and aggression*. Hillsdale, NJ: Erlbaum.

Zillmann, D. (1988). Cognition-excitation interdependencies in aggressive behavior. *Aggressive Behavior*, 14, 51–64.

Zillmann, D. (1993). Mental control of angry aggression. In D. M. Wegner & J. W. Pennebaker (Eds.), *Handbook of mental control*. Englewood Cliffs, NJ: Prentice-Hall.

Zillmann, D. (1994). Cognition-excitation interdependencies in the escalation of anger and angry aggression. In M. Potegal & J. F. Knutson (Eds.), *The dynamics of aggression*. Hillsdale, NJ: Erlbaum.

Zillmann, D., Rockwell, S., Schweitzer, K., & Sundar, S. S. (1993). Does humor facilitate coping with physical discomfort? *Motivation and Emotion*, 17, 1–21.

Zimbardo, P. G. (1977). Shyness: What it is and what we can do about it. *Reading*, MA: Addison-Wesley.

Zuber, J. A., Crott, H. W., & Werner, J. (1992). Choice shift and group polarization: An analysis of the status of arguments and social decision schemes. *Journal of Personality and Social Psychology*, 62, 50–61.

Zusne, L., & Jones, W. H. (1989). *Anomalistic psychology: A study of magical thinking* (2nd ed.). Hillsdale, NJ: Erlbaum.

Name Index

Devine, P. G., 110, 111
Dickinson, P., 235
Diehl, M., 234
Diekman, K. A., 366
Diener, E., 208, 380
Dijkstra, P., 243
Dindia, K., 220
Dineen, 404
Dion, K. I., 208
Dion, K. K., 9, 29, 208, 209, 228, 229, 230
Dion, K. L., 9, 29, 185, 209, 228, 229, 230
Ditto, P. H., 107, 108, 127
Dixon, T. M., 132
Dodge, K. A., 320
Dollard, J., 172, 313, 315, 328
Dona, G., 145
Donahue, E. M., 122, 126
Donnerstein, E., 328
Donnerstein, M., 328
Doob, Anthony N., 33, 398
Dovidio, J. F., 98, 178, 179, 194, 196, 213, 214, 305
Downey, J. L., 213
Draguns, J., 148
Drake, M. F., 268
Drigotas, S. M., 245
Driscoll, R., 228
Driver, B. L., 96
Drumm, P., 227
Dubé–Simard, L., 186
Dubro, A., 357
Duck, J. M., 108
Duck, S., 222, 246
Duffy, S.M., 226
Dugoni, B. L., 265
Duncan, N. C., 209
Dunkel-Schetter, C., 220
Dunning, D., 148, 178, 405
Durso, F. T., 178
Dutton, D. G., 33, 228, 242
Dutton, Don, 212–213
Dutton, K. A., 127
Duval, S., 132
Dymond, R. F., 129

E

Eagly, A. H., 27, 86, 102, 165, 166, 168, 261
Earley, P. C., 346
Early, S., 303
Earn, B., 31, 33
Earn, B. M., 185
Easterbrook, G., 377
Ebert, R., 42
Edwards, D., 398
Ee, J. S., 209
Egbert, J. M. Jr., 406
Eggleston, T. J., 113
Eisenman, R., 224
Eisenstadt, D., 129

Ekman, P., 42, 43, 48, 49
Elderton, E. M., 238
Elicker, J., 235
Elizabeth I, Queen of England, 391
Elliot, A. J., 110, 111
Ellison, J., 235
Ellsworth, P. C., 45, 402, 403
Embree, J. M., 304
Emmons, R. A., 384
Endelman, J. R., 264
Epley, N., 22
Epstein, S., 74
Erber, R., 78, 213
Erickson, G. A., 136
Eron, L. D., 323
Esses, Victoria M., 89, 127, 180, 300, 406
Estrada, C. A., 78
Ethier, K. A., 144
Evans, G. W., 379
Evans, M. C., 205
Evans, N., 178
Evans, S., 139

F

Fabrigar, L. R., 222, 277
Falconer, J. J., 142
Farnsworth, C. H., 398
Farrell, A. D., 242
Fazio, R. H., 85, 95, 97, 98, 112
Fedor, D. P., 390
Fein, S., 175, 196
Feingold, A., 29, 143, 207, 208, 406
Feldman, S. S., 240
Felmlee, D. H., 241, 242
Fenigstein, A., 132
Fernandez, D. M., 145
Ferris, 268
Ferris, J. R., 269
Feshbach, S., 313, 328
Festinger, Leon, 23, 24, 89, 109, 113, 205, 217, 223, 340
Fetzer, B. K., 71
Fiedler, K., 79
Fielding, P. J., 224
Findlay, C., 230
Finger, K., 404
Fink, M. I., 298
Finn, J., 142
Fischer, G. J., 63
Fischer, G. W., 174
Fishbein, M., 95, 97
Fisher, H., 165
Fisher, J. D., 47
Fiske, A. P., 296
Fiske, S. T., 64, 65, 66, 132, 146, 161
Fitzgerald, J., 288
Fletcher, B., 385
Flett, G. L., 142

Florian, V., 383
Floyd, K., 234, 235, 237
Flynn, H. A., 128
Foden, B. I. M., 152
Folger, R., 27, 322, 367
Folkes, V., 51, 62
Fong, G. T., 378
Foot, D. K., 91, 311
Forgas, J. P., 65, 77, 78, 79, 213, 223, 275, 296
Forge, K. L., 305
Forston, M. T., 142
Forsyth, D. R., 24
Forsythe, S., 268
Foss, M. A., 9
Foster-Fishman, P. G., 349
Foti, R. J., 392
Fourment, C., 205
Fraczek, A., 326
Frame, C. L., 208
Francis, Charlie, 53
Frank, M. G., 58, 59
Frank, R. A., 404
Franklin, M., 207
Franz, T. M., 349
Fraser, S. C., 271
Fredrickson, B. L., 235
Freedman, J. L., 271
Freud, Sigmund, 265, 309
Fricko, 387
Fried, C., 112, 113
Friedman, H. S., 380
Friesen, W. V., 42, 48
Frieze, I. H., 230, 240
Frijda, N., 312
Fromkin, H. L., 264
Frost, J. L., 177
Frost, P. J., 394
Fry, D. P., 326
Fry, P. S., 61
Fry, W. R., 367
Fujisawa, T., 396
Fujita, F., 208
Fukushima, O., 364
Funder, D. C., 128

G

Gabor, T., 399, 400
Gabriel, M. T., 209
Gaertner, S. L., 194, 196, 214
Gaines, S. O. Jr., 235
Galbraith, John Kenneth, 263
Galileo, 265
Gallup, 121
Galton, Sir Francis, 223
Gamble, W. C., 384
Gangestad, S. W., 133, 134, 135
Ganley, R., 224
Gao, G., 220
Garcia, L. T., 141
Gardner, 197
Gardner, P., 169

Gardner, R. C., 24, 180, 376
Gartner, 398
Gavanski, I., 73
Geddes, D., 321
Geen, R. G., 282, 287, 323, 328, 329, 344
Geertz, C., 145
Geffner, R., 192
Geis, D., 168
Gelfand, D. M., 305
Gelfand, D. N., 316
Genesee, F., 375, 376
Genovese, Catherine (Kitty), 288–290
Gentile, D. A., 137
George, J. M., 40, 93, 392
George, M. S., 213
Gerard, H. B., 256, 258
Gergen, K. J., 25
Gerhart, B., 388
Gerrard, M., 127
Gerton, J., 145
Ghosh, R., 61
Gibbons, F. X., 113, 127
Gier, J. A., 47
Gifford, R., 47
Gigone, D., 349, 353
Gilbert, D., 58
Gilbert, D. T., 51, 58
Gilbert, L. A., 240
Giles, H., 50
Gill, M. J., 226
Gillen, B., 208
Gilovich, T., 58, 59, 73
Gilroy, F. D., 141
Giner–Sorolla, R., 108
Ginsburg, B., 296
Ginzberg, E., 164
Gladue, B., 318
Glass, D. C., 318, 377
Glass Ceiling Commission, 167
Gleicher, F., 73
Goethals, 351
Gold, D. B., 75
Gold, J. A., 225
Goldstein, A. G., 403
Goldstein, M. D., 213
Goleman, D., 382
Goodstein, L., 63
Goodwin, R., 220, 230
Gordin, F. M., 162
Gordon, R. A., 275
Gottman, J. M., 243
Graham, B., 51, 62
Graham, J. L., 50
Graham, S., 56, 407
Gray, P., 228
Graziano, W. G., 135, 208, 242
Green, L. R., 325
Greenbaum, P., 45
Greenberg, J., 27, 59, 111, 129,

315, 322, 329, 336, 365, 366, 367, 368, 386
Greenberg, M. A., 384
Greenberg, M. D., 142
Greenberg, M. S., 403
Greenwald, A. G., 85
Greenwald, J., 377
Grether, J., 305
Gretzky, Wayne, 101
Griffin, D., 19, 20, 256
Griffin, D. W., 226, 233, 262, 263
Griffin, J., 127
Griffin, K. W., 385
Griffitt, W., 228
Groff, D. B., 345
Groom, R. W., 10, 14
Grossman, M., 143
Grote, N. K., 230, 240
Grusec, J. E., 303
Grzelak, A.L., 225
Gudjonsson, G. H., 397, 401, 402
Gudykunst, W.B., 220
Guerrero, L. K., 243
Guild, W., 307
Guimond, S., 60, 61, 186
Gur, R. C., 143
Guydish, J. N., 305

H
Hackel, L. S., 240
Hagborg, W. J., 142
Hahn, A., 379
Haines, S. C., 340
Hair, E. C., 242
Hall, W. S., 162
Hamilton, D. L., 180, 181
Hamilton, G. V., 282
Hamilton, J. C., 142
Hamilton, P. A., 214
Hamilton, V. L., 260
Han, S–P., 104
Hanna, C., 350, 353
Hanna, R., 208
Hansen, C. H., 43
Hansen, J. S., 213
Hansen, K. A., 9, 207
Hansen, R. D., 43, 53
Hanson, E., 77
Hardin, C. D., 71
Hare, R., 303
Hargis, K., 297
Harkins, S., 346, 347, 348
Harre, R., 25
Harrigan, J. A., 45
Harris, M. B., 312, 324
Harris, M. J., 196
Harrison, A. A., 208
Harrison, B., 375
Hartman, 85

Hartmann, D. P., 305, 316
Harvey, J. H., 53, 241
Hashimoto, H., 114
Hashimoto, T., 230
Hastie, R., 349, 353, 362
Hatfield, E., 207, 209, 221, 227, 228, 229, 230, 246
Haupt, A. L., 128
Haward, 397
Hawley, P. H., 380
Hayden, S. R., 305
Hayes, N. S., 77
Hazan, C., 232
Health Canada, 377
Heatherton, T. E., 143
Hebl, M. R., 143
Heffner, T. S., 122
Heider, F., 51, 223
Heider, K., 48
Heilman, D. E., 165
Heine, S. J., 29, 60, 72, 147, 148, 152
Heine, Steve, 114–115
Heingartner, A., 344
Helmreich, 395
Helson, R., 240
Hemenway, D., 400
Henderson, J., 407
Henderson–King, E., 176
Hendrick, C., 227, 230, 231
Hendrick, S. S., 227, 230, 231
Henkemeyer, L., 240
Henry, 162
Henry, F., 164, 191
Henry, W. A. III, 397
Hensley, W. E., 230
Hepworth, J. T., 173
Herbener, E. S., 230, 239
Herman, E. M., 344
Hershberger, S. L., 92, 93
Hewstone, M., 174, 175
Higgins, E. T., 122, 123, 124, 129, 178, 240
Hilgard, E. R., 327
Hill, C. A., 216, 219, 227
Hill, C. T., 220
Hiner, S. L., 379
Hinkle, S., 354
Hinkley, K., 125
Hinsz, V. B., 352
Hirt, E. R., 136
Hitler, Adolf, 394
Hixon, J. G., 132
Hjelt-Back, M., 325
Hobfoll, 379
Hodge, D., 404
Hofstede, G., 29, 33, 91, 152, 395
Hogg, M. A., 108, 224, 340
Hokanson, J. E., 128
Holahan, C. J., 384

Holmes, J. G., 226, 234
Holtgraves, Thomas, 49, 50
Homer, P. M., 91
Homolka, Karla, 397–398
Horowitz, L.M., 233
Hosch, H. M., 403
House, R. J., 392, 393, 394
Hovland, Carl I., 100, 101, 171, 172–173
Howard, G. S., 273
Howell, 393, 395
Howell, J. M., 394
Howells, G. N., 135
Hoyle, R. H., 133, 222
Hozworth, D. W., 224
Huang, I.–C., 129
Hubbard, C., 77
Hudy, M. J., 386
Huesmann, L. R., 323
Huff, C., 22
Hughes, C. F., 384
Humphreys, L. G., 404
Humphriss, N., 217
Hunsberger, 301
Hunt, J. P., 129
Hunter, B. A., 162
Hunter, C. E., 162
Huo, Y. J., 364
Hutcherson, H. W., 53
Hyde, J. S., 29
Hygge, S., 379
Hyman, L. M., 46

I
Iavnieli, D., 241
Ickes, W., 95, 133, 134, 226
Insel, T. R., 229
Insko, C. A., 262
Isen, A. M., 77, 78, 214, 296, 297
Israel, J., 25
Istvan, J., 228, 380
Ito, T. A., 86
Izard, C., 42

J
Jackson, L. A., 169
Jackson, Lynne M., 300
Jackson, T. T., 305
Jacobi, L., 207
Jacobson, Lenore, 66–67
Jaffe, K., 242
Jalil, M., 403
James, K., 387
James, W., 121, 126
James, William, 122, 135
Jamieson, D. W., 234
Janis, I. L., 100, 353
Janoff–Bulman, R., 124, 169
Jemmott, J. B. III, 244, 380
Jensen–Campbell, L. A., 242
Jerusalem, M., 379

Jessor, R., 381
Jex, S. M., 128
Johns, G., 386
Johnson, 208, 245, 406
Johnson, A. M., 225
Johnson, B. T., 27, 106, 113
Johnson, Ben, 53
Johnson, C., 180
Johnson, M. K., 20
Johnson, P., 50
Johnston, C. T., 214
Johnston, V. S., 207
Johnstone, B., 208
Joiner, T. E. Jr., 224, 380
Joinson, 236
Jolibert, A.J.P., 174
Joly, S., 33, 162, 165, 168
Jones, E. E., 51, 58, 59
Jones, M., 135
Jones, W. H., 71, 243
Josephs, R. A., 378
Jourard, S.M., 220
Judd, C. M., 161, 174, 178
Judge, T. A., 389
Jussim, L., 225

K
Kacmar, K. M., 269
Kagan, 140
Kagitcibasi, C., 150
Kahle, L., 91
Kahn, W., 165, 166
Kahneman, D., 69, 72, 73
Kalichman, S. C., 230
Kalick, S. M., 207, 209
Kalin, R., 31, 189, 190, 191, 197
Kallen, Evelyn, 164
Kallgren, C. A., 256, 258, 259
Kalma, A. P., 318
Kambara, T., 319
Kameda, M., 329
Kameda, T., 353
Kandel, D. B., 224
Kaplan, 395
Kaplan, M. F., 214, 350
Karabenick, S. A., 305
Karasawa, M., 148
Karau, S. J., 346, 347, 348
Karraker, K. H., 139
Karuza, J., 367
Kashima, Y., 61
Kashy, D. A., 234
Kassin, S. M., 148, 403
Katz, I. M., 384
Kaufman-Gilliland, C. M., 357, 359
Kaukiainen, A., 29
Kawakami, K., 179
Kedia, 395
Keelan, J. P., 209
Keller, 227

Subject Index

emotion-focused, 382
illness and medical treatment, 384–385
perceived control, 385
problem-faced, 382
social support, 382—384
strategies, 382
with stress, 381–385
correlation, 12–14
correlational method, 13
correlational research, 17
correspondence bias. *See* fundamental attribution error
correspondent inference theory, 51–52
counselling interrogation style, 402
counterfactual thinking, 72–74
courtesy, 390
covert institutional racism, 163–164
crimes of passion, 317–318
cross-cultural psychology, 12, 149–153
defined, 149
ethnocentrism, 149–150
etic *vs.* emic, 150
indigenous psychology, 150
cross-cultural research
development of, 151–153
indigenisation, 152
individualism-collectivism value dimension, 151–152
positive stereotypes about attractiveness, 208
self-enhancing biases, 72
cross-racial facial identification, 182
cultural diversity, 8, 10–11, 27–29
see also cross-cultural psychology
attribution styles, 60–61
vs. biology, 30
Canadian culture, 31–33
cognitive dissonance, 114–115
collectivism, 29
and conformity, 260–261
display rules, 48–49
emblems, 46
feelings, 48–50
individualism, 29
influences on self, 145–146
intergroup friendships, 191–193
leadership, 395–396
obedience, 279
passionate love, 229–230
prosocial behaviour, 306–308
and self-disclosure, 220–221
and social identity, 143–148
social support, 384
cultural mosaic, 31, 92

cultural norms, 10, 48
cultural styles of attribution, 60–61
cultural values
attitude formation, 90–92
and attitude formation, 90–92
and leadership, 395
and persuasion cues, 104–105
culture, 10
acculturative stress, 144–145
and aggression, 326
and conflict, 364–365
defined, 143–144
ethnic identity, 144–145
passionate love, 227–228
self-enhancing biases, 146–148
culture-biased findings, 25

D

deadline technique, 275
death wish, 309
debriefing, 22
deception, 22–23
decision/commitment, 231
decision making, 27, 349–354
defendant
attractiveness effect, 406
characteristics of, 406–407
ethnicity of, 407
gender of, 406
race of, 407
socio-economic status, 406
dependent variable, 15
depersonalized attraction, 340
depression, and attribution, 62
descriptive methods, 12
descriptive norms, 258–260
desensitization effects, 324
destructive criticism, 360
destructive obedience, 277–279
authority figures, 280–281, 282
restricting effects of, 282
social psychological basis, 280–281
deterrent effect of gun availability, 399–400
diffusion of responsibility, 289, 347
directive-permissive dimension, 392
discounting principle, 55–56
discrimination
see also prejudice
covert institutional racism, 163–164
defined, 160
modern racism, 162–163
neosexism, 165–169
prejudice in action, 162
disease. *See* illness
disease-prone personalities, 380
displaced aggression, 329
display rules, 48–49

dissonance. *See* cognitive dissonance
distinctiveness, 52
distinctiveness-based illusory correlations, 180–181
distraction-conflict theory, 345–346
distributive justice, 366, 368
diversity. *See* cultural diversity
divorce, 246
dominant interrogation style, 402
door-in-the-face technique, 272
downward counterfactual thinking, 73
drive theories of aggression, 312–313
drive theory of social facilitation, 343–344
Dubin Inquiry, 53, 54

E

early approach to persuasion, 100
ecological variables, 8, 10
ego-threat, 319
egocentrism, 149
elaboration likelihood model (of persuasion), 102–104
emblems, 46
emic, 150
emotion, and aggression, 316–318
emotion-focused coping, 382
emotional influences on prosocial behaviour, 296–297
empathy, 303–304
encoding process, 66
equal pay, 166
ethics, 18, 22–23
ethnic identity, 144–145
ethnicity of defendants, 407
ethnocentrism, 149–150
Ethnocentrism Scale, 149
etic, 150
evaluation apprehension, 344
evolutionary perspective
affective component of empathy, 303
aggression, 309–310
genetic determinism model, 295–296
jealousy, 243
passionate love, 228–229
evolutionary social psychology, 9, 29–30
excitation transfer theory, 316
expectancy, 347
expectancy-valence theory, 347
expectations, 79–80
experimental method. *See* experimentation
experimentation, 14–17, 18
basic nature of, 15
careful measurement of effects, 15

confounding, 16, 18
constancy of extraneous factors, 16
dependent variable, 15
explanation, 14
independent variable, 15
longitudinal procedures, 323
random assignment of participants to experimental conditions, 16
short-term laboratory, 323
systematic alteration of variable, 15
extended contact hypothesis, 192–193
external validity, 18
extrapunitive response, 184
eyewitness, 403–405
accuracy, 403–404
blank-lineup control, 404–405
increasing accuracy of, 404–405
memory, 403–404
perseverance effect, 404
repressed memory, 404

F

face-in-the-crowd-effect, 43
facial expressions, 42–44
failure to share information, 353–354
fairness heuristics, 368
false consensus effect, 69–70
family relationships, 237–240
faulty attributions, 360
faulty communication, 360
field research, 12
field theory, 23
fighting instinct, 309
firearms, 399–401
first-shift rule, 350
fixed-choice paradigm, 42
fixed-sum error, 362–363
foot-in-the-door technique, 271
foot-in-the-mouth technique, 273–274
forensic psychology, 397
forewarning, 106–107
four-category model of adult attachment, 233
French immersion, 375–376
frustration-aggression hypothesis, 172, 315
Frustration and Aggression, 172
fundamental attribution error, 57–59, 60

G

gazes, 44–45
gender
and aggression, 324–326
defendants, 406
defined, 137
gender-appropriate behaviour,

Photo and Cartoon Credits

Chapter 1
Page 3, Al Harvey; page 6, Robert A. Baron; page 9, left, Grant LeDuc/Stock, Boston; page 9, right, Esbin-Anderson/Image Works; page 12, Catherine Karnow/Woodfin Camp & Associates; page 13, King Features Syndicate, 1990; page 24, *Toronto Sun*; page 26, Canadian Press/Tom Hanson; page 32, Canadian Press/Tom Hanson

Chapter 2
Page 39, Omni-PhotoCommunications/Dinodia; page 41, Lee/The Picture Cube; Allen/Stock, Boston; Putnam/The Picture Cube; McLaren/The Picture Cube; Herwig/The Picture Cube; Sundberg/The Image Bank; page 44, Canadian Press/Jeff McIntosh; page 46, all Robert A. Baron; page 51, Universal Press Syndicate, 1990; page 55, Jack Cornelis; page 67, Corbis Digital Stock; page 70, PhotoDisc Inc.; page 75, Canadian Press/*Kamloops Daily News*/Murray Mitchell; page 76, *Washington Post* Writers Group, 1997

Chapter 3
Page 85, Canadian Press/Jeff McIntosh; page 89, Jeffrey Dunn/Stock, Boston; page 92, Stuart Cohen/Image Works; page 99, King Features Syndicate, 1992; page 101, Reuters/Mike Blake; page 111, Michael L. Abramson/Woodfin Camp & Associates; page 115, left, Fujifotos/Image Works; page 115, right, Michael Dwyer/Stock, Boston

Chapter 4
Page 121, *New Yorker*, September 30, 1996, p. 65; page 125, Bonnie Kamin; page 134, Toyota; page 136, *Victoria Times*

Colonist; page 138, copyright © 1997 by art spiegelman (reprinted by permission)

Chapter 5
Page 159, *Toronto Star*/P. Power; page 165, drawing by Handelsman, © *The New Yorker* Magazine, Inc.; page 168, Canadian Press/*Maclean's* Photos/Rick Chard; page 176, Charles Steiner/Image Works; page 182, Brown/The Image Bank; McConnell/McConnell,McNamara & Co.; de Lossy/The Image Bank; Forest/The Image Bank; Bieber/The Image Bank; Gallant/The Image Bank; page 196, PhotoEdit/Mark Richards

Chapter 6
Page 203, *The New Yorker*, August 4, 1997, p. 61; page 212, Al Harvey; page 217, Canadian Press/Robert Galbraith; page 221, *The New Yorker*, April 15, 1996, p. 72; page 224, The Bettmann Archive; page 226, *The New Yorker*, January 18, 1998, p. 37; page 241, *The New Yorker*, June 10, 1991, p. 89; page 246, Universal Press Syndicate, 1999

Chapter 7
Page 253, *The New Yorker*; page 254, Al Harvey/Dick Hemingway/PhotoDisc; page 257, Goodwin/*Toronto Sun*; page 273, *The New Yorker*; page 274, Rhoda Sidney/Stock, Boston; page 278, pictures from the film *Obedience*, distributed by the New York University Film Library; page 281, Canadian Press/*La Presse*/Robert Mailloux

Chapter 8
Page 287, *New Yorker*, February 23 and March 2, 1998, p. 145; page 294, United Feature Syndicate, March 8, 1998; page 299, Bob Daemmrich/Stock, Boston; page 304, CBC Still Photo

Collection, Toronto; page 306, Philip H. Condit/Tony Stone Images; page 311, Reuters/Corrine Dufka/Archive Photos, page 323, United Artists/Shooting Star; page 328, *Chicago Tribune* News Syndicate, 1980

Chapter 9
Page 335, both photos by Bob Carroll; page 339, left, Rhoda Sidney/Stock, Boston; 339, right, John Coletti; page 352, AP/Wide World; page 355, King Features Syndicate, 1986; page 356, Bob Daemmrich/Stock, Boston; page 367, King Features Syndicate, 1996; page 369, Topham/Image Works

Chapter 10
Page 377, King Features Syndicate, 1995; page 384, Lonnie Duka/Tony Stone Images; page 387, United Feature Syndicate, 1998; page 390, Nubar Alexanian/Stock, Boston; page 391, left and bottom Corbis-Bettmann, right, National Archives of Canada/C5329; page 397, Playboy, 1984; page 406, Canadian Press/Frank Gunn